# THE IRWIN SERIES IN ECONOMICS

*CONSULTING EDITOR*

LLOYD G. REYNOLDS
YALE UNIVERSITY

# BOOKS IN THE IRWIN SERIES IN ECONOMICS

# GOVERNMENT FINANCE

# GOVERNMENT FINANCE

## AN ECONOMIC ANALYSIS

by John F. Due Ph.D.

*PROFESSOR OF ECONOMICS*
*UNIVERSITY OF ILLINOIS*

THIRD EDITION

1963

RICHARD D. IRWIN, INC.

HOMEWOOD, ILLINOIS

*To my wife Jean*

# PREFACE

This study is designed to present a general survey of governmental expenditure, revenue, and debt systems, with emphasis upon their economic effects and their relationships to principles of economic welfare. The standards of expenditure and revenue systems which will most closely attain the generally accepted goals of present-day society are developed as a basis for evaluation of the existing structures. Details of historical development and description of present-day systems are minimized in order to keep the volume within manageable lengths and to insure that the reader will not lose sight of the forest for the trees. Sufficient description is included, however, to provide a general understanding of the present expenditure and revenue structures.

The preciseness and validity of the conclusions are limited by two primary considerations: the inadequacies of contemporary welfare theory in defining in meaningful terms the optimum economic welfare position, and the lack of adequate knowledge of the economic effects of various taxes, especially upon incentives. These limitations make it impossible, for example, to define the particular distribution of tax burden by income class which will allow optimum attainment of economic welfare. Further progress in scientific evaluation and development of government expenditure and revenue systems must await advances in economic welfare theory, and the attainment, by empirical and analytical means, of greater knowledge of the effects upon the economy of various expenditure and tax programs.

Within the confines established by these limitations, stress has been placed upon a unified treatment of the entire field of public finance, each aspect being reviewed in light of its role in the over-all picture rather than as a separate and isolated phenomenon. An effort has been made to allocate space in terms of the financial and economic significance of the various measures, and thus a larger than usual portion of the section on taxation is devoted to income and commodity taxes. The fiscal policy section is devoted about equally to inflation and depression control measures, and is integrated, so far as possible, with the analysis of expenditures and revenues. A chapter on general aspects of government borrowing has been placed ahead of the section on fiscal policy; while this procedure results in some repetition, it should facilitate an understanding of the general role of borrowing in government finance.

The basic structure of the book remains unchanged from the previous edition. The revision has concentrated upon bringing the material up to date, introducing significant elements from new literature in the field, and altering emphasis in conformity with changing patterns of public finance. The chapter on excess profits taxation has been removed, and material on averaging of income for tax purposes significantly reduced. A new chapter on government finance and economic growth, dealing with both mature and developing economies, has been added. The chapters on economic effects of income taxation and on fiscal policy have been rewritten to lessen duplication and improve presentation.

Additional sections on Canada have been transferred to appendices to chapters so that they may more easily be omitted by instructors in the United States who do not wish to use them. This is the only public finance text which has given specific reference to Canada.

The present edition, as the two previous ones, has of course been greatly influenced by the work of various writers in public finance in recent years. The income tax chapters reflect the ideas of Simons and Vickrey particularly; significant recent publications include those of Kahn, and the Ways and Means Committee's *Tax Revision Compendium*. The work of Kaldor and his critics is reflected in the discussion of expenditure taxation. Throughout the new edition the monumental study of Musgrave, which appeared just after the previous edition was published, has influenced the work. The National Bureau volume, *Public Finances*, has contributed to the expenditure material. The work on budgets has been aided greatly by the work of Smithies and Burkhead; on capital gains, of Seltzer; on government debt, of Buchanan and many others. The Harvard Business School studies of corporate income tax effects, and the work of Goode, E. Cary Brown, and others have influenced the work on corporate income taxes. Others to be noted—and the list in not intended to be complete—include Earl Rolph, Gordon Keith, Carl Shoup, Duncan Black, J. W. Maxwell, A. C. Pigou, E. D. Fagan, H. M. Groves, J. Harvey Perry, Milton Moore, and Challis Hall.

The *National Tax Journal* has been a very valuable source of information and ideas, as has the *Canadian Tax Journal* and other publications of the Canadian Tax Foundation for Canadian material.

The author is also indebted to a number of individuals for their specific assistance on the three editions. I should particularly like to express my appreciation to Professor Malcolm M. Davisson of the University of California, whose course in public finance first stimulated my interest in the field. Valuable comments have come from many persons who have used the book as a text over the years, from my colleague at the University, Professor H. K. Allen, and students in the courses in public finance at the University of Illinois.

Urbana, Illinois
February, 1963

John F. Due

# TABLE OF CONTENTS

## PART II. FINANCING OF GOVERNMENT EXPENDITURES—

## PART III. INCOME TAXATION

## PART VI. THE COMMERCIAL PRINCIPLE

## PART VII. OVER-ALL ASPECTS OF GOVERNMENT FINANCE

# INDEX

# PART I

Governmental Activities and

Expenditures

# Chapter 1

# THE ROLE OF THE GOVERNMENT IN THE ECONOMY

The study of government finance is that portion of economics which is concerned with the economic activity of governments, which are the political organizations of society. Thus the study deals with the determination of the levels of government activities and expenditures, with the means by which the funds to carry on these activities are raised, and with the effects of the expenditure and revenue measures upon the private sector of the economy.

In the Western world the governmental sector constitutes a minority segment of the economy, most economic activity being conducted by private households and business firms. But the governmental sector has grown in importance over the last century, until the activities of government have reached such a magnitude that they exercise important influence over the functioning of the entire economy. In some countries of the world the governmental sector has absorbed the great bulk of production activity and has come to exercise substantial direct influence over consumption, so that in these areas government finance, in its broadest aspects, now encompasses virtually the entire field of economics. The scope of the present study, however, is confined to the situation in which governmental activities constitute a limited, although important, sector of the economy.

Since government expenditures are made because various activities are carried on by governments, the study of expenditures and revenues will be facilitated by a preliminary review of the reasons why the governments have undertaken various forms of economic activity. The remainder of this chapter will be devoted to this question. In the following chapter the question of optimum levels of governmental activities and expenditures, or, in other words, the question of the optimum size of the governmental sector of the economy, will be considered. This will be followed by a review of actual trends and patterns in government activities and expenditures and of the problems of the measurement of the size of the governmental sector. Attention will then be turned to the various sources

3

of revenue, to debt management, and to fiscal policy, that is, the program of increasing economic stability by adjusting government revenues and expenditures.

## THE BASIC ECONOMIC DECISIONS

Any type of economic system must perform various functions if personal wants are to be satisfied by the use of available resources. Decisions must be made about the allocation of resources among various products, to determine which goods are to be produced with available resources. Decisions must be made on the extent to which output will be used for immediate consumption or for use in further production, or, in other words, the rate of over-all real capital accumulation for society as a whole. The particular techniques of production must be selected; for example, is coal to be used for fuel for a particular purpose, or oil? Finally, the distribution of the output of society among its various members must be determined. These are universal problems which confront any economic society; if the society is to function, some type of institutional framework which insures the making of these decisions is necessary.

There are three general ways in which these problems can be solved, and while elements of each are found in most economies, one is usually dominant. The first is that of pure convention or custom. For example, a community may concentrate in the production of bananas, with each family receiving an equal share of the crop, simply because tradition dictates this behavior. Custom is dominant in primitive societies and plays a part also at more advanced levels of civilization. Secondly, decisions may be made by some form of authority, designated as the government, which is able to enforce its decisions upon the members of society. The governmental power may rest in the hands of a dictator who has inherited the position or seized it by force, or it may rest in the hands of a group chosen by the members of the community and responsible to them. Thirdly, the decisions may be made automatically through the operation of the market mechanism, whereby, without central control, the separate actions of individuals are co-ordinated by the price system.

The three systems of decision making can be illustrated with a simple example. In a "tradition"-dominated economy, corn is planted this spring because corn is always planted in the spring; each successive generation is taught by the previous one that the appropriate economic activity is the planting of corn, and hence no other crop is considered. With a centrally controlled economy, corn is planted because the central government planning agency decides that corn is to be grown and directs various persons to plant the desired amounts. In a free market economy, persons plant corn because they see an opportunity to make a higher income for themselves by so doing, in light of the existing relationship between two sets of prices—the costs of producing the corn and the prices for which the crop can be sold. Although one system is usually dominant in a particular society, some combination of the systems may occur. In a market economy a farmer may continue to plant corn even though he might make a greater profit from other crops, because his father and his grandfather always planted corn. But in a market economy, he may be compelled ultimately to abandon the growing of corn if the price-cost relationships are such that he cannot make a living if he continues to follow his former practice. Or while the initiative for planting may rest in the hands of the individuals, the government may influence the amounts which they can profitably plant by affecting the market price through purchases of surpluses. Our present economy is dominated by the market mechanism, but with considerable government influence.

## THE MARKET ECONOMY AND THE ATTAINMENT OF ECONOMIC WELFARE

Before the role of governmental influence in the modern economy is considered, it is desirable to review in somewhat greater detail the manner in which the market economy functions in the solving of the basic economic problems and the extent to which it attains desired goals. In such a society, production is carried on primarily (and would be wholly, if the economy were completely of the free market character) by privately owned business firms. These firms acquire units of the factors of production by the payment of sums of money to their owners and utilize these units in the production of goods and services which are sold for money prices. The amounts received from the sale of the products provide the means to make the payments to the factor owners, the residuals constituting the incomes of the owners of the enterprises. The households or consuming units obtain the means with which to acquire the goods produced by the business firms by the sale of the factor units, such as labor services, which the households possess.

### The Making of the Decisions

In a market economy the basic decisions confronting any economy are made through the automatic functioning of the price system, as noted above. Resources are directed toward the production of those goods which will yield the greatest margin of profit, or excess of price above cost, and thus to those for which the households wish to spend their incomes. The relative quantities of various goods produced depend likewise upon price-cost relationships and, ultimately, upon consumer demand. The rate of capital formation, the extent to which production is directed toward the output of capital goods rather than of consumption goods, is basically determined by the extent to which persons divide their incomes between saving and consumption (apart from certain modifications which arise when full employment is not attained). Techniques of production are selected on the basis of relative costs. The distribution of the output of society is controlled by the relative prices paid for various factor units, which, in turn, depend upon the relationship between the quantities of the factor units available and the demand for their services for use in production. The amount of output received by each household depends also upon the quantities of the various factor units which the household is able and willing to supply for use in production.

The price mechanism is the basic regulator of the economy. It guides business firms, factor owners, and consumers in the making of their decisions, and rations scarce factor units and finished goods among purchasers, in order to balance demand with available supply. It provides a simple mechanism for the distribution of the total output among the individual members of society. The price system allows individuals free choice in the expenditure of their money incomes, the manner in which these expenditures are allocated, in turn, influencing the decisions of producers and the composition of total output.

For two centuries or more the principle that the market or free enterprise form of economy is superior to other forms has been generally accepted in the Western world. But nevertheless, no economy has ever been completely free of governmental activity; no society has ever had a universal market economy, with no interference by central authority. Over the years the trend has been toward the development of increased governmental participation in economic activity. Both the explanation of this trend and an evaluation of it must be based upon a consideration of the extent to which a free market society attains or fails to attain the goals of economic welfare which are accepted by the society. To the extent that the undertaking of economic activity by government is based upon the desires of the community, it reflects dissatisfaction with the adequacy of the market economy in obtaining optimum welfare. Objective evaluation of the actual scope of governmental activities must rest upon a comparison, in particular cases, of the relative attainment of the goals of economic welfare with no governmental participation, on the one hand, and various degrees of such participation, on the other.

### The Accepted Goals of the Economy

The goals of the economy are not derived by economic analysis, but are ethical value judgments. However, at any time, in a given society, there exists a substantial consensus about major goals. In modern market economies, there are four which are ordinarily considered to be paramount, so far as economic activity is concerned:

1. Maximum individual freedom of choice.
2. Optimum levels of living, in terms of available resources, and consumer and factor-owner preferences.
3. Attainment of the desired rate of economic growth.
4. Distribution of income in conformity with currently accepted standards of equity.

Each of these will be considered in greater detail.

### Freedom of Choice

Freedom of choice involves the right of the individual to decide which commodities he wishes to acquire and to act in conformity with his decisions, and the right to make decisions about the use of factor units. Individuals must be free to decide whether they wish to work in one type of employment or another, or for one firm or another. They must have freedom of choice over the manner in which they divide their time between work and leisure. Persons must have the right to undertake production activity and carry it on as they see fit, subject to those restrictions which are necessary to protect the interests of others.

### Optimum Levels of Living

By the requirement of optimum levels of living is meant the attainment of highest possible levels of satisfaction of wants for all individuals, given the available factors and techniques, and given the pattern of income distribution. If this optimum is to be reached, three requirements must be met:

1. *Optimum Efficiency in the Use of Resources.* Factor combinations, or techniques of production employed, must be those which allow maximum output, given the factor supplies. In other words, the methods of production selected must be those which will allow maximum output of particular goods, with available technological knowledge and factor supplies.

2. *Direction of Production in Terms of Consumer Preferences.* Given the income distribution and consumer tastes, the pattern of allocation of resources among the production of various goods, and thus the

pattern of the relative outputs of the various goods, must be that which will best satisfy consumer preferences. This result will be obtained only if the marginal units of each type of factor unit result in the same marginal satisfactions to the users of the products in each line of production in which they are employed.[1] If, for example, the relative outputs of automobiles and refrigerators are such that the marginal consumer satisfaction which results from the use of the present quantity of resources in automobile production is greater than the marginal consumer satisfaction which results from the employment of the present quantities of the same factors in refrigerator production, a reduction in the output of refrigerators and an increase in the output of automobiles will result in an increase in consumer satisfaction.

Or in slightly different terms, the relative outputs of the various goods must be such that, given the pattern of distribution of income, the *marginal social benefit* from the production of each commodity is equal to the *marginal social cost* resulting from the production of the commodity. The marginal social benefit is the gain to individuals from the acquisition of the last units of the commodities. The marginal social cost is the real cost to society resulting from the production of additional units, the cost taking the form primarily of sacrifice of output of other goods. If more gasoline is produced from a given quantity of crude oil, the output of fuel oil must be reduced. Thus the real cost to society of the marginal gallons of gasoline is the reduction in the output of fuel oil which results. If equality of marginal social benefit and marginal social cost is not attained, the shifting of resources from the production of some commodities to others will allow over-all higher standards of living, because the units of additional output of the preferred commodities will yield more satisfaction than the units of the less preferred articles which are given up.

Optimum allocation of resources will be attained in a market economy, provided that (*a*) prices of all commodities are equal to marginal costs of production, (*b*) all real costs to society from the production of the goods appear as costs to the business firms producing them, and (*c*) benefits from the consumption of the goods accrue solely to the persons acquiring them, and not to others as well. Under these conditions the actions of the consumers in distributing their expenditures in such a manner that the marginal utilities of the various goods which they buy are proportional to their prices, and the actions of the producers in insuring that

---

[1] In more technical terms, for each consumer the marginal rates of substitution between each two commodities purchased must be equal to the marginal rates of transformation between the two commodities in production.

marginal productivity of each factor is equal to the factor price and that marginal cost is equal to selling price, will insure attainment of optimum adjustment of output (assuming perfect knowledge).

3. *Employment of All Factor Units Whose Owners Wish to Have Them Employed at Prevailing Factor Prices.* If some factor units are un-employed, obviously over-all levels of living are lower than the possible levels which can be attained. This third requirement also necessitates an adjustment of relative work and leisure in conformity with the desires on the part of the workers.

In general, failure to attain these three requirements would result in a situation such that various adjustments would increase the level of living of some persons without lowering that of others and would thus increase economic welfare. A few examples in nontechnical terms will help to clarify this statement. Suppose that a commodity is being produced with obsolete techniques, which require greater inputs of labor and materials for a given output than newer methods. Introduction of the new techniques will allow greater total output of goods and generally higher levels of living. Or suppose that very large quantities of shoes, relative to demand, are being produced, so that the relative preferences of the consumers for the marginal pairs of shoes are much less than they would be for other commodities which might be produced with the same factor units. Society would be better off if fewer units of shoes and more units of other goods were produced.

### Economic Growth

Increased importance has been attached in recent years to economic growth, both in relatively mature economies such as that of the United States and in the underdeveloped economies of the world. In the latter, great stress is placed on a rapid increase in real per capita income, so as to raise these figures to ones comparable to those in developed economies. In the more mature economies the goal of growth in real per capita income is likewise regarded as important, but in addition, stress is placed on the need for stable growth, with the avoidance of lags of the actual rate of growth below the potential rate allowed by technical factors.

### Equity in the Distribution of Income

The fourth generally accepted goal is that of a distribution of income which is regarded as equitable by the consensus of opinion in society. Since equity in income distribution, as in all matters, is based upon value judgments, economics can be of no real assistance in defining it. It is sometimes argued that economic welfare requires a distribution of income such that the marginal satisfactions of all persons are equal, since otherwise a shifting of income from some persons to others would increase total satisfaction. Actually, this statement has no significant meaning, because of the impossibility of making interpersonal utility comparisons, that is, of comparing relative satisfactions obtained by different persons. There is no way in which the satisfaction received by one person from the consumption of a particular good can be compared with that received by another person from the consumption of the same good. It is not possible to say that two persons with the same income, accumulated wealth, numbers of dependents, and other external circumstances receive the same satisfactions and thus are "equally well off" in any subjective sense. It is impossible to show that a person with a million-dollar income receives less satisfaction from the expenditure of an additional dollar than does a person with an income of one thousand dollars.

However, persons make judgments about equity in the distribution of income, on the basis of which they evaluate the actual pattern which occurs with a market economy. Furthermore, in any particular society, there is a substantial consensus of opinion about an optimum pattern; while there are extremists at both ends of the scale, the differences in opinion would typically appear to extend over a relatively narrow range. There is widespread acceptance of the view that the actual distribution of income which develops in a market economy is excessively unequal, and thus that equity requires a closing-together of the extremes, the incomes of the very poor being increased and those of persons at the highest levels being reduced. On the other hand, the general consensus of opinion today is that complete equality of income, or any close approximation to it, is not equitable, because persons who are successful financially would be deprived of most of their gain. Most persons accept the point of view that those who earn more should be able to enjoy a higher level of living than those who earn less, or, in other words, that people should be rewarded for their efforts.

### The Attainment of Optimum Economic Welfare with the Market Economy

In many respects the market economy will attain, at least in part, the accepted economic goals of modern society. On the other hand, the market economy, as it actually operates, has proved to be deficient in certain respects from the standpoint of these goals; these deficiencies have in large measure given rise to governmental activity.

1. *Freedom of Choice.* The market economy offers a maximum of individual freedom of choice and action. Households may spend their incomes in any manner they wish. Factor owners have freedom over the manner in which they employ their factor units, and persons are free to undertake production as they wish. Persons are free to establish new business firms. The requirements of efficiency in production do necessitate some restriction on individual allocation of time between work and leisure. Freedom of choice is interfered with to a certain extent when competition ceases to be entirely perfect. The development of monopoly power, which essentially constitutes a deviation from a completely free market economy, restricts the freedom of persons to undertake new enterprises. But on the whole, the market economy, even with some departure from completely free markets, offers a maximum degree of individual choice.

2. *Optimum Levels of Living.* The requirements for optimum levels of living will be attained only if certain conditions exist in the economy:

*a*) Perfect competition prevails in all markets. For this condition to be realized, there must be complete absence of monopoly power of any form or degree, in both commodity and factor markets. There must likewise be perfect mobility of the factors of production and complete knowledge of relevant conditions on the part of all persons concerned with economic activity. Under these circumstances the prices of all commodities will equal their marginal costs, and the marginal contributions of each factor to consumer satisfaction will be the same in all lines of production in which it is employed. Thus, resources will be allocated among various products in conformity with consumer choices, and no readjustments in the relative output of various goods could increase total consumer satisfaciton. Efficiency in production will be at optimum levels.[2]

*b*) There are no obstacles in the way of attainment of full employment.

*c*) Benefits from the use of various goods accrue solely to those persons who purchase them, and all costs to society from the production of the goods appear as costs to the business firms producing them. In other words, the marginal private benefits—those which accrue directly to the purchasers—must equal the marginal social benefits, the total benefits to society from the use of the goods; and marginal private costs—the costs to the private producers—must equal the marginal social costs, those to society as a whole. Any deviation between marginal private and social costs

[2] Some question may be raised as to whether perfect competition insures an optimum rate of technological change. This problem is considered in the studies in economic welfare listed at the end of the chapter.

and benefits will lead to excessive or inadequate production, as explained in the following section.

Actually, of course, these requirements are not fully attained in the present-day market economy. Many markets are not completely free markets; perfect competition is impossible in markets in which technological considerations require the number of firms to be small. Varying degrees of monopoly power result in a deviation between prices and marginal costs. The artificially high prices of these goods result in restriction of their production and use to uneconomically low levels, and production of other goods is therefore relatively excessive, in terms of consumer preferences. Rigidities in the interest rate and the limited response of investment by business firms to interest rate changes may make the maintenance of full employment difficult if the sums persons wish to save are relatively high compared to the volume of potential investment.

Furthermore, there are various services, such as national defense, which yield substantial benefits to society over and above those which may accrue directly and separately to individuals. If these activities are left to free enterprise, the output will be too small in terms of the best interests of society. The production and use of other commodities, such as liquor, create costs to society which do not appear as expenses to the individual producers.

The recognition that a market economy, with no government participation in economic activity, cannot insure optimum standards of living was the basis for the undertaking of certain types of activity by governments, even in the days in which the philosophy of *laissez faire*—the superiority of the free market economy—was at its highest. During the last century, increased recognition of the inadequacies of the market economy in attaining the accepted goal of optimum living levels has led to a greater scope for the activities of government.

3. *Economic Growth in the United States and Canada.* Considerable concern has been expressed in the United States and Canada in recent years about the lag in economic growth below the levels of the Soviet Union and other areas; prior to that time, it was generally considered that the rate of expansion provided by the market economy was highly satisfactory. There has also been concern about the stability of growth and deviations of the actual rate of growth away from the attainable rate.

4. *Income Distribution.* The market economy, even with relatively free competition, has resulted in a pattern of income distribution among families which opinion in society has typically regarded as inequitable, because of the high degree of inequality. The degree of inequity has been increased still more by the development of monopoly power.

## THE CONSIDERATIONS WHICH HAVE LED TO THE UNDERTAKING OF GOVERNMENTAL ACTIVITY

The previous sections have outlined some of the limitations of the market economy. It is now desirable to review in greater detail the reasons why governmental activities have developed. The analysis will be facilitated by the use of the classification, based on that of Musgrave, of allocation, commercial, distribution, and stabilization functions of government.[3] Each will be considered in turn.

### Allocation Functions

The allocation functions are those designed to bring about a reallocation of resources; they originate essentially out of the failure of the market economy to bring the desired pattern of allocation. There are several aspects:

1. *Social or Community Wants.* The traditional activities of government have been undertaken because the benefits of these activities are social or community in character; that is, they accrue in part or entirely to the members of the community as a group rather than separately to individuals, and individuals cannot be excluded from the benefits. The activities are thus not divisible into units which can be sold to individuals, and thus, if they are to be provided, they must be rendered by the political organization of society. In more technical terms, marginal social benefits from these activities exceed marginal private benefits (which in fact, may be nil); that is, the total gains to society from the services exceed those which accrue directly and separately to individuals.

Some activities yield only social benefits, the services not being divisible into measurable units which directly benefit individuals. National defense, protection of life and property, prevention of fraud and deception, and enforcement of contracts convey very important benefits to the community as a whole, since anarchy would prevail without them and the operation of the modern complex economic system would be impossible. But despite their importance, these services cannot be produced by private enterprise, since they cannot be broken up into segments and sold to individuals, as can the output of apples, bread, automobiles, and beauty parlor services. Private enterprise can realize gain only from those benefits which accrue directly to individuals, since purchases of the services will be

---

[3] See R. A. Musgrave, *The Theory of Public Finance* (New York: McGraw-Hill Book Co., Inc., 1959). This is the modern classic in the field of government finance.

influenced solely by the direct benefits received as a result of the purchase. Because there is no way to prevent all persons from receiving the benefits if the services are provided, a voluntary "subscription" basis of financing is not feasible. Accordingly, if the activities are to be carried on, governments must provide them.

2. *Merit Wants.* Another group of activities convey benefits, in part at least, to individuals, and the activities thus can be provided by private enterprise. They are taken over by governments with the deliberate intent that total provision of them be increased; that is, society considers that they are of such nature that individuals should have more of them available than if they were privately produced. In part, these activities offer social benefits as well as private benefits. Education provides a classic example. Higher levels of education provide economic and political advantages to the community over and above those received by the persons obtaining the education, in the form of more rapid economic growth and greater political stability. Or governmental insistence on larger amounts being provided may reflect the fact that the individuals involved do not see the advantages of the activity to themselves; this may be true of health services in relatively underdeveloped economies.

Municipal transit provides another example. A good transit system reduces traffic accidents, speeds up street traffic and lessens waste of time, avoids the need for street widening, and lessens the necessity for persons living in congested areas. Yet the transit system cannot realize financially from these benefits, which do not accrue directly to the users of the service.

3. *Additional Social Costs.* Some types of economic activity give rise to costs to society from production and use of the good which exceed the costs to the private producer. The sources of these costs are known as external diseconomies. If production is left in private hands, production will be excessive. Thus, for example, the use of liquor to excess results in loss of time from jobs, sacrifices for the person's family, traffic accidents, and perhaps additional crime. Opium almost completely destroys the usefulness of the person to society. A cement plant or a smelter may destroy production on adjacent farms.

In these cases the government's task is to curtail use. It may do so by prohibiting or regulating the use of the good, as in the case of opium. It may levy heavy taxes on the sale of the good. Or it may undertake production and sale, as in the case of the state liquor monopolies, charging prices higher than marginal cost.

4. *External Economies.* The opposite situation is encountered when the costs to the business firm are greater than to society as a whole. The traditional example is that of a decreasing cost industry, in which expansion of output by a firm results in a lower cost for all firms and thus a real

cost to society less than the cost to the individual firm. Output is too small if determined on a private profit-making basis.

5. *Elimination of Interferences with Perfect Competition.* Imperfections in competition represent a major source of departure from optimum resource allocation, and may also produce changes in the pattern of income distribution which are regarded as inequitable.

For example, lack of adequate knowledge interferes with attainment of optimum utilization of income by consumers, as well as most efficient adjustment of production. The government has attempted to assist, to a limited degree, in attainment of the former objective by checking misrepresentation and establishing standard grades. It has sought to facilitate the adjustment of farm output to changing conditions by informational and guidance services, and in some cases by direct or indirect regulation of output. Even in a situation of perfect competition an optimum adjustment of output in response to dynamic changes may not be attained by independent, uncontrolled operation of the market economy. Provision of data of national income trends, output, etc., is designed to aid businessmen in determining output and investment policies. Employment agencies seek to bring together the unemployed and the available jobs.

The most serious interferences with perfect competition arise from the development of monopoly influences. Rarely do these take the form of complete control of supply by one firm; more commonly, some firms will gain limited control over price. As a consequence, output will be restricted below the level at which marginal cost is equal to price, and operation is not necessarily carried on at the point of lowest cost. In some instances, resources are wasted and poorly utilized, while in others, total output will be restricted to less than optimum levels.

When significant monopoly power exists, the task of the government is to restore output and price to competitive levels. In some instances an attempt is made to do this by regulatory action; for example, the antitrust laws prohibit various combinations and practices regarded as detrimental to the preservation of competition. But the governments encounter a fundamental difficulty with this approach; technological requirements in some industries prevent the number of firms from being large if optimum efficiency is to be attained. If there are only a few firms in an industry, they cannot be forced to engage in effective competition. As a consequence, in many cases the antitrust laws have done little more than curb the most extreme departures from competition.

In some fields—especially public utilities—the impossibility of insuring effective competition and the importance of the services to the public have led either to regulation of rates or to outright governmental production of the service.

### The Commercial Function: Greater Efficiency with Government Operation

It is generally presumed that private enterprise can produce more efficiently than governments, because of the effective stimulus provided by the profit motive.[4] However, there are certain situations in which governmental production may be more efficient, in the broad sense of that term. In the first place, certain real costs to society may be avoided if the services are produced by the governments and provided free of charge to the users. The savings are due primarily to elimination of the costs of collecting the charges from the users; the administrative expenses of the taxes used to finance the activities may be much less. For example, if sidewalks were provided by private enterprise, the costs of collection of tolls would far exceed the present costs of collection of property taxes and special assessments to finance sidewalks. This is an extreme example, but the same considerations apply to the financing of highways, since the costs of collection of tolls on all roads must greatly exceed the costs of administering the gas tax.

In other instances, privately regulated monopolies may become lax in efficiency and modernization, and effective government operation may result in substantial improvements. The urban transit field provides examples, such as in Toronto and Seattle, in which government operation brought increases in efficiency. Government operation does not guarantee optimum efficiency, of course; but in some instances, it offers an opportunity if private operation is unsatisfactory.

Another consideration is the ability of the government to undertake long-range investment projects which either necessitate amounts of capital greater than private businesses in the field can raise or offer chances of profitable return only over a period too long for private enterprise to wait. The TVA and other power projects provide examples at the federal level, and municipal water systems at the local level. Many cities found it necessary to take over their water services for the single reason that private enterprise would not make adequate investments in advance and sudden increases in usage or dry years resulted in shortages of water.

### The Redistributive Function

In recent decades a substantial portion of governmental activity has been undertaken for the purpose of increasing the relative economic well-

---

[4] A general denial of this position is to be found in the article by J. E. Fisher, "Efficiency in Business and Government," *Quarterly Review of Economics and Business*, Vol. II (August, 1962), pp. 35–48.

being of certain groups in the economy, particularly those with very low incomes. This action has been based on divergence between the actual pattern of income distribution and that regarded as most equitable by a consensus of opinion in present-day society. It has come to be regarded as inequitable, for example, that many older persons do not have sufficient income to allow them to maintain even a minimum living standard; accordingly, old-age pension programs have been instituted. The tax structures utilized have also been designed in part to lessen the over-all degree of inequality. There are also redistributive effects arising from some of the allocative functions of government; public education, for example, particularly benefits the lower income groups.

### The Stabilization Function

In the last three decades, governments have given increased attention to the task of gaining greater economic stability and more rapid and stable economic growth. The market economy has demonstrated a failure to provide full employment of resources in certain periods, and to maintain a reasonably stable general price level in others. When unemployment occurs, no one business firm or household can take effective action to bring recovery and full employment, even though simultaneous action on the part of a large number of firms or households would produce this result. Increased investment on the part of one firm, for example, while giving some stimulus to higher levels of national income, would primarily benefit other firms more than the one which undertook it. Accordingly, in order to provide a stimulus toward recovery, governments have undertaken various activities, particularly control over the rate of credit expansion and, in recent decades, public works and relief activities. Increases in the general price level, which have many undesirable effects, cannot be controlled by individual producers.

The growth rate has received increased attention, particularly in underdeveloped countries, where primary stress in the formulation of government expenditures is placed upon increasing the rate of growth. The activities involved are primarily allocative ones, but the goal is that of growth.

### Conclusion

These considerations account for the undertaking of the great bulk of present-day government activities. Likewise, they provide a justification for replacement of the market mechanism by central decision making on the part of the government in a portion of the economy. However, it must be remembered that the activities which governments actually undertake are based upon the views of those who are responsible for the determination of government policy. These views may—and, in fact, do in large measure—reflect the general consensus of opinion in the community as a whole. However, in some instances, there may be little obvious consensus, particularly about the exact scope of the government activities; and in others, those responsible for the decisions may act solely on the basis of their own wishes and interests.

The views may be based upon a careful weighing of the merits of the activities, but on the other hand, they may be the products of ignorance, wishful thinking, political ambitions, or personal gain for the interested groups. While the considerations mentioned above provide the primary bases of justification of governmental activities, they do not in themselves justify all activities which governments actually carry on or the manner in which they are performed. All governments perform some functions which obviously benefit small groups at the expense of society as a whole; some government enterprises are run far less efficiently than private businesses would operate the same undertakings. In Chapter 2 the principles which determine the optimum levels of government activity will be analyzed.

## REFERENCES

This chapter is in large measure a survey of certain aspects of the theory of economic welfare. Further analysis of welfare problems is to be found in the following references:

BATOR, F. M. *The Question of Government Spending.* New York: Harper & Bros., 1960.
  A semipopular review of the justification for government activities.
BAUMOL, W. J. *Welfare Economics and the Theory of the State.* Cambridge: Harvard University Press, 1952.
LITTLE, I. M. D. *A Critique of Welfare Economics.* 2d ed. Oxford: Oxford University Press, 1957.
SAMUELSON, P. M. *Foundations of Economic Analysis,* pp. 203–53. Cambridge: Harvard University Press, 1948.
REDER, M. W. *Studies in the Theory of Welfare Economics.* New York: Columbia University Press, 1947.
MUSGRAVE, R. A. *The Theory of Public Finance,* chap. i. New York: McGraw-Hill Book Co., Inc., 1959.
  The modern classic on the economics of government finance.
  See also references to Chapter 2.

# Chapter 2

# OPTIMUM LEVELS OF GOVERNMENT ACTIVITIES

The previous chapter was concerned with the general explanation of why governments have undertaken various activities. A closely related question is that of the optimum levels of these activities: What rules should govern the extent to which various governmental activities and thus expenditures should be extended? These rules, of course, must be determined on the basis of the generally accepted goals of the economic system, noted in the previous chapter.

Obviously, in the discussion of optimum levels a sharp distinction must be made between the allocation activities on the one hand and the transfer activities on the other. The stabilization functions will be discussed in later chapters dealing with fiscal policy rather than in this chapter.

## OPTIMUM LEVELS OF ALLOCATION ACTIVITIES

In a formal sense the basic rule of optimum resource allocation which applies to the private sector of the economy, that of equality of marginal social costs and benefits, is applicable to the governmental sector as well. That is, given the distribution of income, optimum levels of production are attained only if output in all lines is extended to the level at which the marginal social benefit is equal to the marginal social cost. When this position is reached for all goods, the marginal social benefits in all lines of production are equal, and thus the marginal contributions of each factor of production are the same in the output of all commodities. No reallocation of factors among various lines of production could improve economic welfare, given the pattern of income distribution.

### Application of the Marginal Rule to Governments

As applied to governments, this rule requires that each line of governmental activity be extended to the level at which the marginal social

19

benefits from the activity are equal to the marginal social costs. The marginal social benefits (MSB) represent the gains to the members of the community as a whole from the governmental activities; the marginal social costs (MSC) reflect the benefits from private sector production which are sacrificed when the government acquires the factors to carry on its activities. If this level is attained for each of the activities, the marginal social benefits from all the activities (per dollar spent to produce the services) are equal to one another. For example, the benefits to the community from the last dollar spent on education would be the same as those from the last dollar spent on highways, conservation, national defense, or fire protection. In less technical terms the rule means simply that if, at given levels of governmental activity, the marginal dollar spent on one activity—for example, education—is providing less benefit than the marginal dollar spent on another—public parks, for example—society will be better off if some of the money now spent on education (where the marginal benefits are low) is transferred to use on parks (where the marginal benefits are high). Or if the marginal social benefits from all governmental activities, even though equal to one another, are less than those which would be obtained by individuals if they were free to spend the same amount on the output of the private sector of the economy, society will gain if all governmental activities are curtailed and the output of the private sector is allowed to increase.

### Use of the Price System by Governments

So long as governmental activities yield their benefits directly and separately to individuals and equity conditions do not dictate otherwise, the government can utilize the price system in the adjustment of the levels of activity by selling the services for prices equal to marginal costs, and thus attain the MSB-MSC objective without any problem of direct measurement of benefits. If the prices are established at levels equal to marginal costs (taking into consideration any indirect costs to society as well as those directly involved in obtaining factor units to produce the services), individuals will adjust their purchases of the services to such levels that they attain equality of the marginal benefits from governmentally and privately produced goods. Thus, optimum relative outputs of the governmental services and privately produced goods will be attained, so long as prices are equal to marginal costs in the private sector. If they are not, some misallocation of resources will result, but the optimum can be reattained only by modification of output in the private sector.

One requirement must be stressed: The setting of prices on the governmental services at figures equal to marginal costs will insure optimum levels of output of these services only if there are no indirect benefits to the community as a group, distinct from those which accrue separately to individuals. If there are indirect benefits, the output will be too small if prices are set on a marginal cost basis, and an attempt must be made to measure these social benefits and take them into consideration in the setting of prices. The problems of measurement are the same as those with governmental services which yield all their benefits to the community as a whole, which will be discussed below.

A special problem arises when production is carried on under such conditions that price, when equal to marginal cost, is less than average cost. Thus, on a city subway system the marginal cost of carrying additional passengers may be much less than the average cost per passenger if there is unused capacity. In this case a price equal to marginal cost will not cover all the costs of providing the service. This question will be considered in more detail in Chapter 22.

### Measurement of Community Benefits

Most governmental activities, by their inherent nature, cannot be sold to the users, because the benefits accrue to the community as a whole rather than separately to individuals. In other cases, sale is ruled out by society because of a conflict with desired principles of equity in the distribution of income. In these cases the price system cannot be employed directly as a means of determining the optimum levels to which the activities should be extended. Under such circumstances, the MSB-MSC rule, while still having formal applicability, has little meaning or usefulness for policy.

If the government is regarded as an organic unit, acting for society and making decisions for it but being distinct from the individuals who compose society, it can still be argued that the task of the government is to extend all activities to the level at which marginal gains and marginal costs, calculated in terms of the additions to and subtractions from total social utility, are equal. But such a policy requires estimation by the state of relative gains and losses to various individuals from policies followed, and therefore implicitly requires interpersonal utility comparisons, that is, the comparison of relative satisfactions received by different persons. This comparison cannot be made on any meaningful basis. As a practical matter, there is no way in which the marginal social costs and benefits of activities which benefit the community as a whole can be measured; the MSB-MSC rule offers no actual guidance for policy determination.

A more realistic approach is that which regards the state as merely a collection of separate individuals, providing a framework for the making of decisions by individuals as a group but having no ends separate from those of the persons who compose it.[1] Under this concept the optimum levels of governmental activities which benefit the community as a whole are dependent upon the evaluation by the community of the relative importance of the various goals which the activities serve. In other words, the optimum levels of each activity are determined by the collective estimates of the community regarding relative desirability of particular degrees of attainment of various specific goals—protection of the country against foreign attack, education of the people, protection of life and property, provision of a suitable highway system, etc. This approach to the definition of the optimum levels of governmental activities is not only much more realistic but involves no interpersonal utility comparisons. The MSB-MSC rule, though formally correct in all situations, is meaningless and thus useless when the benefits of activities accrue to the community as a whole; the optimum levels are dependent upon the degree of attainment of the objectives of the various governmental activities which the consensus of opinion in society regards as desirable, relative to the desires of the people for the output of the private sector of the economy.

The task of determining community consensus about the desirability of the various degrees of attainment of the goals, and thus of the relative importance attached by society to the activities, rests upon the government. Likewise, the government must determine the exact policies and expenditure levels which will best allow the attainment of the social goals as ranked by the current consensus of community opinion. In a democracy the basic responsibility for determination of policies rests with the legislative body, with guidance from the executive branch of government.

### Estimation of Benefits

Accordingly, a primary task of governments is that of estimating the benefits from various levels of activities and expenditures, in terms of general community goals. While this task is inherently difficult, especially with such activities as national defense, certain considerations are of assistance in the task.

In the first place, with many activities, factual information based upon engineering estimates and studies is available. In a small town, for example, the decision on the installation of a new sewerage system will depend in part upon the relative costs of the system compared to the savings for homeowners through the elimination of the need for provision of their own septic tanks. The decision on a particular irrigation project can be based in part on engineering estimates of benefits relative to costs.

Secondly, it is obvious that the initial expenditures on certain activi-

[1] See the article by J. M. Buchanan, "The Pure Theory of Government Finance," *Journal of Political Economy*, Vol. LVII (December, 1949), pp. 496–505.

ties are more essential, in terms of community desires, than those on others. By virtually all persons, minimum expenditures on fire protection are considered to be more important to community welfare than expenditures on shade trees; elementary education is more important than adult classes in photography.

Thirdly, it is also apparent that the marginal benefit to society from any activity declines as expenditures on the activity are increased. Thus, beyond a certain point, additional expenditures on activities of high initial importance to society will offer less, in terms of accepted social values, than expenditures on other activities of less initial benefit. Thus, one fire truck to a small city is regarded by society as far more important than the expenditure of the same amount of money on a city park. But the purchase of a fifth fire truck may offer very little benefit, if four are adequate for protection against all potential fire hazards, and may be regarded as far less important to the community than the establishment of a park.

However, in many instances the estimation of benefits in terms of desired goals of society is very difficult. With national defense, for example, the actual level of activities necessary to insure the desired degree of protection against attack upon ourselves and our allies is very difficult to ascertain, since the required level depends in part on unpredictable actions of other countries.

### Estimates of Costs

In determining expenditure programs, the government must likewise take into consideration the costs which result from the programs. There are two aspects of costs created by the programs: (1) the sacrifice of output of privately produced goods due to the transfer of resources to governmental production and (2) the effects of the collection of the revenues, and particularly of taxes, upon factor supplies, incentives, and economic development.

1. *Transfer of Resources.* The primary cost to society due to governmental activities is the reduced output of privately produced goods which results from transfer of resources from private to governmental production. The lumber and concrete and brick which go into new government buildings are not available for private housing; steel made into tanks cannot be used for automobile production. So long as resources are fully employed, any increase in governmental production must result directly in a decline in the output of the private sector.[2] This cost is normally mani-

---

[2] There are some exceptions. Certain forms of government activity may directly facilitate production to a greater extent than the private activity which would otherwise be undertaken; the construction by the government of a railway line into an undeveloped area is an example.

fested to the individual in the form of the taxes which are collected to cover the costs of government activities; as a result of the taxes the person is able to buy less than he otherwise could. But the tax system merely determines the manner in which the burden is distributed over individuals, the real burden to the people as a whole being the reduced output of privately produced goods. With full employment, this burden will exist whether taxes are levied or not. If the money is borrowed, the burden is borne through inflation, which reduces the buying power of given dollar incomes.

The preceding argument has been based upon the premise of full employment. If resources are idle, government production may increase without a consequent decline in private production, since governmental activities merely utilize the resources which would otherwise have been idle and, as explained in Chapter 31, may actually stimulate private sector production rather than restrict it. Accordingly, under such circumstances the real cost to society of governmental activities is very much less than it is in periods of full employment. Some of the major public works of the thirties—the Tennessee Valley project, for example—were built at very little real cost to the economy, since the resources involved would otherwise have been idle. While many activities cannot be easily adjusted upward and downward in conformity with changes in business activity, the real costs of those which are adjustable are so much less in periods of depression that substantially higher levels of the activity are justified.

2. *The Frictional Effects of the Revenue System.* In addition to the burden in the form of reduced private sector output due to the transfer of resources, there is a secondary burden which arises from the effects on incentives in the economy due to the collection of the sums necessary to cover the costs of providing the services—normally, taxes. The direct effect of taxes in reducing private spending is merely a corollary of the transfer of resources to the government. But in addition, the taxes, because of their compulsory nature, may affect the functioning of the economy in other respects. They may reduce (or increase) factor supplies, they may alter the relative quantities of different factors, and they may affect incentives and efficiency. These possible effects will be discussed in greater detail in connection with the study of the various individual types of taxes.

As governmental activities are extended, the real costs to society, per dollar of additional expenditure, rise. The initial governmental activities are undertaken with resources which, if used in private production, would serve the least intensive wants. But as successively more resource units are taken by governments, individuals are compelled to sacrifice privately produced goods which satisfy wants of increasing intensity. At the extreme, governmental activities could be extended so far that land was taken from essential food production to provide more parks; persons would be starving to death because most of the farm land had been turned to recreational use.

Likewise, the frictional effects of the taxes are almost certain to become more serious as the sums collected increase. Relatively low taxes are unlikely to have a significant effect upon the economy, while high rates may seriously deter incentives.

### Comparison of Benefits and Costs

For each level of a particular governmental activity, a certain degree of attainment of the desired goals of society is reached, taking into consideration both the benefits from the activity and the costs, in the form of sacrifice of privately produced output. It is the responsibility of the government to select that level which appears to be most closely in conformity with the consensus of opinion in society with respect to various goals. This process requires the careful weighing of the gains from the various activities against one another, in the light of the government's estimate of the consensus of opinion of society toward the desirability of various degrees of attainment of the goals. Likewise, the benefits must be weighed against the real costs to society.

Several factors complicate the tasks of governments in determining optimum expenditure levels. In the first place, there are major problems involved in ascertaining community preferences. There has been extensive discussion in the last decade of the question of the ascertainment of social choice or, in other words, the pattern of ranking of various goals by the people of a country.[3] One inherent problem is the absence of one single solution which will maximize preferences for all persons, since their preferences for community goods will vary; yet, in a sense, equal amounts are available to all. Another is the task of getting persons to reveal their preferences about community goods; as individuals, they will have incentive to understate their preferences in an effort to benefit from the availability of the good yet to minimize tax burden. Various groups will make strategical moves designed to bring them services for which other persons will pay. Further discussion of this problem is beyond the scope of this book.

In addition, there are, as noted, major difficulties in estimating the

---

[3] See R. A. Musgrave, *The Theory of Public Finance* (New York: McGraw-Hill Book Co., Inc., 1959), chap. vi; P. A. Samuelson, "The Pure Theory of Public Expenditures," *Review of Economics and Statistics*, Vol. XXXVI (November, 1954), pp. 387–89; K. Arrow, *Social Choice and Individual Values* (New York: John Wiley & Sons, Inc., 1951).

benefits from particular levels of government expenditures, in terms of estimated community-ranked goals. Primary responsibility rests with the legislative body. Yet the legislators may have little understanding of many of the governmental activities and their benefits to society, and they often cannot easily gain unbiased information. With the parliamentary form of government, the actual decisions are made to a greater extent by persons in direct charge of the administration of the policies. Theoretically, at least, there should be a better opportunity for more intelligent appraisal of benefits and costs. On the other hand, these persons may become over-enthusiastic about their own activities and may give too little weight to the desires of the community itself.

A related difficulty is that the public as a whole may be uninformed about the possible benefits and costs of particular activities and may prevent the government from carrying out policies which would best serve the interests of the community or may insist upon policies which are not desirable in terms of the accepted goals of society. While society must be the ultimate judge of the desirability of the various goals, persons can appraise various policies in terms of these goals only if they are fully informed about the actual results and costs of the programs. If particular policies, even though approved by a majority of the people, are adopted on the basis of inadequate information about the benefits and costs, the levels of activities and expenditures are not necessarily the optimum in terms of the desired goals of society, even though they represent the will of a majority. The situation is comparable to that of an individual who fails to attain maximum satisfaction from his income because he buys, on the basis of inadequate information, a shirt that shrinks or an automobile tire that blows out the first time it is used. One task of the government is to inform the public as completely as possible about the various activities, so that public support will be gained for those programs which offer the best chance of attaining the goals of society.

### Direct Participation by the Public in the Determination of Activities

It has sometimes been argued that optimum levels of activities in terms of the desires of society would be attained more closely if the people were given more direct voice in the determination of policy rather than merely exerting their influence through their chosen representatives and pressure groups. In conformity with this point of view, some states provide for popular voting on issues through initiative and referendum measures.

The basic difficulty with popular voting on such issues is the public's lack of information about the implications of the proposed programs relative to the goals accepted as desirable. While the members of legislative bodies may often lack adequate information, typically they are in a better position to obtain it than the average voter and to recognize the gains to the community as a whole, as distinct from those accruing directly and immediately to individuals. Direct responsibility in the hands of the voters may result in "eat your cake and have it too" legislation, in wasteful extension of activities, in failure to foresee all consequences of proposed action, and in failure to consider costs as well as benefits. If decisions are made by the elected representatives of the people, who stand responsible to the voters for the consequences of their actions, there is a better chance of the weighing of alternatives and the recognition of all implications of action taken. Furthermore, in modern complex societies the issues relating to government activities and expenditures are so numerous that, as a practical matter, they cannot all be submitted to the voters. Technical problems in presenting the issues in such a way that the real consensus of opinion will be determined are also serious limitations.

### Division of Functions among Various Levels of Government

The division of functions among various levels of government complicates the task of obtaining optimum expenditure levels, particularly in a federal governmental structure, with constitutional division of powers between federal and state governments. This division makes the balancing of gains from various expenditures against one another more difficult, since the task is in part performed independently by different governmental units. The problem is aggravated because some of the levels of government are limited, by administrative or legal considerations, in the types of taxes they can employ. Accordingly, the functions performed by these governments may not be extended as far as they logically should be, relative to those of the governments with less limited revenue sources. Further problems arise when various local units have widely varying revenue resources compared to their revenue needs. These problems will be discussed further in Chapter 24.

### Use of Optimum Techniques

Distinct from the question of levels to which the activities of government are extended is that of the extent to which the greatest efficiency is obtained in the conduct of the activities, so that the costs will be minimized. If a government is to produce at lowest cost, it must utilize the best available techniques and obtain maximum efficiency. In the private sector of the economy the pressures on private firms to attain maximum efficiency are very substantial. In perfectly competitive markets, firms which fail to operate efficiently are driven out of business; with imperfect markets the pressure is less strong but still substantial, since inefficiencies reduce profits. With governmental activities the profit motive is eliminated. Some incentive to efficiency is provided by the desire of governments to hold taxes down and provide maximum services from given revenues. But this may prove inadequate. The price system still provides a guide to efficiency, the difficulty being not one of principle but of insuring implementation of the principle.

## OPTIMUM LEVELS OF REDISTRIBUTIVE ACTIVITIES

Since the redistributive or transfer activities of government do not involve the use of resources or the rendering of services to the community, no problems of adjustment of output of governmental services arise. These activities merely shift purchasing power from some persons to others. Accordingly, the consideration of optimum levels must rest primarily upon the patterns of income distribution regarded as most equitable by the concensus of opinion in society. These patterns are value judgments, as are all questions of equity, and cannot be determined or explained on any analytical basis. There exists in society today rather general agreement that the degree of inequality of income which develops in a market society is excessive and that governments should insure some minimum degree of subsistence to all persons. On the basis of this attitude, not only has the tax system been made progressive, but, in addition, various social security programs have been developed. The desirability and the adequacy of these programs can be evaluated only in terms of the pattern of income distribution regarded as desirable at the particular time, apart from certain economic effects discussed below.

It is important to note that the accepted standards of optimum distribution patterns change materially over the years. The principle that persons should not be allowed to starve to death has been accepted for centuries, but the concept of the exact minimum standard of living which should be insured by government has changed greatly. For example, in the last century the generally accepted philosophy was that old people should be taken care of if they could not support themselves, but at a bare minimum subsistence level in a county poorhouse. Today the philosophy is generally accepted that equity requires the provision of a substantially higher level of support, which will enable these persons to live in their own homes. It cannot be argued that one attitude is "better" than another, except in terms of the basic assumption made about equity in the distribution of income. Inevitably, individual opinions differ widely on the welfare programs, because of different notions of equity. Nevertheless, at any time, there is substantial agreement on matters of equity in income distribution, on the basis of which the welfare programs must be evaluated.

While the welfare programs must be judged primarily in terms of value judgments, they may have certain economic effects, which must also be taken into consideration. On the one hand, the transfer activities may retard economic development. The taxes necessary to cover the payments may lessen incentives; relief systems, especially if poorly administered, may lessen the labor supply. On the other hand, improved standards of living of the poor may increase productivity. The shift in purchasing power may aid in the elimination of unemployment. When the programs have adverse economic effects, these must be weighed against the greater equity in income considered to result from the programs; the final decisions must be made in terms of the ranking of the various objectives by the consensus of opinion in society.

While redistributive activities do not directly involve governmental use and thus reallocation of resources, it must be recognized that they do have allocation effects, since the recipients will spend the money in a fashion different from that of the persons from whom the purchasing power is taken. Thus, relief programs financed by income taxes will increase the output of milk and reduce that of furs. But this is presumably regarded as a desirable consequence of the undertaking of the redistributive activities.

## REFERENCES

BOWEN, H. R. *Toward Social Economy,* chap. xviii. New York: Rinehart & Co., 1948.
  A careful analysis of the problems involved in determining optimum levels of expenditures, with emphasis on various techniques of voting.
BUCHANAN, J. M. "The Pure Theory of Government Finance," *Journal of Political Economy,* Vol. LVII (December, 1949), pp. 496–505.
  An examination of the basic problems with respect to the role of government in the economy.
PIGOU, A. C. *A Study in Public Finance,* Part I. 3d ed. London: Macmillan & Co., Ltd., 1947.
  A statement of the marginal rule with respect to government activities.
VANDERMEULEN, A. J. "Criteria of 'Adequate' Governmental Expenditures and Their Implications," *Journal of Finance,* Vol. VI (March, 1951), pp. 19–31.
  A statement of the issues involved in the definition of adequacy.
U.S. FEDERAL INTER-AGENCY RIVER BASIN COMMISSION. *Proposed Practices for Economic Analysis of River Basin Projects.* Washington, D.C.: U.S. Government Printing Office, 1950.

A study of the problems of evaluating the river basin projects and suggestions for evaluating them.

JOINT ECONOMIC COMMITTEE. *Federal Expenditure Policy for Economic Growth and Stability,* Part II. Washington, D.C.: U.S. Government Printing Office, 1957.

Note especially papers by Heller, Musgrave, Poole, and Thomson on the question of optimum expenditure levels.

SAMUELSON, P. A. "The Pure Theory of Public Expenditures," *Review of Economics and Statistics,* Vol. XXXVI (November, 1954), pp. 387–89.

ECKSTEIN, O. *Water Resource Development.* Cambridge: Harvard University Press, 1958.

The problem of economic evaluation of water resource projects.

ECKSTEIN, O., and KRUTILLA, J. V. *Multiple Purpose River Development.* Baltimore: Johns Hopkins University Press, 1958.

An analysis of costs and benefits of federal river basin development programs.

MUSGRAVE, R. A. *The Theory of Public Finance.* New York: McGraw-Hill Book Co., Inc., 1959.

NATIONAL BUREAU OF ECONOMIC RESEARCH. *Public Finances.* Princeton: Princeton University Press, 1961.

A series of papers on the question of optimum levels of government expenditures.

| Chapter | GOVERNMENT EXPENDITURES: |
|---------|--------------------------|
| 3 | PATTERNS AND TRENDS |

Analysis of governmental activities and expenditures in recent decades reveals two features of paramount importance: (1) the great extent to which expenditures are concentrated for a relatively few purposes and (2) the rapid growth of government expenditures.

## MAJOR PURPOSES OF GOVERNMENT EXPENDITURES

### Federal Budgetary Expenditures

In the United States, through most of the years of its history, the most important federal expenditures have been those for national defense, despite the fact that the country has normally maintained relatively small armed forces. As illustrated in Figure 1, in recent years direct expenditures for military services have accounted for over half of the total federal budgetary expenditures. If items related to national defense, including veterans' benefits, atomic research, foreign aid, and interest on debt incurred during the wars, are included, the total is about 77 per cent of total federal budgetary expenditures of $88 billion in fiscal year 1962.[1] In recent decades, only during the depression years of the thirties did defense spending fall to a minority position, accounting for less than 30 per cent of the total, as welfare spending reached high levels.

The second major category of federal expenditures, 15 per cent of the total, consists of various welfare expenditures, designed to increase the economic well-being of certain groups in the economy. In 1962 the farm-aid program, designed primarily to aid farm incomes, was the largest item in the category, followed by the public assistance programs, primarily grants for old-age pensions. Interest on depression-incurred debt may also be regarded as a type of welfare expenditure. Until the thirties the federal

[1] In usual terminology, by the term *1962 fiscal year* is meant the fiscal year ending in 1962 (on June 30).

government did very little in the welfare field, but the depression brought extensive activity, including the provision of substantial sums for direct relief. With the return of prosperity the importance of welfare spending declined, and direct relief assistance was eliminated. The totals are nevertheless still substantial, and a severe depression would bring sharp increases.

FIGURE 1

FEDERAL BUDGETARY EXPENDITURES BY MAJOR PURPOSE,
UNITED STATES, FISCAL YEAR 1962

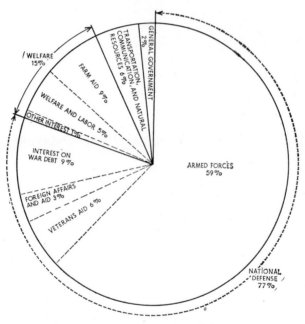

SOURCE: U.S. Treasury, *Treasury Bulletin.*

A third major category consists of expenditures on transportation, communications, and natural resource development, including the postal deficit, aid to the merchant marine, various public works activities, and the like.

The final category, and one which is surprisingly small, 2 per cent of the total, is that for general governmental activities, including Congress, the courts, regulatory agencies, and the various departments other than those such as national defense, included in other categories.

### Federal Nonbudgetary Expenditures

The figures given above include only items which appear in the budget, and exclude expenditures from the various trust funds (and payments into these funds). Expenditures from these funds, however, are essentially governmental in character. The total in 1962 was $24 billion, the two major items of which were $13.3 billion payments under social security old-age and survivors' insurance, and $2.8 billion for federal highways.

FIGURE 1A

FEDERAL BUDGETARY AND TRUST FUND EXPENDITURES BY MAJOR PURPOSE, UNITED STATES, FISCAL YEAR 1962

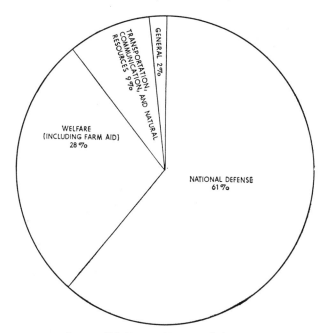

SOURCE:  U.S. Treasury, *Treasury Bulletin.*

If these trust expenditures are added to the totals, the effect is to increase the welfare category (including farm aid) to 28 per cent of the total expenditures, and the transportation category to 9 per cent, and to decrease the other items, including national defense, accordingly, as shown in Figure 1A. But nevertheless, national defense remains as the chief item.

Figure 2 shows the relative importance of various categories for selected years since 1914.

### State Expenditures

At the state level, as shown in Figures 3 and 3A for fiscal years 1961, education, highways, and health and welfare were the most important items. So far as the budgetary expenditures are concerned (Fig. 3), education is by far the most important, accounting for 34 per cent of the total

FIGURE 2

FEDERAL EXPENDITURES BY MAJOR PURPOSE,
UNITED STATES, SELECTED FISCAL
YEARS, 1914–49

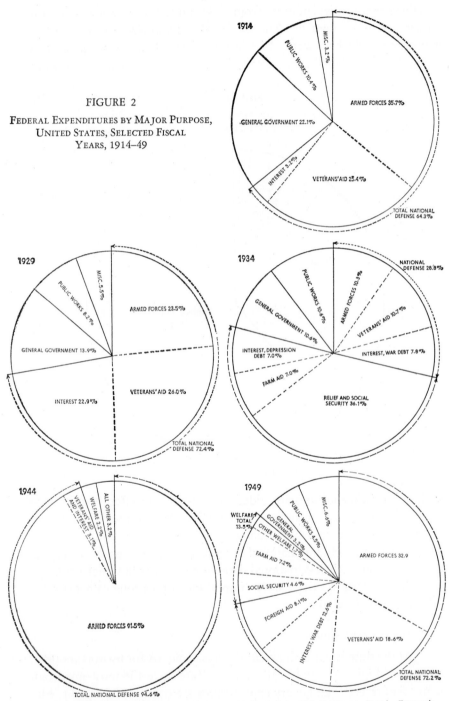

SOURCE: U.S. Treasury, *Treasury Bulletin;* National Industrial Conference Board, *Economic Almanac.*

of $29.1 billion, with highways 26 per cent, and health and welfare 21 per cent. If the trust fund expenditures are added (Fig. 3A), health and welfare becomes the chief item, 31 per cent of the total, since all of the trust fund expenditures, primarily for unemployment compensation, are of the welfare character. Employee retirement benefits are included as welfare expenditures.

FIGURE 3

STATE GENERAL EXPENDITURES BY MAJOR PURPOSE,
FISCAL YEAR 1961

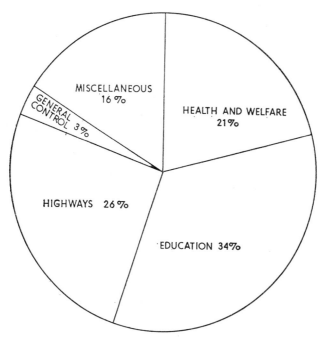

SOURCE: U.S. Department of Commerce, Bureau of the Census, *Compendium of State Government Finances in 1961.*

The figures, as given, include both direct state expenditures and grants to the local governments, which account for about one third of the total. The grants are particularly important in the field of education, in which they exceed direct state expenditures, but are also found in the other fields as well. Practice varies among the states; some, for example, have taken over virtually all highway activities, while others give large grants to the local governments for this purpose.

Examination of the figures of state expenditures over the last fifty years shows several clearly defined trends. All three major functions have grown rapidly, while relative expenditures for general governmental operation have declined. Highway expenditures, negligible before 1900, became the chief item during the twenties, fell in importance in the next two decades, and rose relative to other items in the fifties. Education, by far the chief item prior to 1920, declined in relative importance as high-

FIGURE 3A

STATE GENERAL AND TRUST FUND EXPENDITURES BY
MAJOR PURPOSE, FISCAL YEAR 1961

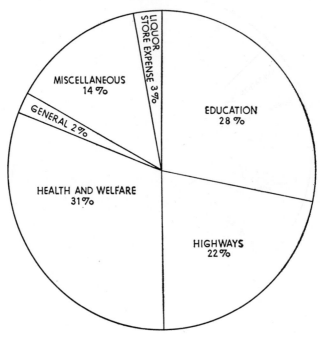

SOURCE: U.S. Department of Commerce, Bureau of the Census, *Compendium of State Government Finances in 1961.*

way and welfare activities increased in the twenties and thirties, and then commenced to rise relative to other items after 1950. Welfare activities gained greatest prominence in the thirties, and have lost some ground, relatively, in recent years. The over-all figures, of course, obscure variation in trends in different states, some of which have pushed certain activities much more than other states. The general patterns, however, have substantial uniformity.

### Local Expenditures

Because of the large number (over 100,000) of local governments, that is, all units below the states, completely accurate data of expenditures at this level are not available. In recent years, however, the U.S. Bureau of the Census has developed estimates on the basis of available data which have a high degree of reliability. In Figure 4, the figures for 1961 are shown; local expenditures totaled $36.8 billion in that year, about $11 billion of which was financed by grants from the federal government and

FIGURE 4

ESTIMATED LOCAL GOVERNMENT EXPENDITURES BY
MAJOR PURPOSE, UNITED STATES, 1961

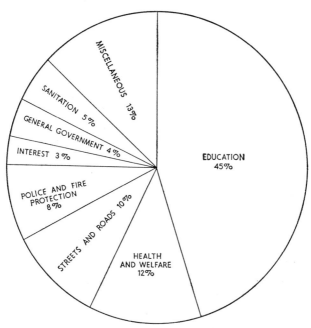

SOURCE: U.S. Department of Commerce, Bureau of the Census, *Government Finances in 1961.*

the states. Nearly half—45 per cent—of the total was spent for education alone, an item which has increased very rapidly in recent years as the school-age population has grown. The other major categories are streets and roads, health and welfare, protection (police and fire), and sanitation and sewage, as well as general governmental costs, which are relatively more important at this level than at higher levels of government.

### The Over-all Picture

Figure 5 shows the combined expenditures of all levels of government by major function, with double counting arising out of intergovernmental grants eliminated. The data on which the chart is based include both budgetary and trust fund expenditures, and the gross expenditures of the postal system and government-owned utilities. Nearly a third of total expenditures are made for national defense and related activities. The health and welfare category, which accounts for 20 per cent of the total, is next in importance, followed by education (13 per cent) and highways (6 per cent).

While military spending has usually dominated the federal expenditure picture, it has been the major item in the over-all pattern only since

FIGURE 5

ESTIMATED TOTAL EXPENDITURES BY MAJOR PURPOSE,
ALL LEVELS OF GOVERNMENT COMBINED,
UNITED STATES, 1961

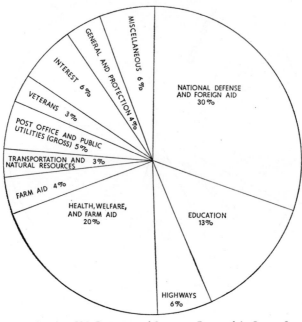

SOURCE: U.S. Department of Commerce, Bureau of the Census, *Summary of Government Finances in 1961*.

World War II, except in war periods. Education, long a major item, declined relatively for several decades, but has grown sharply since 1950. Highway expenditures, which rose rapidly from 1900 to 1929, fell relatively until 1954, and then commenced to rise again. Welfare activities attained their peak in the thirties. Over the years the expenditures for the routine general expenses of government have fallen relative to other items, although increasing in absolute terms.

## RELATIVE EXPENDITURES BY VARIOUS LEVELS OF GOVERNMENT

As shown in Figure 6, a major change has occurred in the relative magnitudes of the expenditures of various levels of government. In the

United States, local expenditures, once more than half the total, are now second in importance. Federal expenditures, on the other hand, have risen to such an extent that they are now greater than state and local expenditures combined, whereas fifty years ago they were the least important of the three. This change is attributable largely to the great increase in defense spending. However, since 1952, local spending has again risen relative to federal.

FIGURE 6

RELATIVE BUDGETARY EXPENDITURES BY LEVEL OF GOVERNMENT,
UNITED STATES, SELECTED YEARS, 1914–61

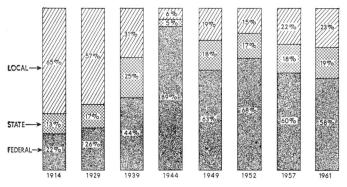

In the expenditure figures for each level of government, grants-in-aid are included, as well as expenditures made from grants received, and the percentages are figured on the combined totals of the three levels. This procedure exaggerates somewhat the relative importance of state and local expenditures combined, compared to federal expenditures.

SOURCE: National Industrial Conference Board, *Economic Almanac*, 1949; U.S. Department of Commerce, Bureau of the Census, *Summary of Government Finances in 1957, 1961.*

Within the general category of nondefense spending, a similar but less marked shift has occurred. Federal nondefense expenditures, expressed as a percentage of total governmental nondefense spending, actually declined from 1900 to 1929; during the depression years the trend was reversed, and the federal nondefense spending rose above state and local spending, when previously it was the lowest of the three. However, since 1940 the federal nondefense spending has declined relative to state and local expenditures; state spending increased the most rapidly of the three for a time; and then, after 1950, local expenditures began to rise most rapidly as educational needs expanded. Today the figures of nondefense spending of the federal and local governments are about equal, with the states somewhat less. Thus the sum of state and local spending is nearly twice the total federal expenditures for nondefense purposes.[2]

[2] This commonly ignored fact was brought to the author's attention by the article by R. A. Musgrave and J. M. Culbertson, "The Growth of Public Expenditures in the United States, 1890–1948," *National Tax Journal*, Vol. VI (June, 1953),

A substantially different picture of the relative activities of the three levels of government is given by the data of employment. In April, 1961, total public employment (with part-time employees adjusted to full-time equivalent) was 9.1 million (excluding military personnel); of these, federal employees accounted for 2.5 million; state employees, 1.6 million; and local, 4.9 million.[3] Even if members of the armed forces are added, state and local employees are almost as numerous as federal, even though the federal government spends much more money. State and local activities are more labor-intensive than those at other levels, no elements of grants given to other governments are involved in the expenditures of local governments, and average salary per employee is less than at the federal level.

The increased relative importance of the federal government over the years can be attributed primarily to two considerations. The first is the rise in defense activities, which affects the federal government alone. Secondly, the depression of the thirties led the federal government to enter the welfare field, previously occupied solely by the other units of government. State employment and expenditures rose relative to those of the local governments because of the tendency to centralize functions. This tendency, in turn, was due partly to administrative considerations (as in the case of highways) but primarily to the inability of the localities to finance the growing demand for various types of services and welfare assistance.

## THE GROWTH IN GOVERNMENT EXPENDITURES

The phenomenal growth in the dollar figures of government budgetary expenditures is shown in Figure 7. Between 1914 and 1961, United States federal expenditures increased over 100 times; state expenditures increased 76 times; and local, about 17 times. If the comparison is made between 1938 and 1961 expenditures, the figures are 12, seven, and six times, respectively. Since 1952 the growth of expenditures at the state-local level has been phenomenal.

These absolute figures of expenditures, however, are somewhat misleading, because of price level and population changes. Furthermore, the economy was expanding rapidly, so that a given dollar expenditure was much less significant in 1961 than in earlier years. Adjustments must be made for these changes, in order to obtain an accurate picture of the increase in governmental activity.

[3] See U.S. Department of Commerce, Bureau of the Census, *State Distribution of Public Employment in 1961.*

## Adjustment for Population and Price Changes

The absolute figures of expenditures exaggerate the real increase because of the rise during the period of both population and the general price level. In the first place, the growth in population—from 76 million

FIGURE 7

TOTAL GOVERNMENT EXPENDITURES BY LEVEL OF
GOVERNMENT, UNITED STATES, 1914–61

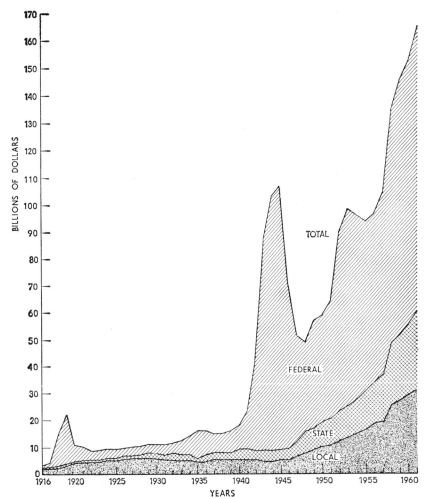

Expenditures from grants-in-aid included in figure of grantor government only. Thus, total expenditures of states and localities as shown are less than actual dollar expenditures of these units.

SOURCE: National Industrial Conference Board, *Economic Almanac;* Tax Foundation, *Facts and Figures on Government Finance;* publications of U.S. Department of Commerce, Bureau of the Census.

in 1900 to 132 million in 1940 and 183 million in 1961—necessitates increased levels of many governmental activities. There are more children to educate, more old persons to care for, for example. Secondly, the general price level has increased sharply, more than doubling since 1939. Thus a given level of governmental activities costs more money, since the yardstick of measurement has shrunk. In Table 1 the absolute figures are adjusted for both price level and population changes for selected years, on a calendar year basis. In the United States, total government expenditures in actual dollars increased 55 times between 1914 and 1961, and 10 times between 1939 and 1961. If the figures are adjusted for price level changes, the increase is 20 times from 1914 to 1961, and four times between 1939 and 1961. If the data are adjusted for price change and placed on a per capita basis, the increase is 11 times between 1914 and 1957, and the 1961 figure is three times that of 1939.

TABLE 1

GOVERNMENT EXPENDITURES FOR ALL LEVELS OF GOVERNMENT, ADJUSTED FOR PRICE LEVEL AND POPULATION CHANGES, SELECTED YEARS, 1914–61, UNITED STATES

| Calendar Year | Total Expenditures (Billions of Dollars) | Total Expenditures (1926 Dollars) (Billions of Dollars) | Per Capita Expenditures (1926 Dollars) |
|---|---|---|---|
| 1914................. | 3.06 | 4.37 | 44.6 |
| 1919................. | 22.13 | 15.96 | 152.0 |
| 1924................. | 9.68 | 9.87 | 87.2 |
| 1929................. | 11.34 | 11.89 | 98.0 |
| 1934................. | 14.57 | 19.45 | 153.9 |
| 1939................. | 16.96 | 22.00 | 168.1 |
| 1944................. | 103.12 | 99.16 | 718.0 |
| 1947................. | 44.04 | 28.98 | 210.1 |
| 1949................. | 59.66 | 38.49 | 262.6 |
| 1952................. | 94.40 | 53.04 | 337.8 |
| 1955................. | 108.60 | 61.70 | 376.2 |
| 1957................. | 124.40 | 66.20 | 389.4 |
| 1961................. | 164.20 | 89.20 | 490.1 |

SOURCE: *Survey of Current Business,* various years; National Industrial Conference Board, *Economic Almanac.*

It must be recognized that the adjustment of the data by the index of wholesale prices is not entirely satisfactory, since the prices of materials and services purchased by governments may not change in the same manner as the general index. There is a tendency for governmental salaries to lag behind those of private industry. Furthermore, the relative importance of the governmental sector depends upon the size of the private sector as well.

## Government Expenditures Relative to Gross National Product

The difficulties of measuring real trends in government expenditures by adjustments in data of dollar expenditures and the desirability of obtaining a suitable measure of the relative spheres of governmental and private sector economic activity have led to a consideration of the relationship between governmental activities and various measures of total income or output of the economy. There are three primary measures of this type which may be used:

1. The ratio of total governmental expenditures to GNP (gross national product).

2. The ratio of the value of the governmental services to GNP. With this measure, transfer expenditures are eliminated from the total of government expenditures.

3. The ratio of net value added through governmental production to national income or the very closely related ratio of income originating in the governmental sector to total national income.

The choice among these alternatives depends in part upon the exact purpose for which the measure is desired. The first is suitable as a measure of the extent to which the spending of income and thus resource allocation are affected in any manner by governmental activity. Accordingly, this measure is useful in measuring trends in the influence of governmental activity compared to private sector activity, and is widely used for this purpose. Figure 8 shows the ratios of total government expenditures to GNP for the United States for selected years. In the years since 1939, while governmental activity has increased rapidly, so has private sector output; and thus, while the relative role of the government in influencing resource allocation has increased somewhat, the growth is not nearly as great as that in government expenditures, as such, even when adjusted for price level and population trends.

While the ratio of expenditures to GNP is useful for certain purposes, and particularly for measuring trends, the figure gives a misleading impression of the actual size of the governmental sector. Governmental expenditure figures include transfer payments, whereas GNP totals do not, and thus the ratios exaggerate the relative role of governmental production in the economy.

The second measure, the ratio of the value of the governmental product to total GNP, eliminates the element of transfer payments and compares actual production activities in the two spheres. The figure for 1961 was 21 per cent. However, this measure, like the first, fails to take into consideration the fact that the government "dispenses" many products which it does not entirely produce, whereas this is much less true with the private sector of the economy. For example, the cost of building a highway is, in its entirety, an element in government expenditures. But the cement, steel, and gravel used to build the roads, and the trucks, graders,

FIGURE 8

RATIO OF GOVERNMENT EXPENDITURES TO GROSS NATIONAL PRODUCT,
UNITED STATES, SELECTED YEARS, 1913–61

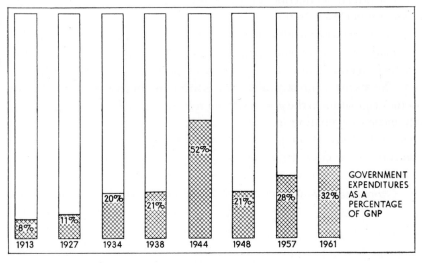

SOURCE: *Survey of Current Business,* various years.

and other equipment used in construction and maintenance, are all produced by private business firms. Even the actual construction work is usually placed in the hands of private contractors. With the strictly governmental types of function, such as police protection, the patrol cars, uniforms, radios, and the like are all privately produced. When a government takes over a transit system, it does not produce its own equipment.

In contrast, relatively few services used in private production are government-produced. Although there are some examples, such as streets, sewers, and fire protection, these, in turn, are largely produced with materials and equipment supplied by the private sector.

The source of the difficulty with the first and second measures lies in the fact that the figure of GNP includes only final products and does not take into consideration the nature of production in the intermediate stages in the production processes. The ratio of governmental output to GNP is useful if the purpose is to measure the extent of the government's role in controlling allocation of resources among the production of various final products. If this is the purpose, the fact that the government has the highway built is the important consideration, and the fact that most of the maerials and equipment are privately produced is not relevant.

If the aim, however, is a measure which will show the relative scope of the public and private sectors in total production activity, the third measure, the ratios of value added, is the most satisfactory. By determining the value added by governmental production, as compared to the value added by private production, a satisfactory measure of relative production activities is obtained. In the case of highways, therefore, the governmental sector's contribution would be the difference between the total expenditures made and the amounts paid for materials, equipment, and contractors' fees. In other words, the amount would be the sum of the actual factor payments made directly by the government and thus would be equal to income originating in the governmental sector of the economy. In practice, only income-originating data are available on an annual basis and thus are used. In 1961, about 13 per cent of all income originated in the governmental sector in the United States.

### Other Measures of the Size of the Governmental Sector

Several other possible measures of the governmental sphere of activities and trends in it have been explored at length in a National Bureau of Economic Research study.[4] One measure is that of government employment; in 1962, total civilian government employment amounted to 14 per cent of the total labor force, and combined civilian and military personnel to 18 per cent. Figures of relative capital investment of government and private sectors are not available, although estimates have been made; a 1946 estimate indicated that governmental assets exclusive of military and highway installations constituted 20 per cent of total capital assets.

### The Causes of the Real Increase in Government Expenditures

Governments spend more money today than they did twenty-five or fifty years ago because they perform more functions and carry them on at

[4] See S. Fabricant, *The Trend of Government Activity in the United States since 1900* (New York: National Bureau of Economic Research, 1952).

higher levels. Apart from the effects of price and population changes, the most important single factor has been the existence of the two world wars during the period and unsettled international relations since 1945. One third of all government expenditures are made for purposes related to national defense. Veterans' aid, interest on the war debt, and foreign aid programs are direct products of the wars. But in addition, costs of conducting war itself increased greatly during the war periods; even in the relatively peaceful period after World War I, regular expenses for maintenance of the armed forces were far greater than they had been prior to the war. During World War II, research into the art of war resulted in extremely expensive tools of destruction, such as atomic weapons, improved tanks, planes, and bombsights, and the like, and postwar research has brought missiles and other weapons. As a consequence, even if we reduced the armed forces personnel to 1929 levels, defense costs would be far greater than they were at that time.

The second major cause of the increase consists of a complex of factors which led to the introduction of the various welfare programs designed to increase the economic well-being of certain groups in the economy. In part, these programs have been due to a gradual change in the attitude of society toward the responsibility of government in assisting those unable to provide themselves an adequate level of living. In part, the depression of the thirties accentuated the trend by increasing the problem of poverty and by transferring control of the governments to groups more sympathetic to welfare activities. Increased urbanization and greater longevity have raised the percentage of the population needing assistance from governments. Finally, the organization of groups of persons using political means to obtain additional government assistance has played a part. The Townsend clubs and other old people's organizations had much influence on the establishment of an old-age pension program in the United States, and the political strength of the farm groups has been an important factor responsible for various forms of farm aid.

Thirdly, the desire for better standards of performance of many government activities has led to greater expenditures.[5] In part, this desire was a reflection of generally higher living standards; when people are able to afford better homes, they also insist on better school buildings. Technological changes have played a major part; the coming of the automobile alone, for example, made better roads imperative. Since roads could not

[5] The importance of this factor is indicated by the studies of relative per capita expenditures by state; there is a very high correlation between per capita personal income by state and per capita state expenditure (see Fabricant, *op. cit.*, chap. vi).

be satisfactorily provided by private enterprise, the governments built them. Expenditures for highways have accounted for a major part of the growth in state and provincial expenditure.

Increased recognition of the indirect social benefits of various activities of government has likewise led to an extension of expenditures. Realization of the gains from providing two additional years of school for those not attending four-year colleges has led to a widespread junior college movement in some states. Recognition of the gains from conservation of national resources and development of recreational facilities has brought an expansion of these activities. The increased complexity of the economy and the tendency of monopoly elements to develop have led to

TABLE 2

| Country | Reported Tax Collections as a Percentage of GNP, 1958 |
| --- | --- |
| United States | 25 |
| Canada | 22 |
| Sweden | 30 |
| Great Britain | 29 |
| Luxembourg | 27 |
| Germany | 24 |
| Belgium | 24 |
| Norway | 24 |
| France | 22 |
| Denmark | 22 |
| The Netherlands | 21 |
| Austria | 21 |
| Finland | 21 |
| Eire | 21 |
| Italy | 20 |
| Spain | 18 |
| Portugal | 15 |
| Rhodesia | 14 |
| Ghana | 13 |
| Kenya | 12 |
| Uganda | 11 |
| Nigeria | 9 |
| Tanganyika | 9 |

SOURCE: Statistical yearbooks and similar documents of the various countries; United Nations, *Yearbook of National Accounts Statistics*. Taxes of all levels of government are included as far as possible.

governmental regulatory activities and, in some cases, to government operation of production. The fact that an increasing percentage of the population dwells in urban areas makes it necessary for governments to provide many services, such as water supply, fire protection, and sewage disposal, that persons took care of themselves or did without when they were country dwellers.

It is sometimes charged that much of the increase has been due to increased graft, inefficiency, "empire building," and multiplication of unnecessary government bureaus. Actually, this charge does not stand up under close scrutiny. In many ways, governmental personnel management and procurement policies have greatly improved over the years. Selection of employees on the basis of political favoritism and outright graft of public funds are much less common than in earlier years. It is easier to talk about duplicating functions and useless bureaus than it is to identify them.

### Comparative Data

Some indication of relative expenditure levels in various countries is provided by Table 2, which shows the tax collections as a percentage of gross national product. Tax data are more satisfactory to use than expenditure data, and give a good comparative picture of the expenditure situation. The figures for the United States and Canada are comparable to those of the European countries, being somewhat less than those of Sweden and Great Britain. The less developed countries have much lower ratios; note, for example, Spain and Portugal, and the African countries listed.

### APPENDIX

The Canadian federal expenditures by major purpose for the fiscal year 1962 are shown in Figure 9. Budgetary expenditures totaled $6.6 billion, while the combined budgetary and trust fund figure was $7.2 billion.

The major trust fund item is the old-age security fund; expenditures from this were included in the data from which Figure 9 was developed. As in the United States, national defense expenditures constituted the major item, but the percentage was relatively much less—37 per cent for the over-all category instead of 61 per cent (including trust fund expenditures in both cases). Welfare activities, including the old-age system, are of somewhat greater importance in Canada if farm aid is excluded, but less with the latter included, since the farm item is of much greater importance in the United States.

The provincial expenditure pattern (Fig. 10) is comparable to that in the United States, highways and other public works, however, outranking the others with 30 per cent, compared to 24 per cent for education and

28 per cent for health and welfare. The direct payment of old-age pensions by the Dominion government lessens the provincial expenditures for this purpose. On the other hand, the provinces have gone much farther in the direction of health and hospitalization activities than have the states.

The local government pattern (Fig. 11) is also comparable to that in the United States.

In the over-all picture, national defense occupies a much less important role than in the United States, whereas the health and welfare and transportation–natural resources categories are more important; highways and education are relatively similar (Fig. 12).

Of total governmental expenditures, including intergovernmental grants, federal expenditures constituted 52 per cent of the total in 1961; provincial expenditures, 27 per cent; and local expenditures, 21 per cent (Figs. 13 and 14). Expenditures from grants are included, as well as those of grants made. Provincial expenditures are thus more important than local, in contrast to the United States picture.

FIGURE 9

FEDERAL EXPENDITURES BY MAJOR PURPOSE,
CANADA, FISCAL YEAR 1962

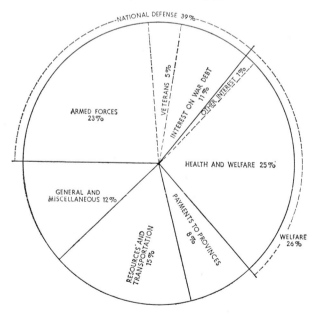

SOURCE: Canadian Tax Foundation, *National Finances, 1962–63.*

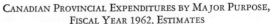

FIGURE 10

CANADIAN PROVINCIAL EXPENDITURES BY MAJOR PURPOSE,
FISCAL YEAR 1962, ESTIMATES

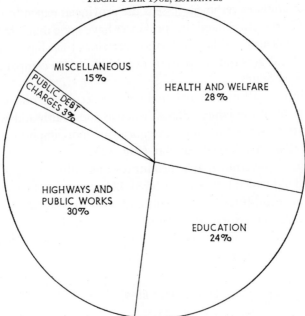

SOURCE: Canadian Tax Foundation, *Tax Memo. No. 29* (1962);
*Provincial Finances, 1962–63.*

FIGURE 11

LOCAL GOVERNMENT EXPENDITURES BY MAJOR PURPOSE,
CANADA, 1962

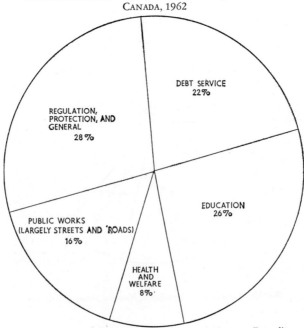

SOURCE: Canadian Tax Foundation, *Local Finances: Expenditures,*
Part II, 1962.

FIGURE 12

EXPENDITURES BY MAJOR PURPOSE, ALL LEVELS OF GOVERNMENT
COMBINED, CANADA, FISCAL YEAR 1959

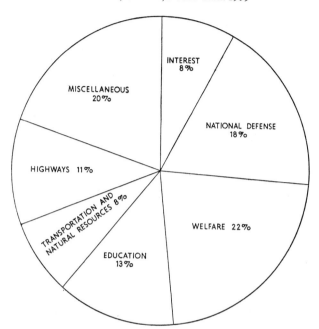

SOURCE: *Canada Yearbook, 1962.*

FIGURE 13

RELATIVE EXPENDITURES BY LEVEL OF GOVERNMENT,
CANADA, SELECTED YEARS, 1929–61

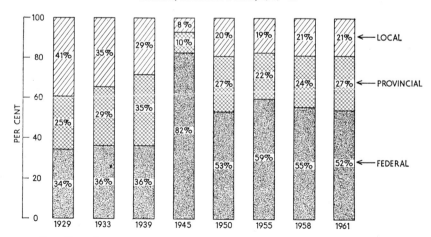

Expenditures from grants are included, as well as those from revenues raised by the particular level of government. As a result, the relative importance of provincial and local expenditures combined, compared to the federal expenditures, is somewhat exaggerated.

SOURCE: Various publications of Canada, Bureau of Statistics, and Canadian Tax Foundation, with some estimation involved in obtaining the results.

Total government expenditures constituted 32 per cent of GNP in 1961 (Fig. 15); the income originating in the governmental sector was 9 per cent of the total.

FIGURE 14

TOTAL GOVERNMENT EXPENDITURES BY LEVEL OF
GOVERNMENT, CANADA, 1929–61

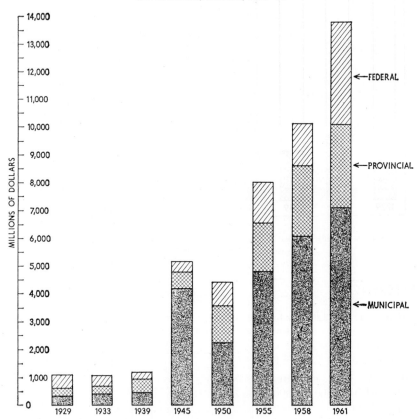

Expenditures from intergovernmental receipts are included in figures of grantor governments only. The figures are thus not directly comparable with those in Figure 13.

SOURCE: *Canada Yearbook;* other publications of Canada, Bureau of Statistics; and Canadian Tax Foundation.

FIGURE 15

RATIO OF GOVERNMENT EXPENDITURES TO GROSS NATIONAL
PRODUCT, CANADA, SELECTED YEARS, 1929–61

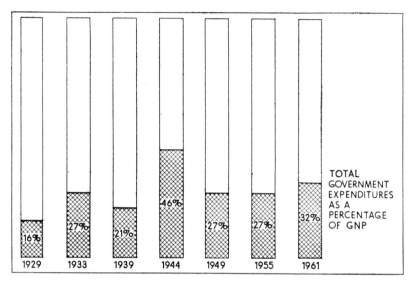

SOURCE: Canada, *National Accounts: Income and Expenditures,* various years.

# REFERENCES

FABRICANT, S. *The Trend of Government Activity in the United States since
1900.* New York: National Bureau of Economic Research, 1952.

A detailed study of various measures of change in the relative importance
of government activity, by level of government and by function.

MUSGRAVE, R. A., and CULBERTSON, J. M. "The Growth of Public Expenditures
in the United States, 1890–1948," *National Tax Journal,* Vol. VI (June, 1953),
pp. 97–115.

A careful survey of changes in expenditures by function over the last fifty
years.

BEROLZHEIMER, J. "Influences Shaping Expenditures for Operation of State and
Local Governments," *Bulletin of the National Tax Association,* Vol. XXXII
(March, April, May, 1947), pp. 170–77, 213–19, 237–44, respectively.

A study of the forces affecting state and local expenditures and the causes of
differences in expenditures in different states.

KENDRICK, M. S. *A Century and a Half of Federal Expenditures.* New York:
National Bureau of Economic Research, 1955.

JOINT ECONOMIC COMMITTEE. *Federal Expenditure Policy for Economic Growth
and Stability,* Part I. Washington, D.C.: U.S. Government Printing Office, 1957.

Several papers on expenditure trends.

CURRENT EXPENDITURE DATA

U.S. BUREAU OF THE BUDGET. *The Federal Budget in Brief* (annual).
A statement of federal expenditures for major purposes in current years.

*Budget of the United States Government for the Fiscal Year* (annual).
The budget document itself.

U.S. TREASURY DEPARTMENT. *Treasury Bulletin* (monthly).
Current expenditure data.

U.S. DEPARTMENT OF COMMERCE, BUREAU OF THE CENSUS. *Revised Summary of State Government Finances, 1942–1950; Compendium of State Government Finances* (annual); *Summary of State Government Finances* (annual) (a preliminary version of the previous series); *Large City Finances* (annual); *Compendium of City Government Finances* (annual); *Summary of Government Finances* (annual); *Government Finances* (annual).

TAX FOUNDATION. *Facts and Figures on Government Finance.* New York (periodic).

CANADIAN TAX FOUNDATION. *The National Finances* (annual); and *Canadian Fiscal Facts*, 1957, and Supplement, 1958.

CANADA, BUREAU OF STATISTICS. *Financial Statistics of Provincial Governments* (annual); *Financial Statistics of Municipal Governments* (annual).

———. *Canada Yearbook* (annual).

CANADA. *Budget Papers* (presented annually to Parliament).

# THE ROLE OF BUDGET
SYSTEMS IN SHAPING
EXPENDITURE LEVELS

*Chapter*
*4*

The actual determination of the extent to which various governmental programs are undertaken and extended is made in two basic steps: (1) the passage of legislation providing for particular programs (or in some fields, especially national defense, the making of commitments by the executive action), and (2) the enactment of specific appropriations for various activities. In modern governmental structures the process of appropriations is encompassed in operation of the budgetary system of the government.

## Responsibilities of Executive and Legislative Bodies

The task of determining the levels of governmental activities and expenditures rests in practice partly with the executive branch of government and partly with the legislative branch, the exact role of each being influenced greatly by the general structure of the governmental system. In all cases, however, the executive branch of government plays an important role. Many proposals for extensions (or contractions) of governmental activities originate with this branch, and in some fields, especially national defense, the actions of the executive essentially commit the legislative branch of government to the financing of certain activities. In most governments today, the recommendations for specific amounts to be spent on various activities originate with the executive, and in large measure are accepted by the legislative body.

On the other hand, a basic principle of democratic government requires that appropriations be made only by the legislative branch, which has final control over both the extension of activities and the precise sums to be spent, as well as the taxes to be collected. Furthermore, the executive branch, in making activity and budget recommendations, is inevitably influenced by its estimate of what the legislative branch will accept.

To a very limited extent, particularly in some states and in New England villages, decisions on expenditure policies are made by the people themselves, through voting on initiative and referendum measures and participation in town meetings.

## THE NATURE OF BUDGET SYSTEMS

A budget, in the general sense of the term, is a financial plan for a specified period of time. A governmental budget, therefore, is a statement of proposed expenditures and expected revenues for the coming period, together with data of actual expenditures and revenues for current and past periods.

Governmental budget systems originated in Great Britain; as early as 1822 the Chancellor presented to Parliament a complete statement of finances and the government's financial plan, and some vestiges of budgeting were to be found in even earlier years. In the United States, budget systems first developed at the municipal level as an element in the general movement shortly after 1900 to reform municipal government and increase popular control. The federal government for many years lacked any systematic budgetary system, Congress acting independently upon expenditure measures for various purposes, with little reference to revenues. Two factors perpetuated this chaotic system: the surplus of revenues relative to expenditures, which made careful reviewing of expenditures unnecessary, and the traditional hostility of Congress toward any change which would increase the role of the executive branch in the determination of policy. However, pressures to control expenditures and improve efficiency developed after 1900. In 1912 the Commission on Economy and Efficiency appointed by President Taft in 1909 recommended the establishment of a budget system. Not until 1921, however, was such a system actually established. Meanwhile, the states and additional municipal governments introduced budgetary systems.

The Canadian budget system dates back to the time of confederation in 1867, when the already well-developed British system was carried over.

### Responsibility for Preparation of the Budget and the Budget Cycle

The exact budgetary practices vary from country to country, and even among the various units within a country. But the cycle, or sequence of events of the operation of the budget system, has certain common steps. The first is that of *preparation* and *submission* of the budget. Typically, this task rests with the executive branch of government; the responsibility is almost always placed upon the chief executive, who in turn has the assistance of a staff established for the purpose. But the initial figures must originate with the various operating agencies; the task of the budget agency and the chief executive is largely that of co-ordination and evaluation of the requests of various agencies in terms of the over-all governmental program, together with the sponsoring of new activities. When the budget document is complete, it is submitted, together with an accompanying summary message which contains recommendations for major changes in various activities, to the legislative body. The establishment of a budget system is significant in itself for the over-all role of the chief executive in the governmental structure, since he is given specific responsibility for the development and presentation of a unified program of activities.

Exception to the role of executive responsibility is found in a few states and many local governments, in which the task of budget preparation is placed in the hands of an agency of the legislative body itself, typically a committee set up for this purpose.

The second step is the *enactment* by the legislative body of appropriations measures based upon the budget. This step may involve extensive review by committees and the making of numerous changes in the recommendations, as in the United States, or mere debate and ratification in unchanged fashion, as is typical in Great Britain and Canada.

The third step is *execution* of the budget by the executive branch, with the making of expenditures by the various agencies under supervision by the central budget agency and the chief executive.

The final step is *audit,* usually performed by an agency independent of the chief executive. Audit is concerned primarily with review of the legality of expenditures made in conformity with appropriations legislation.

## THE BUDGET SYSTEM IN THE UNITED STATES

### The Federal Budget Cycle

In the United States federal budgetary system, responsibility for preparation of the budget is placed upon the President. In practice, the President's role is limited to major policy questions relating to expansion or contraction of activities, and a general review of proposed expenditures. The detailed work involved in the preparation of the budget is carried out by the Bureau of the Budget, an independent agency directly responsible to the President.

The steps in the budget cycle can most easily be presented in outline form:

A.  Preparation.

1. In April of the year preceding the particular budget year (for example, April, 1963, for the 1963–64 fiscal year), each agency commences preliminary work on its provisional budget estimate.

2. In May the Bureau of the Budget requests the preliminary estimates.

3. In June the Bureau of the Budget and the President and his advisers determine the general policy to be followed with respect to new programs and general expenditure levels, in light of economic conditions and other features of the current situation. Departments are then notified of provisional expenditure maxima and the general policies to be followed (for example, *status quo*, retrenchment, etc.) and asked to file their requests.

4. During July and August, each department develops its requests in some detail, together with supporting evidence, and submits these to the Bureau of the Budget. Within the department the requests are built up from various agencies and reviewed and co-ordinated by the higher officials of the department.

5. From September to November the requests are reviewed by the Bureau of the Budget in light of general policy, with hearings involving personnel of the various agencies.

6. In November and December the final budget document is compiled and reviewed by the President, and the summary budget message is prepared.

7. In January the budget is submitted to Congress, together with the budget message.

B.  Enactment.

1. The budget is referred to the House Appropriations Committee. Its various segments are then examined in great detail by the subcommittees of this committee. Close contact is maintained between these subcommittees and the agencies whose expenditures are involved.

2. Following action by the subcommittees, the appropriations measures (of which there are several) are acted upon (usually with little change) by the committee as a whole, and then by the House (usually also with little change). The same procedure is followed in the Senate, although with less detailed examination, and there is a traditional tendency to restore cuts made by the House. In case of disagreements a conference committee works out a compromise.

3. The appropriations measures go to the President for his signature or veto.

C.   Execution.

    1. The funds appropriated are released to the agencies by the Bureau of the Budget, usually with allotments made by quarter of the year.

    2. Expenditures are made by the agencies in conformance with the appropriations legislation. The appropriations are made by agency, but usually not spelled out in great detail with respect to use within the agency, although the latter is expected to follow the pattern indicated in the respective budget items.

    3. Checks are written by the disbursing officer of the agency, and payment is made through the Treasury.

D.   Audit. A post-audit system is employed, with audit by the General Accounting Office to insure that expenditures are made in conformance with the legislation. The office is headed by the Comptroller General, responsible only to Congress.

The budget document itself contains over two thousand pages, specifying proposed use of the requested funds in great detail. To an increasing extent the budget is organized on a performance basis, as explained in a subsequent section, but with expenditures broken down in detail by object (materials, manpower, etc.). Data are given for three years: the past year, the estimate for the current year, and the requested figure for the coming year. Revenue data, prepared by the Treasury, are included, on the basis of existing taxes and tax rates, but most of the volume relates to expenditures. The President's detailed recommendations for tax changes are not included in the budget message, but in a separate subsequent message.

### State and Local Budget Systems

The budget systems of the states are much the same as those of the federal government, except that they are set up for biennial periods. In most states the responsibility for preparation of the budget rests with the governor, who has a staff to assist him with the task. The tendency to earmark certain tax revenues for specific purposes, which is very widespread in some states, lessens the flexibility of budget preparation and enactment. Legislative action is similar to that of Congress; in some states, substantial debate and change in the governor's budget occurs, while in others the budget is typically accepted with little change. In Illinois a budgetary commission made up of members of both houses of the legislature reviews the budget in great detail, and its recommendations are usually accepted by the legislature with little debate. The budget systems of large cities are similar to those of the states, except that frequently the mayor has little responsibility for the preparation of the budget. This tendency is particularly marked in smaller cities and other local governmental units, with the exception of ones using the city manager form of government, which typically place full responsibility for preparation of the budget on the city manager.

### Administrative versus Cash Budgets

A distinction must be made, particularly with the United States federal budget, between the usual or administrative budget and the cash budget, and between gross and net totals in the former. The administrative budget is the usual budget as presented to Congress, and does not include the receipts and expenditures of the government trust funds, such as those for social security, highways, and other purposes. The totals of revenues and expenditures, therefore, exclude these items.

The cash budget, on the other hand, shows the actual cash payments to and from the government during the year (including, however, only the net figures of government commercial enterprises). Thus the cash receipts of the trust funds are included, as well as the cash outlays from them. So long as the trust funds are obtaining receipts in excess of expenditures, the deficit in the cash budget will be less (or the surplus greater) than that of the administrative budget. The cash budget, which has been stressed by the Committee for Economic Development, is of particular use for analyzing the effects upon the economy of governmental activities.

In the administrative budget the totals of revenues and expenditures most frequently employed are figures which include only the net earnings or losses of government commercial enterprises, such as TVA, the post office, etc. However, the budget document and the budget summaries also indicate gross revenues and expenditure figures, which include the total receipts and expenditures of the commercial enterprises. In recent years the gross figures have been about $14 billion greater than the net figures.

A distinction must be made between authorizations and expenditures. It is impossible to obtain exact correlation of amounts actually spent by agencies during a period with the authorizations for expenditure, because of the inevitable time lags in ordering and paying for goods and services. As a consequence, expenditures during one fiscal year are being made in part from authorizations extended in past periods, and authorizations made in the current period will in part be utilized in subsequent periods. Normally, at the federal level, once an obligation is incurred, payment may be charged against the respective appropriation within a two-year period. However, in recent years in the field of national defense, in order to permit long-range planning, Congress has provided authorizations over relatively long periods for particular purposes.

## ATTAINMENT OF SATISFACTORY BUDGETING

The budget system has two primary functions: program review and management control. Program review seeks to develop a balanced over-all program of governmental activities, with adequate comparison of the gains from various alternatives in order to permit attainment of optimum levels of various expenditures. Much of the work in program development must be done at the level of the operating departments, which have the greatest knowledge of the problems and of the need for changes in activities and expenditures. But unfortunately, these agencies are not in a position to balance needs for their activities against those for others, or against costs. This balancing is done to some extent at higher echelons within the departments; but in large measure, it can be done only by the central budget agency, by the chief executive and his advisers, and, in the United States, by the legislative bodies. These groups know less about the specific needs for particular lines of activities, but they are in a position to balance, in a rough sort of way, the various needs against each other and against costs.

Management control seeks to attain optimum efficiency in the performance of the functions. The level of government spending depends, of course, not only upon the scope and extent of various functions performed, but also upon the efficiency with which these have been performed. As with program development, the persons in the best position to increase efficiency are those in direct control of the conduct of particular activities. But these persons often lack incentive to do so, or knowledge of how to do it, or they may have definite preference for certain lines of action contrary to the efficiency goal, particularly that of building as large an "empire" under their own domain as possible. Thus, higher levels in the budgetary system must seek to attain greater efficiency in operation at the lower levels, a task which is not easy to perform. By comparison of costs and results, and study of relative personnel and materials requirements, the central budget agency is able to unearth some inefficiencies, and by intensive and continuing management studies can accomplish more. In practice, the accomplishments have not been spectacular. Congress—spesifically the appropriations subcommittees in the House—frequently try to unearth inefficiencies, but with little over-all success. Both the Bureau of the Budget and Congress are inclined to use the same method of increasing efficiency, that of squeezing the agencies by reducing their appropriations in order to force them to economize. But the results of this approach are frequently the cutting of activities, not the improvement of efficiency. In general, far too little has been done in the way of providing incentives toward greater efficiency at the departmental level. This is admittedly a difficult task, but more attention could well be given to this approach and less to the squeezing technique, which has not proven to be effective.

### Budget Structure

The effectiveness of the budget system is obviously influenced by the manner in which the budget document itself is established. Traditionally, the budgets have been established on the basis of agency, since appropriations are made on this basis, with breakdown, in substantial detail, in terms of objects purchased (materials, equipment, manpower, etc.). Summaries are frequently given in terms of major function (national defense) cutting across departmental lines. The object basis is most suitable for purposes of execution, audit, and Congressional interference with administrative discretion, but it does not provide suitable information for the central budget agency and legislative bodies for intelligent weighing of expenditure alternatives.

In the last two decades, substantial interest has developed in the *performance* approach to budget organization, whereby emphasis is placed upon the objectives to be accomplished, rather than upon the items purchased, as such. The budget is organized on the basis of various programs and activities to be carried on; and in turn, each program is broken down on the basis of the performance of the agencies involved in its accomplishment, in such a manner as to facilitate measure of performance and ascertainment of cost. Information about objects acquired is presented in terms of their use in accomplishing particular programs, not with respect to the objects themselves, per se. Thus, for example, at the municipal level, the portion of the budget relating to expanditure on streets is organized in terms of miles of streets to be paved, to be repaired, etc., rather than in terms of tons of gravel and barrels of cement purchased, number of men hired, etc., as such; data on these items are presented in terms of their use in the paving of a certain mileage of streets, etc.

One basic problem which arises with performance budgeting is that of measuring the units of end product. This is not difficult with some types of activity (removal of dead elm trees, paving of streets, etc.), but is virtually impossible with others, such as operation of the police department.

With the latter type of function, the performance must be measured in terms of extent of conduct of the activity, such as man-hours of patrol duty, etc., which is, of course, only a poor substitute for the actual measurement of results.

Performance budgeting in the United States is largely the outgrowth of recommendations of the Hoover Commission on governmental reorganization.[1] Substantial progress has been made in reformulating portions of the federal budget into a performance basis; and in recent years, extensive use has been made of this approach by municipal governments.

The performance approach offers several advantages. By concentrating on the task to be done, it provides an important tool of executive management. It facilitates the expression of cost of performing various activities on a per unit basis, and thus allows a more satisfactory comparison of cost and output and measure of efficiency. It allows more intelligent action by the central budget agency by reducing unimportant detail and stressing the job to be done and the cost of doing it, and it facilitates legislative review of the budget proposals by emphasizing the programs to be carried out, and permitting a more satisfactory comparison of benefits and costs of various activities. Obviously, there are limitations, particularly that of measuring the output of various types of activities, but in general the development has been a major step in the direction of improved budgetary procedures.

### The Handling of Special Problems

Several problems arise in budgeting for which completely satisfactory solutions are difficult to find.

*Separate Capital Budgets.* Traditionally, governments have treated capital outlays and current expenditures in much the same manner, including both elements in total figures, and considering the budget surplus or deficit to be the difference between total revenues and the sum of current and capital expenditures. As a consequence, no depreciation charges have been established, and no record is kept of the total value of capital assets. The only exception to this rule has been with some commercial enterprises operated by governments. In recent decades, however, there have been two general types of departures, for entirely different reasons.

The first is illustrated by the practice of the Scandinavian countries, particularly Sweden, which have set up separate capital budgets. Steps in this direction were first taken for the purpose of more logical presentation

---

[1] See Commission on Organization of the Executive Branch of the Government, *Task Force Report: Fiscal, Budgeting and Accounting Activities* (Washington, D.C., 1949). Some use of performance budgeting was made prior to this report.

of budget data, but general adoption of the system resulted from the desire of the governments to facilitate the incurring of deficits for purposes of fiscal policy in periods of depression, particularly during the 1930's. By separating the capital expenditures from current ones, emphasis upon balance was directed to the current budget alone and a deficit in the overall budget justified on the ground that the debt incurred for capital outlay was offset by the increased value of the government's assets. After 1940 the divided budget came to be regarded in large measure as a device for facilitating long-range capital investment planning in the interests of economic stability. In no sense did the policy lead to financial irresponsibility and continued over-all deficits, as it might in the hands of governments less responsible than those of the Scandinavian countries.[2]

The second case of separation of capital outlays is to be found in many American cities. There are several reasons for this policy. In the first place, capital outlays are usually the chief source of increase in local expenditures, the items which give rise to the major problems of municipal finance and require the most careful weighing of alternatives, since the demands typically exceed the potential financing. Closely related is the fact that many types of local capital outlays cannot be established on a year-to-year basis, but require careful long-range planning, unlike other local activities. Finally, municipalities frequently resort to borrowing for such purposes, unlike the federal government and the states, whereas there are substantial legal and practical limitations on their ability to borrow for current purposes.

*Trust Funds.* A second problem relates to budgetary treatment of trust funds, to which specific revenues are assigned, and expenditures from which are designated for particular purposes. The establishment of trust funds excludes budgetary control over the activities involved; as a consequence, there is a tendency to exclude the funds from the budget document itself. The United States federal government is a particular offender in this practice; the revenues and expenditures of the old-age annuity and related social security funds and the highway trust fund are excluded from the budget. As a result, the budget totals do not give an accurate measure of the over-all role of the government in the economy, nor of trends in the size of the governmental sector of the economy. The earmarking of revenues for particular purposes does not necessitate the exclusion of the figures from the budget, even though the amounts involved are not subject to budgetary control.

*Government Commercial Enterprises.* Budgetary treatment of gov-

---

[2] See the article by F. M. Marx, "The Divided Budget in Scandinavian Practice," *National Tax Journal*, Vol. VIII (June, 1955), pp. 186–200.

ernmental commercial enterprises, such as public utilities, varies widely among governments and even within particular budgetary structures. The treatment is influenced to some extent by the type of organizational structure employed. Some enterprises, like the post office, are treated as ordinary governmental units and are subject to exactly the same budgetary treatment as other agencies. Others are established as government corporations, such as the Tennessee Valley Authority or the Canadian National Railways, while still others, especially outside the United States, are ordinary stock companies controlled by governments (the Panama Railroad provides an example). A basic problem arises in the budgetary treatment of these enterprises, namely, the need for giving the management of the enterprise substantial flexibility, and at the same time insuring general governmental control over policy. An enterprise of this type does not fit readily into the usual budget framework, partly because its expenditures vary with the volume of business revenues, and partly because greater flexibility is needed to adapt to changing conditions. Rigid budgetary control is also less necessary because of the partial market test of efficiency. On the other hand, it is desirable that major policies of the enterprise, particularly relating to investment, be made to conform with general governmental policy. Excessive autonomy can result in determination of policy without regard to governmental wishes, a charge often levied against the Ontario Hydro Electric system in the days of Sir Adam Beck.

In the United States the federal government corporations enjoyed a very high degree of freedom until change in the basic legislation in 1945. Since that time, such corporations have been required to submit their budgets just like regular agencies, and these are included in the budget, although only the net deficit or surplus is included in the budgetary totals. Usual budgetary review is exercised only over their administrative expenditures and capital outlays, and the appropriations for these agencies likewise control only these aspects, all enterprise revenue in general being available for program operation. This situation contrasts sharply with that of the postal system, which is subject to strict budgetary control, and does not actually receive the revenues from its operations, a situation which has probably restricted the attainment of maximum efficiency.

The municipal utilities likewise enjoy some freedom from usual budget control. The extreme case of autonomy is to be found in the public authorities established in the state governments in recent years, particularly for the operation of toll highways. These are usually completely free of budgetary control, the state governments having no financial responsibility for their deficits, and their profits being used solely for purposes related to their activities. There have been several reasons for the establishment of these autonomous units: the desire to avoid constitutional debt limits and to escape other legal restrictions on the activities performed by strictly governmental units, the notion that political influences can be avoided, and the possibility of overlapping the boundaries of basic governmental units. The authority form of organization has useful purposes, but the need for flexibility does not require complete escape from all controls by the state governments.[3]

### The Problem of Flexibility

One inherent problem of financial management for all types of governmental units is that of maintaining adequate flexibility for the operating agencies, and at the same time insuring control over expenditures. The extent to which flexibility can be obtained is influenced in large measure by the degree of detail in appropriations legislation. If the legislative body insists on substantial detail, agencies may have difficulties in meeting changing conditions, and will experience deficits for some purposes and surpluses for others. Congress has changed its policy on the question of detail a number of times over the years. In general, in recent years, apart from the tendency to prohibit the spending of sums in excess of specified amounts for particular purposes, the acts are much less detailed than the budget itself; agencies thus have substantial leeway, but are expected to keep in line with budget details so far as is feasible. The size of the unit (bureau, department, etc.) for which appropriations are made is also significant for flexibility; Congress has in general been unwilling to make lump sum appropriations by large unit.

Regardless of the precise nature of the appropriations legislation, inevitably some units will run out of funds prior to the end of the fiscal year. Occasionally, especially in the past, this has been a result of poor management, a practice which budget allotments by quarter and establishment of reserves is designed to check. Regardless of the care in management of funds, however, agencies will often run out of funds due to no fault of their own, when the demands for services which they are committed to supply rise, or the costs of labor and materials go up. Thus, certain commitments have been made for the paying of grants to the states for old-age pensions; if the number of persons drawing such pensions increases, budget appropriations will prove to be inadequate.

Three principal techniques are employed to meet the deficiency problem. The first is that of enactment of deficiency appropriations measures, providing supplementary funds. This practice has been very common in

[3] Note the papers in the section "The Authority Device in Present Fiscal Systems," *Proceedings of the National Tax Association for 1957*, pp. 257–97.

the history of federal finance, and every year Congress is called upon to pass measures of this type. These frequently receive little attention or careful study; one of the few instances in which there has been much general notice of the practice arose in the spring of 1957, when Congress balked at providing the Post Office Department with requested deficiency funds, and a sharp temporary curtailment of mail service followed. Extensive use of deficiency measures can of course lead to a breakdown in the whole process of orderly budgeting, and can promote carelessness in the making of expenditures by the departments. On the other hand, some action of this type is necessary. The practice is much less common at the state level, largely because a special session of the legislature would usually be required.

The second method is the establishment of a contingency fund which the chief executive can use to meet the needs of agencies experiencing shortages. This is most common at the state level, about half of the states following the practice. Congress has been unwilling to provide such a fund, such emergency funds as are established being usable for specific purposes only.

The third method is the transfer of funds by the chief executive from agencies having surpluses to those needing additional funds. Traditionally, at all levels of government in the United States, legislative bodies have been reluctant to permit this type of transfer; as a result, the practice is confined almost entirely to transfers from one purpose to another within an agency receiving a lump sum appropriation.

## MERITS AND LIMITATIONS OF THE BUDGET SYSTEMS

The advantages of a budget system are so great that little elaboration is required. The systems not only permit an orderly review of expenditures for various purposes by higher echelons of administration, but they also facilitate a more rational review of proposed levels of activities and a more satisfactory balancing of needs for additional expenditures for various purposes by legislative bodies. They likewise facilitate review of efficiency of operation. At both executive and legislative levels, they permit a consideration of the over-all balance of revenues and expenditures, which is of particular importance in light of increased attention to the effects upon the economy of government revenues and expenditures and the deliberate use of fiscal policy. However, the use of a budget system does not eliminate the inherent obstacles in the path of obtaining optimum levels of government expenditures discussed in Chapter 2; it can only increase the extent to which the obstacles are overcome. There remain the inherent problems of estimating social benefits and social costs, which, for many activities, involve significant subjective elements. Likewise, regardless of the budgetary procedures employed, the task of attaining maximum efficiency in operations is a very difficult one.

### Defects in the U.S. Federal Budget System

Several intensive studies have been made of the federal budget system in recent years, including those of the Hoover Commission and of the Committee for Economic Development. These studies have called attention to various difficulties with the system, which will be summarized briefly:

1. Inadequate correlation of basic legislation and budgetary action on the part of Congress. The enactment of the legislation essentially commits Congress to expenditure of various sums, but it typically undertaken without consideration of needs for funds for alternative purposes.

2. The excessive quantity of detail in the budget, which complicates the task of both the Bureau of the Budget and Congress, while at the same time contributing nothing to intelligent budget action. The emphasis on detail slows down the process of preparing the budget and, more seriously, tends to obscure the more important considerations. The budget document typically gives inadequate description of the major activities of government and the relationship of costs and benefits.

3. The failure in Congress to give adequate attention to the relative needs for funds for various functions; despite the budget, the expenditures for each activity are considered in isolation. This is largely because key decisions are made by the subcommittees of the Appropriations Committee, each dealing with only one type of activity, with little over-all review by the committees themselves, or by Congress as a body, which acts on a series of separate appropriations measures.

4. The failure of Congress to consider adequately the relationships between expenditures and revenues. Tax changes are considered by different committees from those which handle appropriations.

5. The tendency of the Congressional subcommittees to give excessive attention to details, all of which they cannot possibly review, to the neglect of major policy considerations. Emphasis on detail frequently leads to unintelligent action, to the detriment of conduct of the activities involved.

6. The failure to provide review of performance of the agencies once the year is over, at either executive or Congressional levels, and the limited accomplishments in the direction of attaining greater over-all efficiency of operation. Little positive action has been taken to provide

incentives toward greater efficiency or assistance in attaining it. Both the Bureau of the Budget and Congress are inclined to try to force efficiency by squeezing down the appropriations; the net effect of this activity is in many cases merely a reduction in the level of functions performed. There is no systematic process for review of the actual conduct of the activities of the agencies once the year is over.

### Avenues of Reform

Various possible paths of reform have been explored and to a limited degree carried into effect.

1. *The Development of the Performance Budget*.[4]  As noted earlier in the chapter, the introduction of additional performance budgeting on the basis of the Hoover Commission recommendation has constituted a major step in the direction of making the information in the budget more intelligible and useful. But this reform has by no means been fully carried out.

2. *Reduction in Budget Detail.*  Arthur Smithies, in a study for the Committee for Economic Development, particular emphasized the need for reduction in detail in the budget, in an effort to simplify the document, reduce the time necessary for its preparation, and concentrate the attention of the Bureau of the Budget and Congress on major issues of policy rather than details. On the other hand, more information explaining and justifying the various programs, analyzing their cost, and relating costs and benefits would be included. It is not important for Congress to consider how much an agency spends for paper clips, but rather the results of the performance of its functions and an explanation of need for expansion or contraction of them. Greater attention to major elements would allow better review of appropriations by the committee as a whole, with better balancing of alternatives.

3. *Other Efforts to Obtain Greater Co-ordination of Congressional Action.*  Various other proposals have been made to increase the degree of over-all co-ordination, and some have been attempted. In 1946, Congress provided for the establishment of a legislative budget system, whereby a joint committee of the two houses would agree early in the season upon an over-all ceiling for expenditures, to serve as the basis for evaluating appropriations for specific purposes. In part, the move was inspired by a desire to increase Congressional control over expenditures and to bring reductions in total expenditures. The procedure proved to be a complete failure.

---

[4] See R. N. McKean, "Evaluating Alternative Expenditure Programs," in *Public Finances* (Princeton: Princeton University Press for National Bureau of Economic Research, 1961), pp. 337–64.

In 1947 the two houses could not agree on a ceiling, while in 1948 they ignored the ceiling which they had established. No further use was made of the device, largely because it was recognized that an over-all ceiling cannot be set early in the year.

A second attempted reform was the use of the omnibus appropriations bill, starting in 1949, incorporating all appropriations measures in a single bill in an effort to obtain more co-ordinated action. This proved to be a source of excessive delay and was unpopular with committee members because it concentrated power in the hands of the committee chairman; as a consequence, it was abandoned.

Another proposal has been made a number of times, namely, the establishment of a Joint Committee on the Budget, made up of members of both houses, which would be given a substantial staff in order to examine the budget proposals in detail. This change might permit more intelligent action on the part of Congress and permit a better over-all review, but it would result in substantial duplication of work with the Bureau of the Budget. Smithies argues that this essentially would constitute a step in the wrong direction, the need being for less, not more, Congressional examination of detail, with greater emphasis on major programs.

A proposal related in form but very different in substance is that for the establishment of a Joint Budget Policy Conference made up of influential members of both houses, which would review over-all totals and the relationship of revenues and expenditures, but not attempt to examine budget details.

4. *Establishment of a Performance Review, Together with a System of Management Review.* Each agency would make an annual detailed report to the President of its activities, which would in turn be presented to Congress prior to action upon the budget. Increased attention would be given, in conjunction with this review, to the use of detailed management studies of particular units by an agency set up for this purpose, with an eye to obtaining increased efficiency in operation. At the same time, maximum effort would be directed toward increasing incentives in the operating agencies for maximum efficiency.

### The Incremental Approach[5]

It may be argued that the philosophy of an over-all budgetary review, balancing all activities against one another, and against over-all revenues, is completely impractical. The magnitude of the task of decision making

---

[5] See C. E. Lindblom, "Decision Making in Taxation and Expenditures," in *Public Finances* (Princeton: Princeton University Press for National Bureau of Economic Research, 1961).

is so complex as to be beyond the capacities of human problem solving, and the nature of many government activities is such that defining of objectives is difficult. Instead, argues Lindblom, decision making must be incremental, dealing with changes in each activity at the margin. By this means the task becomes manageable, and disagreements over general aims and policies are in large measure avoided. Co-ordination of various activities comes about not by deliberate action, but by what may be called partisan mutual adjustment. Various interested groups, inside government and out, bring pressure to bear with regard to particular expenditures. This procedure allows the ideas of any major group of people to be presented, and weighs interests of various groups. A decision is reached on the basis of the relative strength of these groups. The implications are obvious: Congress should not attempt to deal with appropriation measures as a whole, but only with separate measures spaced over the year to allow more careful examination.

While, in fact, most budget making must be largely incremental, some attempt at over-all review in terms of an assumed set of goals—technically, an assumed welfare function—should contribute to a more balanced picture. Partisan mutual adjustment suffers from one inherent limitation that manifests itself very clearly in present-day budgeting: Those activities which have the support of strong pressure groups (e.g., farm aid) are extended much farther than those which lack organized support but are very significant to the economy (food and drug administration, etc., for example).

## REFORMS IN GOVERNMENTAL STRUCTURE

The attainment of greater efficiency in government depends in part upon careful management control and review of performance, as noted in previous sections. But it depends also upon the structure of governmental organization. Present structures in many cases developed a century or more ago under very different conditions, and unfortunately have undergone little modernization in terms of changing circumstances. Resistance to change is frequently strong, partly merely because of inertia, partly because of vested interests of present officeholders. While a detailed analysis of the problem of governmental reorganization is beyond the scope of this volume, a few general observations can be made.

1. *Reorganization of Governmental Structures, to Eliminate Excessive Small Governmental Units.* The township and the small school district, with its one-room school, are, for the most part, carry-overs from the "horse and buggy" days, when transportation difficulties necessitated

small units in rural areas for the performance of local government functions. Today, these functions can be performed more efficiently and cheaply by larger units, at least of county size. In many states, even the counties are too small for efficient operation, and consolidation would greatly improve administrative effectiveness.[6] Actually, such reorganizations are very difficult to carry through, because of local pride in existing institutions and the desire of officeholders to retain their jobs. In the states of the Far West, where townships have never existed as separate governmental organizations, local government functions very well without them, and no thought is given to the creation of them. But in the eastern states, which have had township organizations from the earliest days, any attempt to eliminate them or transfer their functions to the counties meets with strenuous opposition.

In the field of education, pressure from the states has brought extensive consolidation of school districts.

2. *Internal Reorganization within Governments to Insure More Satisfactory Lines of Responsibility.* Particularly at the state and local levels in the United States, the failure to centralize administrative responsibility in the chief executive has been a continuing source of difficulty. Governors, for example, typically have no control at all over many of the departments headed by elected officials; yet presumably, they have the responsibility for effective operation of the state government as a whole. In other cases the failure to establish a satisfactory pyramidal type of governmental structure has resulted in so many individuals being responsible to one man that effective supervision is impossible. In still other cases, effective control has been checked by failure to establish clear lines of responsibility. Closely related have been the tendency toward development of duplication of work by different agencies and the failure to allocate functions upon a logical basis.

The establishment of a logical administrative structure is a task which cannot be accomplished overnight, and a structure which is logical under certain conditions may be completely illogical under others. Although much has been done over the years to improve organization, many opportunities remain.

3. *Personnel Policies.* The selection and management of personnel are major tasks in efficient operation of government. In earlier years, individuals were selected largely on the basis of political considerations and retained their jobs only so long as their friends were in power. Civil service systems, at the federal and state level and in larger cities, have greatly im-

---

[6] See, for example, the study by the Nevada Legislative Reference Service, *County Reorganization in Nevada.*

proved personnel management. Selection on a political basis, except at top levels, has largely ended in many jurisdictions, and security of tenure has been attained.

While civil service on the whole raises the level of efficiency and eliminates the most flagrant abuses of the older system, it by no means insures effective use of personnel. The protection against arbitrary discharge can easily become protection against discharge for inefficiency. A flexible policy that insures reasonable security without protecting the inefficient is difficult to attain. At the federal level the civil service system has resulted in so much red tape and delay that a recent investigating commission recommended greater autonomy for the agencies in the hiring of personnel.

The establishment of effective supervisory policies to insure maximum utilization of the services of personnel is likewise difficult. Provision of incentive to higher personnel to carry through effective supervision is not easy, and attainment of maximum output from workers is difficult, especially in the face of civil service rules which hamper discharge or demotion for poor work.

Maintenance of qualified personnel at the top levels has always been restricted by inadequate salaries, relative to responsibilities and to opportunities in the business world. Typically, lower level government employees, particularly in the United States, are well paid compared to those of private enterprise, while top officials are poorly paid. A long-standing tradition against high salaries for government officials has made it very difficult to retain top-quality men in government jobs. The cost of providing salaries comparable to those of business would be small in terms of the total expenditure figures and would contribute greatly to effective governmental operation.

4. *Financial Control and Purchasing Policies.* Adequate accounting standards and techniques to insure financial responsibility are essential for effective administration, and great improvements have been made over the years, especially at the federal level. The problem of government purchasing is a highly technical one; purchasing methods have been lax in many cases and in others subject to such rigid rules that maximum economy could not be attained. The armed forces have been particularly criticized in the past for their procurement methods and have been giving serious attention to improved techniques.

*Summary.* The maintenance of maximum efficiency in government operation, to insure that the best results may be attained for the outlay made, is a task requiring constant vigilance and improvement. Inevitably, savings can be made along many lines. The Commission on Organization of the Executive Branch of the Government, headed by ex-President Hoover, in its report to Congress in 1949, recommended improved organization and management techniques which could allow substantial savings to the federal government, in addition to the gains from better standards of performance. Some of these have been carried into effect.

## THE POSSIBILITY OF REDUCTIONS IN GOVERNMENT EXPENDITURES

At the present time, governmental activities have reached such a level that the ratio of government expenditures to national income is a substantial one. A sizable fraction of incomes received by individuals is paid out as taxes, and a significant part of real income consists of governmental services. As a consequence, the questions of the desirability, possibility, and likelihood of reductions in governmental expenditures are of great concern.

To the extent that expenditures can be reduced through greater efficiency in the performance of governmental functions, the reduction is obviously desirable in the interests of optimum economic welfare. But as suggested above, the possibility and likelihood of substantial gains along these lines are not great.

Beyond these limited gains, expenditure reductions can be made possible only by curtailment of governmental functions. Significant reductions at the federal level can take place only if spending for national defense and related items is curtailed; this, in turn, will be possible only if international relations improve over the years. Some curtailment could be made in the welfare field, but strong pressures exist for the expansion, rather than reduction, of these activities. At the state level, curtailment of highway, welfare, and educational activities would be required if total expenditures were to be lowered materially, and at the local level a reduction in educational activities would be necessary. There is grave doubt that the community as a whole desires a reduction in these services. The opposite point of view has been widely publicized by J. K. Galbraith; in *The Affluent Society,* he argues that there has developed a serious unbalance, especially at the local government level, with a relative excess of private sector goods and a serious shortage of public sector goods necessary for the full employment of private sector output. People buy expensive cars, but the streets on which they drive them may be barely passable.

On any objective basis, it is impossible, for reasons previously outlined, to say whether the various expenditures are "too high" or "too low," although a few activities would seem to convey very few benefits to society. On the whole, however, it would appear—given the state of international relations—that the majority of the present activities are desired by society and that wholesale curtailment of functions would be contrary to the accepted goals of the community.

It is important, however, that the sacrifices be kept in mind, as well as the benefits; the governmental activities, with full employment, are necessarily undertaken at the expense of private production. We cannot have more schools, highways, and national defense without reduced output of the private sector of the economy. We cannot give increased old-age pensions and other transfer grants without bringing about lower standards of living for the remainder of the population, given full employment. On the other hand, as technological improvements bring increased general standards of living, greater demands on the governmental sector are to be expected and justified. In all likelihood, the long upward trend of governmental activities will continue, apart from reductions in defense spending which could be made if a general lessening of world tensions could be attained. But every effort must be made to avoid increases which contribute little in the way of benefits to society as a whole, to balance relative benefits and sacrifices, and to maintain vigilance to insure maximum efficiency in the conduct of the performance of the functions of government.

## APPENDIX

### *The Parliamentary Budget System—Canada*[7]

The Canadian budgetary system, modeled very closely after that of Great Britain, provides an excellent illustration of the operation of a budget system under the parliamentary form of government.

Responsibility for preparation of the budget rests with the government, that is, with the cabinet, and specifically with the Minister of Finance. The Minister asks for specific requests from the operating departments during the fall of the year preceding the budget year, the requests being examined in detail and assembled by the Estimates Branch of the Department of Finance. The estimates are then submitted to the Treasury Board, made up of the Minister of Finance and five other ministers, which reviews them with substantial care and attempts to balance the various alternative paths of expenditures. Following Treasury Board action, the cabinet as a whole reviews the estimates.

The estimates of expenditures are presented to Parliament by the

[7] See J. H. Perry, *Taxation in Canada* (3d ed.; Toronto: University of Toronto Press, 1961), chaps. 15, 16; and H. R. Balls, "How to Read a Government Budget," *Canadian Tax Journal*, Vol. VII (September-October, 1959), pp. 379–85.

government—technically by the Governor General; by terms of the British North America Act, following British tradition, only a member of the government may introduce a tax or expenditure measure. The proposals are then subject to debate in the House of Commons, technically sitting as a Committee of Supply. Many detailed questions are asked, which are answered by the minister involved. Members can move for decreases, but never for increases. Various parts of the estimates are approved by resolution; and subsequently, an appropriations bill involving the budget estimates is enacted. In general, the proposals will be enacted in unchanged form, unless the debate leads the government to make adjustments. Failure of Parliament to approve the proposals would result in downfall of the government and, usually, a new election.

Some weeks after the submission of the estimates, the Minister of Finance presents the budget papers, usually on the day before the budget speech. These contain a summary of economic conditions and a preliminary report on the government's financial operations for the year. Next, the Minister presents the budget speech, which contains a survey of the government's finances, together with proposed tax changes. Little is said about expenditures, since these have been given in the estimate. This speech is awaited with great interest because the proposals are almost certain to be adopted (as long as the government has a majority), and great efforts are taken to maintain secrecy of the proposals prior to the date of the budget speech. Many tax changes proposed take effect immediately, as in Great Britain, subject, of course, to subsequent approval by Parliament. The House of Commons, sitting as the Committee of Ways and Means, examines and debates the tax proposals. Resolutions dealing with various provisions, stated in general terms, are proposed and passed; and eventually, amending bills, changing existing legislation, are enacted.

The basic difference from United States procedure is obvious; the executive branch has full responsibility for preparation of the budget, and the budget as prepared is certain to be enacted with little or no change as long as the existing government remains in power. The House of Commons, as such, merely debates the proposals; it cannot in practice reject or modify them without causing the defeat of the government. But it must be remembered that the cabinet is chosen by Parliament and directly responsible to it, in contrast to the situation in the United States. Parliament essentially delegates to the cabinet the task of determining expenditure and tax policy, and confines its own action to examination and debate. So long as it has confidence in the cabinet, the latter is certain that its decisions will be carried out.

The provincial budgetary systems are essentially the same as the federal system, except that they are less complex. Local governmental systems are simpler and more comparable to those of local governments in the United States, with responsibility for preparation of the estimates frequently placed upon the chief financial officer, usually the city treasurer, working in conjunction of the members of the council.

## The Relative Advantages of the Parliamentary Budgetary System

The budget system, without question, functions much more smoothly under the parliamentary form of government than under one characterized by separation of powers. The cabinet has the responsibility for formulation of the requests, and for balancing alternative needs, and expenditures and revenues. There is no possibility of special interest groups raising expenditures during parliamentary action, nor of reductions based on inadequate information, personal prejudices, "meat-axe" techniques, and the like. On the other hand, especially when the party in power has a strong majority and party discipline is vigorous, there is danger of inadequate considerations of the conflicting interests and estimates of the community about the benefits of various types of governmental activities. The decisions are made by a small group of persons without, in practice, adequate review. As a practical matter, the difference between this procedure and that in the United States is probably not as great as might appear, since the legislative review in the United States seldom involves major changes.

## REFERENCES

Two outstanding books have appeared in recent years in the field of budgeting:

BURKHEAD, J. *Government Budgeting*. New York: John Wiley & Sons, Inc., 1957.
  A detailed examination of budget systems and practices.

SMITHIES, A. *The Budgetary Process in the United States*. New York: McGraw-Hill Book Co., Inc., 1955.
  A detailed examination of federal budgetary procedure, and suggestions for reform, prepared for the Committee for Economic Development.

Significant contributions to the subject are also to be found in the following volume:

NATIONAL BUREAU OF ECONOMIC RESEARCH. *Public Finances*. Princeton: Princeton University Press, 1961.

Other works include:

BROWNE, V. J. *The Control of the Public Budget.* Washington, D.C.: Public Affairs Press, 1949.

COMMISSION ON ORGANIZATION OF THE EXECUTIVE BRANCH OF THE GOVERNMENT. *Task Force Report: Fiscal, Budgeting and Accounting Activities.* Washington, D.C., 1949.

*Proceedings of the National Tax Association for 1959*, pp. 267–320.

LANDERS, F. M., and HAMILTON, H. D. "A Survey of State Budget Agencies," *Public Finance*, Vol. VIII, No. 4 (1953), pp. 399–413.

MOSHER, F. C. *Program Budgeting.* Chicago: Public Administration Service, 1954.

McKEAN, R. N. *Efficiency in Government through Systems Analysis.* New York: John Wiley & Sons, Inc., 1958.

JOINT ECONOMIC COMMITTEE. *The Federal Budget as an Economic Document.* Washington, D.C.: U.S. Government Printing Office, 1962.

# PART II

Financing of Government Expenditures—

Introduction

| *Chapter* | THE FINANCING OF |
|---|---|
| *5* | GOVERNMENT EXPENDITURES |

In order to carry on their functions, governments must obtain the services of labor and other factor units and (except in a completely socialist economy) acquire goods produced by private business firms. Governments may simply take these services and goods by force, compelling persons to provide their resources without pay or for less than the current market prices. In earlier centuries, such practices were common; in later years, conquering armies followed the same procedure, and even present-day democracies draft men into the armed forces.

As a usual principle today, however, the taking of factor units by force is regarded as highly inequitable, and is resorted to only in extreme cases. The normal procedure is to obtain factor units and produced goods by paying for them at current market prices.[1] Accordingly, by some manner the government must obtain the funds necessary to make these payments.

## THE SOURCES OF GOVERNMENT REVENUES

### Sale of the Goods or Services

To a limited extent, governments sell the services produced to the users and thus finance the production of the services in the same manner as does private enterprise. The costs of various licensing activities and a portion of the costs of operation of the courts are financed by the charging of fees. The postal services, publicly produced electric, water, and transit service, toll bridges, and the like are financed by charges made against the users. Governments also obtain revenue from the sale of land and royalties from the lease of mineral rights on public land. In most instances, however, either governmental services are of such a character that they cannot

---

[1] Governments may in some instances, however, compel the factor owners to sell their factor units to the government under the powers of eminent domain. Thus a state may require property owners to sell their land for a highway right of way, but pays current market prices.

be sold to the users, or the sale basis is considered contrary to accepted standards of equity.

### Taxation

Taxation is the most common method of financing government activities. The services themselves are provided to the community without charge, and the necessary funds are collected by requiring persons to make compulsory payments to the government in accordance with some established criterion, such as property owned or income received. The payment of the tax does not in itself enable the taxpayer to receive any governmental services to which he would not otherwise be eligible. The basic distinction between taxes and the other sources of government revenues is the compulsory element involved; the individual has no choice in the matter if he is eligible for payment on the basis of the standards established.

### Borrowing

The third method—in a sense a provisional or temporary source—is the borrowing of money. Just as individuals or business firms may borrow in anticipation of other revenues, so may governments. It is ordinarily presumed that the money borrowed will eventually be repaid from other sources, although, in practice, this may not always be the case. Sovereign governments may repudiate their debt, or they may continue indefinitely to refund maturing debt by the sale of new issues. However, private borrowers may follow comparable procedures. While they cannot cancel debt, they may become unable to pay and go through bankruptcy proceedings, or they may reborrow to repay maturing obligations. Railroads traditionally have not attempted to eliminate debt completely. The justifications for borrowing will be analyzed in subsequent chapters.

### Printing of Paper Money

Governments may resort to the printing of paper money as a means of paying their bills. Governments, unlike individuals, have the power to create money and give it legal tender qualities, a sovereign right of governments in the same manner as the power to tax. This method is not substantially different from the borrowing of money from the central banking system, as will be explained in later chapters, since with this type of borrowing purchasing power is also essentially created. The printing of paper money is normally avoided as a source of revenue because its use is too easily abused. Once this method of financing is started, it is difficult to stop, and runaway inflation can easily result. Accordingly, any overt use of it produces adverse psychological reactions in the form of loss of confidence in the stability of the government.

### Intergovernmental Grants

Particular governments may receive revenue from other governments, in the form of grants-in-aid, block grants, and other types, as discussed in Chapter 24. From the standpoint of the governmental system as a whole, this is not a source of net revenue, since the money must initially be raised by other means.

The succeeding chapters will be devoted to an analysis of these various methods of financing. Principal attention will be given to taxation, because it is the most important source of revenue and because its compulsory nature results in greater potential economic effects and more complex problems. The remainder of this chapter will be devoted to a brief summary of constitutional provisions relating to government expenditures, taxation, and borrowing in the United States and Canada, and to the relative importance of various revenue sources.

## THE BASIC EXPENDITURE, TAXATION, AND BORROWING POWERS

The powers to make expenditures, to collect taxes, and to borrow constitute basic sovereign rights of governments, powers which sovereign governments have by the very fact of their existence. In a governmental structure such as that of Great Britain, with no formal written constitution, the powers are unlimited and may, theoretically at least, be used in any manner the government wishes. In countries such as the United States and Canada, however, which have written constitutions, certain restrictions upon the taxing powers of the governments have been placed in the constitutions. While these provisions are subject to change, they are binding on the legislative bodies so long as they stand. Furthermore, both the United States and Canada have federal governmental structures, with the basic powers divided between the national and state governments. As a result, the powers of each level of government are, of necessity, restricted in the field of taxation as well as other aspects of governmental activity.

### Expenditure Powers

The federal Constitution in the United States gives power to Congress to raise money to "pay the Debts and provide for the common Defence and general Welfare of the United States." This power has been interpreted very broadly by the courts, and only on very rare occasions has an expenditure been questioned—in general, only when it is financed by a particular earmarked tax. The major tax of this type held invalid was the processing tax of the original agricultural adjustment program, which was ruled invalid on the basis that the tax was levied for purposes other than the general welfare. So long as expenditures are made from the general revenues, the courts will not entertain suits over the purposes of the expenditures. Agencies can, of course, make expenditures only in conformity with the appropriations voted by Congress, a rule which is enforced by the General Accounting Office.

The situation with the states is somewhat different, however. While ordinarily the state courts will not question an expenditure on the basis of its purpose, there have been a few instances in which state expenditures have been held invalid on the principle that the purposes were not in conformity with the general welfare clauses of the state constitutions. In most cases, these have involved appropriations to undertake certain types of commercial activity.

On the whole, there are very few legal limitations on expenditure powers. The primary restrictions affect taxation.

## POWERS OF TAXATION—THE UNITED STATES FEDERAL GOVERNMENT

Section 8 of Article I of the Constitution gives Congress specific power to levy taxes: "The Congress shall have Power to lay and collect Taxes, Duties, Imposts, and Excises, to pay the Debts and provide for the common Defence and general Welfare of the United States; . . . ." This taxing power rests solely with Congress; taxes can never be imposed by act of an administrative agency. This power is subjected, however, to certain limitations.

### Specific Limitations

There are several limits on the taxing powers imposed by specific provisions in the clauses of the Constitution dealing with taxation.

1. *The Uniformity Clause.* Section 8 concludes with the statement: "but all Duties, Imposts and Excises shall be uniform throughout the United States." This section has been interpreted to mean that any federal tax regarded by the courts as an indirect tax shall be levied at a geographically uniform rate, the rate being the same in all states. In earlier years the

use of progressive rates was contested as a violation of the uniformity clause, but this argument was denied by the Supreme Court when it upheld the use of exemptions and progressive rates under the inheritance tax. The term *excise* has never been clearly defined by the courts. The various taxes on the sale of commodities, plus the death taxes and the original corporation income tax, have been held to be excises. The personal income tax has been held to be a direct tax.

2. *The Apportionment Clause.* Section 9 of Article I states: "No capitation, or other direct Tax shall be laid, unless in Proportion to the Census or Enumeration herein before directed to be taken." Under the terms of this provision the amounts to be collected from any tax interpreted to be direct would have to be apportioned among the states according to population rather than be collected at a uniform rate throughout the country. Thus, if $10 billion were to be collected from a property tax and 6 per cent of the population of the United States were in Illinois, the federal property tax rate in Illinois would be set at such a level that the amount collected in the state would amount to 6 per cent of $10 billion, or $600 million. Thus the federal tax rate would be high in states with low per capita wealth and low in states with high per capita wealth. Because such a provision is extremely inequitable, any tax interpreted to be a direct tax is effectively barred from federal use.

The primary difficulty was encountered with the attempt of the federal government to levy an income tax. The problem centered around the question of whether, at law, the income tax was direct or indirect. In 1872 the Civil War income tax was held to be indirect and thus valid. But portions of the income tax of 1894 were held to be direct and therefore unconstitutional, because the tax was not apportioned among the states according to population. As a consequence, the Sixteenth Amendment was enacted (1913). The amendment provides that "the Congress shall have power to lay and collect taxes on incomes, from whatever source derived, without apportionment among the several states, and without regard to any census or enumeration."

Thus, as the situation stands today, the federal government cannot levy a direct tax on property (including a capital levy or tax on net worth) without use of the hopelessly inequitable apportionment device. It is free, however, to tax income without apportionment.

3. *Exports.* Congress was denied the right to levy taxes on exports, because some of the colonies felt that Congress might destroy their important export business if it possessed the right to tax exports, and because of the dislike of this form of tax as used as an element of the mercantilist tax policies of Great Britain.

### Implied Restrictions

There are additional restrictions on the taxing power of Congress which have been implied from other portions of the Constitution.

1. *The Welfare Limitation.* As noted above, if a particular tax is interpreted by the courts to be levied for purposes other than the general welfare, it may be held invalid. Thus, in a very few instances, taxes were interpreted to be regulatory rather than revenue measures. This occurred with the special tax on industries using child labor and the processing tax of the Agricultural Adjustment Act. However, Congress has imposed other taxes with the primary aim of regulation which have been upheld by the courts.

2. *The "State Instrumentalities" Doctrine.* The Supreme Court long ago held that the basic division of power between federal and state governments required that each level of government be prevented from taxing the "instrumentalities"—the property, securities, and activities—of the other, to insure that the taxing power would not be used to weaken the powers of the other level of government. Thus the federal government has been denied the right to tax interest on state and local bonds, and sales to the states under federal excises. The attitude of the courts has shifted somewhat on the interpretation of this doctrine over the years. At one time, for example, Congress was not permitted to tax salaries of state employees, but the Supreme Court reversed its position on this question in 1938. It is possible that the interpretation of the taxation of interest might likewise be altered, but this cannot be ascertained unless Congress changes the law to make such interest taxable.

3. *The Due Process Requirement.* The federal government is prohibited from depriving persons of "life, liberty or property without due process of law." This provision prevents completely arbitrary classification for tax purposes and retroactive (past the current year) imposition of taxation, and it insures the right of appeal to the courts from the decisions of tax-collecting agencies.

In general, the taxing powers of Congress are, as a matter of fact, restricted only slightly. Apart from property and related taxes, there are virtually no barriers to the use of any form of taxation which Congress might conceivably desire to levy.

## THE TAXING POWERS OF THE STATES

The states, since they have all residual sovereign powers, possess complete powers of taxation without specific designation by the federal

Constitution. However, the Constitution does provide certain specific restrictions on their taxing power, and other limitations have arisen out of the interpretation of provisions of the Constitution not directly relating to taxation. In addition, the states have imposed limitations through their own constitutions on the taxing powers of their legislatures.

### Specific Federal Restrictions on the State Taxing Powers

The federal Constitution specifically prohibits use by the states of three types of taxes: (1) import duties, (2) export duties, and (3) tonnage duties (levies upon ships for the privilege of entering or leaving a port). These restrictions were designed to insure for the federal government complete power over foreign commerce. The framers of the Constitution realized that chaos would result if the individual states were permitted to control, via taxation, imports and exports, and that a unified country could be established only if the federal government had complete power over these activities.

### Implied Restrictions on the Taxing Power of the States

In addition, the courts have interpreted other provisions of the Constitution to limit the taxing powers of the states, in order to prevent infringement upon the various powers given the federal government or destruction of the federal system of government.

1. *Federal Instrumentalities.* In order to protect the powers of the federal government, the states (and their subdivisions) are denied the right to tax federal instrumentalities. Thus, property taxes may not be applied to federally owned property or federal securities, sales to the federal government may not be taxed under state sales and excise taxes, and the interest on federal bonds may not (under existing court interpretation) be subjected to state income taxes. The exact interpretation of the limitations, however, varies from time to time.

2. *The Due Process and Equal Protection Clauses.* The states, by provision of the Fourteenth Amendment, are prohibited from depriving persons of life, liberty, or property without due process of law. This prohibition insures the taxpayer the right of appeal to the courts from the action of tax administration agencies, and it protects against arbitrary procedures. In addition, it has been interpreted to mean that a state may apply a tax only within its territorial jurisdiction. In very rare instances the courts have held taxes to violate due process on the ground that they were con-

fiscatory but, in general, have taken the position that the question of the height of a tax is one within the discretion of the legislative body.

The Fourteenth Amendment also requires that no state shall "deny to any person within its jurisdiction the equal protection of the laws." This clause has been interpreted by the courts in such a manner as to invalidate some state taxes, such as certain ones on chain stores, on the basis of arbitrary classification and thus denial of equal protection. In practice, however, the courts will not interfere with classification unless it is extremely arbitrary.

3. *Discrimination against Citizens of Other States.* Closely related is the prohibition of discrimination against citizens of other states; residents and nonresidents must be treated equally. Thus, property owned by nonresidents cannot be taxed at a higher rate than that owned by residents. This provision applies only to citizens, not to corporations, and thus a state may apply heavier taxes to businesses incorporated outside the state than to those incorporated in the state.

4. *Interstate Commerce.*[2] Some of the most significant restrictions on state taxing powers arise out of interpretation of the clause of the Constitution which gives control over interstate commerce to the federal government. In no circumstances may tax legislation discriminate against interstate commerce; and in some instances, interstate transactions cannot be taxed at all, even in a nondiscriminatory manner. Thus, in effect, states cannot levy discriminatory taxes against goods brought into the state from other states, and thus essentially erect tariff barriers around themselves. They cannot directly tax interstate sales as such under sales or excise taxes, although they may apply use taxes to goods bought outside the state and brought in, at the same rate as the sales tax applying to sales within the state.

Businesses engaged in interstate commerce can be taxed on their gross receipts or net profits only if the total amounts are allocated on some reasonable basis. Serious problems are encountered in taxation of railroads because of their interstate character. The powers of the states to tax interstate motor carriers are considerably broader than over other interstate firms because of the states' proprietary interest in the highways.

5. *Miscellaneous Restrictions.* State taxation must not violate treaties made with other countries by the federal government. The states may not tax in such a manner as to impair contracts. For example, if they issue bonds free from state income tax, they cannot then apply their taxes to the interest on these bonds.

---

[2] An exhaustive study of this question is to be found in the October, 1960, issue of the *Virginia Law Review*, "A Symposium on State Taxation of Interstate Commerce."

*Summary.* In general, therefore, the states have very broad taxing powers. They are free to use any general type of tax they wish, except those on imports, exports, or interstate transactions. Court interpretations of the Constitution have restricted somewhat the exact scope and procedure of individual taxes, but they have not significantly reduced the taxes available for state use.

### Restrictions Imposed by State Constitutions

The state legislatures are subject, in the enactment of tax legislation, to the restrictions imposed by the state constitutions as well as by those of the federal Constitution. In earlier years, these restrictions were minor or nonexistent but were greatly extended during the latter part of the last century. As a result, today in most states the hands of the legislatures are tied to a very considerable extent. The exact degree varies widely, however. In a few states, they have complete freedom. In others, they may levy any type of tax they wish, subject to certain general requirements, such as uniformity of treatment. These uniformity clauses have been interpreted differently in various states, sometimes in such a way as to prevent the use of progressive taxation. Other legislatures are permitted to levy only certain specified types of taxes; and in a few states, such as Louisiana, the whole tax structure is virtually prescribed directly by the state constitution.

The actual significance of these restrictions depends to a very great extent upon the ease of amending the constitution. If amendment is relatively simple, as in California, the restrictions do not prevent readjustment in the tax structure. If amending is very difficult, as in Illinois, the tax structure may be essentially frozen for long periods. On the whole, the practice of freezing the powers of the legislature over tax matters is not desirable, because it interferes with adjustment of tax structures to meet changing revenue needs, conditions, and attitudes toward the desirability of various types of taxes.

### The Taxing Powers of the Local Governments

The local governments, as creations of the states, are subject to the same restrictions imposed by the federal Constitution as are the states themselves. Furthermore, they can levy only those taxes which are specifically authorized for them by the states, since they have no inherent taxing powers of their own.

The taxing powers of the localities may be established by provisions of the state constitution or, more commonly, by general state law. In other cases the powers are granted in the charters of the municipalities, the exact powers varying among different jurisdictions. In practice, virtually all local governments are given the right to levy property taxes; but many, such as school districts, townships, etc., have no other taxing powers. Cities are frequently given additional powers to impose various forms of license taxes and, in some cases, sales, excise, and income taxes.

## BORROWING POWERS

The right to borrow is a sovereign right of government. In the United States the federal government was given unlimited borrowing powers by the Constitution, while the states have this right inherently. In many states, however, the state constitutions have provided very substantial restrictions on the powers of the legislatures to borrow. The local governments have only such borrowing powers as are given to them by state constitutions and state law. The powers are usually restricted as to amounts which may be borrowed, and approval of bond issues by voters is often required.

Just as the federal and state governments have unlimited powers to borrow, so they have unlimited powers to cancel their debts if they wish. While the debts constitute contracts, the fact that sovereign governments cannot be sued without their own consent gives the bondholders no effective redress in case of default. Local governments do not have the power of repudiation, and court action can be taken to compel them to fulfill their obligations.

## THE PATTERNS OF FINANCING

A brief review of over-all financing by level of government in the United States will serve as a useful introduction to the analysis of revenue systems.

### Federal Government

In the fiscal year ended June 30, 1962, the federal government raised a total of $103 billion current revenue. General taxes yielded $85 billion; trust fund levies, $15 billion (mainly for highway and social security purposes); and nontax sources, $3 billion. The general revenue picture is illustrated in Figure 16, while Figure 16A shows the breakdown of general tax revenue by major source. The personal income tax yielded $50 billion, or 49 per cent of the total, and the corporate income tax $21 billion; thus the two together yielded about 70 per cent of total federal

FIGURE 16

FEDERAL GOVERNMENT REVENUES BY MAJOR SOURCE,
1962 FISCAL YEAR

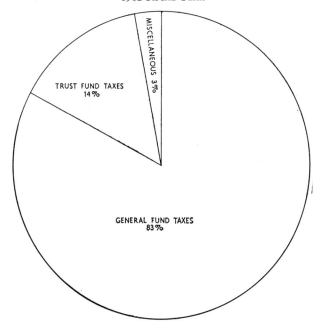

FIGURE 16A

FEDERAL GENERAL TAX REVENUES BY MAJOR TYPES
OF TAXES, 1962 FISCAL YEAR

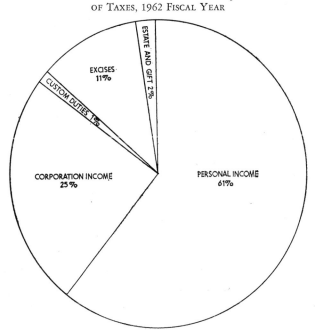

SOURCE: U.S. Treasury, *Treasury Bulletin*, August, 1962.

revenues, or 86 per cent of general tax revenue. Most of the remaining federal revenue is obtained from the excise taxes (about half of this sum being yielded by the liquor and tobacco taxes), with small amounts from the estate and gift taxes and the customs duties. The picture of federal taxation has changed materially over the years. Customs yielded the bulk of the revenue prior to the Civil War, and then shared with excises the dominant role until 1909. The corporation income tax was introduced in 1909 and the personal income tax in 1913, and these soon became the primary elements in the tax system. Excises, although raised sharply in World War II, never regained their previous dominance, and customs duties eventually became negligible in yield. Since 1942 the federal tax system has undergone very little basic modification.

### The States

Figure 17 shows the relative importance of various state revenue sources for the 1962 fiscal year, and Figure 17A gives a more detailed breakdown of state tax revenues. General taxes yielded $20 billion, or 52 per cent of the total; the other major source consisted of grants from the federal government, 18 per cent of the total.

State tax revenues are obtained from a greater diversity of levies than those of the federal government. The sales taxes yield 25 per cent of the total, and the gasoline tax 18 per cent, while the latter's companion in highway financing, the motor vehicle license fees, produce 8 per cent of the total. The two highway levies are used by all states, and the sales tax by 36 states, or 37, if the Indiana gross income tax is included. Income taxes are of lesser importance, the personal tax (35 states) yielding 13 per cent of the total, the corporate levy (37 states) 6 per cent. Liquor and tobacco levies bring in 9 per cent, and various special business taxes, primarily on public utilities and insurance companies, together with the severance taxes, yield 9 per cent. Death and property taxes are of minor importance revenue-wise. The states make little use of excises outside of those on liquor, tobacco, and gasoline. The state systems in general rely much more heavily on so-called "indirect" or commodity and business taxes than does the federal government.

The state systems have changed relatively little since 1940, but underwent substantial modification prior to that time. Traditionally, the states relied on the property tax, plus some minor levies, although they did experiment with income taxes at an early date. Gradually, the pressure of local governments on the property tax led most states to release this source to exclusive local use, and to develop income taxes (from 1911 on through the thirties) and sales taxes (particularly in the thirties). Meanwhile, first

FIGURE 17

STATE REVENUES BY MAJOR SOURCE, 1961 FISCAL YEAR

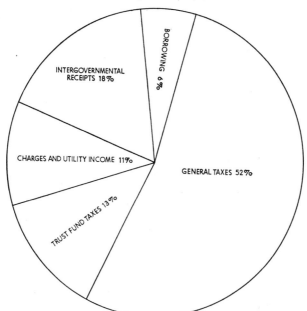

SOURCE: U.S. Department of Commerce, Bureau of the Census, *Compendium of State Government Finances in 1961.*

FIGURE 17A

STATE TAX REVENUE BY MAJOR TYPE OF TAX, 1961 FISCAL YEAR

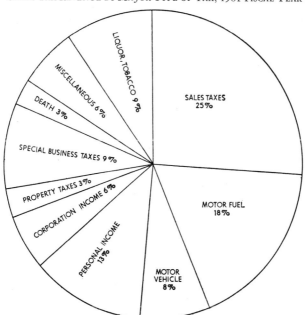

SOURCE: U.S. Department of Commerce, Bureau of the Census, *State Tax Collections in 1962.*

the motor vehicle license fee and then the gasoline tax (beginning in 1919) were introduced for highway finance purposes. In the last decade the only trends have been toward higher rates on various taxes, and introduction of additional sales taxes.

The over-all picture, of course, obscures somewhat the differences among the various states. Some rely much more heavily on the sales tax than others; Washington, West Virginia, Michigan, and Illinois, for example, get the great bulk of their revenue from this source. In contrast, New York and Oregon rely heavily upon income taxes. Several states, such as California, make substantial use of both types of levies. Only one state, Nebraska, has neither sales nor income taxes. Texas gets substantial revenue from severance taxes on petroleum products, and New Jersey from special business taxes. Nebraska alone still relies primarily on the property tax.

### The Local Governments

The local governments rely more heavily on nontax sources than other levels, in 1961 gaining more than half their revenue from such sources, as shown in Figure 18. Intergovernmental grants (mostly from the states) yielded 27 per cent, and various charges and utility revenues 24 per cent. Of the tax revenue (see Figure 18A), virtually all of general character, the property tax yielded 88 per cent (and all of the tax revenue of many local units). Continued property tax rate increases have led to growing pressure for other local taxes, and some money was obtained from sales taxes (particularly in Illinois, California, and New York) and income taxes (primarily in Ohio and Pennsylvania).

### The Over-all Picture

Combined federal, state, and local tax collection figures are, of course, greatly dominated by the federal element. In 1961 the federal government collected $77 billion in general taxes compared to the states' $19 billion and $20 billion for the local governments. Thus, in the over-all picture, as shown in Figure 19, income taxes (personal and corporate) yield about 57 per cent of the total. Second in importance is the property tax, which brings in 15 per cent; this is followed by the gasoline and motor vehicle levies with 6 per cent, the liquor and tobacco taxes with 6 per cent, and the other excises and special business taxes with 5 per cent. The sales taxes yielded 5 per cent and the death taxes 2 per cent.

If the social security payroll taxes are included and the totals revised accordingly, this type of levy yielded about 10 per cent of all tax revenue, and the other percentages are reduced accordingly.

FIGURE 18

LOCAL GOVERNMENT REVENUES BY MAJOR SOURCES, 1961

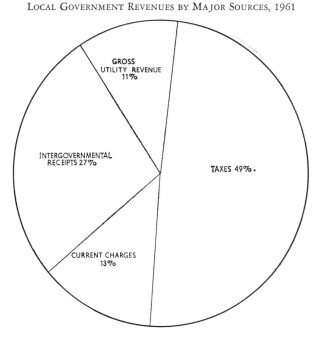

FIGURE 18A

LOCAL GOVERNMENT TAX REVENUE BY MAJOR SOURCES, 1961

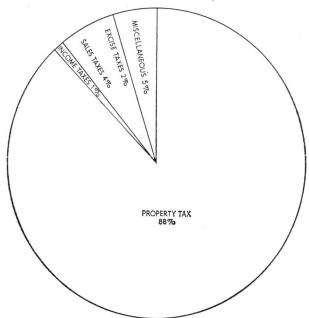

SOURCE: U.S. Department of Commerce, Bureau of the Census, *Summary of State Government Finances in 1961.*

FIGURE 19

FEDERAL, STATE, AND LOCAL TAX REVENUES BY MAJOR TYPE OF TAX, 1961

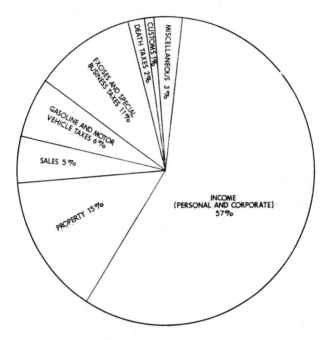

SOURCE: U.S. Department of Commerce, Bureau of the Census, *Summary of Government Finances in 1961.*

## APPENDIX—CANADA

### Expenditure and Taxing Powers

The basic division of powers between the Dominion government and the provinces is somewhat different from the situation in the United States. The provinces have only those powers specifically authorized by the constitution (the British North America Act), while the Dominion retains the residual powers.

*Expenditure Powers.* There are no constitutional restrictions on Dominion expenditure powers. The provinces, on the other hand, are limited to expenditures for "provincial purposes." This phrase has been interpreted broadly to include grants to the local governments and expenditures on provincially owned public utilities.

*The Federal Taxing Powers.* By the terms of the British North America Act the Dominion government was given unlimited taxing powers, being authorized to make laws relating to "the raising of money by any mode or system of taxation." The primary restriction is that against taxing provincial lands and property. This provision is generally interpreted to mean also that purchases by a province for governmental use cannot be taxed. Otherwise, there is no provincial instrumentalities doctrine. Interest on provincial bonds may be taxed. In addition, if a tax is levied for attainment of *ultra vires* purposes, rather than for revenue, it may be held invalid. Beyond these considerations the taxing powers are complete, and the restrictions are thus less significant than those in the United States.

*The Provincial Powers.* The powers of the provinces are more limited than those of the states. The provinces are given the right to levy only direct taxes, being prohibited from imposing indirect levies. In addition, the taxes must be levied for the purpose of "raising a revenue for provincial purposes."

Substantial difficulty has arisen over the years over the meaning of the term *indirect taxes*, particularly when the provinces came to require gasoline and sales tax revenue. In their usual form, these taxes are indirect, in terms of the definition formulated by John Stuart Mill and generally accepted by the Canadian courts, since they are ordinarily shifted from the taxpayer to the purchaser. By the guise of imposing these taxes on the consumer, the vendor being required to collect and remit the taxes as an agent of the province, the provinces have succeeded in making them acceptable as direct taxes in the eyes of the courts. Thus, in practice, the prohibition against indirect taxes has not been as significant as would first appear, but the provinces must take care to insure that commodity taxes are technically imposed upon the final consumer.

The taxing clause limits taxation to persons or property within the province. This clause has been interpreted very broadly; a person may be taxed on his entire income, for example, even though it is earned outside the province. Dominion companies, however, may be taxed only in a fashion nondiscriminatory as compared to other corporations. So far as property is concerned, only that with situs in the province may be taxed.

Taxes must be levied for the purpose of raising revenue; they are invalid if levied in order to gain control over activities which are not subject to provincial control.

In addition to the power to levy direct taxes, the provinces are authorized to impose "shop, saloon, tavern, auctioneer, and other licenses in order to the raising of revenue for provincial, local or municipal purposes." Only limited use is made of this power.

The provinces are not subject to a federal instrumentalities doctrine comparable to that in the United States, although they are not permitted to tax federal property or direct purchases by the federal government. Likewise, they are not subject to restrictions on taxation comparable to those arising out of the interstate commerce clause in the United States except in so far as they are prohibited from levying duties on the importation of goods from other provinces. They can, for example, tax an out-of-province purchaser on an article bought in the province for out-of-province delivery. Their power to compel out-of-province vendors to collect sales taxes for them is less than the power of the states in the United States.

*Local Governments.* As in the United States, the local governments have no inherent taxing powers, but only those which the provinces give them by terms of general laws or charters. The provinces may delegate to them any taxing powers which they themselves possess. The powers actually given are similar to those authorized local governments in the United States.

### The Canadian Tax System

In a general way the tax system of Canada is similar to that of the United States. But there are also a number of differences, particularly the greater reliance by the federal government on commodity taxes, the importance of intergovernmental payments at the federal-provincial level, and the greater over-all integration of the tax systems at the various levels. Figure 20 shows the major revenue source.

*Federal Revenues.* In 1962 the federal government obtained 80 per cent of its revenues from general taxes, 10 per cent from trust fund levies (supplements to the personal and corporate income taxes and the sales tax for the old-age fund), and 10 per cent from various charges, including the net profits of the post office. Of the general tax revenues, the personal income tax yielded 37 per cent and the corporate levy 23 per cent; thus the combined importance is much less than in the United States. By contrast, 15 per cent was obtained from the sales tax and 12 per cent from excises, even though the latter are far less numerous than they are in the United States. Customs duties are likewise far more productive, bringing in 10 per cent of the total, in reflection of the more important status of foreign trade in the Canadian economy. Successions duties are no more important than in the United States.

The Canadian tax system developed in much the same way as the American; early reliance on customs and excises gave way to income and sales taxation as the chief sources in the 1914–20 period. There has been basically little change for a decade, except a tendency to lower rates.

*Provincial Revenues.* The 1962 figures on provincial revenues are

FIGURE 20

CANADIAN GOVERNMENT REVENUES

Federal Revenues by
Major Sources, 1962

Provincial Revenues by
Major Sources, 1962

Federal Tax Revenues by
Major Type of Tax, 1962

Provincial Tax Revenues by
Major Type of Tax, 1962

SOURCE: Canadian Tax Foundation, *The National Finances, 1962–63;* and *Tax Memo. No. 29* (1962).

somewhat misleading because the smaller provinces participated in the tax rental agreements, whereas, for the most part, Ontario and Quebec did not; with the elimination of these agreements the figures will be substantially different in 1963 and later years. In any event, in 1962 the federal payments yielded 21 per cent of the total (but very much higher percentages in some provinces), and taxes 51 per cent. The motor fuel tax was the most important tax, followed by corporate income and general sales taxes.

*Local Governments.* No complete data on local governments are available for recent years. In 1959, 12 per cent of local revenues came from general grants, and 20 per cent from school grants; taxes yielded 61 per cent. The chief tax, the property levy, yielded about 90 per cent of local tax revenue. Municipal income taxes, once widely used, have all been eliminated. Municipal sales taxes are used in Quebec.

### Borrowing Powers

Both the Dominion and provincial governments have unlimited borrowing powers, and the provinces do not have the self-imposed restrictions on borrowing comparable to those of most states. As in the United States, however, the local governments have only such borrowing powers as are authorized by the provinces, and these are subject to restrictions of usage, amount, and the like. In Ontario and some other provinces, larger municipal bond issues require approval of a provincial board, a practice which is not common in the United States.

### REFERENCES

PERRY, J. H. *Taxation in Canada,* chap. viii. 3d ed. Toronto: University of Toronto Press, 1961.
  Limits on provincial taxing powers.
MACDONALD, V. C. "Taxation Powers in Canada," *Canadian Bar Review,* Vol. XVII (February, 1941), pp. 75–95.
  The best review of taxing powers in Canada.
RATNER, S. *American Taxation.* New York: W. W. Norton & Co., 1942.
  An excellent historical treatment of court interpretations of the federal taxing powers.
SHULTZ, W. J., and HARRISS, C. L. *American Public Finance,* chap. vii. 7th ed. New York: Prentice-Hall, Inc., 1959.
U.S. JOINT COMMITTEE ON INTERNAL REVENUE TAXATION. *The Taxing Power of the Federal and State Governments.* Washington, D.C.: U.S. Government Printing Office, 1936.
RATCHFORD, B. U. "Intergovernmental Tax Immunities in the United States," *National Tax Journal,* Vol. VI (December, 1953), pp. 305–32.

An excellent review of the question of restrictions on the taxation of government instrumentalities, stressing the changes in attitudes of the courts on the question.

CANADIAN TAX FOUNDATION. *Local Finance.* A series of memoranda, 1960–63.

Current data on revenues are to be found in the publications listed for expenditure data at the end of Chapter 3. See also:

U.S. DEPARTMENT OF COMMERCE, BUREAU OF THE CENSUS. *State Tax Collections* (annual).

# Chapter 6

# THE PRINCIPLES OF

# TAXATION

Most governmental activities, by virtue of their community benefits, must be financed by taxation rather than by sale to the users. Since these governmental services convey their benefits to the community as a whole, there is no possible way in which they can be divided into segments and sold. As explained in earlier chapters, it is this characteristic of certain activities which initially led governments to undertake them. In other cases the sale of the services, while technically possible, would be regarded as inequitable. When a government enters the welfare field, "sale" is meaningless, since no service is being rendered which could be sold.

Taxation, by definition, involves compulsion; the taxpayers are required to make certain payments, regardless of their individual dispositions in the matter. In a democracy, at least, the taxes will not be imposed unless they meet with the approval of a majority of the representatives of the people. But once they are levied, no individual has the choice of paying or not paying. Because of this compulsory aspect, the collection of taxes may have very significant effects upon the behavior of individuals and the functioning of the economy, which must be taken into consideration in the selection of taxes if the tax structure is not to interfere with the attainment of the economic goals of society. Furthermore, if the goals of society are to be realized, the burden of the taxes must be distributed among various persons in a manner consistent with these goals.

## THE DEVELOPMENT AND NATURE OF THE PRINCIPLES OF TAXATION

The principles of taxation, that is, the appropriate criteria to be employed in the development and evaluation of the tax structure, have received attention from the earliest days of the study of public finance.

Mercantilists and physiocrats advanced doctrines of tax principles; Adam Smith developed his famous canons of taxation, widely quoted down to the present day. McCulloch, Say, and John Stuart Mill dealt with the question at length, as did Edgeworth, Dalton, and Pigou at a somewhat later date. Recent decades have seen relatively little progress, most studies in public finance merely repeating the older doctrines. The development of the principles of taxation is essentially an application of the theory of economic welfare, and further progress must depend in large measure upon advancements in this theory. At the present time, the state of welfare theory is such that it can do little more than assist in the development of very broad principles of taxation. It can provide only limited aid in giving these principles sufficient content that they may serve as a useful guide to policy.

The principles of taxation can be selected only in terms of the goals which are accepted as the appropriate objectives of the economic system. As indicated in Chapter 1, the consensus of opinion in present-day society is considered to regard four goals as of paramount importance for optimum economic welfare: (1) maximum freedom of choice, consistent with the welfare of others; (2) optimum standards of living, in terms of available resources and techniques, and in the light of consumer and factor-owner preferences; (3) an optimum rate of economic growth; and (4) a distribution of income in conformity with the standards of equity currently accepted by society.

In terms of these goals, three major principles or desirable characteristics of the tax system have come to be generally accepted:

1. *Economic Effects.* The tax structure must be established in such a way as to avoid interference with the attainment of the optimum allocation and use of resources and, where possible, to assist in the attainment of the optimum.

2. *Equity.* The distribution of burden of the tax must conform with the pattern of income distribution regarded as the optimum by the consensus of opinion in contemporary society.

3. *Minimum Costs of Collection and Compliance, Consistent with Effective Enforcement.* This rule requires that taxes be established in such a manner as to minimize the real costs of collection, in terms of resources required to collect the taxes and to comply with the tax laws on the part of the taxpayers, as well as in terms of the direct inconvenience caused the taxpayers in the payment of the tax.

Each of these requirements will be discussed at greater length in the succeeding sections.

## ECONOMIC EFFECTS

If taxation is not to interfere with the attainment of optimum standards of living, the taxes must not alter the choices or courses of action on the part of members of society, except in those cases in which interference will allow closer attainment of the goal. Taxes must, of course, reduce total spending; this is their basic economic function, since inflation will result if private spending is not reduced by an amount equivalent to government spending in periods of full employment. But so long as the unregulated functioning of the economy will allow the attainment of optimum output, relative to consumer and factor-owner preferences, in the private sector of the economy, taxes will reduce levels of living below the optimum if they alter consumer or factor-owner choices.

On the other hand, when automatic attainment of the optimum adjustment is not realized, appropriate selection of taxes may allow closer attainment of this adjustment. Thus, for example, if the consumption of liquor becomes excessive relative to the optimum because real costs to society due to drunkenness are not borne by producers of the products and thus do not appear in the prices, a special tax on this product, designed to reduce consumption and production to optimum levels, is justifiable in terms of the goal of optimum adjustment of production. On the whole, since the free market system, despite its limitations, is regarded as the preferred form of economic organization, it can be presumed that any change in behavior produced by taxes is undesirable in terms of optimum living standards, unless it can be demonstrated in each particular case that the changed behavior due to the tax actually allows closer attainment of the accepted goals.

### Unneutral Effects of Taxes

There are several ways in which taxes may alter human behavior. In the first place, they may affect consumer choice. If, for example, a tax is levied on the sale of one commodity but not on that of another, the relative prices of the two are altered, and a readjustment in relative consumer purchases will result. A given dollar expenditure by the consumer will no longer acquire the same quantities of particular factor units regardless of the good purchased, and thus optimum allocation of factors in terms of consumer wants cannot be attained, if the adjustment was the optimum one in the absence of the tax. If the optimum was not attained, because of monopoly influences in the production of one of the goods, for example, the tax may bring the adjustment more in line with the optimum, if it is levied on the good whose output is relatively excessive. On the other hand, if it is levied on the other, the maladjustment will be aggravated. It is assumed thus far that the income distribution is that regarded as optimum; this question will be discussed in the subsequent section.

Taxation may also result in an alteration of the decisions of factor owners with respect to the quantity of factor units which they make available to producers. So far as workers are concerned, taxes may alter the relative desirability of work and leisure. A tax which applies to the return from work but does not affect leisure increases the advantage of the latter as compared to the former. But for those persons who have a relatively inelastic demand for goods and an elastic demand for leisure, the tax will actually result in their working more instead of less. If persons work less, national income is reduced; if they work more, it is increased. In any event, the disturbing of the previous relationship may be charged with loss in economic welfare, under the assumption that the original balance struck between work and leisure was the optimum one. An exception is to be found in underdeveloped economies, in which an increased supply of man-hours is regarded as desirable in order to increase the rate of economic growth. Likewise, various forms of taxes may alter the relative choices of occupations and affect the allocation of labor and other resources among occupations. These problems will be discussed in the chapters dealing with income taxation.

On the other hand, if factor-owner decisions are considered to be contrary to the best interests of society, taxes may be justifiably used as an instrument to bring them into conformity with the accepted standards. If, for example, society wishes to encourage persons to enter the labor market when they would prefer to remain idle, appropriate adjustments in taxes may produce this result.

Finally, taxes may alter the choice of methods of production. For example, taxation may affect the relative advantages of various techniques and cause a shifting-away from those which would allow maximum efficiency in the use of resources. Taxation may affect the relative output of consumption goods and capital goods; if the previous rate of capital formation was that regarded by society as the optimum, a loss in economic welfare results. If a higher rate is regarded as desirable, tax effects which produce this result are advantageous. Taxes may lessen the incentives to maintain maximum efficiency, a charge frequently made against excess profits taxation. On the other hand, if optimum efficiency is not being attained, it is possible that taxes may result in increased effort to gain efficiency.

In the discussion of particular taxes in succeeding chapters, an attempt will be made to discover the extent to which various taxes are likely to have nonneutral effects and to evaluate these in terms of economic welfare. It is not an easy task, and the answers possible on the basis of the present state of knowledge are by no means satisfactory. In some instances the economic effects are very difficult to trace. In other cases the evaluation in terms of economic welfare is not simple. On the whole, virtually all taxes have some nonneutral effects. The necessary aim in the establishment of the tax system is the minimization of the adverse effects, consistent with the attainment of the other desired goals.

## EQUITY IN THE DISTRIBUTION OF BURDEN

The second requirement is a distribution of tax burden among various persons which conforms with accepted standards of equity. Determination of equity in taxation must rest upon value judgments relating to the over-all pattern of income distribution which is regarded as desirable; the most equitable tax system is that which is most closely in conformity with the standards of equity in the distribution of real income which are accepted as most desirable by the consensus of opinion in society. Further discussion of the question of equity in taxation must therefore involve largely an exploration of general social attitudes toward the nature of an equitable distribution.

### The Two Aspects of the Problem of Equity

The problem of equity has two major aspects. The first is that of proper treatment of persons in like circumstances, while the second is the desirable relative treatment of persons in unlike circumstances. For the first problem the rule of "equal treatment of equals," that persons in the same circumstances should be taxed to the same extent, is almost universally accepted, although the question of defining "like circumstances" remains. The answer to the second aspect of the problem is much more complex. The rule that persons who are in some sense "better off" than others should pay more taxes is likewise generally accepted. But the determination of what constitutes "better off" and of the appropriate relative burdens on persons in different circumstances is one upon which the consensus of opinion is much less clear. These questions require careful exploration.

There are two general approaches to the problem of equity in taxation which have dominated thinking and policy determination in the field; these are essentially alternative routes to the definition of "like circumstances" and to the establishment of suitable bases for measuring differences in circumstances and determination of appropriate relative treatment of persons in varying circumstances. The first principle is that of benefit, under which equity is interpreted to require equal treatment of persons who receive equal benefits from government activities and adjustment of taxes on persons who receive different benefits in proportion to the amounts of benefit received. The second is the ability approach, which requires equal treatment of persons regarded as possessing the same taxpaying ability and relative adjustment of taxes on persons in unlike circumstances on the basis of the degree of taxpaying ability possessed.

## The Benefit Basis

The benefit principle involves the application to the entire governmental sector of the private sector, or *commercial*, rule that goods be paid for by the users. Not only would services sold to the users be paid for by them, but the entire tax structure would be erected upon this principle as well, all taxes being adjusted in terms of benefits received.[1]

Perhaps the most basic argument for the benefit principle of distribution of tax burden is simply one of analogy. Since persons pay for the output of the private sector on the basis of the amount of the product which they receive, it is argued that they should do likewise in the governmental sector. To those who accept this point of view, equity requires that persons pay for all goods and services they receive, whether produced in the private or governmental sector, and thus that it is inherently "unfair" to make some persons pay for what others get. In addition, the benefit principle is defended on the basis of incentives, by the argument that any tax structure built upon the ability principle inevitably penalizes success and discourages initiative. The person who has little income or wealth pays little, while the person of ability and initiative who earns a high income and accumulates wealth is penalized heavily by the tax burden imposed upon him. Such a premium on failure, it is argued, curbs incentive and willingness to work and therefore retards the development of the economy.

The benefit approach also serves to emphasize the desirability of basing governmental services on public preferences for them. The benefit basis may also facilitate adjustments of the output of the governmental services, as explained in Chapter 22.

[1] The benefit principle dominated the thinking of many of the earliest writers in the field of public finance. For a later defense of the benefit principle, see the article by H. W. Prentis, Jr., "Taxation and Business Incentive," *Annals of the American Academy of Political and Social Sciences*, Vol. CCLXVI (November, 1949), pp. 70–76. For an historical analysis, see R. A. Musgrave, *The Theory of Public Finance* (New York: McGraw-Hill Book Co., Inc., 1959), chap. iv.

### Objections to the Benefit Basis

The argument that governments should follow the rules of the private sector of the economy is itself of little merit. Reasoning by analogy from the private to the governmental sector is rarely useful, since governments for the most part perform those functions which private enterprise cannot undertake, largely because the output cannot be sold to the individual users. For the same basic reason—the fact that the benefits accrue to the community as a whole rather than separately to individuals—governments cannot sell these services, nor can they measure the benefits received as a basis of taxes. For the bulk of governmental activities the benefit principle encounters a fundamental contradiction. The government produces the services because the benefits do not accrue separately to individuals; it therefore cannot collect charges for them on a benefit basis, because the benefits cannot be identified with individuals. The only way in which the benefit rule could be followed would be through the establishment of arbitrary criteria of benefit; but such a procedure would not involve the taxing of persons on the basis of actual benefit but according to some indicator of it, such as wealth or income, with incentive effects little different from those of the ability principle.

With other governmental services, some direct benefits are conveyed, as is true, for example, of education. But frequently, some of the benefits are social in character. But more significantly, with many of these activities, even though benefits can be identified with individuals, the pattern of distribution of burden that would result is obviously contrary to that regarded by the consensus of opinion in society as equitable. The principle would mean, for many services, the same per capita burden for the poor as for the rich, although the latter have far greater means with which to make tax payments. The lower income groups would give up goods essential to a minimum living standard, while the wealthy would give up only a portion of their savings or marginal luxury spending, a result not in conformity with accepted principles of equity in distribution of burden. In some instances, such as education and recreation, the poor make greater use of the services than the wealthy. Thus the wealthy would pay less for these services than the poor. The benefit principle is contrary to the whole philosophy of governmental welfare activities, designed to increase the economic well-being of the lower income groups. As pointed out many years ago by Adolph Wagner, the German public finance authority of the last century, the entry of governments into the welfare field rendered impossible any universal use of the benefit principle.

## Use of the Benefit Principle

While the benefit principle is unworkable for most governmental activities and unacceptable from an equity standpoint, certain types of activities can be financed on the benefit basis without objectionable results. To the extent that this basis can be employed, the success-penalizing effects of ability-based taxes can be avoided. The cases in which the principle can be used are those in which (1) the benefits received by individuals can be measured and (2) the resulting pattern of burden distribution is regarded by society as equitable; in other words, standards of equity are considered to require that the users pay.

For most governmental services in which these two requirements are met, conditions permit direct sale of the services to the users. As explained in Chapter 22, the sale method often has the further advantages of preventing waste and of guiding the government to optimum output levels. In these cases, no taxes are involved. But with a few services the two requirements for use of the benefit principle are present, but either the sale method is not feasible because of high costs of collecting a charge, or the charging of a price equal to average cost would restrict the use of the services to uneconomically low levels (as in the case of a bridge). In other cases, recipients of the benefits cannot pay in the period in which they receive the benefits, although they can pay at some other time.

The outstanding example of the use of the benefit basis is highway finance. Not only can the benefit be measured reasonably well, but no obvious inequity results from making the users pay. However, tolls are costly to collect, a nuisance to the traveler, and a source of unnecessary restriction of traffic on roads not fully utilized. On the other hand, it is possible to collect taxes on the gasoline used relatively easily and cheaply; gasoline consumed is a better objective measure of highway usage than almost any toll system which can be employed. The old-age annuity system provides another example. While persons receiving the annuities are unable to pay in the years in which they are receiving them, they can pay in the years during which they are at work. The portion of the local property taxes which finances police and fire protection, sewage service, and the like may be justified as a benefit-based levy. The property owners benefit directly from these services, many of which they would have to obtain from private sources were it not for the governmental activity. Special assessments to finance local public works are also based upon the benefit principle.

For most governmental activities, however, reliance must be placed upon the ability principle if the desired goals of equity are to be attained.

## Equity: The Ability Principle

The principle of distribution of tax burden on the basis of ability to pay is the one which conforms most closely with the generally accepted standards of equity. By *ability*, in present-day usage, is meant simply economic well-being or the over-all level of living enjoyed by the taxpayer. The principle that accepted standards of equity require that persons who have the same ability to pay should pay equal amounts of taxes and that the persons who have greater ability should pay more to the government than those who are less well off is today almost universally accepted.[2]

On the basis of earlier theories of economic welfare, attempts were made to justify the ability approach on the grounds of sacrifice. It was argued that the payment of a large tax by a person who was well off involved no more sacrifice or disutility than the payment of a small tax by a person who was less well off. But this argument was based upon the assumption that satisfactions of different persons can be compared; modern welfare theory argues that such comparisons are not possible. The present-day justification for the ability principle is simply the fact that, from all indications, it is in accord with the consensus of attitudes toward equity in the distribution of real income and of tax burden. Equity questions always involve value judgments, and tax structures can be evaluated, from an equity standpoint, only in terms of their relative conformity with the consensus of thought in the particular society.

In addition, the ability principle does have the advantage of being workable. Various measures of ability or economic well-being can be developed, and since these are also to a large extent the means with which taxes are paid, the tax obligations can be met.

It must be granted, however, that the ability-to-pay principle may have some adverse incentive effects and thus may violate the neutrality rule. Taxes imposed on the basis of various measures of economic well-being penalize success and work, reward idleness and failure, and may weaken the incentives of some persons. These problems will be considered in the discussion of various taxes in subsequent chapters.

### The Measures of Economic Well-Being

If the ability principle, as outlined, is to provide workable criteria for establishment and evaluation of tax structures, suitable measures of

---

[2] Some writers, especially the late H. C. Simons and some of his disciples, object to the use of the term *ability* and insist that equity requires simply the establishment of the tax structure in such a way as to reduce the inequality of income. The difference between this point of view and that presented in this section is purely terminological.

ability or economic well-being must be developed. Three primary ones have been utilized: income (usually adjusted for various circumstances affecting expenditures necessary for a given standard of living), personal wealth, and amounts spent, either for certain categories of goods or in total.

### Income as a Criterion of Economic Well-Being

A family's economic well-being depends primarily upon the income of the family during the period. Precise definition of the concept of income must await the discussion in Chapter 7; in general, by the term is meant the amount which the family obtains from activity during the period for consumption or saving. The quantity of goods persons are able to acquire during the period (including the use value of durable consumer goods owned) and the net increase in savings constitute the best measure of how well the family lives or, in other words, its level of living during the period.

However, the actual level of living which can be attained with a given money income depends in part on certain circumstances affecting the amounts that must be spent in order to attain a given level of living. The most obvious is the number of persons in the family; the more children a family has, the lower is the level of living possible with a given money income. Amounts that must be paid for medical expenses provide another example. Accordingly, the most satisfactory criterion of ability is not the figure of income alone, but the income figure adjusted in terms of these circumstances. These will be discussed in the chapters dealing with income taxation.

### The Significance of Wealth

Apart from these circumstances, the economic well-being of the family is influenced not only by the income received during the period but also by the amount of accumulated wealth. To the extent that this wealth is placed in income-yielding investments, the wealth is in part reflected in income. But nevertheless, if two persons have the same income and are in otherwise similar circumstances but have different amounts of wealth, they are not equally well off. The person with wealth is not under the same compulsion to save as is the person without. The person who has little wealth must save in order to attain the same degree of security against risk as the other person and therefore cannot enjoy the same current level of consumption. Furthermore, the person with wealth may, if he chooses, spend a portion of this wealth each year to maintain a higher level of living than that which the person without the wealth can attain.

The problem is much the same if the person with wealth has invested it in durable consumption goods, particularly a home. As discussed in later chapters, while logically the rental value of the home should be included in taxable income, in practice it is not. Accordingly, if income alone is used as the measure of ability, the person who has such wealth essentially enjoys some tax-free income, since he avoids the heavy rental payments of the person who has not yet acquired his home, and he likewise is not under the same obligation to accumulate a reserve.

In general, therefore, both wealth and income are measures of economic well-being. Of the two, income is the better measure, since it, to a greater extent than wealth, determines the level of living. Many persons have high incomes and enjoy high levels of living and yet have little accumulated wealth. Other persons, especially older persons owning their homes, have considerable amounts of wealth but little current income. Thus, primary reliance upon wealth would result in a serious departure from the rule of taxing persons in relation to their economic well-being. But some use of the wealth criterion, along with primary use of the income basis, will adjust the tax structure more closely in terms of over-all economic well-being.

### Consumption Expenditures as a Measure of Economic Well-Being

It has been argued by various persons over the years that the appropriate measure of ability is not total income but the amount of income spent.[3] It is claimed that economic well-being depends upon consumption purchases alone, that wealth accumulated yields no satisfaction until it is used for consumption purposes. This argument goes back to the statement by the philosopher Hobbes, that equity requires the taxation of persons on the basis of what they take out of the product of the economy, not on the basis of what they add to it. The expenditure basis is also defended on the grounds of simplicity and of the avoidance of double taxation of income saved.

On the other hand, the expenditure approach is condemned on the ground that it would favor the miser, the person spending a small percentage of his income, and is difficult to make progressive, or even keep from being regressive, with the use of traditional expenditure-based taxes, such

---

[3] This point of view was expressed by J. S. Mill in his *Principles of Political Economy* (Book IV, chap. ii, sec. 4); it was developed particularly by Irving Fisher, *Constructive Income Taxation* (New York: Harper & Bros., 1942). The most recent presentation is to be found in the book by N. Kaldor, *An Expenditure Tax* (London: George Allen and Unwin, 1955).

as sales taxes. Further evaluation of the expenditure basis must be postponed to Chapter 17, which deals specifically with the question.

## Equity: The Relationship between the Tax and the Size of the Base

Regardless of the measures of economic well-being selected, the question of the appropriate relationship between the amount of tax and the amount of the measure, that is, of the tax base, possessed by the taxpayer must be answered. One aspect of the problem can be solved easily: The "equal treatment of equals" rule requires that persons who are considered to have the same taxpaying ability—the same amount of the base selected as the measure of ability—should pay the same amount of taxes. Thus, on the basis of the income measure, two persons having the same income and being in the same circumstances in other defined respects (numbers of dependents, etc.) must be charged the same amount of tax.

However, the other aspect of the problem—that of the relative burdens on persons having different amounts of the base—is more difficult to resolve. In terms of the primary measure, income, there are three alternative possibilities:

1. A progressive relationship, the percentage of income paid in taxes increasing with increases in income.

2. A proportional relationship, the ratio of tax to income being the same throughout, regardless of the size of the income.

3. A regressive relationship, the ratio of the tax to income being lower with large incomes than with small.

If the tax is levied directly upon income, the nature of the rate itself (progressive, proportional, regressive, relative to the amount of the measure of the tax possessed by the taxpayer) will be the same as the behavior of the tax paid relative to income. But if the tax is not levied on income, there may be a difference between the rate structure and the relationship of tax to income. A sales tax has a proportional rate, but the amount of tax paid, relative to income, is likely to be regressive. The Alaska business receipts tax is one of the few levies to have regressive rates.

## The "Sacrifice" Approach to the Problem

From the middle of the nineteenth century until recent years, a series of attempts has been made to interpret ability in terms of individual sacrifice and to determine the answer to the question of the desirable type of rate structure on the basis of considerations relating to the behavior of utility or sacrifice.

There were at least three distinct approaches to ability in terms of sacrifice. The first idea was that of *equal sacrifice:* that equity required adjustment of tax rates in such a manner that the sacrifice created for all persons should be the same. Others argued that sacrifice should be *proportional* to income rather than equal at all income levels. The rationale of the proportional sacrifice doctrine was the argument that persons with greater incomes received much more benefit from society and thus should bear more tax sacrifice rather than the same amount as persons with smaller incomes. Thus, for example, under the equal sacrifice doctrine, a person with $10,000 income would be taxed so as to bear the same real burden as a person with $5,000 income; with the proportional sacrifice doctrine the former would be made to bear twice the sacrifice. The proportional sacrifice principle would essentially seek to leave utility from national private sector product distributed in the same manner as before the tax.

The third version was the *minimum aggregate sacrifice* or equimarginal sacrifice doctrine, the principle that persons should be taxed in such a manner that the total sacrifice for society would be kept to the minimum possible figure. This, in turn, required that the adjustment of taxes insure that the marginal sacrifice—the disutility arising from the payment of the last dollar of tax—would be the same for all persons. If this point were not attained, the shifting of tax burden from some persons to others would reduce the sacrifice of some persons more than it increased the sacrifice of others, and thus lessen aggregate sacrifice.

All these doctrines were based upon two assumptions: (1) that the law of diminishing marginal utility operates in relation to income, that is, that the marginal utility gained from successive dollars of income declines as income rises, and (2) that all persons have equal capacity for enjoyment of income. The second assumption involves interpersonal utility comparisons, the comparing of relative satisfactions received by different persons.

The earlier exponents of the various sacrifice doctrines maintained that each of the doctrines required progression in taxation. Eventually, however, it was recognized that even in terms of the assumptions above, this did not follow in all cases. Under the first two doctrines, diminishing marginal utility of income (assuming, of course, equal capacities for enjoyment of income) required merely that a larger absolute sum be taken from the rich than from the poor rather than a greater percentage. The proportional sacrifice doctrine is usually interpreted to require progression if marginal utility of income falls with a sufficient degree of rapidity, but not otherwise. On the other hand, the minimum aggregate sacrifice theory, under the assumptions, would require not merely progression but the eventual taking of all incomes in excess of a certain figure, and none from persons with incomes below this figure. This policy is obviously inconsistent with the maintenance of high levels of output and with generally accepted principles of equity in the distribution of income.

### Inadequacies of the Sacrifice Approach

In recent decades, increasing doubt has been raised about the usefulness of any of these sacrifice doctrines. Both the basic assumptions have been questioned.

1. It is widely argued that the principle of diminishing marginal utility does not necessarily apply to income as a whole, even for one individual. As persons' incomes rise, their wants may increase in intensity. As they become accustomed to higher levels of living, their desire to maintain them and increase them further may be just as intense as the previous desires were for the lower levels. The prestige value of progressively higher income levels serves to hinder the operation of the principle. As a consequence, it cannot be argued scientifically that additional increments of income yield persons less satisfaction than earlier increments. A man may feel the loss of 1 per cent of his income as keenly if he receives $10,000 as if he earned $4,000.

2. As indicated previously, modern welfare theory denies the possibility of comparing the utility or disutility experienced by different persons, and the assumption of equal capacities for enjoyment of income is not a realistic one. Even if it be assumed that one person receives greater satisfaction from the first thousand of income than from the tenth thousand, it does not necessarily follow that one individual receiving $1,000 gets greater satisfaction from it than another person gets from an additional $1,000 when he is already receiving $10,000. It cannot even be argued that two persons with the same income and other circumstances receive the same total or marginal utility. Sacrifice or disutility from the payment of tax is not only unmeasurable for one individual, although he may compare it with the sacrifice from payment of other amounts, but it is completely noncomparable among individuals. Any attempt to build a basis for the tax structure upon disutility or sacrifice is therefore futile.

### The Minimum Living Standard Approach

One justification for progression is based upon the relationship between total income and the amount regarded as essential for a minimum living standard. It can be argued that a person has no taxpaying ability until he obtains sufficient income to allow him to live and therefore that he should not be taxed upon this minimum. If this argument is accepted, ability would be measured by the portion of income over and above the minimum. Since this excess constitutes a higher percentage of high incomes than of low, a tax structure progressive according to income is justified. In other words, progression is required because persons with relatively low incomes require all or most of the income for a bare minimum standard of living; and the higher the income is over this minimum, the greater is the surplus, and thus the greater the percentage of income that can equitably be taken by taxation. Acceptance of this principle, however, does not justify progressive *rates* but merely the degree of progression that arises when a certain sum is deductible from the incomes of all persons.

### Progressive Rates and Accepted Standards of Equity in the Distribution of Income

The significant justification for progressive rates, as distinguished from the progression created by the exemption of a certain amount of income, is based on accepted standards of optimum patterns of income distribution. The strongest argument for progression is the fact that the consensus of opinion in society today regards progression as necessary for equity. This general acceptance of the desirability of progression is, in turn, based upon the point of view that the pattern of income distribution, before taxes, involves excessive inequality from the standpoint of the best interests of society. This conclusion is, of course, a value judgment, based upon accepted attitudes toward an optimum distribution of income. It does not necessarily rest upon an assumption of interpersonal utility comparisons; excessive inequality can be condemned on the basis of inherent unfairness in terms of the standards accepted by society, upon the inequality of opportunity which results, and upon the effects of inequality in creating social and political instability.

But as a matter of fact, this principle is accepted in large measure upon an implicit comparison of relative satisfactions gained from incomes in various income groups. Most persons would agree, for example, with the statement that a marginal 1 per cent of income is "worth less" or is "of less importance" or a source of less satisfaction to a millionaire than an additional 1 per cent of income is to a person with a $1,500 income. The fact that there can be no "proof" of this or, in fact, any really significant meaning to the statement does not alter the influence which such beliefs have upon popular attitudes and thus on the development of the generally accepted principle that equity in taxation requires progressive rates.

To the opponents of progression, of course, the consensus argument has no validity, but is a mere rationalization for a policy which is followed because the majority of the people support it.[4] This group seeks to find some absolute and fundamental concept of fairness which is independent of personal preferences. But such a point of view fails to recognize that questions of fairness are by their inherent nature ones on which there can be no scientific answer, and under the principles of democracy the only acceptable criterion is that of consensus of thought on the part of the population.

### The Degree of Progression

Since the justification for progression rests upon community consensus about standards of equity in the distribution of income, the desired degree of progression must rest upon the same basis. Thus, there are no objective criteria for the establishment of the scale of progression, which must be determined on the basis of the interpretation of the exact degree of income inequality which is regarded as most acceptable by a consensus of thinking in society. At one extreme the taking of all income earned beyond any particular figure is almost universally regarded as inequitable; at the other, most persons accept the principle that considerable lessening of inequality is desirable. Within these limits, it is impossible to make any categorical statements about the exact degree generally desired. Most of the discussion of the problem is in terms of relatively minor changes in existing schedules; popular thinking is undoubtedly greatly influenced by the degree of progression which has been in use over recent years.

To some critics of progression the lack of any objective standard for determining the degree of progression is a decisive argument against any deviation from proportional taxation.[5] However, if the principle is accepted that some progression is definitely more equitable than none at all, the lack of an objective standard of progression is no conclusive argument against its use. But determination must rest upon the personal opinions of those responsible for the framing of the tax laws in regard to the con-

[4] For a strong criticism of the point of view expressed in this section, see the paper by A. K. Eaton, "Ability to Pay Revisited," *Report of the 1961 Conference of the Canadian Tax Foundation* (Toronto, 1962), pp. 9–16.

[5] Note the classic statement of J. R. McCulloch: "The moment you abandon, in the framing of such taxes, the cardinal principle of exacting from all individuals the same proportion of their income or of their property, you are at sea without rudder or compass, and there is no amount of injustice and folly you may not commit" (*A Treatise on the Principles and Practical Influence of Taxation and the Funding System* [2d ed., 1865]).

sensus of opinion about desired patterns of income distribution, as well as a consideration of the possible incentive effects of the various degrees of progression.

### The Possible Conflict of Equity and Neutrality Considerations

It has been widely argued by persons opposed to progression or to a high degree of progression that progressive tax rates, by interfering with incentives, curtail economic development and lower national income below potential levels. That some conflict between equity considerations and adverse effects on the economy is possible cannot be denied. From the standpoint of economic neutrality (with optimum economic welfare in the absence of the tax), the most desirable form of tax is one which is completely independent of the economic activities a person undertakes. A poll tax, the burden of which is unrelated to marginal activity, is thus the ideal of all levies. But such taxes are obviously inequitable under usually accepted standards. There is little evidence that highly progressive rate structures are having disastrous effects on the economy; so long as such evidence is lacking, the case against progression is weak. But the possibility of adverse incentive effects must not be ignored.

## MINIMUM COSTS OF TAX COLLECTION AND PAYMENT

A final principle of taxation is that of minimizing the costs and difficulties of collection of the taxes. Effective and inexpensive administration is important if the use of resources to effect the transfer is to be minimized, since, to the extent that resources are used for this purpose, the output of goods and services in the economy is curtailed. Likewise, effective administration is essential for maintenance of equity. No matter how equitable a particular tax structure appears to be in theory, it will not actually conform with accepted standards of equity if substantial numbers of persons are able to evade or avoid the tax.

### The Factors Affecting Administrative Efficiency

Effective administration can be obtained only if the tax base is clearly defined and the tax liability ascertainable with reasonable ease by both the taxpayer and the tax-collecting agency. Ambiguities in the definition of the base make application of the tax difficult for the taxpayer and greatly complicate the task of the government in checking upon the correctness of tax payments made. Ambiguities, as a rule, center around the problem of drawing the line between the taxable base and closely related items which are excluded.

The ability to check upon tax liability depends in large measure upon the general nature of the tax base. The larger the number of tax-payers, obviously, the harder is the task. Whenever the base of the tax consists of a large number of small transactions, or when the transactions do not have clearly ascertainable values, the problems of administration are increased. Almost all broad-based taxes encounter these difficulties to a greater or lesser degree. They must be recognized, however, as inevitable problems with such levies as the income and property taxes, and administrative procedures must be developed to meet them.

Effective enforcement likewise necessitates the establishment of the tax base in such a fashion that persons are unable to escape from the tax by readjusting the manner in which they conduct their activities. It is essential that tax structures be framed to insure completeness of intended coverage; there have been many loopholes, for example, for avoiding federal income taxes. Elimination of these loopholes is not always easy, since drastic measures to close them may create new inequities. But every effort must be made to insure that avenues of escape are minimized so far as possible.

### Costs to the Taxpayer

Effective collection from the standpoint of the economy as a whole requires minimum cost not only to the governmental units but to the taxpayers as well. Simplicity in tax legislation and provision of adequate, clearly worded information are of the greatest importance. Likewise, convenience of payment is greatly increased if the tax is payable in small amounts during the year, so that persons will not have to accumulate large sums for payment at infrequent intervals.

### The Administrative Staff

Effective collection obviously requires an efficient administrative organization. The tasks in the establishment of such an organization are comparable to those involved in the development of any governmental agency. The exact level to which the staff of the tax-collection agency should be extended is not always easily determined. It is obvious that the aim is not the minimum possible staff; if the force is too small, the government will lose directly in revenue through outright evasion more than it saves in collection costs. The rule is generally accepted that the administrative force should be extended at least to the point at which an additional dollar spent on administration is equal to the additional revenue received, because if the government stops short of this point, it is suffering a direct and immediate financial loss.

Actually, however, there may be substantial justification for extending the administrative organization beyond this point. Improved enforcement not only brings in more revenue directly from the persons checked but likewise insures more complete payment from other persons who realize that they are likely to be caught if they seek to evade the tax. At some point, of course, the gains, both direct and indirect, will no longer exceed the additional cost, and further expansion would be undesirable. This point represents the goal, but determination of it may be difficult.

## THE BURDEN OF TAXATION

Under conditions of full employment, when governments divert resources from the private sector of the economy in order to carry on their activities, private sector output is reduced below the levels otherwise attainable. This reduction is the burden or real cost of the governmental activities; from the standpoint of society, it is, of course, offset, and presumably more than offset, by the benefits from the governmental services. This private sector burden exists whether or not taxes are imposed to finance the government expenditures. When taxes are used, as they normally are, the type of tax will control the pattern of distribution of the burden among various persons in society. This pattern is frequently called the *incidence* of the tax. In nonfull-employment periods, no reduction in private sector output is necessary to free resources for governmental use; but if taxes are collected to finance the governmental activities, private sector output will be reduced below levels otherwise attainable, and thus, again, a real burden exists, the nature of the distribution of which depends upon the type of tax employed.

In some instances the tax may be borne directly by the persons who pay it to the government; the dollar disposable income of these persons falls by the amount of the tax, and if no changes in prices of commodities or factor services occur, the real burden rests entirely upon the initial taxpayers, in proportion to the amount of tax they pay. In other cases, however—as, for example, with an excise tax, or an income tax which affects the supply of labor—changes in relative prices will occur, and essentially shift some of the burden of the tax onto other persons. Thus, if the seller of a commodity subject to an excise tax is able to raise the price of his product, he may be able to maintain his own real income more or less unchanged, while the purchasers of the product will find their real incomes reduced, since they cannot buy as many goods with their given dollar income as before. While some persons prefer to ignore factor price changes in the discussion of burden, a much more meaningful concept of incidence is one which takes them into consideration.

Knowledge of the distribution of the burden of a tax is of paramount importance in evaluating the tax in terms of the standards noted earlier in the chapter. Equity considerations must be reviewed in terms of the actual distribution of burden, not the direct monetary payment of tax to the government. Unfortunately, the present state of knowledge does not provide adequate information on the distribution of burden of the major types of taxes. The problems with respect to the incidence of each type of levy will be analyzed in the chapters dealing with these taxes.

## REFERENCES

KALVIN, H., and BLUM, W. J. *The Uneasy Case for Progressive Taxation.* Chicago: University of Chicago Press, 1953.
   The most complete survey and evaluation of the literature on the question of progression in taxation.

FAGAN, E. D. "Recent and Contemporary Theories of Progressive Taxation," *Journal of Political Economy,* Vol. XLVI (August, 1938), pp. 458–85.
   An analysis of the various approaches to the problem of progression.

PIGOU, A. C. *A Study in Public Finance,* Part II. 3d ed. London: Macmillan & Co., Ltd., 1951.
   A careful study of principles of taxation, but based in part on older theories of economic welfare.

SIMONS, H. C. *Personal Income Taxation,* chap. i. Chicago: University of Chicago Press, 1938.
   A very critical analysis of usual theories of desirable distribution of tax burden.

BLOUGH, R. *The Federal Taxing Process,* chap. xv. New York: Prentice-Hall, Inc., 1952.
   A discussion of equity in taxation.

BRYDEN, M. H. *The Costs of Tax Compliance.* Toronto: Canadian Tax Foundation, 1961.
   An analysis and empirical study of the question.

# PART III

## Income Taxation

# Chapter 7

# THE TAXATION OF INCOME:
# THE CONCEPT OF TAXABLE
# INCOME

Income is generally regarded today as the best measure of ability, in the sense of economic well-being, since income is the primary determinant of the level of living which a family enjoys. In a broad sense the term *income* may be defined as the economic gain to the person in a particular period of time. But if the tax structure is to attain the desired goals, a more precise definition of income is necessary, to serve as the basis for the determination of the exact coverage of the tax. This chapter will consider the question of the definition of income and will review present coverage of income tax laws in terms of the definition. In the succeeding chapters, attention will be given to other problems encountered in developing a satisfactory income tax structure. Special problems for income taxation created by the existence of corporations will be considered in Chapter 13.

## THE DEFINITION OF INCOME

In the explanation of the concept of income, the procedure will be followed of presenting, first, the definition which is most logical in terms of the goals of income taxation and then comparing this definition with the interpretation of the term used in current tax legislation.

### Income as Consumption Plus Increase in Net Wealth

Income, as the economic gain received by the person during the particular period, may be defined as the algebraic sum of two items: (1) the person's consumption during the period and (2) the net increase in the individual's personal wealth during the period, each measured in dollar terms. At the beginning of this period the person has net personal wealth of a certain value. He enjoys a certain amount of consumption during the period; and at the end of the period, he has a certain figure of net wealth, which may be different from that at the beginning. If there has been an increase, his total economic gain from the period is measured by the value of his consumption during the period plus the increase in the value of his wealth. If his net wealth has decreased, his net gain is the value of his consumption less the decline in the value of his wealth; in this case, his consumption has exceeded his income.

This definition may seem somewhat awkward and backhanded, but it provides an unambiguous concept which reflects the entire economic gain received during the period. Expressed in somewhat different terms, income consists of:

1. The total amount received from other persons during the period, less the expenses involved (other than personal living costs) in gaining this amount.

2. The value of consumption activity enjoyed by the person which does not involve receipt of money or goods from other persons during the period. As explained in a later section, this element includes such items as the use value of consumer durables, such as homes owned, and the value of home-produced goods and services, such as vegetables.

3. The increase in the value of assets held during the period.

The sum of these three items must equal income measured as the sum of consumption plus increase in net wealth, since all elements entering into the three items must either be used for or constitute consumption activity, or manifest themselves in a change in the person's net wealth during the period. It must be emphasized that income has not been defined simply as the net flow of wealth to the person during the period. This is only one item (No. 1 above) in the total economic gain received by the person during the period.

The definition given is, of course, not that actually found in tax legislation but rather the one which is most logical in terms of the general intent of income taxation, that of adjusting the burden of the tax upon the basis of net economic gain during the period.

### The "Flow of Wealth" Definition in Tax Legislation

Actual tax legislation in the United States and Canada, as well as that in most (but not all) other countries, interprets the concept of income in terms of flow of wealth—of receipts in money or goods—to the taxpayer during the period. For factor incomes actually paid out during the period, such as wages, salaries, interest, and the like, plus the profits of business enterprise, the use of the "flow of wealth" definition produces the same results as the "consumption plus increase in net wealth" definition.

However, in two primary respects, the flow method produces important differences in tax treatment:

1. Taxation is established on a realization rather than on an accrual basis. Increases in the value of capital assets are taxed only when the property is sold and the increased value is reflected in a flow of money to the owner, rather than on the basis of an annual revaluation of the assets.

2. The tax applies only when a transaction occurs between other persons and the taxpayer, as only in this case is there a flow of wealth to the taxpayer. Thus the value of consumption activity enjoyed by the person without an exchange transaction having occurred is not taxable. Accordingly, the use value of an owner-occupied home is tax-free, as well as vegetables grown by a person in his garden and similar items.

The use of the "flow of wealth" definition is a result of expediency. The problems of determining values of income when no market transactions are involved are so great that the tax structure has been established in such a manner that these items of income are completely excluded. Complete use of the "consumption plus increase in net wealth" definition would create hopeless administrative problems. Yet the surrender to expediency, even though necessary in the interests of effective administration, does give rise to inequity and to illogical features in the tax structure. There has been an unfortunate tendency to regard the "flow of wealth" definition as the most logical; if it is recognized that this interpretation of the concept is chosen as a matter of expediency and that consumption plus increase in net wealth is the basically desirable rule, one to be attained so far as is possible, the establishment of a logical income tax structure is facilitated.

Further explorations of these deviations in the tax structure from the broad definition of income will help to point out the difficulties which arise from the use of the flow concept of income.

## THE ENJOYMENT OF INCOME WHEN NO MARKET TRANSACTION IS INVOLVED

One major difference between the actual treatment of income and the basic definition is the failure to tax the portion of income which arises without a market transaction being involved, the person enjoying consumption activity and thus income without the receipt of wealth from other persons during the period. Let us consider, first, the scope of such activities which would logically be subject to tax under the broad definition developed above. The significance of the failure to tax all such income under present tax laws can then be developed.

### The Concept of Consumption

The first step in this analysis is a review of the meaning of the concept of consumption. By this term is usually meant the utilization of goods and services in the satisfaction of wants. Consumption in this sense takes four major forms:

1. The use of goods purchased during the period with money income received or with previously accumulated funds.

2. The use of durable consumption goods acquired in a previous period.

3. The consumption of goods and services produced directly by the person himself, such as home-grown vegetables, dairy products, or flowers.

4. The enjoyment of leisure and recreational activities provided within the family, such as games, walks in the woods, etc.[1]

In the broad sense of the term, all four classes constitute consumption. But the fourth class has no monetary value, since the activity has no capacity to command other goods in exchange. The activity, in large part, involves simply the utilization of free goods. Thus, there is no dollar value to be included in the total consumption or income. While this class must be excluded from taxable income, this procedure inevitably causes the income tax to increase the relative advantage of leisure compared to other forms of consumption activity and therefore to alter relative choices of individuals.

While the first three classes should logically be included within the total of consumption during the period and thus within the category of taxable income, present tax legislation applies only to the first category; the income which a person enjoys from the production and consumption of goods within the family and from the use of durable consumption goods is not subject to tax. This treatment, which essentially draws the line between some consumption activities and others, gives rise not only to departures from the accepted principles of equity but to adverse economic effects as well. These will be considered separately for the two major classes—items 2 and 3 above—which are excluded from the tax.

### The Case in Which Goods and Services Are Produced and Consumed by the Same Household

The failure to include within taxable income the real income which arises when goods and services are both produced and consumed by the

---

[1] The mere enjoyment of idle time is frequently excluded from the definition of consumption. But in the broadest sense of the term, it can logically be included.

same family discriminates against persons who are unable or unwilling to undertake such activity and gives an artificial stimulus to performance of the activity by those who are willing to undertake it. If a plumber and a carpenter work for each other for a price, each is taxed upon the income received. Yet if each does his own work for himself, neither is taxed. Yet (apart from the fact that each is presumably more skilled in his own occupation) they are equally well off in either case, so far as economic well-being is concerned. The result is discrimination. Furthermore, persons are given an artificial tax advantage and encouragement to do such things for themselves, when they are likely less skilled than others. Total output of society would be greater if each person specialized in his own occupation and hired other specialists to paint and repair his house and grow his vegetables.

The problem is particularly serious with farmers, who are in a better position than other occupational groups to provide a substantial amount of their own food if they wish. Canada has attempted to meet this problem by requiring the inclusion in farmers' incomes of the value of the portion of the crop consumed at home, but the provision is hard to enforce. Although a few states use the same procedure, the United States federal government specifically excludes from the tax the value of home-consumed farm produce.

Another example of this problem is presented by routine housework. If a person hires housework done, no deduction from income is allowed; yet if the work is done within the household, no taxable income is created. The result is a certain amount of discrimination against persons who live in hotels and apartments or whose circumstances, such as illness, prevent them from doing their own work. The tax treatment also encourages wives to devote their activities to housework instead of obtaining a job and hiring a maid.

However, any attempt to include activities of this type, with the possible exception of home-consumed farm produce, would encounter serious complications. In the first place, many of the activities are carried on in time which would not be used for other employment; they are not substituted for regular cash-yielding employment but for leisure or other forms of recreation. Many of the activities, although yielding a tangible product, in the form of vegetables or flowers, for example, are undertaken largely as means of utilizing spare time and provide substantial enjoyment (completely apart from the product) to the person carrying them on. Since it is not possible to tax other uses of leisure time, it may be argued that it is not equitable to tax this particular use. Any attempt to distinguish between the activities on the basis of intent—the use of leisure, on the one hand, and the desire for the product, on the other—would be completely futile.

Furthermore, the attempt to tax the results of this type of activity, when leisure cannot be taxed, may easily have greater adverse effects upon the economy than those resulting from the encouragement now given by the tax laws to do one's own work. Leisure and various forms of home work activity are very close substitutes for one another, and the attempt to tax the latter, when leisure is not taxed, may lead to substitution of leisure for work. This effect may be far greater than that which the taxing of money income has in causing persons to forgo regular employment for either leisure or work at home. Marginal activities are likely to be very sensitive to a tax on the real income gained from them, to a much greater extent than is the money income from the regular employment. Since a very large portion of all work at home is carried on in spare time rather than at the expense of regular employment, it represents a net contribution to national income which could easily be reduced by a tax upon it.

As a practical matter, administrative considerations completely preclude taxation of most activities of the type under discussion, because the absence of a market transaction makes it difficult to place a value on the goods and services produced, and many are difficult to detect. Even when the products have a commercial value, such as vegetables, the valuation of the entire crop at the commercial figure may produce quite inequitable results, as the person may end up with far more vegetables than he would conceivably buy if he had to purchase them from his money income.

### The Imputed Income from Durable Consumption Goods Owned[2]

A related problem is the treatment of the imputed income received from durable consumption goods, particularly homes. The purchase of a home is essentially a type of investment in which the return takes the form of the use value of the property rather than a dollars-and-cents income. Because of the possession of a home, a person avoids the necessity of having to pay rent, and thus the return in monetary terms is very immediate and obvious, even though it does not take the form of a dividend or interest check. Accordingly, a portion of a homeowner's income, his economic gain during the year, is the rental value of the home.

Under present American and Canadian law, however, the rental value of homes is not in any way taxable, because it does not fall within the "flow of wealth" definition. As a consequence, persons placing wealth

---

2 See R. Goode, "Imputed Rents of Owner-Occupied Dwellings," *Journal of Finance*, Vol. XV (December, 1960), pp. 504–30.

in homes are favored over those acquiring cash income-yielding investments. Suppose, for example, that two persons have the same current income from salaries and the same amount of wealth. One rents a home and invests his wealth in bonds, which yield $1,200 a year income. The other person buys a home with his money. The former is taxed on the $1,200; not only is the latter not taxed on the rental value of the home, but in the United States, he can deduct property taxes upon the home as well. The first person will pay (with the figures in the example) perhaps $400 more income tax than the second, even though their real economic status—in terms of level of living enjoyed—is the same. The gain is, of course, greater in the high income levels than in the lower ones, and those persons having strong preference for expensive housing are particularly favored. Also, strong incentive is given to purchase a home instead of renting. While such a result may be justified on the basis of social goals, there is serious objection to a policy of accomplishing an end by a means which discriminates against those persons who, for one reason or another, are either unable or unwilling to undertake the action.

The logical solution is the inclusion in income of the rental value (minus cost of repairs, depreciation, property taxes, and interest) of owner-occupied homes. This practice was long followed in Great Britain. There are, of course, some problems of determination of the appropriate rental sum, but this task is not an insuperable one, because of the large amount of rental housing. An alternative method used by Australia is the application of a specified interest rate to the owner's equity to determine annual use value. Such procedures, in addition to raising the income tax base materially and allowing a lower tax rate, would greatly improve the equity of tax treatment between homeowner and tenant. However, regardless of the merits of including rental values of homes, the principle that they should not be regarded as income has become so widely accepted in the United States and Canada that any change in the law is most unlikely. Even Great Britain is abandoning the policy in 1963.

Other durable consumer goods give rise to the same type of problem, but to a lesser degree. If a person invests in furniture, he receives an annual use value in the sense that he does not have to pay the higher rent for a furnished apartment. But estimation of the annual rental value would be more difficult than with homes. If he buys a car, the use value of the car is a source of satisfaction during the period and constitutes a portion of the economic gain. However, the only feasible method of determining use value is by the application of an interest rate figure to the owner's equity. The gain from the use of property of this type is perhaps more suitably reached by a tax on the value of the property itself.

## INCOME RECEIVED IN KIND

Incomes in kind are closely related to the incomes which take the form of goods produced and consumed by the same person and to imputed values of consumer durables. There is no general reason why income in kind should be excluded from income. If a grocery store pays its clerks partly in potatoes or a distillery distributes whiskey to its stockholders, these goods constitute income just as much as their cash equivalents. Since they fall within the "flow of wealth" category, they are subjected to tax.

Frequently, however, the issue is less clearly defined, particularly when the recipient would not acquire the items if their cash value were paid instead. Thus a logging worker may be offered free housing, but he does not take it, preferring instead to drive daily from a distant town, where he finds living more congenial. A railroad worker who travels on a pass might not take the trip were he paid the cash value of the ticket. These cases suggest the classic conundrum of Kleinwächter's *Flügeladjutant*, who, in addition to his salary, received the privileges of going to the operas and attending elaborate dinners with the king—but unfortunately, he detested operas and formal dinners. Was the value of the opera income to him?

Logically, the figure to be included in income is the amount the person would be willing to pay for the services or goods, if this is less than their commercial value. But since this sum cannot be determined, it is necessary to draw a somewhat arbitrary line between those payments which have significant value to the recipient and those which do not. In the United States and Canada, taxation is limited to payments in kind which are made in tangible commodities, plus the value of board and room when these are furnished at the convenience of the taxpayer—that is, when the circumstances of employment are not such that the room and board must be furnished by the employer if the employee is to be able to perform the required work. This rule of convenience is not easy to interpret, and the net effect is to allow the escape of substantial income that logically should be taxed.[3]

The problem has become more serious in recent years as corporations have sought means to increase their employees' incomes in a tax-free fashion. Thus, incentive is given to supply various types of services free of

---

[3] For a time, all such gains, even the value of trips taken on railway passes, were taxable under the East African income tax law. Administrative problems resulted in the exemption of ones under £50.

charge, such as parking space, health insurance, and even paid vacation travel, although the last-named practice has in some instances been disallowed by the Internal Revenue Service. In stores, employees' discounts are often of substantial value.

## THE PROBLEM OF CAPITAL GAINS

Under the basic definition of income as consumption plus increase in net wealth, any increase in the value of property held would be taxable as regular income in the year in which it accrued. But under the flow definitions of income tax laws, such increases are not taxable income, since there is no receipt of wealth from the mere unrealized increase in value. Only at the time the property is sold and the gain realized is there any possibility of application of the tax. Specific inclusion of such gains is necessary if they are to be included in the tax base, and serious complications arise in attempting to provide satisfactory treatment. More complete discussion of the problem of capital gains taxation must await analysis of other aspects of income taxation, and thus is postponed to Chapter 11.

## SPECIAL TREATMENT OF CERTAIN FORMS OF INCOME

The "equal treatment of equals" rule requires that all income be subjected to tax and to a uniform rate structure, except in those circumstances in which there is strong justification for exemption or differential treatment. A case does exist for special, but not necessarily favorable, treatment of capital gains, at least under the type of income tax which we have at the present time. In addition, however, it is argued that certain other forms of income should not be subjected to tax on the same basis as usual income.

### Recurrence as a Criterion of Taxable Income

The argument is raised that recurrence should be a criterion of taxable income and thus that nonrecurring income should not be subject to tax. In the United States, as a matter of practice, recurrence is not relevant to tax status. In Great Britain, however, the original concept of the tax was that of a levy on recurrent income, and the tax was applied to five schedules or classes of incomes, any item not falling within one of the five schedules not being subject to tax. Gradually, the tax was extended to virtually all incomes, now including many capital gains, although the schedule system has been retained, but a few items still remain outside the scope of the law because of their irregular nature. The Canadian legislation followed American rather than British practice, except for the exclusion of capital gains.

There is little logic in excluding particular items because they are not regular sources of income, since these represent gain to the taxpayer, and in some instances take on the form of a windfall. Admittedly, enforcement is somewhat difficult, but this feature does not justify exemption. However, the irregularity may result in an unreasonable burden under progressive rates unless averaging of income is permitted, as discussed in Chapter 10.

### Gifts and Inheritances

The receipt of wealth through gift or inheritance constitutes income within the defined meaning, since the gift or bequest constitutes an economic gain to the recipient. For a variety of reasons explained in Chapter 20, however, it is preferable to treat these items under a separate tax.

### Social Security and Pension Benefits, Annuities, and Insurance[4]

Several types of receipts create problems because they involve simultaneous return of capital and payment of income, the two elements not being sharply distinguished. Benefits received under social security, pensions from private systems, and annuities all have this characteristic. Logically, the portion of the receipts which represent income should be taxed, while that consisting of return of capital should be excluded. But in practice, this is difficult to accomplish. Tax treatment in the United States varies. All social security benefits are exempt, while pensions from private systems are exempt to the extent to which they are derived from payments by the recipients. In addition, retirement income from investments is free of the basic (20 per cent) tax rate, up to the sum of $1,200, subject to various requirements. This system is not only complex, but is by no means satisfactory, since it discriminates in favor of social security benefits relative to others. As application of social security becomes more general, the discrimination will become less serious. Under the Canadian system, all amounts paid into pension systems, including, after 1957, most retirement schemes, are deductible in the years earned, but all pension payments are fully taxable. This method reduces the total tax from

---

[4] See U.S. Treasury, Division of Tax Research, *The Income Tax Treatment of Pensions and Annuities* (Washington, D.C., 1947).

these sums, because the total incomes received by the persons in the years in which they obtain the pensions are typically lower than in the years they were working. It also discriminates somewhat against other methods of saving for old age.

Even when retirement benefits are taxed to the recipient, some opportunities for tax avoidance are created for persons who are employees, compared to the self-employed, such as professional men. There has been a growing trend for corporations to provide substantial retirement benefits for their executives in lieu of salary increases, and thus essentially to shift income from high-tax years to lower-tax years. In contrast, no similar alternative is available for a person who is not an employee. Since 1957, Canada has permitted deduction of amounts paid by the self-employed for certain types of annuities; and in 1962, Congress approved a plan of this sort for the United States.

Annuities give rise to particular problems, since they constitute in part a return of money previously paid in, and in part interest earnings on this sum, the relative size of each element depending upon the number of years the person lives after starting to draw the annuity, and thus indeterminable prior to death. For some years, in the United States an arbitrary rule, involving taxation of the sum of 3 per cent annually on the original cost of the annuity, was employed. In 1954 the law was changed to permit an annual deduction from the amount of the annuity received based upon life expectancy. This rule is more equitable, but highly complex. The Canadian procedure of taxing each year the portion representing interest on the remaining capital discriminates against those persons living relatively short periods after commencing to receive the annuities.

The general question of the taxation of life insurance is a related, though somewhat distinct, one whose complications cannot be dealt with at length here. Insurance policies are in part protection against risk, and in part a form of investment. Under present tax laws the earnings on the investments are never taxed under the income tax, unless the policy is realized upon by the person himself. Accordingly, wealthy persons are given a great incentive to invest in insurance, since by so doing, they can increase the amount which will be available to their heirs over what would be possible if the money were placed in other securities yielding taxable income. It would not be impossible to devise a method of reaching annual interest earnings. But the taxing of these earnings when the policyholders do not actually receive them creates a host of equity and constitutional problems, and would add one more complication to the calculation of tax liability. The practical solution must, of necessity, provide liability at time of death. The present treatment, unfortunately, like several other features of the tax system, encourages wealthy persons to put their funds into safe investments instead of developing businesses or purchasing common stock.

### Interest on Government Bonds

A long-debated issue is the question of the income tax treatment of interest on government bonds. To the extent that such income is not taxed, the government can borrow more cheaply, so that the tax loss is offset in part by the interest saving. But so far as the taxing government is concerned, it was long ago recognized that the interest gain would equal the tax loss only if all the bonds could be sold in the highest bracket income class. Since this is not possible, the interest rate must be sufficiently high to induce persons in lower brackets to purchase the bonds; for all bonds held in income classes higher than this marginal one, the tax loss to the government exceeds the interest gain. Thus, in 1942, in recognition of this fact, all interest on new United States federal issues was made taxable.

When, however, the bonds are those of a jurisdiction different from that applying the tax, the issues are altered. In the United States, for example, the exemption of interest on state and local bonds benefits these governments, since it allows them to borrow more cheaply (about one percentage point less than otherwise), while the tax loss is borne by the federal government. The tax loss far exceeds the gains through lower interest rates. But this gain is very important to the state and local governments, and they have thus gained a strong vested interest in continuation of the exemption. A recent estimate indicates that the rate on municipal issues would rise from 1.2 to 2.0 percentage points if the exemption were removed.[5] Not only is the present situation very inequitable, since persons in the high income brackets can escape a substantial tax burden to which they would otherwise be subject, but the incentive given these persons to buy state and local bonds instead of equity issues lessens funds available for economic development. The objections are strengthened by the fact that a substantial portion of state and local borrowing is undertaken for essentially commercial purposes and, in part, for providing assistance to private business.

The present exemption of state and local bond interest is one of the most glaring defects in the tax structure; yet the opposition of the state and local governments to a change is so strong that reform is unlikely,

[5] David J. Ott and A. H. Meltzer, *Federal Tax Treatment of State and Local Securities* (Washington, D.C.: Brookings Institution, 1963).

especially if a constitutional amendment proves to be necessary.[6] In Canada, no such exemption exists.

## Other Exclusions

A few other exclusions are permitted under present income tax laws. Compensation received for damages or receipts from casualty and health insurance policies are never taxable, on the basis that they do not constitute income but merely offset losses. Most benefits paid to veterans are exempt, largely on the basis of a deliberate policy of assistance to this group. The United States has, during World War II and the Korean War, exempted a portion of the pay of servicemen as an indirect means of increasing the net service pay.

The most recent exclusion is that authorized for certain portions of sick pay, that is, compensation paid by the employer during illness. The exclusion is limited to $100 a week, and the amounts paid become eligible for deduction only after the illness has continued for one week. There is no delay in the event of accident or hospitalization. A special line is provided on the tax forms for this deduction, which is designed, of course, to ease the tax burden when the wage earner is incurring special expenses because of illness, and to equalize tax treatment of those receiving pay from their employers when ill and those receiving insurance compensation to cover lost wages. Logically, however, the sick pay should be taxable and the premiums paid for the insurance made tax-free.

## Labor versus Property Income

One type of deliberate discrimination sometimes favored is that of providing a lower rate on labor income, or at least on such income below a certain figure; until 1943 the tax on so-called "earned" income[7] was 10 per cent less than that on other income. Until 1961, Canada levied a flat 4 per cent additional tax on all investment income in excess of $2,400. Some persons argue for this discrimination on the basis of sacrifice—that

[6] It can be argued that the states and localities are far more hard pressed for revenue than the federal government. But they already receive extensive federal grants and could be given one roughly equal to the interest loss which they would suffer. The gain to the financial position of the states and localities under the present treatment cannot possibly justify the tax avoidance created. But the state and local governments are determined to fight to the last on the issue, despite all logic of the case.

See the article by George Lent, "The Origin and Survival of Tax Exempt Securities," *National Tax Journal*, Vol. XII (December, 1959), pp. 301–10; and Ott and Meltzer, *op. cit.*

[7] The term *earned* is unfortunate, as it implies that in some sense other incomes are not "earned." Within the framework of our economy, these other incomes can be considered "earned" as well as labor incomes.

persons who must work for a living sacrifice leisure that persons who are sufficiently fortunate to be able to live on investments can enjoy. The significance to be attached to this argument, which involves interpersonal utility comparisons, is strictly a matter of personal judgment. More important is the argument of income stability; labor incomes continue only if a person is able to work, while safe investments yield an income regardless of the personal status of the owner. Third, working entails certain costs—for transportation, clothes, etc.—which can be avoided if a person's livelihood does not require work.

It is likewise argued that workers should be allowed a reduced rate to compensate for the fact that they receive no depreciation allowance on their productive capacities, which will ultimately be exhausted. Particularly, the worker is under an obligation to save for old age, while the person who has an investment income already has his reserve built up. Finally, it is argued that most of the avenues of tax avoidance are open only to recipients of property income.

The importance to be attached to these considerations is difficult to assess. So far as additional costs due to employment are concerned, direct deductibility of these might be preferred, while increased social security is in part an answer to the "need for saving" argument. Administration and tax compliance are inevitably complicated somewhat by any differentiation provision. The Canadian and American (prior to 1942) procedures of assuming that all income under a certain figure is earned, regardless of its source, greatly simplifies the task of the taxpayer but lessens the justification for the differentiation system.

### Global versus Schedular Taxes

The income taxes of the United States, Canada, and most continental European countries lump all income (except exempted items) into a single category, subject to a single rate structure. Losses in one category are therefore deductible against gains in others. These taxes are known as *global* taxes. By contrast, the original taxes of France, Italy, Belgium, and other continental countries, plus those of most Latin American countries, were *schedular* taxes, with various types of income (wages and salaries, profits of business, etc.) subject to different rates, and with no deductibility of losses in one category from gains in another. These typically had proportional rates. Ultimately, a single progressive surtax was added, applying to all income. There has been some tendency to shift toward the global form, which is now accepted as being the simplest and most equitable form. Great Britain still retains separate schedules, but all taxable income is lumped and given uniform treatment.

# REFERENCES

### General References on Income Taxation, Chapters 7–12

Several major studies of income taxation relate to the material in chapters 7–12:

Vickrey, W. *Agenda for Progressive Taxation*. New York: Ronald Press Co., 1947.

Although now out of date, this remains as the most thorough theoretical analysis of income tax structure.

U.S. House of Representatives, Committee on Ways and Means. *Tax Revision Compendium*. 3 vols. Washington, D.C.: U.S. Government Printing Office, 1959.

A series of papers, many of high quality, on income tax questions, prepared at the request of the Ways and Means Committee.

Simons, H. C. *Personal Income Taxation*. Chicago: University of Chicago Press, 1938.

An historical and analytical treatment of personal income taxation.

Goffman, I. J. *Erosion of the Personal Income Tax Base*. Toronto: Canadian Tax Foundation, 1959.

A comparative analysis of exclusions and deductions in the United States and Canada.

Ott, David, and Meltzer, Allan H. *Federal Tax Treatment of State and Local Securities*. Washington, D.C.: Brookings Institution, 1963.

A thorough analysis of the question of exemption of state and local bond interest.

McGurran, H. D. "Principles of Income Tax," a series of eight articles, in *Canadian Tax Journal*, Vols. VI and VII, September-October, 1958, through November-December, 1959.

Analysis of Canadian income tax.

### Current Income Tax Information

U.S. Internal Revenue Service, *Your Federal Income Tax* (annual).

Current income tax information.

Commerce Clearing House. *Commerce Clearing House Federal Tax Service*. Chicago (annual).

Loose-leaf volumes providing detailed information.

Prentice-Hall, Inc. *Prentice-Hall Federal Tax Service*. Englewood Cliffs, N.J. (annual).

CCH Canadian, Ltd. *Canadian Tax Service*. Toronto (annual).

Canadian Tax Foundation. *The National Finances*. Toronto (annual).

# Chapter 8

# INCOME TAX DEDUCTIONS

# AND EXEMPTIONS

The figure of a taxpayer's total receipts during the period is clearly an unsatisfactory measure of taxable income regardless of the definition of income employed. For persons operating businesses of any type, including farms, the professions, and provision of rental housing, total receipts, or *gross incomes*, to use the phrase of tax terminology, in large measure are required to cover the expenses of conduct of the business. Such expenditures do not result in the satisfaction of personal wants, and thus do not constitute consumption, in terms of the basic definition of income as consumption plus increase in net wealth. In terms of the "flow of wealth" definition, the portion of total receipts which must be paid out in the conduct of the business does not constitute a part of the net flow of wealth to the person during the period. Accordingly, income tax laws universally permit the subtraction from gross income of *business deductions*, expenses necessary to gain the income. In the United States the figure of gross income minus business deductions is known as *adjusted gross income*.

While the tax could be applied to the figure of adjusted gross income, in practice further refinements are permitted in order to arrive at a figure which is regarded as a more satisfactory measure of taxpaying ability than the income figure itself. There are two types of deductions permitted from adjusted gross income in arriving at the figure of *taxable* income:

1. *Personal deductions*, various expenses which are considered to reduce taxpaying ability, such as medical expenses.

2. *Exemptions*, or *credits for dependents*, designed to adjust taxable income in terms of the size of the family.

Each type of deduction will be reviewed in subsequent sections.

## BUSINESS DEDUCTIONS

If persons are to be taxed upon the basis of the net economic gain they enjoy during the period, it is obviously necessary to allow them to subtract from their gross income the amounts they must spend in order to obtain the income. For the most part, these items are clearly distinguishable from consumption expenditures. In the conduct of a business, payments for wages, materials and goods sold, heat, power, and transportation, and interest on money borrowed for use in the business are not expenditures which in themselves yield satisfaction to the owner but are necessary for the conduct of the business. These items are universally deductible from gross income.

On the other hand, it is equally obvious that expenditures by a person for food, clothing, housing, recreation, etc., are personal consumption expenditures, since they constitute use of income in the satisfaction of personal wants. Thus, they are not properly deductible as expenses necessary to gain the income. There are, however, a number of items of a borderline character, which may be regarded as either business or consumption expenditures, depending upon intent, or which may be used in part for both purposes.

### Dual-Use Commodities

Commodities do not fall clearly into categories of consumption goods on the one hand and capital goods on the other. Many articles are capable of either type of use, and may be purchased by persons for use in part for both purposes. This is particularly true of purchases by farmers, professional men, and operators of small businesses. A farmer buys a truck for hauling his produce to market but also uses it for personal shopping and recreational driving. A professional man uses a portion of his home as an office. A farmer acquiring a set of tools for use in farming buys a much more expensive set than he needs because of his fondness for high-quality equipment. In all such cases the separation of the expenditures into business and personal elements is very troublesome, largely because an appropriate division depends upon intent, which cannot easily be discovered or proved.

Similar problems are encountered with hobbies which take the form of business operations. A farmer raises show animals, primarily as a hobby and only incidentally for supplementary income. The expenses are likely to be in excess of any income from the activity; should the loss be deductible from other farm income? Logically, it should not be deductible, to the extent that the real intent of the enterprise is personal pleasure, not income. But actual determination of intent in such cases is almost hopeless.

Apart from the question of establishing a logical dividing line is that of preventing deliberate tax avoidance or evasion by the taxpayer treating essentially personal expenses as business deductions. Without doubt, this is one of the most important sources of escape from tax and inequity in the income tax structure, a problem of particular importance because this escape route is available only to persons gaining income from sources other than wages and salaries. Farmers, professional men, and operators of small businesses are in the best position to escape taxes by this means. A farmer or a doctor deducts all of his car operating expenses instead of only those properly attributable to his business activity. Expenses of vacation travel are deducted as costs of travel necessary for business, as are those of entertainment. By contrast, the average worker, dependent upon wages or salary, has no possibility open to him of comparable deductions. Corporation executives, however, receive similar gains in the form of nontaxable fringe benefits, noted in the previous chapter.

### Education

Perhaps the most troublesome question, from the standpoint of principle, relates to the treatment of expenses for education. To the extent that education is a source of greater income in the future, payments for it are expenses necessary to gain the income. Deduction can be justified on the grounds of incentives and equity, and failure to allow it may have some adverse effect upon the flow of labor into those occupations which require substantial expensive training. Yet an attempt to allow deduction of costs of education encounters serious difficulties. One problem is that of timing. If the deductions are allowed during the years in which the education is being received, most persons would receive little benefit, since they are making little or no income. Frequently, the gain would go to the parents, who might or might not be made more willing to finance and encourage additional education for the children. If amortization of the costs of education were allowed during the subsequent years in which the person was working, determination of tax liability would be complicated, and the privilege of amortization might have little effect upon decisions on choice of occupation. There is a further problem of determining the amount to be deducted. Tuition costs are often a minor part of the total costs, while the living expenses are a major item. These are not easily calculated, and full deductibility is scarcely warranted, since a person must live whether in school or not. Actually, the most significant cost of obtaining advanced training is that of the sacrifice of the income which could otherwise be earned during the period, and calculation of this loss is almost impossible.

Accordingly, any system of general deductibility of educational expenses appears to be impracticable. On the other hand, there is strong justification for allowing parents to treat children in college as dependents, when they otherwise meet the eligibility requirements. Under original income tax laws, persons lost dependency status once they reached the age of eighteen. The age requirement was later removed; and then, in 1954, continued dependency status was authorized for full-time college students even if they made more than $600 a year themselves. There is also a valid case for permitting adults who are required to obtain additional education to remain in their current occupations and receive promotions to deduct the expenses involved. Thus, for example, the expenses incurred by schoolteachers in attending summer sessions are appropriately deductible. Since 1958, deduction is permitted of educational expenses incurred to further the person's status in the particular line of work—but not to move to a higher position. The dividing line is inevitably arbitrary regardless of where it is drawn.

### Care of Children

Another borderline case is that of expenses of having the children or home looked after if all adults in the family are working. The problem is particularly serious for a widow or divorcee who must work in order to support her small children and must hire someone to care for them. For many years, no deduction was allowed; but because of many complaints, in 1954 Congress authorized a deduction of amounts paid by a widow or widower for care of dependents under twelve or incapacitated, up to the sum of $600 a year.

A somewhat similar case is that of the family in which both husband and wife work. The expenses of having the children taken care of, incurred only because the wife works, are expenses which are necessary if the income is to be obtained. If no deduction is permitted, in many cases little is left of the wife's income after these expenses and taxes are deducted, and thus wives are discouraged from obtaining work. Such a policy might be regarded as justifiable on the grounds of general social policy, but this was not the reason; Congress was unwilling to open another loophole for the deductibility of living expenses. In 1954, Congress did provide limited relief by applying to working wives the same rule as applied to widows and widowers, provided that the combined income of the husband and wife is less than $4,500 a year (with partial relief up to $5,100).

This problem is closely related, of course, to that of the taxation of the imputed value of the work of housewives. If this work were taxed, there would be no need to consider the deduction of expenses of having the home and children cared for if the wife works, since there would be no discrimination against the working wife. But since this policy cannot be followed, some deduction of the expenses is justifiable.

### Travel Expenses

The only business deductions permitted a person who is working as an employee are those for transportation and travel necessitated by the occupation, such as those incurred by an outside salesman, and not reimbursed by the employer.

Expenses of commuting to and from work have never been recognized as expenses of gaining the income, but rather as personal living expenses, despite complaints and litigation. The case for nondeductibility is substantial, because a person has the choice of living close to work or far from it; and presumably, the latter offers certain advantages, such as lower housing costs, better living conditions, and the like. If the commuter were allowed to deduct the traveling expenses but the downtown dweller was allowed nothing to compensate for his higher living costs, discrimination would result.

The question of moving expenses necessitated by changing jobs, however, is a substantially different one. The failure to permit this deduction is an obstacle in the path of labor mobility and optimum use of resources, and the dollar amounts of tax revenue involved are not great.

### Miscellaneous Items

Under American (and since 1951, Canadian) law, workers are permitted to deduct union dues and fees of membership in professional societies, as well as certain expenses of work clothes of a type not suitable for general wear, tools, etc. These are legitimate deductions of the character of business expenses; but for simplification of tax returns, they are authorized only as personal deductions and thus are not available to a taxpayer using the standard 10 per cent deduction.

### The Legitimacy of Business Expenses

A further problem in determination of income is that of the propriety of certain expenses incurred in the operation of a business. Primary difficulty is encountered when over-all tax liability may be reduced by making certain types of payments. A farmer may lessen his tax liability by paying his small son for work which may or may not have been done by the son, for example. With the corporate form of organization discussed in Chapter 13, tax liability may be reduced by paying out larger sums as salaries to the owners, instead of paying them as dividends.

The general rule established by law is that payments made must be "reasonable." Thus, payments of salaries to persons who are also owners must be commensurate with the position, although no close check is made except in obvious cases of intent to avoid tax. Payments to minor children are deductible only if made for work actually done, a rule necessary to prevent tax evasion but difficult to enforce. The Internal Revenue Service, in practice, rarely questions the legitimacy of payments and has not attempted to use the tax laws to penalize persons for making unwise expenditures which do not benefit the business or to control the amount of expenditures on advertising and similar activities.

Similar questions arise with expenditures on fringe benefits to executives and employees, as noted in the previous chapter.

### The Depreciation Deduction

The business deduction which gives rise to the greatest amount of controversy is that of depreciation. Firms are not permitted to charge the costs of capital equipment (any assets with expected life in excess of one year) as expenses in the year in which the equipment is purchased. Instead, they are permitted to deduct an annual depreciation charge, designed, over the life of the equipment, to allow the recovery of the dollar sum invested in the equipment tax-free. The major problems relating to depreciation center around the question of the allocation of the total capital sum over the various years of the use of the equipment; thus, discussion will be postponed to Chapter 10, which deals with a variety of problems relating to the time interval for income taxation.

## PERSONAL DEDUCTIONS

As noted in the introductory paragraph to this chapter, adjusted gross income, that is, net income in the usual sense of the word, could be used as the basis for application of the income tax. But a given sum of income does not necessarily represent the same tax capacity, because persons have widely varying demands upon this income. Accordingly, income tax legislation makes some effort to adjust the tax burden more closely in terms of tax capacity by permitting the deduction of certain types of personal expenses. These include the *credits for dependents*, noted in the following section, and various *personal deductions*. In addition, a few additional personal deductions are authorized primarily for the purpose of encouraging certain types of expenditures.

1. *Medical Expenses.* Substantial medical expenses, which are largely out of control of the taxpayer, can materially reduce the level of living attainable from a given dollar income. If two families have the same incomes and numbers of dependents, and one has no sickness while the other has very heavy medical bills, obviously the second family cannot enjoy as high a level of living as the first. Thus, its economic well-being and its taxpaying ability are less. If all families had about the same medical expenses relative to income, there would be no need for a specific deduction, but this is not the case. Because illness is distributed very unevenly, some families find it necessary to spend very disproportionate amounts for medical bills, which do not actually constitute elements in a higher level of living but are necessary to overcome the misfortunes of illness.

In recognition of this problem, both the United States and Canada allow a deduction of medical expenses in excess of a minimum (3 per cent of income in Canada, 3 per cent of adjusted gross income in the United States) regarded as more or less normal, and subject in the United States to a maximum designed to prevent unnecessary reduction in the tax liability of wealthy persons. This deduction has very strong justification.

It may be argued that a tax credit would be preferable to a deduction from income in order to equalize the tax saving among all income classes.

2. *Other Taxes Paid.* A much more controversial issue is that of the deductibility of other personal taxes paid. Canada allows no deduction at all, while the United States allows no deduction of federal taxes but authorizes deduction of almost all state and local taxes, including property, income, gasoline, and sales taxes (when quoted separately by the vendor), excise taxes if levied on the sale to the customer, and motor vehicle license "fees," which are actually taxes.

A case can be made for the deductibility of state income taxes, to avoid any chance of the combined state-federal burden exceeding 100 per cent. Even so, the deductibility greatly reduces the progressivity of the state taxes. There is no real justification for allowing the deduction of other taxes. While they represent necessary expenditures, so do the minimum amounts paid for food, clothing, shelter, and other items, payments which are presumably covered by the exemption allowed each taxpayer. On the whole, the deductibility of other taxes lessens the progressivity of the income tax (since the low-income groups cannot, in effect, deduct them). Deductibility of the property tax tends to discriminate between the tenant and the homeowner. Deductibility is largely a product of a mistaken notion that failure to provide it is "double taxation" or a "tax on a tax," phrases which have no significant meaning in this instance for tax policy.

3. *Interest.* Interest payments, in a sense, reduce taxpaying ability, because they are mandatory once the obligations are incurred. But most persons incur the interest obligations voluntarily, so that they can enjoy a car or the ownership of a home before they have the necessary funds to pay in cash. In a sense, the interest can be regarded as negative income. But since the imputed income from consumer durables is not taxed, the interest should not be deductible. However, in the United States, all interest is deductible. The deduction was authorized initially because of the difficulty of separating personal and business interest. In the case of homes the interest deduction does equalize the tax burden slightly between the person who owns his home outright and the one who has only a small equity. But it creates a discrimination between the person who has borrowed to buy and the person who lives in rented property, since the latter bears his landlord's interest burden, yet cannot make any deduction.

4. *Casualty Losses.* Losses of property due to fire, theft, accident, etc., are reasonable deductions, because they represent a decline in net wealth and thus a necessary subtraction in the calculation of the actual income of the period. These are authorized in both the United States and Canada. The failure to allow deduction of insurance premiums on casualty insurance in a sense discriminates against the person who insures compared to the one who does not and loses his property. But this is not a serious matter.

5. *Contributions.* Charitable and other eleemosynary institutions perform essentially governmental functions, ones which the governments would otherwise have to undertake. In order to further the work of these private institutions and lessen the need for the transference of their work to the governments, deduction of contributions (up to 20 per cent of adjusted gross income in the United States, with an additional 10 per cent for contributions to churches, educational institutions, and hospitals; 10 per cent of net income in Canada) is allowed and can easily be justified. Unfortunately, the privilege has at times been abused; pseudocharities have been established primarily for the purpose of benefiting the persons who set them up. For example, a charitable trust would be established by the owners of a business and the real property of the firm transferred to it. The trust would receive a rental from the firm for the use of the property,

from which it would pay a nominal sum to charity, and then reinvest the remainder in additional plant facilities for the firm. The business therefore essentially obtained tax-free use of the portion of the profits needed for expansion. Attempts have been made in recent years to strengthen the safeguards against this type of abuse.

With religious organizations the situation is slightly different; the general philosophy in the United States and Canada has been that the governments do not directly support the churches financially but can properly encourage them by means such as allowing deduction of contributions. This is a value judgment of which no scientific evaluation is possible.

6. *Miscellaneous.* Certain other deductions are permitted in the United States. These include losses from bad debts, alimony (which is taxable income to the recipient), and certain expenses connected with employment noted in the preceding sections, which are logically business deductions, but which, for simplification of the tax returns, are defined as personal deductions.

Other deductions are occasionally suggested, such as those of insurance premium payments. Most of these proposals have little merit, and would further erode the income tax base.

### The Optional Deduction

One peculiarity of the United States income tax structure is the provision of the optional or standard deduction, equal to 10 per cent of adjusted gross income, up to a maximum of $1,000, available as an option for all taxpayers. This option, placed in the income tax law in 1942, was designed to simplify determination of tax returns and make possible the use of tax tables, with which no listing of deductions or calculation of tax by the use of the tax rates is required. As the law stands today, therefore, every taxpayer is assured a deduction equal to 10 per cent of adjusted gross income, subject to a $1,000 maximum. Accordingly, those taxpayers at each income level whose deductible expenditures are less than 10 per cent of income are all placed in the same position, taxwise, regardless of the actual size of their expenditures on deductible items. Persons who have relatively greater expenses which are deductible (but totaling less than 10 per cent of income) pay no less tax than persons with much smaller deductible expenses.

Approximately the same result could be attained more simply by eliminating the optional deduction, allowing persons to subtract only the portion of the sum of deductible items in excess of 10 per cent of their incomes, and readjusting the tax rates downward. At present, real benefit is attained from the deductions only if they exceed 10 per cent of income. For all other persons the gains from the deduction are fictitious, since the granting of the allowance requires comparably higher tax rates to raise a given amount of revenue. The only benefit from the present system is a purely psychological one; persons believe the optional deduction to be of real benefit to them and may thus be somewhat less hostile to the tax. A proposal by President Kennedy in 1963 to limit deductions to amounts in excess of 5 per cent of income encountered violent opposition and very little support.

The philosophy of allowing a standard deduction or accomplishing the same result in other ways may be condemned on the ground that it contradicts the whole basis upon which the deduction system is established— that of adjusting actual burden in terms of certain expenditures which affect the living levels obtainable from a given income. On the other hand, it may be argued that there is no need for adjusting these items unless they become substantial relative to total income.

There are two incidental benefits from the present system. In the first place, the optional deduction offsets some of the inequities in the system of permissible deductions; thus the discrimination against the tenant compared to the homeowner is reduced, because the former can use the optional deduction. Secondly, the amount of petty "chiseling" in the form of overstatement of deductions is greatly reduced. And of course, the filing of tax returns is simplified.[1]

## EXEMPTIONS

The third type of deduction from gross income, known as *exemptions* or *credits for dependents*, is designed to exclude from taxable income the sum required for a minimum standard of living, on the ground that this portion of total income does not reflect any taxpaying ability. There are two major consequences of the provision of exemptions: the complete exclusion from tax of families with very low incomes, and the variation in tax burden on the basis of size of families, for those subject to tax. In addition, the exemption gives rise to a certain amount of progression in the distribution of the burden of the tax.

Perhaps, logically, each family should be permitted to deduct the actual amounts spent to obtain a minimum living standard, as defined. But since this procedure is not administratively feasible, the deduction of

---

[1] The percentage of taxpayers using the standard deduction has fallen steadily, from 82 per cent in 1944 to below 62 per cent in recent years. In Canada in 1959 68 per cent used the option of deducting a flat $500 from tax.

a flat sum is permitted regardless of actual expenditures. This approach is reasonably satisfactory because there is a high degree of uniformity in amounts various families must spend in order to subsist. But the uniformity is not complete; a family in Minnesota, for example, must spend more for fuel than one in Florida, while a given quantity of food will cost more in New York City than in country towns. In other words, a flat dollar deduction means more in real terms in some areas than in others. Adjustment for these differences, however, is not practicable.

The most important source of variation in the amount that must be spent to enjoy a given living level is the size of the family. The larger the family, the lower is the living level which can be attained from a given income. Accordingly, the "minimum living expenses" exemption which is allowed each family is made dependent upon the number of persons in the family, and the amount of tax paid at a given income level therefore varies inversely with the size of the family.

The general desirability of this type of adjustment cannot be questioned; one of the greatest merits of the income tax is the ability to adjust the burden in terms of the size of the family, and thus the living level which can be enjoyed at a given money income level. However, there are several issues about the exact nature of the adjustments.

1. *The Size of the Exemption.* The height of the exemption not only controls the over-all coverage of the tax, that is, the extent to which low-income groups are exempt, but also the magnitude of the variation in burden on families of different size, and the degree of progression within the lower income brackets. In terms of the general intent of the exemption, it may be argued that the size should be dictated by the sum required for a minimum living standard for families of various sizes. However, it is impossible to derive such a figure by any scientific means, and attitudes of various persons differ widely about the appropriate magnitude. In practice, the selection of the figure has been controlled largely by revenue requirements of the government. The $600 figure in the United States in 1963 is certainly below the amount required for any sort of typical minimum living standard. The Canadian figure, $1,000 for a single person, $2,000 for a married couple, and $550[2] for each dependent, is somewhat more realistic in terms of living standards. The use of a relatively low figure is often defended on the ground that virtually all families should make some contribution to the support of government, however small.

Since the exemptions are fixed in dollar terms, they do not change

---

[2] Three hundred dollars if eligible for family allowance, which is not taxable income.

as the general price level varies. Thus, continued inflation greatly reduces the real value of the exemption, and deflation increases it. As a consequence, the exemption system contributes to economic stability, since in inflationary periods the governmental revenues rise faster than national income, while in depressions they drop more rapidly.

2. *Exemption versus Tax Credit.* The exemption for dependents may be established as a given dollar deduction from income or as a specified dollar deduction from the amount of tax. Thus the taxpayer might be allowed to deduct $600 from income for each dependent, or he might be allowed to deduct perhaps $120 from his tax bill for each dependent. If the exemption is established as a deduction from income, the dollar tax saving resulting from a dependent is greater in the higher income levels than in the lower, since the tax rates are higher. With the second method the allowance is the same, in dollar terms, regardless of the income of the family. It may be argued in favor of the "deduction from income" method that the dollar cost to the family resulting from an additional dependent will be greater for high-income families than for those with low incomes. This method also equalizes the burden more satisfactorily among families of different sizes at a given income level. On the other hand, the "dollar credit from tax" method is regarded as more equitable by some persons, on the basis that the wealthy should not be allowed more tax savings for each dependent than the poor. This issue can be resolved only in terms of consensus of opinion about equity, which appears to favor the "deduction from income" method. This technique is used at the federal level and in most states, although a few use the tax credit method, as do some other countries, as, for example, Rhodesia.

3. *Uniformity of Size of Allowance.* A further issue is the question of whether or not the exemption should be uniform per dependent, regardless of age or number of dependents.

Under present American law the allowance is $600 for each dependent, including the taxpayer. For many years, however, the amount was greater for the taxpayer and spouse than for additional dependents. This latter method is used by many states and by the Canadian federal government, which allows an exemption of $1,000 each for the taxpayer and spouse, but only $550 for each dependent. The dependent allowance is reduced to $300 if the child is under sixteen, on the assumption that the family allowance is received. The family allowance is not included in taxable income.

Since certain basic living costs are more or less independent of the size of the family, it is reasonable to allow a larger credit for the taxpayer and spouse than for succeeding dependents, who do not add proportional amounts to the expenditures necessary for a given living level.[3] In the United States a couple without children pay tax if their income after other deductions exceeds $1,200, while a couple with four children pay only if their income exceeds $3,600. The latter family can certainly enjoy a better level of living than the former.

The United States system has the merit of simplicity and provides a type of subsidy for large families. If such a policy is deliberately followed, the United States treatment can be justified. If this end is not sought, the Canadian system has greater merit.

The question of whether the amount should be adjusted according to age of the dependent is not easily answered, in the absence of any very satisfactory data of relative costs of maintenance of children at different age levels. The unfortunate provision in the original American law denying dependency status for children over eighteen was finally removed. Canada still limits the credit to children under twenty-one unless they are attending college or are infirm. In Great Britain, the East African countries, and elsewhere, the allowance does vary with the age of the dependents.

4. *Definition of Dependents.* The concept of a dependent is not at all clear-cut, the possible cases extending all the way from the 100 per cent dependence of a month-old baby to the limited dependence of an adult son living at home, or the derelict brother who sponges off the family. Fairly rigid rules are necessary to prevent serious tax avoidance, and splitting of the exemption figure on the basis of degree of dependence is usually regarded as too troublesome administratively to warrant permitting it. The United States rules prior to 1954 were particularly rigid; considerable liberalization was provided in that year, at the expense of greater complexity in the operation of the tax. The basic rules require:

1. Provision of more than one half the dependent's support, with modifications for joint support by two or more persons.

2. Income of the dependent less than $600, with the exception of children under eighteen and college students.

3. Relationship of the dependent to the taxpayer within the categories defined by law.

The exemption status is an "all or nothing" proposition; for example, if a baby is born on December 31, the parents are entitled to the exemption for the entire year.

The Canadian law is even more rigid, although sharing of the ex-

---

[3] For empirical evidence, see the article by Reed R. Hansen, "The Diminishing Exemption—A New Look at Equity," *Quarterly Review of Economics and Business*, Vol. II (November, 1962), pp. 7–16.

emption is permitted in the event of support by several persons. Parents and adult brothers and sisters are eligible for dependency status only if infirm.

## TAX CREDITS

Distinct, technically, from the deductions and exemptions, but often very similar in effect, are the *tax credits*, deductions permitted from the figure of tax payable. The principal distinction between the credits and the deductions is that the former offer the same dollar gain to the taxpayer regardless of his income, whereas subtractions from income benefit the taxpayer according to the marginal tax rate to which he is subject. The principal tax credits in the United States are listed below:

1. Certain foreign taxes paid. The credit is designed to eliminate international double taxation. This deduction is permitted only to persons not using the optional 10 per cent deduction, under one of the most unjustifiable provisions of the legislation.

2. An amount equal to 4 per cent of dividends received, as explained in Chapter 13. This rule is designed to reduce double taxation of corporation income.

3. Retirement income, to the extent of 20 per cent of the sum received, up to $240. The aim is essentially to exclude this income from the basic tax rate, for reasons noted in Chapter 7.

Amounts withheld from wages, and those paid on the basis of declarations of estimated income, are of course credits against tax due at the time of filing of the return.

## SOME GENERAL CHARACTERISTICS OF THE DEDUCTIONS

In 1960 the standard deduction was used by 60.5 per cent of all taxpayers. The returns showing itemized deductions reported adjusted gross income in total of $181.1 billion. Deductions for contributions totaled $6.8 billion; for interest, $8.4 billion; for taxes, $10.5 billion; for medical care, $5.2 billion; and the remainder, $4.4 billion. These total $35.3 billion.[4] Various studies show that the ratio of personal deductions to income is relatively constant at various income levels, with some increase at the higher levels; thus, at the latter the deductions reduce progression to some degree. The particular items vary; with contributions the percentage is substantially higher at high income levels. Medical deductions

[4] U.S. Internal Revenue Service, *Statistics of Income for 1960: Preliminary—Individual Income Tax Returns.*

vary inversely with income. The total magnitude of the deductions is substantial; if none were provided, the income tax rates could be about five percentage points lower (a beginning rate of 15 per cent instead of 20 per cent).

## REFERENCES

See general income tax references listed on page 000, particularly Vickrey; Goffman; and *Tax Revision Compendium*, pp. 365–473.

KAHN, C. Harry. *Personal Deductions in the Federal Income Tax.* Princeton: Princeton University Press, 1960.

McGREGOR, G. *Personal Exemptions and Deductions.* Toronto: Canadian Tax Foundation, 1962.

A review of the various categories, with comparative reference to the United States, Canada, and Great Britain.

LEVY, M. E. *Income Tax Exemptions.* Amsterdam: North Holland Publishing Co., 1960.

# Chapter 9

# INCOME TAX RATE STRUCTURE; INCOME TAX ADMINISTRATION

There are two major questions relating to the rate structure, namely, the definition of the taxpaying unit to which the rates are applied, and the actual system of rates.

## THE TAXPAYING UNIT

The most logical unit for the application of an income tax is obviously the income-earning and income-spending unit, which in modern society is the family. While each individual could be treated as a separate entity for tax purposes, such a procedure would disregard the basic cultural pattern. In many families the wife and the children would have no income tax liability, and treatment of them as separate units would deny to the wage earner, and thus to the family as a unit, the tax benefits appropriate on the basis of the greater expenditures necessary for a given level of living. While it is therefore customary to treat the family as the unit, the exact definition and the tax treatment of its members require attention.

### Treatment of Husband and Wife

So far as the husband and wife are concerned, in the United States today they are treated as partners in the earning of the income, which for tax purposes is divided equally between them regardless of which person actually earned the money. If a husband and wife wish, they may treat themselves as separate units for tax purposes by filing separate returns. But except in rare instances, it is not advantageous, taxwise, for them to do so. The present principle is in accord with the typical family situation in which incomes are pooled and used jointly for family welfare. The procedure does, however, result in a much heavier relative burden on the single persons. Beyond the first bracket of tax, if a person marries, not only does he receive an additional exemption, but he also gains the advantage of tax brackets twice as wide as those provided for single persons. In the United States, with 1962 tax rates, the tax saving due to marriage (in addition to the added dependency credit) is $680 at $10,000 income, $4,060 at $32,000, and $13,680 at $100,000. Likewise, the procedure creates a serious problem for the satisfactory treatment of unmarried persons who maintain a family household, as, for example, a child supporting his parents, or a widow or widower with minor children. If a man's wife dies, for example, his tax burden materially increases, even though his expenses (with minor children) are as great as, or greater than, before. Changes in the federal tax law mitigated this problem by providing that a single person qualifying as the head of a family may use a special rate table yielding a result intermediate between the tax liability of a single person and that of a married couple.

An alternate practice used in Great Britain and other countries is the requirement that husband and wife file a single return, the combined income being taxed on the same rate schedule as that of a single person, except for the additional dependency credit. This procedure has the unfortunate result of increasing the total tax burden of two income-earning persons when they marry. In the United States an additional argument raised against such a policy is the fear that it would encourage couples to live together without benefit of a marriage ceremony.

The third alternative is to allow husband and wife to file joint or separate returns if they wish, with no splitting of income if joint returns are used. Thus, if both husband and wife earn substantial incomes, they can file separately to advantage; if one earns most of the income, no splitting is possible. This system protects the revenue at a given tax rate, without increasing the tax burden on a working couple when they marry. But it has the unfortunate disadvantage of favoring persons having property incomes over those having labor incomes, because the former, by placing some of the property in the name of the wife, can reduce income tax liability.

The Canadian system resembles this third alternative. If the wife's income is small, joint returns may be filed, but with no income-splitting feature. But if the wife's income exceeds $1,000, the filing of separate returns is mandatory. The most objectionable feature of this system is the advantage given to families gaining income from property, since they can reduce tax liability by dividing the property among various members of the family.

### Other Members of the Family

A related problem is that of the family unit in which persons other than the husband or wife earn considerable income, even though they are an integral part of the family. Thus a child, minor or adult, may continue to live at home, although earning substantial income, or a brother or sister may live in the family unit. Under present treatment in the United States, so long as these persons are legally dependents for tax purposes, their own income up to $600 is tax-free, and they provide a dependency credit for the principal taxpayer. Thus, essentially, there is a double exemption. If the income of these persons exceeds the maximum, or if they otherwise do not qualify as dependents, they are treated as independent taxpaying units, completely distinct from the family unit of which they are a part. This somewhat arbitrary treatment results in some persons paying relatively too much tax and others relatively too little, if their expenditure needs as well as their incomes are taken into consideration. Thus, if a child becomes self-supporting but lives in the family, he receives the same credit as a single person living alone, although the expenses necessary for a given level of living are much less. The complete exclusion from tax of income earned by dependents has little justification and facilitates tax avoidance. However, the worst feature of the present treatment is the ability of persons with property incomes to reduce tax liability by transferring property to the minor children and lessen the operation of progression. Each child becomes a separate taxpaying unit, though he is still an integral part of the family unit.

A complete solution to this problem is difficult to find. The first step is closing the double exemption loophole by reducing a dependent's own personal exemption to perhaps $200. Mandatory inclusion of the income of the children in the family income would close this avenue of avoidance. But determination of whether the children actually are integral parts of the family creates problems. The use of age alone as a criterion is insufficient, because some minor children may be essentially self-supporting units, whereas children over twenty-one may be integral parts of the family. Some countries partially meet the issue by requiring inclusion of income from property transferred to the child.

One alternative, as proposed by William Vickrey and others, and used in France, is that of regarding all members of the family household as partners in the earning of the income, just as the husband and wife are now treated. The incomes of all members of the family household are summed, and then divided among the various members, the children being treated as partial partners, with a quotient less than one (in France a child is counted as one half). The effect of this system is to eliminate the present discrimination in favor of property incomes relative to wage income. But it increases the tax advantages of larger families (although this can be offset by exemption adjustments), and gives rise to problems about delimitation of the family household.

## THE STRUCTURE OF RATES

An income tax may have a proportional rate, all taxable income being subjected to the same figure, as is the case with several state income taxes. But the principle is generally—but by no means universally—accepted that the rate structure should be progressive. Limited progression is of course created by the use of an exemption, but significant progression in distribution of burden also requires the use of progressive rates, since the effect of the exemption in giving rise to progression is significant only in the relatively low taxable income brackets.

While there is widespread acceptance of the view that the tax rates should be progressive, there is disagreement about the appropriate degree and speed of progression. These questions must be resolved on the basis of general attitudes toward equity in the distribution of income accepted in the particular society and on an evaluation of the significance of any economic effects which may be produced by the progression. So far as the first question is concerned, there are great variations in attitude, but the general view supports the principle that a fairly rapid progression which continues to a high rate is desirable in the interests of equity. Other persons believe that progression should be very much less.

The question of economic effects will be analyzed in the next chapter. Again, there are substantial differences in opinion but little conclusive evidence of any kind. The present degree of progression, although very severe, has not prevented a high degree of investment and general prosperity during the last fifteen years, but the effects might have been greater had there been fewer loopholes. In future years, additional information should become available about the actual effects of various degrees of progression upon the economy.

It must be emphasized that the case for progression is based upon the consensus of opinion in a particular society with respect to equity in the distribution of real income. It cannot be argued that progression or any particular degree of it is inherently desirable or undesirable upon the basis of economic principles. Primarily, apart from possible economic effects, progression must be evaluated on an ethical basis.

Table 3 shows the rates in effect in the United States and Canada for the 1962 year for selected income levels. Table 4 shows the actual income tax burden at different income levels, for a single person and for a couple in the United States and Canada, on 1962 income. In the lower income groups the burden in Canada is less, because of the higher exemption. For a single person in the United States the burden remains above

TABLE 3

MARGINAL INCOME TAX RATES, UNITED STATES AND CANADA,
1962, SELECTED INCOME LEVELS

| Taxable Income Exceeding: | United States* | Canada† | Taxable Income Exceeding: | United States* | Canada† |
|---|---|---|---|---|---|
| $     0.......... | 20% | 11% | $ 25,000......... | 43% | 50% |
| 1,000.......... | 20 | 14 | 60,000......... | 62 | 60 |
| 2,000.......... | 20 | 17 | 125,000......... | 78 | 70 |
| 5,000.......... | 22 | 22 | 225,000......... | 89 | 75 |
| 10,000.......... | 26 | 35 | 400,000......... | 91 | 80 |
| 15,000.......... | 30 | 45 | | | |

\* For a married couple filing a joint return.
† Before abatement for provincial taxes.

that in Canada throughout. But with married couples the Canadian burden rises above that in the United States, where the operation of progression is slowed down by the income-splitting provision, but falls behind at very high levels. The Canadian figures are those before abatement for provincial taxes.

TABLE 4

RELATIVE INCOME TAX BURDENS, UNITED STATES AND CANADA, FOR 1962*

| INCOME | SINGLE TAXPAYER | | MARRIED COUPLE, NO DEPENDENTS | |
|---|---|---|---|---|
| | Canada | United States | Canada | United States |
| $     700........... | $      0 | $      6 | $      0 | $      0 |
| 1,000........... | 0 | 60 | 0 | 0 |
| 1,500........... | 44 | 150 | 0 | 30 |
| 2,000........... | 99 | 240 | 0 | 120 |
| 2,500........... | 166 | 330 | 44 | 210 |
| 3,000........... | 236 | 422 | 99 | 300 |
| 5,000........... | 591 | 818 | 403 | 660 |
| 10,000........... | 1,840 | 2,096 | 1,544 | 1,636 |
| 15,000........... | 3,630 | 4,002 | 3,230 | 2,960 |
| 20,000........... | 5,825 | 6,412 | 5,357 | 4,532 |
| 30,000........... | 10,520 | 12,228 | 10,020 | 8,434 |
| 50,000........... | 20,965 | 25,668 | 20,415 | 19,002 |
| 100,000........... | 50,855 | 65,928 | 50,205 | 52,056 |
| 200,000........... | 119,550 | 155,380 | 118,850 | 132,726 |

\* The old-age security taxes are omitted.
SOURCE: Canadian Tax Foundation, *The National Finances, 1962-63*, p. 25.

Certain general observations can be made about the schedules. The initial brackets are narrower ($1,000) in Canada than in the United States, so that progression (beyond that produced by the exemption) becomes effective more quickly. In the United States, about 80 per cent of all income taxpayers have incomes within the first bracket (under $2,000 for single persons, under $4,000 for married couples) and thus are not subject to progressive rates at all. In both countries the degree of progression is very rapid once it commences. For example, in the United States, for 1962 the marginal rate is 47 per cent on an income of $15,000 and 75 per cent on one of $50,000 for a single person. The progression becomes more gradual as the higher levels are approached, reaching a maximum rate of 91 per cent in the United States at $200,000 for a single person. All these rates are marginal rates, applying to the income in excess of the stated figures, not to the person's entire taxable income.

The very high figures in the top brackets are not of much significance from a revenue standpoint because of the relatively few taxpayers in these brackets. In 1960, for example, there were only about 5,700 returns with adjusted gross income in excess of $200,000, and obviously many less returns with taxable income over this figure. There are only about 295 with incomes in excess of $1 million.

The actual degree of progression is very much less than it would appear to be from the rate table. The income-splitting provision in itself slows down progression very markedly for a person who is married; for example, a married person who is earning $50,000 taxable income is paying tax only at the marginal rate applicable to a $25,000 income of a single person. A considerable portion of the income at the high levels, furthermore, consists of capital gains, which are subject to a maximum rate of 25 per cent (and are not taxable in Canada). The various means of avoidance open to wealthy persons, such as division of property among various members of the family, use of family partnerships, purchase of state and local bonds, etc., further reduce the operation of progression.

A study based on 1956 data showed that those persons with annual incomes (adjusted gross income) under $2,500 paid an average tax of 5.4 per cent of their incomes, while those from $2,500 to $5,000 paid 12.7 per cent. Other typical figures were: income from $10,000 to $15,000, 15 per cent; $50,000 to $100,000, 35 per cent; $500,000 to $1 million, 49 per cent.[1]

The present rate structure is criticized on two bases: The great majority of taxpayers are subject to the basic proportional rate, the tax being progressive only to the extent brought about by the exemptions; and on the other hand, the top rates bring in very little revenue. Given present-day typical money income levels, the vast majority of all families fall within the first bracket. In 1957, 70 per cent of all taxable income was obtained by persons in the first tax bracket, and the basic 20 per cent rate yielded 87 per cent of the tax revenue.

---

[1] See U.S. House of Representatives, Committee on Ways and Means, *Tax Revision Compendium* (Washington, D.C.: U.S. Government Printing Office, 1959), p. 2226.

The easiest solution to the problem of establishing additional progression in the lower brackets is to divide the first bracket in half, applying, perhaps, a 10 per cent rate to the first portion and 20 per cent to the second. The extreme progression at the top levels could be cut back to 50 per cent without any significant loss in revenue, particularly in light of the fact that the lower rate would lessen pressures to avoid tax. More complete evaluation of present progression must await a review of economic effects of the tax; but in terms of revenue and equity considerations, it is rather difficult to defend the extremely high top-level rates, ones to which very few people are subject because of avoidance possibilities, yet which offer greatest dangers to the economy.

## CURRENT COLLECTION

Traditionally, in conformity with customary procedure in the calculation of income, the year has been the basic unit for income tax payments. But for many individuals the need for making payment of tax in one lump sum on income earned throughout a year period proved to be a serious burden, which was only partially mitigated by allowing payment in four instalments. The latter procedure, in turn, resulted in a very long delay between the receipt of income and the payment of tax on it, to the disadvantage of the government and, in many respects, to the taxpayer himself.

Accordingly, at the time income tax rates were raised and exemptions lowered at the beginning of World War II, a system of withholding was established, both in Canada and in the United States, to insure payment of at least the bulk of the tax on a current basis. Employers are required to withhold tax from the wages and salaries paid their employees; persons with significant income not subject to withholding are required to file declarations of estimated income and pay in four quarterly instalments. In the United States a declaration must be filed if (1) income not subject to withholding exceeds $200 a year, provided that total income exceeds a specified figure, or (2) all income exceeds the figure of $10,000 for a married couple, or $5,000 for other taxpayers. In Canada a declaration is required simply if less than one quarter of the income is obtained from wages and salaries. Special rules are provided for farmers in both countries.

The withholding system has several very important merits. It lessens the burden on the taxpayer by insuring that the tax is paid as income is earned and no large liability is accumulated. Delinquency and evasion are reduced, and tax payments vary currently with changes in national income and respond quickly to tax rate changes. These last two considerations are of great importance in facilitating fiscal policy. Under the old system, when tax rates were raised sharply, a year or more elapsed before tax revenues showed the effect of the increase. When a depression came and incomes dropped sharply, persons were saddled with high income taxes on the previous year's income in the year in which their incomes were reduced; not only were they hard pressed to pay, but their consumption was reduced still further by the tax payments.

The current collection system has certain limitations, however. The costs of compliance on the part of employers are not negligible, although from the standpoint of society these costs are offset by the lessened real burden on the individual taxpayers. More seriously, withholding, by removing the tax from the paycheck before the worker receives it, has the effect of reducing the take-home pay and may encourage unions to demand higher wages than they would otherwise settle for and thus essentially shift some of the income tax burden from the particular workers. Such shifting not only lessens the equity of the distribution of the burden of the tax but greatly weakens its anti-inflationary effects. Finally, the system does not work with complete effectiveness on persons other than wage earners, since the system of payments on declarations of estimated income does not insure payment by these persons on exactly the same current basis as workers. On the whole, however, current collection represents a major improvement in the operation of income taxes, particularly by producing a continuous flow of tax revenue concurrently with the earning of the income.

## ADMINISTRATIVE FEASIBILITY

No tax can conform with accepted standards of equity if it cannot be administered with a high degree of effectiveness. If persons are able to escape, by legal or illegal means, the tax to which they should logically be subject under the general scope of the tax, the theoretical equity of the tax is to a large measure lost.

### Evasion

The basic limitation of the income tax is the inability to check with complete accuracy the reported incomes and the amounts claimed as deductions. When incomes are paid from sources which can be easily checked, the chances for evasion are slight, as is true, for example, with most wage, salary, and dividend receivers. But there are certain groups of persons whose incomes are obtained from sale of goods or personal services in relatively small transactions. Since accurate check upon reported income in such cases is virtually impossible, these groups in the economy, particularly farmers, professional men, and operators of small businesses, are able to escape with considerable understatement of income and overstatement of business expenses. A test audit by the Internal Revenue Service has shown that over 70 per cent of the misstatements of tax liability arise from underreporting of adjusted gross income, in most cases involving understatement of receipts. Deduction of essentially personal expenditures as business expenses is a major source of evasion. Many persons fail to report miscellaneous casual income from irregular sources.

The magnitude of the evasion from underreporting income is difficult to assess. One effort has been made to determine the amount of evasion in quantitative terms by comparing incomes reported by various occupational groups on their tax returns with the Department of Commerce estimates of total incomes received in these occupations. On this basis the income tax returns were shown to report 95 per cent of wages and salaries, 87 per cent of nonfarm entrepreneurial income, 76 per cent of dividends, 37 per cent of interest, 45 per cent of rent, and only 36 per cent of farm income.[2] These estimates were based upon 1944–46 data. A study of dividend reporting by Daniel Holland showed evasion on 14 per cent of all dividends and about 30 per cent of interest.

A 1959 study (for 1957 incomes) shows comparable results.[3] The estimates showed 97 per cent of all wages and salaries to be reported, 86 per cent of dividends, 42 per cent of interest, 74 per cent of entrepreneurial income, and 40 per cent of farm income. These figures are, of course, not entirely accurate, but are of significance in showing the wide range of variation by type of income. It is probable that most underreporting of dividend and interest income occurs in the lower income groups, since the information reporting by corporations of larger sums paid serves to check evasion in the higher levels. In the future, more complete reporting will greatly reduce understatement of dividends and interest; all amounts of interest and dividends in excess of $10 must be reported. Use of electronic data-processing equipment will allow much more complete check of information returns against tax returns.

Evasion from overstatement of personal deductions is limited to persons not employing the optional deduction and is probably not great in

---

[2] See Selma F. Goldsmith, "Appraisal of Basic Data Available for Constructing Income Size Distributions," Part VI in Vol. XIII, *Studies, Conference on Research in Income and Wealth* (New York: National Bureau of Economic Research, 1951); and W. W. Heller, "Limitations of the Federal Individual Income Tax," *Journal of Finance*, Vol. VII (May, 1952), pp. 185–202.

[3] See the article by C. H. Kahn in *Tax Revision Compendium*, pp. 1439–59.

magnitude, although limited overstatement of some items is likely to be fairly widespread. Some overstatement of dependents also occurs; in latest test audits of the Internal Revenue Service, about 16 per cent of all errors discovered involved misreporting of dependents.

As time has passed, improved enforcement standards have been developed and have gradually cut down the amount of evasion. Audit control programs have been identifying those types of returns most likely to show error, and greater attention has been given to these. But the fact remains that only a small fraction of the returns receive any actual audit. In 1962, about 3.5 million returns were examined out of 96 million total returns. While most income is reported, largely because it originates in sources such that check is either automatic (through withholding or information returns) or is relatively easy, evasion continues. But it would not appear to be sufficiently great, either in the United States or in Canada, to destroy the basic equity of the tax. Yet the leakages do require ever-vigilant check upon returns and do suggest that continued increases in income tax rates will intensify the problems.

### Avenues of Avoidance

The equity of an income tax can be lost through legal means as well as by illegal escape. The income taxes of both Canada and the United States, but particularly that of the latter, have so many avenues of avoidance that the actual burden is much less severe than it appears to be from the rate tables. It is not feasible to examine these avenues in detail; a few can be outlined briefly.

1. *Capital Gains.* The tax-free status of capital gains in Canada and the favorable treatment in the United States pave the way for substantial tax avoidance through conversion of other income, especially earnings of closely held corporations, into capital gains. Congress has attempted to check some of the more flagrant techniques, such as the use of collapsible corporations, but considerable avoidance is inevitable so long as capital gains receive favorable treatment. This problem is discussed in Chapter 11.

2. *State and Local Bond Issues.* In the United States the purchase of state and local bonds insures a safe method of avoidance for persons in all but the lowest income brackets.

3. *Depletion Allowances.* The liberal depletion allowances on natural resources, and the exclusion from tax of earnings used for further exploration and development, have frequently been utilized as a method of reducing tax liability.

4. *Division of Property among Members of the Family.* A com-

mon technique is the division of ownership of property among various members of the family, in order to escape the effects of progression. This is difficult to prevent; the problems in treatment of members of the family were outlined above, and as indicated, no entirely satisfactory solution is possible. Family partnerships are also used to reduce the effects of progression.

5. *Trusts.* Judicious use of trusts also reduces liability; each trust, under both Canadian and United States law, is treated as a separate taxpaying unit, the income being taxable neither to the donor nor to the donee, but to the trust itself. Thus the operation of progression is reduced. The person, of course, must be willing to freeze his property in an irrevocable trust.

6. *Insurance.* Use of insurance as a form of investment can reduce materially the total tax paid on property which is to be transferred to one's heirs, since the interest return on the investment is never reached by the income tax.

7. *Executive Compensation Plans.* In recent years, extensive use has been made of various techniques of increasing the incomes of executives in a tax-free fashion. One method is through stock options, whereby the executive is given the right to buy stock of the company at a specified price. When the stock has risen in price, he exercises the right, being taxed only on the capital gain when the stock is sold. Deferment of partial compensation until retirement is another. Provision of various tax-free real benefits, such as health insurance, can often increase real income materially without increasing tax payments. These techniques are not necessarily objectionable, but they do enable some persons to reduce tax liability.

8. *Self-Incorporation.* By incorporation a person may be able to escape high personal rates, his earnings becoming subject to the lower corporate rate to the extent to which they are held in the business. They may ultimately be withdrawn via capital gains, or in years of low earnings. This technique has been barred, so far as investment income is concerned, by the placing of a severe penalty tax on personal holding companies. But movie and TV actors and other professional entertainers earning very high salaries have found it possible essentially to incorporate their activities, the corporation selling their services. To avoid penalty taxes, the corporation must do more than merely sell the services of the one person owning it, but it is usually not difficult to broaden the activities to provide other services as well.

In a few cases, these avenues are products of the inherent problems of a satisfactory definition of taxable income and the taxpaying unit, as is the case with division of property among various members of the family. But many of the leakages are products of defects in the law; this is true with respect to capital gains, state and local bond interest, depletion, treatment of trusts, and insurance. A foolproof solution to the last two problems is difficult. Canada has avoided opening a few of the loopholes, especially in respect to government bond interest, but allows most of the remainder. In the United States the Treasury has long recognized these defects and has tried to get several of the major loopholes closed, but with only limited success, because of the strong political pressures to retain them.

## REFERENCES

See general income tax references listed on page 139: Vickrey, chaps. iv, x, xi, xiii; *Tax Revision Compendium*, pp. 473–538, 1397–1536, 2223–80.

Federal income tax enforcement problems are discussed in detail in two papers presented at the Conference on Tax Administration in Buenos Aires, October, 1961:

OLDMAN, OLIVER. "Controlling Income Tax Evasion."

SURREY, STANLEY S. "Automatic Data Processing and Tax Administration."

The September, 1961, issue of the *National Tax Journal* (Vol. XIV) is devoted to the question of the use of electronic data processing in tax administration.

# Chapter 10

# THE TIME PERIOD PROBLEM UNDER INCOME TAXATION

Income is essentially a flow or continuous stream, which goes on from the time the person earns his first dollar or, for tax purposes, the time he becomes an independent taxpaying unit, until he ceases to earn an income because of death, retirement, or other causes. If it were possible to tax persons on this entire flow over their lifetimes, many complications would be avoided. But as a practical matter, it is necessary to divide the flow into segments and apply tax to the amounts of income between the dividing lines which are drawn. The segments into which the income stream is divided are normally one year in length.

Three major problems arise from the segmentation of the income stream. The first two relate to the determination of business profits in a particular year. A considerable lag exists between the time when expenditures are incurred by the firms and the time when the goods purchased or produced are sold. Thus, in any time period the purchases made by the business are not entirely identifiable with the sales made by the business during that period. Part of the goods sold were produced with items purchased in previous periods, while part of the purchases during the period will be used for the output of future periods. No serious problems are created if the volume of business, the price level, the profits of the firm, and the tax rate are relatively constant. But variations in any of these give rise to complications. The most serious difficulties occur with durable capital equipment; but in periods of rapid changes in prices, troubles are also encountered with the valuation of inventories.

The third time period problem is of more general scope, that of providing suitable treatment of incomes which fluctuate from year to year.

## DEPRECIATION

Capital equipment purchased in one period may be used over a period of years. Accordingly, the cost of the equipment must be allocated

167

among the various years in which it is in use, the share allocated to each year being known as the *depreciation* charge. This is the sum necessary to maintain intact the money capital of the firm during the period, that is, to cover the actual depreciation, which is the decline in the value of the capital assets which occurs from usage or passage of time. A portion of the gross receipts of a firm each year consists of the return of invested capital, which is obviously an expense, and not income, since it does not constitute economic gain to the owners. Failure to exclude it from income would result in taxing the owners of the business on receipts which represent merely a change in the form of assets rather than income as defined.

### The Problems of Determining Depreciation

Total depreciation charges over the life of the equipment must equal the original cost of the equipment if all of the money capital of the firm invested in the equipment is to be recovered tax-free. But at the time the equipment is installed, it is impossible to predict with any high degree of certainty the usable life of the equipment. Thus, any figure chosen is essentially an estimate, and if it proves to be longer than the actual life, the depreciation charges will be inadequate. Furthermore, there is no necessary way in which the total capital cost must be allocated year by year over the life of the equipment. Since it is impossible to ascertain the actual depreciation, in the sense of the decline in value of the equipment year by year, the total sum is allocated to the various years on the basis of arbitrary accounting conventions. A business firm can never be certain of the "correct" depreciation charges for any particular year, and thus of the amount of its profits for the year; only when the business is liquidated or all equipment now in use has been replaced can the actual profit for the period of years be ascertained.

In some cases the allocation of depreciation by year is not very significant, since the method of allocation will affect merely the tax payments in particular years but not the total over a period of time. This is true with a firm which is not expanding and has stable earnings from year to year, provided tax rates are also stable. The only difference in this case is the interest benefit from delaying tax payments. But in other cases the depreciation methods are very significant. If carry-over of losses from one year to another is severely restricted, and earnings fluctuate sharply or are subject to a significant upward or downward trend, the allocation method will influence tax liability. In years of heavy losses, depreciation charges will not be covered, and thus portions of the firm's money capital will not be recovered tax-free. If equipment suddenly becomes obsolete in years of losses, the same will be true. If tax rates fluctuate substantially, or earnings do so and tax rates are progressive (even though no losses are incurred), the long-period tax payments will be affected by the methods used to allocate capital costs over the various years.

Furthermore, the general system of allocation is highly important to a growing concern. So long as a firm continues to expand, its tax liability will be less, over the period of time in which growth continues, to the extent to which it can depreciate on a basis which allows relatively high deductions in the early years of the life of the equipment. The firm never catches up with itself so long as it continues to add capital equipment.

On the one hand, it is important, in terms of the general intent of income taxation, that firms be permitted to recover all capital tax-free; failure to do so is not only inequitable and discriminatory against firms with fluctuating earnings, but may impede investment unnecessarily. On the other hand, complete freedom on the part of firms to allocate depreciation by year would result in deliberate tax avoidance, since a dollar of deduction represents more tax saving to a firm in one year than in another.

### United States Practice

The United States has been relatively rigid in its control of depreciation policies, but there has been substantial relaxation in the last decade. Two basic rules have governed the procedure: (1) No asset can be depreciated beyond 100 per cent of cost, regardless of changes in replacement cost, and (2) depreciation allowable in one year but not covered cannot be charged in later years, except as results in effect through loss carry-forward. In addition, for many years, the Internal Revenue Service strongly favored the use of the straight-line method, which allocates a uniform sum of the capital cost to each year of the expected life, and frowned upon the use of any method which concentrated a heavier portion of the total in the early years of the life of the equipment. Many business firms favored the latter methods, under the argument that the actual decline in value is more rapid in early years than late.

In 1954, in response to many demands for change, Congress specifically authorized the use of the diminishing balances method, and its simplified relative, the "sum of year digits" method. These have the effect of virtually doubling the amounts deductible in early years of life of the equipment and cutting them in later years. The effect was to accelerate materially the over-all rate of depreciation. A primary goal of the change was the desire to stimulate new investment, the goal of better measurement of income being secondary. Some effect on investment is likely, but in total magnitude is probably small,[1] while the dollar tax loss to the government, in a growing economy, is very substantial. So long as the economy continues to grow, the revenue never catches up (although it does on any one capital asset); it is permanently less than the amount obtained with the straight-line method.

Internal Revenue has likewise controlled rather rigidly the rate at which property may be depreciated, in many cases holding firms to a longer period (and thus to a lower annual charge) than the firms believe to be desirable. However, deduction of extraordinary obsolescence or loss upon retirement of depreciable assets is allowed when the actual life is less than the originally expected life. But unfortunately, when equipment becomes obsolete, the firm is likely to show a loss for the period; the limited carry-back of losses may make it impossible to shift these losses into years of profit, and thus the firm has actually been taxed on recovery of capital. In 1962 the Treasury materially liberalized the depreciation time periods.

The Canadian treatment of depreciation is now more rigid than that in the United States. The law provides schedules of annual depreciation percentages for various classes of assets, the schedules based upon the diminishing balances method. The taxpayer no longer has any choice in the matter, from the standpoint either of method or of period of depreciation, except in that he is not compelled to depreciate at the maximum rate. The diminishing balances method does have the advantage of making the depreciation charge higher in years in which the equipment is new. Only in recent years have deductions for obsolescence been authorized; and even now, they are less liberal than in the United States.

### Inflation and Depreciation

The rapid increase in the general price level after 1939 has created a new depreciation issue. Since capital equipment increased greatly in cost, the sum of the depreciation allowances upon the old equipment is not sufficient to cover the cost of the new equipment necessary to replace it when it wears out. Accordingly, it has been argued that for tax purposes as well as others, firms should be allowed to depreciate upon the basis of replacement rather than original cost, or to adjust original cost upward by an index number of the general price level. Adjustments of this type have actually been allowed in countries such as France and Belgium, in which inflation was much more severe. The issue has been debated very extensively in the accounting profession and elsewhere.

[1] See E. C. Brown, "The New Depreciation Policy under the Income Tax Act," *National Tax Journal*, Vol. VIII (March, 1955), pp. 81–98.

Regardless of the merits of the replacement cost basis for nontax purposes, it can be justified for tax purposes only as a deliberate policy of facilitating the task of firms in obtaining additional money capital necessary to replace worn-out capital equipment. However, so long as a business is prospering, the additional money capital required for the more expensive equipment can be obtained, since a normal return can be earned upon the funds. If the enterprise cannot earn such a return, reinvestment is not warranted. There is no evidence in recent years that firms have actually encountered difficulty in obtaining additional money capital required for replacement of old equipment.

Considerations of equity require merely that the owners be allowed to recover, tax-free, the capital originally invested; the fact that a greater amount of capital is now required to continue operation on the same basis does not in itself justify a policy of allowing the owners to obtain a certain amount of income tax-free. Added cost of equipment is a manifestation of general increases in the price level; since there are no feasible tax adjustments which will compensate all persons suffering from inflation, there is no obvious reason for doing so for the owners of businesses whose equipment has become more expensive. In a sense, these persons benefit for a substantial period from being able to use equipment purchased at lower prices to produce goods selling at current high prices and hence are squeezed by inflation much less severely than many other persons.

### Special Depreciation Allowances and Tax Credits

In part because of the problems of increased cost of capital equipment, and in part because of the desire to minimize the effects of the income tax on investment, several countries have introduced special tax concessions for investment in the past decade. One approach is that of *initial allowances*, as developed in Great Britain in the late forties, whereby an additional sum over and above regular depreciation is deductible in the first year in which new equipment is acquired, but the subsequent deductions for depreciation are reduced accordingly. This system was introduced on a small scale in the United States in 1958, with an initial 20 per cent allowance on industrial equipment, subject to a dollar maximum. The net effect of the initial allowance approach is to delay payment of tax and thus to provide working capital to the firm and to reduce annual tax liability so long as the firm is expanding.

A more positive measure to encourage investment is the *investment allowance* or tax credit for investment, first introduced in Great Britain in 1954, and in modified form in the United States in 1962. It is also used in Rhodesia, in the East African countries, and at times in various

European countries. The investment allowance, established as a percentage of the amount invested in new equipment, is deductible in full in the year the equipment is acquired, and does not reduce the subsequent allowable depreciation charges. Under the United States version, 7 per cent of the investment outlay is a direct credit against tax due, but the sum eligible for subsequent depreciation charges is reduced by the amount of the credit. Thus the system has features of both the initial allowance and the investment allowance plans;[2] in effect, for a firm subject to the maximum corporate income tax rate of 52 per cent, it constitutes an initial allowance of roughly 3.5 per cent and an investment allowance of roughly 3.5 per cent.

The usual investment allowance system, including that in the United States, is provided on the gross amount of the types of investments covered, rather than the net amount over and above depreciation charges on existing equipment, as sometimes proposed. The net approach should provide maximum incentive to new investments for a given amount of revenue loss, but provides no incentive for modernization, as distinguished from expansion, and is generally unpopular with business groups because of its limited range of impact. One basic difficulty with all these concessions is that most of the investment would be undertaken without the allowance, and it is difficult to determine the marginal amount influenced by the tax concession.

### Depletion

One of the most extreme cases of special favors in the federal income tax legislation is that of the very liberal depletion allowances permitted the oil, gas, and mining industry. Such enterprises, in addition to normal depreciation deductions on their capital equipment, are allowed an annual deduction, known as depletion, designed to reflect the declining value of an exhaustible asset. Firms in the industries affected are given the choice of cost or percentage depletion, the latter typically being the most advantageous. The cost method involves dividing the number of recoverable units of output into the total value of the resources owned, and multiplying this figure by the year's output. The percentage depletion authorizes the deduction of a specified percentage of *gross income* for tax purposes, year after year, without end. As of 1962, the percentage allowed was 27.5 for oil and gas, 23 for a number of metals such as lead and zinc, 10 for coal, 5 for gravel and sand, and 15 per cent for most other minerals. This extremely liberal provision greatly reduces the taxes

---

[2] Full credit is given only if the equipment has a prospective life in excess of eight years.

of the companies in these fields and makes the old statement that millionaires grow only in Texas more fact than fiction.

The strong tug of war has gone on over depletion allowances for a number of years, with continued successes for the pressure groups benefiting, and failure for the Treasury and the taxpayers as a whole. On the one hand, these allowances are defended as essential for continued exploitation and development of the natural resources. On the other, they are bitterly condemned as grossly discriminatory in favor of the owners of the firms in the industries involved, and as unnecessarily expensive to accomplish the desired purposes. Their basic defect arises from their application to all firms in the fields affected in order to aid the few marginal operations. The cost to the Treasury has been estimated to be over $500 million a year. The concession can easily produce misallocation of productive resources. In some fields, serious question can be raised about the desirability of encouraging a rapid rate of exploitation and thus depleting resources available for the future.[3]

## INVENTORY VALUATION

The second problem of determining income in a particular year is that of the treatment of the changes in the value of inventory. A firm has on hand a given stock of goods at the beginning of the year; it buys additional amounts, sells a certain quantity, and ends the year with a certain amount on hand. If the prices of the goods purchased do not change, no problem is encountered. Beginning and ending inventories and cost of goods sold during the period will all be valued at the constant figure. When price levels are changing, however, a problem is created. If prices are rising and the costs of goods sold are figured on the basis of the cost at the end of the period, the total cost of goods sold will appear to be greater, and the profit less, than if they had been valued on the basis of the cost at the beginning of the year.

### FIFO and Its Limitations

For many years, conventional accounting practice has required that the cost of goods sold be figured on the basis of the cost of the earliest acquired portion of the inventory on hand at the beginning of the period and (if sales exceed the beginning inventory) on the earliest acquisitions

---

[3] See pp. 933–1060 of the *Compendium* volumes of the U.S. House of Representatives, Committee on Ways and Means, listed at the end of the chapter; and articles on the subject in Vol. XIV (December, 1961) and Vol. XV (June and September, 1962) of the *National Tax Journal.*

during the period. Closing inventory, in turn, is valued at cost or market value at the end of the period, whichever is lower. This procedure is based on the assumption that goods are sold in the order in which they are purchased—first in, first out (FIFO). Thus, if the replacement cost of inventory rises during the year, the cost of goods sold is still figured on the basis of the original cost of the stock on hand at the beginning of the year (and thus at figures less than actual cost of additional amounts). Thus, total profit includes gains from increased value of the stock in trade held during the period of the price increase, as well as ordinary merchandising profit. The reverse is true when profits decline.

The limitations of this approach to the calculation of income, for both tax and other purposes, have long been recognized in periods in which prices fluctuate rapidly. In industries with substantial inventories subject to price fluctuations, attempts were made in the earlier years of the income tax to eliminate the effects of the inventory price changes from income by carrying inventory at a fixed value. When this procedure was held invalid for income tax purposes in 1930, various firms sought a different approach.

### Development of LIFO

Out of this situation evolved the LIFO (last in, first out) procedure, under which it is assumed that the sales are made from the last addition to inventory rather than the first. Thus, cost of goods sold is determined by the cost of the last units purchased. If total units sold exceed the amount purchased at the latest price, the price on those acquired at the next earliest time is used on the remaining units. The inventory is valued at the end of the year on the basis of the cost of the earliest acquired units. As a consequence, in periods of rising prices, no inventory profits—gains from selling goods acquired at low price levels in a period in which prices are higher—are included in income; in periods of price declines, no inventory losses are subtracted. Thus, profits appear to be lower than those shown with the FIFO procedure when prices are rising, and higher when they are falling. Over a long period of time, total profits and total tax liability would be about the same, regardless of the method employed, so long as tax rates were constant and not progressive. Primarily, the choice of method would affect the timing of tax payments under these circumstances. But with fluctuating and progressive rates the total long-run tax bill will be affected as well.

LIFO accounting was first legalized for tax purposes in the United States in 1938 and allowed broader application in 1939. While a substantial number of firms have adopted it, others have been deterred from doing so because, once LIFO is introduced, it cannot be abandoned without specific approval of the Internal Revenue Service. Many firms fear the consequences of its use in periods of falling prices. LIFO is not permitted in Canada. The primary objection to the LIFO system is the fact that tax revenue will rise less rapidly during periods of inflation than under FIFO, and thus the anti-inflationary effect of the tax will be less.

## THE PROBLEM OF IRREGULARITY OF INCOME

The complications which arise in the determination of the earnings of business firms in any particular time period are actually only manifestations of a much broader problem which arises out of the segmentation of the flow of income into time periods, namely, that of obtaining equality of treatment between fluctuating incomes and those which are relatively regular from year to year. If this general problem could be solved, the manner in which business expenses were allocated to particular years would be of relatively little importance, and the problems of taxing capital gains would in large measure be eliminated without providing special treatment for this type of income.

### The Source of the Problem

When a person's income is constant from year to year, segmentation for tax purposes into annual amounts creates few problems; it makes little difference how the income stream is split into pieces if it flows at a uniform rate. But when incomes fluctuate, this is no longer true. Part of the problem arises from the provision of exemptions in the tax laws. If a person has no income or a very small income in one year, he loses the benefit of the exemption to which he is entitled, although his necessary expenses go on, regardless of the income. If he receives a large income the following year, he receives no credit for the exemption lost in the previous period. Thus, for this reason alone, two persons with the same total income over a period of years will pay different amounts of taxes if the income of one falls below the exemption figures in some years, while the income of the other is regular.

The seriousness of the problem is greatly increased by the progressiveness of the rate structure. If a person's income fluctuates sharply, he will be penalized in his high-income years because he reaches high brackets, without a corresponding offset in low-income years. Suppose, for example, that two persons received a total of $100,000 taxable income over a ten-year period, one receiving the entire amount in one year, the other receiving $10,000 per year. Under 1962 rate schedules the first person will pay a $67,320 tax, the second a total of $26,400 over the ten years. The result is a penalty on persons whose incomes fluctuate substantially. This group includes particularly the owners of risky types of businesses with greatly fluctuating earnings. Workers whose wages are irregular are likewise discriminated against, as well as persons such as actors, professional ballplayers, novelists, etc., whose incomes tend to concentrate in a relatively few years of their lives.

Apart from the discrimination, the effect of the present treatment is to encourage persons to alter the realization of income from one period to another, where possible, to minimize tax liabilities. Thus, there is a tendency to avoid realization of income in years in which other incomes are high or the tax rates are high and to concentrate realization of expenses in high-income years. The difficulties in providing a satisfactory treatment of capital gains are largely a product of the segmentation of income into annual periods, as explained in Chapter 11.

### Present Treatment of Irregular Income

Under the present United States and Canadian law, little recognition is given to the irregularity problem. Business firms are allowed to carry losses back three years and forward five years (one and five in Canada); this has the effect of averaging out the income when losses are incurred, but not otherwise. In Great Britain and some Commonwealth countries, unlimited loss carry-forward is permitted. Capital gains receive special treatment in the United States and are not taxed in Canada. Both countries have limited provisions applicable to authors and persons in related types of endeavor in which a large sum is received in one year for work done in several, but the restrictions are so severe that few persons benefit. Canada allows farmers and fishermen to average their income over a block of five years and recalculate tax for each year on the basis of the average income for the period. Once the privilege has been taken, it cannot be employed again for another five years. Beyond these rather limited, although desirable, provisions and a few other minor ones, no averaging of income over a period longer than one year is permitted in either country.

The basic difficulty with the present treatment is that to an excessive extent the year is regarded as an absolute, closed period for tax purposes. There is a tendency to regard the year's income, as determined, as final, with complete disregard of the fact that the division of the income stream into annual segments is essentially arbitrary. The use of the year period is essential, but it does not have to be regarded as final for tax purposes. To the extent that longer periods can be taken into consideration, the distribution of the tax burden will be brought more closely into conformity with the intent of the tax, and many of the complications and arbitrary features of the present structure will be avoided.

## Some Alternative Solutions

Any complete solution to the problem of irregular incomes requires substantial departure from the annual basis of calculation of income, and is difficult to attain. There are several partial solutions, in addition to those now in use for special cases.

1. *Moving Average.* The calculation of tax on a moving average basis (perhaps five-year) would smooth out the irregularities, but would produce a substantial tax liability in a year in which income fell sharply, and cause collections to lag behind increasing incomes in a period of inflation.

2. *Optional Recalculation, as Now Permitted for Farmers and Fishermen in Canada.* This system, if universally permitted, would reduce materially the discrimination against irregular incomes and permit the taxation of capital gains as regular income. However, there are substantial complications for the taxpayer and tax administrator, and an element of guessing in the selection of the blocks of years to use for recalculation. However, some further extension of the system has merit.

3. *Cumulative Averaging—the Vickrey Proposal.* A system of cumulative averaging which would avoid the problems of the first two alternatives has been proposed by William Vickrey. A person's total income would be cumulated from year to year, the total tax on the cumulated sum ascertained each year (on the basis of the number of years over which the accumulation had occurred), and the total tax paid in previous years plus compound interest subtracted to determine this year's tax. The cumulative averaging and the compound interest feature would eliminate the discrimination arising from irregularity, the gains to the taxpayer from postponing realization of income, and the need for recalculating the returns of previous years. The main obstacle is the conceptual complexity of the system; it should not be difficult to implement in practice.

The system has one limitation in principle: The tax yield lags behind increases in incomes. To meet this problem, some writers have suggested that the tax rate be based on the current year's income but be applied on the basis of cumulated income. Even so, the tax yield would be less responsive to tax changes and income changes than the present method.

Some students of the question have suggested that long-range averaging is neither essential for equity nor desirable. Shorter time intervals are of greater significance with respect to planning the use of income, and there is no particular justification for attempting to equalize the tax of two persons with the same lifetime income but allocated very differently over the years. If this point of view is accepted, optional recalculation is preferable to cumulative averaging.

4. *Carry-over of Unused Exemptions.* For most lower income taxpayers the loss in some years of the full benefit of personal exemptions (due to the fact that their incomes are less than their exemptions) is more serious than the effect of graduated rates on fluctuating incomes, as demonstrated by H. M. Groves with respect to the Wisconsin experience. This problem can be met without any elaborate averaging system by allowing taxpayers to carry over unused exemptions from one year to another. Some time limit would be required, partly to simplify administration, partly to insure that persons with long periods of low incomes did not escape taxation almost indefinitely once their incomes rose. With this modification the system has few objections and very real merit; for most taxpayers, it would accomplish as much as a complete averaging system.

## REFERENCES

### DEPRECIATION AND INVENTORY VALUATION

BUTTERS, J. K. *Effects of Taxation: Inventory Accounting and Policies.* Boston: Harvard University Graduate School of Business Administration, 1949.
A study of inventory valuation problems.

BROWN, E. C. *Effects of Taxation: Depreciation Adjustments for Price Changes.* Boston: Harvard University Graduate School of Business Administration, 1952.
A review of the problems created for the determination of depreciation by changes in the general price level.

GREAT BRITAIN. *Report of the Committee on the Taxation of Trading Profits.* London: H.M. Stationery Office, 1951.
One of the most complete studies of the problem of depreciation allowances in periods of rising prices.

U.S. HOUSE OF REPRESENTATIVES, COMMITTEE ON WAYS AND MEANS. *Tax Revision Compendium,* pp. 793–932 (depreciation); pp. 933–1060 (depletion). Washington, D.C.: U.S. Government Printing Office, 1959.

CHASE, S. B. "Tax Credits for Investment Spending," *National Tax Journal,* Vol. XV (March, 1962), pp. 32–52.
An analysis of various proposals to stimulate investment by investment credits.

### AVERAGING OF IRREGULAR INCOMES

WILLIS, J. *The Mitigation of the Tax Penalty on Fluctuating or Irregular Incomes.* Toronto: Canadian Tax Foundation, 1951.

The most complete survey of the averaging problem, with a very extensive bibliography.

VICKREY, W. *Agenda for Progressive Taxation*, chap. vi. New York: Ronald Press Co., 1947.
The cumulative averaging proposal.

GROVES, H. M. *Postwar Taxation and Economic Progress*, chaps. vii and viii. New York: McGraw-Hill Book Co., Inc., 1945.
A discussion of the problem of irregularity and of various solutions.

HOLT, C. C. "Averaging of Income for Tax Purposes," *National Tax Journal*, Vol. II (December, 1949), pp. 349–61.
Presentation of a modification of the Vickrey system.

SIMONS, H. C. *Federal Tax Reform*. Chicago: University of Chicago Press, 1950.
The overemphasis on annual time periods in the tax legislation is shown to be the source of many of the difficulties of the income tax.

# Chapter 11 THE TAX TREATMENT OF CAPITAL GAINS

One of the most troublesome problems of income taxation is that of devising a suitable method of taxing capital gains, in a system in which tax liability is based upon realization, and rates are progressive. If such gains could be taxed on an annual accrual basis, regular income tax rates could be applied without difficulty, and many of the problems created by the present treatment would be avoided. However, this practice is not only contrary to the general philosophy of the present income tax systems, but is not administratively feasible, since annual valuation of the assets of all taxpayers would be necessary. The task in practice is that of determining a workable compromise within the framework of the income tax structure.

## THE TREATMENT OF CAPITAL GAINS

### The Nature and Sources of Capital Gains

Capital gains consist of all increases in the sale value of property held, except merchandising profits on goods regularly bought and sold as a business activity. Thus, if land, buildings, capital equipment, stocks, bonds, and the like can be sold for prices higher than the amounts originally paid for them, a capital gain has occurred.

In dollar terms the major element of capital gains is made on common stock of corporations, with real estate a poor second, and other property of minor importance.[1] A primary source of the gain on stock is the reinvestment of earnings by the corporation. In addition, gains may arise as the earning capacity of a business increases due to improved management, development of new products and techniques, lessened competition, etc. Growth in population and economic activity increase both corporation profits and land value, and pure speculation may have the same effect.

[1] See L. H. Seltzer, *The Nature and Tax Treatment of Capital Gains* (New York: National Bureau of Economic Research, 1951), chap. x.

Urbanization is the prime source of increased land values. Capital gains are also in part the product of increases in the general price level, and of declines in the market rate of interest.

Capital gains are distributed in a highly progressive fashion among income groups, although with great individual variation. They constitute a major source of income of the higher income groups. Accordingly, any favorable treatment given them tends to reduce the progressiveness of the tax structure. On the other hand, capital losses concentrate heavily in the middle income groups; thus, limitation of the deductibility of losses from income particularly injures persons in these groups.[2]

### Capital Gains as Income

Capital gains logically fall within the category of income, whether income is defined as consumption plus increase in wealth or as flow of wealth, so long as they are not merely manifestations of general price level increases. The increase in the value of property held increases the person's economic well-being in the same manner as does ordinary income, unless the general price level has risen in the same proportion and, in some cases, unless the interest rate has fallen. If a person buys a piece of land for $5,000 and sells it for $10,000, the $5,000 gain is available for consumption or for increase in the person's net wealth just as surely as if he had received the $5,000 as salary or as profits from a business.

Accordingly, if capital gains were not taxable, persons receiving this form of income would be favored compared to persons receiving other forms of income. It is very difficult to justify such differential treatment on an equity basis; few persons would regard as equitable the exclusion from the tax of gains from stock speculation or from the ownership of land which increased sharply in value while other persons are taxed on wages, salaries, and the earnings from the conduct of business activity. It is likewise hard to justify complete exclusion of capital gains on the basis of economic effects; while taxation of them may lessen the supply of capital for business expansion, so does all taxation of the earnings of business enterprises.

The argument sometimes advanced that capital gains are not income represents simply an effort to redefine income in a manner different from the usual concept and one which is inconsistent with the general goals of income taxation. It is true, of course, that capital gains have certain characteristics different from many other types of income; they are nonrecurrent, and the taxpayer has considerable choice over time of re-

[2] *Ibid.*, chap. viii.

alization. But these considerations, while suggesting that special tax treatment may be desirable, do not alter the fact that capital gains are income, as defined.

As explained below, the issue is complicated when the gains are due to price level or interest rate changes. These cases will be considered separately.

### The Use of the Realization Basis

Much of the difficulty in the field of capital gains taxation arises from the need for taxing at the time of realization of the gain, rather than at the time of the accrual. In the first place, the gains are made much more irregular than they would otherwise be on an accrual basis. Since the property may be held for a number of years before realization, taxation of the entire gain in one year at progressive rates would be seriously discriminatory. Secondly, the time of realization can be adjusted to suit the convenience of the taxpayer. As a consequence, the taxation of the gains on a realization basis may lead persons to hold onto property which they would otherwise sell or, when losses have occurred, to sell it sooner than otherwise.

The first of these problems would be avoided and the second lessened in severity (relative to taxation at full income tax rates), by a general system of averaging of income, as discussed in Chapter 10, although the second problem would in part remain. However, since Congress has been unwilling to allow general averaging, some special treatment for capital gains was imperative if they were to be taxed at all.

### The Special Tax Treatment of Capital Gains

Present (1962) law in the United States gives the taxpayer two options: He may include half of all long-term capital gains (those on property held more than six months) in his regular income, or he may apply a flat 25 per cent tax rate to all such gains. Short-term capital gains, those on property held less than six months, are taxed in the same manner as regular income. On the long-term gains the present treatment not only avoids the penalty which would arise because the gains accrue over a period of years, but in addition, in many cases provides a much lower burden on capital gains than on other income. Capital gains on property held until death, or given to charitable and similar organizations, are not taxable at all.

While the special treatment of capital gains was largely a product of their irregularity, the continued provision of particularly favorable treatment has been a reflection of fear on the part of Congress that application of higher rates would impede the flow of money capital into investment outlets, and would aggravate the "locked-in" problem discussed below—the tendency of high taxes on capital gains to freeze existing investments. The capital gains treatment has also been regarded as a type of safety valve in the income tax structure, designed to lessen the dangers to the economy of highly progressive rates.

The net effect of the present tax treatment is to reduce materially the typical tax burden on persons in the higher income groups compared to what it would be under full application of the progressive rates to all incomes. Any type of investment on which gains can be realized via the capital gains route is rendered relatively more attractive than other forms of investments.

In Canada, capital gains are even more strongly favored, since they are not subject to income tax at all. In part, this treatment is an outgrowth of the historical development of the British tax system, and in part, especially in Canada, a deliberate policy designed to aid economic development. The scope of the definition of capital gains, however, is substantially less than in the United States, since many transactions which enjoy the favorable capital gains rate in the United States are fully taxable. These are primarily transactions of a more or less isolated character, not carried on as a part of regular activity, but definitely undertaken for the purpose of benefiting from increases in value of the property acquired.[3]

Great Britain did not tax capital gains until 1962, and many are still free of tax. Under the 1962 legislation, only "speculative" ones are taxable: those on land owned less than three years, and on other property owned less than six months. On the Continent, only Sweden, Finland, and Germany tax capital gains of individuals, and then only if the property is held a relatively short time.

## THE CONSEQUENCES OF FAVORABLE TREATMENT

The application of tax rates to long-term capital gains which are lower than the basic income tax rates gives rise to several important consequences. These are, of course, of greater significance in Canada, where

---

[3] The literature on Canadian treatment is extensive. Most of it centers around interpretation of the present treatment, with little question raised about the basic policy of exemption. Note R. Tresilian, "The Capital Gains Scare," *Canadian Tax Journal*, Vol. III (November-December, 1955), pp. 396–98; "Can Capital Gains Confusion Be Removed by Legislation?" *Proceedings of the 1956 Tax Conference, Canadian Tax Foundation*, pp. 29–63; F. M. Covert, "Capital Gains," *Canadian Tax Journal*, Vol. VI (September-October, 1958), pp. 348–59.

the gains are completely tax-free, than in the United States, but they are serious even in the latter.

### Borderline Problems

Application of special treatment to any form of income inevitably gives rise to problems of delimitation of the category affected and other income. A few of those arising with capital gains can be noted briefly.[4]

1. Is the person involved engaged in a trade or business? In other words, has he bought the property as an investment from which to gain an income, or has he bought it in the course of conduct of a business activity of dealing in the commodity? Regularity is an important criterion, but not necessarily conclusive. In Canada the requirements for obtaining capital gains treatment (and thus tax-free status) are more severe, the test being essentially whether or not the "badge of trade" can be applied. Tax status thus depends in large measure upon intent; even though the person does not regularly carry on a business activity in the property, the purchase of it for the purpose of gaining from an increase in value renders the gain taxable, whereas in the United States it may not be if the transaction is an isolated one. Many of the borderline cases arise in real estate transactions, since almost never are gains on securities held to be regular income, except for a dealer.

2. Is the property a "stock in trade" of a type normally handled in the course of the business? Even though the person is clearly carrying on a business activity, the gain from the sale of property not normally bought and sold by the enterprise may be treated as a capital gain. Ordinary merchandising profits are, of course, regular income. Special rules are provided for farm livestock and some other categories.

3. Is a particular payment by a corporation to its stockholders a dividend or merely a distribution arising from total or partial liquidation of the business, and thus entitled to capital gains treatment? There is strong incentive for corporations to attempt to distribute surplus in the form of liquidating payments in order to reduce tax liability.

4. Is a particular gain the result of an investment or of personal effort? For example, if a person develops a patented device and sells it, or writes a novel and sells the right, is the amount of the nature of a capital gain? In earlier years, capital gains treatment was often obtained in such cases, but the incentive given to convert wage or salary income into capital gains led to a tightening of the policy, so that today only the receipts from patents are eligible.

[4] Note the article by R. Slitor, "Problems of Definition under the Capital Gains Tax," *National Tax Journal*, Vol. X (March, 1957), pp. 26–37.

### Conversion of Other Income into Capital Gains

Because of the favorable treatment given to capital gains, strong incentive is given to convert regular income into the legal form of a capital gain. The most common method is the retention of profits in the corporation and subsequent realization of them as capital gains through the sale of the stock, or through some device which allows the owners to gain the benefit without sale of the stock. If the stock is held until the person's death, even the capital gains tax is avoided. The use of a special tax on accumulated earnings, discussed in Chapter 13, has not been successful in preventing this practice. In earlier years, until prevented by legislation, the personal holding company technique was even more effective; a person could essentially incorporate himself, and thus reinvest the earnings from his securities without their being subject to the high-bracket personal income tax rates.

The more extreme form of conversion involves the use of collapsible corporations, which essentially permit the conversion of the output of the firm into a capital asset subject to capital gains treatment. A group of persons form a corporation to produce a single motion picture, and then sell the stock of the company—and thus the picture— to a distributing company, realizing on the profits from the picture in the form of capital gains. Congress attempted to outlaw capital gains treatment for the collapsible corporation in 1951, but not with complete success.

Another common device, designed to lessen the tax burden on corporate executives, is the stock option technique. Corporate officials are given the right to buy additional shares of stock of the company at a relatively low figure; when they exercise this option and then sell the stock, the gain is subject only to capital gains rates. Similarly, bonds may be sold at substantial discount in lieu of higher interest payments.

Congress has made an effort to close the more obvious loopholes as they appear. But this is often difficult to do effectively, as, in Surrey's terminology, the property soon appears "under another shell." The basic problems of corporate accumulations is inherently difficult to solve, and attempts to lessen these avenues of avoidance seriously complicate the tax laws.

### Capital Gains Taxation and Investment

While the favorable treatment of capital gains is a source of both complexity and outright tax avoidance, it does offer one advantage: It encourages persons in the higher income brackets to invest in new and venturesome enterprises in order to realize the gain in the form of capital gains rather than ordinary dividend income. The tax saving is of course tremendous for such persons. The study by Butters *et al.*, in the Harvard Business School series on the effects of taxation, concluded that the tax treatment of capital gains was an important factor in encouraging venturesome individuals to "shift funds out of relatively conservative investments offering little or no opportunity for capital appreciation, and into more venturesome types of investment. . . ."[5] This is not necessarily a justification for lower taxes on capital gains, since a general reduction in highly progressive rates might be preferable. But at least the lower rates on capital gains do constitute a safety valve.

At the same time, the special treatment of such gains may encourage speculation in extremely risky ventures to an undesirable degree. Undertaking of new enterprise serves the interests of the economy so long as there is a reasonable chance of success, but wild speculation, particularly in stock of highly risky ventures, may accomplish little and interfere with the orderly flow of money capital into useful channels.

### Limited Deductibility of Capital Losses[6]

Since capital gains are provided favorable treatment, inevitably capital losses are limited as to deductibility. In the United States, such losses can be deducted only against capital gains, and against other income up to the sum of $1,000 per year, with a carry-forward of five years permitted. Capital losses on owner-occupied homes and other nonincome-yielding property are not deductible at all. Unrestricted deductibility of capital losses is not feasible, because of the possibility of adjusting the timing of the realization in terms of total income. But the present treatment is highly discriminatory against persons who suffer serious net capital losses, which reduce their taxpaying ability materially. Unfortunately, gains and losses are not necessarily realized by the same persons, and thus the favorable treatment given the former does not offset, person by person, the unfavorable treatment given the losses. Limitations on loss deduction increase somewhat the penalty from failure of a business venture, and thus offset, at least for persons inclined to be pessimistic, the advantages of the capital gains treatment in encouraging the development of new ventures.

The nondeductibility of losses on durable consumer goods, such as homes, can be defended only by the argument that the decline in value is

---

[5] J. K. Butters, L. E. Thompson, and L. L. Bollinger, *Effects of Taxation on Investment by Individuals* (Boston: Harvard University Graduate School of Business Administration, 1953), p. 42.

[6] See George F. Break, "On the Deductibility of Capital Losses under the Income Tax," *Journal of Finance*, Vol. VII (May, 1952), pp. 214–29; and U.S. Treasury, *Federal Income Tax Treatment of Capital Gains and Losses* (Washington, D.C., 1951).

a manifestation of consumption of the goods; since the use value is not taxed, there is no justification for allowing deduction of the decline in value. This procedure, however, discriminates against those persons unfortunate enough to own homes which decline sharply in value, beyond normal depreciation.

## OBJECTIONS TO ANY TAXATION OF CAPITAL GAINS

While, on the one hand, present treatment of capital gains is criticized for its leniency, on the other hand the argument is frequently advanced that any taxation of capital gains is undesirable. The case is largely built around the "locked-in" problem, but also in part on the argument that many capital gains are not actually income because they result from price level or interest rate changes.

### The "Locked-In" Problem

By the term *locked-in problem* is meant the effect of the tax in encouraging investors to hold onto securities or other property on which gains have accrued, rather than selling them and reinvesting in other property. Clearly, the tax must have some effect of this type, since the margin of gain from the shift in investment must be somewhat greater to make it worth while. The tax is certain and immediate, while the gains from the shift in investment are always uncertain. Apart from the logic of the case, some investors may be reluctant to change simply because they resent the tax. Greatest incentive to hold exists for older persons, since capital gains on property held until death are not taxable at all under the income tax laws. Also, particular incentive is provided for persons to hold short-term investments up to the six-month borderline.

Two adverse effects are claimed for the "locked-in" effect: It tends to aggravate fluctuations in stock prices and to restrict the flow of funds to new ventures. When prices have risen, investors are less willing to sell their stock; thus the supply is restricted, and the price rises more than is justified by market conditions. A decline is aggravated as persons seek to realize on their capital losses. So far as new ventures are concerned, persons who have accumulated capital gains are made reluctant to sell the property and provide funds for new undertakings, and the result is a slowing-down in the rate of economic development and a restriction of the flow of funds from declining industries to expanding ones.

The significance of the "locked-in" argument is often exaggerated. Without question, as demonstrated by various empirical studies, the six-month rule does cause some deferment of realization of gains, but this is of very limited significance. Apart from this effect, the Butters study referred to in a previous section showed that only a very small percentage of investors in the sample studied (6 per cent) indicated that the timing of their investment transactions was affected by the capital gains tax.[7] A more recent study by Holt and Shelton also shows that the tax does not produce a significant locked-in effect.[8] The existence of a tax with a maximum rate of 25 per cent will not deter most investors from making a shift when there are substantial gains from doing so, although, of course, the margin is altered slightly.

Furthermore, there is some doubt about the significance of such locking-in as may occur on security prices and the flow of capital. Persons selling securities because of an increase in their prices may very well simply reinvest in other securities and thus help to push the general level upward, and the elimination of the tax would increase the funds they have available for this purpose. Furthermore, the more lenient the tax treatment of capital gains, the greater the flow of money capital into stock speculation. The effects of locking-in on the flow of capital to new firms are likewise dubious. While the presence of the tax undoubtedly reduces the mobility of capital somewhat, this is likely to be much less significant than the effect of the relatively favorable treatment of capital gains in luring additional capital into venturesome investments. Obviously, complete elimination of tax on capital gains would encourage investment still more, but it is questionable if this is either desirable or warranted by the additional inequity and tax avoidance which would result. And provision of further incentive to investment would inevitably provide further incentive for pure speculation in securities.

While locking-in may reduce the individual mobility of investment dollars, it does not necessarily reduce the flow available to new ventures. The sale of securities on which capital gains have occurred does not create new money capital, but merely takes it away from other persons; the net effect depends upon the relative uses which would have been made of it by these persons, compared to the actions of those who sell their securities. If the former would have placed the funds in new ventures to the same extent, there is no effect at all in reducing the flow of money capital to such ventures.

Finally, it must be recognized that such locking-in as occurs is attributable in large measure to the exemption from tax of capital gains held until death. If these were taxable, the freeze on the investments of older persons would be greatly reduced.

---

[7] Butters *et al.*, *op. cit.*, p. 339.

[8] C. C. Holt and J. P. Shelton, "The Lock-in Effect of the Capital Gains Tax," *National Tax Journal*, Vol. 5 (December, 1962), pp. 337–52.

## The Price Level Problem

A second complaint against capital gains taxation is the argument that in large measure, capital gains are fictitious, because they merely reflect the increase in the general price level. Certainly, in the last two decades, many capital gains, on both stock and real property, have been of this character, although by no means all of them. If an attempt is made to separate the two types by means of some sort of index number adjustment, serious problems are encountered in the selection of the appropriate index and the administration of the system. In inflationary periods the sale of securities which had not risen in price would result in losses once adjustment by the index number was made.

It may also be argued that the gains involved are less fictitious than they look; if comparison is made between investors holding securities which have risen in price and those holding bonds which have not, the taxation of the gain serves to equalize somewhat the position of the two groups. In other words, stockholders and landowners benefit from inflation compared to bondholders, even though they do not gain in the sense of increased purchasing power, and thus taxation of their gains may be regarded as desirable. There is considerable merit to the argument of Vickrey and others that the evils produced by inflation are so great that taxation of capital gains arising from inflation cannot add seriously to them and may offset them in part.

Present United States federal law makes only one concession to the problem of price level changes—the provision added in 1951 which excludes from tax (or more correctly, defers from payment of tax)[9] the capital gain on a home, provided that the amount received from the sale is invested in another home within a specified period. This change has substantial merit, but it does discriminate against persons who sell their homes because they wish to move into apartments, rented property, or cheaper homes. Complete exemption of capital gains on homes can be justified as a more equitable solution, since rarely do significant increases in the value of homes, as such, occur, except in response to general price level changes.

## Capital Gains Which Reflect Interest Rate Changes

It is also argued that capital gains which reflect general changes in the rate of interest are fictitious, and do not constitute income. If the interest rate falls, the market prices of existing bonds rise, and thus a person who sells such bonds makes a capital gain. However, if he reinvests the

---

[9] In fact, often the effect is to exclude the gain completely, to the extent to which the gains are never realized until death.

money in other bonds, he will make no greater income than before. No improvement in his economic well-being has occurred, and thus, if he is taxed upon the gain, he is worse off economically than before the transaction occurred. Suppose that after a person has bought $10,000 worth of 6 per cent bonds at par, the market rate for this type of investment falls to 3 per cent. The market price of the bonds will almost double in price if the length of time until maturity is substantial. If he sells the bonds and reinvests in other bonds, he must reinvest the entire sum (almost $20,000) to maintain his previous interest earnings. If he is taxed on the capital gain of nearly $10,000, he cannot retain his old rate of earnings. The gain is, in a sense, fictitious and not actually income under the definition employed. On the other hand, if the market rate rises, existing issues will fall in price. Yet there is no real loss to the owners, so long as they continue to invest in bonds. However, if losses are deductible from income, the owner can sell, deduct his loss from other income, reinvest the money, and thus experience a net gain.

Suppose, however, that when the interest rate falls, the person who sells the bonds which have increased in value uses the money to buy consumption goods or nonfixed-income investments. In this case, he is essentially better off economically than he would have been if he had not held the bonds during the period in which the market prices rose. If the interest rate rises and bond prices fall, and he sells his bonds and uses the money for purposes other than reinvestment in bonds, he is likewise worse off than he would be if he had his wealth in bonds.

The basic issue is whether equity requires maintenance of the capital sum or of income received before taxable gains are considered to occur. The best case can be made for use of the capital maintenance approach and thus taxation of the gains without respect to the change in interest rates, in order to maintain equality in treatment between the holder of this type of investment and the owners of ones yielding a rate of return which varies with the market rate. A decline in the rate injures these persons; unless they are to be allowed to deduct a capital loss, which is not feasible, those persons who held fixed rate securities can justifiably be taxed, since they have gained relative to the second group.

Furthermore, any attempt to distinguish between gains due to interest changes and others would result in complications, since there is not one interest rate but a whole complex of rates, and bond prices are affected not only by interest changes but by changes in the credit strength of the corporations and other factors. The prices of other properties besides bonds are affected, in diverse ways, by interest rate changes. There appears to be no ideal solution to the problem that is administratively feasible.

## REFORMS OF CAPITAL GAINS TAXATION

As suggested in the preceding review of criticisms of the present tax treatment, there are two potential lines of reform. The critics of the taxation of capital gains urge complete elimination of the tax, or at least a reduction in the holding period necessary to obtain favorable treatment, or a reduction in the rate. British and Canadian experience is cited in favor of this approach. Those who condemn the tax for being unduly lenient argue that further reduction in the tax would increase still more the inequity and avoidance dangers, which they regard as very serious even at present, and is completely unnecessary in terms of economic effects. They argue for a lengthening of the holding period, and for a readjustment of rate structure.

In terms of an ideal income tax structure, capital gains would be taxed as they accrued, with averaging over a period of years permitted. Some have argued for at least partial use of the accrual basis. But usually, this approach is regarded as not being administratively feasible, and thus the realization basis must be continued. In the absence of a strong case to the contrary, the tax treatment should be designed to place the same burden on capital gains as on other income. But the irregularity problem is so serious that some form of averaging is imperative, whether this treatment is provided for other irregular incomes or not. Thus, gains would be made fully taxable (and losses fully deductible), but with averaging permitted (and perhaps required with capital losses). If this approach is rejected for administrative reasons, the next best alternative is an adjustment of the rate on the gains in terms of the number of years the property has been held.

Apart from these basic changes, two simple modifications would reduce inequity and the "locked-in" problem. The first is an increase in the holding period necessary for special treatment to at least one year, since no possible inequity (except that from irregularity) can be created for property held for a period less than the normal income tax interval. The second is the elimination of the exemption from income taxation of capital gains held until death. This is one of the most serious sources of locking-in and is completely unnecessary. The application of the estate tax in no way compensates for the present income tax exemption, since the estate tax applies whether the amounts have previously been subject to income tax or not. Full taxation would create some problem of lack of adequate liquid assets to pay the tax, but most persons would avoid this by realization prior to death. Constructive realization without actual sale of assets could be authorized.

If the tightening of the capital gains loophole is found to reduce investment significantly, the appropriate corrections should be made in the basic personal and corporate income tax rates, not in the capital gains treatment. Safety valves are not necessary on boilers in which the pressure is automatically held to tolerable limits. If the "locked-in" problem comes to be regarded as highly significant, one suggested solution is that of permitting "roll-over" from one investment to another (similar to the present treatment of homes) without incurring liability for tax. Locking-in would be reduced, but so would tax revenue, and the policy is of doubtful desirability in terms of general income tax goals.

## REFERENCES

SELTZER, L. H. *The Nature and Tax Treatment of Capital Gains.* New York: National Bureau of Economic Research, 1951.

    A thorough analytical and statistical study of tax problems relating to capital gains.

U.S. TREASURY. *Federal Income Tax Treatment of Capital Gains and Losses.* Washington, D.C., 1951.

    An analysis of the capital gains problem.

U.S. HOUSE OF REPRESENTATIVES, COMMITTEE ON WAYS AND MEANS. *Tax Revision Compendium,* pp. 1193–1300. Washington, D.C.: U.S. Government Printing Office, 1959.

    A series of papers on capital gains taxation.

SOMERS, H. M. "Reconsideration of the Capital Gains Tax," *National Tax Journal,* Vol. XIII (December, 1960), pp. 289–309.

GREAT BRITAIN, ROYAL COMMISSION ON THE TAXATION OF PROFITS AND INCOME. *Final Report,* pp. 25–39, 365–81. London: H.M. Stationery Office, 1955.

    The case for and against capital gains taxation.

SMITH, D. T. *Federal Tax Reform,* chap. v. New York: McGraw-Hill Book Co., Inc., 1961.

| Chapter 12 | INCOME TAXATION: INCIDENCE AND ECONOMIC CONSEQUENCES |

The preceding chapters have given only incidental mention to the possible effects which income taxes may have upon the functioning of the economy. To the extent that the tax violates the principle of economic neutrality and produces consequences for the economy which are undesirable in terms of the accepted goals, the advantages of the tax as the most satisfactory means of taxing persons according to economic well-being are in part offset. Economic consequences, as well as aspects of equity, must be taken into consideration in determining the appropriate role of the income tax in the tax structure. Furthermore, the reactions to the tax may alter the pattern of incidence, and the burden may not rest entirely upon those who pay the tax, as has been assumed in the preceding chapters. Such shifting has inevitable implications for equity.

The income tax may affect the functioning of the economy in two general ways. In the first place, it may alter the supplies of the factors of production which are made available to business enterprise. Secondly, it may alter the decisions of business firms and thus the demand for the factors. Both these effects will alter the level of national income, its composition, and its distribution. Not only are these changes of significance in themselves for economic welfare, but they may alter the pattern of distribution of the tax as well.

The succeeding sections of this chapter deal, respectively, with the effects of the tax upon factor supply and factor demand, and the consequences of these effects (1) for the incidence of the tax and (2) for the functioning of the economic system.

## CHANGES IN FACTOR SUPPLIES

An income tax reduces the direct monetary gain to factor owners from the supplying of units of the factors for use in production. The effect which this will have upon the quantities of the factors available for use in production depends upon the nature of the factor supply schedules. If a schedule is perfectly inelastic, the quantity supplied will not be altered. If the curve is positively sloped, the quantity supplied will fall. If the curve is negatively sloped, that is, if more units are available at low prices than at high, as may be the case with certain types of labor, the tax will cause the quantity supplied to increase. The exact nature of the supply schedules is likely to vary according to the type of factor.

### The Supply of Labor

The effects of an income tax upon the supply of labor have been debated for years, with little conclusive evidence developed. An income tax affects the relative gain from work and leisure by reducing the rewards from work, and thus lessening the cost of leisure, in the sense of the gain from labor which is forgone because of the failure to work. If an income tax takes 50 per cent of the wages of a worker, the amount the person sacrifices by enjoying leisure instead of working is cut in half. Thus the substitution effect should encourage workers to seek more leisure and less work, since the former is relatively more advantageous than the latter, compared to the situation before the tax.

On the other hand, the income effect produces the opposite tendency. Because the tax reduces the income available for consumption, it gives the workers an incentive to curtail leisure and work more, in order to restore their incomes to previous levels. In other words, the tax will, on the one hand, discourage work by lessening the reward from work; on the other hand, it will encourage persons to work more in order to maintain usual living standards. But the issue is complicated still further by the fact that the gains from leisure are not independent of the gains from work but are in large measure dependent directly upon them. Leisure is of little benefit to many persons unless the gain from work is sufficient to allow enjoyable (and costly) use of the leisure. This effect tends to reduce the likelihood of substitution of leisure for work.

The two conflicting reactions may be illustrated with an example. Suppose that a plumber who works for a manufacturing plant during the regular working day also has a chance to do some additional work in the evenings for friends and neighbors. He has little choice of hours in his regular occupation but is entirely free to do the extra work or not as he pleases. If a tax is imposed upon his income, will he be more or less inclined to do the evening work? On the one hand, the tax, by reducing the amount of income he has left after taxes, will encourage him to do this work in order to maintain his old living standard. This reaction is the income effect. On the other hand, his net gain, after taxes, from doing the extra work is reduced by the tax, and thus the compensation he obtains for sacrificing the leisure of his evenings is now less. He may therefore figure that it is not worth his while to sacrifice the leisure for work when the compensation for the work is reduced. Leisure thus is relatively more attractive, compared to work, than before, and the substitution effect will encourage him to substitute leisure for work and thus work less. Whether he actually will work more or less in the evenings will depend on the relative strength of these two conflicting forces and thus upon the relative importance he attaches to leisure, on the one hand, and the strength of his desire to maintain accustomed living standards, on the other.

While it is not possible to generalize about the relative strength of the income and substitution effects, certain relevant considerations which influence them in various situations can be noted.

In the first place, a reduction in the exemptions of an income tax, with the marginal rates unchanged, is particularly likely to encourage persons to work more, since the tax on the marginal income is not affected, while the lowered exemptions cut into the existing living levels. An increase in the basic rates, the marginal rates on additional income being left unchanged, will have a similar result. On the other hand, sharp increases in marginal rates, without much change in the basic rates to which most incomes are subject, are likely to reduce labor supply, since living standards are not materially affected, yet a heavier penalty is placed on gains from the marginal hours of work.

Secondly, the tax is much more likely to affect supplementary activities, such as overtime work or jobs outside the person's regular employment, than the work on the primary job. The worker not only has more freedom in the adjustment of hours in these extra jobs, but income from them is often not regarded as necessary for the basic living standard enjoyed.

Thirdly, the general attitude of the population toward the relative merits of maintaining existing living standards as compared to their desire for additional leisure is of primary significance. If there is a strong desire to retain existing living levels, and if additional leisure is regarded as being of little value, there is no great likelihood of a significant reduction in labor supply. If the desire for leisure is stronger, a reduction is more likely. Likewise, the presence of strong motives of other types encouraging persons to work to the maximum, such as those which arise in war periods, will lessen the likelihood of reduced labor supply. When persons are subject to substantial fixed commitments, the tax will tend to make them work more.

Current trends in income are also relevant. If incomes have been falling, persons are much more likely to seek to work more in response to the tax, in order to retain accustomed living standards, than they are if their incomes have been stable or rising. If incomes are rising rapidly at the time the tax is introduced, so that old living levels can be retained despite the tax, there is much more likelihood of a curtailment of labor supply or, at least, no increase. The behavior of marginal utility of real income is also a factor; if it does not fall as income rises, the possibility of a reduction in the supply of labor is much less, since the relative value to the workers of additional real income, compared to leisure, will be higher than it would be if marginal utility of income fell rapidly.

The chances for a significant effect on the labor supply are reduced by the fact that the average worker has relatively little control over his hours of work, which are set at a certain figure by the employer or through union negotiation. The worker must accept this figure if he is to work in the particular plant. However, the worker does have some leeway by varying overtime worked, absenteeism, and the amount of work supplementary to the regular job which is performed. Furthermore, other members of the family, in addition to the principal wage earner, may enter or drop out of the labor market as wages change. Professional men, farmers, and operators of small business have considerably greater leeway.

A final consideration is what Musgrave calls the "spite" effect; a person may react differently to a tax increase than to a reduction in wages because of his dislike of taxation as such. As a consequence, he may reduce his work more than he would in response to a wage cut. Or on the contrary, if he regards taxation as payment for governmental services which he considers to be important, the tax may have less effect than a change in income produced by market forces.[1]

### Empirical Studies

A few empirical studies of the effects of income taxes upon the supply of labor have been attempted. One of the more careful was that made by George Break, of solicitors and accountants in Great Britain, where marginal rates of tax affecting typical members of these occupational groups are much higher than in the United States. About 40 per cent of the respondents reported some influence of taxation on their working lives, the most common effect being that of postponement of retirement, but for the most part the effects appeared to be minor. A small number were induced to do less work because of the tax. The general conclusion reached was that the net effects were of very minor significance, despite

---

[1] R. A. Musgrave, *The Theory of Public Finance* (New York: McGraw-Hill Book Co., Inc., 1959), p. 240.

the fact that these persons were relatively free to vary the amount of work they did. Fixed commitments and fondness for the work played a part in minimizing the effects of taxation.[2]

A more limited study of the effect of income taxes upon doctors in the United States by R. Davidson revealed that there was very little effect upon incentives to work, the influence of the tax being primarily reflected in rather incidental matters, such as the taking of longer vacations combined with attendance at medical conventions.[3]

The British Royal Commission on the Taxation of Profits and Income conducted a survey of the effects of the income tax upon work incentives by interviewing a large number of industrial workers. While a substantial number maintained that the tax affected productivity, the evidence indicated that the actual effect on hours worked was very small. Few workers knew enough about their marginal tax rates for the tax to have any possible effect. About as many believed that the tax increased their efforts as the number which maintained that the tax reduced them.[4]

The Sanders study on the effects of taxation on executives is noted in the following section.

### The Relative Supplies of Particular Types of Labor

The effects of the taxes on wages and on the economy are influenced not only by the reaction of the total supply but also by the changes in relative supplies of various types of labor. The tax lessens the differential return between various types of labor, the net gain from the higher paid occupations being reduced. It has long been argued, therefore, that persons will not be willing to undertake the greater responsibilities of the higher paying jobs if the net gain from them is less.[5] The study by T. H. Sanders, *Effects of Taxation on Executives*,[6] has attempted to explore these effects in some detail, so far as executives are concerned, primarily through interviews. The general conclusions indicate that the taxes have not seriously reduced the work and effort of business executives but that in some cases they have been definitely responsible for persons refusing promotions or job offers which entailed substantially greater responsibility but

---

[2] See the article by George F. Break, "Income Taxes and Incentives to Work," *American Economic Review*, Vol. XLVII (September, 1957), pp. 529–49.

[3] See R. Davidson, "Income Taxes and Incentive," *National Tax Journal*, Vol. VI (September, 1953), pp. 293–99.

[4] Great Britain, Royal Commission on the Taxation of Profits and Income, *Appendix I to the Second Report* (London: H.M. Stationery Office, 1954).

[5] For a good presentation of this point of view, see the paper by C. H. Greenewalt in Joint Committee on the Economic Report, *Federal Tax Policy for Economic Growth and Stability* (Washington, D.C.: U.S. Government Printing Office, 1955), pp. 185–91.

[6] Boston: Harvard University Graduate School of Business Administration, 1951.

little net increases in pay after taxes. The author concludes: "There is unquestionably some loss of energy and service to the economy from this kind of cause, though probably the loss is smaller than is sometimes supposed."[7] On the whole, the nonfinancial advantages of more responsible jobs and the social and business compulsions to accept them are sufficient to insure an adequate supply of executive personnel despite the taxes.

In general, the same considerations which apply to executives apply to other jobs as well. The nonpecuniary compulsions to take better jobs are strong, and the existence of the tax, by cutting into living levels, gives incentive to seek better employment. The narrowing of the differential gain from better jobs as a result of the tax is of doubtful significance in the majority of cases. There are certain conditions, however, in which the relative labor supply of particular types of labor may be altered:[8]

1. *Differences in Expenses.* If transfer to a higher paid occupation results in substantial expenses, such as those of moving, living in a more expensive neighborhood, etc., the willingness to take the job will be reduced. Since these costs are not deductible under income tax laws, the gain from the move is reduced by the tax, and the margin at which moving becomes profitable is altered. The mobility of the labor supply would be increased if such moving expenses were deductible, as could easily be authorized. It is impossible, however, to adjust income tax deductions in terms of differences in living costs.

Similarly, since the costs of training and education are not deductible, the advantages of entering a high-pay occupation requiring substantial training are reduced. Again, however, the motives attracting persons into these occupations are not solely pecuniary, and the actual effects of the tax may be slight.

2. *Differences in the Extent to Which the Gains from the Various Occupations Are Subject to Tax.* Some types of occupations give rise to incomes which, in part or in entirety, are not taxable. Since the gains from housework are tax-free, wives may be encouraged to stay home and do their own housework rather than take paying employment. This tendency could be lessened somewhat by adjustments in the income tax laws, as noted in Chapter 7.

Likewise, the existence of the tax increases the relative attractivness of jobs with substantial nonpecuniary (and nontaxable) benefits, such as prestige, independence, living conditions, etc. The penalty for taking such a job at relatively low pay is reduced.

3. *Income Irregularity.* So long as the income tax structure does not

---

[7] *Ibid.*, p. 13.

[8] See R. Goode, "The Income Tax and the Supply of Labor," *Journal of Political Economy*, Vol. LVII (October, 1949), pp. 428–37.

allow general averaging, a regular income is rendered relatively more attractive as a result of the tax than an irregular one, which is penalized by the present tax structure.

4. *Differences in Effectiveness of Tax Enforcement.* As noted in Chapter 9, the tax cannot be enforced on some occupations as easily as on others, and thus greater relative advantage is enjoyed by the former.

As a result of these factors, some altering of the relative supplies of various types of labor is inevitable. In some instances, if there are more persons qualified for particular work than can find employment of that type, there will be no general alteration of wage levels but simply the employment of different individuals in the higher paid jobs. Such a situation is possible, of course, only with imperfections in competition; otherwise, the excessive supply of the high-pay type of labor would reduce the wage level for this group. But in practice, at the managerial level, such restrictions on competition are likely. While there maye be five men in a plant more or less equally capable of being superintendent, there is no way in which the four who do not get the job can compete against the one who does. If one is not willing to take the job because of the effect of the tax on the net gain, others of the group probably will, with no real sacrifice of efficiency or resource allocation. If some persons are not willing to enter the medical profession because of the effect of the tax, others, now prevented from entering by limited training facilities, will do so.

However, in other cases the supply of qualified persons may be reduced below the number of available jobs at existing salaries. In this case the salaries paid will tend to rise; this increase will offset the tax, in part at least, and serve to retain the capable workers in the employment.

### Capital Supply

The income tax inevitably has some effect upon the supply of money capital available to business firms. In the first place, the taxpayers are certain to absorb a considerable amount of the tax out of the portion of income that would otherwise be saved. This is particularly true in the higher income levels, in which saving is in large measure a residual. Since the tax is progressive, the portion of the tax borne out of savings is almost certain to be greater than that of other taxes which rest more heavily on those income groups which have a narrow margin of savings and thus will reduce consumption to a greater extent. Accordingly, the income tax will reduce the capacity of persons to supply money capital, to a greater extent than other taxes, per dollar of revenue.

Secondly, the fact that the returns from lending money capital or advancing it to business on an equity basis (whether in the person's own business or through the purchase of stock) are reduced will lessen somewhat the incentive to make the money capital available for use. Since the tax does not apply to the liquidity gains from holding wealth in liquid form, it tends to increase the advantages of keeping wealth in this form. In part, however, this effect may be offset by the same considerations determining the reactions of the supply of labor. The total money income from the person's investments is reduced by the tax; it is this income, and not the liquidity gain, which provides the means with which to acquire goods. Accordingly, some persons may be more willing to advance their money capital because of the existence of the tax, in order to maintain present levels of living.

It is likely, however, that the net effect of the two considerations is to lessen the supply of loanable funds forthcoming from individuals from a given flow of income to a somewhat greater extent than with other taxes. However, there are several complicating factors. The actual supply of money capital is also affected by central bank credit policies. If, for example, the government is committed to the maintenance of a given interest rate level, any tendency for the rate to rise will be offset by central banking action, involving, in the United States, open-market purchases of securities by the Federal Reserve System. This step essentially prevents any real decline in the quantity of money capital available, since additional bank credit replaces the amount which is not forthcoming from individuals. A second complication arises out of the fact that if total money capital is reduced as a result of the tax, there may occur a decline in the level of production and national income, which will materially alter the supply of capital. The question of the possible effects of the tax and expenditure program upon national income will be discussed in Chapter 25.

The preceding discussion has not distinguished between funds loaned and those advanced on an equity basis; the effects of the tax upon the supply of equity funds available may be quite different from those upon the supply available in the form of loans. Equity investments offer greater chance of high return but greater risk of loss. Loans, on the other hand, have some of the nontaxable advantages of holding wealth in monetary form, such as greater security and, typically, greater liquidity. To the extent to which persons are certain that their equity investments will be successful, and they discount heavily the possibility of losses, the tax will lessen the relative advantages of equity investments compared to loan investments, and retard economic development. But to the extent to which investors take losses into consideration, and these are deductible, the income tax does not discriminate against risk taking or equity investments compared to more secure types. In practice, however, the losses may not be fully deductible, particularly because of the failure to allow general averaging of incomes over a period of years. The income effect may make some persons more willing to take the risks of equity investments in the hope of obtaining a higher return and maintaing their after-tax income.

Musgrave has demonstrated rather conclusively[9] that an income tax with full loss offsets and a proportional rate will increase, rather than decrease, the total amount of risk taking in the economy. With losses fully deductible from other income, the net amount of risk taken by an individual with given investments is reduced as a result of the tax, and the investor will presumably seek to restore the old risk position; thus, he will be encouraged to undertake additional risk investment. Or in other words, with full offset the marginal return on additional risky investment is not reduced by the tax, while the tax reduces the over-all potential risk. Thus a person is encouraged to invest more in risky undertakings. However, under present income tax laws, not only are losses not always fully offset, but the tax rates are progressive. Both of these considerations increase the possibility that the tax will have a net disadvantageous effect on risk taking.

*The Harvard Study of Effects upon Investment.* The most thorough empirical study of the effects of the tax structure upon investment policies and the supply of money capital was one made in 1953 under the auspices of the Harvard Business School, based upon extensive interviews. The major conclusions are noted below.[10]

1. Most equity capital comes from the higher income groups. While their ability to supply the capital has been reduced by the tax, they are still able to supply very substantial sums, in part because of the ways in which they can accumulate capital without the earnings being subject to full income tax rates.

2. The tax definitely affects the investment policies of persons in the higher income groups. The tax causes a majority to shift to more secure types of investment, but a substantial percentage shift to more risky types in order to obtain the favorable capital gains treatment.

3. The tax encourages greater use of trusts, and thus lessens the supply of equity capital.

4. The net supply of funds for new ventures is probably increased because of the desire to obtain capital gains treatment.

## THE INCIDENCE OF THE PERSONAL INCOME TAX

In the preceding chapters, it was assumed that the burden of the income tax is borne by the persons upon whom it is levied, in the sense that

[9] *Op. cit.*, chap. xiv.
[10] J. K. Butters, L. E. Thompson, and L. L. Bollinger, *Effects of Taxation: Investments by Individuals* (Boston: Harvard Graduate School of Business Administration, 1953).

their real income is lowered because a portion of their money income is taken away from them by the tax. The entire evaluation of the tax in terms of equity has been based upon this assumption. However, the possible effects of the tax upon factor supply and demand, as outlined in the earlier paragraphs of this chapter, suggest that some shifting of the tax may take place. Shifting will be considered to occur if the various reactions to the tax serve to restore in part the real incomes of the taxpayers and reduce those of other persons in the economy. The final pattern of incidence or distribution of burden rests on various persons in proportion to the extent to which their real incomes are reduced as a result of the tax.

### Changes in Quantities of Factors Available

Shifting of the tax may occur if the tax produces changes in the quantities of various factors available. To the extent to which the quantity of labor available falls as a result of the tax, wages will tend to rise, and a portion of the tax will shift from workers as a group onto the owners of business enterprises. But the wage increase raises the costs of the firms and will lead to upward readjustments in prices, assuming that appropriate monetary adjustments take place. As a consequence, the tax in part shifts forward onto persons in their capacity as consumers. Thus a portion of the burden originally on workers, as such, is transferred onto other groups in the economy, although, of course, a large portion comes back onto the workers in their capacity as consumers. Prices of labor-intensive products will rise more than those of capital-intensive ones; thus, consumers with relatively high preferences for the former will be subjected to a disproportionately high percentage of the total tax burden.

If the total quantity of labor available increases, the results are much more complex. Hourly wage rates will tend to fall, while the behavior of per capita real wages will depend upon the elasticity of demand for labor. If per capita real wages fall, other factor owners will benefit through lower prices for consumer goods purchased. The total real burden, in the sense of the reduction in the output of the private sector of the economy, will be less than the real value of the tax revenue at the original prices, but labor will suffer an additional burden reflecting the alteration of the work-leisure ratio from the preferred pretax position.

The picture of incidence is complicated by the fact that the supplies of different types of labor are likely to react in different ways. If the willingness of persons to take more responsible jobs is reduced by the tax, the supply of persons in these occupations will be reduced, and those in other occupations increased; this will lead to salary increases in the former occupations and decreases in the less responsible occupations, with consequent readjustment in relative real incomes in different occupational groups. In any occupational groups in which the primary goal of the workers is to maintain a given income level after taxes, the tendency of persons to work more as a result of the tax will tend to depress wages.

Similar influences affect the price of money capital. If the total supply is reduced, the interest rate and the earnings on equity capital will tend to rise. However, as indicated above, the nature of the total supply schedule of money capital depends very largely upon central bank policy. In periods in which the central banking system seeks to maintain a given interest rate level, the supply will be highly elastic, and there will be little or no increase in the interest rate. To the extent that the relative supply of equity capital is reduced, compared to the total supply of money capital, it would be expected that over a period of time the rate of profit would tend to rise, assuming that full employment is maintained. If the result of the tax and expenditure program is to lessen investment and reduce national income below full-employment levels, the rate of profit will, of course, fall.

The tax may likewise reduce the relative flow of money capital into certain types of industries. On the other hand, the present tax structure, which gives favorable treatment to various types of industries (particularly mining and oil production) tends to increase the flow into these fields. These reactions will result in modifications of the prices of the products and thus alter the over-all pattern of distribution of burden.

### Significance for Incidence of Changes in Factor Demand

Effects of the tax upon factor demand are complex. The income tax, just like any tax, will reduce the private sector demand for factors below what it would be if government expenditures were given, as well as revenues from other taxes. But this comparison is not ordinarily a significant or useful one. When taxes and expenditures are both increased, the increased governmental factor demand will tend to offset the reduced private sector demand, and the over-all effects can be considered only in terms of the significance of both the tax and expenditure policy. If the income tax is compared with other levies, it will be recognized that the relative demand reductions for various factors will be different, and thus changes in relative factor prices will be somewhat different. Particularly, demand for specialized factors necessary to produce goods consumed primarily by the higher income groups will be reduced to a greater extent by the income tax than by other levies, and thus the prices of these factors will be reduced relatively more by the income tax. But generalizations about the over-all differential effects are difficult to make.

### Effects of Nonperfectly Competitive Elements in Factor Markets

So long as markets are perfectly competitive, factor or commodity prices can readjust, and thus the tax can be shifted only as a result of changes in supply or demand schedules. Actually, of course, many factor and commodity markets are not perfectly competitive. The imperfect elements may allow direct and immediate shifting without prior changes in supply or demand schedules.

1. *Labor.* Direct changes in wages are particularly likely, since wages are determined largely on the basis of employer-union bargaining. As in any case of bilateral monopoly, the wage levels as well as the changes due to a tax are indeterminate on the basis of analytical principles. But certainly, the tax on income from wages, which reduces the net gain to the workers, is likely to be a factor which encourages the unions to insist on higher wage levels than they would otherwise obtain. This is particularly true when taxes are withheld, since the income tax directly reduces take-home pay, the consideration of paramount importance to the typical worker. It is impossible to determine, either empirically or analytically, the actual extent to which unions can succeed in obtaining higher wages as a result of the tax. But certainly, the general tendency would be in the direction of money wages higher than otherwise.

On the other hand, another element which enters into the bargaining picture is the profit level of the employer; to the extent that this is reduced by the tax, the ability of the union to get higher wages is lessened. At the same time, the fact that the wages are deductible expenses reduces materially the net cost to the employer from a wage increase if he is earning substantial profit, and weakens his resistance to the wage increases.

The net effect, then, is likely to be some tendency for the portion of tax on labor income to shift forward, particularly when unions are strong but have not previously pushed wages to the maximum which they can succeed in compelling the employers to pay. The increased costs to business firms will, in large measure, be reflected in higher prices, and the ultimate incidence will be comparable in part to that of a sales tax. Monetary readjustments will of course be required for a general increase in the price level to occur. If the increase does not occur, money wage levels will tend to fall, but those workers whose unions have pushed their relative wages upward will still be freed of a portion of the burden, which will essentially rest in proportion to consumer expenditures, since the price level will be relatively higher, compared to other factor prices, than before. The main difference between the case in which the price level rises and that in which the wage level falls is the placing of greater burden, in the first case, on fixed income groups or those living off accumulated wealth, compared to the second case.

2. *Money Capital.* So far as interest rates are concerned, imperfections play a minor part in the markets in which the basic long-term rates are determined. With some specialized types the tax on the interest return might influence the lenders' interest rate policy. On the other hand, so far as profits on equity investments are concerned, imperfections may be very significant. In most lines of activity today the prices of the products are set by the business firms in essentially imperfect markets, the degree of imperfection, however, varying widely. In terms of strict marginal economic analysis the imposition of a tax on the net income of the business would not alter the optimum profit price level. But in practice, the tax may cause firms to readjust prices to higher levels and actually attain greater profits, provided that competitiors react in the same way. In similar fashion, persons renting out capital equipment or buildings may increase their rental charges. In a perfectly competitive market, no increases could occur without a prior reduction in supply. Readjustments of prices by business firms will be considered at greater length in the chapter on corporation income taxes.

*Summary.* The generally accepted conclusion that the income tax is borne by the persons upon whom it is levied is likely not to be universally true, even though, as a statement of a general tendency, it may be reasonably accurate. Neither empirical evidence nor contemporary economic analysis allows precise statements to be made about shifting. The effects which the tax may have on labor supply are completely unpredictable. But present-day bargaining methods of determining wage levels suggest that in some instances, union activity will result in wages being higher with the tax than they would be in its absence. The lessened desirability of high-pay, high-responsibility jobs may result in higher salaries in these fields and partial shifting of the tax. Likewise, in some instances, business firms may succeed in passing on to their customers a portion of the tax on their earnings through price increases, but not with the ease with which a sales tax can be shifted. The reduction in the supply of money capital may lead to higher interest rates, unless prevented by governmental action.

To the extent that certain groups in the economy shift the burden forward, the tax is reflected in higher costs of production and prices, and borne in relation to the consumption of taxed articles, apart from further modifications comparable to those which occur with a sales tax, as discussed in Chapter 16. If shifting by labor is widespread, workers as a whole do not actually escape the tax, as it is shifted back to them in the form of higher prices. But the relative burdens on various individuals will be altered materially; those persons who are unable to shift will be burdened not only with their own tax but with a portion of that levied upon others as well. The net effect is probably to make the tax somewhat less progressive than it would otherwise be. However, the progressive element, which affects individuals very differently even in the same occupation, is probably the portion least likely to be shifted.

## ECONOMIC CONSEQUENCES

Apart from the adjustments involved in the shifting of the tax the various reactions to the tax considered in the first part of the chapter may have important consequences for the functioning of the economy.

### Effects upon the Level of Production

Perhaps the most important adverse effect which an income tax may produce is a reduction in the real level of national income. As a result of the use of income taxes, the government shares in the receipts of activity and enterprise, by requiring relatively greater payments from those persons who are successful financially than from those who are not. Thus, in one sense an income tax is an inevitable penalty upon financial success. From the standpoint of society the tax represents payments for govermental services which benefit the members of the community. But the significance of this consideration is reduced by the lack of a direct relationship for individuals between the services received and the taxes paid. More specifically, there are several ways in which the income tax may alter the level of national income.

1. *Changes in Factor Supplies.* In the first place, any changes which the tax produces in the quantities of the various factors available for use in production will affect the total volume of output. If labor supply falls, the combined public and private sector output will be reduced below the optimum, if previously the actual ratios of work to leisure reflected the relative desires of workers for the two. Thus, if persons are discouraged from working overtime, absenteeism is increased, marginal workers leave the labor market, output will fall, and the over-all level of living will be reduced. On the other hand, to the extent that persons seek to work more, national income will tend to rise rather than fall. But such an increase in national output does not necessarily constitute an increase in economic welfare. Welfare depends not solely on the absolute magnitude of output but also upon the realization of an optimum balance between leisure and work. If it can be assumed that persons, within the limits in which they have individual control over working hours, have obtained an optimum

adjustment previously, any disturbance in this adjustment as a result of the tax, whether output is increased or decreased, may be considered to reduce economic welfare.

Particularly serious consequences could result if the tax greatly lessens the supply of executive talent or the desire of businessmen to expand and develop their businesses. As noted earlier in the chapter, there is little conclusive evidence of serious effects upon the behavior of executives and persons in other highly paid occupations. To the extent, however, that persons of exceptional ability are discouraged from taking the more responsible jobs, the results, in terms of optimum economic development, may be very serious.

2. *Effects on Unemployment.* Secondly, an income tax may alter the level of national income by reducing total spending and thus affecting the volume of employment. All taxes curtail private spending; this is, of course, their primary economic function. In part, the income tax does this by curtailing private consumption by taking money away from persons; in part, it does so by lessening both the funds available for investment and the desire to undertake investment. On the other hand, the expenditure of the tax revenue by the government serves to offset the conractionary effects of the taxes. Whether any net decline occurs in employment and national income depends upon the relationship between the net expansionary effect of the use of the revenues and the net contractionary effects of the collection of the tax. Since income taxes are borne out of income which would be saved to a larger extent than other taxes, and thus the direct effects on consumption are less, it is likely that the income tax will have less severe effects on total spending and national income than most other taxes. However, if the tax does have substantial effects upon incentives, particularly to undertake and expand businesses, the net result may be deflationary.

From a long-run standpoint, real levels of national income will be affected by changes in the rate of capital formation caused by the tax; this question will be discussed in the section below and in Chapter 13. Complete analysis of the effects of the present income tax structure upon investment must take into consideration the corporation income tax as well as the tax on personal income; thus, further discussion of the question will be postponed to the following chapter.

### The Effects on Resource Allocation

Income taxes may produce some effects upon over-all resource allocation (and thus composition of gross national product), apart from the effects upon the level of national product. We are concerned at this point with the effects of the taxes alone rather than with those of the expenditure program, which are independent of the methods of financing.

The primary effect will come through the influence upon the supply of various types of labor. To the extent that such relative supplies are altered, the relative costs of producing particular commodities will be affected, with consequent changes in relative outputs. Thus, if persons are discouraged from entering medicine because of the high tax on the additional income, the costs of medical service will tend to be higher, and less of the service will be available to society. The tax will also affect the attractiveness of various types of industries because of risk differences and thus alter relative output.

Likewise, the division of total product between consumption goods and capital goods will be altered in favor of the former. The income tax is likely to be borne to a greater extent than most other taxes out of savings. Thus the rate of capital formation would be slowed down, so long as full employment was maintained, whether the government expenditures were undertaken or not. The question of the desirability of the slowing-down of capital formation, in terms of the goals of economic welfare, is not easily answered. A high rate of capital formation allows a rapid improvement in living standards over a period of years, although lessening the volume of consumption goods currently available. However, capital formation could become so rapid that the level of living for the majority of persons would be reduced to bare subsistence. In general, the higher the rate of capital formation, the greater is the extent to which present consumption is sacrificed for the benefit of persons in the future. The question of the extent to which this sacrifice should be extended can be answered only in terms of the general consensus of opinion in society wtih respect to the relative claims of present and future generations.

### Effects on Income Redistribution

As noted above, the use of income taxes to finance government expenditure programs results in some over-all redistribution of income after taxes. This is a major factor affecting the rate of capital formation, the level of investment and thus the level of employment, and the allocation of resources among the productions of various goods. Evaluation of such redistribution is, of course, a value judgment.

## CONCLUSION TO THE DISCUSSION OF INCOME TAXATION

The personal income tax is generally regarded as the most equitable means of distributing the burden of the costs of government. Its burden is correlated with economic well-being more satisfactorily than that of any other tax; not only is the tax based directly upon income, the primary determinant of economic well-being, but it can be refined in terms of family size, medical expenses, and other considerations affecting the level of living which may be enjoyed with a particular income. Although some very fundamental problems arise with respect to the definition and adjustment of income and the segmenting of the income stream into time periods for purposes of application of the tax, nevertheless a reasonably satisfactory structure can be devised. The degree of progression must always be based on consensus of attitudes of society on equity in the distribution of income.

From a practical standpoint, the most serious limitation to the tax is the inability to prevent some evasion on the part of certain groups in the economy. From the standpoint of economic effects, the chief danger is that of adverse effects upon incentives, particularly to develop and expand businesses and to take more responsible positions. There is little conclusive evidence of serious adverse effects of this character, despite the highly progressive rates that are now in use. But these may appear over a longer period. On the other hand, the income tax has much less restrictive effect on consumption than do sales and excise taxes, and in this respect is less of an obstacle to the maintenance of full employment than are commodity taxes which raise the same amount of revenue. The present income tax structures contain unnecessary loopholes, which create inequity and lessen the degree of effective progression; on the other hand, some of these loopholes probably lessen the adverse economic effects of the tax. A general overhaul of the tax, to close loopholes and lessen the severity of the rates on income which is fully taxed, has great merit. The present degree of progression, introduced during war emergency and never carefully reconsidered, is open to serious question, in light of the relatively little revenue produced by the top brackets, the pressure of the high rates in leading persons to seek avenues of avoidance, and the potential but as yet unproven dangers of the high rates upon economic development. In the author's opinion the income tax system would be much more satisfactory if the numerous loopholes were closed and the higher rates sharply reduced. Substantial attention has been given in the last decade to tax reform along these lines; but as of 1962, there has been no action. Numerous proposals for a "package" reform of closed loopholes and a broader base coupled with lower tax rates encounter the major obstacle that those groups benefiting from concessions in the present laws will fight strongly to retain them, since they gain more from the concessions than they would from lower tax rates.

## REFERENCES

COOPER, G. "Taxation and Incentive in Mobilization," *Quarterly Journal of Economics*, Vol. LXVI (February, 1952), pp. 43–66.

A mathematical analysis of the effects of income taxes on labor supply.

SANDERS, T. H. *Effects of Taxation on Executives*. Boston: Harvard University Graduate School of Business Administration, 1951.

The results of interviews with executives about the effects of taxation on their behavior.

BUTTERS, J. K.; THOMPSON, L. E.; and BOLLINGER, L. L. *Effects of Taxation: Investment by Individuals*. Boston: Harvard University Graduate School of Business Administration, 1953.

A study of the actual effects of the tax upon individual investment decisions.

GOODE, R. "The Income Tax and the Supply of Labor," *Journal of Political Economy*, Vol. LVII (October, 1949), pp. 428–37.

An analysis of the effects of the tax upon labor supply.

BREAK, GEORGE F. "Income Taxes, Wage Rates, and the Incentive to Supply Labor Services," *National Tax Journal*, Vol. VI (December, 1953), pp. 333–52.

The most exhaustive study of the relation of the income tax to labor supply.

————. "Income Taxes and Incentives to Work," *American Economic Review*, Vol. XLVII (September, 1957), pp. 529–49.

Report of an empirical study.

JOINT COMMITTEE ON THE ECONOMIC REPORT. *Federal Tax Policy for Economic Growth and Stability*, Parts III, IV. Washington, D.C.: U.S. Government Printing Office, 1955.

A series of papers on the economic effects of federal income taxes.

U.S. HOUSE OF REPRESENTATIVES, COMMITTEE ON WAYS AND MEANS. "Income Tax Rates and Incentives to Work and to Invest," *Tax Revision Compendium* (Washington, D.C.: U.S. Government Printing Office, 1959), pp. 2247–55.

MUSGRAVE, R. A. *The Theory of Public Finance*, chaps. x–xiv. New York: McGraw-Hill Book Co., Inc., 1959.

An advanced analytical study.

# Chapter 13

# CORPORATION INCOME TAXATION

The preceding discussion of income taxation has abstracted completely from the problems created by the existence of corporations, under the assumption that all income is received directly by individuals. Actually, of course, most business activity is carried on under the corporate form of organization, with a separate legal entity between the income-producing unit and the individual persons who own it. The income accrues directly to the corporation and may or may not be paid out currently by it to the individual owners. Thus, if taxes are applied only to individuals on income realized, the corporate earnings which are not paid out as dividends would completely escape current taxes. The corporation would thus be a device which would allow profits to be reinvested without being subjected to tax.

On the other hand, treatment of the corporation as a person for tax purposes and application to it of ordinary personal income tax rates would violate the accepted principles of distribution of tax burden. The concept of ability to pay relates to burdens borne by individuals and cannot appropriately be applied to corporations. The use of usual progressive rates would result in serious discrimination against low-income owners of stock of large high-total-profit corporations. Great incentive would be given to split the enterprise into many small corporations, to escape progression. Despite these disadvantages, a few countries, including Venezuela, have taxed corporations and individuals under the same levy.

If the income tax were based upon the "consumption plus increase in net wealth" definition of income, the problem created by the existence of corporations would be lessened, to the extent that the reinvested earnings of corporations were reflected in increased values of the stock and thus included in the current accrued income of the owners. But since this adjustment in stock prices is not fully attained, the problem would remain in part. The use of the "flow of wealth" definition of income merely aggravates the problem; it does not create it.

211

## THE TWO PHILOSOPHIES OF INCOME TAX TREATMENT OF CORPORATIONS

While it is almost universally recognized that the personal income tax cannot be applied directly to all corporate income, there are two distinct philosophies about the desirable treatment of this income.

### Integration

The first, or integration, point of view would disregard the existence of the corporate structure so far as possible and attempt to place the same tax upon income earned within a corporation as would apply to the income if it were earned by noncorporate enterprises. There are two primary arguments for this point of view. On the basis of equity, it is argued that the existence of the corporate form should not be allowed to obscure the fact that tax burdens ultimately rest upon individuals, and principles of ability must be interpreted solely in terms of personal burdens. It is argued that there is no reason to tax income earned through the corporate form more (or less) heavily than that earned in other ways. If differential treatment is given, the "equal treatment of equals" rule will be violated, and the actual progression in the tax structure will be different from the intended degree.

Secondly, it is maintained that the tax can be completely neutral and avoid adverse economic effects only if the tax burden is independent of the form of business organization. Any attempt to tax the corporation more heavily will discourage the use of this form of organization, interfere with economic development (since the corporate form is essential for larger undertakings), and affect business policy in many respects. This approach requires close integration of the corporate and personal income taxes, along the lines indicated later in the chapter; it is the underlying philosophy of the Canadian system of providing credit for corporate tax paid against individual income tax liability, and is the original basis for company taxation in Great Britain and the African countries of British background.

### The Separate Entity Approach

The second approach, which has dominated practice in the United States for several decades, apart from the very limited degree of integration introduced in 1954, is that of the treatment of the corporation as a separate entity, with the corporate net income being regarded as a suitable base for taxation, without respect to tax paid on dividends by individuals.

The corporation is thus divorced from the individuals who own it, the taxes upon it being adjusted in terms of its own special characteristics. The basic argument for this point of view is that the corporation is, in law and in fact, distinct from its owners. The average stockholder has no direct control over its policies, which are determined typically by its salaried managers. The earnings do not accrue directly to the stockholders and may be held in the corporation regardless of the wishes of particular stockholders. A further argument for separate treatment is that much more revenue can be gained in this manner (at given tax rates); if additional burden is not placed on the corporation, the money must be raised in some other manner, with possible effects worse than those of the corporate tax.

Before evaluating these points of view, attention will be given to the actual tax treatment of corporate income in the United States, which was for many years based entirely on the second philosophy, and still is today in large measure, despite the limited step toward integration introduced in 1954.

## THE PRESENT CORPORATE INCOME TAX

The present treatment of corporation income is based in part upon the recognition that the corporate income cannot suitably be taxed by the personal income tax, and it is influenced to a substantial extent by the philosophy that the corporation, as such, is a suitable base for tax distinct from that on its owners. The corporation income tax in the United States applies to all corporate profits, after deduction from gross receipts of all ordinary business expenses, depreciation, and interest. Contributions to charity up to 5 per cent of net income are also deductible, but there are no other personal deductions or exemptions comparable to those of the personal income tax. No dividends paid, whether on common or preferred stock, are deductible, with minor exceptions. The base of the tax is therefore profit in the accounting sense rather than in the economic sense of pure profit, since no deduction is allowed for the necessary return on the owners' investment or other imputed costs.

The rate structure varies from time to time as revenue needs change. As of January 1, 1963, the basic rate, applying to all taxable profit, is 30 per cent; there is, in addition, a surtax rate of 22 per cent on profit in excess of $25,000. The maximum rate, therefore, is slightly less than 52 per cent. The progression is not based upon the usual concept of ability but is designed to facilitate the growth of new businesses, which is particularly restricted by the income tax, since these firms must expand largely with reinvested earnings.

Three-year carry-back and five-year carry-forward of losses are permitted. This rule is of great value to new enterprises and those with sharply fluctuating earnings, and greatly reduces the adverse effect of the tax upon the incentive to undertake investment. Great Britain and some Commonwealth countries allow unlimited carry-forward.

The base of the Canadian tax is substantially the same, except for the prescription of more rigid rules relating to depreciation. The base rate is 18 per cent on the first $35,000 of net income, with a rate of 47 per cent applying to income in excess of $35,000. These figures do not include the 3 per cent tax on corporate income for social security puposes.

In the United States, dividends paid to stockholders were fully taxable until 1954. In that year, two concessions were made:

1. The first $50 of dividend income was excluded completely from tax.

2. Taxpayers were permitted a credit against tax due of 4 per cent of dividends received.

The net effect was to eliminate entirely the double taxation on persons with very small amounts of stock, and to reduce it to a limited extent on other stockholders. In 1958, Congress authorized small corporations, as defined by law, to elect to be taxed on a basis similar to that of partnerships, as explained on page 231.

Thus, despite the change, the individual stockholders in the United States are typically subject to a substantial element of double taxation, to the extent to which the corporate tax is not shifted forward to the consumers and is reflected in lower dividends and/or stock prices. While all other incomes are subject to federal income tax only once, the portion of corporate income paid out as dividends is subject to both personal and corporate levies. Low-income stockholders receiving dividends in excess of $50 a year are taxed indirectly by the corporate levy, even though their total incomes are less than the exemption figures of the personal income tax. To the extent that dividends are not reduced because the tax is absorbed out of undistributed profits and thus is reflected in a slower increase in the value of the stock, the direct double taxation is less severe, since the gains from the increases in stock prices receive the lighter capital gains tax treatment. But the smaller amount of undistributed profits will lessen the corporation's earning ability and burden the stockholders, directly or indirectly, through reduced profits in the future.

The portion of the profits not distributed to stockholders is currently taxed at a higher rate than the personal income tax rate to which the owners are subject if they are in the lower income brackets and at a lower rate if the owners are in high income brackets. For the high-income owner of stock, the separate entity treatment of the corporation results in under-taxation, compared to other income, rather than double taxation, since the top corporate rate is much lower than the high-bracket personal rates.

The reduction in dividends and in future earning power due to the tax will be discounted by prospective stock purchasers and will result in some decline in stock prices, provided, of course, that the income taxes as a whole do not reduce the over-all rate of return on investment. Accordingly, in a sense the future shareholders are relieved of a portion of the real burden, since they paid less than they otherwise would have for their stock.

## THE SHIFTING AND INCIDENCE OF THE TAX

Further discussion of the equity and significance of the present tax structure requires a knowledge of the extent to which the tax is shifted and thus the final incidence of the tax. No precise answers can be given to this question with the present state of knowledge, but some progress toward an answer is possible.

### The Traditional View

Under the traditional analysis of the problem, accepted for many years, a corporation income tax could not be shifted. A tax which takes a constant percentage of net income of a firm will not affect the optimum level of output or price, since the output level which yielded the greatest profit before tax will continue to do so after tax. If a series of figures is reduced by a given percentage, the figure that was highest before will still be the highest. Or in other words, neither marginal revenue nor marginal cost are affected by the tax, and price and output adjustments are not advantageous. Firms in purely competitive industries will not reduce output, and thus price cannot rise; firms in nonpurely competitive fields will not find price increases to be advantageous.

In terms of the traditional argument, shifting is likewise not possible over a longer period of time. To the extent to which the tax is confined to pure profit, as was implicitly assumed in the earlier analysis, it would exercise no influence on investment policies of new or old firms, since the necessary return element would not be subject to tax. In practice, however, corporate income taxes are not confined to pure profit, and therefore this reasoning is not valid. But an alternative argument was advanced, that since the tax (together with the personal income tax) applies to all income, there is no alternative to which to turn, and thus investment will remain the same despite the lower after-tax rate of profit.

### The Possibility of Shifting: Direct Reactions of Business Firms

Against this point of view, increasing criticism has been advanced in recent years. There are two major lines of argument, one relating to the direct reactions of business firms, the other to the longer period effect of the tax upon the volume of investment. The traditional argument that firms in perfect competition cannot directly shift an income tax is, of course, valid; the same is true of a complete monopolist who has already maximized profits. In the short run, this conclusion is valid even if the taxes apply to profits in the accounting sense, including imputed return to the owners, since this element is a fixed cost rather than a necessary return in the short run, apart from possible effects of the tax on investment in working capital. But most markets today are characterized by neither of these extremes but by a considerable degree of imperfection and of mutual interdependency or oligopoly. Although the theory of oligopoly pricing is by no means entirely complete or satisfactory, certain generalizations about the reaction to an income tax can be made. The ultimate goal of the firms in any oligopoly situation is that of maximization of the joint profits of the group, since only the price-output combinations which will allow this are optimum from the standpoint of the firms as a group. But as Fellner has demonstrated in detail, rarely do conditions allow the firms to attain this goal.[1] Firms will often deliberately avoid trying to attain 'the maximum profit figure for the group. If the corporation tax is imposed or increased and the firms treat this tax as an expense item, they may adjust prices upward as a result. If the dominant firms, those whose price policies largely determine the price level in the industry, behave in this manner, and if they have roughly the same tax burden per unit of output, all will be better off as a result of the increase, so long as the prices previously set did not maximize profits for the group. The question may be raised as to why the firms did not make the increases prior to the tax if they were profitable. The answer is that the competitive circumstances did not permit any one firm to raise prices for fear others would not follow, or the firm did not wish to raise prices because of fear of entry of new firms, public relations, etc. But the introduction of the tax made each firm willing and able to move upward, because each was reasonably certain that the other firms would react in like manner. The tendency to shift will be increased if prices are determined on a price leadership basis and the leader readjusts as a result of the tax.

[1] See W. Fellner, *Competition among the Few* (New York: Alfred A. Knopf, Inc., 1949), chaps. v, vi.

The various markup and full-cost pricing practices encourage the same type of adjustment, so long as the firms treat the tax as an element to be considered in determination of full-cost or markup percentage. The likelihood of shifting is also increased if the persons responsible for pricing policy aim for "reasonable" or "satisfactory" profits, a practice which many students of pricing believe to be common. With such a policy, if prices are below the level which would give maximum profit, the income tax, which cuts into profits, will almost certainly encourage firms to make upward adjustments. Very little information is available about the extent to which firms do treat income taxes as expenses for purposes of price setting; in fact, the firms may not always be aware of the extent to which the tax actually affects their prices. The increased tendency for firms to include in cost for price calculation purposes a given after-tax return on investment furthers the likelihood of direct shifting.

### Obstacles to Direct Shifting

On the other hand, there are serious obstacles in the way of exact and complete shifting.[2] In the first place, the amount of income tax per dollar of selling price of the product may vary widely among the firms. This is due partly to the obvious fact that some firms earn more profit, relative to sales volume, than others. But in part, it is due to the fact that when numerous products are made, as is typically the case, the profit margins on particular products will vary among the different firms. This is especially true when a product is produced by firms whose other products are not the same. Thus, one brand of refrigerator is produced by a firm which is primarily an automobile producer, another by a firm which is solely an electrical equipment manufacturer. Inevitably, the profit margins on refrigerators and the allocation of income tax by product will differ. Even if two firms are earning about the same rate of return on investment, the ratios of sales to investment will vary. Finally, the extent to which capital has been obtained from borrowing will affect the tax-sales ratio, because of the deductibility of interest for income tax purposes.

These differences make it almost impossible for firms to shift the entire tax. When products are sufficiently similar that prices must be reasonably uniform, those firms subject to greater tax per unit of sales could not possibly shift this differential. But even more significant is the fact that the differences create uncertainties about competitors' reactions. Each

---

[2] See Carl Shoup, "Some Considerations on the Incidence of the Corporation Income Tax," *Journal of Finance*, Vol. VI (June, 1951), pp. 187–96.

firm is more reluctant to shift because of doubt as to the amount of tax borne by competitors and the price adjustments they are likely to make. In some cases the consequent uncertainties may be so great that no shifting at all will occur.

*Summary.* Under the type of competition which is most prevalent, some shifting of the tax, especially in periods of strong demand relative to capacity, is almost inevitable. The typical analysis of traditional economics ignores the realities of the situation so far as the exact nature of competition is concerned. On the other hand, complete shifting by direct action of the firms is certainly not possible. In more highly competitive markets or with complete monopoly[3] or oligopoly so tight that joint profits are already maximized, direct shifting is unlikely. Even with the more common oligopoly situation, the nonuniformity of the ratio of tax to sales of various products makes exact shifting impossible and increases uncertainty about competitors' reactions, thereby lessening the likelihood of general price increases.

### Effects on Capital Investment

The second general line of criticism of the nonshifting theory is based upon an analysis of the effects of the tax upon capital investment and relates to long-run adjustments.

To the extent that the tax is not immediately shifted, it reduces the net return from capital invested. The corporation management may be unwilling to undertake expansion if the government is to share heavily in the profits. The double taxation of dividend income lessens the attractiveness of equity investments and makes purchase of fixed return securities and the holding of cash relatively more attractive. Thus the flow of equity capital is reduced. This result comes about essentially because the actual corporation tax applies to necessary cost elements, particularly the return on the owners' capital, rather than to pure economic profit, and because of the differentially higher burden against corporate profits than other investment income, which results in a shifting toward alternatives.

From a short-run standpoint the reduced return on investment is likely to produce unemployment, with complex consequences upon distribution of burden. But over a longer period of time, if full employment is maintained, the before-tax rate of return must become higher than it

---

[3] With public utilities, the corporation tax is usually regarded as an expense by regulatory commissions, and thus the companies are permitted to shift it forward in the form of higher rates. The companies will seek to do so, however, only if the regulated rates are actually below those which would maximize profits.

would be in the absence of the tax, in order to insure an adequate supply of money capital on an equity basis and adequate incentives to undertake investment. Essentially, the before-tax return is increased by the effects of the tax in curtailing investment, to the extent to which it does not occur from direct price increases by the business firms.

In a static industry characterized by high fixed investment, the period of time necessary for shifting may be very long. But in a dynamic economy, with a constantly growing volume of investment, the effects of the tax upon investment may be felt very quickly as the tax reduces the volume of new investment being undertaken, and thus the tax will shift, provided that investment is restored to levels adequate for full employment.[4] Even in the short-run period, some shifting may occur through the effect of the tax upon the investment in working capital.[5]

## Empirical Studies

Several attempts have been made to study empirically the shifting of corporate taxes, primarily by analyzing trends in rates of return on investment over a period of years in which tax rates changed significantly. A study by E. M. Lerner and E. S. Hendriksen reviewed the effects of changes in the corporate tax rate between 1927 and 1952.[6] So far as short-run adjustments were concerned, they found substantial evidence that tax increases and tax cuts were typically not passed on, at least in full, as evidenced by substantial changes in the after-tax rate of return on investment consequent to tax rate changes. On the other hand, for the twenty-five-year period, the after-tax rate of return on investment was found to fluctuate around a level trend line despite the substantial increase in the corporate tax. While, clearly, other factors were at work, the evidence strongly suggests that the tax did tend to shift through higher before-tax profit rates.

A similar study was made by Kaldor on the basis of British data;[7] at first glance, in terms of industry as a whole, there appeared to be evidence of a sharp rise in before-tax rate of return between 1937 and 1948–50,

---

[4] See the article by D. Bodenhorn, "The Shifting of the Corporation Income Tax in a Growing Economy," *Quarterly Journal of Economics*, Vol. LXX (November, 1956), pp. 563–80.

[5] See E. C. Brown, "The Corporate Income Tax in the Short Run," *National Tax Journal*, Vol. VII (September, 1954), pp. 240–41.

[6] See their article entitled "Federal Taxes on Corporate Income and the Rate of Return in Manufacturing, 1927 to 1952," *National Tax Journal*, Vol. IX (September, 1956), pp. 193–202.

[7] N. Kaldor, *An Expenditure Tax* (London: George Allen and Unwin, 1955), pp. 149–52.

and thus of tax shifting. But when the data are reviewed by industry group, it is rather obvious that the increase was largely confined to a group of industries badly depressed in 1937, and thus was due to forces other than the tax.[8]

Another similar study by Clendenin for the United States, for the period from 1926 to 1955, produced comparable results;[9] the before-tax margins widened after 1940 to absorb the tax in large measure; that is, the tax shifted forward in the form of higher prices. Again, however, it is impossible to be certain about the extent to which nontax forces produced this increase in margins.

One study, that of Adelman, produced entirely opposite conclusions.[10] Adelman studied the behavior of the percentage of corporate profits before tax to income originating in corporate enterprise in the period between the 1920's and 1946–55 in the United States, and found no significant change; thus, he concluded that the tax did not shift. However, this criterion of measurement is open to serious question, because important changes occurred in two other relevant variables over this period: the rate of interest and the ratio of sales to investment. The fall in the former and the rise in the latter tended to reduce the income generated in the corporate sector, and thus, in the absence of the tax, the over-all percentage would have fallen; the effect of the tax was to prevent the fall, and thus presumably make the before-tax rate of return higher than it would have been in the absence of the tax.

A very extensive study of the question on an empirical basis by Musgrave and Krzyzaniak, not yet published at the time of writing, yields substantial evidence of short-run shifting of the tax; on the whole, before-tax rates of return in the fifties were roughly double those of the twenties, while net returns have remained about the same, despite an increase in the corporate tax rate from 5 to 52 per cent.

The basic limitation of all these studies, however, is the inability to isolate the tax effect from other effects. The long-range distribution of burden of the tax depends in large measure upon the effects of the tax upon economic growth, and this is particularly hard to determine.

---

[8] A study by R. P. Collier of the red cedar shingle industry, one characterized by substantial price competition and declining capacity, concluded that the corporate tax was not affecting price or output decisions, and thus was not shifting in the short run. See his article, "Some Empirical Evidence of Tax Shifting," *National Tax Journal*, Vol. XI (March, 1958), pp. 35–55.

[9] J. C. Clendenin, "Effects of Corporate Income Taxes on Corporate Earnings," *Taxes*, Vol. XXXIV (June, 1956), pp. 391–95.

[10] M. A. Adelman, "The Corporate Income Tax in the Long Run," *Journal of Political Economy*, Vol. LXV (April, 1957), pp. 151–57.

## The Burden on the Stockholders

To the extent that the corporation is not able to shift the tax forward, the direct and immediate burden rests upon the funds which the corporation has available after other expenses are covered. There are three steps which the company may then take:

1. Certain types of expenditures, such as those for maintenance and research, may be reduced. Since the gain from such activities is very difficult to determine, firms are influenced with respect to the amounts which they make available for such purposes by the current rate of profit. The burden of the tax in this case rests directly upon the persons whose incomes are cut off or reduced as a result of the reduction in these activities. These persons, however, will find other employment under ordinary circumstances. If the activities would have been beneficial to the company, the ultimate burden will rest upon the stockholders, through reduced profits earned. If the activities were not profitable, the burden is essentially absorbed through elimination of wasteful use of funds by the business.

2. Dividends may be lower than they would otherwise be. If most of the earnings are being paid out as dividends, the company has little choice; it must cut dividends. If management is anxious for a continued supply of internal funds for expansion and feels that the stockholders are agreeable, it will likewise reduce dividends even if they constitute only a small portion of earnings. On the other hand, if funds are not needed so urgently in the business, dividends may be left unchanged and the tax borne entirely out of profits which would otherwise have been added to surplus. The general policy will depend primarily on the urgency with which the enterprise requires additional funds and the attitude of the stockholders.

To the extent that dividends are reduced, the burden rests very directly on the stockholders, and double taxation of dividend income results.

3. The tax may be borne out of undistributed profits. To a substantial extent, corporate taxes are probably borne out of funds which would otherwise have been retained in the business. If dividends are left unchanged, there is no direct double taxation of dividend income. However, the reduced surplus will tend to lower the selling prices of the stock and thus reduce the capital gains which the stockholders would ultimately have enjoyed. If the tax seriously restricts profitable expansions, the ultimate burden on the stockholders may greatly exceed the dollar sums of taxes paid. On the other hand, the market value of the stock does not always accurately reflect the amounts being added to surplus, and the reduction in these sums due to the tax may therefore not be manifest in

an equivalent decline in stock prices. In this case the stockholders do not suffer the full tax burden. A portion of the tax, in a sense, does not rest on individuals at all but on the undistributed profits as such. However, except in the unlikely case that the surplus had been allowed to lie idle, the earning power of the enterprise would have been reduced, and the stockholders would eventually have experienced lower returns than they could otherwise have received.

Studies by D. M. Holland have attempted to assess the typical differential burden on stockholders in various income classes arising out of the present treatment of corporate income, on the basis of data of income and tax liability published by the Internal Revenue Service.[11] The assumption is made that the tax is not shifted; to the extent that it is, of course, the differential is altered. The evidence clearly shows that many stockholders are undertaxed, compared to the burden which would rest on them if all income were subject to current personal tax rates. In contrast, lower income stockholders are typically overtaxed. The relative tax burden is very uneven and indiscriminate among various persons in the same income groups, depending upon the magnitude and nature of their investments in stocks. The tax does not clearly make the tax system more progressive than otherwise, as is commonly argued. The additional revenue arising from double taxation is relatively small; in 1955 a three percentage point increase in the personal tax rate would have yielded as much revenue as the net contribution of the present corporate tax, if all corporate income were treated as personal income of the stockholders. The studies also show that the 1954 changes offered the average stockholder very little relief from double taxation.

### Summary

Despite the limited knowledge about the exact distribution of the burden of the corporate income tax, some generalizations can be made.

1. The traditional argument that the tax cannot be shifted is valid under the assumptions that perfect competition or complete monopoly prevails and that the tax does not apply to the necessary return to the owners of the businesses. However, the latter assumption is not a valid one.

2. In industries characterized by imperfect competition and oligopoly, direct and immediate shifting by the firms may occur. But there are serious obstacles in the way of complete shifting, and probably the bulk of the tax rests upon the owners of the corporations.

---

[11] See D. M. Holland, *The Income Tax Burden on Stockholders* and *Dividends under the Income Tax* (Princeton: Princeton University Press for National Bureau of Economic Research, 1958 and 1962).

3. Because the tax applies to the necessary return to the owners, it may check investment. Over a period of time, under the assumption of the maintenance of full employment, the consequence will be an increase in the rate of profit before tax, and thus a shifting-forward of the burden from the stockholders to the consumers of the products.[12]

## ECONOMIC EFFECTS

The levying of special taxes on corporate income may produce significant effects upon the functioning of the economy. The effects to which greatest attention has been given are those upon investment; there are other possible effects upon methods of corporate financing, corporate organization, and consolidation.

### Effects upon Investment: Curtailment of Funds Available

The chief criticism advanced against the corporate income tax has been the adverse effect upon investment. There are two distinct effects—those upon the funds available to finance expansion and those upon the incentives to expand. The effects upon the capital available from earnings for use for expansion are very real,[13] to the extent that the tax is not shifted, since a substantial portion of earnings is taken from the firms. While, in part, dividends may be reduced, almost certainly a substantial portion of the tax will be borne out of funds which would otherwise be available for expansion. If the amount of these funds which remains after taxes is less than the amount the firm would actually use for expansion, the volume of investment will be reduced unless the firm is willing and able to obtain outside capital. But firms are often more willing to undertake expansion with their own funds than with amounts obtained by borrowing or the sale of additional stock. The effect is particularly severe on new and growing enterprises, which may have great difficulty in raising capital from outside sources even if their owners are willing to follow this course. The tax aggravates the problem of raising outside capital by reducing the prospective earnings.

[12] A. C. Harberger has recently attempted to analyze the problem with the aid of general equilibrium theory, concluding that the tax is borne primarily by owners of capital. See "The Corporation Income Tax: An Empirical Appraisal," in U.S. House of Representatives, Committee on Ways and Means, *Tax Revision Compendium* (Washington, D.C.: U.S. Government Printing Office, 1959), pp. 231–50; and "The Incidence of the Corporation Income Tax," *Journal of Political Economy*, Vol. LXX (June, 1962), pp. 215–40.

[13] The significance of the tax with respect to funds for expansion is developed at length by J. K. Butters and J. Lintner, *Effect of Federal Taxes on Growing Enterprises* (Boston: Harvard University Graduate School of Business Administration, 1945).

Apart from the direct effects upon undistributed profits available for expansion, the combined corporate and personal income tax structure checks the amount of equity capital available. If persons invest in stock, the return is essentially taxed twice, and thus the possible net return is reduced. Accordingly, stock prices are depressed, and the sale of new stock is made more expensive to the company, since a higher yield rate must be offered, and thus the dilution of earnings with the new stock-holders will be greater. Therefore the willingness of the firms to expand through the sale of additional stock is reduced. There is only one exception to this tendency. The favorable treatment afforded capital gains increases the desire of wealthy persons to buy stock in new ventures. But this is a product of the peculiar treatment of capital gains in the present tax structure rather than of the corporate tax as such.

### Incentive Effects

Secondly, the tax may reduce the incentives of the business managers to undertake expansion. The tax reduces the net return which will be available to the firm as a result of expansion, and as a consequence, some marginal projects will not be undertaken. So far as the small, closely held corporation is concerned, the effects of the corporate tax are not particularly different from those of the personal income tax. In fact, to the extent that retained earnings are subject to a lower rate than that of the personal income tax on the income of the owners, the incentive is less adversely affected. But in the larger corporation the income tax on the earnings of the owners is of little concern, because the persons actually making the corporation decisions are likely to be primarily interested in the earnings of the corporation as such rather than in the income of the owners. Since these earnings are affected by the tax, the managers may be less willing to undertake marginal investments, which run the risk of severely reducing the earnings of the company, yet can increase them only by the amount of profit net after corporate income tax in case of success. There is reason to believe that the typical management of a corporation places a very high priority on avoiding any action which might impair the solvency of the company and thus endanger its own position; this consideration may be much more important than an actual maximization of profit.

### Effects upon Economic Progress

Closely related to these considerations is the possible effect of the tax upon economic progress. New firms are particularly hampered by the tax, because they require earnings for expansion. These firms may be the ones most likely to develop new products and new techniques and thus aid economic development. The restriction upon their growth tends to protect the existing firms against additional competition, and thus the tax helps to perpetuate monopoly and semimonopoly positions. Even with established firms, it may be argued that the tax especially discourages venturesome undertakings because of the high risk and the heavy tax penalty placed upon the possible rewards which will be received if the undertaking is successful, without a fully offsetting tax reduction in case of failure.

### Resource-Allocation Effects

The tax produces various effects on the allocation of resources, by its differential impact upon various forms of investment. The tax rests directly upon the return from corporate equity capital; since the rates of return from various types of investment must equalize (with appropriate adjustments for risk), the prices of goods produced with relatively heavy equity capital will tend to rise, and consumption will be shifted from these lines to others. Thus, allocation of resources will be directed from the pattern presumed to be the optimum.

### The Validity of the Arguments

Against this general line of reasoning, several questions may be raised. In the first place, in large measure the result noted cannot be attributed to the present corporate tax structure, as such, with its peculiar treatment of corporate income, but rather to any tax levied upon the earnings of business enterprise. The collection of any tax upon business earnings will inevitably reduce the amount available for expansion. Even taxes levied on wages and salaries will deter investment by absorbing funds which workers would otherwise save and eventually use to develop new enterprises. However, the corporate tax, as such, is significant in three respects: (1) Because the tax impinges directly upon the corporation, it may affect the decisions of the managers much more than a tax on the income (or the distributed part) after it reaches the stockholders. (2) Because the tax reaches the earnings before they are paid out, the funds directly available to the corporation are affected more than they would be if the tax structure impinged to a greater extent at the personal level. (3) The corporate tax, with the consequent double taxation of dividend income (assuming no forward shifting), may particularly check the flow of equity capital.

Secondly, and more significantly, the usual arguments in regard to the corporate tax ignore completely the fact that the major function of taxes, from the standpoint of the economy, is to curtail private spending, in order to free resources for government use. It is perfectly obvious that in the absence of any tax on corporate earnings, business investment could be (although it might not be) much greater than it is. But if investment were at a higher level and other taxes did not reduce consumption spending, resources would not be freed to a sufficient extent for governmental use, and the excessive competition of the governmental and private sectors for the resources would produce inflation, under the assumption of full employment. The real check to a higher level of investment under conditions of full employment, just like that to higher levels of private sector output consumption, is the spending of the money and thus the use of the resources by the government, rather than the taxes which raise the revenue. The usual criticism of the corporate income tax—that it reduces the total amount of investment—completely ignores the fact that the major economic function of any tax is to reduce private spending in order to prevent inflation. Central banking systems attempt to lessen investment in inflationary periods by various credit control measures for exactly the same reason. The legitimate criticism of the tax, on the basis of economic effects, is not its absolute effect in curtailing investment but its relative effect in slowing down the rate of long-run capital formation to a greater extent than other taxes.

In periods in which full employment is not attained, the criticism of the effect upon investment becomes more serious. Actually, however, the criticism should be directed against all taxes which reduce private spending in any way in such periods; the effects of the corporate tax are likely to be less than those of other taxes. In depressions, business firms are undertaking little new investment and, typically, are not using all the liquid funds they have available. Accordingly, a corporate tax will be absorbed largely out of idle funds and will reduce total spending to a lesser extent than a tax which impinges directly on consumer spending.

Thus, in general, the "effect on investment" argument in its usual form has little merit. In inflationary periods the checking of investment is an anti-inflationary measure and is essential as a part of a general program of curtailing spending. It is true that the corporate tax is not selective in distinguishing between those investments which are particularly inflationary and those which indirectly check inflation by leading to an increase in output of particularly scarce goods. But most other taxes are likewise not selective. In depression the effects of the corporate tax in curtailing expansion are probably less serious than those of other taxes.

### Long-Run Capital Formation

There remains the question, however, of the long-run effects of the tax upon the rate of capital formation. If it is assumed that aggregate demand is sufficiently great to insure full employment, the significance of the tax for capital formation can be approached only by considering its effects on the consumption-savings ratio. To the extent that the tax is not shifted, the corporation income tax, without doubt, cuts the percentage of national income saved more than most other taxes. In part, the tax is absorbed out of undistributed profits and thus directly reduces saving; the portion which rests upon the stockholders is likely to be borne largely out of savings, because of the concentration of stock ownership in the higher income levels. Accordingly, the potential rate of capital formation is reduced more sharply than by other taxes which impinge more largely upon consumption.

If investment opportunities are limited, the rate of capital formation depends not only on the consumption-savings ratio but on the volume of profitable investment as well. If the corporation income tax has a greater effect on investment than other taxes, it could be charged with restricting the rate of capital formation, as well as aggravating unemployment, by reducing capital formation below the potential level. But as indicated above, in periods of less than full employment the restrictive effects of the tax are not likely to be great, unless there are serious "incentive to invest" effects; the over-all restrictive effect is probably less than that of taxes which impinge directly on consumption and less than the expansionary effect of the government expenditures which the revenues finance. In this situation, only replacement of the tax by borrowing would aid investment and employment; the criticism is really, therefore, one not against the type of tax, but one against the use of taxation instead of borrowing in such a period.

Economic development depends, however, not only upon the rate of capital formation, but also upon the nature of the investment being undertaken. Growth requires not merely the investing of more money in capital goods, but also the introduction of new methods and the development of new products. These may come from long-established firms, but they often are developed primarily by newcomers—newly established firms. But it is this group of firms which is particularly affected by the tax, because of the need for expansion from retained earnings. Rate concessions for smaller profit firms are made in the current tax law, but these may be entirely inadequate to meet the problem. One of the most serious charges which can be advanced against high income taxation generally is that of retarding new developments; the effect of the corporate tax is merely one manifestation of this more general problem.

### Effects upon Corporate Financing

Not only may the corporate income tax affect the volume of investment, but it also may alter the methods of financing.[14] The tax gives some incentive toward reliance upon borrowing and less reliance upon sale of stock. Since interest is deductible, the tax does not increase the difficulty or cost of financing from this source. But in the case of stock the reduced prospective return makes the sale of additional stock more expensive from the standpoint of the present owners, in the sense that it dilutes the prospective earnings per share and may also endanger control. Actually, however, available statistics do not show any marked trend toward debt in preference to equity financing; while the incentive given to the use of debt is undesirable, the actual consequences do not appear to have been serious.[15]

In other ways as well, the tax may influence the general corporate structure. The combination of high corporate rates plus the favorable treatment of capital gains may be a factor which increases mergers; study has indicated that in a number of instances, tax considerations have greatly encouraged persons who have developed new businesses to sell out and realize on the profits in the form of capital gains. The encouragement is not so much given by the corporate tax alone as by the existence of the corporate form of business organization, which allows the accumulation of capital free of personal income taxes, yet results in the earnings being subject to taxation twice if they are paid out as dividends. The incentive to realize on the earnings as capital gains is so great, especially if there is danger of large estate taxes at death, that many persons are influenced to sell their businesses.

### Effects upon Efficiency

A final possible effect of the corporate tax is that of lessening efficiency of operation and increasing waste. If a corporation is subject to a 50 per cent tax rate, for example, the government bears one half the cost of any unnecessary expenditure or inefficiency in operation. The net result

---

[14] The most complete discussion of this problem is to be found in D. T. Smith, *Effects of Taxation: Corporate Financial Policy* (Boston: Harvard University Graduate School of Business Administration, 1952).

[15] See J. K. Butters, J. Lintner, and W. L. Cary, *Effects of Taxation: Corporate Mergers* (Boston: Harvard University Graduate School of Business Administration, 1951).

may be some decline in incentive to maintain maximum efficiency. On the other hand, some firms may be stimulated by the tax to attain greater efficiencies, in order to maintain old levels of profits after taxes. It is very difficult to assess the actual effects along these lines; an excess profits tax probably has much greater effect in increasing waste than the corporate income tax itself.

## EQUITY CONSIDERATIONS

From the standpoint of accepted standards of equity, the present treatment of corporate income in the United States has serious limitations.[16]

1. To the extent that the corporate tax reduces present or future dividends, a discriminatory double burden rests on stockholders, since this particular part of the income stream is singled out for double application of income taxes, whereas other incomes—including other property incomes—are taxed but once. Or in terms of the "consumption plus increase in net wealth" definition of income, the corporate tax reduces the income of individuals thus defined below the levels that would otherwise be attained; the income is then subjected to regular income tax rates. Thus the tax rate structure reduces the income from dividends twice but that from other sources only once.

2. To the extent that dividends are received by low-income stockholders, they are subject to income tax from which, on the basis of the exemptions of the personal income tax, they should be free.

3. On the other hand, the undistributed profits of corporations owned by persons in the high income brackets are subjected to lighter tax burden than that to which they would be subject if the personal income tax rates applied to this income.

4. To the extent that the tax is shifted, it becomes essentially a sales tax, inferior in its pattern of tax burden to the usual sales tax, because the burden is distributed unevenly on expenditures on various commodities.

In defense of the corporate tax on an equity basis, it may be argued that on the whole, the tax is distributed in a progressive fashion, because the bulk of stock is owned by persons in the higher income brackets. As demonstrated by Goode, the tax structure as a whole is more progressive with the corporate tax than it would be without it.[17] But this considera-

[16] The inequity aspects are developed at length by W. L. Crum, "The Taxation of Stockholders," *Quarterly Journal of Economics*, Vol. LXIV (February, 1950), pp. 15–56.

[17] R. Goode, *The Corporation Income Tax* (New York: John Wiley & Sons, Inc., 1951), chap. v.

tion, while not unimportant, obscures completely the inequity which results among persons within various income classes. However, this inequity is mitigated by two considerations.

1. In the small, closely held corporation the owners are often able to realize on the profits of the enterprise through the form of capital gains and thus escape the full burden of the personal income tax. This possibility, while reducing the double burden, by no means insures equality of treatment of these taxpayers with other persons.

2. In the larger corporations, it is likely that the tax is frequently borne primarily out of funds which would otherwise be retained in the business. To the extent that this occurs, there is no direct burden on the stockholder through reduced current return, although ultimately, in a rough fashion, the reduction in undistributed profit will be reflected in lower stock prices.

Despite these mitigating circumstances, however, the basic discrimination against the receivers of dividend income remains in large measure. From the standpoint of equity, there would be substantial merit in a policy of taxing corporate earnings on exactly the same basis as that on which they would be taxed if they were earned directly by individuals. If this could be accomplished, the double taxation of dividends, on the one hand, and the favorable treatment now given to undistributed corporate profits (when the corporation stock is owned by the wealthy), on the other, would be avoided. Equity considerations definitely favor the integration approach to corporate taxation rather than the separate entity approach.

## INTEGRATION OF THE PERSONAL AND CORPORATE TAXES

If the basic principle is accepted that income should, so far as possible, be taxed at the same rate regardless of the form of business organization through which it is earned, some form of integration of the tax on corporate income with the personal income tax is required. Complete integration, if it could be attained, would eliminate all inequity due to the arbitrary elements in the tax structure unrelated to personal ability to pay which arise from separate taxation of income earned in the corporate form of organization and should facilitate the flow of outside equity capital to the corporations. It should likewise lessen the shifting of the income taxes to the consumers.

### The Partnership Approach

Complete integration can be obtained only if the corporation is completely ignored, all earnings of the corporation being taxed directly to the owners. Under the partnership technique, all taxes on corporations would be removed, dividends would be taxed as regular income, and undistributed profits allocated to individual stockholders and taxed to them, even though not currently received by them. The tax burden would thus become the same on all corporate earnings as on other income, and the tax liability would be unaffected by the dividend policies of the corporation.

The partnership method is entirely feasible for small, closely held corporations and has been employed for them by Great Britain and Australia for some years. These corporations are not fundamentally different from partnerships. The earnings can easily be allocated among the various owners, and since the latter have a direct voice in the dividend policies of the corporation, they can avoid any hardships which might arise from taxation of income which they had not actually received. The partnership treatment would be particularly advantageous to closely held businesses which were not growing rapidly and whose owners thus would prefer to withdraw earnings as dividends.

On the other hand, the partnership approach is not feasible for larger corporations. The first difficulty is that of allocation of earnings; when a corporation has diverse security issues outstanding, the task of allocation would be, as a matter of principle, a very difficult one. In addition, the mechanics of the task of allocation and notification of the stockholders would not be negligible. Secondly, the average stockholder of a large corporation has no influence upon dividend policy. If the corporation retained large amounts of profits, the stockholders would be subjected to tax on money which they had not received and over whose disposition they could exercise no real influence. Hardships would result, and persons would be discouraged from buying stock in such enterprises.

The feasibility of the partnership method for closely held corporations and its nonsuitability for ones with widespread ownership suggest the possibility of using the procedure for the first group only, either on an optional or on a mandatory basis. If an option was allowed, the taxpayers would, of course, employ it only where tax relief would result. But the main difficulty lies in the drawing of a satisfactory line between the two classes of corporations. Any such line, based, for example, upon the number of stockholders, would of necessity be highly arbitrary. Essentially, the net result would be the drawing of a sharp line between one type of corporation and another rather than between partnerships and corporations. Yet the line would be somewhat more realistic than the present one, since the basic differences between widely held and closely held corporations are far more fundamental than those between partnerships and corporations.

In the 1958 tax legislation designed to aid small business, Congress authorized corporations having no more than ten stockholders to elect the partnership basis for income taxation if they wish. The privilege includes the right to pass through operating losses to the stockholders.

### The "Dividend Received Credit" Approaches

The second general approach would allow the stockholder a credit for taxes paid by the corporation on the portion of profits paid out as dividends. This approach takes three forms. The first is the withholding method, as used in Great Britain and various Commonwealth countries, including Nigeria and Rhodesia. So far as dividends are concerned, the portion of the income tax applying to corporations is treated simply as a withholding levy, comparable to the withholding collections for the personal income tax on wages and salaries. When the stockholder determines his income tax liability, he includes in his income both the dividends and the tax paid by the corporation on the dividend income (which is reported to him by the corporation). After calculating his tax liability, he subtracts from his tax his reported share of tax paid by the corporation. If his total income is such that the amount thus "withheld" exceeds his total income tax liability, he is entitled to a refund. Undistributed corporation profits are taxed at the usual corporate tax rate. This method insures completely equitable treatment of dividend income. It does not, of course, result in taxation of undistributed profits at the same rate as would be applied in the absence of the corporate form of organization. But it eliminates very effectively the inequitable treatment of individual stockholders. Great Britain also imposes a 15 per cent profits tax on corporations, which is not integrated with the personal tax.

The second form, which Canada employs, allows a partial credit to the stockholder for corporate tax paid. In calculation of income tax liability, the taxpayer includes all dividends in taxable income; after he determines the amount of tax due on this income, he subtracts from it an amount equal to 20 per cent of the dividends received from Canadian corporations. The credit covers the entire tax paid by the smaller corporations, but only a portion of that paid by the ones with larger profits. The maximum corporate rate is 47 per cent on profit in excess of $35,000. The amount of tax paid by the corporation on the sum paid out as dividends is not included in the stockholder's income. No refund is allowed to low-income stockholders. This system is a much less complete form of integration than the British system and by no means eliminates all inequity. Particularly, it does not alleviate the burden on the very-low-income stockholder. The method was selected by Canada primarily because it was somewhat simpler and involved less revenue loss than the British approach. The primary intent of the Canadian program (adopted in 1949) was not so much improved equity as primarily a means of lessening the danger that the heavy personal and corporate levies would impede business expansion.[18]

In January, 1954, the use of the Canadian system was recommended to Congress by President Eisenhower. As the Revenue Act of 1954 was finally adopted, a limited version of the Canadian credit system was provided, with complete exclusion from tax of the first $50 of dividend income received by each taxpayer, and a credit against tax liability of 4 per cent of the amount of dividends in excess of $50. The "credit against tax" system was used instead of a "deduction from income" system to provide the same tax saving per dollar of dividends in all income brackets. While there were originally plans for increasing the figure of the credit to 15 per cent, this has never been done. As a result, the credit removes only a small portion of the double taxation.

A third, and closely related, method was employed in the United States prior to 1934; corporation dividends were exempt from the normal tax rate of the personal income tax but were subject to the surtax. Since during most of the period the corporate tax rate and the personal income tax normal rate were similar, the effect was to avoid the discriminatory taxation in relatively effective fashion. This approach does involve some complication of the personal rate structure and requires that the basic rates of the two taxes be similar, if full relief is to be obtained. As in the Canadian system, no relief is given to low-income stockholders having no personal tax liability.

Of these three forms of "dividend received credit" approach, the British system is by far the most satisfactory, although it is somewhat more complicated than the other forms. None of the methods accomplishes complete integration, which can be realized only by the partnership approach. In addition, there are two serious limitations to any of the "dividend received credit" approaches. Since the burden on the corporation is left unchanged, any effects which the tax may have in encouraging debt financing are not mitigated, and there is no elimination of any adverse effects which the corporate tax may have on incentives of the managers of the larger corporations or the willingness of all types of businesses to undertake risky developments. As indicated above, these problems may not be too serious, but they may be significant in some particular instances. Secondly, and of greater concern, is the fact that this approach gives the stockholder a completely unwarranted bonus in the cases in which the tax is shifted by the corporation to the consumers of the prod-

---

[18] This intent was made clear by the Assistant Deputy Minister of Finance, A. Kenneth Eaton, in an article in the *National Tax Journal*, "Recent Developments in Corporate Taxation in Canada," Vol. III (March, 1950), pp. 75–81.

ucts. In this instance, there is at present no doubt taxation of dividend income and no need for relief; the credit essentially frees this income completely from any income taxation. On an equity basis, such treatment is completely unjustifiable. At best, it could be defended only as a stimulus for business expansion. This problem suggests that a more satisfactory solution to the question of integration lies in the direction of adjusting the tax burden at the corporate level. Thirdly, this approach does nothing to provide equality of treatment of undistributed profits and other income.

### The Undistributed Profits or "Dividend Paid Credit" Approach

The final alternative is that of allowing corporations to subtract amounts paid out as dividends in determining taxable profits. This procedure would, of course, have the effect of retaining the corporate tax only on undistributed profits, while the dividends would be fully taxed to the stockholders. As a result, the dividend income would be treated in the same manner as other income, and no refunds would be necessary for low-income dividend receivers. Since this portion of the tax would be removed from the corporate level, the chances of shifting, and thus of unwarranted bonus to stockholders when shifting occurs, would be eliminated. All incentive for debt financing would be eliminated, as well as the effects of the tax on management policies (except as noted below). This method would not result in the same burden on the undistributed profits as that which would be imposed on them by the personal tax. Otherwise, the tax would be completely integrated with the personal income tax.

There are, however, some questions about the effects of the procedure on corporate dividend policies and possible competitive disturbances among various firms. Some additional incentive would be given to pay out earnings as dividends, especially in those cases in which the decisions were made by corporation management, as distinguished from the major owners. The economic effects of such a policy vary according to circumstances. In depression the action would facilitate recovery, to the extent that the dividends were spent and the undistributed profits were not being used for business expansion.[19] In inflation, with the same assumptions, the economic effects would be undesirable. From a long-range standpoint the action might slow down the rate of capital formation. It is doubtful, however, if firms would commonly pay out earnings as dividends, if there were good opportunities to use these funds for expansion of the business, merely in order to reduce corporate tax liability.

---

[19] The undistributed profits tax of 1936-37 was a supplement to the regular corporate tax designed to accomplish this result. But it functioned badly, penalized firms which were using earnings for expansion, and became so unpopular that it was repealed.

The question of the effects on new, growing firms and their competitive relationships with older firms is a more serious one. Since growing firms require earnings for their expansion, they would be subject to heavier corporate tax, relative to sales, than their established competitors which no longer required funds for expansion and could pay out larger amounts as dividends. The real complaint, however, is not so much one of discrimination, since the higher tax would not interfere with the ability of the new firm to compete, but of effects on expansion; and it suggests once more the principle that if encouragement of new businesses is the primary goal of tax policy, the solution is the use of policies which deliberately favor earnings of such businesses, without regard to equity considerations. It is true that the tax would check the growth of new firms, but no more so than the present tax. However, the complaint of discrimination could be met in large part, without serious loss of equity, by exempting the first $50,000 of earnings from the corporate tax, whether it was actually distributed as profits or not.[20]

In the immediate postwar years, there was substantial attention to the integration question. Since 1955, however, the issue has ceased to be a major one, with more pressure in the United States to eliminate the present concessions on double taxation than to extend them. Thus the basic rule of treating the corporation as a separate entity has been in large measure reaffirmed. Great Britain has been moving in the direction of greater use of the separate entity approach; and two African Commonwealth areas, Ghana and the East African countries, have likewise moved away from the traditional integrated approach.[21]

## SPECIAL PROBLEMS OF CORPORATE TAXATION

Several special problems relating to the corporate tax warrant brief attention.

[20] The late Henry Simons advanced an additional proposal. Once capital gains were made fully taxable, all taxes would be removed from the corporations, and stockholders would be taxed on their dividends and upon the undistributed profits when they realized upon them through sale of their stock. This proposal is not acceptable to most students of the problem. Undistributed profits would completely escape taxation on a current basis, a consideration of great importance with respect to the fiscal aspects of the tax structure, and corporations would be encouraged to hold more earnings in the form of undistributed profits. Funds earned by a corporation and invested unsoundly would never be subject to tax. Stock prices do not reflect reinvested profits sufficiently closely to insure equitable treatment by this means.

[21] In continental Europe, some integration of the corporate taxes is provided in Germany and Belgium by placing a lower corporate rate on profits distributed as dividends, and Italy and Finland reduce the personal tax on dividend income. Eire follows the traditional British pattern of avoiding double taxation.

### Unreasonable Accumulation

In a tax system in which the personal income tax rates applying to many persons are higher than the corporate rates and capital gains are taxed lightly or not at all, the owners of small, closely held corporations are encouraged to retain earnings in the corporation and eventually realize on them as capital gains. The United States income tax law has for many years contained a provision which provides for penalty taxes on "improper accumulations" of surplus designed to lessen the tax liability of the owners. Because of the vagueness of the statute and the difficulties of determining "unreasonableness" of accumulation, the provision has been of greater significance as a threat to business firms than as an actual penalty on firms which accumulate for the purposes indicated.

Studies of the effects of the penalty tax suggest that it does exercise real influence on the dividend and investment policies of small corporations.[22] The number of assessments has been relatively small, the Internal Revenue Service following a rather conservative policy and applying the penalties only in the most obvious cases. Nevertheless, many corporations pay out more in dividends than they would prefer to pay because of fear of possible application of the provision. The effectiveness of the section was weakened still more in the 1954 Revenue Act.[23]

While the aims are desirable, the rule has not proven to be an effective means of accomplishing the result. The task is inherently difficult because of the problems of drawing the line between accumulations for purposes of legitimate business use and those for tax avoidance. The vagueness of the statute creates unnecessary fears on the part of many business firms that they might be subjected to it. More precise wording is very difficult, because of the considerations of intent which are relevant. In the light of the difficulties, Canada repealed a similar provision and replaced it with a novel rule designed in part to check unreasonable accumulation and in part to handle the problem of payments to stockholders at the time of liquidation of corporations. Since Canada does not tax capital gains, the owners of small corporations have had tremendous incentive to add earnings to surplus and then withdraw them as capital gains. As a consequence, it became necessary to define as income various types of withdrawals of previous earnings of corporations in capital gains

---

[22] See Joint Committee on the Economic Report, *The Taxation of Corporate Surplus Accumulations* (Washington, D.C.: U.S. Government Printing Office, 1952); Tax Institute, *Economic Effects of Section 102* (Princeton, N.J., 1951).

[23] A description of the revised section is to be found in the book by R. S. Holzman, *The Tax on Accumulated Earnings* (New York: Ronald Press Co., 1956).

form, a policy which in some cases resulted in heavy tax burdens and in continued attempts to avoid the provisions. Accordingly, in 1949 and 1950, new legislation allowed corporations to pay a 15 per cent tax on existing surplus and on future additions to surplus (over and above the current corporate tax) and then to distribute these amounts to individual stockholders at a later date tax-free. On subsequent additions to surplus the firm has the right to use the procedure only if it pays equal amounts in cash dividends.

Some countries apply a special tax on the portion of undistributed earnings in excess of a specified percentage of total profit.

### The Tax Treatment of Co-operatives

One of the most difficult problems is the taxation of the earnings of co-operatives.[24] The profits of co-operatives, apart from a fixed return on shares and amounts added to surplus, are distributed on the basis of the purchases or sales of the members. One basic problem is whether the amounts returned to the customers represent refund of overpayment of prices (or additional payments for goods handled, in the case of marketing co-operatives) or income in the usual sense. There is likewise the question of whether any or all of the earnings of the co-operative should be taxed to the co-operative itself.

While arguments can be advanced on both sides of the issue, two principles emerge:

1. The patronage refund is essentially not income but merely a return of an overcharge, so long as it represents economies in operation rather than return on invested capital. By the same line of reasoning, it is not taxable income so far as the co-operative is concerned. Any attempt to tax these amounts at either level would encourage the co-operatives to reduce prices in order to pass on the gain directly or pay higher prices for goods handled, a practice generally felt to be detrimental to the operation of the co-operatives.

2. On the other hand, the earnings of the co-operative from invested capital and the payments of these to the members are certainly income, in the usual concept of the term. The difficulty arises, however, in distinguishing these elements from the ones which represent economies in operation.

There remains the question of amounts added to surplus. The members do not directly have claim to any portion of these amounts and are

[24] See U.S. House of Representatives, Committee on Ways and Means, *Tax Revision Compendium*, pp. 1867–1982; and R. C. McIvor, *Recent Growth in Canadian Co-operatives* (Toronto: Canadian Tax Foundation, 1962).

not permitted to withdraw a proportional share in them if they cease to be members. Accordingly, it would seem reasonable to tax these amounts as earnings to the co-operative. This is the general procedure now applied by the United States and Canadian income tax laws. In Canada, co-operatives are subject to tax, but any corporation, including co-operatives, may deduct patronage refunds from income for tax purposes; the net results are thus much the same as in the United States. Patronage refunds are taxable income to the recipients, except in the case of consumer co-operatives.

### Intercorporate Dividends

Dividends received by one corporation from another in which it holds stock receive special treatment, in order to minimize double taxation. In Canada, these dividends are not taxed at all; in the United States, 15 per cent of such dividends received are taxable.

## REFERENCES

GOODE, R. *The Corporation Income Tax.* New York: John Wiley & Sons, Inc., 1951.
  The most complete analysis of the corporation income tax.
SMITH, D. T. *Effects of Taxation: Corporate Financial Policy.* Boston: Harvard University Graduate School of Business Administration, 1952.
  A study, in part empirical, of the effects of the tax structure on corporate financing policies.
BUTTERS, J. K.; LINTNER, J.; and CARY, W. L. *Effects of Taxation: Corporate Mergers.* Boston: Harvard University Graduate School of Business Administration, 1951.
  The effects of the tax structure in encouraging corporate mergers.
PETRIE, J. R. *The Taxation of Corporate Income in Canada.* Toronto: University of Toronto Press, 1952.
  A review and analysis of Canadian experience.
U.S. HOUSE OF REPRESENTATIVES, COMMITTEE ON WAYS AND MEANS. *Tax Revision Compendium,* pp. 231–50, 1537–1652, 2281–2330. Washington, D.C.: U.S. Government Printing Office, 1959.
SCHLESINGER, E. R. "Corporate Income Tax Shifting and Fiscal Policy," *National Tax Journal,* Vol. XIII (March, 1960), pp. 17–28.
HOLLAND, D. M. *The Income Tax Burden on Stockholders.* Princeton: Princeton University Press for National Bureau of Economic Research, 1958.
  Analysis of the burden on stockholders arising from the corporate income tax, and of related problems.
RATCHFORD, B. U., and HAN, P. B. "The Burden of the Corporate Income Tax," *National Tax Journal,* Vol. X (December, 1957), pp. 310–24.

A critical review of recent literature on the question of the shifting of the corporate income tax.

JOINT COMMITTEE ON THE ECONOMIC REPORT. *Federal Tax Policy for Economic Growth and Stability,* Parts XII, XIII. Washington, D.C.: U.S. Government Printing Office, 1955.

A series of papers on corporate income taxation.

*Annual Proceedings of the National Tax Association.*

These contain extensive discussions on the question of corporation income taxes, federal and state.

# Chapter 14

# STATE AND LOCAL

# INCOME AND BUSINESS

# TAXATION

The same arguments which justify income taxation by the federal government can be used to justify use of the tax by smaller jurisdictions. In practice, use has been made of the tax by the states for many years, and in recent years by a number of local governments. Several states experimented with income taxation in the last century, long before the federal government permanently established the levy. But these early taxes were not successful, due primarily to poor enforcement, and for several decades the tax was regarded as impossible of state administration. In 1911, however, Wisconsin successfully imposed an income tax, and the introduction of the federal tax paved the way for revived state usage. The spread of the tax continued through the thirties, but came to a dead end as the federal tax was raised sharply. Not until 1961 did any other states impose the tax.

## PRESENT STATE USE

As of January, 1963, the personal income tax is imposed by thirty-five states, although in two of these it applies only to income from investments, in lieu of application of the property tax to intangible property. The New Jersey tax is limited to commuters to New York. In addition, the Indiana gross income tax applies to incomes of individuals. The taxes yielded 13 per cent of state revenue in 1962, with only five states—Oregon, New York, Wisconsin, Alaska, and Hawaii—obtaining more than 20 per cent of their revenue from this source. Typically, but not in all cases, the states relying heavily on income taxes are ones not imposing sales taxes.

All except four states now use graduated rates, but most have only a few (five or six) brackets, and graduation usually stops at a relatively low figure (in many cases $10,000 or less). Rates typically run from 1 to 5 or 6 per cent. Exemptions are in some cases comparable to those of the federal tax; in other states, higher. On the whole, the burden of the state levies is very light compared to that of the federal government. The concept of income and the deductions are comparable to those of the federal government, but not in all cases identical, particularly in the treatment of capital gains and other special cases. The consequence is a substantial amount of nuisance for the taxpayer. A few states experimented for a time with giving the taxpayer the option of paying a sum equal to a certain percentage of his federal tax liability, but for the most part have given this up. Alaska and West Virginia provide the simplest rule: The amount of tax due is simply 10 and 6 per cent, respectively, of the federal tax. States differ in their policy of allowing deductibility of federal income taxes paid; those which permit this generally have higher tax rates than those which do not. Some states now permit simplified forms, but a number still require itemization of deductions.

There has been an increasing trend toward withholding in order to improve administration. In 1958, 11 states had used it; by 1963 the figure had reached 27.

The states encounter one problem to a much more serious extent than the comparable problem of the federal government, namely, that relating to interstate income. Substantial amounts of income are earned by persons resident in other states, and residents of one state will earn income in other states. Initially, the states followed two patterns: Some taxed residents on all income but did not tax income earned in the state by nonresidents, while others simply taxed income earned in the state, regardless of residence of the recipients. Gradually, most states combined the two methods, taxing all income of residents, and income earned in the state by nonresidents. The result was a substantial amount of double taxation of interstate income. Gradually, however, most states introduced reciprocal clauses into their tax legislation, whereby a credit is permitted for income tax paid another state, provided the latter state employs a comparable rule.

## MERITS AND LIMITATIONS

A state income tax introduces a degree of progression into the relatively regressive state tax systems, and distributes the tax burden in a more equitable fashion among individuals than the alternative state sources. However, several major objections are raised, which have served to restrict the scope and magnitude of the state levies.

The first is the interjurisdictional problem noted above, which complicates administration, makes evasion easier, and in some instances results in double taxation of the same income by more than one state. It is difficult for a state to learn of income earned by nonresidents, or earned in another state by its residents. The states have access to federal income tax returns for purposes of audit of their own income taxes, and several states have made co-operative audit agreements with the Internal Revenue Service. But nevertheless the interstate complications are still troublesome.

A second limitation is the possible effect—or fear of the effect—of the taxes in causing shifting of resources, particularly labor, from the area. The state legislatures have frequently feared that high state taxes will cause a loss of population and business from the state, though there is little evidence of such a tendency.[1] But the fear makes the enactment of high income tax rates difficult.

Thirdly, use of the tax at the state level results in duplication of tax-collecting machinery and unnecessary work for the taxpayer, who must compile and file two or more returns. Theoretically, this task could be reduced to a minimum by close correlation of the bases of the state and federal taxes; but in practice, such correlation is difficult to attain.

Fourthly, independent use of income taxes by several jurisdictions may prevent logical development of the tax structure. If state and local rates are established without regard to the federal tax, the combined rates may exceed those which would be regarded as reasonable on an equity basis and may result in serious adverse consequences for the economy. With present federal rates in both countries as high as they are today, any attempt on the part of the states to rely heavily on the income tax could easily produce combined rates which would be regarded as excessive. In practice, the state rates are sufficiently low that this problem is not serious.

Against these objections, there remains the primary consideration that the income tax is the best single means of reaching persons on the basis of their economic well-being. But as will be explained in later chapters, the use of some other bases in conjunction with the income tax may produce a more satisfactory over-all tax structure than the income tax alone. Use of other taxes in lieu of the income tax, or in conjunction with a low-rate income tax, appears to be the most logical solution to state financial problems.

---

[1] A study by Vickrey of population growth in various parts of metropolitan areas extending into more than one state, with state income tax in some areas and not in others, shows no evidence which can be detected statistically of any effect of the state taxes upon population growth (see W. Vickrey, *Agenda for Progressive Taxation* [New York: Ronald Press Co., 1947], pp. 446–48). Most other studies of the question of tax effects upon location of industry conclude that these effects are minor. A summary of the studies is presented in an article by the author, "Studies of State-Local Tax Influence on Location of Industry," *National Tax Journal*, Vol. XIV (June, 1961), pp. 163–73.

## MUNICIPAL INCOME TAXES

The use of income taxation at the municipal level is a relatively new development in the United States. Apart from a few experiments, municipalities entered the field only after World War II, when they were seeking additional revenue sources to complement the existing inadequate levies. The pioneer levy was that of Philadelphia, which became effective in 1940, and served as the model for other local levies. As of 1962, there were over 1,200 municipal income taxes, primarily employed by the cities, but including school districts in Pennsylvania. Most of these, however, were to be found in two states, Ohio and Pennsylvania, plus St. Louis, Detroit, and a few Kentucky cities. The total yield in 1961 was $258 million. In many Ohio cities the income tax yield exceeds that of the property tax.

The municipal levies differ sharply from the federal and state taxes. They do not apply to all income, but only to wages and salaries, plus the net profits of business enterprises (in Pennsylvania, to noncorporate businesses only). Thus, investment income is completely excluded, primarily for administrative reasons and to prevent migration from the city. Secondly, with a very few exceptions, no exemptions are provided, and no deductions from income are permitted (except, of course, expenses of doing business). Thirdly, the rates are very low, 1 per cent being the most common, and 0.5 per cent next in importance. The range is from one eighth of 1 per cent to 2 per cent. No progression is employed. Income earned in the city by nonresidents is included, as well as taxable forms of income earned outside the city by residents. State law usually prevents double taxation of the same income by more than one city. Withholding of tax on wage and salary income is almost universal, and important as a means of preventing evasion.

These municipal income taxes are open to serious criticism. It is difficult for the cities to prevent some evasion, especially on income earned outside the city. The base of the taxes is such as to discriminate seriously against wage and salary income, and the usual equity of an income tax is in large measure lost by the failure to provide exemptions and deductions. On the whole, the municipality is too small a unit to administer a true income tax effectively, and any increase in scope and rate could easily have serious effects in driving people and industry outside the city limits. The adding of a third layer of income tax causes further duplication of tax returns for both business firms and individuals. The use of the municipal levies can be explained almost entirely in terms of revenue needs and the desire to reach persons working in the city but residing outside, and only by confining it to certain types of income can the tax be made workable at all.

## STATE CORPORATION INCOME TAXATION

As of January, 1963, thirty-seven states imposed corporation income taxes which, in 1962, yielded 6 per cent of state tax revenue. The typical rates are 5 and 6 per cent, with a range from 1 to 10.23 per cent. Six states apply graduated rates. The base of the tax is comparable to that of the federal levy, but with some differences, particularly in respect to loss carry-over.

These state levies involve the same discrimination, from an equity basis, that occurs with the federal tax. Yet failure to tax the corporate income would allow the undistributed profits to go free from state income taxes, while none of the integration plans discussed in Chapter 13 are feasible for the states because of the interstate income complications. The state taxes have one major justification: Only by this means can a state obtain tax revenue from the earnings of corporations owned by nonresidents. It would appear reasonable that a state in which a corporation does business is entitled to some revenue from its earnings, but it cannot reach this revenue except by some type of levy on the corporation itself.

One inherently difficult problem with a state or provincial corporate tax is that of the allocation of interstate income, and any solution must be somewhat arbitrary. Unfortunately, the states have never used uniform methods, and some discriminatory double taxation results. The federal courts have for many years allowed a state to tax corporations chartered by the state on their entire income but have permitted taxation of other corporations only on income earned in the state. But the courts have never defined "income earned in the state" in terms of any one formula of allocation. About half the states use the "Massachusetts formula," which gives equal weight to the percentages of total payrolls, sales, and property which are in the state in determining the percentage of total income considered to be earned in the state.

These problems of treatment of interstate income, plus the fears of injuring business development in the state if the rates are raised to high levels, seriously restrict the revenue potentialities of the state corporation income taxes.

### Alternative Approaches to State Business Taxation

Those states which do not employ corporate income taxes attempt to attain the same objectives by other levies on corporations. These take several forms.

1. *Gross Receipts.* A few states, including Washington, West Virginia, and Alaska, tax corporations on the basis of their gross receipts, at rates of less than 1 per cent. In some instances the rates vary according to the type of business. These taxes are sometimes defended on the basis of ease of determination of gross receipts compared to net income and as a means of insuring some payment from all business regardless of earnings. But such a procedure, while it might be justified on a strict benefit doctrine, raises serious questions of equity. But more significantly, these taxes are almost certainly shifted to the consumers of the products and thus do not actually accomplish the primary purpose of state business taxation at all. From the standpoint of shifting, there is no basic difference between a gross receipts tax and a sales tax, except in so far as the low rate of the former lessens the urgency of readjusting prices.

The unique Indiana gross income tax is basically a combination of a gross receipts business tax and a personal income tax. As of January, 1963, wholesalers and retailers were subject to a rate of $\frac{3}{8}$ per cent on gross receipts, while individuals, service establishments, and manufacturers were taxed at a $1\frac{1}{2}$ per cent rate. Major changes were made in the tax in April, 1963.

2. *Capital Stock.* A number of states, including several which also use corporate income taxes, tax corporations on the basis of their capital stock. Methods of determining the value vary widely. This type of tax is highly inequitable, since the value of the capital stock, regardless of the basis chosen, is not a satisfactory measure of income earned. When par value is used, the results, from the standpoint of equity, are little short of absurd. Very-low-rate capital stock taxes might be justified as continuing compensation for the privilege of incorporating, but they are completely unsatisfactory means of reaching income earned in the state by corporations.

3. *Occupational Levies.* Several southern states continue to reach corporations and other business firms by means of special occupational levies, applied to particular industries, but of sufficient scope that virtually the entire range of business is covered. Some have flat rates; others are graduated on some very rough basis related to the amount of business. All are very unsatisfactory and inequitable means of reaching business earnings.

4. *Value Added.* The state of Michigan uses a unique form of business tax, somewhat similar to the French sales tax, but at a much lower rate. This levy is imposed upon value added, that is, gross receipts less cost of goods sold, materials, and similar items. Unlike most business taxes, it applies to both incorporated and unincorporated businesses, although with substantial exemptions, which free most farmers and many

small businesses from liability. The rate is under 1 per cent. The tax is defended as simpler and less injurious to business efficiency than a net income tax, and more equitable than a gross receipts tax, in the sense that value added, rather than gross recepits, is a better measure of the economic activity of the firm.

On the whole, these alternative methods are much less satisfactory than the corporate income tax as a means of reaching income earned in the state. In part they may be shifted, while in part they bear very inequitably upon the owners of different forms of business. Their only redeeming feature is the relatively low rate. For the most part, they represent crude and obsolete methods of reaching business income.

## APPENDIX

### Provincial and Local Income Taxes in Canada

Provincial personal income taxation was used as early as 1876, but at the time of World War I, only two provinces imposed the levy. The depression of the thirties brought a sharp increase in use; and by 1940, seven provinces collected the tax. The history of provincial corporate income taxation was essentially the same. In 1941, in order to insure complete control of income taxes by the federal government, the provinces were induced to abandon their income taxes in exchange for federal tax rental agreement payments. After the war, these arrangements were continued on a voluntary basis, although Quebec, and for the most part, Ontario, did not participate. In these postwar agreements, technically the provinces continued to levy the corporate taxes, but the federal government collected them. Ontario and Quebec imposed and collected their own corporate taxes, and Quebec did so with the personal income tax; Ontario did not levy a personal tax.

In 1962 the federal government eliminated the tax rental agreement system, but offered instead to collect personal and corporate income taxes imposed by the provinces, provided that the coverage conformed with that of the federal tax. The federal personal income tax was reduced by 16 per cent (the figure to rise to 20 per cent by 1966), and a tax abatement of 9 per cent provided for provincial corporate income taxes against the federal tax. All provinces except Ontario and Quebec accepted the federal offer to collect the taxes and Ontario did so on personal income tax. The eight provinces plus Ontario impose their personal taxes at rates equal to 16 per cent of the federal tax (22 per cent in Manitoba and Saskatchewan) and corporate tax rates (as of 1962) of 9 per cent in six provinces and 10 per cent in two. Ontario and Quebec operate their own corporate income taxes with 11 and 12 per cent rates, respectively, and Quebec its own personal income tax, at rates from 2.5 per cent to 13.2 per cent of taxable income.

Municipal income taxes were imposed widely for many years until the establishment of the tax rental agreements in 1941, primarily in the maritime provinces, and to some extent in Ontario and Quebec.

### Local Income Taxes Elsewhere

Income taxes of the usual form are major sources of revenue of the municipalities in Norway, Sweden, and Denmark. These taxes are for the most part collected by the national government in conjunction with its own tax. The rates are substantial, typically from 10 to 15 per cent. In Norway the city income taxes yield over 90 per cent of the revenues of these units, and thus compare with the property tax in the United States in relative importance. The success of these taxes and the little adverse criticism of them on economic grounds result primarily from their relative uniformity and the collection of them in conjunction with the income taxes of the national governments.

## REFERENCES

SIGAFOOS, R. A. *The Municipal Income Tax.* Chicago: Public Administration Service, 1955.
  A review of municipal income taxation in the United States.
QUINTO, L. J. *Municipal Income Taxation in the United States.* New York: Mayor's Committee on Management Survey of the City of New York, 1952.
  A description of the major municipal income taxes.
STUDENSKI, P. "Toward a Theory of Business Taxation," *Journal of Political Economy,* Vol. XLVIII (October, 1940), pp. 621–54.
  One of the most complete studies of business taxation, from the standpoint of principle.
PENNIMAN, G., and HELLER, W. W. *State Income Tax Administration.* Chicago: Public Administration Service, 1959.
  A detailed study of administration.
TAYLOR, M. C. "Local Income Taxes after Twenty-one Years," *National Tax Journal,* Vol. XV (June, 1962), pp. 113–24.

# PART IV

## The Consumption Basis of Taxation

# TAXATION BASED

# UPON CONSUMPTION

# EXPENDITURES

A major alternative to income as the basis for taxation is consumption expenditure. Despite the general acceptance of income as the most suitable measure of economic well-being, substantial use has been made of the expenditure base as well, and arguments have often been advanced for increased, or even exclusive, reliance upon this basis in preference to income. The debate over the relative merits of the income and the expenditure bases has continued for centuries and has been reflected in the varying importance of the two bases in various periods.

In terms of the basic definition of income presented in Chapter 7, a consumption-based tax would apply only to one segment of total income, namely, consumption, while increases in net wealth would be excluded from the base of the tax. In terms of the "flow of wealth" definition of income employed in the tax laws, only the portion of the flow employed for consumption purposes would be taxed. For persons who are spending more than their incomes, the potential tax base is greater under the expenditure approach than under the income approach.

## THE CASE FOR THE EXPENDITURE BASE

The general argument for the use of the expenditure base can be developed independently of the particular type of tax to be employed to implement the base. The most complete case for the expenditure basis appears in the book by N. Kaldor, *An Expenditure Tax,*[1] and the presentation below has been influenced materially by this work.

### Income Defined as Consumption

A group of writers over a long period of time has argued that income is appropriately defined for tax purposes as consisting only of consumption expenditures, because economic well-being is determined by con-

[1] London: George Allen and Unwin, 1955.

sumption alone. The chief exponent of this doctrine in later years was Irving Fisher,[2] but the idea is to be found in earlier writings. Classical economists such as John Stuart Mill and Pigou followed a similar line of reasoning in arguing that the taxation of both the portion of income saved and the subsequent earnings from the sums saved constitutes double taxation, since the principal is reduced by the amount of the tax, and then the earnings on it are taxed.

This terminological approach is not particularly fruitful. The definition of income which includes sums saved as well as sums consumed is more generally accepted, in line with the point of view that saving a portion of income constitutes a contribution to the person's economic well-being and reflects a deliberate choice. The double taxation argument is also not convincing; the argument over the desirability of excluding saving from the base of taxation can be resolved only in terms of the merits and limitations of doing so, not by labeling the failure to do so as "double taxation."

### Equity Considerations

The key argument on equity grounds for the expenditure base dates back several centuries to the statement of Hobbes that equity requires the taxation of persons on the basis of what they take out of the common pool (national product), rather than what they put into it. A person's direct and immediate level of living depends upon his consumption expenditure; when he saves now and consumes later, he will be caught at the time of ultimate consumption. If a person currently consumes from previously accumulated or inherited savings, equity requires that he make some current contribution to government on the basis of this expenditure, especially in periods of severe shortages and inflationary pressures.

Furthermore, the income tax ignores the different spending capacity of various incomes; spending capacity, rather than income, is the best measure of taxpaying ability. The differences arise in part out of the varying wealth status of the recipients. A person who has not yet accumulated and must put some of his income aside does not have the same consumption power as another person with the same income who has already accumulated. Thus, income taxation tends to discriminate against persons gaining their incomes primarily from wages, compared to those gaining them from already accumulated savings. This discrimination can be offset in various ways, but with the expenditure basis, it does not arise at all. In addition, spending power is dependent upon expected regularity. A non-

2 *Constructive Income Taxation* (New York: Harper & Bros., 1942).

recurrent income or one expected to last only a few years will not offer the same spending possibilities as one expected to continue indefinitely.

Similarly, only the expenditure basis insures equitable treatment of capital gains without hopelessly complex administrative problems. Some capital gains represent income, whereas others do not, reflecting merely price level or interest rate changes, as explained in Chapter 11. Satisfactory segregation of these elements is impossible under the income tax, whereas under the expenditure basis they are reached by taxes to the extent to which the taxpayers themselves regard them as incomes and adjust their expenditures accordingly.

In general, under the expenditure basis, no attempt is necessary to adjust for the varying degrees of spending power, since these are automatically reflected in the expenditures which persons actually make.

### Effects upon Savings

Further defense for the expenditure basis is built on the argument that income taxes, by reducing the net income from savings, distort the choice of the individual between present and future consumption, by making the latter less attractive than it would otherwise be. Persons are prevented from making their choices in terms of the relative costs to society of providing goods at various times, as reflected in the interest rate. In simple terms, persons are given added incentive to consume now. When marginal income tax rates are very high, the income gain from additional savings is extremely slight, while the income loss from dissaving is equally slight. Kaldor argues that the higher income groups in Great Britain have ceased to save because of the present tax treatment. By contrast, the expenditure basis would eliminate this bias, and even reverse it if persons believed the tax to be temporary or discount future tax payments. Apart from these incentive effects, an expenditure tax, especially one imposing substantial burden on the lower income groups, tends to reduce consumption to a greater extent than the income tax by concentrating its burden on persons who must reduce consumption because they have inadequate savings margins from which to absorb the tax.

The validity and significance of this argument depend in part upon the motives which influence saving. To the extent to which persons seek to obtain a given dollar income from their savings, the income basis leads them to save more, not less, and to the extent to which they save for purposes unrelated to the return, the effect of the two bases of taxation may be the same. It must be kept in mind that taxes based on consumption expenditure may be absorbed out of the portion of income that would have been saved just as well as taxes based on the entire income.

The significance of the argument also depends in part upon the desirability of additional savings. A higher rate of savings is clearly undesirable in periods in which investment is inadequate to absorb higher levels of planned savings. Even if full employment can be maintained, however, a higher rate of capital formation is not necessarily desirable in terms of economic welfare standards. With the present state of knowledge, definition of the optimum rate of capital formation is impossible, except within very broad limits. In an undeveloped economy, in which a higher rate of capital formation would allow a very sharp increase in consumption goods output in a reasonable period of time, the case for the higher rate is substantial; in a more mature economy the case is less obvious. An answer can be given only in terms of the prevailing consensus of opinion on the question of the relative claims of present and future generations to current output.

The case for a higher rate of savings is of course increased when inflationary tendencies are present; as explained in a subsequent section, the case for the expenditure basis is strongest whenever strong inflationary trends are encountered.

### Effects upon Investment and Risk-Taking Incentives

Distinct from the question of the relative effects of the expenditure basis upon the incentives to save is that of the relative effects, compared to the income basis, on the incentives to undertake investment and to take risks in a broad sense. The income basis, particularly with present progression, not only takes away a substantial portion of the incomes of corporations and wealthier persons who are in a position to undertake the risks of business development, but also reduces the incentive to do so, since the government will absorb most of the possible gains. The expenditure basis, which does not apply to earnings so long as they are saved and used for further business expansion or other purposes, avoids the excessive draining of savings away from investing groups and the incentive penalties.

The significance of this argument depends upon several factors. Musgrave, E. C. Brown, and others have shown that the income tax does not necessarily cause persons to shift away from risky investments, since the government shares in the losses as well as the gains.[3] As noted in previous chapters, there is little evidence as yet that the income tax is having serious incentive effects on investment. The relative advantage for the expenditure basis is largely lost if persons typically seek additional income from business expansion primarily for the purpose of consumption expendi-

[3] E. C. Brown, "Mr. Kaldor on Taxation and Risk Bearing," *Review of Economic Studies*, Vol. XXV (October, 1957), pp. 49–52.

tures. Furthermore, investment can become excessive as well as inadequate; in inflationary periods, restrictive effects of taxes on investment are merely alternatives to more restrictive monetary policy. Finally, the significance of consumption for investment levels must not be ignored; in periods of lagging investment, a tax which has a greater restrictive effect on consumption than savings may seriously affect the volume of investment by lessening the sales of consumption goods.

### Effects upon Work Incentives

The expenditure base, it is argued, may have less severe effects upon work incentives than the income base, since the taxes imposed upon the former can be escaped, at least temporarily, by saving, whereas the taxes based upon income cannot be. This difference is particularly important if people believe the expenditure-based tax to be temporary. Even if they believe it to be permanent, they may tend to regard a tax liability at some distant date as of lesser importance than one payable now. The significance also depends in part upon the relative desires of persons for consumption and savings; if they wish all additional income to spend on goods subject to the expenditure-based tax, this basis may have just as much effect, per dollar of revenue, upon work incentives as the income-based tax. Even Kaldor grants that the superiority of the expenditure basis from the standpoint of work incentives is probably not very great.

### Solving the Corporate Tax and Capital Gains Problems

Kaldor and others have argued that the use of the expenditure basis would avoid the troublesome problems of the treatment of corporate income and capital gains (which in large measure reflect reinvested corporate earnings). The corporate income tax is defective in many ways, as noted in Chapter 13; it is likely shifted in part, and to the extent to which it is not shifted, it is distributed among various persons in a fashion not in conformity with desired standards of uniformity of tax treatment of all income, in the absence of complicated and troublesome integration systems. The tax also encourages retention of earnings, and retards the growth of new firms, to the benefit of the position of existing ones.

The use of the expenditure basis exclusively would permit elimination of the corporate tax. No consumption occurs at the corporate level. Distributed profits would be reached directly as they are spent by the recipients, and undistributed profits in part when reflected by a higher rate of spending because of the improved wealth position, and ultimately when actually received and spent. As noted above, no effort would be required to distinguish among various capital gains to determine which ones constitute income, since to the extent that the recipients regarded them as income and spent the sums, they would be reached by the tax.

The defects of the present tax treatment of corporate income and capital gains are obvious. But exclusive reliance on expenditure-based taxes would allow very large sums to go untaxed on a current basis, a result regarded as questionable at best.

### Greater Efficiency of the Expenditure Basis in Checking Inflation[4]

A major function of taxation, in terms of the economy, is the prevention of inflation, particularly that which would result from government expenditures in a full-employment situation. The income basis is a somewhat clumsy way of accomplishing this result, since it strikes all income in order to reduce spending. Saving, as such, does not contribute to inflation, and the curtailment of savings does not necessarily bring about an equivalent reduction in the volume of planned investment. The income basis gives no incentive to reduce consumption. The expenditure-based taxes strike only at the portion of income spent, and provide incentive to consume less; thus, per dollar of revenue, they are more effective in checking inflation, and the total revenue which must be collected to obtain a given anti-inflationary effect is less. The larger collections necessary with the income base increase the dangers of adverse incentive effects on the economy.

This argument is one of the most significant defenses of the expenditure basis of taxation, and will be discussed again in Chapter 29 in connection with fiscal policy. But it has relevance, of course, only in periods of inflationary pressures; the greater anti-inflationary effect of expenditure-based taxes is a definite disadvantage in other periods, as noted later in the chapter.

## THE OBJECTIONS TO THE EXPENDITURE BASIS

There are several arguments advanced against the use of the expenditure basis, particularly against exclusive reliance upon it.

### Discrimination in Favor of Persons Saving High Percentages of Their Incomes

The primary objection raised against the expenditure basis on equity grounds is the discrimination, so far as current tax payments are con-

---

[4] For a discussion which minimizes the greater efficiency of the expenditure base, see A. Morag, "Deflationary Effects of Outlay and Income Taxes," *Journal of Political Economy*, Vol. LXVII (June, 1959), pp. 266–74.

cerned, against persons who spend relatively high percentages of their incomes. Not only does this basis favor the high-income groups generally, since they are in a better position to save relatively large amounts, but also persons at all income levels who save disproportionately large percentages of their incomes. If the expenditure-based taxes apply to all consumer expenditures at proportional rates, the burden is almost certain to be distributed in a regressive fashion, and will discriminate against large families and others in such circumstances as to require the spending of most of the income. The discrimination would be much less severe if an expenditure-based tax could provide for exemptions based upon family size and other factors affecting need, and could employ progressive rates. The feasibility of such a tax will be discussed later in the chapter.

Even with exemptions and progression, however, the expenditure basis still favors the miser—the person who deliberately saves large amounts of income. High-income families could accumulate tremendous sums without incurring tax liability by continually reinvesting earnings rather than spending them. A substantially improved system of death taxes would improve the situation, but would not insure adequate current collection. This is not a conclusive argument against partial use of the expenditure basis, but it is a significant one against sole reliance upon this basis of taxation.

### Greater Deflationary Effect

The greater potential deflationary effect of an expenditure-based tax is an advantage in strong inflationary periods, but it is a detriment in other periods. If there is a tendency toward unemployment, the use of the expenditure basis will aggravate the tendency, and require a larger deficit to eliminate it. Even in periods in which there is no deflationary tendency in the private sector of the economy, the use of the expenditure basis might require a continuing government deficit, with the consequent problems of adverse psychological reactions and the management of the debt. Under such circumstances, the less "efficient" income taxes have the merit of raising considerable sums without creating an equivalent deflationary effect, and thus minimizing the growth of the debt. If a deficit is regarded as of no consequence, as it is by the extremists of functional finance, this argument against the expenditure basis has no merit. But if it is regarded as undesirable, the case for the expenditure basis is weakened.

Closely related is the superior built-in flexibility contribution of the income tax, to the extent that income falls more rapidly than expenditures in periods of decline, and rises more rapidly in inflationary periods.

### The Dilemma of Implementation of the Expenditure Basis

The primary difficulty of implementing the expenditure basis is that of developing a tax which is feasible of administration and is at the same time capable of fully attaining the merits of the approach. There are two basic approaches. A tax may be levied directly on the sum of expenditures made during the year, collected in the same manner as the income tax by means of returns filed by individual taxpayers. Such a levy is known as a *spendings* tax or, in Great Britain, as an *expenditure* tax. The second alternative is to use commodity taxes, levies imposed upon the sale of commodities and collected from the vendors, but presumably shifted forward to the consumers and thus borne in relation to consumer expenditures.

Examination of each of these approaches is necessary before an evaluation of them is possible, but a few generalizations can be made. The spendings tax would most closely attain the objective of expenditure-based taxation, since the distribution of burden would conform with the desired pattern, and the use of exemptions and progressive rates would allow the realization of desired standards of equity and maximum anti-inflationary effects. But unfortunately, it is much more difficult to administer than the usual commodity tax, and governments are completely unfamiliar with it. The commodity taxes, on the other hand, are relatively simple to collect, but they produce a haphazard and often regressive pattern of burden distribution, they cannot easily be made progressive, and their anti-inflationary influence is greatly weakened by the lack of progression relative to total spending, and by their tendency to generate wage increases.

In conclusion, the case for the expenditure basis for taxation is strongest:

1. In countries in which a higher rate of capital formation is essential for economic development, and the income taxes are clearly holding down the rate.

2. When inflationary pressures continue over a period of time, and income taxes high enough to check them are not politically feasible, or would cause serious adverse effects upon incentives. The case is particularly strong if much of the inflationary pressure is being generated by consumer spending from previously accumulated funds, as, for example, in a postwar period.

The case will be strengthened if increasing evidence develops of adverse effects of income taxes upon incentives, and if a feasible spendings tax can be developed. The case for partial use of the expenditure basis is much stronger than that for exclusive use, since the latter would permit large segments of income to escape completely the payment of current taxes.

The spendings tax will be examined briefly in the remainder of this chapter and the commodity taxes in the three succeeding chapters.

## THE SPENDINGS TAX

A spendings tax has never been employed in the United States, Canada, or western Europe; to date, the only countries to use the tax have been India and Ceylon.[5] However, the tax has been proposed on several occasions, as early as 1921 by Congressman Ogden Mills (later Secretary of the Treasury), two decades later by Irving Fisher, and in 1942 by the United States Treasury as a wartime anti-inflationary measure. None of these proposals received serious consideration. In 1955, as noted, the British economist Kaldor proposed such a tax in Great Britain, partly as a result of his work on the Royal Commission on the Taxation of Profits and Income, and the plan has received considerable favorable reaction, especially from the Labour Party.

### The Structure of a Spendings Tax

A spendings tax would be collected through the use of tax returns filed by individuals, supplementary to, or a portion of, the regular income tax return. The taxpayer would determine his net savings during the year, that is, the net change in his total savings, as indicated by larger security or real property holdings, larger bank deposits or cash holdings, payments on life insurance, reductions in debt, etc. He would then subtract this figure of savings from taxable income to determine the amount of expenditures made during the year. Expenditures for expansion of a business owned by the person would be regarded as a form of savings and thus would not be taxed. Should the figure of net savings be negative, the sum would be added to income. Exemptions comparable to those of the income tax would be allowed to exclude minimum necessary expenditures from the tax and adjust the burden in terms of family size. Certain other deductions, such as expenses for medical care and education, could be permitted. The tax rate could be made progressive, and very steeply so, if the tax were intended primarily as an anti-inflationary measure. The amounts due would be paid in conjunction with income taxes at the end of the year.

[5] Only about eight thousand taxpayers were affected in India. See O. Prakash, "An Indian View of the Expenditure Tax," *Manchester School of Economic and Social Studies*, Vol. XXVI (January, 1958), pp. 48–67. See also R. Goode, "New System of Direct Taxation in Ceylon," *National Tax Journal*, Vol. XIII (December, 1960), pp. 329–40.

A declarations system could be employed to distribute the burden over the year.

### Evaluation

In general, the use of the spendings tax would allow the attainment of the goals of the expenditure basis much more adequately than the commodity taxes. The desired pattern of burden distribution could be obtained in much more precise fashion than by the use of commodity taxes, with their capricious and in part unascertainable burden pattern. The use of exemptions and progressive rates would not only eliminate regressiveness, but also allow the attainment of desired degrees of progression. The relative burden on various persons would conform much more closely with desired standards of equity than that of sales and excise taxes. The progressive rates of the spendings tax make it a much more effective anti-inflationary device than the sales tax, which, at tolerable rates, cannot offer much incentive to curtail consumption. The spendings tax is likewise much less likely to generate wage increases. In Kaldor's terms, the spendings tax makes possible the attainment of the desired degree of progression in the tax structure without the potentially dangerous effects on economic development of high income taxation, a result not obtainable with commodity taxation.

The objections to the spendings tax are twofold. In part, they include the basic objections to the expenditure basis, particularly exclusive use of it, noted earlier in the chapter—the failure to reach on a current basis the large accumulations of wealth made by persons saving high percentages of their incomes, the lessened built-in flexibility, and the greater deflationary effect, a disadvantage in noninflationary periods. The other basic objection is that of administrative complexity. There has as yet been very little experience with the tax, in itself a drawback but not a fundamental objection. Several problems, however, must be solved:

1. In addition to the problems of income taxation, one additional step is required, namely, the calculation of net savings during the period. This is not an insuperable task, but is an additional source of nuisance, error, and evasion. In some instances, troublesome valuation of assets might be required.

2. Special treatment must be given to consumer durables, to avoid the inequities consequent to irregularity of expenditures with progressive tax rates. The purchase of homes is the most significant case; treatment of these as investment expenditures and inclusion of an annual rental figure in expenditures would be the most logical procedure, but one troublesome administratively. Failure to tax house purchases at all would neces-

sitate exclusion of rental payments from the tax. Averaging of expenditures on other major consumer durables, such as cars, would be necessary.

3. The delineation of consumption expenditures from those for investment and for business purposes would be troublesome. The incentive for persons in higher expenditure brackets to treat personal expenses as business expenses would be tremendous, as well as that to have business firms controlled by the persons provided benefits in goods and services rather than cash income. If marginal rates went well over 100 per cent, as they might in periods of severe inflation, these incentives would be tremendously greater than they now are under income taxes.

4. The treatment of gifts is troublesome, in part since these can lead to outright tax evasion.

5. The anticipatory effects of introduction of the tax and changes in the rates could be very troublesome to the economy. Expenditures are much more subject to personal discretion, timewise, than is the acquisition of income. Prolonged discussion of the levying of the tax could bring a mad scramble for durable goods, and expectation of a rate reduction would bring purchases of these articles to a standstill. The hoarding of cash in anticipation of the tax (the cash not being reported initially and then brought forth as evidence of savings) could be serious, and might require the calling-in and reissue of all paper money.

These administrative problems are not insuperable. But they, plus the general lack of familiarity with the tax, constitute a serious obstacle to its use.

### Deductibility of Savings

A less far-reaching deviation from the income basis, as proposed by Slichter and others, would involve the authorization to deduct from taxable income the amounts currently saved. This measure would thus convert the income tax, at least partially, into a tax upon the portion of income spent. Amounts spent from previously accumulated savings would not be included in the base of the tax, as they would be with the spendings tax. In part, the plan was devised as an anti-inflationary measure, designed to curtail spending by providing a tax incentive to save; in part, it was intended to be a permanent element in the tax structure, with the purpose of increasing the rate of capital formation.

As an anti-inflationary measure, the basic weakness of the proposal is that the exemption of savings from taxes has both an income and a substitution effect, as have all price changes. The substitution effect would encourage replacement of consumption by saving, that is, persons would be encouraged to consume less and save more. But the freeing of income from tax would make possible a greater amount of both consumption and savings, and the net effect might well be an increase in consumption rather than a reduction, to the detriment of inflation control. Furthermore, from a long-range standpoint, as indicated above, an increased rate of saving does not necessarily result in an increased rate of capital formation but merely makes it possible; it may, instead, aggravate unemployment.

The other inherent weakness in this approach, unlike the spendings tax, is that no penalty is placed on dissaving. This not only greatly weakens the anti-inflationary effects, compared to those of a spendings tax, but opens a great avenue for tax avoidance by allowing persons to save tax-free in one year and spend the amount in subsequent years. Furthermore, the tax may provide very little incentive toward permanent increase in savings. Persons save, in part at least, in anticipation of future consumption or for accumulation of a reserve; if the tax structure is to discriminate permanently in favor of saving, a person gains little by stepping up his current rate of saving. As Tobin has pointed out, if the plan could be modified to provide tax reduction only on additional savings over and above amounts normally made, it would be much more effective in increasing the percentage of income saved. This result is very difficult to accomplish.

Finally, the plan would materially reduce progression in the tax structure, because of the higher percentages of saving in the higher income levels; this would be difficult to compensate for by rate changes.

On the whole, the savings deductibility plan is not only a very doubtful means of checking inflation but an even more questionable element in the permanent tax structure; it not only suffers from all the limitations of the spendings tax but, in addition, has potentially greater loopholes of escape.

## REFERENCES

KALDOR, N. *An Expenditure Tax*. London: George Allen and Unwin, 1955.
   The most complete analysis of the case for the expenditure basis.
PIGOU, A. C. *A Study in Public Finance*, Part II, chap. x. 3d ed. London: Macmillan & Co., Ltd., 1947.
   The argument that taxation of income saved results in double taxation.
VICKREY, W. *Agenda for Progressive Taxation*, chap. xii. New York: Ronald Press Co., 1947.
   An analysis of the spendings tax.

   Much of the discussion of the relative merits of taxation of consumption expenditures compared to income taxation is to be found in the references on sales taxation listed at the end of Chapter 17.

# Chapter 16

# COMMODITY TAXATION: SHIFTING AND INCIDENCE

From the standpoint of tax burden, commodity taxes are presumed to do indirectly what a spendings tax would do directly, namely, to distribute the cost of governmental activity in proportion to consumption expenditures. Commodity taxes are levied upon the sales (or output) of commodities and collected from the vendors. To the extent that the taxes are reflected in higher prices, individuals are essentially bearing the tax in the form of a tax supplement to the prices of the goods they buy and thus in relation to their consumption expenditures, so long as their incomes are not affected by the tax.

A commodity tax may reach all or a wide range of consumption expenditures or only those made for particular commodities. The former type is known as a *sales tax*, the second type as an *excise tax*.[1]

Since the intended distribution of burden of sales and excise taxes will be realized only if the taxes are actually passed on from the vendors upon whom they are levied to the ultimate consumers without change in persons' money incomes, the question of the shifting and incidence of these taxes is one of fundamental importance. If the taxes are not shifted, a capricious distribution of burden may result which cannot be justified under usually accepted principles. Accordingly, attention must first be turned to the question of the shifting and incidence of commodity taxes. In the two succeeding chapters the structure and operation of these taxes will be reviewed.

The analysis of shifting and incidence is essentially an application of the theory of price and output determination to the reactions which occur in response to an increase in cost, since the tax constitutes an addition to the costs of the firms upon which it is levied. The procedure em-

[1] Occasionally, a general sales tax will be referred to as an "excise"; thus the National Association of Manufacturers has long argued for what it calls a "manufacturers' excise tax," which under the more common definitions would be a sales tax. In the United States, certain other taxes are legally designated as excises for constitutional reasons. The meaning given above is the distinction usually made outside legal circles.

ployed will be to consider, first, the direct effects upon the prices of particular commodities which result from the imposition of a tax on their output or sales and then to bring into the picture possible modifications of factor prices and the significance for shifting of the general character of sales taxes. Care must be taken in making the step from special to general levies to avoid the fallacy of composition.

## DIRECT REACTIONS TO THE TAX BY THE VENDOR

When a tax is imposed upon the sales of a firm, this tax constitutes a direct increase in the expenses of the firm, one which varies in direct relationship to sales of taxed articles and one which must be currently met. The reactions of the firms will depend in large measure upon the nature of competition in the markets in which the firms are selling and must be analyzed in terms of these market types.

### Purely Competitive Markets

If a tax is levied upon a commodity sold in a purely competitive market, the individual sellers, who, by the definition of this type of market, have no control over market price, cannot directly shift the burden of tax from themselves. Thus, if a tax were levied upon the sales of a wheat producer, he would not be enabled thereby to increase the price he receives for his wheat. However, some market price adjustments may occur through readjustments in market supply. If reservation prices remain unchanged, the lower price received (after payment of tax) by the seller will result in his placing fewer units on the market, and the market price will rise, from $p$ to $p'$ in Figure 21–*A*. However, if there is a fixed stock of goods on hand (wheat, for example, after the year's harvest), the market cannot be cleared in the necessary period of time, and price will sink back to the pretax level for the remainder of the given market period. In other words, if, in the market period, a given quantity must be cleared out before the new output becomes available, the entire burden must rest upon the owners of the business firms, a general result whenever supply is perfectly inelastic. If production were a continuous process, reduced market supply would come about more quickly, and the market period and the short-run period would be identical.

As time passes, downward adjustment in output will occur as firms restore equality of marginal cost (which is increased by the tax) and price; in Figure 21–*A*, output will fall to *OA*, and price to *pS*, the point of equality of demand with the new short-period supply, which is controlled by marginal cost. A portion of the tax is now borne by purchasers of the product, a portion by the owners of the business enterprises and other factor owners who are unable to withdraw their factor units from the industry in the short-run period. Since the short-run supply schedule of the product is not perfectly elastic, complete shifting of the tax is impossible.

FIGURE 21

SHIFTING OF A TAX ON OUTPUT—PURELY COMPETITIVE INDUSTRY

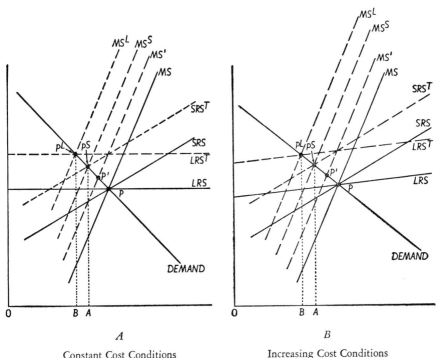

|     |     |
| --- | --- |
| *A* | *B* |
| Constant Cost Conditions | Increasing Cost Conditions |

*MS:* Market supply before tax.
*MS':* Market supply immediately after tax.
*MS^B:* Market supply after short-run adjustments.
*MS^L:* Market supply after long-run adjustments.
*SRS:* Short-run supply; *SRS^T:* short-run supply after tax but before long-run adjustments.
*LRS:* Long-run supply before tax; *LRS^T:* long-run supply after tax.

Over a long-run period, more complete shifting becomes possible as some firms quit the industry because they are not making a normal return. Ultimately, all the tax burden must be shifted from the owners of the businesses and an average rate of profit restored. If the industry is one of constant cost conditions, as shown in Figure 21–*A*, essentially all factors are completely mobile, the long-run supply of the good will be perfectly elastic, and complete shifting will occur. Price rises to *pL* in Figure 21–*A*, as output falls to *OB*. This result is independent of the elasticity of demand for the product. On the other hand, if the industry is one of increasing cost conditions, the long-run price increase will be less than the amount of the tax, as shown in Figure 21–*B*. A portion of the tax burden will be borne by the owners of the specialized resources which are not perfectly mobile.[2] The relative division of burden between this group and the consumers depends upon the relative elasticity of demand for the product and the relative elasticity of supply of the product. The latter, in turn, depends primarily upon the mobility of the factors used to produce it, that is, their ability to move out of the industry if the return received from them falls. The more elastic the long-period supply, that is, the closer the industry approaches constant cost conditions, the greater will be the shifting of the tax. On the other hand, the more inelastic the demand, the greater will be the shifting, because a smaller reduction in output (and thus absorption of the tax by nonmobile factors) will be necessary to restore equilibrium. By contrast, in a constant cost industry the elasticity of demand is not relevant because supply is perfectly elastic. In this case the entire amount of the tax will shift in the long-run period, regardless of the nature of the demand schedule.

This discussion has abstracted from any effects of the use of the tax revenues on the demand schedules or any adjustment in nonspecialized factor prices; these questions will be discussed in subsequent sections.

### Complete Monopoly

At the other extreme in the range of competitive conditions is complete monopoly. As shown in Figure 22, immediate price adjustment is likely as the monopolist restores equality of marginal cost and marginal revenue. Price will be increased from *p* to *pT* in Figure 22. With constant marginal cost and a linear revenue curve or one without substantial curvature, the price will rise by less than the amount of the tax, since average revenue will rise less than marginal revenue. The output reduction must be sufficient to raise marginal revenue by the amount of the tax, since marginal cost is raised by this amount. A portion of the tax will rest upon the consumer, a portion on the receivers of the monopoly profits.

The extent of the price increase will depend on the nature of the monopolist's demand schedule at levels above the old price and on the be-

---

[2] Theoretically, a third case, that of decreasing cost conditions due to external economies, is possible but is not sufficiently important to warrant attention. Price would rise by more than the tax in such cases, the consumer being burdened not only with the tax but with the higher per unit cost due to loss of external economies. The more elastic the demand, the greater the loss of these economies, and thus the greater the price increase.

havior of marginal cost in the range in which the firm is operating. Price increase will be greater if marginal cost is decreasing than if it is increasing, since the necessary output reduction will be greater. With increasing marginal cost the price increase will be greater, the more inelastic the de-

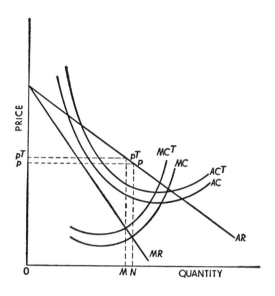

FIGURE 22

SHIFTING OF A TAX ON OUTPUT—COMPLETE MONOPOLY

mand; with decreasing cost the reverse is true. With constant marginal cost, elasticity of demand does not affect shifting, so long as the demand curve is linear. In any cost situation a sharp decrease in elasticity above the old price will encourage shifting, because once the firm gets into this relatively inelastic range, a substantial price increase, perhaps in excess of the tax, is profitable.

### Nonpurely Competitive Conditions

The typical market situation today is characterized neither by pure competition nor by complete monopoly, but by the intermediate zones, which may be called nonpurely competitive conditions. Firms exercise some individual control over price, but are subject to competition in varying degrees from other firms. This type of competition is much more difficult to analyze, because it is a spectrum of many special cases rather than a single clear-cut situation, and specific policies followed by particular businessmen greatly influence the reaction of price to cost changes.

If the firms act completely independently of one another, as in the model of monopolistic competition developed by Edward Chamberlin, the firms would readjust prices upward in response to a tax, to re-establish equality of marginal revenue and marginal cost. With the relatively elastic demand curves characteristic of this situation, the price increases would transfer little of the burden to the customers, and most would rest temporarily upon the owners of the business firms. As a consequence, firms would leave the industry until price and average cost were again at least equal for the remaining firms. Theoretically, if the average revenue curves did not change slope as they moved upward when some firms left the industry, price would rise by the exact amount of the tax in a constant cost industry, as shown in Figure 23.[3] If the slope of the curve became steeper, price would rise by more than the amount of the tax; if it became less steep, some of the burden would be absorbed through economies of large-scale operation.

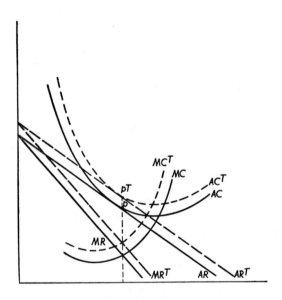

FIGURE 23

Shifting of a Tax on Output—The Case of
Monopolistic Competition

The much more typical case in nonpurely competitive conditions is that characterized by oligopoly in one degree or another, that is, by a feeling of mutual interdependence among the various firms in the industry. Firms, in reacting to changes in costs, will typically not disregard the

[3] In Figure 23 the amount of the tax (the vertical distance between $AC$ and $AC^T$) is equal to the amount of price increase ($p$ to $pT$).

probable responses of competing firms to the changes in costs and to the readjustments they make in their own prices. Under such circumstances, the most likely reaction to an excise tax is an immediate increase in price by the firms, by the amount of the tax. The tax represents a cost increase to each firm; each seller knows that competitors are likewise affected and that they are likely to increase, especially if the firm in question does so as well. Accordingly, each firm increases price, and each finds the increase profitable, provided that prices had not already attained the levels which would maximize profits for the firms as a group. The tax provides an impetus for movement closer to the maximum total profit level, a movement which the firms could not make prior to the tax because the degree of cooperation among them was not sufficiently strong.

If the total profits of the group of sellers had been maximized prior to the establishment of the tax, increases by the full amount of tax would be profitable only under the same circumstances as those which would lead a monopolist to make the full increase. But it is likely that firms in typical situations rarely find it feasible to attain this point, given the exact competitive circumstances, particularly because of diversity of interests among various members of the group. Or they may deliberately avoid maximizing short-run profits in order to lessen the danger of the entry of new firms into the industry. The tax serves as an impetus to move closer to the maximum point and lessens the danger that the price increase will encourage additional competition.

In some cases the demand schedules of the typical oligopolist may be kinked at the level of the prevailing price. Any price increases will cause drastic loss of sales, as competitors will leave their prices unchanged. Price reductions will cause little increase in sales, because competitors will meet the reduction. Thus, price, of necessity, must be set at the level of the kink ($p$ in Fig. 24). But when the tax is imposed, a price increase that was not previously possible becomes profitable. So long as each seller knows that other firms will now raise prices by the amount of the tax provided that he does, the point of the kink is moved upward by the amount of the tax, and thus price increases by the amount of the tax occur and are profitable. In Figure 24 the new price is $p'$.

Various practices which develop in oligopoly situations designed to lessen uncertainty and simplify price setting facilitate direct shifting. If outright agreements on prices are made, the tax is very likely to be taken into consideration, with a new agreed-upon price selected which is higher by the amount of the tax, unless sharp losses in sales are anticipated. If price is set by one firm acting as price leader, this firm is likely to readjust price upward by the amount of the tax, and other firms will follow. Standard markup percentage systems, under which prices are set by adding a certain percentage figure to direct labor and materials costs or purchase prices, simplify shifting, as they encourage uniform treatment of the tax. Shifting of the exact amount of the tax is greatly facilitated by the practice, which is particularly common with retailers, of charging the tax to

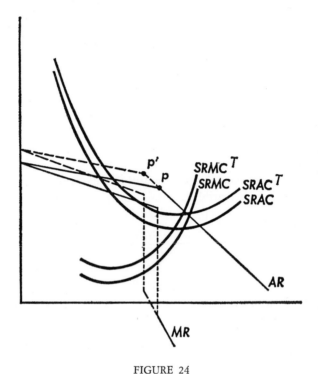

FIGURE 24

SHIFTING OF A TAX ON OUTPUT—OLIGOPOLY CONDITION
WITH KINKED DEMAND CURVE

the customer as an item separate from the price. General acceptance of the practice lessens the uncertainty about competitors' reactions and reduces the opportunity for changing the price by amounts greater or less than the amount of tax. Separate quotation, even if required by law, is no absolute assurance that the tax will be borne by the consumer, as prices net of tax may be adjusted as a result of the effect of the tax. But the practice definitely facilitates shifting.

On the whole, oligopoly is characterized by direct and immediate shifting; the burden of a tax on output or sales is passed directly on to the consumer and thus is borne in proportion to consumption expenditures on the taxed product. While few careful empirical studies of shifting have been made, there is considerable evidence of this rule. A study by the author of the reactions of sellers to the 1954 reduction in federal excise taxes on electrical appliances revealed that in the great majority of cases, immediate changes in list and catalogue prices were made. In the sample studied, involving twenty-nine manufacturers and two large mail-order houses, prices were cut by the manufacturers on 212 of 224 models of larger appliances, and 47 of 50 smaller appliance models. The mail-order houses reduced prices on all of 114 models of various appliances covered in the sample. Typically, but not universally, the price reduction at the manufacturing level approximated the amount of the tax reduction.[4]

*Exceptions to Shifting.* Without question, there are certain circumstances in which complete immediate shifting is not possible.

1. *Highly elastic total demand.* If firms believe that the total demand for the product is highly elastic, they may hesitate to shift because of the effects upon sales volumes and per unit costs. This situation is particularly likely to occur if substitutes are not taxed. Essentially, this is a case in which joint profits of the group have been maximized prior to the tax and further price increases would lessen profits. Even if the total demand is not highly elastic, further increases by the full amount of the tax are not likely to be profitable if the firms had already maximized joint profit.

2. *Severe competition.* If price competition is very severe, some firms may seek to gain volume by failing to raise prices while other firms are increasing. If this practice is widespread, it may prove unprofitable for any of the firms to maintain the increase. This result is much more likely in periods of depression than in those of prosperity.

3. *Low tax rate.* If the tax is very low, many firms may not take the trouble to readjust, especially on articles sold for a standard price. This result was indicated in early studies of the shifting of sales taxes in the states and is particularly evident in Indiana, in which the fractional rate tax on retail sales is generally not shifted as a separate item and is not shifted at all on many articles with standard national prices.

*Longer Period Adjustments.* Over a longer period of time, some modification of the initial pattern of shifting is likely. This is particularly true if there was no immediate shifting, but it may occur even when the tax is directly passed forward. If shifting did not take place initially or was incomplete and firms are unable to cover costs, some further readjust-

---

[4] See J. F. Due, "The Effect of the 1954 Reduction in Federal Excise Taxes upon the List Prices of Electrical Appliances," *National Tax Journal*, Vol. VII (September, 1954), pp. 222–26.

ments must occur. Some firms may cease production, and as a result, the remaining firms will either raise prices or benefit through increased sales volume and lower per unit costs. In the latter case the consumers are never burdened with the full amount of the tax; some is absorbed through cost reductions from more efficient use of resources.

Even if initial shifting occurred, the firms may not be able to cover their costs if their sales fall and they had been earning only an average return before the tax. Direct secondary shifting may be possible, particularly if competition is not strong and demand not too elastic; the firms may merely raise prices a second time. But differences among the various firms in cost patterns, reactions of sales, and times of realization of the need for further adjustments may interfere seriously with these increases, which are certainly less likely to occur than the increases in direct response to the tax. Otherwise, in this case as well as in that in which no initial shifting occurs, departure of some of the firms may be necessary.

If excess profits exist in the industry, the tax may in part be absorbed from them. If the profits are substantial, either the entire tax, if there is no initial shifting, or the higher cost per unit due to loss in sales volume, may be borne by the owners, with no long-run adjustments.

There is likewise some possibility that the tax on the sale of one commodity will be shifted to the consumers of another good. If the demand elasticities of various products sold by a firm are substantially different, there may be a tendency to raise the prices of those with inelastic demand (perhaps even though these items are not taxed at all) and not to increase the prices of those with elastic demands. Multiplicity of products also lessens the need for the departure of firms from the industry in the case of partial shifting, because the taxed line may represent such a small part of the firm's business that reduction in profits may not be of sufficient importance to cause the firm to leave the industry. On the other hand, when a firm produces a number of items, it may be very simple for it to drop a particular item which is no longer profitable.

Whenever a general reduction in output occurs because of the tax, the cost conditions of the industry will modify the final distribution of burden in the same manner as in conditions of pure competition. Under increasing cost conditions a part of the burden will rest permanently on the owners of specialized nonmobile resources, such as land, which is most suited for this particular purpose.

*Summary.*  Price will tend to rise by more than the amount of the tax if the following conditions prevail:

1. Secondary price increases, to pass on higher unit cost due to re-

duced sales, are successfully made. In this case the consumer is burdened with both the tax and an additional element which allows the retention of unneeded factors in the industry.

2. The industry as a whole is one of decreasing cost conditions.

3. The tax on another commodity is shifted to the one in question, due to differences in elasticities of demand schedules for the products.

Price will rise by less than the amount of tax if the following conditions prevail:

1. The tax is not fully shifted initially, and some firms quit the industry, allowing lower cost per unit for the remaining firms through greater sales volume. The unshifted portion is borne through greater efficiencies in operation.

2. The tax is in part absorbed out of excess profits.

3. The industry as a whole is one of increasing cost conditions, and sales volume falls; a portion of the burden is borne by owners of specialized factors.

4. The tax is shifted to the consumers of other goods.

It should be noted that even if the tax is fully reflected in prices, some indirect burden may remain, either on monopoly profits or on owners of specialized resources in the field.

These exceptions do not appear to be of sufficient significance to destroy the basic rule: For the most part, any tax on sales or output tends to shift directly to the consumers of the products and is borne primarily in relation to consumer expenditures on the taxed goods. This conclusion is of course based upon the assumption that no change occurs in factor prices and thus money incomes, apart from the exceptions noted. If the effect of the tax is to reduce total spending in the economy by an amount greater than the additional expenditure arising out of the governmental use of the funds, factor prices will tend to decline and unemployment to develop. Thus the prices of nontaxed articles will fall somewhat, and consumers of them will enjoy benefits, while the prices of the taxed goods will rise by a sum less than the amount of the tax. A portion of the burden is borne in proportion to factor incomes received, consumers of the taxed articles bear less than the amount of the tax, and consumers of untaxed goods, as such, will experience a net gain, to the extent that their expenditures on these goods are such that the gain from the lower prices exceeds the reduction in their money incomes. The likelihood of factor price adjustments depends upon the use made of the funds, which will be discussed later in the chapter. It may be argued, however, that any net deflationary effect resulting from the levying of the tax should not be regarded as an element in the determination of the incidence of the tax but an effect of over-all fiscal (tax and expenditure) policy.

### Pyramiding

When a tax is levied at an earlier stage in the distribution channels than retailing, there is a tendency for the tax to pyramid, with resultant price increases to the consumer in excess of the amount of tax collected by the government. Pyramiding is almost solely a result of the percentage markup system common in wholesaling and retailing; the markup percentage is applied to a purchase price figure which includes the tax and thus essentially to the tax itself. The consumer is burdened not only with the tax but with an additional amount which accrues either to the owners of distribution establishments in the form of added profits or, if sales volumes fall, to the owners of the resources which would otherwise be forced out of the industry. To a limited extent, pyramiding will be necessary to cover added expenses caused by the tax, such as interest on additional working capital required. Beyond this, if the tax-induced price increases reduce sales, the costs of the retailers, per dollar of sales, will tend to rise. Some retailers would normally be forced out of business, and the costs of the remaining retailers would then fall, per dollar of sales, because of their larger volumes of sales. But pyramiding, by increasing the revenue of the firms sufficiently to cover the higher per unit cost, may make the departure of the firms unnecessary. There is substantial evidence of pyramiding with the Canadian manufacturers' sales tax.[5]

There are some exceptions to the tendency toward pyramiding. If markups are typically calculated as fixed amounts of money per unit of product (as is true with gasoline, for example), no pyramiding will occur. If manufacturers set resale prices, they may allow an increase in the retail price by only the amount of the tax, in order to lessen the loss in sales volume.

Even when pyramiding does occur, over a period of time competitive forces should tend to eliminate it, except to the extent that it is necessary to compensate the retailer for various expenses created by the tax. This point of view is frequently expressed by Canadian government officials in

---

[5] In the author's study of the effects of the 1954 reduction in excise tax rates, it was found that on the larger electrical appliances, typically the retail list prices were reduced by amounts reflecting the actual tax reduction at the manufacturing level pyramided by typical margins. Thus the dollar price reduction to the consumer substantially exceeded the dollar tax reduction to the manufacturer. This suggests, of course, that when the taxes were imposed, they were pyramided, and that the pyramiding remained throughout the years the taxes were in effect. (See Due, *op. cit.*)

minimizing the significance of pyramiding under the manufacturers' sales tax. Some tendency in this direction is inevitable, especially if the pyramiding creates temporary excess profits. But competition in retailing is by no means perfect. The tendency to use the same markup percentage for long periods is in itself an obstacle to elimination of the pyramiding. If the pyramiding does not create excess profits but merely enables some firms to stay in business when they should leave the field, it is likely to continue more or less indefinitely.

### Ad Valorem versus Specific Taxes

The discussion of shifting has been based upon the assumption that the tax is levied as a fixed amount per unit of output, as is the gasoline tax. Actually, however, most excises and all sales taxes are levied as percentages of the selling price, and any adjustment made in the selling price therefore alters the amount of tax due. The fact that amounts collected by the vendor to cover the tax are not themselves usually included in the figure of taxable sales lessens the complications and increases the similarity of the ad valorem and specific taxes. But nevertheless, there is some difference in the exact price adjustments that will occur. This difference does not alter the basic initial reactions or the ultimate distribution of burden. Analysis of the exact difference is very technical.

### Price Increases and Burden Distribution

Whenever the price of a commodity increases as the result of the imposition of an excise tax, the particular commodity is made more expensive relative to others not so affected, and to factor incomes, so long as the latter remain unchanged. Thus, to the extent to which people buy the commodity, they are bearing the burden of the tax, in the sense that they pay more for the commodity than they would have had the tax been absent. Thus, they have less income available with which to buy this and other goods, and to save. This is simply the income effect of the price increase arising from the tax. The net result, from the standpoint of distribution of burden, is exactly the same as if the consumers had been required to pay directly to the government an annual sum based upon their expenditures on the particular good during the year. Persons who do not buy the commodity bear no portion of the burden of the tax, and an individual can vary the amount of burden he carries by altering his expenditures on the taxed good. Thus, it may appropriately be said that the tax distributes the burden (which arises out of the diversion of resources to government) in relation to consumption expenditures on the taxed good.

## THE SIGNIFICANCE FOR DIRECT SHIFTING OF THE GENERAL CHARACTER OF A SALES TAX

The analysis of the preceding pages is directly applicable to excise taxes. In large measure, it is also relevant to the question of the shifting of a sales tax, which in a sense is merely a combination of a wide range of taxes on the sales of particular commodities. But for the explanation of the direct shifting of a sales tax to be complete, the significance for shifting of the general character of the tax must be considered.

### The General Character of a Sales Tax and Demand Elasticity

The general nature of a sales tax inevitably results in a somewhat different response of sales to price increases induced by the tax than would otherwise occur. If a tax is levied on the sale of one commodity, some purchasers will shift to untaxed products. Thus, immediate shifting may be restricted; some firms will be reluctant to raise prices because of the fear of a heavy loss in sales. But if the tax is general, applying to all or most expenditures, the potential loss in sales is much less, since the prices of substitute commodities will be rising as well, and thus firms will be much less reluctant to shift. When the tax is imposed at the retail level, the ability of the vendor to apply a flat percentage to the customer's entire bill greatly simplifies application of the tax, since the individual prices on various commodities do not need to be readjusted.

### Variations in Burden Arising from Nonretail Sales Taxes

If a sales tax is imposed on the final retail sale, and confined to consumption goods, the tax burden will constitute a uniform percentage of consumption expenditures on all goods, provided the tax is shifted in full and exact amount. But when the tax is levied at earlier levels, this result will not be attained. If the tax is imposed upon the manufacturers, and the exact amount of the tax shifted forward, the tax burden, expressed as a percentage of consumption expenditures, will be relatively heavy on goods having relatively low wholesale and retail margins, and relatively light on goods having high margins. Further distortions will result if pyramiding occurs.

If the sales tax is levied in the turnover form, on all transactions through which a commodity passes on its path from initial production to final consumption sale, the final burden on each commodity will depend upon the number of sales transactions involved. Production and distribution channels with relatively large numbers of independent links will be placed at a serious competitive disadvantage relative to integrated systems, and complete shifting of the tax will be almost impossible.

### Departure of Firms from the Industry

The general character of a sales tax may also influence shifting by affecting the departure of firms from various industries presumably required for complete shifting. As indicated above, in some cases the firms will directly shift the tax in full, without prior departure of firms from the industry. In other instances, however, prior departure of firms is necessary. Even in the case of direct shifting, consequent losses in sales may make it necessary for some firms to quit the industry. But when the tax is general, the opportunities for transfer to other industries are lessened, especially if complete immediate shifting is not widespread. Essentially, therefore, the general character of a sales tax lessens the mobility of the factors out of various industries, since there are no untaxed fields to which to go. Consequently, it would appear that factor prices would fall and the burden would be removed from the consumers as such and would rest upon persons in relation to the declines in their factor incomes. Because of rigidities in many factor prices, the owners of the businesses would be particularly affected.

However, this analysis ignores completely the uses of the revenue by the government and the effects of this use upon the demand for factors. Essentially new avenues for factor employment are opened up by the government expenditures, and thus transfer of business firms and of other factors becomes possible. This adjustment is analyzed in the following section.

## CHANGES IN EMPLOYMENT AND FACTOR PRICES

A complete theory of shifting of commodity taxes must take into consideration possible general modifications in factor prices. This is especially true with a general sales tax, but is partly true even with taxes on particular commodities. Analysis of this aspect of incidence theory is greatly complicated by the inadequacies of general equilibrium theory and by the lack of adequate empirical landmarks as guides in the choice of appropriate assumptions.

The controversial aspects of the question of shifting and incidence of a sales tax center around the potential effects upon the general level of factor prices. There are several points of view on the question, the differences arising primarily from the nature of the assumptions made about the use of the funds collected from the tax, and the precise meaning given to the concept of incidence.

### Maintenance of Real Factor Demand

The traditional approach is based upon the assumption that the governmental expenditure of the funds insures that there is no net decline in actual demand for factor units. The tax revenues are employed by the government to acquire factor units; the governmental demand replaces the private sector factor demand lost because of the higher commodity prices, and thus there are no general deflationary influences upon factor prices. Firms increase prices in response to the tax; fewer goods are purchased, and thus fewer factor units are used in private sector production, but these factors are used either directly by the government or in producing goods which the government needs. If the government pursues a general over-all policy of maintaining full employment, as is a reasonable assumption, the general level of factor prices is maintained, and the tax is borne in relation to consumer spending. There may be shifting of relative demands for various types of specialized factors, since the government's demands for particular factors are different from those of the private sector; thus, some shifting of relative factor prices will occur as a result of the over-all expenditure and tax program, but this reaction is best regarded as not being an element in the picture of the sales tax incidence, but a result of the over-all fiscal program.

### General Factor Price Decline

The opposite point of view is reflected in the writings of Earl Rolph and others, who have long argued that a sales tax is not shifted to consumers. This conclusion is reached as a result of ignoring the use of the revenues collected by the government. Under this assumption, and further simplifying assumptions of pure competition in factor and commodity markets and perfectly inelastic supplies of each type of factor, the conclusion is reached that the tax will be borne in a fashion proportional to factor incomes received, and thus is identical in incidence to a proportional income tax. Quite apart from the unrealistic nature of the assumptions of pure competition and inelastic factor supplies, the basic objection to this point of view is the improper assumption about use of funds. Some use must be made of the tax revenue collected; it may be used to finance additional expenditures, to replace another tax, or to retire debt, for example. But there must be some use, and to ignore this use is to provide a most misleading picture of impact of the tax on factor prices.

The most realistic assumption is that the money is spent on government activities. A government undertakes an activity and requires factor units for this purpose; it imposes a sales tax to provide the funds to acquire the factor units, and thus to reduce private sector demand for the factor units. The real burden (apart from frictional effects of the taxes on the functioning of the economy) is the loss of these factor units for private sector production. The tax determines the pattern by which this burden is distributed in the economy. Thus the assumption that real factor demand (and thus the level of employment) is maintained is a much more satisfactory one than one which ignores the use of the funds.[6]

### Declines in Employment

Suppose, however, that as a result of the sales tax method of financing, the level of employment does fall below the level prevailing prior to the introduction of the tax and use of the funds. This may occur, for example, if the tax is used to replace an income tax or for purposes of debt retirement. Should this decline be considered to result from the tax, and thus be regarded as an influence on the incidence? Or should it be regarded as a product of the over-all tax and "use of funds" program? Are those workers who lose their jobs, for example, bearing a portion of the burden of the tax through the loss of their incomes? Or should this loss be regarded as a product of the over-all fiscal policy involved? This is largely a definitional matter; but on the whole, it would appear to be more satisfactory to regard the loss in employment as a consequence of the over-all program, and not an element in the burden of the tax. Thus, incidence is considered in terms of the level of employment prevailing before the tax expenditure program is instituted.

### Tax versus Monetary Causes of an Increase in the General Price Level

Other proponents of the doctrine that sales taxes are not borne by consumers, particularly J. M. Buchanan, argue that a sales tax cannot cause an increase in the general price level, since such an increase can, by definition, result only from adjustments in the money supply. It is true, of course, that an increase in the price level cannot occur unless there are monetary adjustments; either the supply of money (including bank deposits) or the velocity of money must change. These, however, are almost certain to occur in response to the introduction of a sales tax. In the first

---

[6] If the tax money were, in fact, "sterilized" and not used at all, continuous deflation would result, rather than adjustment to a new equilibrium at a lower level of factor prices. The Rolph conclusions would appear to be valid only under the assumption that total *money* demand for the factors remained unchanged.

place, when a government introduces a sales tax, it typically assumes that the burden will be borne in relation to consumption expenditures, and thus will assure that the necessary monetary adjustments will be forthcoming. Secondly, given the institutional rigidities against wage reductions, failure to allow an adjustment in money supply would in fact produce unemployment, and the use of fiscal policy to eliminate it.

The basic element in the reasoning of Buchanan and others that only monetary changes can cause price level changes is unacceptable under more commonly accepted explanations of causal relationships; the tax increase is the direct and immediate change which produces the reactions indicated, while the monetary adjustments, together with others, are merely elements in the reaction to the initial change. The Buchanan argument is primarily a terminological one, and is not helpful in an analysis of the repercussions occurring in response to the tax.

### Absolute versus Relative Price Changes

Further review of the question by Musgrave and others has suggested that the absolute direction of change in commodity and factor prices is not basically significant for the incidence of the tax. Even if commodity prices remained unchanged and factor prices fell, it could still be argued that the tax is borne in relation to consumption expenditures, since once the adjustment has taken place, each person can vary the amount of tax burden by varying the amount he spends on consumption. On the other hand, varying his factor income would not alter the tax burden unless the person also altered his consumption. If, in contrast, net factor income is reduced by an income tax, change in the amount of income will directly alter the tax burden, whereas change in consumption at given income levels will not directly do so.

However, given the institutional factors of the modern economy, the direction of absolute change is of substantial significance. Many factor incomes, especially of unionized labor, are highly rigid, and any general downward trend in factor incomes would encounter substantial resistance and could easily result in unemployment. Changes in the general price level alter the purchasing power and the share of real income of holders of fixed income assets. The money illusion itself will result in different behavior in response to various changes in the general price level. As a matter of actual practice, a rise in commodity prices, with given factor prices, is the most likely result.

### The Significance of the Taxation of Capital Goods

As explained in the next chapter, the usual sales tax is not confined entirely to consumption goods, but applies, mainly for administrative reasons, to a substantial range of capital goods. There are two approaches to the question of the shifting of the tax on these goods. According to one point of view, the tax on them becomes an element in the cost of goods made with them, and thus rests on the final consumers of the consumption goods produced, directly or indirectly, with the use of the equipment. Thus the pattern of burden distribution is the same as that of the portion of the tax resting on the consumption goods, except for the fact that different goods require varying amounts of taxable goods in their production.

According to the opposite point of view, as reflected in the writings of Musgrave and others, a tax on capital goods should be regarded as a tax on savings, which reduces the return per dollar of savings. Thus a general sales tax applying to all final capital goods as well as consumption goods would be roughly equivalent to a tax on all income. Persons would bear the tax on the portion of income spent through higher prices of consumer goods relative to factor incomes, and on the portion of income saved through reduced return on saving. However, this argument is both oversimplified and unrealistic, ignoring the variety of factors which influence the return on capital, and the consequences of the tendency of the firms to include the tax element on capital equipment in the cost on the basis of which prices are set.

### Tax-Induced Increases in Factor Prices

The imposition of a sales tax may raise factor prices, instead of lowering them, through the effect of the initial increases in commodity prices upon the cost of living. Wages particularly may be affected. At the present time, many labor contracts contain escalator clauses. When a sales tax is introduced and prices rise, wages covered by these contracts will automatically rise. Even without such contracts the higher cost of living tends to encourage unions to demand higher wages. If the wage increases take place, the prices of the commodities produced tend to rise, and the tax burden is in part shifted from the groups of workers who succeed in getting higher wages to other groups. If the tendency is widespread, much of the burden will come back again to the same groups of workers in the form of higher prices, and some further wage adjustments may occur. The net result is to concentrate a greater share of the burden on those income groups which are least able to obtain income increases when the cost of living rises.

This escalator effect could be checked if cost-of-living indexes were modified to exclude price increases due to sales taxes. But some question can be raised about the desirability of manipulating the indexes in this manner, and political pressure against the exclusion would be tremendous.

## CONCLUSION

Thus, in answer to the question with which this chapter has been primarily concerned—with the sales taxes which are today employed, the prevalent forms of competition, use of the revenues, and the monetary policies—it would appear that most typically, the burden of sales taxes is distributed in proportion to consumption expenditures on the taxable goods. The retail sales taxes of the states and the provinces are clearly shifted directly to the consumers; the manufacturers' sales tax in Canada is not only typically shifted but is inclined to pyramid, at least for short periods, on the way to the final consumer. There are, however, important exceptions:

1. Whenever excess profits exist, there is always the possibility that a portion of the tax may be absorbed out of them; this is especially true if the price has already reached full monopoly levels.

2. In a few cases a portion of the tax may be absorbed through economies in production when output is concentrated in the hands of fewer firms.

3. Where the net effect of the tax program is to curtail output in increasing cost industries, some tax will be borne by the owners of the specialized resources.

4. In pure competition and in other cases in which initial shifting is difficult, the burden will rest for a time on the owners of the businesses involved.

In almost no cases do the present-day taxes used actually fall on firms selling in purely competitive markets; when a retail tax is imposed, however, on the sale of a product which is initially produced under purely competitive conditions, the reduced demand will tend to lower the price of the product, and thus the tax will not actually shift, though nominally it appears to, until readjustments are complete in the primary industries.

5. When factor owners are able to obtain money income increases as a result of the higher cost of living due to the tax, a general redistribution of burden occurs, with transfer of a portion to factor owners not able to obtain such increases.

6. A general decline in employment and in factor prices due to the tax and expenditure program is best attributed to the over-all program rather than included as an aspect of incidence of the tax.

## REFERENCES

Due, J. F. *The Theory of Incidence of Sales Taxation.* New York: King's Crown Press, 1942.
An analysis of shifting, utilizing the theory of imperfect competition.

BROWN, H. G. "The Incidence of a General Output or Sales Tax," *Journal of Political Economy*, Vol. XLVII (April, 1939), pp. 254–62.
  The pioneer article emphasizing the effects of the tax on factor prices.

RECKTENWALD, H. C. *Steuerinzidenzlehre.* Berlin: Duncker and Humblot, 1958.
  A recent German review of tax incidence theory.

ROLPH, E. R. *The Theory of Fiscal Economics*, chaps. vi, vii. Berkeley: University of California Press, 1954.

BREAK, G. F. "Excise Tax Burdens and Benefits," *American Economic Review*, Vol. XLIV (September, 1954), pp. 577–94.

ROLPH, E. R., and BREAK, G. F. *Public Finance*, chap. xiii. New York: Ronald Press Co., 1961.

JASKARI, O. V. *A Study in the Theory of Incidence.* Helsinki: Suomalainen Tiedeakatemia, 1961.
  An analysis of incidence on a general equilibrium basis.

MUSGRAVE, R. A. *The Theory of Public Finance*, chaps. xiii, xv, xvi. New York: McGraw-Hill Book Co., Inc., 1959.
  A high-level analysis of the question.

BUCHANAN, J. M. *Fiscal Theory and Political Economy.* Chapel Hill: University of North Carolina Press, 1960.
  The Buchanan point of view on shifting.

# Chapter 17  SALES TAXATION

The most important type of consumption-based tax in present-day tax structures is the sales tax, a tax applied to the sale of a wide range of goods and services. To the extent that the tax is shifted to the purchasers of the products, as is typically presumed, its burden is distributed in proportion to the consumption expenditures upon the taxable goods and services. A universal sales tax would reach all consumption expenditures; those actually in use apply to a considerably narrower range, because major items of expenditures, particularly for housing and various personal services, are almost never included within the scope of the tax. The sales tax is the major source of state revenue, and is the most important element in the tax structures of many countries in Europe, South America, and elsewhere.

In terms of the principles of taxation, the sales tax is defended as an administratively feasible method for distributing a portion of the tax burden in proportion to consumption expenditures, and thus in lessening the reliance upon excessively high progressive income taxes, with their potential repressive effects upon incentives. Under the assumption of complete forward shifting, the sales tax can do, at least in part, indirectly and with less administrative difficulty, what the spendings tax would do directly. In practice, a primary reason for the introduction of sales taxation has been its greater administrative feasibility compared to income taxation, especially in countries with relatively low standards of tax morality and administration. Another has been its relatively high revenue productivity, in situations in which political pressures and economic difficulties have made the collection of equivalent sums from income taxation impossible.

### Requirements for an Optimum Sales Tax Structure

If a sales tax is to attain the goal of distribution of tax burden in proportion to consumer expenditures in a manner consistent with the gen-

erally accepted principles of taxation, several requirements must be fulfilled:

1. The burden of the tax must be distributed uniformly on consumer
expenditures for all purposes, except when deliberate deviation from uniformity is desired for purposes of economic or social policy. Nonuniformity results in discrimination against those persons having particular
preference for the more heavily taxed goods, and leads to uneconomic reallocation of resources, in the same fashion as with excise taxes, as discussed in the next chapter.

Uniformity requires that the amount of tax constitute a uniform percentage of the selling prices to the final consumers, that full and exact
shifting occurs, and that the tax does not affect factor prices.

2. The tax must be neutral in its effects on production and physical
distribution methods. Optimum efficiency in production will be lost if the
tax favors certain methods of production, organizational structures, or
distribution channels. If, for example, the tax (as a percentage of retail
price) is lower if goods are sold directly from manufacturer to retailer
than if they are sold through wholesalers, integration in distribution channels is artificially encouraged.

3. The tax must be feasible of administration, with tolerable levels
of enforcement attained at reasonable costs of collection and taxpayer
compliance.

### Forms of Sales Taxes

Sales taxes fall into two general classes. The single-stage levies apply only once to each commodity as it passes through production and distribution channels. This type of tax may be imposed on the final retail
sale, as in the states, the Canadian provinces, and Norway and Sweden, in
the form of the *retail sales tax*. It may be imposed as a *wholesale sales tax*,
on the last wholesale transaction through which a good passes, that is, on
the sale to the retailer, whether by a manufacturer or wholesaler, as in
Australia and Switzerland. Finally, the tax may be imposed upon the sale
by the manufacturer, in the form of a *manufacturers' sales tax*, as in
Canada.

The other major form, the multiple-stage or *turnover* tax, applies,
in pure form, to all transactions through which commodities pass, at all
production and distribution stages. In practice, as the tax is used in Germany, Italy, and elsewhere, some types of transactions are excluded. Finally, the *value-added* tax, which combines features of both single- and
multiple-stage taxes, applies at each transaction, but only to the value

added (selling price less the cost of taxable goods). The French sales tax takes this form.

Sales taxes also differ widely in exact coverage, in rate structures, and other features. Experience with the major forms will be reviewed briefly.

## THE RETAIL SALES TAX IN THE UNITED STATES

The retail form of sales tax involves application of the tax to the final sales transaction through which commodities pass, that is, the sale to the final consumer. This form is the basis of the taxes employed by all states using the sales tax, although a few states apply low rates to non-retail businesses. The tax has become the most important state revenue source, yielding, in 1962, about 25 per cent of total state tax revenue, and over 40 per cent of the tax revenue of several states employing it. As of January 1, 1963, thirty-six states impose the tax.[1]

### Development of State Sales Taxes

The state sales taxes originated as means of eliminating deficits which arose from the depression of the thirties and of meeting the demand for lower property tax rates. The depression reduced revenue from other state taxes and increased expenditures for relief and public works, while the local governments sought increased state aid and urged the states to free property taxes for their sole use. Potential yields from state income taxes and other possible sources were limited. Thus the states turned to the sales tax essentially as a last resort. Precedents for the tax were to be found in low-rate taxes levied by several states on the receipts or sales of business firms, essentially as business-occupation taxes. By confining this type of tax to retail sales and employing a rate of 2 or 3 per cent instead of a fractional figure, the states obtained substantial amounts of revenue. Mississippi imposed the first sales tax of this type in 1932, and 13 states enacted the levy in 1933. By 1937, 29 sales taxes had been introduced, and 23 remained in operation. Almost all the original taxes were levied as temporary emergency taxes, and a few actually were allowed to expire. But most of them became permanent elements in the tax structures. The war period improved state financial positions, and no new sales taxes were

---

[1] Excluding the Indiana gross income tax, which applied, as of January 1, 1963, to wholesale and retail sales at a ⅜ per cent rate, and to other sales, services, and personal income at a 1½ per cent rate. In April, 1963, Indiana imposed a 2 per cent retail sales tax, to bring the number of states using the tax to 37.

added until 1947. Since that time, inflationary pressures and increased state activities have brought 13 additional levies.[2]

### Structure of the Taxes

The state sales taxes, with minor exceptions, are strictly retail sales taxes, since interstate complications prevent collection of the taxes at earlier stages in the distribution channels. Four states couple low-rate gross receipts taxes on nonretail businesses with their retail sales taxes, but these are essentially designed as business-privilege taxes. Two other states, West Virginia and Washington, levy low-rate gross receipts taxes on all businesses, distinct from their sales taxes. Alaska, which does not levy a sales tax, does use a gross receipts tax.

Retail sales are defined, for tax purposes, as sales for purposes of use or consumption rather than for resale. Sales for resale, which are free of tax, include those of goods purchased for the purpose of resale in unchanged form, and, under what is called the *physical ingredient* rule, sales of goods, such as materials and parts, which will become physically incorporated into goods which will be sold. Under these definitions the tax not only applies to sales to individual consumers for personal use, but also to sales of machinery, equipment, supplies, and other items to business firms for use by the firms, since these items do not become physically embodied in the products of the firms. The consequence is a certain amount of multiple taxation of the final consumption goods, since the tax on goods used to produce them is reflected in their selling prices, and then, in turn, they are fully taxed when sold. In order to lessen this multiple taxation, several states specifically exempt certain classes of producers' goods, such as industrial machinery, fuel, and some farm equipment. Only four states—Ohio, Michigan, Pennsylvania, and West Virginia—attempt to exclude most producers' goods from the tax.

The taxes are applied to the sales of tangible personal property; thus, real and intangible property is universally excluded, as well as services, except as specifically included. A number of states confine the levies strictly to commodities, but many include a few services, particularly public utility services, amusements, and hotel and motel rentals. A small group of states extends the tax also to charges for storage, dry cleaning, repair service, and similar items. Only New Mexico and Hawaii tax professional services. As a consequence of the limited taxation of services, a major portion of consumer expenditures, perhaps one third on the average, escapes the tax.

Apart from the exclusion from tax of expenditures on services, some

[2] Hawaii entered the union with a sales tax imposed in depression years.

states have exempted certain major categories of expenditures on tangible goods, of which food is the most important. Only three states imposing sales taxes prior to World War II exempted food, but seven of the postwar acts did so, to bring the total to ten. This exemption is designed to lessen the regressiveness of the tax. Several states exempt medicines and articles such as gasoline which are subject to state excises.[3]

The majority of the taxes are technically imposed upon the sale to the consumer, while the others are imposed upon the retailer in the form of a business-occupation tax. With both forms, however, the tax is collected from the retailer; and with both, it was clearly the intent of the legislatures that the tax should rest upon the purchasers of the taxed commodities rather than upon the owners of the establishments. In all of the states imposing the tax on the *sale*, and in most of the other states, the vendor is required by law to collect the tax as an element separate from the selling price and to shift the tax forward to the consumer. Only three say nothing at all about tax shifting or quotation. These rules, placed in the laws to lessen the hostility of retailers toward the taxes, do not, of course, insure shifting, since a retailer can escape them if he wishes by reducing his price exclusive of tax, and then adding the tax. But they increase uniformity of action on the part of retailers, and thus facilitate shifting. Some of the states originally issued mill tokens to permit shifting of the exact amount of the tax on each purchase; but because of the nuisance, these were abandoned in favor of the bracket system, which allows the retailer, on the average, to collect about the same amount from his customers as he must pay the state. The tax rate as of January 1, 1963, is 2 per cent in 10 states, 2½ per cent in two, 3 per cent in 20 states, 3½ per cent in one, and 4 per cent in three.

The experience with the administration of the sales tax has been favorable, although collection costs are somewhat higher than those of some other taxes. Costs of collection have averaged about 1½ per cent of revenues; the figure is about doubled if compensation is given to retailers for handling the tax. The efficiency of collection is generally believed to be good so long as an effective auditing program is used. The high percentage of total sales made through large retailers lessens the evasion of tax. When necessary, sales of retailers are checked against their purchases from suppliers in order to determine if substantial evasion is occurring. Experience has shown that much of the underreporting of tax arises through overstatement of sales of exempt commodities, failure to

---

[3] The Pennsylvania and Wisconsin taxes are unique in that they apply to specified classes of commodities, rather than to all except ones specifically exempted.

report tax on goods purchased by the vendors tax-free for resale and then used for taxable purposes by the firm, and simple failure to record all sales, on the part of small firms.

Compliance costs on the part of retailers are fairly substantial. Application of the tax requires time of clerks and bookkeepers and often more expensive cash register equipment.[4]

### Out-of-State Purchases

One of the most troublesome aspects of state sales taxation is the handling of out-of-state purchases. If these are not reached by the tax, loss of revenue occurs, and incentive is given to avoid the tax by buying outside the state.

The states are barred by constitutional interpretation from applying their sales taxes, as such, to interstate purchases. However, all states using sales taxes have introduced supplementary use taxes, which apply the sales tax rate to goods bought outside the state and brought in. These are technically levied on the purchaser and are actually collected from the purchaser in some cases, as, for example, when a person buys a car in another state and brings it in for licensing. More commonly, the tax is collected from the vendor; payment can be enforced if the firm also carries on business in the state. The constitutionality of the use taxes was upheld in 1938, with the qualification that the taxes can be employed only as supplements to a state sales tax and at the same rate.

Actually, however, the use taxes cannot be universally enforced, since it is not possible for a state to trace all outside purchases made by residents. The problem is especially serious when some cities in the state are located close to the state borders. In practice, the taxes can be enforced only on the purchase of automobiles (which must be registered in the state), on purchases from the large mail-order houses, and on purchases of goods by business firms for taxable uses.

It is widely recognized that further improvements in enforcement of the use tax require more effective collection from the out-of-state vendors rather than from the in-state customers. Several states have been highly successful in obtaining voluntary registration and collection of tax by out-of-state firms. The power of the states to require collection from out-of-state vendors has been broadened in recent years as a result of vari-

---

[4] A study by Yokum in Ohio shows ratios of direct costs of sales tax collection to sales tax payments averaging 3.93 per cent, ranging from 1.23 per cent in department stores to 10.77 per cent in grocery stores (food being exempt). See J. C. Yokum, *Retailers' Costs of Sales Tax Collection in Ohio* (Columbus: Ohio State University, 1961).

ous Supreme Court decisions; the exact scope of the power is by no means clear at the moment.[5]

### Municipal Retail Sales Taxes

The use of sales taxes by municipalities in the United States is largely a postwar phenomenon, although New York City had imposed the tax in 1934. After World War II, many municipal governments were hard pressed financially by rising price levels and increased demands for services in the face of resistance to substantial increases in the property tax. As a consequence, the legislatures of several states authorized the cities to impose sales taxes, and a number have done so.

The municipal sales taxes fall into three patterns. In the first place, in several states, particularly New York, cities levy and administer their own sales taxes even though the state does not have such a tax. The New York City 3 per cent tax, by far the highest of any municipal levy, is comparable to the sales taxes of the states, and yields more than the sales taxes of all except two states.

Secondly, in some states the municipalities levy and collect their own sales taxes independently of the state sales tax, resulting in duplicating administration. This is the situation in Colorado, for example.

The third pattern is found in Illinois, in which state collection of locally imposed sales taxes is mandatory, the bases of the local and state taxes are identical, and municipal rates are in practice uniform (0.5 per cent). Thus, enforcement and compliance problems are minimized, and the incentive to shop outside the city has been lessened by the use of county sales taxes in areas outside the cities. Over 1,100 out of 1,188 municipalities in Illinois have imposed the tax.

## THE CHOICE AMONG VARIOUS FORMS OF SALES TAXATION

On the basis of the experience of various countries with different forms of sales taxation, explained in greater detail in Appendix I and Appendix II at the end of this chapter, some general observations can be made about the relative merits of the various types.

The most objectionable is the turnover tax. In pure form, applying to all transactions at all stages in production and distribution, it discriminates severely against nonintegrated business firms, makes subcontracting in manufacturing prohibitive, encourages integration, and aids large firms

---

[5] The entire issue of out-of-state collection is being reviewed (1963) by a subcommittee of the House Judiciary Committee, as a basis for possible federal legislation affecting state powers in this field.

at the expense of small ones. In practice, modifications are introduced to lessen the discrimination; not only do they not fully succeed in attaining this goal, but they severely complicate the application of the tax. In addition, the turnover tax results in substantial variation of burden on different commodities because of differences in average number of transactions through which goods pass, and complete shifting is impossible because of the varying burden on competing firms. The tax must be collected from an unnecessarily large number of firms, and equitable relative treatment of imports and domestic goods is impossible. In countries in which the tax is still used, such as Germany, it is subjected to widespread condemnation.

The development of the European Common Market has necessitated review of the various forms of sales taxes used in the countries involved, and it is likely that the turnover tax will be abandoned in favor of the value-added tax.

The turnover tax has only two advantages, ones of little significance, but having substantial influence on governments. The tax requires a lower rate than a single-stage tax, and the impact is spread out over a wider range of firms. The former is not significant from the standpoint of equity or administration, and the latter in many ways is a disadvantage. But nevertheless, because of these considerations, governments which have used this form of tax for a number of years are very reluctant to make a change.

All of the single-stage taxes are far superior to the multiple form, because they avoid the undesirable effects of the latter. The higher rate required is no serious handicap. Among the single-stage taxes, the wholesale and manufacturing forms have one major advantage: There are many more retailers than manufacturers and wholesalers, and on the average they are smaller firms, with less adequate record systems. This consideration almost alone has led most countries to reject the retail type of tax, and in the United States has caused the National Association of Manufacturers, the chief exponent of a federal sales tax, to support the manufacturing-level tax. In practice, this argument is much more significant in countries in which standards of tax morality are low and retailing is a family rather than a commercial activity than it is in such countries as the United States. State experience has clearly demonstrated the ability to administer retail taxes effectively in a favorable environment, provided an adequate auditing program is used.

The retail form of tax has several important advantages over ones levied at earlier stages in the distribution channels. Only this form of tax can insure uniformity of tax burden per dollar of consumer expenditures (assuming complete shifting), because with other forms, nonuniformity of distributors' margins will cause variation in the ratios. If specific departure from uniformity is desired as a matter of general policy (to place a heavier burden on luxuries, for example), only the retail tax, hitting the final sale, can accomplish the desired result. Secondly, only the retail tax avoids pyramiding, which is inevitable to some degree with the other forms. Thirdly, only the retail tax can be applied to the actual selling prices in all instances, without the types of price adjustments which have proven to be very troublesome with both the Canadian tax at the manufacturing level and the British purchase tax. In many ways the retail tax is by far the simplest levy to apply, and the least disturbing to competitive relationships. There are several other advantages as well. Separate quotation of tax to the consumer is feasible; thus, shifting is facilitated, and the bearer of the tax is made aware of his burden.[6] Tax rate changes produce fewer disturbances, since losses (or gains) on merchants' stocks are avoided, and retailers are given no incentive to reduce inventories in anticipation of a tax cut. Finally, in the United States, interstate complications are minimized. In total, these advantages of the retail tax are very significant and warrant its use whenever the retailing environment permits.

The issues involved in the choice between the manufacturing tax and wholesale taxes are not clear-cut.[7] Either form can be used with reasonable satisfaction, and both suffer from the same limitations relative to the retail tax. The wholesale tax allows a somewhat more uniform burden relative to consumer expenditures than the manufacturing tax, import and export transactions can be handled more easily, and it may be possible to apply the tax to the actual selling price in more cases, particularly if there is little backward integration by retailers. On the other hand, there are fewer small manufacturers than wholesalers. Furthermore, when price adjustments must be made for tax purposes because retailers assume wholesale functions, experience suggests that they are more difficult to make, partly for the purely psychological reason that the adjustment is upward rather than downward and thus is resisted rather than favored by the taxpaying firms directly involved.

---

[6] This is regarded as a disadvantage in Germany and some other countries, in which concealment of the tax in the price is considered to be an advantage, since it reduces popular opposition to the levy and thus increases the politically feasible yield.

[7] This problem is discussed in the *Report of the Sales Tax Committee* (Canada), (Ottawa: Queen's Printer, 1956), and in the article by the author analyzing this report, entitled "Report of the Sales Tax Committee," *Canadian Tax Journal*, Vol. V (March-April, 1957), pp. 88–105. See also the article by G. E. Lent, "Manufacturer's v. Wholesaler's Sales Tax Base," *Taxes*, Vol. XXXVI (August, 1958), pp. 573–601.

The final alternative, the value-added tax, has the great merit of avoiding the evils of the turnover tax, since it is not discriminatory against nonintegrated forms. In over-all effect, it is essentially a single-stage tax with multiple points of collection. It involves more taxpayers and collection complications than the single-stage taxes, but offers one major advantage over the latter: The impact of the tax is spread more widely. This is not significant in many countries, but it is, at least politically, in others. The value-added form does facilitate auditing of taxpaying firms, since deductions reported by one firm should show up as tax payments by others. It also may facilitate the exclusion of producers' goods from the tax.

## OTHER PROBLEMS OF SALES TAX STRUCTURE AND OPERATION

Regardless of the level at which the tax is imposed, certain general questions relating to structure and operation must be resolved.

### The Tax Treatment of Producers' Goods

If a sales tax is to be a truly single-stage levy, applying only once to each commodity in its path from initial production to final consumption, it should apply only to goods to be used for personal consumption purposes. Application of the tax to producers' goods is objectionable in several ways. The over-all sales tax burden per dollar of consumer expenditures will not be uniform on all goods, since the ratios of cost of taxable capital goods to final selling prices of consumption goods will vary widely on different products. Shifting of tax is likely to be less perfect, and some pyramiding will be inevitable. Complete exemption of certain consumption goods, if desired, cannot be attained, since articles used to produce these goods will be taxed. The tax will discriminate against capital-intensive methods of production, and make modernization of industry more expensive.

In practice, however, sales taxes typically apply to a wide range of capital equipment and other producers' goods. A few states, Canada, Australia, France, and Great Britain have attempted to minimize the taxation of producers' goods, but in no case are they completely excluded. The reluctance to exclude producers' goods is due to lack of understanding of the objections to taxing them, to the desire to maximize revenue at a given tax rate, and to administrative considerations which virtually preclude complete exemption. Many commodities are sold for both consumption and production use, often to the same buyers, and delimitation of the two transactions is difficult and may lead to outright evasion. If the exemption is made conditional upon specific usage in a particular case, determination of actual use by sellers and tax auditors is difficult. But any general unconditional exemption by type of commodity is impossible when the articles are used in part for consumption purposes. Complete exemption is impossible, but many governments could do much more than they have.

An opposite point of view is expressed by Musgrave and others. It is argued that failure to tax capital goods when consumption goods are taxed makes investment relatively more attractive than consumption, and thus resource allocation will be altered from the optimum. However, this approach ignores the likelihood that any tax on capital goods will be reflected in the prices of the consumption goods made with them, and thus no advantage is given to investment. Furthermore, the basic issue involved is whether the curtailment of private sector resource allocation should take place primarily in consumption, or to some extent in investment. If government spending is regarded as of the nature of consumption, then the existing rate of capital formation can be maintained only if capital goods are kept free of tax. Furthermore, if failure to tax capital goods does increase the over-all rate of capital formation, this is not contrary to optimum resource allocation if a faster rate of growth is regarded as desirable in the particular economy.

### Coverage of Consumption Goods

If the burden of the tax is to be uniform relative to consumption expenditures on all goods and services, the coverage of the tax should be complete, with no exemptions at all. Any exemption discriminates in favor of persons having relatively high expenditures for the exempted articles, and most exemptions complicate administration by creating problems of delimitation of taxable and exempt articles, and pave the way for misapplication of the tax and outright evasion. Revenue is reduced at a given rate. The sales tax, on the whole, is a simple levy if it applies uniformly to all sales at a certain level; it soon becomes complicated if many special categories are established. This is particularly true of a retail tax, because of the wide range of goods carried by many retailers and the nature of retail record systems. There is great merit in avoiding exemptions except in those cases in which strong justification exists. Most of the controversy has centered around a few classes of goods:

1. *Services.* Many sales taxes are confined largely or entirely to physical commodities. This is true of the state levies, all manufacturers' sales taxes, and the turnover taxes of Belgium and other countries. While, of course, services rendered to business firms are not suitable for inclusion within the scope of the taxes because they are producers' goods, there is

no justification for blanket exclusion of consumer services, since expenditures on them satisfy personal wants just as do those on commodities. Failure to tax services is often a source of administrative problems, since some services are rendered in conjunction with the sale of goods, and separation of the two elements in the price is often troublesome. Some of the greatest headaches with the retail sales taxes as they operate in the states and provinces are encountered by repair and other service firms. General exclusion from tax tends to favor the higher income groups, which on the average spend greater percentages of their incomes on services.

On the other hand, blanket inclusion of all services is impossible, partly because many are rendered to business firms, partly because many are unsuitable for reasons of general social and economic policy, as, for example, medical and hospital services. Taxation of real property rentals would give rise to inequity between tenant and homeowner. Therefore, taxation of services requires enumeration of specific types to be included, a task which many governments have been reluctant to undertake. However, a good case can be made for including ones typically rendered by commercial establishments, such as repair, laundry, dry cleaning, etc.

2. *Food and Other Necessities.*  Many sales taxes exempt food, but a substantial number, including those of most states, France, Germany, and other countries, do not. Food exemption materially reduces the regressiveness of the tax and the absolute burden on the lower income groups, as has been demonstrated in a number of studies.[8] On the other hand, the exemption favors persons with particularly high preferences for food, materially reduces revenue at a given tax rate, and gives rise to some administrative problems, although it avoids others, such as the collection of tax from numerous small food vendors common in some countries. The food exemption issue must be resolved in terms of equity considerations primarily; the case for it is strengthened if the tax rate is high and the tax system does not contain important progressive elements.

A stronger case can be made for exemption of medicines, particularly because the distribution of expenditures for them by family is so uneven. Some problems, however, are created in defining the category, as the Canadian provinces have discovered. The case for excluding other necessities, such as soap, is weak, because the sums of tax involved are not sufficiently important to warrant complicating compliance and administration.

Exemption of articles subject to excises is particularly objectionable because of the complications created for compliance and administration. If the combined sales-excise tax burden is regarded as excessive, adjustments should be made in the latter, not the former.

[8] See page 298.

## GENERAL EVALUATION OF SALES TAXES

### The Case for Sales Taxes

The case for sales taxation rests on several primary considerations: (1) the general arguments for basing a portion of the tax on expenditures rather than income, as outlined in Chapter 15; (2) the consideration that a sales tax appears to be the most feasible means of reaching persons on the basis of expenditures, without the discriminatory effects of excises, unless in the future a workable spendings tax can be developed; and (3) the administrative advantages relative to the income tax (*a*) for reaching persons who escape income taxation, (*b*) for use by states and provinces in a federal system, and (*c*) for use in countries of low tax morality and enforcement standards, and inadequate record systems.

The argument for the use of the expenditure basis was evaluated in Chapter 15 and need not be repeated here. As noted, the case becomes strong only if there develops significant evidence that the income taxes are having serious adverse effects upon the economy. Such evidence does not exist at the present time, although it is possible that if all revenue now being raised from expenditure-based taxes were obtained on an income basis, the effects would be noticeable.

Secondly, if the use of the expenditure basis is desired, it must be granted that the sales tax is administratively more feasible than the spendings tax.

Thirdly, the sales tax is an effective means of reaching those persons who escape income tax liability by legal or illegal means. This consideration is of particular importance in countries in which standards of tax morality are relatively low, standards of enforcement are not high, and use of checks and recordkeeping systems is limited. These conditions are found not only in relatively undeveloped countries, but also in other areas, such as southern Europe. Under present conditions, for example, it is impossible for a country such as Italy to gain large sums of revenue from a personal income tax. The problems of income taxation are aggravated when there are very large numbers of persons earning low incomes and subject to only small amounts of income tax.

The sales tax offers significant advantages for the states and similar units of government in other countries. They can administer sales taxes more easily than income taxes, and there is less fear that the former will drive people and business out of the state. With high federal income taxes the economic and political obstacles in the way of high state income taxes are substantial; if the states are to retain financial autonomy, they are virtually compelled to turn to sales taxation.

Support for sales taxes also comes from groups which wish to see a greater proportion of total governmental costs imposed upon the lower income groups than that which results from the usual income tax. It was once argued by these persons that the sales tax is a more efficient way of reaching the low-income groups than the income tax. The development of withholding systems and the reductions in the exemptions in the personal income tax have demonstrated that the income tax can reach down into the lower levels satisfactorily. However, for those who still seek greater burden on the poor and tax relief for the wealthy, a sales tax appears to have greater political feasibility than further reductions in income tax exemptions. But this general point of view with respect to distribution of tax burden would appear to be a minority one.

Evaluation of the use of the sales tax as a temporary anti-inflationary measure in periods of severe inflation will be undertaken in Chapter 29.

### The Objections to Sales Taxation

The objections to the use of sales taxation are in part the objections to the use of any expenditure-based levy, as outlined in Chapter 15, and in part reflect the inadequacies of this type of tax relative to other expenditure taxes.

1. *Economic Effects.* As with any expenditure-based tax, the greater deflationary effect of the tax, per dollar of revenue, compared to the income tax is objectionable in any period in which difficulty is encountered in maintaining full employment. While the tax may have less adverse direct effects on incentives to invest than an income tax, it has greater effects on consumption, and the volume of investment, in turn, is influenced by consumption goods sales.

To the extent to which a sales tax applies to producers' goods, as in practice is almost inevitable to some degree, a tax penalty is placed upon investment, and some uneconomic alteration in methods of production is inevitable. To the extent to which the sales tax burden is relatively greater, per dollar of expenditures, on some goods than on others, a reallocation of resources which may interfere with attainment of optimum economic welfare will result. If the turnover tax is used, serious interference with attainment of optimum organization of production is inevitable.

2. *Equity.* The most significant arguments against sales taxation are those based on equity considerations. As with any expenditure-based tax, the tax favors those persons who accumulate as savings unusually high percentages of their incomes. In addition, unlike the spendings tax, it is extremely difficult to make the over-all burden progressive by adjustment in the rate structure, and if the tax is applied uniformly to all consumption expenditures, it is likely to be regressive. On the average, the

larger the income, the greater the percentage of income which will be
saved, and, with the usual form of sales tax which excludes most services,
the greater the percentage of income spent on nontaxable services. This
conclusion has been demonstrated empirically by D. G. Davies and others,[9]
and is illustrated on Figure 25.

FIGURE 25

PERCENTAGE OF INCOME SPENT ON TAXABLE GOODS,
ILLINOIS RETAILERS' OCCUPATION (SALES) TAX, 1950

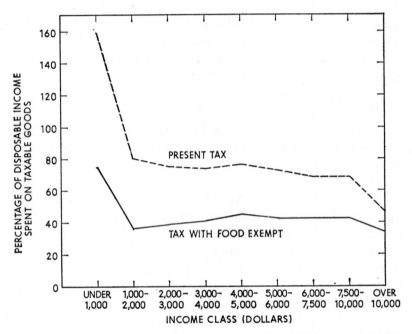

SOURCE: *Study of Consumer Expenditures, Income and Savings* (Philadelphia: University of Pennsylvania Press, 1955).

The budget data on which these studies are based are by no means
entirely accurate, and suffer from the limitation that at any particular time,
some families in various income groups have been in the group only a short
time. Various efforts have been made to meet this difficulty by using disposable receipts or permanent component income rather than income in
the usual sense as the basis for measuring regressivity. The disposable
receipts basis provides recognition for past and expected future income,

[9] See D. G. Davies, "An Empirical Test of Sales Tax Regressivity," *Journal of Political
Economy*, Vol. LXVII (February, 1959), pp. 59–71; and Division of Research and Statistics,
California State Board of Equalization, *Distribution of the Burden of California Sales and
Other Excise Taxes* (Sacramento, 1958).

since disposable receipts include sums derived from liquidating previously acquired assets and from borrowing on the basis of anticipated future income. Since excess of disposable receipts over income is greater in the lower income levels than in the higher levels, the regressivity is less; with food exempt, the tax is progressive. However, since net savings constitute a deduction in ascertaining disposable receipts, disposable receipts and consumption are identical, and the progressivity is not surprising nor too significant in terms of usual standards of ability to pay. A more satisfactory approach is one in terms of the permanent income component, as developed by Milton Friedman; income is defined in terms of longer periods, and temporary fluctuating elements are omitted. On this basis, under which the incomes of most of the low-income groups are higher than the actual incomes for the year because past incomes were higher, the sales tax is found to be progressive whether food is exempt or not.[10]

Evaluation of the regressivity argument is a complicated task. Primary reliance upon regressive taxes is obviously contrary to accepted standards of equity in distribution of burden. On the other hand, the regressiveness of one particular tax is not a conclusive argument against its use in a tax structure which contains highly progressive elements. However, the present income taxes do not produce a progressive distribution of burden within the lower and lower-middle income classes, and sales taxes therefore tend to bring about a regressive over-all burden within these classes. Apart from the question of regressiveness, the absolute burden placed upon the poor may be regarded as undesirable. This is not serious, in dollars-and-cents terms, with the low-rate taxes now in use in the states. It becomes progressively more objectionable as rates are increased and sales taxes are used by more than one level of government.

### Other Problems of Burden Distribution

In addition to the charge of regressiveness, the distribution of the burden of a sales tax is subject to criticism in other respects.[11] In general, the taxes, which cannot, for administrative reasons, be made to apply to all consumption expenditures, favor those persons whose expenditures concentrate heavily on untaxed items, such as personal service, foreign travel, or expensive apartments. On the other hand, the tax discriminates against persons whose circumstances compel them to spend disproportionately high percentages of their incomes for taxable purposes. Thus, large

[10] See D. G. Davies, "Commodity Taxation and Equity," *Journal of Finance*, Vol. XVI (December, 1961), pp. 581–90.

[11] See Reed R. Hansen, "An Empirical Analysis of the Retail Sales Tax with Policy Recommendations," *National Tax Journal*, Vol. XV (March, 1962), pp. 1–13.

families are discriminated against, as compared to smaller families with comparable incomes. Although the former have less, rather than more, taxpaying ability, they pay more tax. Food exemption lessens the discrimination, because a high percentage of expenditures of the large families is made for food. In the same fashion, to the extent that the taxes do not constitute uniform percentages of consumer expenditures for various goods, they discriminate on the basis of relative preferences. Studies show that rural families are favored over urban families because of use of home-produced items.

Another source of inequity is the failure of the tax to shift fully in all cases, as explained in the previous chapter. To the extent that a portion of the tax rests upon monopoly profits, the modification in distribution arising from the failure to shift may be regarded as desirable. But to the extent that a portion of the burden rests indiscriminately on the owners of certain businesses or other nonmobile factor owners, purely extraneous and accidental factors cause the over-all pattern of burden to depart from the intended one.

Finally, to the extent to which sales taxes bring about wage increases, the final distribution of burden is likely to be highly capricious and unrelated to desired standards of equity.

### Attempts to Improve the Burden Distribution

Various efforts have been made to lessen the regressiveness of sales taxes and improve the over-all burden distribution relative to usually accepted standards. As noted, food is commonly exempted. The effect is to reduce the regressiveness, as illustrated in the relative burden on large families compared to small, and the absolute burden on the lower income groups. However, the exemption creates a peculiar sort of discrimination of its own, favoring persons who have particularly strong preferences for purchase of expensive foods. Extension of the coverage of the tax also lessens regressiveness and inequities among families arising from differences in preferences.

Proposals have been made for a system of personal exemptions, which would remove the burden more effectively than food exemption from the lower income groups, and could perhaps be used to make the tax progressive. There are various possible alternative approaches, all of which have the effect of exempting a certain minimum amount of expenditures from the tax, the amount varying according to the size of the family. The most workable approach is one which would treat the sales tax essentially as a partial withholding system for the income tax. Each taxpayer would be allowed to subtract from his income tax *liability* a certain amount of sales tax paid during the year. Persons with incomes so low that they owed no income tax would be entitled to a refund of the appropriate amounts. All taxpayers could be allowed the deduction, or it could be confined to those with incomes below a certain level, as proposed by Morton. Apart from the problem of handling the additional income tax returns, the only real administrative problem created is that of preventing persons in the lower income brackets from filing more than one refund-yielding return. The procedure would very effectively improve distribution of the sales tax burden, in terms of accepted standards of equity.

A number of countries have sought to make their sales taxes more progressive by rate differentiation, higher rates being applied to luxury items than to those regarded as necessities. This system is used in the British purchase tax (although partly for purposes of restricting spending on certain items), in Australia and New Zealand, and to a lesser extent in other countries. By contrast, the state sales taxes and many others have uniform rates. The basic objections to differentiation are those of the added compliance and enforcement difficulties created, and the inevitable discrimination against particular consumers on the basis of preferences. There is no workable rule for classification of commodities by degree of "luxury," and arbitrary dividing lines are inevitable. If some differentiation is sought, it can probably be accomplished more satisfactorily by coupling a few excises with the uniform rate sales tax.

## CONCLUSION[12]

The sales tax is the most feasible method, from an administrative standpoint, of distributing tax burden on the basis of consumption expenditures, provided, of course, that the tax is shifted forward to the consumers. The case for the tax therefore rests in large measure upon the merits of the expenditure basis of taxation, and the argument that the spendings tax itself is not feasible of administration. In addition, the case for the sales tax rests upon its superiority, relative to the income tax, in raising revenue under circumstances in which highly productive income taxes are not administratively feasible, as in undeveloped countries. Finally, the case rests in part on the need for autonomous revenue sources for the states in a federal system. The objections to the tax center around its somewhat capricious incidence, its tendency toward regressiveness and discrimination against certain groups in society, its greater deflationary

---

[12] For a review of the question with somewhat different conclusions, see H. M. Somers, "Theoretical Framework of Sales and Use Taxation," *Proceedings of the National Tax Association for 1961*, pp. 607–25.

effect in periods of unemployment, and the difficulties in the establishment of sales tax structures in conformity with desired standards.

The strength of the case depends upon the actual adverse incentive and development effects of the income tax, which are by no means proven; upon the extent to which a higher rate of capital formation is regarded as desirable; upon the administrative difficulties in the way of effective collection of income and spendings taxes; and upon alternative taxes available. Specifically, the sales tax can be defended in three primary situations:

1. When the expenditure basis is regarded as essential to avoid adverse incentive effects of income taxes or to allow a higher rate of capital formation, yet the spendings tax is regarded as infeasible.

2. When economic, administrative, and educational considerations prevent the collection of adequate revenues from income taxation.

3. When an autonomous revenue source for the states in a federal system is regarded as essential.

Thus the case for the tax is strongest in relatively underdeveloped countries, in the states in a federal system, and in countries in which the over-all tax burden is so great that the income tax is failing to check inflation without serious repercussions on the economy. As will be explained in Chapter 29, the success of the sales tax as an anti-inflationary measure depends in large part on the ability to prevent it from generating wage increases.

## APPENDIX I—CANADIAN SALES TAXES

### *Retail Sales Taxes in the Canadian Provinces*

Eight of the ten Canadian provinces impose retail sales taxes as of January, 1963, at rates ranging from 3 to 5 per cent. Only in Quebec and Ontario is the designation *sales tax* applied to the tax, the taxes in the other provinces being designated on the basis of the uses to which the tax revenues are put. Municipal sales taxes are used extensively in Quebec.

Unlike the state taxes, these taxes are imposed technically upon the consumer, the retailer being designated as an agent of the province for purposes of collection. This procedure, which is necessary for constitutional reasons, does not result in fundamental differences between these taxes and those used in the United States. The taxes apply to retail sales, which, as in the United States, are defined to exclude sales for resale and sales of materials. Exemptions are somewhat broader than in the states. Exclusions of producers' goods include materials, catalytic agents or consumables used in industry, farm and fishing equipment, and most fuel. Ontario, the maritime provinces, and, in part, Quebec, exempt industrial machinery. All of the laws apply the tax to out-of-province purchases, but the term *use tax* is not employed.

Food and most drugs and medicine are exempt in all provinces, and some or all fuel. Several exempt children's clothing, books, soap, and other items. No services are included in the tax except those of certain utilities, such as electric power and telephone service.

The first provincial taxes originated in the depression; six of the present eight, however, were introduced in the postwar period, when rising costs and pressure for increased welfare and other activities necessitated additional revenue sources. Greater reliance on income tax is in effect restricted by the amount of the federal rebate for provincial income taxes.

## The Manufacturers' Sales Tax in Canada

A major alternative to the use of the retail level for the sales tax is the imposition at the manufacturing level. This form of tax has been used by the Dominion government in Canada for a number of years, and is also used in Finland and various South American countries.

### Development

The sales tax was first levied in Canada in 1920 as a modified turnover tax, applying to all transactions except those at retail. Protests of discrimination by nonintegrated business firms led to modifications, and finally, as of January 1, 1924, to the replacement of the old levy by one confined to the manufacturing level. The tax was still highly unpopular, however, and in 1927 a program of gradual elimination was commenced. But the depression of the thirties led to rate increases, and gradual acceptance of the tax as a permanent source of revenue. The rate remained at 8 per cent from 1936 to 1951, when it was raised to 10 per cent. In 1959 the rate went to 11 per cent, of which three percentage points are allocated to the old-age security fund.

### The Present Tax

The present tax is levied upon all sales by manufacturers, except those of commodities specifically exempted. The term *manufacturing* is interpreted in the usual sense, including such borderline activities as blending and assembling. Some small manufacturing plants are exempted. Imported goods are subject to tax at time of importation. For direct sales by manufacturers to retailers or consumers, an attempt is made in most cases to apply the tax only to the price which would have been charged had the goods been sold to a wholesaler. Firms are allowed to use their actual wholesale prices for these sales, or to reduce the sale price by a specified discount.

There are a number of exemptions from the tax. In the first place, in order to eliminate double taxation so far as possible and avoid tax burden on business development, major categories of producers' goods are exempted. These include the following:

1. Materials, partly finished goods, and other items which become parts of finished products. Thus, only finished products are taxed.

2. Industrial consumables: items such as bleaches, abrasives, and acids which are consumed in the process of manufacturing but do not become physical ingredients.

3. Industrial machinery, used directly in production.

4. Farm implements and machinery.

5. Fuel and power.

6. Building materials.

A second major class of exemptions is designed to bring the distribution of tax burden by income group more closely into line with accepted principles. The major exemptions of this type include the following:

1. Almost all food products.

2. A limited number of medicines.

3. Books and other items of educational and religious use.

4. Household fuel and power and building materials, as well as those used for other purposes.

Services are in no instances subject to tax.

### Problems

The principal problems encountered in the operation of the tax have centered around delimitation of various exemptions, and the determination of the suitable price for tax purposes on direct sales by manufacturers to retailers or consumers. If the basic tax rate were applied to such transactions in all cases, firms making such sales would be placed at a competitive disadvantage compared to firms performing fewer distribution functions and selling to wholesalers at lower prices. To meet the problem, the government has permitted downward adjustments of tax on direct sales. But such adjustments have seriously complicated the operation of the tax, equity has been difficult to attain, and taxpayers have lacked any right of appeal because of the absence of a statutory basis for adjustment.

## APPENDIX II—OTHER FORMS OF SALES TAXES

The other forms of sales taxes can be illustrated from the experience of various countries.

## The Wholesale Form of Sales Tax and the British Purchase Tax

Another alternative is the imposition of the tax on the last wholesale transaction, that is, on the sale to the retailer, whether by manufacturer or by wholesaler. This procedure is used in Australia, for example, which modeled its tax on that of Canada, but selected the wholesale level instead. The tax has numerous exemptions, and rates differentiated by type of commodity, and thus resembles a series of excise taxes more than a sales tax. The wholesale tax in Switzerland is basically a uniform rate tax, more similar in coverage to the Canadian tax.

The best known of the wholesale-level taxes is the British purchase tax, first imposed in 1940. Its most distinguishing feature is the extremely high differentiated rate structure. The tax applies only to specified categories of goods, with food and other basic necessities being tax free. The taxed goods are grouped into several classes, seven in recent years, with rates at times as high as 125 per cent. Many consumer durables, including automobiles, have been taxed at rates of 50 and 60 per cent. Almost all producers' goods are excluded from the tax. A primary goal of the tax at times has been that of deliberately discouraging the use of various goods, in an effort to lessen inflationary pressures and free output for export. In recent years, rates have been substantially reduced.

The usefulness of the tax during the years of most severe inflation has been generally accepted; but ultimately, the criticism increased, particularly from the industries whose products were subject to high rates. One difficulty centered around the delimiting of the various rate classes and the discrimination between various closely related items placed in sharply different rate classes. A very extensive itemization of articles in various rate classes has been necessary. Some of the most troublesome problems centered around the determination of taxable price in fields of diverse distribution channels, with attempts to gain greater equity resulting in serious complications and taxpayer protection. A final major problem has centered around the disturbance to buying during periods of anticipation of rate changes. Since no refunds are allowed for stocks on hand, retailers as well as consumers have tended to reduce buying whenever tax cuts were expected.

From the standpoint of principle the tax undoubtedly avoids the regressiveness characteristic of the usual sales tax, and is a more effective anti-inflationary device. But the high, differentiated rates are frequently regarded as discriminatory among various consumers and industries, and the high level of rates has greatly aggravated the problems of taxable price and disturbing effects of rate changes. As a permanent revenue measure the tax is open to serious question.

### The Turnover Tax

The multiple-stage or turnover tax, in its pure form, would apply to all transactions in all commodities—raw materials, parts, finished products—at a uniform rate. In practice, however, all such taxes deviate somewhat from the pure variety. This is the form which the Spanish *alcavala* of past centuries took—a levy regarded by some as a major cause of the economic decline of Spain. The modern turnover tax began with the levy imposed in Germany at the time of World War I, and copied by neighboring countries, by Italy, and for a few years by Canada. The present turnover tax provides the German federal government with about half of its total revenue.

Complaints of discrimination against nonintegrated production and distribution systems have led to certain modifications designed to lessen the discrimination to some extent. In Germany, for example, the rate on wholesalers is only 1 per cent (compared to a basic tax of 4 per cent). In the Netherlands, production of some goods by manufacturers for their own use is taxable. Belgium and Italy apply special substitute single-stage taxes in those industries in which the discrimination is particularly severe. Some of the countries exempt retail sales for administrative reasons. The net result of these modifications is to lessen somewhat but not to eliminate the discrimination, and they very seriously complicate the operation of the taxes. The turnover tax is a simple levy so long as it is completely uniform; when it is not, it becomes much more complex to operate than a single-stage tax. Despite the difficulties, Germany and other countries continue to use the tax because of the political objections to the shifting to the higher tax rate required with a single-stage tax.

### The Value-Added Tax

The most recently developed form of sales tax is the value-added tax, introduced in France in 1954.[13] This levy applies to all firms engaged in manufacturing and wholesaling (and could be applied to retailers, but is not, for administrative reasons), but only to the value added, that is, gross receipts during the period less amounts paid for commodities, including, in France, capital equipment, subject to the tax. Thus the tax, while applying to all transactions, does not discriminate against particular distribution channels or favor integration. At the same time, it permits the spreading-out of the impact of the tax over a wide range of firms, an important political advantage with a tax whose rate exceeds 20 per cent. A major reason for introducing the tax in France was the desire to facilitate the

---

[13] The state of Michigan uses a low-rate value-added tax as a general business tax.

exclusion of producers' goods from the sales tax, in order to stimulate investment and industrial modernization.

The development of the European Common Market has resulted in review of the various forms of sales taxes used in the countries involved; it is likely that the turnover tax countries will abandon this form of tax in favor of the value-added form.

## REFERENCES

### GENERAL

DUE, J. F. *Sales Taxation*. London: Routledge and Kegan Paul; and Urbana: University of Illinois Press, 1957.

ORGANIZATION FOR EUROPEAN ECONOMIC COOPERATION. *The Influence of Sales Taxes on Productivity*. Paris, 1958.

*Report of the 1962 Conference of the Canadian Tax Foundation* (Toronto, 1963).
Contains two major papers on turnover taxation and the value-added tax, by CLARA SULLIVAN and MARTIN NORR, respectively.

### UNITED STATES

OSTER, C. V. *Retail Sales Taxation*. Columbus: Ohio State University Press, 1957.

HAIG, R. M., and SHOUP, C. *The Sales Tax in the American States*. New York: Columbia University Press, 1934.
A description of the development of sales taxes in the United States.

JACOBY, N. H. *Retail Sales Taxation*. Chicago: Commerce Clearing House, 1938.
A survey and evaluation of the state retail sales taxes (now out of date).

U.S. TREASURY, DIVISION OF TAX RESEARCH. "Considerations Respecting a Federal Retail Sales Tax," published in *Hearings of the Ways and Means Committee on Revenue Revision of 1943*, pp. 1095–1272.
A detailed Treasury study of the question of a federal sales tax during wartime.

NATIONAL INDUSTRIAL CONFERENCE BOARD. *Consumption Taxes and Tax Reform*. New York, 1953.
A symposium on the question of a federal sales tax.

"A Symposium on Sales Taxation," *Vanderbilt Law Review*, February, 1956.
A series of papers, primarily on legal questions relating to sales taxes.

### CANADA

DUE, J. F. *The General Manufacturers' Sales Tax in Canada*. Toronto: Canadian Tax Foundation, 1951.
A detailed description and analysis of the Canadian tax.

——. *Provincial Sales Taxes*. Toronto: Canadian Tax Foundation, 1953.
A survey of the provincial retail sales taxes, based in part on interviews with business firms. A new edition is scheduled for 1963.

# Chapter 18 EXCISE TAXATION

Excise taxes are levies imposed upon the sale of particular commodities or groups of commodities. To the extent that an excise tax is shifted forward to the consumers of the products, the final burden is distributed in proportion to consumption expenditures on the taxed articles. The difference between excise taxes and sales taxes is, of course, one of degree rather than of kind; an extensive system of excises closely resembles a sales tax with numerous exemptions. But most excise systems in use are confined to a relatively small number of categories, with varying rates, and thus differ substantially from the sales taxes.

## THE BASES OF EXCISE TAXATION

There are four major bases upon which the taxation of particular classes of consumer expenditures may be justified. In the first place, the consumption expenditures for particular articles may be regarded as a better measure of taxpaying ability than total consumption expenditures. Accordingly, if some use is to be made of the expenditure basis of taxation for reasons outlined in Chapter 15, excises may be regarded as preferable, in terms of equity, to the sales tax. Excises designed to distribute the burden of taxation in proportion to consumption expenditures which are considered to constitute suitable measures of taxpaying ability are known as *luxury excises*. The federal excise tax structures in the United States and Canada are built upon this basis in large measure.

Secondly, excise taxation may be based upon the deliberate desire to curtail the consumption of commodities whose use results in costs to society over and above those incurred in their production and/or to penalize those persons who continue to use the commodities despite the tax. Such excises are known as *sumptuary taxes*. The liquor and tobacco taxes are the most important examples.

Thirdly, excises may be based upon the principle of allocating tax burden in relation to benefits received. If a close correlation exists between the benefits from a particular government activity and the consumption of a certain commodity, the levying of an excise tax on the sales of the commodity will provide an effective means of distributing the burden in relation to benefit and will facilitate the determination of optimum levels of the service to be provided. The gasoline tax is the outstanding example of a benefit-based levy.

Fourthly, in war and other inflationary periods, excises may be used as rationing devices, to curtail the use of particularly scarce commodities without the necessity of direct control measures.

In practice, the present excise tax structures have been based to a large extent upon these considerations, although by no means in an entirely logical fashion. In addition, some excises have been introduced for the sole purpose of gaining revenue, without justification on any other basis.

## PRESENT EXCISE TAX STRUCTURES

The excise tax structures will be reviewed briefly. The excises, except the gasoline tax, are primarily federal levies.

### The U.S. Federal Excises

In Table 5 the excise structure of the federal government is summarized, as of January 1, 1963. For the fiscal year 1961–62 the excises yielded $12.8 billion, or about 13 per cent of the total federal tax revenue. Of this sum, the liquor taxes yielded $3.3 billion and the tobacco taxes $2 billion, almost 40 per cent of the total. In addition, the highway user excises, in part allocated to the Highway Trust Fund, yielded $4.8 billion. The majority of the taxes on commodities are imposed at the manufacturing level, but four—namely those on jewelry, cosmetics, fur, and luggage —are collected from the retailers.

### State Excise Tax Systems

The states have not developed extensive excise tax systems but collect substantial revenues from a relatively few items. The most important is the benefit-based gasoline tax, levied in all states. This tax is discussed in Chapter 23.

All states have some form of liquor taxes or earn profits from state liquor monopolies. Forty-seven states tax cigarettes, at rates ranging from 2 cents to 8 cents per package. The liquor and tobacco taxes have low rates compared to the federal levies. The state excise structures are limited to the three categories mentioned, plus taxes on amusements and a few other items.

Thus the over-all excise tax picture includes three primary elements: (1) very heavy sumptuary excises on liquor and tobacco, (2) lower rate excises on commodities whose use is considered to be a suitable measure of taxpaying ability, and (3) substantial benefit-based taxes on gasoline, primarily at the state level, as a means of financing highway construction. Some of the present taxes generally regarded as luxury excises were actually introduced during World War II to lessen the use of scarce articles and have never been repealed. In addition, the tax system contains a few elements, such as the tax on business machines, which were introduced almost solely as revenue measures and have a broad distribution of burden somewhat comparable to that of a sales tax, although haphazard and uncertain.

TABLE 5

MAJOR UNITED STATES FEDERAL EXCISES

| Type of Excise | Rate, January 1, 1963* | Revenue Yield, 1961–62 Fiscal Year (Millions of Dollars) | |
|---|---|---|---|
| *Sumptuary:* | | | |
| Whiskey and other distilled spirits | $10.50 per gallon (proof) | $2,423 | |
| Wine | $0.17 to $2.50 per gallon, according to alcoholic content | 100 | |
| Beer | $9.00 per barrel (31 gallons) | 818 | |
| Cigarettes | $0.08 per package of 20 | 1,957 | |
| Cigars | $2.50 to $20.00 per 1,000 according to selling price | 50 | |
| Other tobacco products | $0.10 per pound | 19 | |
| Slot machines | $250 per year ⎱ | | |
| Wagers | 10% ⎰ | 21 | |
| Total, sumptuary | | | $ 5,388 |
| | | | |
| *Luxury:* | | | |
| Manufacturing level:† | | | |
| Radio, TV, etc. | 10% | $ 197 | |
| Electrical appliances | 5% (air conditioners 10%) | 121 | |
| Musical instruments, etc. | 10% | 19 | |
| Sporting goods, etc. | 10% (firearms 11%) | 38 | |
| Cameras, film, etc. | 10% | 25 | |
| Light bulbs | 10% | 34 | |
| Pens, etc. | 10% | 8 | |
| Matches | $0.02 per 1,000 | 5 | |
| Playing cards (stamp) | $0.13 per pack | 9 | |
| Retail level: | | | |
| Luggage | 10% | 69 | |
| Jewelry | 10% | 174 | |
| Furs | 10% | 31 | |
| Toilet preparations | 10% | 143 | |

TABLE 5 (*Continued*)

| Type of Excise | Rate, January 1, 1963* | Revenue Yield, 1961–62 Fiscal Year (Millions of Dollars) | |
|---|---|---|---|
| Services, etc.: | | | |
| Admission and cabarets . . . . . . | 10% | 73 | |
| Club dues . . . . . . . . . . . . . . . | 20% | 68 | |
| Telephone and telegraph . . . . . | 10% | 834 | |
| Passenger transport (air) ‡ . . . . | 5% | 260 | |
| Safe deposit boxes . . . . . . . . . | 10% | 7 | |
| Total, luxury . . . . . . . . . . | | | 2,115 |
| *Highway:* | | | |
| Allocated to Highway Trust Fund: | | | |
| Trucks and busses . . . . . . . . . . | 10% | $   256 | |
| Truck use tax . . . . . . . . . . . . . | $3.00 per 1,000 pounds | 80 | |
| Gasoline and diesel fuel . . . . . . | $0.04 per gallon | 2,510 | |
| Tires, tubes, etc. . . . . . . . . . . . | $0.05 per pound, and others | 360 | |
| Total . . . . . . . . . . . . . . . . | | | 3,206 |
| To general revenue: | | | |
| Automobiles and parts . . . . . . . | 10% (parts 8%) | $1,497 | |
| Lubricating oil . . . . . . . . . . . . | $0.06 per gallon | 73 | |
| Total . . . . . . . . . . . . . . . . | | | 1,570 |
| *Miscellaneous:* | | | |
| Business machines . . . . . . . . . . . | 10% | $     82 | |
| Stamp taxes on transfers of | | | |
| securities, etc. . . . . . . . . . . . . | Various | 151 | |
| Total, miscellaneous . . . . . . | | | 233 |
| Other . . . . . . . . . . . . . . . . . . . . . . . . | | | 102 |
| Total . . . . . . . . . . . . . | | | $12,752§ |

* Percentage of selling price of the firms subject to tax, except where otherwise noted. There are exceptions to some of the rates listed.
† The highway levies (except the truck use tax), the business machines tax, and the liquor and tobacco taxes are also imposed upon the manufacturer.
‡ During the 1962–63 fiscal year the tax applied at 10 per cent rate to all intercity passenger transport.
§ After adjustments for depository receipts.
SOURCE OF REVENUE DATA: U.S. Treasury, *Treasury Bulletin,* September, 1962.

## EVALUATION OF EXCISE TAXATION

Because of the variety of bases upon which excise taxes are justified, the various categories must be evaluated separately, and few general statements are possible. However, all excises have the merit of reducing the reliance on high income tax rates, with their possible adverse incentive effects, and most excises are relatively easy to administer, largely because they are collected from relatively small numbers of firms.

### The Benefit-Based Levies

The excises which are designed to finance a particular governmental activity by placing a charge on those benefiting from the activity and measured by the amount of benefit are the most widely accepted of all excises. Essentially, these are substitutes for direct charges or tolls on the users of the service, employed because they are more convenient and economical than the direct charges. The gasoline tax is the primary example of this type of levy. These taxes will be reviewed later in Chapter 23.

### The Sumptuary Excises

The argument for the liquor, tobacco, and other sumptuary excises rests primarily upon the contention that the output and use of the commodities involved would reach levels beyond those regarded as optimum were it not for the taxes imposed upon them. In other words, the use of the commodities, it is argued, gives rise to certain real costs to society which do not appear as costs to the producers, and therefore are not reflected in the prices for which the articles are sold. Evaluation of the sumptuary taxes actually used requires an estimate of these indirect social costs. For liquor, especially that of higher alcoholic content, there is substantial evidence. The effects of excessive use of liquor upon the person's wife, his dependents, his work, and possible crime and automobile accidents are too well known to require elaboration. With beer and wine the argument is much less strong; for tobacco, it is even more doubtful. While some disutility may be created for nonsmokers by tobacco smoke, fire damage may be increased, and some possible—though not clearly demonstrated—adverse effect upon health produced, it is difficult to argue that there are very substantial additional real costs to society arising from the use of the product.

While the taxes may have merit in checking excessive use and thus production of the articles, at the same time they place a very heavy burden on the great majority of persons who use the commodities only moderately. This pattern of distribution cannot be justified on the basis of economic effects but must be evaluated in terms of equity considerations. On the one hand, it may be argued that consensus of opinion in society accepts the principle that persons should be penalized taxwise for using the articles, even in moderation. Accordingly, it is argued, the heavy burden which rests on the moderate users is in conformity with the standards of equity in distribution laid down by society, even though it is not consistent with the principles which are generally accepted as the primary basis for distribution of tax burden. The widespread acceptance of these taxes provides support for this point of view.

Nevertheless, the sumptuary excises have been subjected to sub-

EXCISE TAXATION · **313**

stantial criticism on equity grounds. It is argued that the basis of the taxes is the moral judgment of persons responsible for tax legislation that the users "don't really need" the commodities and could just as well get along without them, or that the use of the commodities is in some sense "sinful." The use of a morality basis for taxation is often regarded as somewhat flimsy at best. Furthermore, the taxes on cigarettes and beer are criticized for the regressive distribution of burden which results. The amount which a person spends on cigarettes is not dependent upon his income (beyond a certain level) if he smokes regularly. With the present tax rates, the absolute burden upon the lowest income groups from the tax is very substantial; the federal tax in the United States amounts to $30 a year if the person smokes one package of cigarettes a day. The taxes upon liquor appear to be progressive. A final argument against the taxes is that of evasion; present taxes are so high that strong incentive is provided for illicit production of liquor and smuggling of cigarettes. Bootlegging has many undesirable social effects and reduces tax revenue. Increases in Canadian cigarette taxes in 1951 led to wholesale smuggling from the United States, which was difficult to check and became so serious that eventually the rate was reduced.

On the whole, the portion of the sumptuary excise tax structure which checks use of commodities whose social costs exceed their private costs can be justified on the basis of the improved allocation of resources which results, as well as on equity grounds. However, a portion of the liquor taxes and the great bulk of the tobacco taxes rest upon moderate users. This policy can be justified only on the basis that even moderate use of the commodities is regarded by society as warranting the imposition of a heavy tax penalty. But the discrimination among individuals and the regressiveness of distribution of burden, especially of the cigarette tax, suggest that the taxes deviate from the generally accepted standards of equity in taxation. However, the taxes are so strongly entrenched in the tax structures and so widely supported that it can be argued that society regards the consequent distribution of burden as equitable, even though it is contrary to principles accepted for other portions of the tax structure. The high revenue yield makes the taxes particularly attractive to governments.

### The Luxury Excises

The basic justification for luxury excises is the argument that these taxes allow the attainment of the general advantages of expenditure-based taxes with a more acceptable distribution of burden than that which results from a sales tax. By a proper selection of commodities for taxation, it should be possible to avoid the heavy burden on the poor and the regressiveness of the usual sales taxes, although, as pointed out below, in practice this result is difficult to accomplish. The case for luxury excises is also based in part upon the philosophy that some goods are more necessary for a reasonable living standard than others (in the eyes of the persons who frame the tax laws); thus, expenditures on the less necessary ones are more suitable bases for taxation than total expenditures.

On the other hand, the principle of luxury excise taxation is subject to very severe limitations, apart from objections which may be raised against the present selection of items for taxation.

1. *Discrimination According to Preference.* The first limitation is that of discrimination on the basis of relative preferences. A fundamental argument against any form of selective expenditure taxation is based on the wide variation in preferences among persons for different commodities. Thus, no matter how carefully a list of commodities for application of excise taxes is chosen, those persons who happen to have a relatively high preference for the commodities which are taxed are penalized. Thus, persons who are in essentially the same economic circumstances, except for the fact that they have preferences for different goods, are not taxed equally, and the relative burden on persons in different circumstances is not in proportion to their economic well-being. The luxury taxes are not deliberately designed to penalize persons who purchase the commodities but merely to distribute the relative tax burden in proportion to certain criteria of taxpaying ability. But since the actual consumption will vary widely among different persons according to individual preferences, the effect is a penalty burden upon the person who prefers the taxed commodity. In contrast, an "ideal" general sales tax does not discriminate among persons on the basis of individual preferences, although actual sales taxes do so to some extent.

2. *Finding Suitable Measures of Ability.* A second and related limitation is the difficulty in selecting categories of commodities which are suitable measures of taxpaying ability. There are relatively few commodities on which expenditures are progressive relative to income, with relatively small amounts purchased by the lower income groups. The few commodity groups which meet these requirements are of such limited importance that the revenue yield would be insignificant. In practice, it is necessary to select goods which are widely used; as a consequence, the over-all distribution of burden becomes similar to that of a sales tax, yet discriminatory among individuals according to personal preferences. In other words, the goal of a luxury excise tax structure—of taxing those

specific consumption expenditures which are better measures of taxpaying ability than total consumption expenditures—is not possible of attainment, if any significant amount of revenue is to be obtained. It appears to be impossible to establish taxable categories of consumption expenditures which will yield substantial revenue and at the same time provide a general distribution of burden regarded as superior to that of a sales tax.

The present excise tax systems contain many commodities of very widespread use, such as cosmetics, household appliances, automobiles, telephone service, etc. While expenditures on some of these, such as expensive jewelry, are relatively progressive in relation to income, others are very obviously regressive. A study by Musgrave illustrates the regressiveness of the distribution of the United States federal excise tax structure as a whole, including sumptuary as well as luxury and other excises. The results are illustrated in Figure 26. Considerable estimation is involved in the establishment of these figures; nevertheless, they should be sufficiently accurate to give a fair indication of the over-all distribution of excise tax burden, under the assumption of forward shifting of the taxes.

It is sometimes suggested that the regressiveness should be reduced by varying the tax rate in terms of the value of the product and exempting completely the cheapest items. This method, while suitable for some commodities, often discriminates against the person who buys long-lasting,

FIGURE 26

FEDERAL EXCISE TAX PAYMENTS AS PERCENTAGES OF
INCOME, UNITED STATES, 1954

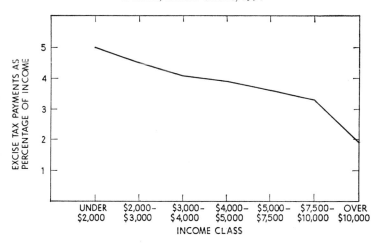

SOURCE: R. A. Musgrave, "The Incidence of the Tax Structure and Its Effects on Consumption," in Joint Committee on the Economic Report, *Federal Tax Policy for Economic Growth and Stability* (Washington, D.C.: U.S. Government Printing Office, 1955), p. 97.

high-quality items and greatly complicates compliance and administration, because of the necessity of applying a more elaborate rate schedule.

3. *Reallocation of Resources.* The chief argument advanced against the excises on the basis of economic effects is the tendency of the taxes to bring about a reallocation of resources away from the optimum. The sumptuary excises are deliberately designed to check production of goods the output of which is excessive in terms of economic welfare, and thus are justified on this basis. However, the luxury excises are not intended to bring about this result, except when used as wartime measures to "ration" scarce goods, but they almost inevitably do so. When a tax is imposed upon the sale of a particular good, some persons will cease to buy the commodity or will buy less of it and buy other things instead. They have failed to obtain optimum satisfaction from their incomes, yet the government has gained no tax revenue. Thus, production of other goods will increase, and that of taxed goods will decrease; if optimum allocation of resources was previously attained, a poorer allocation will result.[1]

The argument assumes, of course, that other excise taxes are not being employed. It can easily be demonstrated that if one excise is already being used, the placing of an additional excise on another commodity may be preferable, from the standpoint of resource allocation, to the introduc-

---

[1] This argument, long recognized, was explicitly developed by H. Hotelling, "The General Welfare in Relation to the Problems of Taxation and of Railway and Utility Rates," *Econometrica*, Vol. VI (July, 1938), pp. 232–69. It was developed more specifically with respect to taxation by M. F. W. Joseph, "The Excess Burden of Indirect Taxation," *Review of Economic Studies*, Vol. VI (June, 1939), pp. 226–31.

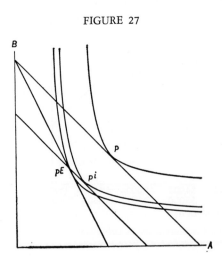

FIGURE 27

This argument has frequently been demonstrated by the use of indifference curves. In Figure 27 the original equilibrium of commodities $A$ and $B$ is at $p$. An excise tax is introduced and is shifted; the equilibrium is moved to $p^E$. If, instead, an income tax yielding the same revenue had been levied, equilibrium would have been at $p^i$, and thus on a higher indifference curve. Or in other words, the individuals' rates of substitution of the various goods for one another are no longer equal to the transformation rates in production of the goods.

A different diagrammatic approach is employed by Milton Friedman to produce the same conclusion, in his article, "The Welfare Effects of an Income Tax and an Excise Tax," *Journal of Political Economy*, Vol. LX (February, 1952), pp. 25–33.

tion of an income tax. Also, the entire analysis is based upon the assumption that optimum resource allocation is attained in the absence of the excise taxes. But several factors may prevent this adjustment. Imperfections in commodity and factor markets cause substantial deviations between marginal costs and prices; excessive quantities of some goods are produced and inadequate amounts of others. Outputs are restricted below optimum levels in fields with monopolistic restrictions and become excessively great in others. Deviations of marginal social costs and benefits from marginal private costs and benefits interfere with attainment of the optimum adjustments of output, as do immobilities and other frictions. Accordingly, the fact that an excise tax distorts resource allocation is not necessarily an a priori argument against the tax; the distortion may bring the allocation closer to the optimum instead of farther away from it. If, for example, a tax restricts the use of a commodity whose use creates significant social costs which do not appear as costs to the producers, resource allocation is improved. This is the intended result with the sumptuary taxes, but it may occur with luxury excises as well.

However, the present excise systems have been developed without any regard to allocation effects, and there is no evidence that they actually do improve the pattern of allocation. It is reasonable to conclude that, almost certainly, some net adverse effect results from the present structure.

Examination of the present tax structure suggests one major aspect in which the effects on allocation are particularly likely to be objectionable. A number of major excises, such as those upon automobiles, appliances, etc., are imposed upon the sales of industries which are operating under conditions of highly imperfect competition. The output of these commodities is likely to be less than the optimum, and the taxes therefore aggravate the misallocation of resources.

Another criticism advanced against the "distortion of resource allocation" argument is based upon considerations of income distribution. A particular resource allocation can be considered to be optimum only in terms of a given income distribution. Even if an excise tax system does distort resource allocation away from an existing optimum, it may be justified if the distribution of real income is brought more in line with the standard accepted as desirable. Thus, if excises reduce the output of goods primarily used by the higher income groups, relative to the output of those consumed largely in the lower income groups, the adjustment may be regarded as desirable on the basis of greater equality of real income which results. But as pointed out in earlier sections, the establishment of an excise system which accomplishes these results is very difficult.

A final criticism advanced against the distortion argument is that income taxes also distort resource allocation by altering the relative desirability of work and leisure, by checking the flow of labor among occupations and localities, and by increasing the relative desirability of noncash income-producing activities and of occupations which offer non-monetary income advantages, such as prestige.[2] But it has been pointed out by Henderson and others that excises and sales taxes have these effects as well, because they reduce the real value of money income and, in addition, produce distortion of allocation of resources among various commodities.[3]

This, however, is not a conclusive answer to the criticism, as has been demonstrated by Little.[4] Direct taxes with highly progressive rates may have such a drastic effect upon labor supply that the net results may be worse than those of the excise taxes, even though the latter produce two types of adverse effects, namely, those upon the work-leisure ratio and those upon relative output of various goods. It does not appear that the present direct taxes have such drastic effects, but there is always the possibility that they may have. On the whole, the theoretical case against the excise taxes is valid only if the supply of labor is highly inelastic, so that the marginal rates of the direct taxes have little or no effect upon the choice between work and leisure.[5]

In summary, the argument that excise taxes are inherently undesirable because they will distort allocation of resources away from the optimum does not have the general validity once claimed for it. The over-all significance of the argument depends very largely upon the actual reactions of factor supplies to direct taxes, discussed in previous chapters. But the analysis does provide a tool for evaluating particular excise taxes; the present system has been established with little consideration of allocation effects, and casual review suggests that many undesirable allocative effects can be found.

4. *Effects upon Owners of Businesses and Other Factor Owners.* The discussion thus far has assumed complete and exact forward shifting

---

[2] See H. Wald, "The Classical Indictment of Indirect Taxation," *Quarterly Journal of Economics*, Vol. LIX (August, 1945), pp. 577–96.

[3] See A. Henderson, "The Case for Indirect Taxation," *Economic Journal*, Vol. LVIII (December, 1948), pp. 538–53.

[4] See I. M. D. Little, "Direct vs. Indirect Taxes," *Economic Journal*, Vol. LXI (September, 1951), pp. 577–84. Little suggests that from the standpoint of resource allocation alone, a case could be made for taxing necessities, since persons are unlikely to substitute leisure for these commodities, and then subsidizing luxuries, in order to increase incentives. But there are, of course, serious equity objections to such a policy.

[5] For a review of the long controversy, see the article by D. Walker, "The Direct-Indirect Tax Problem," *Public Finance*, Vol. X, No. 2 (1955), pp. 153–76.

of the taxes, without effect upon factor prices. Actually, however, this result may not be attained. Business firms may find shifting difficult, especially when substitute products are not taxed, and a portion of the burden may remain upon the owners of the firms for substantial periods. The firms forced out of business may experience loss of capital. The decline in the output of the taxed goods will reduce prices of specialized factors used in their production, and thus lower the incomes of these factor owners, a portion of the burden thus being removed from the consumers of the products.

Apart from the problems of shifting, compliance with the tax laws may involve considerable nuisance and cost, the burden of which may rest for a time on the owners, and the tax may create competitive disturbances and alter methods of production.

Finally, it should be noted that the basic economic objection to all expenditure-based taxes in noninflationary periods—their tendency to encourage saving and discourage spending—applies to excises as well as to other taxes in the group. The relatively high rates of the excises will have particularly strong deflationary effects if the taxed goods have a relatively high elasticity of demand, and the income not spent on them is in large measure saved. This argument is, of course, not valid in inflationary periods.

## Defects in the Actual Excise Tax Structures

The objectionable features of excise taxation are aggravated in practice by the failure to adhere carefully to accepted standards in the establishment of the excise tax systems. Too often, such taxes are imposed primarily for the purpose of raising more revenue, with little attention to economic effects and inequities. The present federal excise tax system is defective in several ways.

1. *Taxation of Goods and Services Used in Production.* The present United States tax structure includes several excises which apply primarily to expenditures by business firms rather than to consumption expenditures. This is true in part of taxes generally regarded as luxury excises, such as those on telephone service, plus the tax on business machines, which has been levied for no purpose other than revenue. These items become business expenses and are likely to be shifted to the customers of the firms acquiring the taxed goods and services. The ultimate burden is distributed in a haphazard fashion, with no relation to ability to pay in any sense. Part of the tax can be shifted only with difficulty and burdens the owners of the businesses inequitably. The portion that is shifted reaches basic items of consumption, such as bread and milk.

2. *Use of Specific Rates.* The taxes on liquor and tobacco, plus a few others, have specific tax rates, which do not vary with the value of the product. This method places a disproportionate burden on the users of the cheaper types, increases the regressiveness of the taxes, and tends to drive the cheaper brands off the market. Tax treatment of cigarettes has apparently been a significant factor in checking the development of the so-called "economy" brands. The maintenance of a uniform relationship between consumption expenditures and tax is lost completely when the specific rate is used, if there is substantial variation in price. However, with the gasoline tax the relative uniformity of prices and the benefit basis of the tax justify the use of a specific rate.

3. *Pyramiding.* Since the excise taxes are for the most part levied at the manufacturing level, considerable direct pyramiding probably occurs. Excise taxes on most commodities, however, are difficult to impose at the retail level, because retailers cannot easily keep records of sales of particular commodities. The federal excises on cosmetics, luggage, jewelry, and furs are levied at retail, in part because the very high margins on these commodities intensify the effects of pyramiding, and in part because firms tended to disperse packaging and related functions away from the manufacturing level when the taxes were collected from the manufacturers. However, enforcement is by no means complete.

Apart from pyramiding, the collection at the manufacturing level results in the taxes being hidden in the prices of the products rather than directly evident to the consumer.

4. *Technical Problems of Operation.* Many of the excise taxes were enacted hastily, with little careful wording of legislation; the tendency to regard them as temporary lessened the interest in revising the legislation or in developing extensive regulations. As time passed, criticisms of the operation of the taxes increased, and led, in 1956 and 1957, to extensive hearings by the Forand Subcommittee of the House Ways and Means Committee, and recommendations for extensive technical changes in the code, which were made in 1958. Several of the major problems can be noted briefly:

*a*) A satisfactory legal basis was lacking for determination of taxable price on direct sales by manufacturers to retailers. In practice, firms selling directly have frequently set up sales subsidiaries to which sales were made at figures lower than those paid by the retailers, but this method has not been entirely satisfactory. The 1958 legislation took a limited step in the direction of providing an improved legal basis, and further change has since been made.

*b*) Some of the classes of taxable goods, especially those subject to the retail excise, have not been clearly defined.

*c*) The term *manufacturing* has not been clearly defined, particularly with regard to such activities as rebuilding, and the treatment of private brand merchandise.

*d*) Regulations have been inadequate, and excise tax rulings have frequently not been published. Appeal procedures are unsatisfactory, and auditing of taxpayers has been entirely inadequate.

## CONCLUSIONS

Excise taxes are clearly justifiable and desirable (1) if they serve as a means of distributing the costs of a governmental activity in terms of benefit, when circumstances are such that the use of the benefit principle is desirable, and (2) if they restrict the output of goods whose production will otherwise be carried to uneconomically high levels. If partial reliance upon the expenditures basis of taxation is desired, and if it is possible to devise excises which will provide a more acceptable over-all distribution of burden than a sales tax, the case for additional excises beyond those justified on the first two bases is strengthened. But in practice, it is extremely difficult to develop a system of excises which will accomplish this result. Even if it were possible, discrimination against individuals according to preference and possible misallocation of resources from the pattern allowing optimum economic welfare would occur.

The present excises on gasoline and on liquor can be justified on the basis of the first two criteria above. However, the heavy taxation of tobacco on a sumptuary basis is questionable at best. The luxury excise systems include so many goods of very widespread use that the distribution of burden is likely regressive and not superior to that of a sales tax. Substantial burden rests on business firms. In addition, the present structure includes some items, such as business machines, the taxation of which has no conceivable justification.

Finally, excise taxation, like all expenditure-based taxes, suffers from the limitation of being more deflationary than other taxes. On the other hand, like any expenditure-based tax, it is less likely to produce serious adverse incentives to work and to expand businesses than is a progressive income tax.

The most vigorous opponent of excise taxation in recent decades was the late H. C. Simons; his classic, if somewhat exaggerated, statement about excise taxes will serve as a fitting conclusion to this chapter:[6]

Fifth Proposal [for reform of the federal tax structure]: *Elimination or radical reduction of excise taxes (especially on beer, liquors, tobacco, admissions, etc.) as an element in the federal revenue system.*

These taxes, to my mind, are the worst elements in our revenue system. They are much more regressive than sales taxes. They are almost wholly concealed, precluding real awareness by individuals of their actual annual burden. They pander to misguided demands for sumptuary legislation, deriving strong support from alleged purposes which they are carefully designed *not* to serve. They pose as levies upon "luxuries," while serving to divert expenditures not from the objects taxed but from "necessities." Like corporation taxes, they are the revenue devices of political cowards who live in terror of voter-taxpayers and of government by intelligent discussion. The only cogent defense of them rests on the Calvinist premise that poor consumers of the objects in question are obviously damned for the next life and may properly be prepared now for their fate, by carrying what would otherwise be tax burdens of the elect.

## APPENDIX

### Canadian Excise Taxes

The importance of excise taxation in Canada has varied from time to time in recent decades to a much greater extent than in the United States, primarily because greater use has been made of this type of tax as a deliberate instrument of fiscal policy, as explained in Chapter 29. The excise tax structure as of January 1, 1963, is shown in Table 6, together with the yield for the preceding fiscal year. The excise taxes currently yield about 12 per cent of total budgetary tax revenue. These levies, are, of course, imposed in addition to the 10 per cent manufacturers' sales tax. The excise taxes, strictly speaking, are collected in conjunction with the latter at the manufacturing level. The excise duties, the basic taxes on liquor and tobacco, are imposed at specific rates and administered separately, with a close supervision exercised over the manufacturers of the products.

The Canadian excise system is less broad in coverage than the American, partly because it is accompanied by the sales tax. The Canadian levies on cigarettes are much higher than the American—almost twice as high—while the taxes on liquor are roughly the same.

The Canadian provinces make roughly the same use of excise taxes as the states; gasoline is universally taxed, as well as liquor (primarily

[6] *Federal Tax Reform* (Chicago: University of Chicago Press, 1950), pp. 36–37. Reproduced by permission of the University of Chicago Press.

TABLE 6

CANADIAN EXCISE DUTIES AND TAXES*

| Levy | Rate, January 1, 1959 | Yield, 1962 Fiscal Year (Millions of Dollars) | |
|---|---|---|---|
| *Sumptuary:* | | | |
| Liquor, duty .............. | $13 per gallon | | |
| Beer, duty .............. | $0.38 per gallon | $211 | |
| Wine, duty .............. | $0.25 to $2.50 per gallon | | |
| Cigarettes: | | | |
| Duty ................. | $4.00 per 1,000 | 159 duty | |
| Excise ............... | $0.015 per 5 | 220 excise | |
| Other tobacco products, duty and excise ......... | Varying | | |
| Total .............. | | | $590 |
| | | | |
| *Luxury:* | | | |
| Jewelry, etc. .............. | 10% | $ 26 | |
| Matches, lighters .......... | 10% | | |
| Toilet articles, cosmetics ..... | 10% | | |
| Radios, TV, etc. ........... | 15% | 18 | |
| Repealed levies ........... | | 28 | |
| Total .............. | | | 72 |
| Over-all total ..... | | | $662 |

\* The duties are applied to both domestic and imported articles. The taxes are applied at the manufacturing level.

SOURCE: Canadian Tax Foundation, *The National Finances* (Toronto, 1962).

through the device of profits of provincial liquor stores) and amusements. Tobacco products are taxed in four provinces.

# REFERENCES

There have been few general discussions of excise taxes. Most of the analysis in the literature of economics has dealt with a few specialized aspects, such as the "distortion of resources" arguments.

Hu, T. Y. *The Liquor Tax in the United States.* New York: Columbia University Press, 1950.

A history and analysis of liquor taxation.

Law, W. A. "Tobacco Taxation in the Revenue System," *National Tax Journal,* Vol. VI (December, 1953), pp. 372–85.

A thorough study of the tobacco tax problem, stressing administrative aspects.

Marbach, F. *Luxus und Luxussteuer.* Bern: A. Franke, 1948.

The most complete study of luxury excises ever published.

PERRY, J. H. *Taxation in Canada*, chaps. vii, xii. 3d ed. Toronto: University of Toronto Press, 1961.

The Canadian excise tax system.

ROZENTAL, A. A. "Selective Excises and the Federal Tax Structure," *Southern Economic Journal*, Vol. XXIII (April, 1957), pp. 421–33.

An argument for expanded use of excises.

CALIFORNIA SENATE INTERIM COMMITTEE ON STATE AND LOCAL TAXATION. *State and Local Taxes in California*, chaps. x, xi. Sacramento, 1951.

A survey of excise and gasoline taxation by the states.

DISCHAMPS, JEAN-CLAUDE. *Compartements economiques et distortions fiscales.* Paris: Presses Universitaires de France, 1960.

The most complete analysis of the resource distortion arguments.

# PART V

The Taxation of Wealth
and Transfers of Wealth

| Chapter | TAXES ON |
| --- | --- |
| 19 | GRATUITOUS TRANSFERS |
| | OF WEALTH |

The receipt of a gift or a bequest constitutes an economic gain to the recipient and thus increases his economic well-being. Such receipts constitute income under the "consumption plus increase in net wealth" definition explained in Chapter 7 and would fall within the "flow of wealth" definition of income in the present laws, were they not specifically excluded. Traditionally, gratuitous transfers have never been subjected to income taxes.

However, governments have applied separate taxes to gratuitous transfers, particularly to bequests. These levies are known as death taxes or death duties. They take two major forms: estate taxes, imposed upon the entire estate as a unit, and inheritance taxes, imposed upon the shares to each heir. The use of these taxes has been motivated by two primary considerations. The first is the recognition of the ability to pay involved in the acquisition of wealth by bequest or gift. The second, which has often played an important political role, has been the deliberate desire to break up large fortunes for reasons of general social policy. Particularly in the United States, the death taxes have never been important, revenuewise, partly because of high exemptions, partly because of numerous loopholes.

### The Reasons for Separate Tax Treatment of Gratuitous Transfers

There are several reasons why gifts and bequests have been excluded from the scope of the income tax and provided separate treatment instead. In the first place, a large number of bequests pass from the decedent to his widow or to minor children. In this case the receipt of title to the property does not represent a real improvement in the economic well-being of the recipient. The beneficiaries had full use of the property prior to receipt of title, and the occurrence which led to the transfer in many cases eliminated the chief source of family income, thus making the beneficiaries worse off economically. Accordingly, taxation of the bequest at regular income tax rates would result in departure from the rule of distribution of tax burden in relation to economic well-being. On the other hand, some bequests represent completely unexpected or windfall gains, which may be considered to represent greater taxpaying ability than usual income.

Secondly, receipts of bequests are highly irregular from year to year. So long as the income tax allows no general averaging of irregular incomes, taxation of gifts and bequests as income would result either in serious complication of the returns or in gross inequity.

Thirdly, gifts in smaller amounts are very difficult to detect. Small gifts within the family, especially in kind rather than cash, would be especially troublesome; yet any exemption of such gifts would pave the way for avoidance of tax on other gifts. Taxation of gifts within the family would raise some very difficult questions over the distinction between normal support of dependents and gifts to them.

Finally, gifts and bequests, being mere transfers, would in many cases not "stand up" if they were taxable as income. The primary problems arise when one person is both a potential donor and a donee. If this person is short-circuited, the tax can be reduced materially. Thus, if a father leaves property to his son, who in turn leaves it to his son, the amount involved would be taxed twice. But if the father left the property to his grandson, the first tax would be avoided, yet the same final transfer of property would be attained. This procedure may have socially undesirable results, especially when the property is passed to minor children and is essentially "frozen" until they come of age.

These considerations suggest that any attempt to tax gifts and bequests as income is not desirable.[1] While some of the difficulties might be avoided in part by appropriate modifications in the income tax, serious complications in the structure of the tax would result. To argue that bequests and gifts should be taxed under separate laws is not to maintain, however, that there should be no integration of the taxes on these transfers with the income tax. This problem will be discussed in the next section.

The problem of death taxation, therefore, is that of devising a satisfactory means of reaching bequests and gifts in light of their four major characteristics:

1. The significance for taxpaying ability of the relationship of the heir to the decedent.

---

[1] One of the few persons to argue for inclusion of gifts and bequests in income for income tax purposes was the late H. C. Simons (*Personal Income Taxation* [Chicago: University of Chicago Press, 1938], chap. vi). To Simons, inclusion in income was essential if all persons were to be treated equitably under the income tax and arbitrary distinctions between earned and gratuitous income be avoided.

2. The irregularity. Most persons receive significant bequests only at very rare intervals and frequently only once.

3. The voluntary character. Possibilities of short-circuiting intermediate generations must be taken into consideration.

4. The small size of many gifts and the ease of concealment.

## Integration versus Isolation in the Treatment of Gratuitous Transfers

A very fundamental question must be raised before progressing further: Should the tax on gifts and estates be regarded as a supplement to the income tax, designed to reach directly the additional accretions to economic well-being represented by gratuitous receipts? Or should the gifts and bequests be regarded as separate elements suitable for taxation, to be taxed quite independently of the income tax, with rates graduated in terms of the bequests themselves and bearing no relation to the income of the recipient?

The former method, though not employed, actually has much merit. If the economic gain represented by a gift or bequest is considered to be affected by the current income of the recipient, direct integration of the taxes, with the tax rate dependent upon the income of the recipient, is the most logical approach. In terms of accepted standards of desirable patterns of income distribution, it is justifiable to tax a $5,000 gift more heavily if it is received by a person who has an annual income of $50,000 than if it is received by a person who has a $2,500 annual income. The tax could be collected in conjunction with the income tax, in much the same way that the self-employment tax for old-age annuities is now collected in the United States. A separate return form would be filed with the income tax return, listing gifts and bequests received during the year. Individual gifts under a certain figure, perhaps $100, could be excluded, since they cannot actually be detected. The tax rate would be ascertained from a table which would take into consideration the amount of other income which was received or, preferably, the average income of the preceding period of years. The person would not be taxable at all on gifts received if the combined earned income plus gift income was less than the exemption figure of the income tax; only the excess of the combined earned and gift income over the exemption figure would be taxable in any case.

The burden on widows and minor children would be reduced, either by a substantial exemption for them or by a lower rate table. Some differentiation could also be introduced in favor of other direct heirs, although this is less necessary. The problem of irregularity would also require consideration. Some method of spreading irregular bequests over a substantial period of years would be essential if the tax rates were at all progressive; otherwise, persons receiving gifts over a period of years would be favored over those receiving one bequest of the same size as the total of the gifts.

By this means, close integration of the two taxes could be obtained, without complicating the income tax and with due regard being given to most of the special characteristics of gratuitous transfers. The adjustment of the tax burden on the basis of the income of the recipient would result in more equitable burden, in terms of accepted standards, than that attainable with any system in which the tax on bequests and gifts is determined independently of income tax liability. It does not, however, meet the problem of short-circuiting intermediate generations. Such a measure could be introduced, along the lines of the "bequeathing power" approach advanced by Vickrey, but only at the expense of serious complications in the structure of the tax.

The major obstacle to the use of the integration approach is that of tradition. From time immemorial, bequests have been regarded as a suitable separate base for taxation, quite independent of the income or wealth of the recipient. The philosophy that bequests and gifts must be treated as separate entities, with the amount of tax being determined on the basis of the size of the bequest (or total estate) alone, has become so generally accepted that a change would be very difficult. The logical case for this "isolation" approach would appear to be weaker than for the integration approach; nevertheless the weight of history so strongly favors it that a shift to an integrated tax, however desirable, can at best be attained only over a substantial period.

In subsequent sections the present taxes, based upon the "isolation" or "separate entity" doctrine, will be reviewed in terms of the intended objectives of this approach.

### Inherent Problems of Death Taxation[2]

Any system of death taxation encounters several basic obstacles, which are not easily overcome in a logical and feasible fashion.

In the first place, the tax must apply to a base which does not involve a market transaction, in contrast to income and expenditure taxes. As a consequence, no automatic valuation is possible; a deliberate administrative valuation of property must be made, as with the property tax. With complex estates, this task is an inherently difficult one.

Secondly, the transfer of property is not limited to the occasion of

---

[2] Note the article by C. L. Harriss, "Sources of Injustice in Death Taxation," *National Tax Journal*, Vol. VII (December, 1954), pp. 289–308.

death; the existence of a death tax will stimulate the making of gifts prior to death, and thus the tax must be supplemented by one applying to gifts *inter vivos*—between living persons. But these transfers are difficult to detect, and effective progression is difficult to attain.

Thirdly, transfers of property are not always clear-cut; there are various actions which result in partial transfer of interest, or of interest for a limited period of time (during the person's lifetime, for example).

Fourthly, persons recognize death as inevitable, but they do not know the time of death. Thus, they will adjust their property holdings in light of anticipation of both death and death taxes, but they will inevitably gamble to some extent on the time—and the outcome of their gamble will greatly determine the final tax liability.

## ESTATE, INHERITANCE, AND GIFT TAXATION IN THE UNITED STATES

The federal government employs an estate tax and a supplementary gift tax; all states except Nevada levy some form of death tax.

### The Federal Tax

The federal estate tax applies to estates in excess of $60,000, with rates ranging from 3 per cent upward to 77 per cent on the excess over $10 million. The taxable estate includes not only the estate in the usual sense, but also the proceeds of insurance policies on the life of the deceased. Contributions to charitable and similar organizations, costs of transference of the estate, and debts outstanding are deductible. In addition, a marital deduction, consisting of the portion of the estate (other than community property)[3] left to the surviving spouse, up to the amount of one half the estate, is granted. Thus, in effect, if the deceased has left half or more of the estate to his or her surviving spouse, the tax does not apply until the estate exceeds $120,000.

A tax credit, known as the state tax offset, is permitted against the federal tax liability for state death taxes paid on the estate or shares in the estate, up to specified amounts (which constitute 80 per cent of the portion of the tax as it stood in 1926). This rule was introduced in order to insure for the states a share of death tax revenue, and to stop the practice of certain states, primarily Florida, of seeking to lure elderly wealthy people to the state by avoiding the use of death taxes. With the offset rule, on estates large enough to be subject to the federal tax the tax bur-

---

[3] Under the community property laws of several states, half of all family property belongs to the wife.

den will be much the same whether the state involved has a tax or not.

The federal gift tax is levied on gifts *inter vivos*—between living persons—at rates three fourths the height of the estate tax rates. No offset for state gift taxes paid is allowed. The exemption system is dual:

1. A person may give a sum of $3,000 per year per recipient tax-free, regardless of the total which he gives in the year or has given in the past.

2. The amounts given in excess of $3,000 per year per recipient do not become taxable until the cumulative total of these amounts exceeds $30,000. A person has only one of these $30,000 exemptions during his lifetime; all gifts in excess of the annual $3,000 figure are cumulative against this $30,000 exemption. Once it is reached, all amounts given in excess of $3,000 per year per recipient become taxable.

Under a provision comparable to the marital deduction rule of the estate tax, one half of the amount of a gift given by a person who is married is considered to come from the spouse. For a married couple, therefore, the effective exemptions discussed in the preceding paragraph are $6,000 and $60,000, respectively.

Gifts held to be in contemplation of death are defined to be a portion of the taxable estate and are taxed by estate, rather than gift, tax rates. While under the present law, gifts given during the period of three years prior to death are considered to be in contemplation of death unless proved otherwise, the courts have in general been rather lenient to the taxpayers regarding proof that death is not "in contemplation."

### The State Taxes

All states except Nevada impose some form of death tax. The majority of the states (thirty-nine) use the inheritance form, in which the tax is levied on the separate bequests, the exemption and the rate depending upon the relationship of the heir to the decedent. The rate is progressive according to the size of the bequest. The variations among the taxes are so great that generalizations are difficult. There are frequently at least four classes of heirs: widows and minor children, other direct heirs (including parents), other related persons, and unrelated persons. The differences in exemptions are often very substantial; for example, in California, the exemption for a wife is $24,000; for an uncle, $500; for unrelated persons, $50. Rates in California range from 2 to 10 per cent (graduated according to the size of the bequest) for widows to 7 to 16 per cent for unrelated persons. Typically, the exemption figures are lower than those of the federal tax, but the total exemption on a particular estate may be greater when there are several heirs. The state rates are much lower than the federal rates on larger estates. The inheritance tax form has one great advantage over the estate tax, namely, that of adjusting the burden more precisely in terms of relationship of heir to decedent. On the other hand, it is somewhat more complicated to administer, particularly when bequests involve contingent interests. Some of the state inheritance tax laws classify heirs into an unnecessarily large number of groups.

With the use of the inheritance tax form, the states cannot obtain full benefit of the federal offset rule and at the same time not run the amount of the state tax over the offset figure, because the tax liability in each case will depend upon the number and relationship of the heirs. Accordingly, all except four of the states using the inheritance tax form impose supplementary estate taxes, the amount of tax liability on an estate being the difference between the sum of the inheritance taxes due on the various shares of the estate and the amount of the federal offset credit allowed. By this means the states can get the maximum possible amount of tax from each estate without creating a burden greater than that existing in other states.

Ten states levy estate taxes in lieu of, rather than as supplements to, the inheritance form. Five of these are based closely upon the federal tax, being designed in general to take exact advantage of the federal offset. Only twelve states use gift taxes; more would probably do so if the offset provision were extended to gift taxes. The federal gift tax alone, however, if effective, would be sufficient to discourage wealthy persons from giving away property to escape death taxes.

One problem peculiar to the state taxes is that of possible double taxation of the same property by more than one state. So far as real property is concerned, the rule is clear: Only the state in which the property is located may apply tax. For both types of tangible property, however, the possibility of double taxation arises. With tangible personal property, Supreme Court decisions have established the rule rather firmly that only the state of physical location can apply the tax. With intangibles, however, the situation is less clear. A series of Supreme Court decisions largely limited taxation to the state of domicile, denying the state in which the securities happened to be located or the state of incorporation, in the case of capital stock, the right to tax. After 1940, however, the court reversed its previous position, allowing the state of incorporation to apply the tax as well as the one of domicile. This problem is minimized by the reciprocal clauses in the laws of most states, under which one state will not tax intangibles of the residents of another state, provided that the latter follows the same policy with respect to residents of the first state.

Some multiple taxation has also arisen from multiple domicile; in some cases, more than one state has claimed a person to be a resident, and this claim has been upheld by the Supreme Court. Few persons, however, now allow their estates to be trapped in this manner.

The great complexity and nonuniformity among the various state death taxes have been sources of complaint for many years. To meet this problem, the Advisory Commission on Intergovernmental Relations, a federal commission established in 1959 for the purpose of improving relations among various levels of government, recommended a substantial increase in the size of the federal offset, coupled with the requirement that the states convert their death taxes to the estate tax form, in order to obtain greater uniformity. It was also recommended that the credit be graduated in two steps, higher on small estates than on larger ones, to provide greater aid for the poorer states.[4]

## THE LIMITATIONS OF THE PRESENT TAXES

As previously indicated, the taxation of estates and inheritances without reference to the income-wealth status of the recipients results in a distribution of burden which, it may be argued, is not in conformity with usual concepts of ability. Thus an estate of a given size going to a poverty-stricken friend will be subject to the same (or under many of the state taxes, greater) tax burden as that on an estate of the same size going to a millionaire brother. This objection can be avoided only by integration of the tax with the income tax. Apart from this basic question, there are several serious limitations of the present taxes, in terms of their objectives.

### Lack of Integration of Gift and Death Taxes

A basic avenue of avoidance and inequity arises out of the treatment of gifts; the death and gift taxes are distinct, with no real integration between them. Thus a tremendous incentive exists to give property away before death. There are several sources of savings. First, the gift tax rates are lower. While this differential was designed to compensate for the fact that the tax is paid at an earlier date if the property is given away prior to death, it often allows a material net gain. Secondly, progression is lessened. Since the death and gift taxes are levied separately of one another, the gift of a part of the property (so long as the gift is not held to be in contemplation of death) will divide the property into two segments and

---

[4] See Advisory Commission on Intergovernmental Relations, *Coordination of State and Federal Inheritance, Estate, and Gift Taxes* (Washington, D.C.: U.S. Government Printing Office, 1961); and J. A. Maxwell, "A New Proposal for Coordination of Death Taxation," *National Tax Journal*, Vol. XIV (December, 1961), pp. 382–87.

materially check the operation of progression. Thirdly, an additional exemption is gained. Fourthly, the amount of gift tax paid comes out from the base completely. This sum is not a portion of the base for either tax, whereas if all the property is held until death, there is no comparable exclusion. In addition, the exemptions for the gift tax are liberal; by judicious spreading of the gifts over a number of years, a tremendous amount of death tax liability can be avoided. The relatively small yield of the gift tax suggests that most tax-stimulated gifts are made in such a way as to avoid any gift tax liability at all.

There are two general types of solution to this problem. The simplest one would involve merely a direct integration of the gift and estate taxes. Each taxpayer would be required to cumulate the figures of his gifts (tax being paid upon each gift if above the exemption figure), as at present. At the time of death the total cumulated figure of gifts would be added to the estate, the total tax on the entire amount determined, and credit given for gift taxes already paid (plus interest). The difference would be the figure of estate tax payable. By this means the tax burden would be the same whether property was given away prior to death or not. The present avenues of avoidance would be closed, and the artificial stimulus to give away property prior to death eliminated. The change would involve relatively little modification of the present tax structures and would lessen their complexity, since the problems of distinguishing between bequests and gifts would be eliminated.

A more far-reaching solution, and one which would modify the present taxes more fundamentally, is the replacement of the present levies by an *accessions tax*, imposed directly upon the recipients of gifts and bequests. The base of the tax would be transferred from particular gifts and bequests to the cumulative total sum received as gifts or bequests by an individual during his lifetime. Each individual would be required to cumulate the figures of gifts and bequests received, regardless of the source. The tax would be applied to the cumulated total on a progressive basis. This procedure would bring the tax more closely in line with usually accepted standards of equity. At present, if one person inherits $100,000 from one person and another inherits $150,000 in six sums of $25,000 each from different donors, the tax burden will be greater in the first case than in the second, although the total amount received is less. The accessions basis would result in greater tax in the second case than in the first. It would complicate the administration of the tax, however, and involve a much more fundamental departure from the present taxes.[5]

---

[5] The most complete discussion of the accessions tax is to be found in the article by H. J. Rudick, "What Alternative to Estate and Gift Taxes?" *California Law Review*, Vol. XXXVIII (March, 1950), pp. 150–82.

### Effects of the Taxes upon the Methods of Transfer

A related but more fundamental problem is the tendency of the taxes in their present form to alter the methods of bequeathing property, since the amount of tax due is affected by the particular method chosen. One result is short-circuiting; intermediate generations are skipped in order to lessen the over-all burden. An elderly man, wishing his estate to reach his grandchildren, is given a strong incentive to leave the property to them rather than to his middle-aged son, since the tax will apply only once rather than ultimately twice. Secondly, the tax treatment encourages the use of complicated methods of leaving property, particularly the establishment of trusts and powers of appointment. Under the present tax, for example, if property is left for use during the recipient's lifetime, to pass to a third party at the latter's death, the tax applies only to the first transfer. One consequence is great complication in the methods of transfer, which produces disputes and litigation over tax liability. A death tax structure should result in the same total burden regardless of the exact manner in which the property is left and the number of steps through which it goes between two particular generations. Thus the final burden should be the same whether property is transferred from father to son to grandson or directly to the grandson. Such a result would avoid the freezing of property in the names of minor children, which is contrary to the best interests of the economy.

The accomplishment of these results, however, is extremely difficult. Adjustment of tax according to the difference in age between decedent and recipient would lessen the tendency to short-circuit intermediate generations. The greater the difference, the greater would be the tax burden, because the greater would be the likelihood that the property would not be transferred again for some years. However, complete equity cannot be attained, and incentives to use complicated forms would remain.

Vickrey has developed a more complicated solution[6] with the use of the "bequeathing power" technique, which would adjust the tax in terms of the excess of the age of the decedent over that of the heir, in such a manner that the burden would be exactly the same, regardless of the path the estate follows. The tax would be greatly complicated by such a procedure, however.

### Capriciousness

In part as a result of the considerations already noted but also because of the general complexity of the laws, particularly the federal estate

[6] W. Vickrey, *Agenda for Progressive Taxation* (New York: Ronald Press Co., 1947), chap. viii.

tax law in the United States, the distribution of the burden of the death taxes is capricious. Careful planning can reduce death tax burdens tremendously; as pointed out by Lowell Harriss, few activities are so profitable for elderly wealthy persons as ferreting out means of reducing estate tax liability.[7] The heirs of other persons who are less careful or who die prematurely are subjected to very heavy taxes, if the estates are large. With no other tax does the liability depend to such a large extent (in an inverse fashion) on the ingenuity of the persons involved. The great complexity of the taxes makes the planning of estates and the determination of tax liability difficult, and places a great premium on the use of the best legal talent.

In one other way the tax is capricious: It tends to discriminate against the heirs of persons who die relatively young. The receipt of a given sum of money is of less value to a widow with small children who must be educated than it is to an older widow whose children are grown. Early death involves a greater sacrifice of earning power.

## GENERAL EVALUATION OF DEATH AND GIFT TAXES

The problems mentioned in the preceding section are for the most part products of the peculiar structure of the present death taxes, which could in large measure be alleviated by changes in the taxes. But there remains for consideration the more fundamental question of the appropriate role of death taxation in the tax structure; the answers are influenced by the estimates of the economic effects of the taxes, both in their present form and with possible modifications.

### Incidence

Shifting of the taxes by the recipients of inheritances or gifts is almost inconceivable. Some questions have been raised about the relative burdens on decedent and recipient. In the case of gifts, since the tax is on the donor and he is still alive, it may be reasonable to assume that he bears the burden, except to the extent that he reduces the net gift because of the tax. In the case of bequests, it is difficult to argue that the burden is on a person no longer living, although he may have sacrificed consumption during his lifetime in order to leave a given net estate to the heirs. The relative burden on each heir is largely within the control of the decedent at the time he made his will, since he can adjust the bequests in light of the tax. If specific bequests are made to various persons, and the

---

[7] See "Public Finance," in B. F. Haley (ed.), *A Survey of Contemporary Economics,* Vol. II (Homewood, Ill.: Richard D. Irwin, Inc., 1952), p. 289.

remainder left to a residual heir, the entire burden will rest upon the latter, unless the amounts of the bequests are appropriately adjusted.

### Economic Effects: Incentives

The question of the economic effects of death taxes has been debated for many years. Three aspects are of particular importance: the effects upon incentives, upon the rate of capital accumulation, and upon liquidity of estates.

With respect to incentives, it is rather generally agreed that a tax on estates is not likely to deter many persons from working, taking more responsible positions, or developing and expanding businesses, because of its remoteness. The influence is certainly less than that of income taxes, which directly and immediately reach the returns from the activity involved. It is possible that in some cases, persons may be deterred from building up their estates because of the tax; on the other hand, other persons may accumulate more than otherwise in order to be able to leave an estate of a given size after tax to their heirs.

### Effect on Capital Accumulation

Despite the lesser incentive effects, it is argued that the tax has severe effects on capital accumulation, because it takes funds which would otherwise be available for business expansion. It is undoubtedly true that the tax is borne primarily out of accumulated funds rather than out of current income. But the contrast with the income tax is more apparent than real, although the death tax probably has somewhat greater effect, per dollar of revenue. The income tax checks capital accumulation by taking funds which would otherwise be added to accumulated savings, while death taxes take the funds after accumulation. Both income and death taxes have greater effects in reducing the over-all percentage of income saved than have sales and excise taxes, and thus lessen the potential rate of capital formation to a greater extent. But the death tax has much less effect in curtailing consumption, and thus, if deflationary pressures are present, the net effect of the death taxes upon the actual rate of capital formation may be less than that of sales and excise taxes. The net effects of a reduction in the rate of capital formation have been discussed in earlier chapters.

### Effect on Liquidity of Estates and Forced Liquidation

A much more significant effect of death taxes is that upon the liquidity of estates. A person with substantial investment in his own business and little liquid capital is in a highly vulnerable death tax position. Forced liquidation, with severe losses to the heirs, transfer of control of the business, and general disorganization of the enterprise could easily result. In the earlier days of the estate tax, great fear was expressed of dire consequences of this character.

In practice, however, forced liquidation has not proven to be a serious problem except in isolated cases. The tendency to transfer property prior to death lessens the problem, as does the provision that, upon request, heirs can be allowed up to ten years in which to make payment if forced liquidation will otherwise result. With a few large estates—that of Henry Ford being an outstanding example—a major portion of the estate has been given to a charitable foundation in order to avoid public sale of the stock of the enterprise. But primarily, the problem is avoided because of the care taken by persons with large estates to insure that sufficient liquid funds are on hand. A study by Lowell Harriss has demonstrated the fact that on the whole, taxable estates have more than sufficient liquid assets with which to pay the tax.[8]

However, while forced liquidation may not be serious, the steps taken to avoid it may have significant repercussions. On the whole, the tax causes persons to keep their estates in more liquid form than they otherwise would. As a consequence, funds which might be used for expansion are placed in government bonds and similar assets. While it is impossible to demonstrate the actual magnitude of this effect, it is probably considerable, even under present relatively light estate tax burdens on the typical estate.

The need for liquidity of the estate has also encouraged mergers. A study in the Harvard Business School series on effects of taxation concluded that the estate tax has been a factor in encouraging the owners of closely held businesses to sell their enterprises to other firms in order to avoid any danger of forced liquidation at the time of death.[9] In addition to the desire for liquidity, these persons have also been influenced by fears that the valuation placed upon the stock of closely held companies by the Internal Revenue Service at the time of death may be unreasonably high. There is little evidence that such a policy has been followed, but the fear has definitely influenced the actions of some persons.

The Harvard study showed that the pressure to sell was especially strong if one person held securities in a closely held corporation in excess of $500,000 and had few other assets. In the sample taken, the authors

---

[8] "Liquidity of Estates and Death Tax Liability," *Political Science Quarterly*, Vol. LXIV (December, 1949), pp. 533–59.

[9] J. K. Butters, J. Lintner, and W. L. Cary, *Effects of Taxation: Corporate Mergers* (Boston: Harvard University Graduate School of Business Administration, 1951).

found that when the companies had assets of between $15 million and $50 million, taxes played a part in motivating the sale in about two fifths of the cases. If the assets were between $1 million and $5 million, taxes were significant in from one fifth to one third of the cases. Taxes were less important if the property was worth less than $1 million. The estate tax was not the only relevant factor, but one of major importance in the decisions. It should be noted that the tendency of the tax to encourage mergers is greatly facilitated by the low taxes on capital gains. If these were fully taxable, the income tax penalty on the sale of the business would often be so great that the sale would not be advantageous.

### Summary of Economic Effects

On the whole, the adverse effects of present death taxes do not appear to be serious; the most significant considerations are those of greater liquidity of estates and increased incentive given to mergers. If, however, rates were increased and exemptions lowered in order to raise substantially greater amounts of revenue from the tax, the magnitude of these effects would increase greatly. A high-level tax on the transfer of property, almost regardless of its form, would inevitably raise serious problems for the transfer of family-owned businesses; the present law causes little serious trouble, primarily because of the high exemptions and the numerous ways of escaping from the tax.

On the positive side the primary advantage of death taxes over those levied upon income is the lesser adverse influence exerted upon incentives—to work, to take more responsible positions, to undertake business development and expansion. This consideration suggests that the tax structure as a whole might justifiably be based to a greater extent upon transfers of property at death, with somewhat lessened reliance on income taxes. This consideration would appear to outweigh the problem of the transfer of family-held businesses, which, incidentally, would be less serious if income tax rates were lower.

### Equity Considerations

From the standpoint of equity the basic justification for death taxes is that the receipt of bequests or gifts represents an improvement in the economic well-being of the recipient, upon which he can justifiably be taxed. Since relatively few persons are fortunate enough to receive significant bequests or gifts during their lifetimes, there is particular reason to require those who do to make additional tax payments on this basis. Since the receipts are supplements to regular income, taxation does not cut into usual levels of living.

In addition, death taxes have the effect of breaking up large fortunes, a consideration which has brought much of the political support for these taxes. Many persons regard as highly inequitable the fact that some individuals are sufficiently fortunate to inherit so much property that they never need to work or otherwise contribute toward the welfare of the economy. Reasonable equality of opportunity requires that limits be placed upon the amounts which persons can inherit, and death taxes are the most effective means of accomplishing this result. Also, the breaking-up of large fortunes lessens the danger of continuing monopoly power.

In the present tax structures of both Canada and the United States a further advantage of the use of death taxes is that they reach capital gains, which in large measure escape income taxation. Because capital gains are not taxed until realized and gains on property transferred at death are not taxable at all as income, many estates contain substantial accumulated capital gains, which completely escape income taxes. The use of death taxes does at least place some burden upon these amounts, although not an adequate amount compared to the combined income and death tax burden on amounts received as regular income and added to the estate. In Canada, in which capital gains are not taxable at all, the death taxes provide the only means by which this form of addition to wealth is reached by taxation. Reform of the capital gains treatment under the income tax laws would be the logical step; but so long as this action is not taken, the death taxes perform an important function in placing some tax burden upon the gains.

On the other hand, the present tax structures result in highly inequitable treatment among individuals subject to the taxes, for reasons indicated in preceding paragraphs. In particular, those persons who devise various means of giving away their estates prior to death escape the payment of appropriate amounts. Some question may also be raised about the tax-free status of grants to charitable trusts and foundations, which allow substantial amounts to escape taxes. While the heirs lose the income from the property, they retain control over the property itself, and one aim of the tax, that of breaking up large concentrations of wealth, is not attained. It is true, of course, that very useful ends may be served by the charitable institutions set up, and the deduction of grants to them lessens the possibility of breaking up family-owned businesses. But nevertheless, some doubts may be raised on an equity basis.

### Administrative Considerations

Since all property transferred at death must (legally) pass through the hands of the courts, the chances of evasion are limited to those items of property, such as cash or jewelry, which the heirs simply take without the courts being aware of them. With gift taxes, there is greater chance of evasion, especially with smaller amounts.

There are, however, some difficult questions of valuation. The general intent is that the property be valued on the basis of its market value at an open sale with free exchange. With many types of property, no difficulty is encountered. But in some cases, particularly with large blocks of stock of small corporations, sale would depress the price of the property. For years, no recognition of losses due to this "blockage" problem was made; but in more recent years, some adjustment is authorized when warranted by the circumstances.

A related problem, that of the date as of which the value for tax purposes is determined, becomes serious in a period of depreciating values, such as between 1929 and 1933. Because several months may elapse between the time of death and the time of completing the closing of the estate and the payment of taxes, an heir could find himself in the position of having to pay more in taxes than the estate was currently worth. The use of a single-day valuation increases the seriousness of the blockage problem noted above. In order to lessen the danger of inequity, present federal law gives the heirs a choice of several options, including value at date of death and that one year later.

With closely held businesses, direct valuation is necessary, since there is no market price for the stock. The task is in some cases very difficult, especially when the value of the business has been greatly dependent upon the work of the deceased.

## CONCLUSION

In the establishment of a logical system of taxes upon gratuitous transfers of property, a basic question must first be resolved: Are the transfers to be regarded as separate indicators of taxpaying ability in themselves, distinct from the income and wealth of the recipients? Or are the taxes to be regarded as supplements to the income tax, designed to reach accretions of wealth which, because of their gratuitous and irregular nature, do not fit well into the scope of an income tax itself? The latter approach appears to be basically the most equitable. But by long-standing tradition the transfers are regarded as distinct and separate measures of taxpaying ability.

Even in terms of this approach the present tax treatment is by no means satisfactory. The separation of the gift and estate taxes paves the way for tax avoidance and inequity, and could easily be solved either by cumulating gifts and estates or by shifting over to a tax on cumulated accessions of recipients. The other basic problem, and one more difficult to solve, is the encouragement given to the short-circuiting of particular generations and selection of some methods of transferring property in preference to others. Only by adjustment of tax on the basis of the length of time between transfers can this be avoided.

From the standpoint of general economic effects, the major problem arises with transfers of family-held businesses. In order to avoid forced liquidation, the owners find it necessary to keep a larger portion of the estate in liquid form than they might otherwise wish, and in some instances find it advantageous to sell the enterprise as a unit prior to death. On the other hand, the adverse effects of death taxes on incentives are undoubtedly less than those of income taxes, which directly affect the profitability of particular actions.

## APPENDIX

### Canadian Death Taxes

In Canada, major changes have occurred in the structure of death taxes since 1941, the date of the enactment of the first federal tax. Prior to that time, only the provinces used the levies; since that time, all provinces except three (British Columbia, Ontario, and Quebec) have relinquished their levies in exchange for federal payments.

Prior to 1958, both federal and provincial governments used successions duties, which are hybrids of the estate and inheritance tax forms, the tax being based partly on the shares to particular heirs and partly on the total size of the estate. After several years of study, in 1958 the federal successions tax was replaced by an estate tax, largely for the purposes of simplification.[10] Under the present estate tax the basis for taxation is the entire estate, without regard to its disposition, and one rate schedule is applied. The only concession to the relationship of the heir to the decedent is the provision of a larger deduction (exemption) for a widow ($60,000 instead of the basic $40,000 figure) and an additional sum for each dependent child ($10,000 in certain cases, $15,000 in others). Rates range from 10 per cent to 54 per cent on the excess over $2 million. A tax credit of one half the provincial death taxes paid is granted. Gifts given within three years of death, plus any others held to be in contemplation of death, are defined to be portions of the taxable estate.

[10] See "The New Estate Tax Bill," Canadian Tax Foundation, *Tax Memo. No. 16* (Toronto, 1958); W. I. Linton, *A Review of the Estate Tax Act* (Toronto: Canadian Tax Foundation, 1961).

Other gifts are subject to the gift tax, which was introduced prior to the successions duty, and originally designed to check transfers of property within the family to lessen income tax liability. Like the United States tax, it is a separate levy, not integrated with the death taxes. There is no cumulative exemption feature, as in the United States law; gifts in excess of $1,000 are taxable, provided that total gifts during the year exceed $4,000, or more than one half the income of the taxpayer in the preceding year, whichever is lower. Rates range from 10 to 28 per cent. Liability for payment is on the donor.

Provincial successions taxes are employed by Ontario and Quebec and, as of 1963, by British Columbia. The taxes are hybrids, rates depending on the amount of the estate, the size of the individual bequest, and the relationship of the heir to the deceased. Exemptions are based upon the same factors. The rates are highly complicated and similar in level to the federal taxes. Because of their greater height, the taxes are more important revenue producers than the inheritance taxes in the states. The other provinces receive 50 per cent of the federal estate tax yield in the province.

## REFERENCES

BLOCH, H. S. "Economic Objectives of Gratuitous Transfer Taxation," *National Tax Journal*, Vol. IV (June, 1951), pp. 139–47.
  An analysis of economic effects and objectives of the tax.
"Federal Estate and Gift Taxes," *California Law Review*, Vol. XXXVIII (March, 1950).
  A series of papers on federal death tax problems.
VICKREY, W. *Agenda for Progressive Taxation*, chaps. vii–ix. New York: Ronald Press Co., 1947.
  An analysis of death taxation and a presentation of the "bequeathing power" system.
HARRISS, C. L. "Sources of Injustice in Death Taxation," *National Tax Journal*, Vol. VII (December, 1954), pp. 289–308.
JOINT COMMITTEE ON THE ECONOMIC REPORT. *Federal Tax Policy for Economic Growth and Stability*, pp. 819–71. Washington, D.C.: U.S. Government Printing Office, 1955.
  A series of papers on federal estate tax questions.
PERRY, J. H. *Taxation in Canada*, chaps. v, x. 3d ed. Toronto: University of Toronto Press, 1961.
  A survey of the Canadian death taxes.
LINTON, W. I. *A Review of the Estate Tax Act*. Toronto: Canadian Tax Foundation, 1961.
  A detailed review of the federal tax.

ADVISORY COMMISSION ON INTERGOVERNMENTAL RELATIONS. *Coordination of State and Federal Inheritance, Estate, and Gift Taxes.* Washington, D.C.: U.S. Government Printing Office, 1961.
  A study of intergovernmental relations in the field of death taxation.

# Chapter 20

# THE TAXATION OF WEALTH:

# A TAX ON INDIVIDUAL

# NET WEALTH

In the preceding chapters the discussion has been centered on the establishment of tax structures on the basis of income, gratuitous transfers, and the portion of income spent. An alternative measure of economic well-being is personal wealth, in the sense of the value of goods, claims, and property rights owned. This measure is not a flow during a period but the value of the stock of wealth of a person at a particular moment of time. The basic justification for the use of this basis of taxation is the dependence of economic well-being on personal wealth as well as on income. If two persons have equal incomes but one has a considerable accumulation of wealth, he enjoys several advantages. He has a means to maintain his level of living, should his income cease; he is not under compulsion to save, as is the person who has not accumulated; and the mere possession of wealth may be regarded as a source of satisfaction in itself, particularly because of the prestige value. There is substantial justification, therefore, for placing a somewhat heavier burden on this person, while under the income tax, in its usual form, the tax burdens on the two will be the same.

## INADEQUACIES OF THE INCOME TAX IN REACHING WEALTH

The argument has been advanced that an entirely logical income tax structure would solve the problem without a separate tax on wealth. The portion of the wealth consisting of securities and business property is taxed indirectly through the yield; the investment in homes might be taxed through inclusion in income of their rental value. If it is desirable to place a heavier burden on property income, this can be accomplished by differential rates in the income tax structure.

### Wealth Yielding Little Cash Return

This approach, however, cannot be entirely satisfactory. Suppose, for example, that four persons have each accumulated $10,000. One person places the sum in common stock which yields 6 per cent; a second places it in a savings account at 3 per cent; a third holds it in cash or in a checking account; a fourth buys a home. The first person is reached satisfactorily by the present income tax; the fourth would be, if the imputed rental value of the home (or interest on the investment) were included in taxable income. But the third person is not reached at all by the income tax, no matter what adjustments are made in it. Yet this person obviously is better off economically than he would be if he did not have this wealth, even though it yields him no income during the period.

Likewise, the second person, who earns a small interest return on his savings deposits, is taxed very lightly compared to the first. Essentially, a portion of his return takes the form of liquidity and risk avoidance, on which he pays no income tax. The person who buys common stock is taxed upon the full return, while the person who buys securities of lesser risk or who holds his wealth in liquid form escapes with considerably less tax burden.

Not only is a tax upon property important as a means of reaching wealth which yields no cash return or a relatively low one, but it is likewise a more effective means of reaching the wealth represented by a person's home than is an income tax adjusted to reach the imputed income from the home during the year. Any attempt to include the rental value of homes in income for income tax purposes encounters numerous problems, as discussed in Chapter 7. Likewise, the use value of consumer durables, such as automobiles, which are also measures of economic well-being, can be reached more easily by a tax on wealth.

### Evaluation of a Wealth Tax on an Equity Basis

Thus, on an equity basis the use of a tax on wealth as a supplement to the income tax would accomplish three results:

1. The placing of heavier over-all burden on persons receiving property incomes than on those receiving labor incomes, on the principle that the possession of the property is a measure of economic well-being apart from the income earned from it.

2. The provision of means of reaching nonincome-producing property, such as idle land, cash, checking account deposits, etc., and of taxing low-yield, minimum-risk investments more adequately.

3. The provision of a more equitable means of reaching the wealth represented by homes than inclusion of imputed rental value of the homes in taxable income.

By adjusting the burden in this manner, the over-all tax structure would be more equitable than one consisting of an income tax alone, and the lessened relative burden on the higher rates of earnings on equity capital should reduce the over-all adverse incentive effects of the tax structure. The income tax inevitably allows the owners of low-interest, high-grade securities, cash, and the like to pay too little relative to their actual economic well-being, and places too much burden on the persons willing to take the risks of business development.

The major objection, on an equity basis, to the net wealth tax is the burden placed upon persons who have wealth but little or no current income. Particularly if the amount of wealth possessed were small, serious hardships could result. Even owners of large estates could be penalized severely if they were compelled to sell property to pay taxes in periods in which property values were depressed. These problems suggest the need for a minimum exemption from the tax and for a relatively low rate. Likewise, the taxpayer could be allowed a period of years in which to pay, at only small penalty, when serious losses might result from forced sale of property. The exemption could be established in terms of property owned or in terms of income received, or a combination of both. For example, a person could be exempted from the wealth tax on property of a value less than a certain figure, if his current year's income were less than a designated amount. These problems arise, of course, from the fact that income is the primary criterion of economic well-being and suggest that under no conditions should the wealth tax become the primary source of tax revenue. But they do not preclude the gaining of considerable revenue from this source.

## THE STRUCTURE OF A TAX ON NET PERSONAL WEALTH

A tax on net personal wealth would differ substantially from property taxes now in use in the United States and Canada.[1] The aim would be to reach all persons on the basis of the net value of their wealth. Accordingly, the tax would be levied upon *individuals*, and individuals only. No attempt to levy on property as such, without respect to the owners, can ever result in a satisfactory distribution of burden. Secondly, the tax would be imposed upon the net wealth of each person (or family)—the current value of all wealth, less debt outstanding. Mortgages against homes would be deductible from the value of the home and would be taxable to the holders or, if the owner of the mortgage were a corporation, indirectly to the stockholders. The value of corporation stock would be included in the net worth of the owners; the corporation property, as such, would not be taxed. In other words, the corporate property would be reached via a tax on the value of the securities outstanding, not on the property of the

---

[1] Net worth taxes are imposed in the Scandinavian countries and elsewhere in Europe.

corporation as such. To include both would involve discriminatory double taxation; to tax the corporation as such would allow the stockholders to escape the burden if the tax were shifted to the customers. The value of proprietorship and partnership businesses would be assessed directly to the owners. All intangibles—mortgages, bonds, stock, bank deposits, cash —would be taxable, as well as all tangible property of individuals (less claims against it). The value figure sought would be the current market value, so far as this could be ascertained.

An exemption could easily be employed if the tax were nationwide in scope. It would be particularly desirable to avoid a heavy burden on older persons or others with little current income but with a home and some other property. The use of an exemption would raise the question of definition of the taxpaying unit, with problems similar to those under the income tax. Establishment of the exemption on a per capita basis would be simpler than use of the family basis and would avoid attempts of persons to separate themselves out of a family, but would give inadequate exemptions to single persons maintaining their own homes, compared to single persons living with their families.

The question of rate structure is not an easy one to answer. Progression might be justified on the basis of the same arguments as those which support it for income taxation. A progressive rate would also tend to break up large fortunes. But some question may be raised about the possible economic effects of the use of progressive taxes upon both income and wealth. As a more practical matter, progression would aggravate the problems of delineating the taxpaying units. There would be even greater tendency than with the income tax to spread property among various members of the family in order to escape progression. Since the tax is intended only as a supplement to the income tax, rather than as the primary means of insuring a progressive tax structure, a proportional rate structure, with limited progression due to the exemption, may be preferable.

## SHIFTING AND INCIDENCE

For the most part, a tax on personal net wealth would remain upon the persons upon whom it was levied. Relatively few persons would be in a position to shift forward a tax levied in relation to the amount of property they owned. This is particularly true of residential property and most intangibles. So long as all intangibles were taxed, there would be no alternative to which to turn (as there is with the income tax, which does not reach money holdings and reaches high-grade securities only very lightly). Only if the tax influenced the total supply of money capital would any general shifting by the owners of stocks and bonds be possible. It is much more likely that the over-all interest rate might be reduced (with given monetary policies), since the tax would give some incentive to shift away from holding of cash to the purchase of securities. Some shifting in investments from low-yield to high-yield securities would be encouraged, with a consequent increase in the yield on the former and decline on the latter. If the tax discouraged savings, there might be some long-run tendency toward a higher interest rate, which would offset the initial shift to securities from cash. But the likelihood of any very significant influence on the propensity to save is not great, because of the wide variety of motives which influence savings patterns.

In nonperfectly competitive markets, such as those for real estate mortgages, there would be more possibility of shifting. In the case of business property operated on a proprietorship or partnership basis or by a closely held corporation, some shifting is possible, again because of nonperfectly competitive elements in the markets. But the absence of any untaxed alternatives and the competition of widely held corporations, which could scarcely shift the tax burden on their stockholders, would seriously interfere with shifting. On rental housing the imperfect condition of the market would again make possible some shifting to tenants. The limited amount of shifting would interfere somewhat with the desired distribution of burden but should not reduce seriously the general equity of the tax.

## ECONOMIC EFFECTS

A tax on net wealth, just like an income tax, would increase somewhat the relative advantage of consumption as contrasted to saving, since the latter would give rise to additional tax liability. Since all wealth would be taxed, the effect might be greater than that of the income tax, since the income tax can be avoided if the savings are placed in noncash-yielding investments. The significance of these incentive reactions is lessened by the fact that so many considerations, in addition to the rate of return, influence decisions to save or consume. However, since some liability for the net wealth tax would be incurred by persons who had no current income, the wealth tax would likely be borne out of previously accumulated savings to a greater extent than would the income tax. Thus the potential rate of capital formation might be checked to a greater extent than it would be by an income tax with a burden distributed in a similar manner by income group. But the high progressivity of the actual income taxes might more than offset the fact that the wealth tax burdened some persons with no current income.

The wealth tax does not discriminate against high-return investments compared to those offering maximum liquidity and security with low cash return, as does the income tax. Accordingly, the wealth tax should have much less effect than the income tax in lessening the relative supply of equity capital. The collection of the tax on nonincome-yielding property would encourage some persons to buy equity investments in order to maintain their current income at the old levels, and tend to reduce the cost of equity funds.

The tax would likewise have less effect upon business policy than the income tax. Corporation property as such would not be subject to the wealth tax at all, and the tax on the wealth of the stockholders would not affect the policy of large, widely held corporations. The owners of noncorporate businesses or closely held corporations would be subject to tax, but tax liability would be incurred whether they used savings to expand their business or for other purposes.

The wealth tax, however, does affect the relative desirability of various forms of consumption expenditures. Since the purchase of durable consumables increases tax liability, incentive is given to buy more nondurables and fewer durables. In particular, heavy expenditures on housing facilities would be discouraged.

## PROBLEMS OF A TAX ON NET PERSONAL WEALTH

A tax on net wealth used as a supplement to the income tax offers significant advantages from the standpoint of equity. But unfortunately, the operation of such a tax would encounter serious difficulties.

### Valuation

Any tax based upon current value encounters more severe problems of valuation than a tax based on income or receipts, since no market transaction which automatically provides a value is involved. When property sells frequently in open markets, as is true of stocks and bonds of larger corporations, valuation is not difficult. Values can be placed easily upon cash, notes and mortgages not in default, and bank deposits. Assessment of farm land and homes of common types which sell frequently is feasible. Tangible personal property gives rise to some problems. But the major difficulties arise with stocks of closely held corporations, businesses operated as partnerships or proprietorships, and residential property of a somewhat unique type. These problems are not insuperable if the task is attempted on a scientific basis. Since corporate physical property would not be taxed, many of the most troublesome problems of present-day property tax administration would be avoided.

One question of principle would arise in the case of corporations whose property, valued on any logical basis, exceeds the current value of outstanding securities. Under the strict logic of the net wealth tax, this problem would be ignored, since the stockholders could in no way currently realize on the higher value of the corporation property. But it does suggest that some wealth in the economy would go tax-free.

### Reporting of Intangibles

A second problem is that of insuring correct reporting of intangibles. With administration of a net worth tax on a national basis, it would not be impossible to check upon ownership of most security issues. Some difficulties would arise with coupon bonds, but tracing of interest payments could enable a check even upon these. In general, for income-yielding securities the problems of finding the securities are no more difficult than those of reaching the income from them under present income tax laws. Bank deposits likewise could be determined easily. On the other hand, cash holdings are difficult to trace, and any failure to reach them would provide an incentive to hold wealth in this form. If this form of evasion did prove to be serious, it could be lessened by changing all money at intervals of several years, but only with substantial nuisance and cost. A related problem is that of checking upon tangible personal property. While automobiles and furniture can be discovered, other items, particularly valuable jewelry, can be concealed relatively easily.

A third problem, one inherent in any tax on accumulated wealth, in contrast to one on income or spending, is that relating to the selection of a particular date for application of the tax. For real property, this problem is not serious, since any one date during the year would be satisfactory. With bank deposits the use of an average of monthly balances would be advantageous. Yet if one date is chosen for some property and an annual average for others, complications are inevitable. So long as all wealth is reached regardless of its form, the one-date procedure is probably satisfactory.

### The Problem of Governmental Units

The most serious limitation to the use of a tax on net wealth arises from the distribution of powers and activities among various levels of government. Only the federal government could feasibly administer a net wealth tax, since only the federal government is in a position to obtain adequate information about intangibles. Likewise, any use of an exemption or of progressive rates would make a federal system mandatory. Yet in practice, the taxation of property has become the primary source of local government revenue, in large measure because it is the one major tax which—in a form considerably modified from the net wealth tax discussed above—can be administered locally. But any attempt to transform the present type of property tax into one on net wealth of individuals would run into insuperable obstacles. It would be impossible for the local governments to check upon intangible property, and the tax would result in a jurisdictional distribution of revenue very different from that of the property tax. Local units with extensive corporation property would lose a large portion of their tax revenue, to the benefit of those jurisdictions in which the stockholders live. But the areas in which the businesses are located have a reasonable claim—and often a great necessity—for revenues from them, whereas the areas of residence of the stockholders may have very much less need.

While a tax on net wealth is not feasible at the local government level—the level at which some form of property tax is the only major type of tax which can be administered—this tax serves as a useful standard for analysis of present-day property taxes, and study of it may suggest reforms in the present property tax which will increase equity and reduce adverse economic effects.

## THE CAPITAL LEVY

Related to a tax on net wealth is the capital levy—a tax imposed upon all wealth, but only once. It is not a recurrent tax, like the net wealth tax or the usual property tax, but a "once and for all" levy. Chief attention to capital levies has generally been given in the periods immediately after wars, as a means of reducing the national debt in one drastic step. It is expected that such a tax would be paid not out of income but out of accumulated wealth.

The primary advantage of such a tax is that it would eliminate the need for continued use of other taxes at high levels to meet commitments on debt accumulated during the war period. Likewise, the tax would place a heavy burden on persons who had greatly increased their wealth as a result of the war and would, in a sense, eliminate a substantial amount of "fictitious" personal wealth, in the form of government bonds issued during the war. It was also argued that such a measure would aid in checking postwar inflation.

In practice, however, the difficulties created by such a tax are serious.

Many persons are unable to meet their liabilities from liquid assets and must sell property; the consequent depressing of prices causes serious inequities and disorganization in the economy. If all persons held sufficient government bonds to meet their liabilities, this problem would not be serious, since essentially the capital levy would merely wipe out a part of the debt. But this is by no means true. There are also tremendous problems of valuing property, which are of extreme importance because of the high rates necessary if the tax is to accomplish the intended purpose. The tendency of the tax to lower property prices complicates the task. Finally, if many persons must borrow to meet tax liability, the consequent expansion of credit may produce inflationary, rather than deflationary, effects. Since World War II, much less attention has been given to capital levies, partly because of increased recognition of the problems which they created and partly because it is now realized that continuation of the national debt has less serious effects than was once believed. The question of the debt will be considered in later chapters.

## REFERENCES

Only limited attention has ever been given to the possibility of a tax on net wealth.

Vickrey, W. *Agenda for Progressive Taxation*, pp. 362–66. New York: Ronald Press Co., 1947.

Rolph, E. R., and Break, G. F. *Public Finance*, chap. ix. New York: Ronald Press Co., 1961.

"Net Wealth Taxation," *Public Finance*, Vol. 15, Nos. 3 and 4 (1960).
A symposium volume on the question.

# Chapter 21

# TAXATION OF WEALTH: THE PROPERTY TAX

Taxation of wealth has played a major role in the over-all tax structures of the United States and Canada since colonial days. The taxes, however, have not been imposed on the net personal wealth of individuals but on all property, or certain types of property, regardless of ownership, and on gross value without deduction of any claims outstanding against the property. The property tax yields about 87 per cent of the tax revenues of the local governments in the United States and about 85 per cent in Canada. Many local units have no other tax sources than the property tax. This tax was once also a primary source of state revenue and an important one for the provinces, but these governments have now largely abandoned it. In recent years, only about 3 per cent of state revenues have been obtained from property taxes, much of this coming from taxes upon specific types of property, such as automobiles.

## DEVELOPMENT

In the United States the property tax originated in colonial days as a series of separate levies upon particular types of property, such as land, homes, carriages, and merchants' stocks of goods. During the early part of the last century the taxes were consolidated and extended to all property, to form what was called the *general property tax*. Theoretically, the tax applied to all property in a uniform fashion. The property, for administrative purposes, was grouped into three classes:

1. Real property: land and permanently attached improvements, such as buildings.

2. Tangible personal property: property which has intrinsic value, but is readily movable, in the sense that it is not attached permanently to real property. This category included such items as merchants' stocks of goods, household effects, vehicles, farm livestock, personal effects such as diamonds, etc.

3. Intangible personal property: property whose value rests not upon any intrinsic worth of the objects themselves but rather upon a claim against tangible property, ownership in tangible property, or means of acquiring tangible property. Bonds, stock, mortgages, notes, bank deposits, and money represent major classes of intangible property.

All of these classes were taxed at a uniform rate. To the extent that both tangible property and claims against it were taxed on a gross basis, double taxation resulted. Partly because of this feature but primarily because of the difficulties of locating intangible property for tax purposes, the tax gradually became, in fact, a tax on physical property. Eventually, most states adapted their laws to the realities of the situation, by exempting some or all intangible property or taxing it at a very low rate. Certain forms of tangible personal property are also often exempt.

In Canada the tax did not go through this cycle of widened and then narrowed scope. The Canadian property taxes have always been confined to tangible property and primarily to real property.

## PRESENT STRUCTURE

A brief description of the structure and operation of the present property taxes will provide a basis for an evaluation of their role in the tax structure.

### General Nature

The present-day property tax in the United States is in fact, and in many states by law, a tax upon tangible property, and largely on real property. In 1961, total assessed valuation of all taxable property in the United States was $367 billion, of which $310 billion consisted of real property and $57 billion of personal property, mostly tangible.[1] As a consequence, individuals for the most part escape any direct tax burden on intangible property, such as securities, cash, bank deposits, etc., which they own. On the other hand, property owned by corporations is taxed as well as that owned by individuals. The tax is applied to property regardless of the personal status of the owner, with a few exceptions. The tax is imposed upon gross value, without adjustment for any debts or claims which may be outstanding. Since the tax on real property is assessed against the property rather than against the owner, it becomes a lien upon

---

[1] See U.S. Department of Commerce, Bureau of the Census, *Assessed Value for Property Taxation* (Washington, D.C.: U.S. Government Printing Office, 1962). The real property figure given includes a small amount of state-assessed personal property of railroads and utilities.

the property, and liability passes with the title at the time of sale. Thus, if the tax is not paid prior to sale, the liability rests upon the new owner. In three major respects the property tax differs from the tax on net wealth discussed in the previous chapter:

1. Individuals are, with minor exceptions, taxed only upon their tangible property rather than upon all their wealth.

2. The tax is imposed upon gross value rather than upon the owner's equity, no allowance being made for debts outstanding.

3. The property of corporations is taxed directly rather than indirectly through the value of the securities outstanding.

No exemptions of small amounts of property are provided, with one exception. Six states allow so-called "homestead" exemptions of owner-occupied homes under a certain value; Florida is the best-known example. Fifteen states exempt homes owned by veterans so long as they do not exceed a certain value, a seriously objectionable policy since it benefits only those veterans who are able and willing to purchase homes rather than to rent. Several states authorize local governments to exempt new industries from tax for a period of years, a policy which could result in serious uneconomic location of new plants, and is self-defeating if widely extended. Studies suggest that the provisions have had little over-all effect on location.[2] The only general exemptions are those of property of governments and of religious and charitable organizations, and even these vary somewhat among the states.

### Steps in the Operation of the Tax

The administrative operation of the tax differs from that of all other levies in the tax structure. The operation can be explained most satisfactorily by outlining the various steps in the process.

1. *Assessment.* The first step is that of assessment of the property, that is, of the placing of a value for tax purposes upon all property in the taxing jurisdiction. This task is performed by a local tax assessor, frequently chosen by election. The assessor is typically a county official in the West and South,[3] and a township official in the East and in much of Canada. In some cases, cities assess property for the purposes of city taxes separately from the county or township assessment.

The initiative in the assessment of the real property rests with the assessor, who places a value upon all such property, using the title records

[2] See W. D. Ross, "Tax Concessions and Their Effects," *Proceedings of the National Tax Association for 1957*, pp. 216–24.

[3] Plus Ohio, Delaware, Maryland, and West Virginia.

of the property as a guide to the ownership. In most states the initiative in the assessment of personal property rests upon the taxpayer, who must file a statement of such property owned and place a value (subject to change by the assessor) upon it. Assessment is performed as of a certain date, usually early in the spring. Annual assessment is often required by law but rarely occurs in practice, the figure of the preceding year being carried on to the next.

2. *Review or Appeal.* The taxpayer has the right to appeal any assessment to a board of review, usually the county commissioners or a similar body sitting ex officio for this purpose for a few days during the year.[4] Following this appeal, the taxpayer may contest the assessment in court, but rarely is this action successful, unless the procedure of assessment has been faulty or the property is clearly assessed in excess of its sale value. The courts typically, but not universally, take the position that the property owner is not entitled to legal redress of assessment so long as his assessment does not exceed the percentage of value specified by law, even though his assessment may be relatively much higher than that of other property in the taxing jurisdiction. However, in 1957 the Supreme Court of New Jersey took the opposite position, in requiring assessors to raise the over-all level of assessment in conformity with the law.[5]

3. *Determination of the Tax Rate.* Once assessment is complete, the total assessed valuation of all property in each taxation jurisdiction—county, township, city, town, or village, school district, special district, etc.—is determined by totaling the individual assessments. Each of these jurisdictions then determines its own property tax rate by dividing the figure of the total assessed valuation in the area into the sum to be collected from the property tax. The rate, which is a percentage, is usually expressed as mills of tax per dollar of assessed value, or dollars per $100.

The figure set must not exceed the maximum rate allowed by state constitution or law, or city charter. Furthermore, in determining expenditures, the local legislative body will be influenced by political repercussions which may arise from any change in tax rate which will be required. Thus the process of determining the rate is not in fact merely a process of arithmetic, as might at first appear. If the planned expenditures require a tax rate which exceeds the legal or politically feasible limit, either the

---

[4] The unimportance of review is illustrated from Washington experience in the article by J. K. Hall, "Assessment Equalization in Washington," *National Tax Journal*, Vol. IX (December, 1956), pp. 302–25.

[5] For a survey of the question of judicial review of assessments, see the article by J. R. Hellerstein, "Judicial Review of Property Tax Assessments," *Tax Law Review*, Vol. XIV (March, 1959), pp. 327–52; and the May, 1962, issue of the *Harvard Law Review*, pp. 1374–95.

expenditures must be reduced, or other sources of revenue must be found. After the rate is ascertained, the legislative body of the respective governmental unit technically levies it. Each of the units follows this same procedure.

4. *Calculation of Each Tax Bill.* In most states, each of the local units in the area reports its rate to a county official, who then figures the total tax bill on each piece of property by summing the various rates (school district, city, county, etc.) to which the property is subject and applying this figure to the assessed value. The bill is then mailed to the owner. Payment is made to the appropriate official, usually the county treasurer, who in turn allocates the money to the various taxing jurisdictions.

5. *Treatment of Delinquency.* If the tax is not paid by the due date, the tax becomes a lien against the property, which is ultimately sold at public auction. The buyer usually receives only a temporary deed for a period of years, during which time the original owner has a chance to redeem the property by paying the taxes due and penalties. Eventually, in most states the buyer obtains a clear title, if no redemption occurs.

### State Assessment

At a relatively early date, it became apparent that local assessors could not adequately determine the value of segments of railroad lines and, later, public utility facilities within their jurisdictions. A five-mile stretch of railway line crossing a county has no value distinct from its role as a segment in the entire system. As a consequence, toward the end of the last century, most states assumed the task of assessing railways and in many states all public utility property. State assessment, often called central assessment, permitted the task to be performed by experts in the field and the use of the unit rule, that is, assessment of the entire railroad or utility as a unit. Following assessment, the property is allocated back to the local units, largely on a mileage basis, for taxation along with other property.

State assessment gave rise to numerous debates over the question of the appropriate method of valuing the property of the enterprises involved. The aim is to obtain a figure for which the property would be sold in an open market sale, but since such property rarely sells, the task of ascertaining a suitable figure is a troublesome one. The states stress the capitalization of earnings basis, largely on the premise that the selling price of a property basically depends upon the amount the property can earn. In order to insure some tax revenue from enterprises yielding no profit, an arbitrary minimum figure, per mile in the case of railways, is frequently employed for such companies. In 1961 the states assessed $28 billion of the total assessment of $367 billion.

### Defects in Administration

Of all major taxes, the property tax, as it actually operates, is the most poorly administered. The consequence is not only a loss in potential revenue at rates regarded as tolerable, but also gross inequity in distribution of burden. The difficulties are partly inherent in the tax, arising out of the use of a base which does not involve a market transaction and therefore requires administrative discovery of the taxable items and establishment of value figures. But they are also in part a result of failure to establish suitable administrative organization and procedures for the task.

In the first place, tangible personal property and such intangibles as remain subject to the tax escape assessment in large measure. Much personal property has no recorded title; taxpayers do not report it, and assessors make little serious effort to find it. In many jurisdictions, assessors seek to include only automobiles, a nominal amount of furniture, farm livestock, and merchants' inventories. Even cars frequently escape, despite the possibility of airtight control through requirement of payment of tax as a requisite for licensing, as is done in some states. The consequence of mass escape of personal property is gross discrimination in favor of persons who have relatively large amounts of personal property, and relative overtaxation of the owners of real property. The taxation of intangibles raises special problems discussed in a subsequent section; in the states in which intangibles are still nominally taxable at full rates, few get on the tax rolls, and almost all taxpayers commit perjury annually when they file their property tax returns.

Secondly, the assessment of all property, personal and real, is often highly unsatisfactory, with a wide range of variation in the ratios of assessed values to reasonable appraisal figures. A number of studies have been made of the assessment patterns, frequently by comparing assessed values with actual sale prices of pieces of property sold during the year; universally, they have shown a great variation in the ratios. One of the most complete studies was that made in conjunction with the 1957 Census of Governments.[6] For the purpose of measuring the variation, a coefficient of dispersion was developed; this is the percentage which the average of the deviations from the median ratio of the assessment ratios of properties sold during the period bears to the median ratio. Only 8 per cent of the areas studied had coefficients under 15, and over half had figures over 30; one sixth had figures in excess of 50 per cent.

[6] See F. L. Bird, *The General Property Tax: Findings of the 1957 Census of Governments* (Chicago: Public Administration Service, 1960).

The results of a typical study (of King County, Washington, which includes Seattle) are shown in Table 7. This Washington State study showed an over-all range of the ratio of assessed value to sale value on residential property from less than 2 per cent to over 900 per cent. Many of the state studies show substantial numbers of parcels of property assessed under 25 per cent, while many others in the same county are assessed at over 75 per cent. The consequence is gross inequity among various property owners. Some of the studies, including that of the 1957 Census of Governments, show a tendency for less expensive property to be assessed nearer sale value than more expensive property, but others show exactly the reverse. There is also frequently a tendency to assess some types of property relatively more heavily than others; the Washington survey, for example, shows that in the state as a whole, single-family dwellings are typically assessed at 19 per cent of sale value, while industrial property is assessed at 33 per cent. A similar tendency is found in the 1957 Census of Governments study. A few states—particularly New Jersey—notoriously overassess railroads.

TABLE 7

RATIOS OF ASSESSED VALUES TO SALES VALUES,
KING COUNTY, WASHINGTON
1953

| Ratio of Assessed Value to Sale Value | Number of Properties |
| --- | --- |
| Under 10 | 857 |
| 10– 20 | 3,601 |
| 20– 30 | 586 |
| 30– 40 | 132 |
| 40– 50 | 62 |
| 50– 60 | 27 |
| 60– 70 | 12 |
| 70– 80 | 15 |
| 80– 90 | 8 |
| 90–100 | 5 |
| Over 100 | 36 |

SOURCE: State of Washington, Report of the Subcommittee on Revenue and Taxation of the Washington State Legislative Council, *A Study of Real Property Assessments in the State of Washington*, 1953, p. 17–2.

Another feature of poor asessment is a chronic tendency toward gross underassessment. This is shown in a number of state studies; in California, for example, in 1955, the typical ratio of assessed to sale value was 22 per cent; in Washington in 1956, 20 per cent. The Census of Governments study for 1957, with a nationwide sample involving 700,000 pieces of property, found the over-all typical assessment for residential property to be 30 per cent of sale value, with a range from 7 per cent in South Carolina to 66 per cent in Rhode Island.[7] In eighteen states the figure is under 20 per cent.

[7] *Ibid.*, p. 39.

Underassessment is a product of several factors. Assessors feel that they cultivate good will if they underassess (although it does the taxpayer no good, unless his property is underassessed more than the average), and they wish to make sure that the assessments do not go over 100 per cent of sale values. Failure to reappraise property at frequent intervals has resulted in a lag of assessed values behind rapidly increasing sale values. When the states used property taxes, the counties had a further reason for undervaluing, namely, to lessen the burden of state property tax (which was levied on the local assessed valuations) on residents of the county. In some states, greater underassessment increases school-aid grants for the locality. Underassessment, in itself, is not inequitable; it merely results in higher tax rates. But individual inequities are greater the higher the degree of underassessment, as shown by the 1957 Census of Governments study, in part because the assessors lack well-defined figures as a goal. General underassessment robs the taxpayer of any effective review of his individual assessment in most cases and may deprive the local governments of needed revenue when there are rigid tax-limit laws.

As noted above, poor assessment and consequent inequity are in part results of the inherent difficulties—of finding personal property, and of placing values on property, particularly those of types which do not sell frequently. But a large part of the trouble is the result of the methods of selection of assessing personnel and the procedures of assessment used. The assessing unit in a number of states is the township, a unit which is often too small to allow the use of full-time personnel. The assessment is thus performed on a part-time basis by a person whose main interests are in other pursuits. Even in the larger cities and in the counties of the western and southern states, the personnel have often been unqualified. The assessor himself is almost always elected, and his subordinates have in many cases been selected on a political basis. Only in recent years have personnel been selected and retained on a merit basis, and as yet only in limited areas. The assessors have worked largely on a guesswork basis, with only gradual introduction of scientific appraisal methods developed long ago by banks, building and loan companies, and the like.

One of the greatest sources of difficulty has been the failure to revise assessments from year to year. Even when the law requires annual reassessment, assessors tend to continue to use the same assessment, year after year, sometimes for decades.

### Improvements in Administration

Great strides have been made in recent years in property tax administration, although much remains to be done. A gradual trend toward improved selection of assessment personnel and toward use of better methods of tax assessment has been evident. Scientific appraisal techniques have been introduced and extensive reappraisal programs undertaken. Where the township is the unit of assessment, increased assistance has sometimes been given by the county to the township assessors.

Apart from the locally initiated improvements, the states have played an increasingly important role in improving local assessments. For many years the state activity was confined to assessment of railroads and utilities, and equalization of assessment levels among counties. Equalization, which was designed to prevent competitive undervaluation by counties to lessen state property tax burden, was largely abandoned as the states eliminated their own property taxes. The increased state participation in recent years has involved increased aid for local assessment rather than any significant increase in state assessment. In part, this aid consists of the holding of schools for assessors, preparation of assessors' manuals, and the like. Other states have gone farther in offering direct assistance in assessment, in some instances providing personnel to aid in general reappraisal programs. Some states, including Washington, have gone still farther, in attempting to force local assessors to reappraise all property, under supervision of state agencies.

There has also occurred substantial revival of interest in state equalization by county, in an effort to obtain more uniform valuation throughout the state and lessen individual inequities. Even without a state property tax, intercounty uniformity is desirable to insure equity between centrally assessed utility property and locally assessed property, and to permit equitable allocation of equalizing grants of state funds to local school districts in the systems in which local property valuation is a factor in determining the share for each district. The need for such equalization has been revealed by the work of tax study commissions in several states, which showed great intercounty variation, as well as great individual inequity. California, in which no effective state equalization had been attained in many years, commenced in 1955 to require changes in assessment levels in various counties to bring them to the state-wide average. The program was bitterly criticized by some groups, particularly by persons who thought that the program increased their tax bills.[8]

In Illinois a somewhat similar system was placed in operation in 1947. The state revenue department was authorized to increase the general level of assessment in each county to bring the level to 100 per cent valuation; in carrying out the program, however, the department has,

[8] See the article by Ronald Welch, "Intercounty Equalization in California," *National Tax Journal*, Vol. X (March and June, 1957), pp. 57–66, 148–57. A South Dakota equalization program proved to be so unpopular that the legislature in 1957 severely limited the equalization powers of the state board.

from all indications, aimed in recent years at 55 per cent of sale value.

These programs require state determination of the ratio of typical assessed values to commercial values. The determination in some states is made on the basis of a sample study of properties actually sold during the period. In California a scientifically selected sample was subjected to careful direct appraisal by the state. While state equalization in itself does not eliminate individual inequities in assessment within counties, it does help to lessen them, because with the higher over-all ratios, those properties relatively overassessed have a better chance of attaining readjustment, since the overassessment is much more obvious. If typical 100 per cent assessment could be attained, the system would be much more effective in lessening inequities, since the owner of any property assessed in excess of 100 per cent could obtain revision relatively easily. But in no states have the taxing authorities actually had the courage to attempt 100 per cent valuation—even though this is typically required by state law.

Despite these developments, there is much room for additional improvement. While it is not possible to consider this question in detail, several general lines of reform particularly appear to offer chances of success.

1. Transfer of assessment from the townships to larger units. Unfortunately, the political pressures against this shift are tremendous in some states. Iowa has been one of the first to make the change.

2. Elimination of duplicating assessment by counties and cities where this practice is still followed.

3. Increased selection of assessing personnel on a merit basis.

4. Further use of scientific appraisal techniques, with additional attention to tangible personal property, which has been largely neglected in recent assessment reform programs.

Regardless of the reforms, perfect assessment can never be obtained, in light of the inherent problems of valuation. But a much better result can be attained than has been typical in the past.

## SHIFTING AND INCIDENCE

The analysis of shifting of the property tax must be made in terms of the various classes of property which are subject to the tax. No over-all generalizations are possible, because the shifting of some portions will differ substantially from that of others.

### Owner-Occupied Homes

Shifting of the tax upon owner-occupied homes would appear to be impossible. Certainly, there is no direct way in which the owner can shift the tax to persons to whom he sells his own factor services. The only possible way in which shifting could come about is via changes in the selling prices of the homes. The direct anticipated burden of the tax may deter some persons from buying their own homes; the lessened demand for houses would tend to depress somewhat the prices of existing houses and, by lessening the demand for sites for houses, lessen the land value element. Thus, subsequent buyers would be freed of some of the burden. The effects along these lines are not likely to be significant, since persons must have a place to live and the rents which they pay if they do not buy will reflect the landlord's tax. But there may be some net reduction in demand for separate homes and sites for them, because the tax encourages persons to get along with less expensive housing. Prices of new houses are not likely to be affected unless the land value element is reduced, because the prices must cover costs of construction.

### Rental Housing

The property tax upon rental housing is a direct expense to the landlord, one which he must cover over a period of time if he is to continue to supply housing accommodations. Accordingly, the tax tends to shift forward to the tenants, in proportion to the rent which they are paying. There are, however, certain exceptions.

1. If there is a relative oversupply of rental housing units, the income of the landlord will be below the figure which will allow a normal return. Accordingly, property tax increases will be difficult to shift, so long as the supply remains excessive.

2. The portion of the tax which rests upon the land value rather than on the cost of the buildings will be difficult to shift, since dwelling units in poorer locations will not be subject to comparable tax. The share of income going to the landowner will tend to fall, and the tax will in part be capitalized, as discussed in the section below dealing with land rent.

3. On the other hand, if rental housing is very scarce and landlords are able to earn much more than a normal return, increases in property taxes may not result in full increases in rentals, for the same reason that monopolists will not shift a tax on their net income.

### Income-Producing Land

The most complete discussions of shifting of the property tax have dealt with the portions of the tax on income-producing land, narrowly defined as indestructible resources of which a fixed supply is available. It is generally argued that the tax will tend to capitalize, that is, to reduce, the selling price of the land by the capitalized sum of the tax. Thus, if a parcel of land has been yielding an annual net income of $400, its selling price would have been roughly $8,000, if 5 per cent is considered by investors to be the appropriate return on investments of this degree of risk and liquidity. But if a tax of $100 is imposed on the value of the land, the net yield will be cut to $300—under the assumption that no forward shifting is possible—and the selling price will drop to $6,000. The future burden, as well as the present, is on the person owning the land when the tax is imposed or the rate is increased, as subsequent owners are in a sense freed of the burden because they were able to buy the land at a lower price. Capitalization will occur only if two assumptions are realized:

1. The tax cannot be shifted. This is likely to be true under purely competitive conditions. The tax on the land itself will not affect the supply of land, which is perfectly inelastic, nor the output upon it, and thus prices of the products will not increase. But under other circumstances, if the various firms treat the portion of the tax on the land as an expense, they may succeed in shifting it forward.

2. The over-all rate of return on capital is not affected. If the income from all types of investments were reduced by the property tax, the percentage return on the basis of which the land yield is capitalized will be lower, and the land value will not necessarily fall. Suppose, for example, that the average rate of return is reduced from 5 to 4 per cent by a property tax which reduces the net yield on a particular piece of land from $1,000 to $800. The capitalized value of $800 at 4 per cent is the same as the capitalized value of $1,000 at 5 per cent. But the present property tax does not reach all types of property, and the burden on some types is almost certain to be reflected in higher consumer prices. Accordingly, the over-all return may not be reduced materially, and at least some capitalization can occur.

To the extent to which capitalization occurs, persons owning the land at the time the tax is imposed, or when the rate is increased, are burdened not only with the tax they pay but also with the reduction in the selling price which occurs. If they sell, the purchaser is in a sense freed of the tax burden, since he is able to obtain the property at a lower price than otherwise. The imperfections in the markets for land, however, are so great that exact adjustments of this type are very unlikely.

Just as the tax on land may capitalize, so may the tax on capital improvements during a relatively short period. When purely competitive market conditions prevent immediate forward shifting, the reduced rate of earnings on the capital goods will result in a decline in their selling prices. If they are sold, persons buying them are thus freed of the property tax burden during the remainder of the life of the goods, because the buyers were able to acquire them at prices lower than otherwise. Over a period of time, however, the supply of capital goods will fall, and forward shifting and restoration of a normal rate of return on the capital invested will result, as explained in the following section.

### Other Business Property

A substantial portion of the property tax rests upon capital goods, including buildings, used in production. Since the tax is a direct expense, in nonpurely competitive markets immediate shifting of the tax is likely to be the rule, except to the extent that some firms are burdened more than others per dollar of sales. Firms in a high-tax area cannot shift the differential portion of the burden upon them with any ease, and over a period of time will tend to move out of the area. Actually, property taxes are usually such small elements in cost that they are not likely to have much influence on location, except in encouraging firms to build outside city limits.

To the extent that the tax is shifted, it will rest upon the consumers of the products in relation to their expenditures on the goods produced, and thus is borne in much the same way as a sales tax. Since the ratio of property employed to sales will vary widely in different industries, the final burden will vary greatly among expenditures on different commodities. Thus the incidence is in part similar to that of excises.

### Shifts in Rate of Return

The property tax bears very unequally on various types of property, and therefore produces shifts from one type of property holdings to another. Real property, generally, is made less attractive relative to many intangibles. The result will be some increase in the prices (decrease in yield) of intangibles, and declines in the prices of real property. Thus, some of the burden passes off onto the holders of untaxed property, and a portion is removed from the owners of the taxed form.

Since cash is not actually subject to tax, the advantage of liquidity relative to the types of property reached by the tax becomes greater, with possible effects on the rate of return. But the availability of untaxed income-yielding property lessens the significance of this reaction compared to that with a net wealth tax.

## EVALUATION OF THE PROPERTY TAX

The case for the property tax must be considered in terms of four factors: revenue requirements of the local governments; equity, in terms of both ability and benefit principles; economic effects; and administrative feasibility.

## Local Government Revenue Needs

The property tax has for many years been the mainstay of local government finances. In 1961, local governments in the United States collected $17.2 billion from property taxes. Many local units, such as school districts, have no tax sources at all except the property tax. Relatively few taxes are suitable for local government use, in light of administrative and economic considerations. Local income, sales, or excise taxes of any magnitude are difficult to enforce adequately, and lead to migration of population and business activity outside the taxing jurisdictions. These taxes are also extensively utilized by the higher levels of government. A property tax, centering on real property, is almost imperative for the local governments if they are to retain some financial autonomy.

## Equity Considerations—Ability

The case for property taxation on an ability basis is essentially the same as that for a general net wealth tax outlined in the previous chapter. Wealth, as manifested by property ownership, is a measure of economic well-being, and partial use of this basis serves to offset the discrimination of income taxation in favor of persons who have accumulated wealth. Particularly, the tax places a more equitable burden on persons who place their wealth in expensive homes instead of income-yielding investments reached by the income tax.

However, as the tax actually operates, it is substantially different from a true net wealth tax; and as a consequence, much of the equity is lost.

1. *Application to Certain Types of Wealth Only.* The fundamental difficulty with the tax from an equity standpoint is its application to the gross value of only certain forms of wealth, rather than to all wealth on a net basis. No adjustment is made for debt outstanding against property, and thus a person with a $2,000 equity in a $20,000 home will pay the same property tax as a person owning a home of equivalent value debt-free. Furthermore, the tax concentrates on real property and some types of personal property. Thus, persons with their wealth in intangibles go largely tax-free. The tax on corporate real property is likely to shift to

the consumers of the products sold by the firm, rather than resting on the stockholders. To the extent that the stockholders are burdened, the relative amounts on ones in different companies will vary widely. Since the holders of bonds, mortgages, cash, bank deposits, and the like will bear little or no burden, in no respect does the property tax accomplish a major goal of a tax on wealth, that of placing a greater relative share of the total tax burden on the persons who have considerable wealth in forms which yield little or no cash income subject to the income taxes.

The tax does have the merit of placing a heavier tax burden on persons who have a relatively large share of their total wealth in their homes. But the property tax does not equalize the tax burden satisfactorily between the average tenant and homeowner, since the tenant is typically burdened with the property tax collected from his landlord.

2. *Regressiveness.* The burden of the property tax is probably distributed in a regressive fashion. A large portion rests upon housing expenditures, which are typically believed to be regressive relative to income.[9] Much of the remainder of the tax rests upon business firms and is shifted forward in large measure to the consumers of the products. Accordingly, this portion of the tax tends to be regressive for the same reason that sales taxes are regressive and, in addition, places a very unequal burden on the consumption of different commodities.

Figure 28 presents the estimated distribution of the entire property tax burden by income class in the United States, as developed in the Musgrave study of distribution of tax burden by income class for 1954. A more detailed 1948 study shows the portions of the property tax on owner-occupied residences, personal property, rental housing, and business improvements to be distributed in a regressive fashion throughout the income scale, while that on farm and business land (which is assumed not to be shifted) is progressive in the higher income brackets.[10] The over-all distribution is highly regressive. Figure 29 shows the relative expenditures for housing (rental and owner-occupied) by income class in Canada.

The tendency toward regressiveness will be increased if assessors tend to underassess more expensive houses to a greater degree than cheaper houses.

3. *Burden on Persons with Small Current Cash Incomes.* With present-day property taxes the burden on persons who own their homes

---

[9] This conclusion is disputed by the work of Margaret G. Reid; see her recently published *Housing and Income* (Chicago: University of Chicago Press, 1962).

[10] See R. A. Musgrave *et al.*, "Distribution of Tax Payments by Income Group," *National Tax Journal*, Vol. IV (March, 1951), p. 37.

FIGURE 28

DISTRIBUTION OF PROPERTY TAX PAYMENTS BY
INCOME CLASS, UNITED STATES, 1954

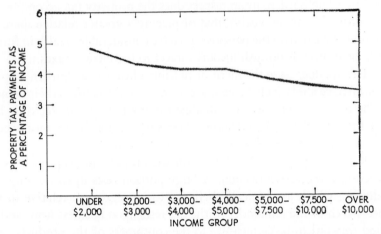

SOURCE: R. A. Musgrave, "The Incidence of the Tax Structure and Its Effects on Consumption," in Joint Committee on the Economic Report, *Federal Tax Policy for Economic Growth and Stability* (Washington, D.C.: U.S. Government Printing Office, 1955, p. 98.

FIGURE 29

HOUSING EXPENDITURES AS A PERCENTAGE OF
TOTAL FAMILY EXPENDITURES BY
INCOME GROUP, CANADA, 1948

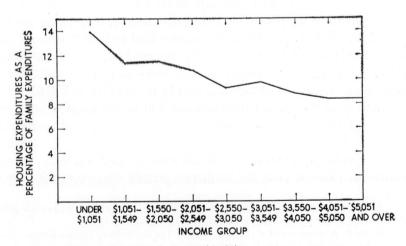

SOURCE: Data compiled by Canada, Bureau of Statistics.

but have small current cash incomes is substantial. The burden is particularly felt by older persons living on accumulated savings or pensions, as well as by widows with small children and by many persons during a depression period. It may be argued, of course, that these persons are better off than others who have the same incomes but do not own their homes. This is true, of course, but nevertheless the hardships placed upon these persons may be very severe. If their cash incomes fall below certain figures, they have essentially no taxpaying ability unless they sell their homes. A tax policy which compels them to do so is generally regarded as highly inequitable and socially undesirable. During the thirties, so many families were unable to meet property tax payments that the states were finally compelled to ease their laws relating to the sale of property for tax delinquency.

Under a net wealth tax operated in conjunction with the income tax, this problem could be met with an exemption based on the amount of property or on the amount of income. With the usual form of property tax, however, a solution is very difficult to find. A few states have provided homestead exemptions, which exclude from the tax owner-occupied homes of less than a certain value. But this approach discriminates against the tenant who bears property tax in the rent which he pays. It likewise creates very serious problems for those municipalities in which most of the property consists of homes of values below the exemption figure. Since there is no completely satisfactory solution, the argument for holding down property tax rates so that the burden on the low-income groups will be tolerable is strengthened.

4. *Inequity from Poor Administration.* Finally, as noted in preceding sections, poor administration has allowed large amounts of tangible personal property to escape tax completely, and has brought great inequities of assessment and thus of tax payments among the owners of real property. The situation has improved somewhat, but even so, such equity as the tax might otherwise have is seriously reduced by the poor administration.

*Summary.* As the property tax actually operates, it deviates from usually accepted standards of ability to pay in many ways, producing serious discrimination among various persons on the basis of the type of property they own and the specific treatment they receive at the hands of the assessors, and tending to be regressive in over-all distribution of burden. It fails completely to attain the goals of wealth taxation of reaching wealth which yields limited or no current return more effectively than income taxation, and while it does reach wealth in the form of homes, it does not adjust for varying degrees of debt outstanding, and it does not equalize burden between tenant and homeowner.

### Equity—The Benefit Principle

As an ability-based tax, the property tax is seriously inequitable. But it may be argued that to some extent the tax can be justified on the benefit principle, in terms of which the concentration on real property and the use of the gross basis can be justified (but not, of course, the uneven assessment). A considerable portion of local government activity directly benefits property, in the sense that if the activities were not carried on, the property owners would have to provide the services themselves or incur great risks or nuisance.

Fire protection is an excellent example, as well as sewer construction and operation, drainage facilities, sidewalk and street improvements, street lighting, and a portion of police protection. Both individual homeowners and business firms directly benefit from these activities. The benefit is not necessarily in direct proportion to the value of the property but can be presumed to be roughly so.

In this situation the two conditions necessary for the employment of the benefit principle are fulfilled: Benefit can be measured reasonably well, and no serious inequity, in terms of accepted standards, will result, so long as the expenditures involved are kept at such levels that the burden is moderate relative to incomes. From the standpoint of economic effects, the assessment of the costs of these activities against business firms on the benefit basis has a definite advantage. Optimum allocation of resources in the economy requires that the costs to society of rendering the services should also appear as costs to the business firms which are responsible for the need for them and thus enter into the prices of the finished products. For example, the building of a new factory requires extension of sewer lines, new streets and sidewalks, and additional fire and police protection. If these services were not provided by the town, the business enterprise would have to provide them at its own expense. The costs of providing the services are real costs for society which arise out of the particular business activity, and assessment of the charges against the firm is justified, in terms of best use of resources.

### Limited Scope of the Benefit Principle

The benefit basis for property taxation is applicable only for the financing of those activities which directly benefit property owners as such in dollar-and-cents terms, such as police and fire protection, streets, sidewalks, lighting, sewerage facilities, and the like. The "benefit to property owners" basis cannot be used as a justification for financing the costs of education by the property tax, since there is no direct relationship between the ownership of property and the benefits gained from education. The long-standing tradition in both the United States and Canada of financing education from property levies is largely a product of circumstances rather than logic. Education was regarded as a local government function, and its provision was placed in the hands of school districts, which had no other tax source except the property tax. But the use of the levy for this purpose can be based only upon the ability principle, and, as indicated, the tax is so defective from the standpoint of ability that the case for its use—on the basis of any other consideration than financial expediency—is very weak. One unfortunate result of financing education on the basis of property ownership is that in many rural districts a large part of the costs of education is borne by the railroads, and thus in large measure ultimately by the shippers and their customers. The final incidence is distributed in a completely haphazard manner, unrelated to ability.

### Economic Effects

From the standpoint of economic effects, the property tax has the general advantage over income-based levies that it does not place a direct burden on the results of current economic activity, and thus may have less adverse effects upon incentives toward economic activity. However, the property tax is likely to have greater effects than a net wealth tax in influencing business decisions, largely because it is imposed upon corporation property, as such, rather than being confined to the net wealth of individuals. The tax lessens the profitability of some marginal projects which will create heavy property tax liability. More significantly, the tax increases the relative costs of those lines of production which require particularly large amounts of taxable property per dollar of sales, increases the prices of these products, and thus may cause an uneconomic curtailment of their output. Particularly, the tax will tend to curtail the relative production of housing facilities, which give rise to large property tax liability. Individuals will be encouraged to invest less in their housing and increase their consumption of other goods and services which do not give rise to comparable tax liability. These consequences are undesirable in terms of generally accepted social values, except to the extent to which the property taxes reflect higher governmental costs (such as for streets or fire protection) incurred as a result of the existence of the particular property.

In addition to these effects, the differences in tax rates in various areas create artificial barriers to the most economic location of industry, unless the higher property taxes are offset by comparable increases in government services of direct benefit to the industries involved or are offset by lower burdens of other taxes. Business firms are encouraged to locate their stores and factories outside large cities in surrounding rural low-tax areas.

One of the most serious effects of the higher property tax rates in larger cities is the encouragement given persons to build homes in suburban areas outside the city limits. This very widespread tendency aggravates the tax problems of the large cities, increases the total cost of governmental services, and interferes with effective planning of the development of government facilities. The belief that lower taxes can be obtained by building outside the city often proves to be a delusion, as various special districts must be formed to supply services and any initial tax saving is often quickly offset by higher fire insurance and sewage disposal costs.[11] But the belief that there will be a saving influences the behavior of many persons. Some of the most critical present-day problems of metropolitan areas have been produced by this tax-stimulated migration outside the city limits.

A final effect of property taxes arises from the relative lack of responsiveness of property tax yields to changes in national income, particularly because property assessments tend to lag behind changes in sales values. As a consequence, fluctuations in economic activity are aggravated. Continued high property tax collections in depressions take purchasing power that would otherwise be spent and also cause serious individual sacrifices. In inflationary periods the lag in property tax collections creates problems for the local governments and aggravates the inflationary tendencies.

## REFORMS IN THE PROPERTY TAX

Readjustment of the property tax to bring it in line with a logical tax on net wealth and improve the over-all equity of the tax structure would require the extension of the tax to all intangibles, the exemption of corporate property, the allowance of subtraction of debts owed, and greatly improved assessment standards. But changes of these types (except the last noted) are impossible so long as the tax remains a local levy. The changes are not administratively feasible and would result in an extremely

---

11 For a sample study, see R. B. Andrews and J. J. Dasso, "The Influence of Annexation on Property Tax Burden," *National Tax Journal*, Vol. XIV (March, 1961), pp. 88–97.

unsatisfactory redistribution of tax revenue among various local units.

So long as the property tax remains a local levy—and almost of necessity it will—it must continue to be largely an *in rem* tax, levied on physical property without respect to the owners, and intangibles must receive some form of special treatment. The difficulties of the tax have long been recognized, and some reforms have been instituted and others considered. Administrative reforms, of utmost importance, have been discussed in a preceding section, and do not require reconsideration here. Other reforms include the limitation of the height of property tax burdens, the provision of special treatment of intangibles, and possible classification and differential treatment of other property.

### Restrictions on Property Tax Burdens

Continued increases in the tax rates result in increasingly severe burdens on low-income homeowners and unreasonable distribution of total tax burden on the basis of ownership of particular types of wealth. With full-value assessment a $2 tax rate results in an annual tax burden of $200 on a $10,000 house—certainly a modest dwelling at present-day price levels. For a retired couple living on a pension of $2,000, for example, this tax is a very significant expense. Local government expenditures today have typically reached levels which cannot be financed by property taxes at tolerable rates.

In an effort to check property tax increases, almost all states have imposed property tax rate limitation laws. They may be divided roughly into two classes. The first, or over-all, limitations, such as those imposed in Ohio and West Virginia, are established by provisions of the state constitutions and set a maximum combined rate (the sum of the rates of all the taxing jurisdictions in which a piece of property is located) which may apply to any piece of property. The second type, established usually by state legislation, establishes separate limits for each type of local governmental unit (school district, city, etc.). These are much more flexible than the over-all limits and are changed from time to time. Even the more rigid type is subject to some flexibility, since the limits may often be exceeded by a sufficient vote.

The tax limitation laws have by no means been fully successful, although they have exercised a restraining influence on property tax rates. The flexible type has done little harm but, on the other hand, has exercised only a mild restraining influence. This form has sometimes resulted in the multiplication of special districts, formed to perform particular tasks when the existing units reached their tax rate limits. The more rigid over-all limitations, on the other hand, have in a sense accomplished too much.[12] They have prevented local governments from obtaining adequate revenues to provide the services demanded and have resulted in excessive borrowing, failure to retire debt, use of other taxes unsuited for local governments, and, in limited instances, the crippling of vital services.

The primary weakness of the rate limitation programs has been their failure to provide substitute revenues. The limitation of the property tax burden, however desirable in itself, results in an intolerable situation if it prevents the local governments from raising funds necessary to carry on the functions which the residents desire. If the limitations are flexible, they will not be effective at all if no other sources are provided, because the pressures against them will bend them. If they are rigid, the consequences are likely to be worse than the high property tax burden. The additional revenue must come primarily from state assistance, since so few taxes can be administered effectively and without adverse economic effects at the local level.

### Special Treatment of Intangibles

The general property tax in its original form applied both to real property and to intangible property. As a consequence, when property had debt outstanding against it, or was owned by a corporation, the tax applied twice—to the real property, and to the evidences of indebtedness or title representing it. Thus the mortgaging of a house would give rise to additional property tax liability, even though the amount of wealth had not increased at all. The incorporating of a business potentially doubled the property tax liability of its owners. Such treatment constituted discriminatory double taxation in its worst form. Partly because of the obvious inequity, and partly because intangibles were so easy to conceal from the assessor, few intangibles ever reached the tax rolls. The pressure to conceal them was increased by the fact that ultimately tax rates reached levels which would more than confiscate the earnings from bank deposits, bonds, and the like so long as they were assessed at or near full value. Since the prices of these were obvious in many cases, there was less tendency to undervalue them than tangible property, and so when they were caught, the tax was extremely severe. Thus, gradually assessors ceased to look for the intangibles, and they disappeared almost completely from tax rolls, except for a very few unfortunate persons.

---

[12] A study of the effects of the West Virginia limitation, one of the most rigid, is to be found in H. J. Shamberger and J. H. Thompson, *Operation of the Tax Rate Limitation in West Virginia* (Morgantown: University of West Virginia Bureau of Business Research, 1950), summarized in the article by J. H. Thompson, "Effects of Property Tax Limitation in West Virginia," *National Tax Journal*, Vol. IV (June, 1951), pp. 129–38.

From the standpoint of the logic of a wealth tax, reform would have involved exemption of the real property and the taxation of the intangibles. Homes, for example, would be taxed to the owner to the extent of his equity in it, and to the mortgage holder to the extent of the mortgage (a practice which a few states tried). Corporate property, as such, would have been exempted, and tax applied to the securities held by the stock and bond holders. But this approach was completely impossible from an administrative standpoint for the local governments, and so the states proceeded to provide special treatment of intangibles. Many states have exempted some or all intangibles completely, while others have subjected them to low rates, in an effort to keep them in the tax base and obtain some revenue from their owners.[13] The general philosophy is that a low-rate tax avoids the objectionable multiple taxation of the use of the full rate and encourages persons to report the intangibles, which they will not do and often cannot afford to do if the intangibles are subject to the regular rate. The success of these programs has been somewhat limited. Without question, more intangibles are reported when they are subject to a low tax rate than when the regular property tax rate applies. This is clearly demonstrated, for example, by the Ohio experience, in which various studies have indicated that the majority of intangibles were reported.[14] with over 10 per cent of the property tax yield from this source. However, complete listing is still difficult to attain, especially if a long tradition of failure to report has grown up. If the state uses an income tax, the earnings from intangibles can be reached more satisfactorily by this means. If no income tax is used, the case for a low-rate tax on intangibles is stronger. Certainly, it is greatly to be preferred to the futile and undesirable attempt to include intangibles within the scope of the general property tax.

### Special Treatment of Tangible Personal Property

The effectiveness of enforcement of the tax on tangible personal property is typically much less than on real property. Some forms, such as jewelry, are difficult for the assessor to find, and others, such as used furniture, are difficult to value. Assessment depends in large measure upon the honesty of the taxpayer, and when it is widely known that much property of this sort is not on the rolls, even the most honest person is inclined to "forget" to report some of his property. As a consequence, Delaware, New York, and Pennsylvania exempt all such property from tax, and

---

[13] Only seven states subject intangibles to the general property tax rate. Fourteen states tax them at lower rates.

[14] See G. W. Thatcher, "Taxation of Intangible Personal Property in Ohio," *National Tax Journal*, Vol. IV (December, 1951), pp. 351–61.

some forms are exempted in a number of other states. There is a wide variation in the ratio of personal to total assessed property, ranging from none in the three states named and 3 per cent in Maryland to 45 per cent in South Carolina. Nineteen states exempt motor vehicles from the tax.

There are, however, good reasons for including major classes of tangible personal property within the tax. Motor vehicles represent a particularly suitable basis for taxation, since many families own automobiles but have little other taxable wealth. In general, the broader the base of the property tax, the lower the rates, and the less discrimination against those persons whose wealth is concentrated in real property. An effective enforcement program can increase the amount of personal property on the tax rolls substantially; there is no excuse for escape of motor vehicles, since the taxation can be linked up with the issuance of licenses.

### General Classification

A few states—Minnesota and Montana particularly—have carried classification much further. In these states, property is grouped into several classes, such as urban and farm land, improvements, mining property, personal effects, intangibles, etc., and different effective rates are applied to the various classes. The basic intent was to bring the tax more in line with "taxable capacity." Actually, there is little logic to the classifications used. Those types of property, such as household furnishings, which are considered to show little capacity are ones whose taxation is particularly justifiable, because they do not yield money income subject to the income tax. More seriously, there is no conceivable way in which different tax capacity can be determined for various property, except on a basis of income. If this were accepted as the criterion, an income tax would be preferable. As a practical matter, any general classification almost certainly will give rise to endless political disputes over relative burdens, and the latter will be determined on the basis of political influence of various groups, rather than on standards of tax policy.

### Special Treatment of Certain Types of Property

Distinct from general classification is the policy of providing special treatment of certain types of property which give rise to difficulties if the general property tax is applied to them. In most cases the intent is not so much to alter the burden on the property, but to provide a more satisfactory procedure for taxing it. Major examples of special treatment are noted below.

1. *Forest Property.* The property tax has never been entirely satisfactory when applied to commercial timber holdings. The levying of a

property tax each year on standing timber encourages premature cutting and, in some instances, logging of all trees, large and small, followed by abandonment of the property. As a consequence, poor utilization of natural resources results, and the tax base is destroyed. Some of the most serious cases of tax delinquency have been encountered in areas with large acreages of cutover timberland. In order to avoid these consequences, several states which have extensive forest lands have made special provisions for taxing this property, with adjustment of tax burden primarily in terms of yield, and a very small burden on the standing timber itself.[15] Recent studies suggest that this procedure is less satisfactory than improved treatment of forest land within the framework of the property tax.

2. *Mining Property.* In part, the same problems are encountered with mines as with forests. But the primary difficulty with taxation of mines, especially precious metal mines, is the determination of the value of the property, in view of the fact that the size of the ore bodies is not usually known. As a consequence, a number of mining states have provided special measures for mine taxation. In some cases the value is determined as a multiple of the annual proceeds from operations (gross or net), and the general property tax rate is applied. In other cases the output is taxed on a per unit or proceeds basis by a direct *severance* tax independent of the property tax but designed to impose comparable burden. All these methods are somewhat arbitrary, but they are at least workable and do not encourage wasteful exploitation.

In addition to the levies used in lieu of the property taxes, a number of states apply additional severance taxes upon the output of mines and other extractive industries (except farming). These are designed to recover for the states an additional portion of the profits from the exploitation of exhaustible resources, over and above that collected from other taxes. These severance taxes have been subject to bitter debate in many states. On the one hand, they are defended as a means of providing a more equitable burden on those persons who profit from the development of scarce natural resources. On the other hand, they are condemned as obstacles to the production of minerals and oil.

3. *Banks.* In the United States the states have been seriously restricted in their taxation of banks by the fact that the national banks, being federally chartered, may be taxed only in the manner authorized by Congress. For many years the banks were taxed, under such authorization,

---

[15] For a recent review of the question, see E. T. Williams, "Trends in Forest Taxation," *National Tax Journal*, Vol. XIV (June, 1961), pp. 113–44.

For Canadian practice, see A. M. Moore, *Forest Tenures and Taxes in Canada* (Toronto: Canadian Tax Foundation, 1957).

on the value of their real estate plus the value of the shares of their stock. But those states which exempted other intangible property, or taxed it at low rates, were eventually denied the right to continue to tax bank shares at property tax rates, because the latter would be taxed at a higher rate than other "moneyed capital," in violation of the provisions of the federal legislation. In 1926, Congress authorized the states to apply franchise taxes measured by bank net income, a procedure now generally used. While the states are not restricted in the taxation of state-chartered banks, they have usually treated them in the same manner as the national banks. This problem with banks emphasizes once again the inherent difficulties in attempting to develop a logical *in rem* property tax. With a true net wealth tax, bank stock would be taxed to its owners, like any other investment, and no particular complications would arise.

4. *Insurance Companies.* The property tax places little burden on insurance companies as such, since they own little real property relative to their total assets. In order to obtain additional contributions from them, most states have introduced specific levies, as a rule on gross proceeds or gross premiums received. There is no particular logic in this procedure. Again, no entirely satisfactory application of the present type of property tax or any supplement to it is possible. Even the application of the income tax to insurance companies and insurance policy proceeds encounters fundamental problems of principle.

## CONCLUSIONS ON WEALTH AND PROPERTY TAXATION

A tax levied on all individuals—but only individuals—on their net wealth would be a useful complement to the income tax. It would increase the equity of the tax as between the holders of various forms of wealth and the earners of property and labor income. Such a tax would have less adverse incentive effect than the portion of the income tax it would replace. Some of these results, but not all of them, could be obtained by modifications in the income tax discussed in earlier chapters. There are, however, two serious obstacles in the way of the use of such a tax. Even if it were administered by the federal government, problems of enforcement, especially with respect to cash holdings, would be serious, although probably not insuperable. But it is the local governments which have urgent need of property tax revenues, and these governments could not possibly administer a tax on net wealth. If the present property tax were transferred to the federal level (a step which would require a constitutional amendment in the United States), the financial autonomy of the localities would be completely destroyed. On the other hand, to add a federal net wealth tax on top of the present local property taxes would increase the already excissive burden on certain types of property. Despite these serious obstacles, however, from a long-range point of view further consideration should be given to the possibility of a federal net wealth tax as a means of lessening some of the possible adverse effects of other forms of federal taxation on the economy.

The general property tax, as it stands, deviates from a net wealth tax in several respects. It taxes individuals on only a portion of their wealth and makes no allowance for debts, while it does apply to corporate property and is in part shifted, with much the same incidence as a sales tax. In part, it rests in an inequitable fashion on the owners of various businesses. Thus the tax departs very sharply from the ability principle, bearing heavily on persons who have put their wealth into real property, making no allowance for debts, allowing the owners of intangibles to go largely tax-free, and severely burdening persons with homes but little current income—a phenomenon of particular seriousness in depression periods. Such equity as the tax might have is lost in part through poor administration. The burden it places on housing unquestionably lessens the volume of housing facilities below the levels which would otherwise be attained, while, from a general social point of view, it is generally considered that increased, not decreased, housing facilities are desirable.

However, a portion of the property tax may be justified on the basis of the benefit principle, since the activities financed are of direct financial benefit to the property owners. Beyond this—and particularly with respect to the primary function of education—the present tax can be justified only on the basis of expediency; the local units cannot finance their activities by other means. So long as the tax remains in local hands, no general modification of the structure of the tax which would bring it more in line with an ability-based net wealth tax is feasible. The major improvement which can be made is that of further reform in assessment methods, to lessen individual inequities and place more personal property on the tax rolls. But the inherent limitations of the tax suggest that its rates must be kept within reasonable bounds, to insure against excessive burdens on those against whom the tax discriminates.

## APPENDIX I

### Special Assessments

The benefits of some of the local government services to particular property owners are so obvious that they are financed by direct charges rather than by the property tax. These charges, called *special assessments,* are imposed upon property owners to cover the costs of public improvements directly benefiting the property. They have some characteristics of both fees and taxes. Like the former, they are directly related to benefit and, as a rule, are not imposed (and the improvements are not made) unless the majority of the property owners involved approve. On the other hand, payment is compulsory once they are imposed. They are almost always assessed on a physical unit basis, as, for example, front footage of the lots in the case of street improvements, instead of on the value of the property. They are usually assessed against land only, with no consideration of improvements.

The special assessment system does have the merit of associating the charge with the benefit more closely than does the property tax basis, and especially of associating the benefits from a particular improvement with payment of the costs. The assessment of the entire burden on the basis of land is not without merit. However, special assessments result in a somewhat incomplete and irregular provision of the services; if street improvements are financed on this basis, there will be missing links—unpaved segments—in the street system which may be a source of great nuisance. Furthermore, the allocation of benefits is often difficult, the bases actually used being even more arbitrary than the value basis of the property tax. Perhaps the main objection to special assessments is the piecemeal approach which results with respect to the improvements. If, over a period of years, all, or almost all, of the streets in a city are to be paved, little is gained by assessing the costs of particular streets against the specific property owners involved. Since all persons will benefit over a period of time, the specific benefits from the paving of particular streets can be ignored and all improvements financed from general revenues.

Some inequity arises in an attempt to shift over from the present system to a general tax system, since those persons who have already paid for their improvements directly will also have to bear a portion of the costs of the improvements in other areas. There is, however, considerable merit in restricting the use of the assessment basis and financing the activities involved, so far as possible, on the basis of the property tax itself, viewed as a benefit-based tax.

## APPENDIX II

### *Special Features of Canadian Property Taxes*

The Canadian property tax never assumed the general, universal form of the United States taxes, being confined to tangible property.

There has also been a tendency over the years to eliminate tangible personal property, so that today the levy is imposed almost solely upon real estate. Some personal property, however, is taxed in the three maritime provinces and Manitoba. In the eastern provinces, land and improvements are taxed at the same rate. In the western provinces, however, improvements and land are differentiated, the former being taxed at a lower rate. The exact practice varies widely among the provinces. In part, the heavier taxation of land is a reflection of the desire to encourage improvements; in large measure, it is a product of the single-tax movement, which received wide acceptance in the western provinces early in the century.[16]

The assessment system is comparable to that in the United States, with much the same difficulties and inequities. One major exception to the use of the "value of property" basis is St. John's, Newfoundland, which levies its property tax on the annual income from the property, in conformity with the English tradition.

The assessors in Canada are usually municipal or township officials and are appointed rather than elected. The provinces have increased their assessment assistance to the localities in recent years, and in Saskatchewan, Prince Edward Island, British Columbia, and Manitoba, substantial assessment of local property is performed by the provinces themselves.

Most provinces supplement the property tax on real estate by occupancy taxes on business firms which are based upon the value of the property occupied but are collected in addition to the taxes paid by the owner upon the property itself. Rental value, floor space, and sales are used as the base in various provinces. The property tax rate is frequently employed as the basis for these occupancy taxes, the actual rate being varied according to the type of business. These taxes largely take the place of the taxation of the tangible personal property (chiefly inventories) of businesses in the United States.

[16] The single-tax movement, based upon the writings of Henry George, proposed use of a tax on land value as the sole source of government revenue. The plan was based upon the argument that increases in land values were the products of growth of the community and constituted a form of "unearned increment" or surplus, the taxation of which would have no adverse economic effects and would check the development of extreme inequality of wealth. At the same time, the freeing of improvements from tax would eliminate a major deterrent to economic growth.

The single-tax doctrine had considerable political appeal in the United States, but the only significant use of the plan in modified form has been in the city of Pittsburgh, which taxes land at a higher rate than improvements.

The taxation of land values rather than both land and improvements has been used extensively in Australia and New Zealand, in Kenya and Tanganyika, and in modified form in Rhodesia. See F. H. Finnis, "Site Valuation and Local Government," *Canadian Tax Journal*, Vol. 11 (March–April, 1963), pp. 118–26; and J. F. Due, "Taxation of Property in Developing Economies: The African Experience," *Land Economics*, Vol. 39 (February, 1963), pp. 1–14.

# REFERENCES

## GENERAL REFERENCES

BIRD, F. L.  *The General Property Tax: Findings of the 1957 Census of Govern-ments*. Chicago: Public Administration Service, 1960.

An excellent survey of the property tax.

JENSEN, J. P.  *Property Taxation in the United States*. Chicago: University of Chicago Press, 1931.

This is the outstanding discussion and analysis of the property tax. Although some of the descriptive material is out of date, the volume is still very useful for its analytical treatment.

MORTON, W. A.  *Housing Taxation*. Madison: University of Wisconsin Press, 1955.

An extensive study of property taxation as it applies to housing.

NEWCOMER, M.  "The Decline of the General Property Tax," *National Tax Jour-nal*, Vol. VI (March, 1953), pp. 38–51.

TURVEY, R.  *The Economics of Real Property*. London: George Allen and Unwin, 1957.

The annual *Proceedings of the National Tax Association* virtually always contain papers on property tax problems and developments.

Extensive discussions of property taxation are to be found in the reports of tax study commissions in various states. See the following:

*Report of the Revenue Laws Commission* (Illinois), 1949, chaps. iii, iv.

*Report of the Tax Study Commission* (Indiana), 1952.

*Report of the [California] Senate Interim Committee on State and Local Taxation, Property Assessments and Equalization in California*, 1953.

*A Report of the Subcommittee on Revenue and Taxation of the Washington Legis-lative Council, A Study of Real Property Assessments in the State of Washing-ton*, 1954.

*Michigan Tax Study Staff Papers*, 1958.

## CANADIAN PROPERTY TAXATION

GROVES, H. M.  "The Property Tax in Canada and the United States," *Land Eco-nomics*, Vol. XXIV (February and May, 1948), pp. 23–30 and 120–28, re-spectively.

A comparison of Canadian property taxes with those of the United States.

PERRY, J. H.  *Taxation in Canada*, chap. 14. 3d ed.; Toronto: University of Toronto Press, 1961.

A description of Canadian property taxes.

DUPRÉ, J. S.  "The Property Tax in Canada," *Proceedings of the National Tax Association for 1958*, pp. 77–83.

FINNIS, F. H.  *Real Property Assessment in Canada*. Toronto: Canadian Tax Foundation, 1959.

A detailed description of Canadian practice.

SHIFTING AND INCIDENCE

SHOUP, C. "Capitalization and Shifting of the Property Tax," *Property Taxes*, pp. 187–204. New York: Tax Policy League, 1940.

BUEHLER, A. G. "The Capitalization of Taxes," *National Tax Journal*, Vol. III (December, 1950), pp. 283–97.

STOCKFISH, J. A. "The Capitalization, Allocation and Investment Effects of Asset Taxation," *Southern Economic Journal*, Vol. XXII (January, 1956), pp. 317–29.

# PART VI

## The Commercial Principle

| Chapter | THE SALE OF GOVERNMENT |
| 22 | SERVICES: FEES AND |
| | COMMERCIAL REVENUES |

Governments can sell their services to the users only in those cases in which the benefits accrue directly to individuals, the services being of such character that they can be segmented into amounts which can be provided separately to particular individuals and withheld from those persons who do not wish to pay for them.

Most governmental services, such as national defense, police and fire protection, etc., convey their benefits indivisibly to the community as a whole. They cannot be divided into amounts which can be sold to individuals, and the benefits cannot be withheld from those persons who do not wish to buy them. The governmental transfer activities provide no service which can be sold, since they merely shift purchasing power from some persons to others. Accordingly, the sale method of financing cannot be employed for most governmental activities. Nevertheless, the group of services for which this method is feasible is not unimportant. This chapter is concerned with the methods of financing these services.

## THE TYPES OF DIRECT BENEFIT SERVICES

For purposes of analysis, those services which yield benefits separately to individuals may be classed into several groups. In the first place, there are certain services of a basically governmental character—which, if performed at all, must be provided by government—which yield direct personal benefits. Many of these services consist of the regulation of certain activities, which, in the best interests of society, persons cannot be permitted to undertake without community sanction. When they do receive this permission, they are directly benefited. Examples include the granting of the right to fish, to operate certain types of businesses, to drive a car, to marry, to keep a dog, and so forth. Closely related are certain services which do not convey permission to carry on an activity but provide direct benefit in other ways, such as the recording of deeds. If titles to property are to be secure, it is essential that the government perform this function.

Secondly, there are several major activities in which the services are of such a character that they might be provided by private enterprise but which governments have typically undertaken for a long period of time, primarily because of the importance of the benefits to the community as a whole which accrue along with the direct benefits to the individuals. These community benefits may be called external economies. The postal service, education, and highways are primary examples.

Thirdly, there are the distinctly commercial activities, ones which are frequently performed by private enterprise, governmental operation being the exception rather than the rule. In general, the relative importance of the community benefits, as distinct from the direct benefits, is less with these activities than with the second type. Provision of water, electric power, transportation, and other utility services are the primary examples. There is no clear-cut line between the second and the third categories; the provision of highways is not fundamentally different from the provision of city transit services, for example. Nevertheless, the classification is useful because of common differences in methods of financing.

Because of the direct benefits to individuals, it is possible to sell all these classes of services to individuals if such a policy is considered desirable. The charges for the first category—the strictly governmental services—are known as *fees;* when the activity sanctions a particular action on the part of the individual, the fee is often called a *license* or *license fee.* The charges for the third category—the strictly commercial activities—are known as *rates, prices,* or *commercial revenues* or *charges.* To the extent that charges are made for the second category, the name applied varies according to the exact nature of the service and the circumstances of sale. The terms *fees, commercial revenues,* and *tolls* are employed in various cases.

## THE DESIRABILITY OF GOVERNMENTAL PROVISION OF THE SERVICES

The general question of the desirability of governmental undertaking of various activities has been considered in Chapter 1. But some additional exploration of this question with respect to those services which could be produced and sold by private enterprise is warranted before the problem of the methods of financing them is analyzed. Four major factors must be considered in each particular case:

1. Are there substantial social or indirect benefits, or, in other terms,

external economies arising from the activity, beyond the direct benefits obtained by those using the services, or persons benefiting from the activities of the users? If so, private provision of the service will result in inadequate output compared to the quantity which will allow optimum levels of living from given resources. Governmental provision of education, for example, can clearly be justified on this basis, as well as the building of a railway to aid in the economic development of a remote area.

In such cases an alternative to governmental provision of the services is the subsidization of private enterprise to allow a greater output than would otherwise be profitable. Such a procedure may be feasible in some cases. But it suffers from one basic difficulty, as shown by experience, that is, the inevitable conflict between private and public interests. The business firm is interested in getting the maximum governmental aid for the minimum provision of unprofitable activities. Substantial governmental supervision becomes almost inevitable if public interest is to be served, and clashes between business and governmental policy may paralyze action.

2. Can the government provide the services more efficiently than private enterprise? The generally accepted assumption in the United States is that private production is more efficient than governmental production, because of the profit motive and the absence of political interference, unless the evidence is to the contrary in the particular case.[1] But there are several situations in which government production may be more efficient. Private enterprises protected by monopoly position may be operated by persons of limited managerial ability, who fail to attain optimum efficiency. Private enterprise may fail to undertake expansion far enough in advance or provide adequate service. Unnecessary duplication of facilities may sometimes occur. Or private operation may result in unnecessarily high costs of collection of the prices. These considerations, as well as that of social benefits, justify governmental provision of highways, for example.

If governments do undertake a particular activity, attainment of efficiency requires that management policies be designed in terms of attainment of the desired goals, not in terms of strictly political considerations. If personnel are chosen on the basis of political patronage and policies dictated by small pressure groups or political interests of the group in power at the moment, efficiency will be seriously impaired. To avoid this situation, government enterprises are frequently separated from the direct control of legislative bodies and government executives and placed

[1] For the opposite point of view, see J. E. Fisher, "Efficiency in Business and Government," *Quarterly Review of Economics and Business*, Vol. II (August, 1962), pp. 35–47.

under separate commissions. These, unfortunately, sometimes lose touch with public interest and operate in much the same fashion as private monopolists.

3. Does monopoly result with private enterprise, and is the attempt to regulate the monopoly unsuccessful? Monopoly is likely to cause mal-allocation of resources due to the restriction of supply and to cause greater inequality of income distribution. Effective regulation of private enter-prise is basically difficult, because of the inevitable clash of interests.

4. Do the circumstances warrant the undertaking by government of the risk of failure of the enterprise? A primary function of private entre-preneurship is that of undertaking the risk of failure of an enterprise; in the event of failure the burden rests upon those persons who undertook the risk in the hope of earning profits, not upon the community as a whole. When government undertakes an enterprise that fails, the burden rests upon the taxpayers of the community as a whole; the debts created by the establishment of the project may be carried on long after the project has been liquidated. There is little or no possibility of "writing off" the losses through bankruptcy, as there is with private enterprise.[2] The entire capital of the government enterprise is essentially obtained on a debt basis, with no equity cushion in the case of a decline in business.

Each individual situation must be studied in terms of these questions. With respect to education and highways, the case for governmental oper-ation is almost universally accepted. With the strictly commercial activi-ties, no one general answer can be given. A presumption is ordinarily ac-cepted against government ownership in industries in which most benefits are individual in character and in which some degree of effective competi-tion is maintained or regulation is reasonably effective. When the service has significant social benefits or is of particular importance to the users and neither competition nor regulation can be made effective, the case for governmental operation is stronger. Thus, public ownership has been confined largely to the public utilities field, in which these conditions are most often found. But even in this field the answer to the question of government versus private ownership must be determined separately in each case, in terms of careful study of differences in efficiency and service to the community with public, as contrasted to private, ownership, the undesirable effects of monopoly in private hands and the relative effective-

---

[2] An example is provided by the experience of certain Ontario municipalities with elec-tric railways in the period after World War I. Some of these proved to be complete failures and were liquidated, but the municipalities were saddled with the debt which had been in-curred to acquire and modernize the properties.

ness of regulation, and the general attitude of the community toward the philosophy of government ownership.

## The Extent of Government Ownership

In practice, the scope of governmental production of commercial services is relatively limited in the United States. The most important case at the federal level is the postal service, other examples being federal reclamation and power projects, the national forests (primarily acquired for reasons of conservation), and the Alaska Railroad, plus certain defense production plants. In most other countries the scope of government ownership is much broader; railroads particularly are generally government-operated. Peculiarly, the chief example of governmental operation of railroads in the United States is that of rail lines in this country owned by the government of Canada, namely, the Grand Trunk Western and Central Vermont systems.

The states, of course, operate the highway systems, including toll roads and bridges, but provide very little strictly commercial service. In earlier years, they experimented with railway operation but withdrew from this field, although some trackage is still state-owned. A number of states operate liquor stores. Some years ago the state of North Dakota undertook a number of commercial enterprises, including banks, flour mills, elevators, and cement plants, but has discontinued most of them.

The local governments, in addition to providing roads and streets, have entered the field of water service to a major extent, only one major city now having a privately operated water system. There is considerable municipal operation of electric power and transit systems.

Government ownership is considerably more widespread in Canada. For many years a portion of the railway system was operated by the government, largely because the earlier lines serving the maritime provinces were not able to operate profitably. Between 1900 and 1920 an excessive mileage of railway lines was constructed far in anticipation of need, partly because of a competitive struggle between the Grand Trunk Pacific and the Canadian Northern. The government itself built the National Transcontinental through the wilderness from Winnipeg to Quebec and Moncton in an effort to provide a short cut to the seaboard for prairie wheat. None of these lines were able to cover their expenses, especially when costs rose faster than rates at the time of World War I, and the government was not only compelled to keep the National Transcontinental but to acquire the Canadian Northern and the entire Grand Trunk system to keep them operating. All of the government-owned lines were merged into the Canadian National Railways in 1923 and operated as a Crown corporation, in competition with the somewhat smaller but more profitable privately owned Canadian Pacific. The Canadian National, after serious initial deficits, benefited from the growth of the economy, and has not fared too badly, financially, since 1940.

The Canadian federal government has not entered the electric power field. Apart from the railways and the principal air transport system (Trans-Canada Airlines), the federal activities have been concentrated in certain defense and developmental industries. The provinces, on the other hand, have played a major role in the development of electric power systems. Most power in Ontario is produced by the Ontario Hydro-Electric Power Commission, and in other provinces as well, substantial amounts are provided by provincial enterprises. Two provinces operate railways of considerable size. The prairie provinces, especially Saskatchewan, have carried public ownership still further, to include telephone and intercity bus systems, insurance companies, and other enterprises. The Canadian local governments have entered the public utilities field to a greater extent than in the United States. Water is almost universally provided by the cities, and electric power and transit services in many cities.

## THE CHOICE BETWEEN TAXATION AND CHARGES

In the financing of the types of services of such nature that they may be sold, a government must make the choice between the tax and charge methods. The choice must be made in terms of several considerations:

1. Will the use of the charge method facilitate determination of optimum amounts of the service to supply? One basic objection to the use of taxes in any situation in which other financing methods are possible is the inability to insure that each individual attains an optimum balance between private and public sector outputs, and thus that governmental output of the service is determined in an objective fashion. The decision about output must be made in terms of usual budgetary principles, with the inevitable subjective elements involved in estimating and comparing benefits and costs. On the other hand, if charges are made, each individual can acquire the amount of the service which he wishes—in terms of his relative desires for this service and privately produced goods—and the output of the service can be adjusted automatically to the amount which users will buy at the prices established. The investment in the facilities necessary to provide the service, in turn, can be adjusted in terms of consumer demand, in the same fashion as in the private sector of the economy.

The usefulness of a charge in facilitating optimum adjustment of output depends in part upon the extent to which the charge prevents waste of the service, which either results in production of more than is economically justifiable, or prevents other persons with greater need from obtaining it. Some services, such as the provision of marriage licenses, and in large measure, education, are not susceptible to waste because of the nature of the wants for them. In other words, demand is perfectly inelastic, even at a zero price. In other instances, once facilities have been provided, the demand for their use at zero prices is less than capacity. As a consequence, marginal cost is little or nothing, and the collecting of admissions charges would result in uneconomic restriction of usage. An example of this would be a park not used to capacity.

On the other hand, many services are likely to be wasted if persons do not have to pay for them. If water is provided free of charge, persons will be careless with it, and use far more than they would if they had to pay for it. In other cases, charges may facilitate the rationing of facilities not easily increased, such as parking facilities in downtown areas of large cities, among the various persons seeking to use them, on the basis of their willingness to pay for them. In both of these types of cases the charges received give some indication of the desirability of additional investment in the facilities. In general, whenever demand for a service has any elasticity and marginal cost is more than negligible, the charging of prices facilitates output adjustment.

The usefulness of a charge in the determination of optimum output depends to some extent upon whether or not the service gives rise to indirect benefits or external economies. If so, care must be taken in pricing not to cause uneconomic restriction of use. If most of the benefits are indirect, collection of a small part of the cost from charges may not be worth while, while collection of larger amounts will results in sacrifice of the indirect benefits.

A special case is that in which the users cannot be given the choice to use or not use the service, since the indirect benefits are of sufficient importance that in the interests of the community all persons must be required to make use of it. This is true in large measure of education, sewage service, and garbage disposal. In such cases the charge takes on the nature of a tax, since persons must pay it, and contributes nothing toward resource allocation. The decision about the use of the charge must be made solely in terms of equity considerations discussed below.

2. Can the charges be collected without costs to the government and the user being substantially greater than the costs of collecting taxes?

Relatively high collection costs, such as would be incurred if all roads were financed on the toll basis, constitute a serious argument against the use of this method of financing.

3. Does the use of the charge method result in a distribution of burden which is regarded by the community as equitable? In part, the answer to this question depends upon the scope of the benefits. If they are widespread and do not differ greatly among various persons, the case for the charge basis is less strong than it is if relatively few persons benefit. The case for a charge is particularly good if a relatively small group receives all the benefit and can easily pay for the service without inequity.

Even if the benefits are widespread, the pattern of burden distribution which results from charges may not conform with accepted standards of equity. If the use of the service is largely independent of income, the burden distribution of a charge will be regressive, and the tax form may be regarded as preferable, especially if the dollar magnitudes are substantial. If charges materially reduce the use of the service by the lower income groups, the distribution of burden may not be regressive, but the consequent resource allocation may be regarded as undesirable by the community.

The question, from an equity standpoint, therefore resolves itself into the following issue: Is it more equitable to make all persons pay for these services which they receive, or is it more desirable, in terms of accepted optimum patterns of income distribution, to provide these services free of charge and cover the costs by taxation, in order to improve the living levels of the poor? The answer to this question hinges in part upon the exact nature of the pattern of income distribution regarded as optimum. But it also depends upon the relative desirability of various techniques of improving the economic position of the poor. The choice of the method of providing the services free of charge to the poor results in relatively greater use by these persons of the services and smaller use of other goods than would occur if greater use was made of transfer payments, such as relief. The transfer payment method has the advantage of allowing greater freedom of choice of consumption patterns by the poor, while the free services method is advantageous if it is considered desirable to encourage the use of these services because of indirect benefits rendered to society.

In summary, the case for charging most or all of the costs against the users is strongest if—

*a*) Substantial waste of the service will result if it is provided free of charge.

*b*) The benefits are primarily individual in character rather than benefiting the community as a whole.

*c*) The prices for the services can be collected easily.

*d*) The method does not result in burdens on individuals which are considered to be contrary to accepted principles of equity.

In contrast, the case for providing the services free of charge and covering their costs from taxation is strong if—

*a*) The services are of such nature that little waste will occur if they are made available without charge.

*b*) The benefits accrue in part to the community as a whole, so that the charging of a price will result in unnecessary restriction of use of the service.

*c*) Costs of collection of prices are high.

*d*) The pattern of distribution of burden which would result from charging for the services is one which would be regarded as inequitable.

### Special Benefit Taxes in Place of Charges

With some types of services the case for the collection of a charge may be strong, but the costs of collection may be excessive, and the direct imposition of the charge may have certain undesirable consequences, such as the uneconomic restriction of the use of particular facilities. This situation is most likely to arise when the benefits from the service concentrate in certain groups in society which, in terms of usual standards of equity, can justifiably be made to pay for them, yet collection of the charges is not feasible. In such instances the activity may be financed by taxes established on the basis of the charge or commercial principle, that is, collected from the users of the service on the basis of some measure of their use. The primary application of this principle is in the field of highway finance, which will be discussed in the following chapter.

### The Optimum Level of Prices

If prices are to be charged to the users, some very difficult issues must be solved in the determination of the pricing policies to be followed. If optimum allocation and use of resources and thus optimum standards of living are to be attained, given the pattern of income distribution, the general rule of pricing requires that the price be set at a level equal to marginal costs of production, provided that three requirements are met:

1. The marginal monetary costs of producing the service cover all marginal social costs; that is, there are no indirect costs to society in addition to those directly incurred in producing the service.

2. There are no indirect community benefits from the service, in addition to the benefits received directly by the users.

3. Prices are equal to marginal costs in other sectors of the economy.

FIGURE 30

OPTIMUM PRICE LEVEL FOR A GOVERNMENT ENTERPRISE

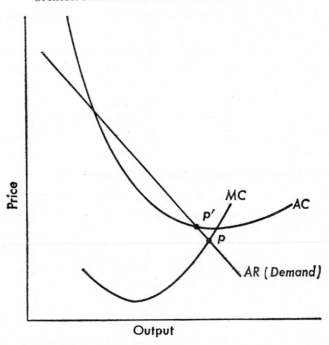

Given these conditions, price must be equal to marginal cost, at point $p$ on Figure 30, if output of the service is to be optimum. However, several considerations may complicate the use of this rule.

1. *Additional Social Costs.* The production and use of some commodities and services are responsible for certain costs to society which do not enter directly into the costs of production. The consumption of liquor to excess may result in suffering to members of the person's family, in loss of the person's contribution to economic activity, and in crime. In such cases the price (as, for example, of liquor sold by a government liquor store) can justifiably be set well above marginal cost, in order to restrict the use of the commodity more closely to the optimum level in terms of marginal social cost.

2. *Additional Community Benefits.* If a service conveys benefits to the community as a whole, in addition to those derived directly by

individuals, pricing on a marginal cost basis results in restriction of production below the optimum; prices should be set below marginal cost in order to insure greater use. Thus, for example, if the services of higher education are to be charged for at all, the indirect benefits justify the setting of prices below marginal cost and the covering of the remaining cost by taxation. The exact extent to which price should be set below average cost can be determined only upon the basis of an estimate of the significance of the indirect benefits.

3. *Nonoptimum Adjustments in the Private Sector.* The failure of price to equal margin cost in parts of the private sector of the economy suggests that the use of the rule in the governmental sector will result in an excessively large output of the governmental services. The only completely satisfactory solution to this problem is the reattainment of equality of marginal cost and price in the private sector, which is almost impossible to accomplish.

4. *Considerations of Equity.* A particular allocation of resources can be regarded as optimum only in terms of the given pattern of income distribution. But this pattern may not be regarded as equitable by the consensus of opinion in society, and some readjustment in resource allocation as a deliberate policy to increase the real income of the lower income groups may be regarded as justifiable. Thus, prices on certain services may be set below marginal cost with the direct intent of increasing the amounts of the services used by persons in the lower income groups.

The use of the marginal cost principle requires not only the establishment of the general level of charges at the marginal cost level, but also the variation of the charge on various classes of users on the basis of the marginal costs for which each class is responsible. Thus, if the marginal cost at peak hours is much greater than at other times, the charges for peak load use should be higher.

### Decreasing Cost Conditions and Marginal Cost Pricing

The analysis to this point has assumed that a price equal to marginal cost will cover average cost of production, and thus the total amount received from the sale of the services will cover the entire costs of providing them. However, this situation will not be attained if the output at which price is equal to marginal cost is in the range in which average cost is decreasing, since in this range marginal cost is below average cost. This is the situation shown in Figure 30, in which the price, $p$, is below the average cost curve. Thus a basic dilemma is encountered: If price equals marginal cost, a deficit is incurred, which must be made up from taxes. If price is set at the average cost figure ($p'$ on Fig. 30) and all costs are covered, price exceeds marginal cost, and output is held to uneconomically low levels.

There are two related situations in which average cost may exceed marginal cost. The first is the case in which the plant capacity that was most economical to build (or was actually built) is greater than that required for current demand, so that marginal cost, at the level at which it is equal to price, is extremely low, because additional services can be provided without an increase in most of the factors employed. Short-run average cost is declining, and thus marginal cost is less than average cost. If a bridge has been built and is not used to capacity, the marginal cost of additional vehicles crossing it is almost nil. This is the situation with many highways, with transit facilities during parts of the day, and with electric power systems in some instances.

The second situation is that in which, even though existing plant may be used to capacity, long-run average cost would decline if plant capacity and output were increased, because the economies of large-scale production are not yet fully realized. In this case, long-run marginal cost may be very low (compared to average cost). This is less likely to be a troublesome case than the first. The generation and distribution of electric power may in some instances be an example.

What is the best solution to the dilemma? Several opposing points of view have developed. Those adhering strictly to the marginal rule maintain that the deficit is unimportant and that any attempt to eliminate it by a higher rate would lead to uneconomic restriction of use. This point of view is best illustrated with the example of a toll bridge. If the bridge is not used to capacity and its depreciation and maintenance do not depend on traffic, any toll charged would discourage some persons from using the bridge unless the demand was perfectly inelastic. Thus, some persons would lose the advantages from the use of the bridge, while the real cost to the economy of this use is nil.

Several objections have been advanced, however, against this point of view. The deficit must be covered from some source; if it can be covered by a tax which in no way alters economic behavior, resource allocation will be better if this method is used than if a charge high enough to cover all costs is placed on the users. But actually, it is very difficult to insure that additional taxes to cover these deficits do not have effects upon the economy even more serious than the misallocation which results from making the users pay all the costs.

Secondly, it is charged that those persons who use the facility are given an inequitable share of total purchasing power. When the facilities were built, it was assumed that the users as a group would be willing to pay a sufficient amount to cover the costs. But if the users are not charged these amounts and a portion of the burden is placed upon all taxpayers, the users benefit from the service, yet have the money they would otherwise pay for it available for other purposes. Thus a redistribution of income results, with some persons worse off and others better off. The users of the service gain at the expense of those who pay the tax to provide the facilities. Thus, there is no assurance that economic welfare has been increased, unless it is assumed that the consequent redistribution of income is more in line with the pattern of income regarded as optimum by society, or unless a system of compensations could be devised whereby those benefiting would compensate the taxpayers for their tax payments in support of the activity. But this policy would contradict the basic foundation of pricing on the marginal cost basis, unless some method can be devised of making the users pay without their payments being made directly dependent upon the amount of use. If this can be done, they can just as well pay in this manner initially, without use of taxes at all. This possibility is discussed in subsequent paragraphs.

Thirdly, from an administrative standpoint, it is argued that the failure to price at average or full cost leaves the administrators without a guide to investment policy and thus encourages "empire-building" expansion. Pressure to maintain maximum efficiency in operation and to resist unreasonable demands of employees is lessened because of the reduced emphasis on deficits. At the same time, because of the need for covering the deficits by governmental appropriations, political interference with the policies of the enterprise is almost inevitable, to the detriment of efficiency in operation.

Finally, difficulties arise in the determination of marginal cost, and the rapid fluctuation of marginal cost from time to time—particularly between peak-load and nonpeak-load periods—creates serious complications for rate setting. For example, a toll bridge may have very light traffic during most of the day but be overcrowded during rush hours; thus the rate should be much higher in the latter period. But precise adjustment may be impossible.

### Alternatives to Marginal Cost Pricing

One alternative solution to strict marginal cost pricing would involve establishment of a rate structure which would make the users pay the entire cost, yet their payments for particular quantities would cover only marginal costs.[3] Thus, only marginal costs would influence the amount of the services which they acquired. For example, each electric

---

[3] In a sense, their over-all payments would approximate long-run marginal cost, which is typically more than the short-run marginal figure after the facilities have been built and are not used to capacity.

power user would pay a substantial stand-by charge, whether he used any power or not, but would pay only a low rate, equal to marginal cost, per kilowatt-hour actually used. For the privilege of crossing a toll bridge, a person would pay a toll bridge pass fee, which would entitle him to cross the bridge an unlimited number of times, but he would pay no tolls for individual crossings. This rule works satisfactorily on a type of service which potential customers will continue to use despite the stand-by charge; otherwise, the desired results are not attained. If the service is of such type that the quantities which various persons use differ widely, a heavy stand-by charge may be regarded as inequitable, since the average cost for those making relatively little use of the service is high. This problem may be partly avoided by giving the user the choice of paying the stand-by charge plus a price equal to marginal cost on actual usage or an amount equal to average cost without the stand-by charge if he uses the service to a very limited extent.

This method is really a simplified version of perfect discrimination of rates, whereby charges on each user would be adjusted to obtain the entire amount that the person would pay for the service and still use it or, in other words, to tap fully the benefits to each user from the service. While discrimination may have substantial advantages from the standpoint of resource allocation, it is generally regarded as inequitable among the various customers, because some persons would be paying much more than others for the same service. Likewise, the establishment of a system of perfectly discriminatory rates is administratively very difficult.

A completely different approach suggests that over a period of time the appropriate escape from the dilemma is that of adjusting the quality of the service until the rates set can equal both marginal and average cost. For example, if a reduction in service quality lowers cost more rapidly than demand, an equilibrium will shortly be attained. Or if an improvement in quality raises demand more rapidly than cost, the equilibrium will be attained by changes in this direction.[4]

An answer to the dilemma is not simple, regardless of which alternative is followed. If marginal and average cost are not substantially different and the demand is highly inelastic, little harm will be done by setting price equal to average cost and thus avoiding a deficit. If marginal cost is almost nil, as with a toll bridge, there is a strong case for avoiding tolls and covering the costs from taxation. With some types of enterprises the stand-by charge plus low-price policy may be suitable. The basis of the difficulty lies in the fact that prices have two functions: They serve

---

[4] See the paper by P. Thomson, "Prices versus Taxes in the Allocation of Public Resources," *Proceedings of the National Tax Association for 1955*, p. 152.

as rationing devices to prevent excessive use of the goods (and thus shortages or excessive allocation of resources to the product), and they also provide means of covering the costs of rendering the services. As long as marginal cost is equal to average cost, the price serves both functions properly. But if marginal cost is nil, a price is no longer needed for rationing purposes. If one is charged to cover the cost (and the demand is at all elastic), it will interfere with optimum resource utilization. But if it is not charged, the costs must be covered from other sources, with consequent redistribution of income and possible effects upon resource allocation. Over a peroid of time the service variation alternative may be useful in some cases.

### The Case in Which Marginal Costs Exceed Average Costs

In some instances the reverse of the decreasing cost case may be encountered, with marginal cost in excess of average cost. If prices are set at marginal cost levels, a profit will be earned; if they are set at average cost levels, demand will exceed output, and price will no longer effectively ration output. In such instances the use of the marginal basis is clearly justified. One example of this occurs when the demand for the service is so high that the plant is overutilized; marginal cost in the short run is well beyond average cost, as the enterprise is operating on the rising portion of its average cost curve. Price must exceed average cost to hold down usage until the plant can be expanded. Thus, if traffic on a bridge exceeds capacity, marginal costs, primarily arising from loss of time and a high rate of accidents, may increase rapidly. Although most of this marginal cost will actually be encountered not by the government but by the motorists, it is nevertheless a real cost to society. Thus the use of a relatively high toll during rush hours to hold usage down to a feasible figure—in other words, to ration the space—is certainly justifiable.

A policy of charging in excess of average cost, particularly at certain time intervals, is often strongly resisted by the users. Partly, this opposition results from continued overemphasis on the prices as a means of recovering the average costs, rather than as a means of rationing use when demand exceeds potential output. Furthermore, the policy may run counter to accepted standards of equity. If the peak-load, high-marginal-cost time periods are those in which the service is used primarily by commuting workers and the nonpeak users are largely tourists, the charging of high tolls or charges in the peak hours will be condemned as grossly unfair.

Profits will also be earned by a government enterprise when marginal social costs exceed marginal private costs, and prices are, justifiably, set on the former basis. The apparent profit is, from the standpoint of society, a compensation for the additional social costs created.

### Deliberate Profit Maximization

Government enterprises, particularly at the local level, sometimes deliberately seek to maximize profits in order to provide a "painless" means of covering other governmental expenditures. Some municipal power systems point with pride to their high profits, which allow the city to operate with lower taxes and in a few instances with no taxes at all. Several major objections can be advanced against this policy. In the first place, the setting of a price above marginal cost, which almost inevitably occurs in such cases, interferes with optimum use of resources, the consumption of the service being held to artificially low levels. Secondly, the policy amounts essentially to a tax on the users of the service, comparable to the excess profits of a private monopolist. It is difficult to justify the distribution of municipal tax burdens on the basis of power consumption under usual standards of equity. The concealment of the tax may be regarded, in itself, as undesirable; and as a practical matter, residents of the community lose the benefits of deductibility of local taxes for federal income tax purposes. It may be more desirable for monopoly profit to accrue to the government than to a private company (on the basis of the effects upon distribution of income), but it is clearly undesirable for either to gain such a profit, except in the cases noted above.

### Cases in Which Costs Cannot Be Covered

A final situation is that in which, regardless of the pricing policies followed, it is impossible to avoid deficits, because the relationship of demand and cost is such that there is no price level or pricing technique (with tolerable degrees of price discrimination) which will allow the covering of all costs. Several observations can be made about such situations. In the first place, if the deficits are due to failure to hold cost schedules down to optimum figures, because of poor management or monopoly policies of unions of the employees (such as union insistence on the use of unnecessary numbers of men), the obvious solution, though one not always politically feasible, is a reduction in costs.

Secondly, if costs could be covered if completely perfect rate discrimination could be followed, the undertaking is economically justifiable, even though equity and administrative considerations prevent the use of rate discrimination, and thus all costs are not, in practice, covered. That is, if costs could be covered if each user were paying the largest amount that he would be willing to pay for the service, the undertaking is economically justifiable, even if this method of financing cannot be used. Some railroads, for example, would be able to cover all their costs if they were able to use a discriminatory rate system which tapped fully the economic advantages of the road to each shipper. But considerations of equity prevent the use of such a rate structure, and thus deficits are incurred. Continued operation of the railroad, which would be impossible if it were privately owned, is clearly warranted.

Thirdly, if substantial indirect benefits accrue to the community, the enterprise may be economically justifiable even if it shows a deficit. The enterprise itself cannot realize financially on the indirect benefits; if it is estimated that the real benefits to society exceed the real costs, operation of the enterprise is warranted. Thus a city subway system, which is almost never financially profitable, may be entirely justified if the gains from lessened traffic hazards and avoidance of loss of time for motorists and transit riders are estimated to offset the burdens of the taxes necessary to cover the deficit. Evaluation of relative benefits and relative costs is of necessity, of course, a matter of community judgment. In like manner, operation of a railroad that facilitates economic development, such as portions of the Canadian National, the Ontario Northland, and the Pacific Great Eastern, or one that is essential for national defense, may easily be justifiable, despite deficits.

Fourthly, if efficiency is maximized and there are no community benefits from the projects or advantages to users for which payment cannot be obtained because of the inability to use discriminatory rates, the loss is evidence of the fact that the project should have never been undertaken in the first place. Once the equipment wears out and replacements are necessary, liquidation is desirable.[5] Meanwhile, if variable costs, that is, the direct costs of operation, are covered, continued operation is preferable to immediate abandonment, since the specialized resources cannot be effectively utilized for other purposes.

There is a great tendency to condemn as a failure and a source of economic waste any public commercial enterprise which shows a financial loss, whereas similar standards are never applied to many government activities, such as highways, which are financed on a tax basis. There is good reason to believe that a large portion of the highway network could never "pay for itself" on a toll basis, yet the economic desirability is never questioned. This is even more true of river improvements. In the evaluation of government enterprises, complete emphasis must not be

---

[5] In practice, abandonment of service may be very difficult politically, an illustration of one of the inherent limitations of government operation of such enterprises.

placed upon the profit position, but attention must be given to other factors which affect the usefulness of the undertaking to society.

### The Actual Pricing Policies

In the actual setting of prices, almost no direct attention has been given to margin cost considerations. Typically, government-owned utilities have followed the same general patterns as the rate regulation policies applied to private utilities: They have set rates sufficiently high to cover average cost, in many cases including an "average" rate of return. In a few cases, they seek to maximize profits. Controlling legislation often requires the enterprises to cover costs, denying them resort to taxes to cover deficits. In setting rates on particular types of service, marginal considerations have played a part, as is manifest in the low rates charged industrial users by municipal power systems and the developmental rates of the TVA. But even in most of these cases the over-all goal has been the covering of average cost. In Canada the Canadian National Railways has essentially no independent rate policy of its own at all, merely following the rates of the Canadian Pacific, which serves as the yardstick.

The United States postal system has used a type of pricing discriminatory by class of mail, based on the implicit (and largely incorrect) assumption that the marginal cost of handling additional second- and third-class mail is relatively low, and thus rates much lower than those on the basic first-class mail are imposed. As a matter of actual policy, the low rates on second-class mail (periodicals, etc.) have arisen largely out of Congressional policy designed to disseminate information and thus presumably reflect indirect benefits to the community. The low rates on third-class mail (advertising circulars, etc.) have rarely been explained and, in fact, largely are attributable to the pressure brought upon Congress by the benefited groups. The net result of the low rates on these two classes of mail is a continuing over-all postal deficit, which is rather obviously due to the setting of rates well below marginal cost, not to a deviation between marginal cost and average cost. Justification for the deficit in terms of indirect benefits is difficult to find. As one student of the question concludes, "Postal pricing policy is chaotic, if not bizarre."[6] Much of the difficulty has arisen out of the unwillingness of Congress to permit the postal system to have greater freedom in rate setting, and from the influence of pressure groups on Congressional action.

The operation of the federal reclamation projects presents an example of the problems of pricing with a decreasing cost operation. The

---

[6] See Jane Kennedy, "Structure and Policy in Postal Rates," *Journal of Political Economy*, Vol. LXV (June, 1957), p. 208.

general procedure has been to set the charges for water on an average cost basis after deducting cost elements attributed (in rather arbitrary fashion) to other functions, such as flood control. But none of the projects can cover their costs on a strictly uniform average cost price, given the capacity of the farmers to pay and continue farming. As a consequence, the Bureau of Reclamation has established a block pricing system, which constitutes a step in the direction of marginal cost pricing. The lands served by a project are grouped into blocks, and the rate for water for each block is adjusted in terms of the net increment in farm income resulting from the use of the water. Unfortunately, however, the diversity of land in the various blocks prevents any close adjustment of benefit and charge, and interferes with efficient use of the water. But the resistance of the farmers to more complete classification prevents the use of more scientific pricing which would permit the projects to cover their costs. Congress has, in practice, not insisted that they do so and, as a consequence, has allowed perpetuation of unsatisfactory pricing methods.[7] Federal electric power projects typically price on an average cost basis.

Policies on indirect benefits have varied widely. Typically, municipal utilities ignore these completely and attempt to make the users pay all of the costs.[8] As suggested in the examples above, the federal government has frequently established rates which do not cover costs and thus has in a sense recognized indirect benefits, although the motive for the relatively low rates was often quite different.

In contrast to the utilities, the government liquor monopolies have typically aimed at the earning of a very high rate of profit. This excess profit, which essentially constitutes a type of tax, may be justified on the same (somewhat weak) bases as the excise taxes upon liquor discussed in Chapter 18.

On the whole, the pricing policies, except those for liquor, have left much to be desired, particularly in those instances in which marginal cost is much lower than average cost and in those in which social benefits are substantial. Lower rate policies in these cases would have facilitated optimum allocation of resources, even if deficits had resulted. On the other hand, excessive use of the marginal principle, without careful considera-

---

[7] See J. Margolis, "Welfare Criteria, Pricing, and Decentralization of a Public Service," *Quarterly Journal of Economics*, Vol. LXXI (August, 1957), pp. 448–63.

[8] In some cases an attempt is made to require the users to pay for aspects of the service which are provided for purposes other than benefit to the users, as such. Thus, San Francisco retains its cable cars primarily for reasons of tradition and tourist attraction, but attempts to cover the somewhat higher costs of this form of transport from the users of the system, not from general tax revenues, as would be appropriate.

tion of the taxes necessary to cover the deficits, could produce even more undesirable consequences. In some instances, governments have been reluctant to make effective use of prices as rationing devices, particularly with respect to overcrowded highways and bridges. There are cases, for example, in which tolls have been collected on bridges during the years in which they were used only to a fraction of capacity, and thus marginal costs were almost nil, and then removed (because the bridge was now paid for) at the very time that the bridge had become congested and tolls were needed to prevent unnecessary use. Governments have often been reluctant to adjust rates in terms of varying costs of serving different classes of users.

## REVENUE IMPORTANCE

In the United States, charges are of primary importance at the local government level. In 1961, municipal utilities yielded a gross revenue of $3.9 billion, with a net from operations of $2.4 billion. Water service was the chief source of both gross and net revenue. Nonutility charges yielded $3.7 billion, or 9 per cent of municipal revenues, and special assessments $392 million. The total of the charges of all types, in gross figures, was $9 billion, or 23 per cent of local government revenue. This is a gross, not a net, figure; much of it goes to cover the costs of the specific services rendered. The states gained $2.85 billion from charges and $1.1 billion from liquor stores. The federal government received about $10.8 billion, much of it from the postal service.

## REFERENCES

The literature on price policies of government enterprises centers largely around the question of the desirability of marginal cost pricing.

HOTELLING, H. "The General Welfare in Relation to the Problems of Taxation and of Railway and Utility Rates," *Econometrica,* Vol. VI (July, 1938), pp. 242–69.

The pioneer article in the modern controversy over marginal cost pricing.

MEADE, J. E. "Price and Output Policy of State Enterprises," *Economic Journal,* Vol. LIV (December, 1944), pp. 321–28.

HARBESON, R. W. "A Critique of Marginal Cost Pricing," *Land Economics,* Vol. XXXI (February, 1955), pp. 54–74.

BACKMAN, J., and KURNOW, E. "Pricing of Governmental Services," *National Tax Journal,* Vol. VII (June, 1954), pp. 121–40.

THOMSON, P. "Prices versus Taxes in the Allocation of Public Resources," *Proceedings of the National Tax Association for 1955,* pp. 140–56.

RUGGLES, N. "The Welfare Basis of the Marginal Cost Pricing Principles," and "Recent Developments in the Theory of Marginal Cost Pricing," *Review of Economic Studies*, Vol. XVII, Issues I and II (1949–50), pp. 29–46 and 107–26.

A complete summary of the marginal cost controversy.

LITTLE, I. M. D. *A Critique of Walfare Economics*, chap. xi. 2d ed. Oxford: Oxford University Press, 1957.

A review of the issues of marginal cost pricing and other aspects of pricing by government commercial enterprises.

BROWNLEE, O. H. "User Prices vs. Taxes," *Public Finances—Needs, Sources and Utilization*, pp. 421–38. Princeton: Princeton University Press for National Bureau of Economic Research, 1961.

| Chapter 23 | HIGHWAY FINANCE: A CASE STUDY IN THE USE OF THE COMMERCIAL PRINCIPLE |

The provision of highways is a type of activity which can be financed either under usual budgetary principles from general tax sources, or through the use of the benefit or commercial principle, whereby the users are required to pay the costs of the activity and the annual expenditures are determined in light of user demand, rather than through budgetary principles of weighing relative benefits and costs of various governmental activities. In turn, the commercial principle may be implemented either by direct charges on the users or by taxes imposed upon them in relation to use, under a version of the benefit principle of taxation. In practice, both the budget and commercial principles have been employed, as well as both the user tax and the pricing (toll) methods of implementing the commercial basis. Strict use of the commercial principle is largely confined to the United States. Other countries impose road user levies, but provide little direct tie between the yield and highway expenditures. A review of the experience in this field in the United States provides an excellent illustration of the operation of the commercial principle, and also examines one of the most pressing problems of government finance in recent years.

### Historical Development

In postcolonial days, local streets and roads were provided, in a primitive fashion, by local government units, in large measure by the "working-out" of the road tax by adult male members of the community. Intercity routes were provided primarily by private turnpike companies subject to some supervision by government. Numerous plans for federal building of through roads were impaled on the spikes of the anti-internal-improvements and states' rights movements, and only one significant project was actually undertaken, the building of the National Road from Cumberland to Vandalia between 1811 and 1836. This route was eventually turned over to the states.

By mid-century the federal government was completely out of the highway field, virtually all toll roads had been driven out of business by the railroads, and the states had departed from such participation in road-building as they had undertaken. Long-distance travel by road vanished in the sections of the country served by rail, and the old turnpikes reverted to purely local access routes, and in part were completely abandoned. Provision of roads and streets was now exclusively a local function, financed by the property tax.

Toward the end of the nineteenth century began the redevelopment of the rural road systems, initially as a result of the demand of farm and village dwellers for greater mobility, and of the boom in the use of bicycles. Shortly thereafter the development of the automobile made extensive intercity travel by road feasible again, and brought great demands for road improvements. The local governments were capable neither of efficient intercity roadbuilding nor of financing the expanded road program. Since there were strong prejudices against return to the old private turnpike system, the states gradually took over the task of building the major intercity routes and commenced to aid the local governments in the financing of secondary roads and city streets.

## Emergence of the Commercial Principle of Financing

Prior to the period around 1910, road activities had been regarded as a normal routine function of local government, to be treated in the same fashion as other activities, and the states followed the same policy when they first took over highway construction. Roads were financed from regular tax sources, and in part from borrowing, in view of the belief that highway construction was a "once and for all" problem. But the difficulties of this approach became increasingly apparent, and led to gradual transition to the commercial principle. One reason for the change was the inadequacy of traditional revenue sources in financing the sharply rising demand for highways, and the strong opposition against increases in general taxes for this purpose, especially on the part of property owners, in light of the fact that in this period relatively few persons benefited from the roads. Not for another decade and a half was the family automobile commonplace.

This was clearly an instance in which the benefit principle could be employed, since the two requisites were present: a reasonably satisfactory means of measuring benefit from road usage, and the ability of the users to afford the payment without serious burden. The trend toward user financing was greatly facilitated by the fact that the user groups, particularly the automobile associations, favored the system, in one of the few cases in which groups have supported levies on themselves, rather than trying to get something for nothing. They did so for two reasons: They recognized that in practice only by this means could adequate funds be obtained for rapid highway development, and they saw that products used by motorists, such as cars and gasoline, were likely to be singled out for general revenue levies if they were not subjected to taxes for the specific purpose of highway development.

The adoption of the commercial system involved the development of special levies on highway users which bore some relationship to the extent of highway use, of specific allocation of highway user levies for highway purposes, and of the determination of annual expenditures on highways largely on the basis of the yield of the user levies. The sums involved were thus effectively removed from annual budgetary control (although the figures remained in the budgets), and there was little balancing of needs for additional highways against those for other state activities financed by general revenues. The commercial principle never completely replaced the budget principle; the local governments continued to finance their roads and streets in large part by property tax revenues (aided by state grants from highway user levies), and until 1956 the federal grants for highway purposes, discussed below, were never directly linked with federal taxes on highway use products, which were regarded as general revenue sources. But for most main highway activities, the commercial principle reigned supreme.

The commercial principle offered several significant advantages, from the standpoint of the principles of public finance and economic welfare. In the first place, it facilitated the allocation of resources to various forms of transportation in an economic fashion. Road transport competed with rail lines; of particular importance was the competition between trucks and the railroads for the movement of freight. Were roads financed from general revenues and road haulers provided with highways free of any specific charge for use, while railroads built and maintained their own lines, the former would be given an uneconomic competitive advantage, since they would not be required to cover all costs for which they were responsible. Too much of the total freight movement would be handled by truck and too little by rail, in terms of optimum economic efficiency. Such diversion could easily destroy much of the rail system, because of the inability to reduce costs in proportion to traffic declines below certain levels.

In the second place, the principle facilitated the determination of the annual expenditures to be made for highway purposes. Under the assumption that the level of highway user taxes established in conformity with the wishes of the people of the state reflects the level of expenditures and taxes which the users regard as the optimum, the annual expenditure level is determined automatically by the yield of these levies, and no effort to estimate relative benefits and costs and to compare them with those of other activities is necessary. The principle requires, of course, that all levies imposed for the purpose of highway finance actually be used for this purpose; but at times, particularly in the depression years, some states have diverted such funds to other purposes.

Thirdly, the principle offered some assistance in the allocation of funds among various roads, on the basis of the estimated yield of the levies from traffic on the particular roads. In practice, however, there were serious deviations from this principle. Many roads were built which could not possibly generate enough revenue to cover their costs, in the interests of general mobility of all people of the state, and allocation was in part controlled by political considerations unrelated to optimum allocation of resources, as legislators sought the use of allocation formulas which favored certain areas.

Finally, the widespread acceptance of the principle on the part of highway users and others indicated that the consensus of contemporary opinion regarded the use of the principle as equitable.

### Implementation of the Commercial Principle

The commercial principle of highway finance could be implemented in either of two general ways: by the use of direct charges or tolls upon the users or by the levying of taxes based upon highway use. The former approach was rejected for several reasons, particularly the nuisance and cost of collection of the tolls on a widespread system of roads with many points of access, and the tradition that persons should be free to move on government-supplied roads as they wish without the requirement of paying. Thus, until the modern toll road movement, discussed below, tolls were restricted to a few very expensive bridges and other specialized facilities, and highway user taxes were employed to implement the commercial principle.

The first of these, historically, was the license "fee," initially a nominal charge to cover cost of licensing for regulatory purposes, and then raised to provide substantial sums of revenue.[1] But these charges bore no relation to road usage, and since they were payable in one lump sum annually, there was strong resistance against raising them to levels which would provide funds regarded as adequate. As a consequence, commencing with the state of Oregon in 1919, the gasoline tax was developed as a

[1] The first use was in New York State, 1909.

more equitable and painless method of financing, the burden being adapted much more closely to road usage, and paid in small increments. This became the chief highway user levy, the license fee on cars becoming nominal in most states. However, since gas consumption does not increase in proportion to weight, it was necessary to retain heavy license fees on commercial vehicles in order to obtain from them a compensation regarded as adequate for the use of roads.

Thus, by the 1930's the state and local highway programs had more or less stabilized. The bulk of the funds for state highways came from the gas tax, with a median rate of 4 cents, supplemented by license fees graduated by weight, at least for commercial vehicles. The yield from these levies was largely allocated to highway use (part being granted to the local governments for road use), and annual highway expenditures were determined by the yield of the levies. The local governments supplemented the grants by property tax collections for road purposes, often financing residential nonarterial street pavement by special assessments on the property owners.

### Federal Participation

In 1916 the federal government commenced to provide grants-in-aid to the states to assist in the completion of primary routes, especially links in the interstate systems, some of which were not of much concern to the particular states involved. The federal government left the construction and maintenance in state hands, but gave the grants for specified routes only, required 50–50 matching by the states, and exercised some supervision over state use of the grants. Originally, the grants were made only for major interstate routes designated as federal-aid highways (234,000 miles in 1954); but eventually, funds were provided for secondary routes, by 1954 totaling 483,000 miles.

### The Postwar Breakdown in Highway Finance and the Solutions

By 1940 the problems of highway finance had apparently been solved relatively well, to the reasonable satisfaction of all concerned, although even at this point it was obvious that some routes were inadequate for the traffic which they were carrying. During the years of World War II, it was recognized that a major catching-up problem would exist after the war, but few persons realized its magnitude. By 1950, however, the problem was altogether too apparent; and by 1954, it appeared to be getting completely out of hand in some areas. The problem was simple: Many roads were inadequate, especially at peak hours, to handle the traffic seeking to use them, with consequent delays, frustration, and accidents. In some instances, almost complete breakdown of traffic movement occurred. Many roads had inadequate lanes for the traffic volume; local and through traffic were constantly intermingled, and the latter was subject to the obstacles of traffic signals and flow of traffic onto and off the roadway. Curvature was often excessive, and surfaces were broken. In some states, sharp pavement edges constituted a particularly malevolent hazard. Two serious mistakes had been made in highway planning of the twenties and thirties. Main highways had been routed through the center of every town, partly because of the location of the old access roads, partly because of violent pressure of merchants to prevent by-passing, which gave way only when the traffic became so bad as to choke off business. Secondly, the use of the rule of unlimited access permitted ribbon business developments on new as well as old highways, and greatly slowed down traffic and increased accidents.

The problem, serious as it has been in some areas, was a spotty one; many rural highways were entirely adequate for the traffic which they were likely to bear for many years to come. The problem was also largely a peak-load one, the congestion being concentrated in certain time periods, particularly in rush hours near metropolitan areas, while the highways were adequate most of the day.

### The Causes of the Difficulty

A combination of factors brought about the serious postwar problem. The war had postponed all construction for a four-year period, and thus created a serious backlog. Inflation had increased highway construction costs materially, roughly two and a half times between 1940 and 1956. Car usage had increased very rapidly, total vehicle-miles doubling between 1940 and 1955, and ton-mileage of large trucks increasing fivefold over the period. The increase was far greater than the average on access roads to metropolitan areas, in which suburbs had grown rapidly and public transport had declined. In many instances the increase was so great that the problem could be solved only by building a completely new road to high standards, at a cost per mile many times that of prewar roads.

In the face of this sharp increase in funds required to bring many highways up to standards regarded as acceptable, the system of highway finance under the commercial principle ceased to function satisfactorily; funds were not forthcoming at a rate high enough to satisfy demands of road users. There were several factors responsible, which serve to illustrate the difficulties with the use of the commercial principle for this type of activity. Directly and immediately, the lack of funds reflected the unwillingness of the legislative bodies to make adequate increases in the gasoline tax rate and license fees; the median rate of the tax rose only from 4 cents to 6 cents from 1940 to 1956. The specific nature of the gas tax rate in itself played a part, by aligning the forces of inertia on the side of inadequate revenues. Had the tax been ad valorem, the yield would have increased automatically as the price level rose.

The more fundamental question, however, is: Why did the states not act to provide the desired funds? Were highway users simply unwilling, as a whole, to sanction the higher tax levels necessary for the desired improvements, and thus essentially seeking something for nothing? If so, they of course had no one to blame but themselves; and in a sense, there was really no problem at all, given the use of the commercial principle. To some extent, this was the situation; persons were accustomed to certain tax levels in the field and were unwilling to stand the shock of rates perhaps twice as high. And much of the opposition to increases, which delayed action in the legislative bodies, came from the powerful lobbies of the oil industry and commercial highway user associations, the opposition in part reflecting a general and not entirely logical opposition to any tax increases affecting the industry. Providing a general background for the whole picture was the widespread feeling that all taxes, regardless of their use, were too high, a result primarily of the high federal income taxes.

But the obstacles in the way of financing the desired roads in part reflected a basic weakness in the commercial principle as it operated in the field of highway finance, namely, the lack of any close correlation between the highway user tax yields on particular roads and the expenditures upon improvements of those roads. Thus, highway user groups were more hostile to tax increases than they would otherwise have been, because they could not be sure that the funds would be used where they were most needed. In practice, under the formulas for allocation of highway tax revenues in many states, appropriate use of the funds in terms of highway needs was rendered impossible; far too much of the total was apportioned to rural roads, and far too little to major routes and urban expressways. Thus, only a small portion of any increase would go to the sphere of urgent need. The formulas reflected the situation in the early decades of the century, in which the greatest need was to "get the farmers out of the mud," and the domination of many state legislatures by rural groups, which blocked any change in the formulas.

This problem in part reflected the failure of the states to adjust the relative charges on various users in terms of their contributions to the congestion on the existing roads and the need for additional construction. In many areas, there was no need for additional roads, and little justification for assessing the users of existing roads large additional sums to build highways of no possible benefit to them. The persons using the congested roads were not required to pay additional sums to compensate for the "spill-over" costs arising from their contributions toward congestion, or for an adequate share of the cost of new roads necessary to eliminate the congestion. In many cases, had persons been required to pay the larger sums, the congestion would have been greatly reduced, as car travel would have been curtailed. But in practice, it was not possible to make the adjustments.

Also, the difficulty arose to some extent from the unwillingness of legislative bodies to vote tax increases which highway users who were footing the bill were willing to sanction. This was a result in part of strong commitments on the part of legislators and governors against any sort of tax increases, reflecting the general sentiment of the period, but unfortunately carried over into a field of taxation in which the persons involved might have sanctioned the increases. Legislators were also influenced, as noted above, by vociferous minority groups of road users, whose point of view did not necessarily reflect that of motorists as a whole.

In the absence of adequate tax increases the desired road improvements could be financed only by borrowing, but there were serious constitutional limitations on borrowing in many states, and the experience of the twenties with this method for highway purposes indicated the dangers. The high level of highway needs could well prove to be continuing rather than temporary.

Finally, it must be recognized that in part the problems reflected the inherent shortages of the postwar period, rather than merely financial difficulties. With full employment, it was not possible for highway construction to be undertaken as rapidly as many persons sought, even if funds had been available, at least not without a prohibitive increase in cost and major contributions to inflationary pressures. As it was, many projects were delayed for months at a time for lack of steel, and any major attempt to accelerate the program would have encountered increasingly serious obstacles of this type.

### The Seriousness of the Problem

The measurement of the exact amount of highway inadequacy and the funds needed to eliminate it was not an easy task, and statements varied widely. Typically, the task was left to engineers, who established certain standards, such as the requirement for four lanes on highways exceeding certain traffic densities. But this approach easily leads to an exaggeration of expenditure needs relative to the demand prices for road improvements; it would obviously be "nice" to have four-lane roads connecting all major cities, but motorists as a whole might prefer somewhat less adequate accommodations at substantially lower cost. Value judgments are inevitable in reaching decisions about road standards, and high-way engineers, just like specialists in any field, are apt to err in the direction of excessive perfection. In terms of the economy, needs for highways must be balanced against needs for other private sector and governmental sector outputs; no one would advocate spending so much money on highways, for example, that persons would not have enough income left after tax payments to buy cars to drive on them. Determining optimum highway expenditures is complicated by the peak-load nature of the problem, since roads adequate to meet peak-load demands adequately involve substantial waste of investment at other times. The use of the commercial principle could not provide answers to these questions because there was no direct tie between revenues gained from particular roads and the expenditures on them, and no satisfactory way of determining the users' choices among various alternatives.

Regardless of exact measurement of needs, however, it was obvious by the early fifties that many roads were inadequate in terms of what users of those particular roads were willing and able to pay; yet, in terms of the institutional framework, traditional methods, at least in some states, were failing to find an answer. As a consequence, two major developments took place: the toll road movement and the great increase in federal participation in highway development.

### The Toll Road Movement

The toll principle had long been rejected in the United States; and in fact, federal legislation even prohibited the use of tolls on federal-aid routes (except for special facilities such as bridges). But in the late thirties, the state of Pennsylvania, in an effort to find a solution for the need for an east-west highway to replace grossly inadequate routes, turned to the toll road approach and built the Pennsylvania Turnpike on the right-of-way of a graded but never-built railroad. The financial success of this project led other states into the field, primarily after World War II, until, by 1959, about three thousand miles of toll roads were in operation, the major route connecting the Chicago area with New York City. The routes are shown in Figure 31.

The toll solution allowed the building of the most urgently needed expensive intercity routes without the need for adjustment of gas tax rates or allocation formulas, and thus by-passed the blockade which had developed. The use of revenue bonds allowed escape from constitutional restrictions on state borrowing (which apply only to bonds which are obligations of the taxpayers), and thus immediate completion of major routes, rather than piecemeal building. The toll approach was also particularly attrac-

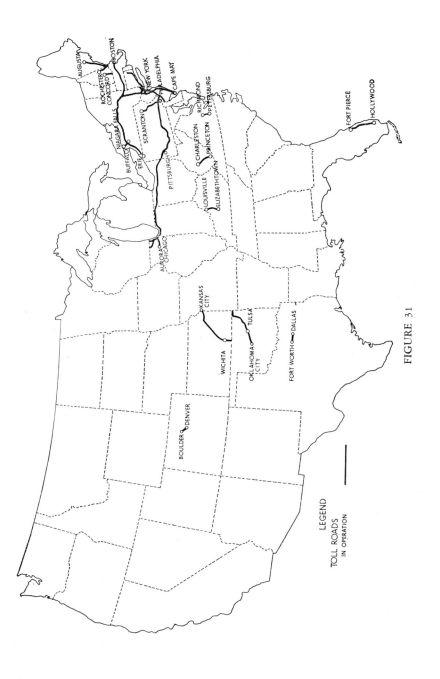

LEGEND

TOLL ROADS
IN OPERATION

FIGURE 31

tive to states such as New Jersey with a very heavy volume of cross-state traffic. Essentially, the toll system, by creating a direct link between user payments and expenditures on particular roads, enabled the users to obtain immediate construction of those facilities for which they were willing to pay enough to cover all costs.

The toll roads were, with minor exceptions, all four-lane roads, with access limited to a relatively few points. Tolls ranged typically from 1 to 2 cents per mile, with charges up to 4 to 10 cents a mile on larger vehicles. Considerable revenue was obtained from concessions to oil stations on the route. The accident rate was very much lower than on roads which they replaced. Financially, most of the first roads built were successful, some much more than anticipated. But several of the later projects were not; and by 1958, one system, West Virginia's, was unable to meet bond interest payments. The inadequate profits of the later routes served as one factor in pricking the bubble of toll road building; in the period around 1954, grandiose schemes developed for toll roads which could not have covered their costs had they been built.

Despite the success of some of these routes in meeting urgent highway needs, the toll road movement suffered serious limitations as an overall solution to the highway problem. Wholesale replacement of the traditional highway user taxes by highway user charges was clearly not the answer, even though the method provided a more direct link between payments and benefits and a more direct guide to allocation of funds for particular projects. In the first place, tolls are more costly to collect than user taxes, and create far more nuisance for the motorist. These problems are not serious on high-density, long-distance-travel routes, but they become progressively more significant as the use of tolls is expanded. Secondly, toll roads are necessarily more expensive to build than their free counterparts, since entry must be restricted more rigidly, existing routes cannot usually be utilized, and greater duplication of other facilities is required. The interest burden, particularly with the higher-interest revenue bonds, is substantial, as compared to tax-financed highways. These three considerations severely limit the scope of toll roads, and only a relatively small portion of the total mileage of the country could be self-supporting on a toll basis.

From the standpoint of resource utilization, tolls on roads which are not utilized to capacity unnecessarily restrict usage, to a much greater extent than the gas tax, and lead many motorists to use the less satisfactory routes instead. The toll method is particularly unsuitable on metropolitan area roads, because of the need for numerous points of entrance and the peak-load problem, yet it is in these areas that the greatest congestion occurs. Some authorities have argued that the toll movement interfered with the development of a rationally planned over-all system by allowing the perpetuation of the obsolete allocation formulas and lessening the need for adjustments in highway user levies.

The peak year of toll road construction was 1955. By the end of 1956 the movement had largely come to an end, partly because of the unhappy financial results of some of the newer roads, partly because of the federal highway program noted below. As of 1963, however, a few projected routes are under consideration.

The pricing policies of the toll road systems have been relatively simple: The various classes of traffic have been charged on the basis of engineering estimates of "what the traffic will bear"—of demand considerations almost entirely, a figure being selected which, it is believed, will maximize revenue. No attempt has been made to set price for various classes of users on the basis of estimated costs to the particular classes. Changes, few in number, have been made only where revenues were proving insufficient and changes (upward in some cases, downward in others) were expected to prove beneficial to revenues.

### The 1956 Federal Highway Program

As noted, ever since 1916 the federal government has aided the states by grants for highway purposes, to the sum of $600 million annually in the early fifties. In September of 1954, in recognition of the problem of lagging highway construction, President Eisenhower appointed a committee known, for its chairman, General Lucius Clay, as the Clay Committee, to study the highway problem. The report, issued in January, 1955, stressed the need for improved highways from the standpoints of military and civil defense and economic development, and urged the spending of a total of $101 billion over the next ten-year period, an increase of $54 billion over the funds available from existing programs. The committee urged a sharp increase in federal participation (from 8 to 30 per cent of the total), and financing via bond issues. The President recommended to Congress in 1955 the enactment of the program envisaged by the committee, but because of a fight over bond versus tax financing, action was not taken until 1956.

As enacted, the new program had several major features:

1. Provision over a thirteen-year period of grants of $27.5 billion for the new 41,000-mile National System of Interstate and Defense Highways connecting the major cities, and for connecting urban expressways and belts. This network, involving largely new four-lane construction, is financed to the extent of 90 per cent by the federal government (up to 95 per cent in some states).

2. Allocation of funds, after 1958, on the basis of amounts needed

to complete the system in each state, in contrast to the old formula of allocation on the basis of mail route mileage, population, and area, which was not satisfactory in terms of relative needs of different states. Federal controls over standards were increased.

3. Continuation of the old grant program on an enlarged basis.

4. Increases in taxes on gasoline, on sale of trucks and busses, and on tires, and collection of an annual use tax on trucks.

5. The establishment of the principle of earmarking these additional revenues for highway purposes into the Highway Trust Fund. This was a completely new departure in federal finance, which had previously treated highway grants as a regular budgetary expenditure and the highway user taxes as "luxury" excises.

The new program involved an increase in highway expenditures of about $2 billion a year, with great emphasis on the 41,000-mile network and urban expressways, not previously aided to any extent by the federal government. By 1962, 33 per cent of the 41,000-mile network had been completed. Since most of the needed major routes are being built under this program, the chances for expansion of the toll routes were largely ended, and the legislation provided for study of possible absorption of the toll roads into the federal highway system.

The program clearly had certain advantages, particularly in helping to break the roadblock in the way of highway expansion, and had merit over the previous federal programs in allocating funds more closely in terms of need and in providing assistance for urban area routes. The adoption of the commercial principle for federal highway finance offers the same merits as at the state level, although the elimination of the sums from the budgetary totals is most unfortunate and results in a serious distortion of figures of trends in government expenditures. Essentially, the enactment of the program reflects the greater willingness of Congress than the state legislatures to meet the pleas of road users for improved highways, and partly the willingness of the user groups to accept the higher levies because of assurance that the funds will be used on the more needed roads. Thus the commercial principle is made to operate somewhat more effectively than it did in state hands alone.

However, the program is open to several objections. The increased role of the federal government contributes little or nothing to greater efficiency in highway construction, toward the opening of new revenue sources, or toward equalization among states. The same revenue sources are used as those employed by the states, and the latter could certainly have financed the program equally well had they been willing to do so. But their inability to surmount the problems discussed in previous sections resulted in federal action and transfer of a large part of responsibility in a traditional state sphere of action to the federal government.

The federal program, as established in 1956, called for a program of expenditures over a thirteen-year period, the annual amounts to be completely independent of business conditions. This aspect of the program was widely criticized in light of the possible contributions which the program might make toward greater economic stability, rather than merely aggravating inflationary pressures. Early in 1958, as business activity continued to decline, Congress provided for an acceleration of the rate of spending. It is very doubtful, of course, whether the expanded federal program will actually come to an end in 1972. Since the earliest days of highway finance in the United States, the notion that the problem is of "once and for all" nature has been widely accepted, yet in the past proven by experience to be incorrect.

### An Alternative Solution—Demand Restriction

Governments have been very reluctant to meet the problem of highway congestion by restriction of demand, the whole emphasis being upon increasing supply, largely because of the tradition that roads must be open to anyone at any time, even when traffic conditions are so bad that the "inalienable right" to use a road meant in practice the right to get caught (and help catch others) in a traffic jam. Particularly as a temporary measure, pending the making of improvements, demand restriction has much to commend it. The congestion problems center on certain bottleneck roads; restriction of trucking on these roads during periods of congestion, such as week ends or rush commuting hours, could in some instances do a great deal to speed traffic without great injury to the truck operators. As a more general solution of this type, in theory at least, tolls could be applied to existing routes used beyond capacity in an effort to restrict usage. Tolls have traditionally been regarded as means of financing, not as means of controlling use, yet from the standpoint of resource utilization, their primary potential function is along the latter lines, as a means of rationing available space and forcing the users of the congested roads to pay for the "spill-over" costs which they create, that is, their contributions toward traffic congestion and consequent higher costs of travel for others. But the task of administering such tolls would frequently be difficult, and an extensive educational campaign would be necessary to impress upon the users the usefulness of the toll system as a rationing device.

From a longer range standpoint the case for general usage restriction (below the level which occurs when no specific tolls or restrictions are applied) is weaker; so long as the road users are willing to pay for the additional road capacity, the production of it is warranted. Unfortunately, however, the lack of a direct correlation between the amounts of highway user taxes collected on particular roads and the expenditures on the roads lessens the direct applicability of the commercial principle in determining optimum expenditures on particular highways. Persons seeking very expensive new routes to eliminate congestion in peak-load periods may well not pay for them in full, the funds being drained in part from other parts of the road system. In view of the great difficulty of establishing a direct link in the absence of the troublesome and expensive toll system, highway users as a whole may well be better off if somewhat less is spent on the routes involved, and steps are undertaken to restrict peak-load demand; otherwise, a tremendous sum of money may be invested in road capacity which is unused most of the time, a sum far in excess of the amount the additional peak-load users themselves would be willing to pay for the facilities.

### Improved Road Utilization

A related alternative, but one much more palatable politically, is that of improving the utilization of existing roads. In many cases, relatively minor improvements, such as rerouting roads around the outskirts of towns and the addition of passing lanes on hills, will tremendously improve the flow of traffic on existing routes at costs relatively small compared to those of building new four-lane highways. Even more important is the need for revision of traffic control policies, with increased emphasis on keeping the flow of traffic moving, rather than constantly attempting to slow it down. In many instances, speed limits are set far below the figures consistent with reasonable safety; while these cannot be effectively enforced, they do have the effect of impeding traffic flow. On the other hand, minimum speed requirements on main highways are urgently needed, yet almost never employed. The notion that a motorist is free to loiter at any low speed he prefers, while he is prohibited from exceeding a certain rigidly set figure, is an obsolete carry-over from earlier decades which is a serious handicap to effective road utilization. In urban areas, excessive use of four-way stop signs, poor timing of traffic lights, and failure to stop double parking are major sources of traffic pile-ups.

### The Urban Area Problem

The most troublesome aspect of the highway problem is that of handling traffic within metropolitan areas. Typically, the arterial and business streets of such areas witness the worst congestion on the highway system, and the solutions are the most difficult, particularly because of the tremendous expense of providing more adequate streets. The building of expressways has facilitated the movement of vehicles between certain sectors of the areas, but unfortunately often aggravates the congestion in the downtown areas. This case, unlike that of intercity highways, is clearly one in which the expense necessary to provide all of the facilities which car users desire (at present levels of charges) would be tremendously greater than the users would possibly be willing to pay. Inherent limitations of space in such areas make provision of adequate street and parking space almost completely prohibitive. Expansion in supply cannot solve the problem in the larger cities, as it can in smaller ones and rural areas; some other approach must be followed to restrict the usage to a level consistent with movement at a tolerable pace. There are three general types of solutions:

1. Over-all planned community redevelopment, which will lessen the concentration of traffic in downtown areas, solving the problem by moving out business and industry, and thus reducing the numbers seeking to use the areas.[2] This is at best a slow and laborious process, one which many persons feel is neither practicable or desirable.

2. Restriction of usage of downtown streets.[3] A second alternative is the deliberate restriction of usage of downtown streets, and thus curtailment of demand to available street space. It is particularly important to cut down on the volume of traffic in rush hours, particularly the use of cars to drive to and from work. Deliberate prohibitions against use of cars are highly unpopular and difficult to administer, although control of truck traffic at certain hours is not impossible. Tolls on access roads are sometimes suggested, but expensive and troublesome to collect, particularly at rush hours. One of the most feasible methods is that of discouraging travel into congested areas by rigid control of parking, with restriction of curb parking which interferes with traffic flow, and the imposition of very substantial charges for parking in the congested areas. By this means, downtown car travel will be restricted to those persons who are willing to pay the price sufficient to ration the downtown area street and parking space. Parking meters and off-street parking represent a step in this direction; but typically, the charges are far too low, in terms of the cost and rationing needs.

3. Improvement of mass transit. The third method is that of provid-

---

[2] The best presentation of this point of view is to be found in W. Owen, *The Metropolitan Transportation Problem* (Washington, D.C.: Brookings Institution, 1956).

[3] See L. Fitch, "Financing Urban Roadways," in *Financing Highways* (Princeton: Tax Institute, 1957).

ing improved mass transportation, to encourage persons to use the far more efficient mass carriers and leave their cars at home. Unfortunately, as car usage has developed, mass transportation has seriously deteriorated in many areas, to the point at which many persons have no alternative except to drive. Urban transit is rarely profitable in itself, but its important contributions to the lessening of automobile traffic congestion make it economically justifiable. Even if some service of this type can cover its costs, the total amount supplied on a profitmaking basis will be too small, in light of the indirect social benefits from the service from which the operators can realize no dollar return. Accordingly, governmental provision of the service is essential, as well as partial support from general revenues, to insure full realization of the indirect benefits. Unfortunately, in many large cities the importance of mass transportation in solving the traffic problem was not recognized soon enough, and efficient systems were allowed to deteriorate badly.[4] By 1963, however, renewed interest in the question led to several experiments designed to improve mass transport.

## THE ALLOCATION PROBLEM

Since the earliest days of the use of the commercial principle of highway finance, one troublesome problem has defied solution, namely, that of the appropriate allocation of highway costs among various groups. There are two main aspects: the allocation of the costs between highway users and general taxpayers, and the allocation among various classes of highway users.

The first problem is essentially an aspect of the question: To what extent should the commercial principle be employed in highway finance? Even in the absence of automobiles, some streets and roads would be required, and thus it can be argued that motor vehicles should not be assessed the entire sum of highway costs. Furthermore, it is argued that highway development offers important secondary benefits to society as a whole through lower costs of transport, lower prices of commodities, and the like. The second argument has virtually no merit, since this type of secondary benefit is characteristic of all industries, and accrues through those directly using the highways; its existence offers no justification for subsidizing highway construction from general levies, any more than it

---

[4] The exact type of service required depends upon the circumstances. In the largest cities, rail rapid transit lines, despite their high initial cost, remain as the most effective carriers. In some instances, busses operated on expressways may be adequate; but unfortunately, these are caught in the same traffic jams as the private vehicles. One of the most effective forms, suburban service on main-line railroads, is still in private hands, but must be taken over by governmental units if it is to survive.

justifies subsidies to the steel industry, the railroads, or department stores.

The first argument has some merit, but it cannot be resolved on any scientific basis. The question can be decided only in terms of general public policy decisions about the relative merits of various degrees of use of the commercial principle. In practice, the tendency has been to apply the commercial principle more or less completely to state highways (under the assumption that the costs are due entirely to motor vehicles), but only partially to local roads, which are largely financed by property tax levies or, for city streets, by special assessments. This practice cannot be condemned in any objective fashion; many of the attempts to develop a more refined allocation are largely futile.

## Standards of Allocation by Vehicle Class

The question of relative charges on different classes of users has received even greater attention for several decades. There are two primary approaches, involving incremental costs and ton-miles, respectively.

1. *The Incremental Cost Approach.*[5] One approach to allocation is that of determining the additional or incremental cost for which each particular class of vehicles is responsible, and adjusting the charges accordingly. After early attempts to use this method proved futile, relatively little use was made of it for some years; but since 1953, it has enjoyed a revival, in studies in Ohio and Louisiana particularly. This method seeks to determine exactly how much each particular vehicle class adds to the total cost of highway construction and maintenance. Those elements which are related to weight are ascertained on the basis of engineering studies of additional costs necessitated by successive weight classes. Other cost elements are allocated on the basis of vehicle-miles or other criteria. From the standpoint of the economics of highway finance the approach has great merit, since it permits the adjustment of highway user charges in terms of marginal social costs for which each type of vehicle is responsible.

However, it is subject to several limitations, the most serious of which is that of ascertaining the actual increments in cost attributable to each weight class. Over the years, engineers have differed widely on this question, although a series of tests of highway wear conducted in recent years helps to throw some light on the question. Inevitably, the method involves some arbitrary allocation, without respect to actual incremental costs, of the large part of the total cost independent of weight, and the making of arbitrary assumptions about the functional relationships involved. The use of weight classes ignores, of course, variations within

---

[5] See W. D. Ross, "The Incremental Method of Allocating Highway Costs as a Basis for Motor Vehicle Taxation," *National Tax Journal*, Vol. VIII (June, 1955), pp. 201–8.

classes, dependent particularly upon the specific roads used. Certain vehicles, driven primarily on roads designed for lower weight, may cause maintenance costs all out of proportion to those caused by the weight class as a whole, and others may be used in such a manner as to contribute materially to delay and congestion.

A major question in the field of incremental costs relates to the desirability of inclusion of "spill-over" costs, the expenses created for other highway users by particular vehicles, rather than for cost of highway construction and maintenance. There are very real costs, indeed; slowly moving vehicles impede the speed of other persons, cause loss of time, and increase accident hazards. Diesel busses in some urban areas add seriously to smoke and smog hazards. Whenever roads are used to capacity, additional vehicles seeking to use the roads create additional costs for other users. To some extent, these are temporary elements, of particular importance in the period before highways are improved; but in part, they are permanent, since standards of construction necessary to eliminate all such delays would be intolerably expensive. In practice, these "spill-over" costs are not taken into consideration, and any precise adjustment in terms of them would be impossible. They may be regarded, however, as justification for imposing higher levies on vehicles used primarily in congested metropolitan areas than those used mainly in rural areas or small towns.

2. *The Ton-Mile Approach.* In light of the difficulties of ascertaining incremental cost, the more common approach to the establishment of standards of allocation by vehicle class is that of ton-miles, all highway costs being allocated uniformly on this basis. This is a very simple solution, involving the implicit assumptions that either cost or benefit, or both, vary directly with ton-mileage. This is, of course, a highly arbitrary assumption, but it appears to be reasonable to many people, in the absence of any more satisfactory incremental cost standard.

### Attainment of the Desired Allocation

Given the standards of allocation regarded as desirable, there remains the problem of how to attain the desired allocation in practice. Motor fuel tax burden does not increase in proportion to weight; and therefore, on the ton-mileage and probably on the incremental cost approach, this tax does not place an adequate burden on the larger vehicles. The attempt to compensate for this by varying the license fees by weight, which is the universal practice for larger vehicles, is not entirely satisfactory, since the charges bear no relation to mileage traveled.

To attain more satisfactory allocation, several states have developed ton-mileage or axle-mileage levies, commonly known as third-structure taxes. These require the payment of an annual tax from larger vehicles based upon the number of miles traveled and either the number of axles (e.g., Ohio) or the declared loaded weight (e.g., New York). Most logically, a true ton-mileage tax would be preferable, but the tasks of keeping and checking records of ton-miles would be so great that the states have used the simpler versions noted above. While the administrative costs have been relatively high compared to many taxes, the states using the levies are well satisfied with them. The trucking associations, however, violently oppose the taxes, partly because of compliance problems, partly because they inevitably increase the taxes on some types of trucks.

A related problem is that of the relative taxes on gasoline and diesel fuel; since diesel trucks obtain more miles per gallon (one third to one half more) than those using gasoline (for a given weight), the tax must necessarily be greater, per gallon, on the diesel fuel. Yet few states (nine in 1962) have followed this policy, and in many of these the differential is inadequate. The argument of the diesel truck operators that a differential discriminates against them and discourages the use of the more efficient diesel motors is absolute nonsense, since the adjustment is necessary to equalize contributions per ton-mile.

The problems of motor vehicle taxation in the United States are greatly complicated by the importance of interstate commercial operations. Typically, the states, through reciprocity agreements, do not require licenses of out-of-state trucks. But this rule has not been entirely satisfactory to some states, and has led in the West to proration of license fees among the various states, and in other areas to the requirement that truck lines prorate their fleet registrations by state. States have also restricted the amounts of fuel that a truck may bring into the state in its tanks without paying tax to the state. The development of the ton-mile taxes has created new problems for reciprocity; in general, the states quite rightfully apply this tax to all truck operations in the state, whether by domestic or out-of-state trucks. The firms claimed this policy violated the reciprocity agreements, and other states canceled their agreements. Gradually, however, the right to collect the taxes regardless of the agreements has been recognized.

## CONCLUSION

The use of the commercial principle in the field of highway finance has demonstrated important advantages. It prevents (or lessens) subsidization of highway transport compared to other forms, insures substantial sums for highway development without the need for constant balancing of the demands for better roads against those for other governmental activities, and avoids further increases in ability-based taxes. The employment of use-based taxation to implement the commercial principle has avoided the expense and nuisance of direct toll collection, and lessened unnecessary restriction in the use of roads not used to capacity. On the other hand, the system failed to respond adequately to the greatly increased need for highway expenditures after World War II, partly because of the lack of a direct connection between additional collections and expenditures on the most needed roads, partly because the road users wanted more than they appeared willing to pay for, and partly because of the failure of legislatures to reflect user will adequately. The result was the toll road movement, and then the federal program, which broke the bottlenecks, in part, in state financing, and applied the commercial principle to the federal sphere. The commercial principle has proven least satisfactory in the area of metropolitan traffic problems, in which restriction of demand and assistance to more efficient mass transit are essential to an adequate solution, since the supply increase approach is inadequate, and the user charges do not fully reflect "spill-over" costs of car use.

## APPENDIX

### Canadian and British Practice

Few countries have gone so far as the United States in the direction of use of the commercial principle of highway finance. Most countries tax motor fuels and collect license fees, but there is rarely any earmarking, or any direct connection between the total of highway charges and highway expenditures.

In Canada, highway construction is primarily a provincial function, with local government provision of local roads and streets. The highway expenditures are treated as a regular budget item, with no earmarking of funds, and no direct adjustment of annual expenditures to current yields of the highway user charges, although in practice there is obviously some rough relationship. In the 1946–51 period, about 80 per cent of all provincial highway expenditures were covered by highway user levies (ranging from 42 per cent in Newfoundland to 116 per cent in Saskatchewan). In 1960 the figure was 57 per cent. The highway user levies themselves are comparable to those in the United States, although gasoline tax rates are higher (about 30 per cent higher in recent years, with a median of 14 cents per gallon, and figures as high as 19 cents). Third-structure taxes are not used, and the toll principle has not been employed. On the whole, Canadian highway development has lagged behind that in the United States, largely because the initial task was a much more difficult one, in terms of mileage required relative to vehicle use. The Dominion government has never established a continuing highway program at all comparable to even the pre-1956 federal program in the United States. Grants have been given at certain times for specific purposes, such as for the not fully completed Trans-Canada Highway.

Great Britain has in practice made even less use of the commercial principle than Canada, although for a number of years it did have a road fund to which highway user levies were credited, and the funds supposedly used for roadbuilding. In practice, the charges were frequently used for other purposes, and in 1936 the road fund system was essentially abandoned. In recent years, highway expenditures have been treated as normal budget items and highway user levies as normal budget revenues. The user taxes are high, the gasoline (petrol) tax being 2s. 6 d. (about 35 cents at current exchange rates) a gallon. The annual highway expenditures have been only about one fourth the yield of the charges, to the continued and bitter complaint of the highway user groups, particularly in light of the hopeless inadequacy of many British roads. Any substantial increase in roadbuilding, at all comparable to the yield of the highway user charges, has been regarded as impossible, in light of other demands on government, and the user charges are considered basically as general government revenues.[6]

## REFERENCES

BURCH, PHILIP H. *Highway Revenue and Expenditure Policy.* New Brunswick: Rutgers University Press, 1962.
 A review of highway finance and administration.
ZETTEL, R. M. "Whither Highway User Charges?" *Proceedings of the National Tax Association for 1961*, pp. 665–92.
 A good summary of the issues.
BUCHANAN, J. M. "The Pricing of Highway Services," *National Tax Journal*, Vol. V (June, 1952), pp. 97–106.
BROWNLEE, O. H., and HELLER, W. W. "Highway Development and Financing," *Proceedings of the American Economic Association for 1955*, pp. 234–64.
JOINT ECONOMIC COMMITTEE. "Federal Expenditures for Transportation, Particularly Highways," *Federal Expenditure Policy for Economic Growth and Stability.* Washington, D.C.: U.S. Government Printing Office, 1957.
 See particularly the papers by H. HOUTHAKKER and R. M. ZETTEL.

[6] See G. Walker, "Highway Finance," *Journal of Industrial Economics*, Vol. IV (June, 1956), pp. 161–77, for a review of British experience.

*Proceedings of the National Tax Association* for recent years.

NETZER, D. "Financial Policy for Highways," *National Tax Journal*, Vol. X (June, 1957), pp. 114–25.

CANADIAN TAX FOUNDATION. *Taxes and Traffic.* Toronto, 1955.
A review of Canadian experience and problems.

TAX INSTITUTE. *Financing Highways.* Princeton, 1957.
A series of papers on highway finance.

### TOLL ROADS

DEARING, C. L. "Toll Road Rates and Highway Pricing," *Proceedings of the American Economic Association for 1956*, pp. 441–52.

NETZER, D. "Toll Roads and the Crisis in Highway Finance," *National Tax Journal*, Vol. V (June, 1952), pp. 107–19.

DUE, J. F. "The Rise and Decline of the Toll Principle in Highway Finance," *National Tax Journal*, Vol. X (June, 1957), pp. 97–115.

OWEN, W., and DEARING, C. L. *Toll Roads and the Problems of Highway Modernization.* Washington, D.C.: Brookings Institution, 1951.

# PART VII

## Over-all Aspects of

## Government Finance

# Chapter 24 | INTERGOVERNMENTAL FISCAL RELATIONS

If all governmental activities in a country were conducted by a single government, the over-all expenditure and revenue policies could be developed in an integrated fashion. Expenditures for all purposes could be weighed against one another to insure an optimum balance in terms of community preferences for the various services. The tax structure could be built up in such a manner as to attain most satisfactorily the accepted principles of taxation. But when activities are divided among various levels of government, each unit making its own decisions on expenditures and establishing its own tax structure, the attainment of the desired expenditure and tax goals is made much more difficult. No longer is the balancing of the gains from various activities against one another performed by a single government; no longer are the expenditures financed from one tax structure. The problems are further complicated when the governmental structure is a federal one, with constitutional division of powers between federal and state governments. The difficulties created by the division of governmental activities among various levels of government are known as the problems of intergovernmental fiscal relations.

## THE PROBLEMS

Further analysis of the problems is necessary before consideration can be given to various solutions. The major ones are reviewed in the succeeding paragraphs.

### Lack of Correlation between Expenditures and Revenue Sources

The most basic problem arising from the division of the conduct of activities and the collection of taxes among the verious levels of government is the lack of correlation between the amounts of expenditures which the particular units of government wish to make, on the one hand, and the

435

potential yield of the taxes which they can use satisfactorily, on the other. The criteria which determine the optimum allocation of functions, and thus of expenditures, among the different levels of government are substantially different from those which determine the optimum use of various taxes by the various governmental units. As a consequence, some units have inadequate revenues compared to their functions and expenditure needs, whereas others have greater potential revenue than they need.

1. *Criteria for the Allocation of Functions.* The primary considerations determining the unit of government which can most satisfactorily perform a particular activity are those of efficiency, need for uniform standards and policy, and adjustment of the activities in conformity with the wishes of the persons concerned.

From the standpoint of efficiency the higher levels of government obtain certain economies of large-scale production, which are lost if the activities are performed by smaller units. Some of the activities, such as education, fully attain these economies at the county level; others, such as national defense, do so only at the federal level. On the other hand, performance at the higher levels produces the inevitable disadvantages of large-scale bureaucracy, such as delay, red tape, wasted administrative personnel, etc. Because of these considerations, there is merit in keeping particular activities in the hands of the lowest units of government which are able to attain major economies of large-scale production. For example, transfer of fire protection from the city to the state or federal level would produce few economies and a substantial increase in bureaucratic inefficiency.

The second criterion is that of the need for uniformity in standards and policy. If the need for a unified policy is very great, as is true with national defense or monetary and fiscal policy, the activity must be carried on at the federal level. In other cases, such as welfare, highways, and education, the need for a unified policy is less essential. Yet even with these activities, minimum standards are desirable, because policies followed in one area do affect persons in another. In the interests of the entire country, children growing up in some parts of the country should not be deprived of educational facilities comparable to those available in other areas, at least up to certain minimum standards. If the activity is of almost purely local concern, such as street lighting, uniformity is not important.

Thirdly, the adjustment of the activities in terms of the wishes of the persons directly affected is desirable, so long as policies thus determined do not conflict significantly with the interests of society as a whole. The retention of activities at the local level increases the extent to which they can be adjusted in terms of the needs and desires of the persons in the localities and insures closer contact between the persons receiving the services and those determining policy. Transfer of activities to higher units of government results in the making of decisions by persons out of touch with circumstances and desires in the particular cases.

On the whole, these criteria suggest that while certain activities must be placed in the hands of the higher levels of government in the interests of efficiency, unified policy, and consideration of the interests of the entire nation, activities should be kept in the hands of the smallest units which can perform them effectively in a manner consistent with the interests of society as a whole. While increased complexity and interdependence of the economy have resulted in greater centralization in government, there is very widespread acceptance of the principle that functions should not be transferred to the higher levels except in those cases in which there is clear demonstration of net gains from doing so.

With certain activities, performance can justifiably be kept at lower levels of government, yet some stimulus to raise standards of performance is needed because some benefits from the activities go to persons in other areas. High educational standards provide benefits which extend far beyond the confines of the particular school district, and good roads benefit motorists from other areas as well as the local residents. But a local government—and even the states in some instances—will take into consideration only the benefits accruing to the residents of the taxing jurisdiction. Especially in the small local governments the persons responsible for policy decisions may not be aware of improved standards and methods or be conscious of the benefits of various activities. Accordingly, a certain amount of stimulus of local activity in the interests of the state and the country as a whole is justifiable and necessary for the attainment of optimum levels of government activity.

2. *Criteria for the Allocation of Taxes among Governmental Units.* There are two primary criteria determining the unit of government which can most satisfactorily utilize various possible taxes and thus the optimum allocation of the use of the taxes among the various levels of government. The first is administrative efficiency, while the second is the nature of the economic effects which result from the tax.

Efficiency of administration depends in large measure upon the ability of the governmental unit to obtain necessary information about the amount of tax base in the hands of particular taxpayers. As a general rule, this is possible only if the activity involved in the base of the tax takes place within the taxing jurisdiction. It is difficult, if not impossible, for example, for a local government to ascertain income earned by residents from investments in distant states or to discover intangibles owned by residents representing claims against property in other areas. Only with great difficulty can a state discover purchases made by its residents from outside sources. In general, the larger the unit of government, the fewer will be the taxable activities not completed within its borders. Thus the larger units of government can administer most taxes more effectively than the smaller units. Not only are transactions made within the taxing jurisdiction easier to discover, but the taxes upon them can be enforced more effectively when they are discovered. For example, the taxation of interstate transactions is restricted not only by constitutional limitations but also by the difficulty of enforcing payment of the tax which is legally due. In other cases, transactions which are made across governmental borders are subject to discriminatory double taxation, with consequent loss of equity.

The possibility of migration of the tax base is the economic consideration of primary importance. Whenever migration is relatively easy, attempts to tax will yield little revenue and will produce economic effects particularly adverse to the taxing jurisdiction. Thus, if a city attempts to use a sales or gasoline tax of any magnitude, some shoppers will transfer their purchases to suburban vendors. Heavy state taxation of income may induce some persons to leave the state. Municipal income taxes applying to all income of residents would encourage persons to move out into the suburbs.

Most taxes can be collected with the highest degree of effectiveness by the federal government, while very few can be administered in even a tolerable fashion by the local governments. The states occupy an intermediate position. But the extent of superiority of the federal government over the other units and that of the states over the localities vary according to the nature of the tax.

Income taxes can, without question, be administered most effectively and with least migration of economic activity by the federal government. State use is feasible, although less satisfactory, while local use is not feasible, because many incomes are earned in one area by persons living in another, migration of economic activity among local units is easy, and the local governments cannot obtain adequate information about total incomes received. A local income tax can be administered only if it is confined to limited types of incomes, such as wages earned within the taxing jurisdiction.

Sales and excise taxes can be administered only by the federal government if they are imposed at the manufacturing level. But at the retail level the advantages of the federal government are weaker, and the states can administer such taxes with a high degree of effectiveness, although with some interstate complications. Local sales taxation is much less satisfactory, because out-of-city purchases will escape tax, and retailers will be encouraged to locate outside the city limits.

Death taxes may be administered almost equally well by the states and the federal government. Only the federal government could administer a tax on all net wealth, but the local governments can tax real property and certain types of tangible property; this is the one major tax which the localities can satisfactorily administer. Information is available to them, migration is difficult, and no cross-boundary problems arise.

As a result of the diverse criteria which determine optimum location of functions, on the one hand, and tax administration, on the other, the local governments are, in general, in the position of requiring far more money than they can raise. They are confined largely to the property tax, which, in light of its basic limitations, is inadequate to provide the funds necessary to finance the activities which they conduct. To a limited extent, they can use other sources, but any extensive use of either income or sales taxes results in inequities and produces adverse economic effects. On the other hand, the federal government and the states have more extensive tax sources. Under ordinary conditions, they are able to finance their activities without serious difficulty and, except in periods of war or depression, can actually raise much more in taxes than the amounts which they are currently spending. A major consequence of this situation is the inevitable tendency for those activities carried on by the local governments to be starved for funds and thus curtailed below levels which are regarded by society as optimum, relative to the levels to which federal and state functions are extended. Accordingly, an optimum over-all pattern of governmental activities and expenditures is less likely to be attained than in a governmental structure which has only one level.

### Unequal Revenue Sources at the Same Level of Government

The second major problem of intergovernmental fiscal relations is the uneven distribution of tax capacity relative to functions among various governmental units at the same level. The most serious problems arise with the local governments, particularly in financing education. The variation in the amount of property per capita among the school districts in a state is as a rule very substantial. The poorer districts must either operate with lower standards or levy higher tax rates than the wealthier areas. While the problem is most serious in the field of education, it arises with other functions as well. A low-income area, for example, is likely to have much greater demand for relief and old-age pension payments, although it has less means with which to pay them, at given tax rates. The problems of the states in highway construction are similar, because some states have greater road mileage per capita and per dollar of total personal income than other states.

The unequal division of tax resources has several undesirable consequences. In the first place, the poorer areas will have great difficulty in maintaining as high standards of performance as the wealthier areas. Roads will be poor, educational facilities limited, old-age pensions low. But many of these functions, while best performed at the state and local level, offer benefits which accrue in part to the people of the country as a whole. Persons from some states take trips into others, and those educated in one state may move to another, for example.

Furthermore, the basic equity rule of equal treatment of equals cannot be attained when the tax resources of the various units differ. If given standards of education require twice as high a tax rate in one area as in another, persons in like circumstances, except for the geographical location of their homes, are not being treated equally. It is hardly in conformity with accepted standards of equity that an old person living in a poor area receive a much smaller old-age pension than one living in a wealthy area, simply because the first unit cannot afford to pay as much.

Finally, unequal tax resources, with consequent uneven tax burdens relative to benefits, will result in uneconomic relocation of economic activity. Businesses will tend to move from the poor, high-tax, low-benefit areas to those in which tax rates are lower and benefits greater. As a result, geographical neutrality of the governmental activities is not attained.

### Overlapping of Tax Sources

The third intergovernmental problem is that of overlapping of use of particular tax sources by different levels of government. There are only a few major taxes which meet the accepted criteria of a desirable tax structure. Most of these taxes can be administered, although not always with maximum efficiency, by more than one level of government. Because of the recognized superiority of some of these taxes over others and the limited number of alternatives, they have been adopted by more than one governmental unit. The political reaction to very high rates on any one tax has encouraged diversity in tax structures, which furthers the amount of overlapping use of particular taxes. Both the federal government and a number of states employ income taxes, and a few municipalities levy taxes on certain types of income. Death taxes, the gasoline tax, and taxes on liquor and tobacco are used by the federal government and almost all states. Although the states have largely withdrawn from the property tax field, some localities have invaded the sales and gasoline tax fields, which have long been state domains.

In Canada the degree of multiple taxation is less. There is little overlap of personal and corporate income taxes or death taxes. On the other hand, the Dominion government and eight provinces levy sales taxes, as well as municipalities in Quebec.

The use of a particular tax by more than one level of government is not necessarily objectionable. If the tax is preferable to alternatives available, can be administered well by both levels, and is necessary to preserve the financial autonomy of the lower government, multiple use may be justifiable. But indiscriminate multiplication of overlapping taxation has several disadvantages. In all cases, some administrative duplication results. For example, in Canada, both the federal government and eight provinces have separate sales tax auditing staffs, in many cases auditing the same firms. In the United States, there is substantial duplication of income tax auditing by the federal and state governments. Secondly, nuisance is created for the taxpayers, who must file separate returns and supply time and information to auditors from both levels of government. Thirdly, from the standpoint of the tax structure itself, if each taxing jurisdiction determines its rate independently of the rate of the other, the combined figure may be excessive in terms of the standards accepted by either government and a source of serious adverse economic effects. For example, marginal income tax rates as high as perhaps 75 per cent might have little adverse effects on incentives. But if the federal government adopted this rate and then the states levied high income tax rates as well, the combined rate might approach 100 per cent, with extremely serious consequences.

More likely, however, the government which first uses the tax may, in fact, pre-empt it to the exclusion of those which follow. If, for example, the federal government uses a high income tax, it is not politically feasible for the states to gain much revenue from this field, even though it might provide a more suitable source than those which they use. This "pre-emption" principle may work in the direction of a more logical over-all tax structure, but it may have the opposite effect. The net result depends largely upon the historical accident of which government arrived on the tax scene first.

A related problem, but one with more serious equity consequences, is overlapping taxation of the same units of the tax base by more than one state or local government. Thus, interstate incomes or estates may be taxed by more than one state, and one purchase transaction may (on rare occasions) be reached by two states. The result in this case, unlike that of over-lapping taxes by governments on different levels, is discriminatory double taxation. Only those persons who are involved in interstate transactions are caught twice, while others are reached but once.

### Perverse Fiscal Policy

A further problem, discussed at length in subsequent chapters, is that of the perversity of the fiscal policy of the states and local governments. Their tendency to cut expenditures in depressions offsets in large measure the efforts of the federal government to bring recovery, while increases in their construction programs in years of prosperity tend to further inflationary pressures.

### The Fiscal Illusion or "Santa Claus" Doctrine

A troublesome factor in the field of intergovernmental problems is one which may be called the fiscal illusion—the belief on the part of many people that additional expenditures from higher levels of government do not cost them anything. Time and time again, persons will turn to the state for aid for a particular function when the local governments do not meet their demands, or to the federal government when the states do not do so, motivated in large measure by the belief that aid from the larger units is costless. Partly, this attitude results from the complexities of budget making at the higher levels, partly from a less direct correlation between expenditures and taxes at these levels. If a new school is built with local funds, a direct and immediate increase in local taxes will result. But if state or federal funds can be obtained, there is no such direct response of taxes, and the community which can get more than its share of state or federal aid permanently benefits. For the people of the country as a whole, aid from the larger units is not cost-free—but it may be for particular communities. The over-all consequence is serious interference with optimum allocation of governmental activities by level of government.

## SOLUTIONS TO THE PROBLEMS OF INTERGOVERNMENTAL FISCAL RELATIONS

The problems of intergovernmental fiscal relationships have been recognized for many years. But there are serious obstacles in the way of solving them. One of the basic difficulties is that of finding means of insuring greater financial resources for the smaller units of government and for those particular units with the least adequate resources, without impairing their autonomy. Virtually any form of feasible assistance almost inevitably involves some loss of financial and political independence, and some methods could completely destroy the integrity of the local governments and the states. This problem is particularly serious with federal systems, in view of the possible destruction of the constitutional allocation of powers between federal and state governments by devices used to improve the financial position of the states. But even within the states, some financial autonomy of the local units is generally regarded as desirable, although in some countries, such as France and the Netherlands, it has largely disappeared.

Apart from the basic autonomy problem, there are other practical obstacles to reform. Constitutional adjustments may be difficult. More serious is the divergency of interests; some types of programs or allocation formulas may be much more favorable to some states or local units than to others, and quarrels over the systems may impede the attainment of any reforms or result in unsatisfactory compromises.

Despite these problems, however, major steps have been made in the direction of reform. The major alternatives are explained in the succeeding sections.

### Increased Separation of Sources

In earlier years, in which expenditure levels were lower, intergovernmental fiscal problems were minimized by extensive separation of tax sources among the various levels of government, each relying on sources not used by other governmental units. In the last century, there was almost complete separation between the federal government and the states, the former using customs and excises, the latter the property tax and other direct sources. The situation in Canada was essentially the same. On the other hand, both the states and localities relied heavily upon the property tax. After 1900 the states and localities began to separate their sources, the states gradually withdrawing from the property tax field. At the same time, however, the movement of the federal government and the states into the income and death tax fields resulted in lessened separation, as has the levying by some cities of sales and earnings taxes.

One partial solution to the present problems, therefore, is an increased degree of separation, particularly through withdrawal by various governmental units from the use of taxes which offer them the least relative advantages. For example, it can be argued that the states should abandon income taxes and cigarette taxes so that the federal government may have exclusive use of these fields, while the federal government should abandon death taxes and the gas tax to the states and the admissions tax to the localities.

Greater separation would avoid waste and administrative duplication, mitigate the danger of excessive tax burdens, and allow more rational selection of taxes by the smaller units. The administrative argument must be evaluated with some care, since duplicating administration may be preferable to the use of separate taxes which have greater combined administrative cost. A more significant advantage arises from the fact that the local units are now restricted from the use of some of the few taxes which they could administer, because the larger units, which do not require these sources, have taken them over. Separation lessens the danger of loss of financial autonomy which may occur with other methods of co-ordination.

On the other hand, separation, while having some merits as a partial solution, cannot possibly meet the basic problems of intergovernmental fiscal relations noted in the preceding sections. Regardless of the system of separation employed, the tax sources which may be allocated to the localities cannot, on the whole, meet their needs. While transfer to them of such levies as the admissions tax would lessen their problems, it could by no means solve them. Separation does nothing to meet the problem of differences in wealth and income relative to expenditures in various local areas. Likewise, the optimum use of the best revenue sources may be prevented. States and localities may, of necessity, be allocated second-best taxes, with consequent excessive reliance upon these in the over-all tax structure. Duplication of taxes may be preferable to lessened reliance on the best revenue sources and to the use of a diverse tax structure which includes some elements difficult to administer. If localities are forced to rely entirely on property tax revenues, the burden of this tax, which is defective at best, may become intolerable.

### Shared Revenues

A second approach to the problem is to share revenues. Under this policy, collection of a tax is concentrated in one unit of government, and a portion of the amount collected is shared with the smaller units on the basis of place of collection. Thus, in some states a portion of the income tax is returned to the local units on the basis of the amounts collected within each area.

A system of shared revenues goes further toward meeting the basic intergovernmental fiscal problems than does mere separation of sources. Like separation, the sharing of revenues eliminates the waste of duplicating collection of the same taxes. But beyond this, sharing gives the smaller units access to revenues from taxes which either are denied them under separation or are difficult for them to use even if they are legally permitted to employ them. Thus the problem of the basic inadequacy of the tax sources of the smaller units is met, at least to a limited extent. The greater utilization of the better revenue sources reduces the reliance on unsatisfactory taxes and, at the local level, lessens the burden on the property tax. Unlike more far-reaching approaches to the problem, there is little interference with the financial autonomy or conduct of the affairs of the smaller units.

Nevertheless, the system does increase the reliance of the smaller units on the larger, since administration of their own revenues is in part removed from them. This may be a relatively small price to pay for the advantages, but nevertheless it is commonly regarded as an objection, especially by those who stress the importance of local autonomy. More fundamentally, the distribution of the revenues on the basis of origin ignores the different relative needs of the various local units, and it does not meet the basic problem of varying degrees of local ability to raise taxes to meet necessary functions. Some areas may receive more than they need, with a consequent tendency toward waste of funds. The distribution of revenues on the basis of origin is not workable in some instances; for example, sharing of the gasoline tax among the counties of collection may be very inequitable for counties in which the gasoline is distributed from bulk plants or refineries in other areas.

On the whole, a program of shared revenues, while incapable of solving all intergovernmental fiscal problems, may prove a useful tool of co-ordination in particular instances. The procedure will work satisfactorily only if three requirements are met:

1. All or almost all of the smaller units must desire revenue from the particular source.

2. The revenue source must be one which is generally regarded as sufficiently desirable to provide support for two levels of government.

3. Allocation on the basis of place of origin of the revenues is feasible.

Furthermore, if the shared-revenue system is to be used extensively, the recipient units must be of sufficiently uniform ability to support their own functions that no equalization is necessary. If grants are used in conjunction with shared revenues, this consideration is not relevant. Perhaps the best argument for shared revenues used in conjunction with grants is that they serve to protect the autonomy of the smaller units to a greater extent than grants alone.

In the United States, some sharing of revenues occurs between the states and localities, particularly with income taxes and to a very limited extent with sales taxes. No sharing between federal and state governments has ever been developed, primarily because of the unwillingness of the states to surrender separate administration of any of their taxes.

### Supplementary Tax Rates

Closely related to the system of shared revenues is one of supplementary tax rates, in which the larger unit collects, in addition to its own tax rate, a supplementary rate for those smaller units which desire it. Thus, in Illinois the state will collect for any city which requests it a sales tax supplement to the state sales tax and give the amount collected to the city. The Canadian federal government collects supplementary income tax rates for those provinces which desire it.

This approach to the problem maintains local autonomy in the determination of the use of particular taxes and thus lessens the danger of loss of financial responsibility. This argument has been stressed in Quebec, in opposition to suggestions that a program of shared revenues replace the present municipal sales tax system. The procedure also avoids any danger of excessive revenues for particular areas. On the other hand, administration of the tax may be seriously complicated, and major compliance problems created for vendors, if sales or excise taxes are used, since the tax rate will likely not be uniform on all the firms' sales. Since the higher rate applies only in those areas which wish the use of the tax, incentives are given for shift of economic activity and avoidance of tax, just as with local collection. If the tax involved is a sales tax, persons still have incentive to purchase outside the local tax rate areas, with consequent escape from the tax and a tendency for retailing to shift away from the areas using the tax.

On the whole, a system of supplementary rates offers only one advantage over local collection of the taxes, namely, that of avoiding duplicating tax administration. As compared to shared revenues, the supplementary rate system does retain the responsibility for imposing the additional tax upon the local government and thus increases financial responsibility and lessens the danger of waste of funds. But on the whole, if local governments reach the point at which most of them must use a tax which they cannot administer satisfactorily, a shared-revenue system has many advantages over supplementary rates. The financial autonomy argument ceases to be significant if circumstances compel the various local units to use the tax source.

### Grants-in-Aid or Conditional Grants

A more far-reaching approach to the problems of intergovernmental fiscal relations is the use of a system of grants, under which the higher governmental unit makes grants of money to the smaller units. These may be *conditional*, granted for specific purposes and their use subject to supervision, as is true of all federal grants in the United States. Or they may take the form of *block grants*, given unconditionally, without specification of purpose or supervision.

Grants-in-aid, unlike shared revenues, are not usually linked to particular taxes but are paid from general revenue funds, and the allocation is made on the basis of some criteria of need rather than of origin of the revenues. The supervision established under the conditional grants usually requires the maintenance of certain standards of performance.

*Bases of Distribution.* There are two primary bases or types of formulas used for the distribution of the conditional grants. The first type of formula takes into consideration only criteria of expenditure needs, without respect to the ability of the recipient governments to finance the activities themselves. When grants for education are made on this basis, for example, the share to each school district is based upon the number of pupils in attendance.

The second, or equalizing conditional grant, takes into consideration not only the expenditure needs but the financial resources of the recipient government as well, the grants being larger (relative to expenditures) for the poorer areas than for the wealthy. For example, many state grants to the localities for education have equalizing features. A certain standard of expenditures, regarded as necessary to allow a reasonable minimum standard of performance, is established on a per pupil basis. For each school district, this figure is then multiplied by the number of pupils in attendance, to find the total sum needed. Next, the ability of each district to finance this expenditure by its own resources is determined by applying a standard prescribed tax rate to the total assessed valuation in the district. The difference between this sum and the figure of the expenditures regarded as necessary is the amount of the grant. For example, suppose that $150 per pupil is regarded as a standard expenditure. If a school district has fifty pupils, the total amount required annually is $7,500. If the total assessed valuation is $400,000, and a $1 per $100 tax rate is established as the standard, $4,000 can be raised. The excess of $7,500 over $4,000, or $3,500, will be the amount of the grant.

The equalizing grant has the merit of meeting more effectively the problem of an unequal distribution of tax resources among various local units or various states than the first type of formula. It is particularly useful if resources vary widely among the units and the function is one of significant state-wide or nationwide importance. If there is a less unequal distribution of tax resources, the equalization basis is less necessary.

*Merits of Conditional Grants.* Conditional grants-in-aid solve the basic problems of intergovernmental fiscal relations more completely than do the other solutions thus far mentioned. Grants allow the functions to remain in the hands of the localities and the states and thus avoid the need for further centralization, while at the same time they provide adequate funds from acceptable revenue sources. Thus the burden on unsatisfactory revenue sources, such as property taxes with rates so high that they impose intolerable burdens on persons with limited incomes, or local sales and income taxes which are difficult to administer, is reduced. The basic problem of the inadequacy of local revenues compared to functions is thus solved more satisfactorily than with any alternative. Likewise, particularly when the equalizing basis is employed for allocation, the problem of unequal tax resources among governmental units at the same level is met. Excessive tax burdens and extremely low levels of service in the poor areas can thus be avoided. Closer attainment of expenditure levels and tax structures which are optimum from the standpoint of the country as a whole becomes possible. Grants can be varied in the light of economic conditions, in order to eliminate the cyclical perversity of local revenue expenditure programs which occurs when the localities must finance their own expenditures entirely. Finally, the grants can be used to stimulate local activities and raise the standards of functions which are of state-wide or nationwide interest, without imposing excessive restrictions on local authorities.

*Objections to Conditional Grants.* Various objections, however, can be raised against grants. While these do not warrant abandonment of grants, they do suggest the need for caution in the extension of the grant system. Perhaps the most widespread charge is that the larger unit uses the grant system to buy control over functions which properly belong in the hands of the smaller units. This charge has only minor significance for state-local relationships, since the states can, if they wish, directly exercise complete control over the localities. But in the field of federal-state relationships the charge is more serious. The basic feature of a federal governmental structure is the constitutional division of power between federal and state governments. If the federal government uses grants to obtain control of matters over which the states are supposed to have jurisdiction, the way is paved for destruction of the states and the breakdown of the federal system.

This objection must be weighed against the very substantial advantages of the grant system outlined above. But it suggests that federal grants should be confined to those activities for which there is a particularly strong case and that the federal government should use the greatest caution in the establishment of standard requirements which accompany the grants. The actual grant systems in use in the United States would not appear to be particularly dangerous from the standpoint of state sovereignty, but they do represent a precedent for possible drastic interference with the functions of the states.

A second objection, and one applicable to all grants, is the possible tendency to cause waste and a loss of financial responsibility on the part of recipient governments. It is likely that on the whole, governments will be inclined to use money which is given them more carelessly than that which they raise themselves. This is difficult to prove, but a tendency in this direction would certainly be expected. Widespread provision of grants may have the effect of lessening the willingness of the local units to raise their own funds and of leading them to cry constantly for more assistance.

Thirdly, when grants are given for particular purposes and matching of them is required, as is common with the federal-state grants in the United States, expenditures of the recipient unit may be distorted from desired patterns. The government finds it difficult to turn down the money, yet the matching requirement may mean that expenditures for other activities are stifled if the necessary matching funds are to be obtained. As a consequence, the over-all budget may be substantially different from that which would most satisfactorily meet the desires of the community. This result may be justified if a high level of performance is essential in the interests of national welfare. But in other cases, it is objectionable.

Fourthly, it may be argued that the grants interfere with optimum use of resources.[1] Grants, especially for social welfare purposes, tend to perpetuate maladjustments in resource distribution, particularly by checking the flow of labor out of areas in which an excessive labor supply holds wages down. While this result may occur in some instances, not all grants will have this type of effect.[2] For example, if lack of capital or skill on the

---

[1] See, for example, the articles by A. D. Scott, "Notes on Grants in Federal Countries," *Economica*, Vol. XVII (1950), pp. 416–22; and "Federal Grants and Resource Allocation," *Journal of Political Economy*, Vol. LX (December, 1952), pp. 534–38.

[2] See J. M. Buchanan, "Federal Grants and Resource Allocation," *Journal of Political Economy*, Vol. LX (June, 1952), pp. 208–17.

part of the workers is responsible for the low levels of income, the grants may help to eliminate the causes and raise the level of production. The grants may facilitate the training of the workers and encourage the flow of capital into the area. Improved educational facilities may increase investment and may also encourage the migration of workers out of the area if there is a basic excess relative to other resources. The pension and relief grants are the ones which are most likely to perpetuate low incomes by checking the outflow of labor.

Finally, it is argued by some that the grant system is wasteful because it merely returns to the states the amounts which their taxpayers pay in the first place, and, on the other hand, that the system results in some states subsidizing others, or some areas within a state subsidizing other areas. The two arguments are, of course, contradictory. The first one is for the most part simply untrue; the grants do not come back in the same pattern as the tax payments. Even if they did, an argument could be made for the grant system on the grounds that the federal government can collect the taxes more effecively and with less economic disturbance than the states, and that the system effectively stimulates state activity. The second argument is, of course, contradictory to the basic intent of those grant systems designed to improve the economic position of the states or localities with relatively inferior tax resources relative to need. In practice, in the United States the federal grants do little in the way of actual redistribution of real income by state, although on the whole they give a very limited relative benefit to the poorer states.[3]

On the whole, the case for conditional grants, if appropriately selected and administered, is strong. It may be admitted that they could be used to break down the division of powers among the various levels of government. But the danger does not appear to be great. Proper standards for the grants will tend to minimize any adverse effects on the financial responsibility of the smaller units and any tendency toward waste. In many instances, grants are the only suitable alternative to direct centralization of functions; if levels of government activity which are optimum from the standpoint of society as a whole are to be attained, some granting of funds from higher levels of government are essential if further centralization is to be avoided. By this means the actual conduct of the functions can be kept in the lower units, and adequate and equitable

[3] See the articles by H. G. Schaller, "Federal Grants in Aid and Differences in State per Capita Incomes," *National Tax Journal*, Vol. VIII (September, 1955), pp. 287–99; and Selma Mushkin, "Federal Grants and Federal Expenditures," *National Tax Journal*, Vol. X (September, 1957), pp. 193–213.

financing be provided by the higher levels. But the inherent dangers of grants, especially at the federal-state level, require the use of great care in their establishment and administration.

*Conditional Grants in the United States.* The United States has made greater use of conditional grants than any other country. The federal government has for many years provided conditional grants to the states for such purposes as aid to agricultural education, support of the National Guard, and highway construction and maintenance. During the thirties, extensive temporary grants were given for relief and public works purposes, and new grant systems established for social security, particularly old-age pensions, unemployment compensation administration, aid to dependent children, etc. Total federal grants to the states in 1961 were $6.3 billion, and to the local governments $0.7 billion. The grants constituted about 20 per cent of total state revenues. All involve some degree of control over state policy and supervision of the conduct of the activity by the state. Most contain no equalizing feature, but several of the programs introduced after 1945 do take tax capacity of the states into consideration in the allocation formulas. Many of the grants require state matching of federal funds, often on a 50–50 basis. Under the new federal highway program, however, the federal government provides 90 to 95 per cent of the funds for the major interstate system. The federal grants have been designed primarily to stimulate state activity, rather than for purposes of equalizing fiscal burdens.

The grants, without question, have brought improved standards of many activities. But they have grown in haphazard fashion; it is generally agreed that there are far too many (about ninety), many very small, and many continued after the original need for them has vanished. Some are accompanied by excessive interference in the conduct of the particular activities. Many have been introduced as a result of the work of pressure groups seeking to by-pass state and local resistance to expansion of the activities, rather than careful examination of the need for them. A major overhaul, with reduction in the number and concentration in a few major fields, such as welfare and highways, is long overdue.

The states likewise make extensive use of grants to the local governments, providing in 1962, about $10.1 billion. This accounts for about one fourth of all local revenues. The money was given primarily for education, but also for streets, welfare, and other purposes. To a much greater extent than at the federal level, these have been designed to improve the general financial position of the recipient units and to equalize relative fiscal capacities, as well as to stimulate the particular activities. Many of the education grants contain equalizing features. Grants are a much more important item in state expenditures than in federal, and in local revenues than in state revenues.

### Block Grants

In contrast to the conditional grant, the block grant is given in a lump sum, without specification of purpose and without supervision. The recipient government is free to use the money as it wishes. The only type of requirement established is that of adherence to certain general policies. Great Britain and Canada have made much more extensive use of block grants than has the United States.

The block grant system is one of the most satisfactory methods of meeting the problem of the unequal distribution of tax resources (relative to expenditure needs) in various areas. By their use the local tax burdens will be equalized, particularly if the grants are given on a basis which takes into consideration the ability of the local units to finance their own activities. Also, the inequities and adverse economic effects produced by unequal tax resources will be avoided. The block grant system interferes much less with the autonomy of the recipient governments than does the conditional grant, since the recipient government is free to use the funds as it sees fit, without supervision. Thus, there is no distortion of expenditure patterns. The only possible danger is that if the amounts of the grants are determined on the basis of bargaining, the recipient units might be induced to make major concessions in the way of loss of autonomy in order to receive larger grants. But once the system has been established, there is no day-to-day supervision or control over the use of the funds.

On the other hand, the unconditional grant provides no stimulus to particular activities of the smaller units and no insurance of raising standards of performance. A primary purpose of grants is the stimulation of activities which are of benefit to the larger area as well as to the smaller; the block grants may be spent for purposes of purely local concern. These considerations suggest that any program of block grants should be supplemented by conditional grants for particular purposes. Finally, it is difficult to find a formula for the allocation of the block grants which meets with general approval, as has been clearly demonstrated by Canadian experience. There is a tendency for the various recipients to argue constantly for revised formulas that will increase their shares.

In Canada, where block grants have been used in preference to extensive conditional grants, they are generally favored as being less destructive of provincial autonomy than the conditional form. By contrast, in the United States the 1955 Commission on Intergovernmental Relations condemned the block grants in favor of the conditional type, on the ground that the former would not satisfy the needs and thus conditional grants would be provided as well, and that the block grants would undermine state financial responsibility.

## The Commission on Intergovernmental Fiscal Relations

In 1953, Congress provided for the appointment of a commission, subsequently headed by Meyer Kestnbaum, to review the problems of intergovernmental relations, fiscal and otherwise, in the United States. The commission was made up of a group of persons of widely divergent attitudes, and the report is in large measure a compromise. Nevertheless, the group found no basic weakening of the federal structure by past grant programs, and recommended no very drastic changes. The basic philosophy is indicated in the following summary statement:

Leave to private initiative all the functions that citizens can perform privately; use the level of government closest to the community for all public functions it can handle; utilize cooperative intergovernmental arrangements where appropriate to attain economical performance and popular approval; reserve National action for residual participation where State and local governments are not fully adequate, and for the continuing responsibilities that only the National Government can undertake [p. 6].

Major recommendations included:

1. Improvements in state governmental structures, to increase the vitality of the states. Legislative reapportionment, increased powers for the governors, and greater home rule were suggested, as well as reduction in the number of small local units.

2. Increased federal-state co-operation in administrative matters.

3. Improved state and local tax systems, with less multiple collection of particular taxes. Separation of sources was regarded as impossible.

4. Continued use of conditional grants-in-aid, in place of block equalizing grants, with the grants limited to cases of obvious national objectives. Grants are in large measure regarded as means of stimulating state activity without the need for direct centralization of functions in the hands of the federal government. While the commission opposed deliberate equalization of the fiscal capacities of the states, it supported use of the equalization element in allocation formulas.

As is common with the work of such commissions in the United States, it has had virtually no influence on actual governmental policy. One consequence, however, was the establishment of a permanent Advisory Commission on Intergovernmental Relations, with twenty-six members, drawn from Congress, the administration, and state and local officials. A permanent staff was established to conduct studies of the questions of intergovernmental relations.[4]

## Miscellaneous Co-ordination Devices

In the preceding paragraphs the major approaches to the problem of intergovernmental fiscal relations have been noted. But several other devices of limited applicability are used to meet particular problems:

1. *Deductibility.* The problem of an excessive combined burden when two levels of government use the same tax is lessened by the deductibility of the tax paid to one unit in the determination of the tax due to the other unit. The net effect is to lessen the combined burden and to equalize to a considerable extent the relative burdens on persons in different areas. Thus the deductibility of state income taxes from income in the determination of federal income tax liability avoids the danger of excessively high combined burden.

2. *Tax Credits or Offsets.* Instead of allowing deductibility of the tax paid the other unit from the tax base, a government may provide the much more liberal privilege of deducting the tax paid the other unit from the tax due to it or, in other words, allow the tax paid to constitute a credit or offset against the tax liability. Thus, in the federal estate tax structure a credit for state death taxes paid is allowed against the federal tax due. As between governments at different levels, this device greatly reduces the combined burden and has the advantage, compared to outright abandonment of the tax by the higher level, that competition among the lower units to lure people or business by failing to use the tax is avoided. Substantial uniformity of tax rate is attained, and all the lower units are assured the possibility of gaining revenue from the tax. Uniformity can be increased if the tax credit is granted only if the tax meets certain standard requirements.[5]

As between units on the same level, this procedure eliminates discriminatory double taxation and is allowed by many states for this reason. Likewise, the United States, like most countries, gives credit to its residents for taxes paid to another country on income earned in that country.

3. *Division of Control over Taxes.* In several federal countries of the world, including Nigeria, the federal government is given the power to establish the structure of the income tax, except for rates and credits

---

[4] For the consequences of the Kestnbaum report, see the article by J. A. Maxwell, "Recent Developments in Federal-State Financial Relations," *National Tax Journal*, Vol. XIII (December, 1960), pp. 310–19.

[5] See J. W. Maxwell, *Tax Credits and Intergovernmental Fiscal Relations* (Washington, D.C.: Brookings Institution, 1962).

for dependents, while the states impose the taxes and administer them. This procedure insures a degree of uniformity and thus lessens the nuisance to the taxpayer and possible adverse effects on location of business. Furthermore, such legislation effectively eliminates double taxation of the same income by more than one state. It does little, however, to meet the other intergovernmental problems.

## CONCLUSIONS

Any division of governmental functions between various levels of government, each exercising a certain amount of autonomy, gives rise to financial problems not encountered in a country with a unified governmental system. The criteria which determine optimum location of expenditures are different from those which determine optimum allocation of taxing powers, and thus some levels of government have inadequate revenues compared to their expenditure needs. The task of attaining optimum expenditure and tax levels and patterns is seriously complicated, primarily because the amounts of income and wealth in various jurisdictions differ widely relative to the sums required to render desired services. In addition, independent selection of tax sources interferes with the attainment of a logical tax structure. The combined burden on particular taxes may be excessive, and smaller units may rely heavily on inferior taxes because they cannot administer other taxes satisfactorily. Discriminatory double taxation may easily occur.

On the other hand, the division of governmental functions is almost imperative in a large country for the attainment of workable democracy and the avoidance of excessive bureaucracy and centralization of government. In order to preserve the advantages of the federal system and the separate conduct of activities by the local units, some price must be paid in the way of complications in financial affairs. But it is desirable to take measures to meet the basic problems of differing resources in various areas and the inability of the smaller units to raise the funds necessary to conduct the functions which are appropriately entrusted to them. The avoidance of use by the federal governments of levies, such as sales and various excise taxes, which can be used by the states and the avoidance of use by the states of the property tax which the localities need will minimize the problems and avoid the dangers of excessive combined burdens on particular taxes. Shared-revenue systems and supplementary rates aid in augmenting the inadequate revenues of the smaller units and lessen the encroachment on local autonomy. But only a grant system can adequately adjust for differences in resources relative to functions and allow closer attainment of optimum levels of government activities and tax structures in accord with the accepted goals. But grants are not without their limitations; judicious use of them is essential if the purposes are to be attained without waste and complete destruction of the autonomy of the lower levels of government. The conditional form of grant is the most satisfactory if the goal is to raise standards of performance of particular activities to nationwide or state-wide levels. The unconditional or block grants interfere with the autonomy of the smaller units to a lesser extent and may be more satisfactory than the conditional type in bringing about an over-all equalization of financial resources compared to expenditure needs.

## APPENDIX

### Conditional Grants in Canada

Canada was much slower to develop conditional grant programs than the United States, primarily because of greater fear of the effects of such grants on provincial autonomy. Quebec, until 1960, flatly refused to accept the grants for this reason. There is as yet, for example, no general highway grant program, and the number of grant systems is much less than in the United States. However, the programs have expanded rapidly in the last five years, and the total sum given in the 1963 fiscal year, $754 million, is several times as great as the unconditional grants. The major grants are those for hospital insurance, welfare, higher education, and the Trans-Canada Highway. The provinces have made extensive use of conditional grants to the local governments for a number of years, primarily for education and roads.[6]

### The Canadian Unconditional Grants

The story of the Canadian Dominion block grant system is an extremely complicated one, and cannot be explained in detail. There are several distinct elements:

1. *The Statutory or Constitutional Subsidies.* When the Dominion was formed in 1867, the powers of the provinces to levy indirect taxes were taken from them. Since they had relied heavily on these taxes, the Dominion gave them annual subsidies to replace the lost revenue. The amounts were intended to remain fixed, but were gradually increased, and have continued down to the present time. The total in 1963, however, was only $24 million.

6 For a detailed review of the grants for education, see K. G. Crawford, *Provincial School Grants* (Toronto: Canadian Tax Foundation, 1962).

2. *Equalization Grants, Designed to Equalize the Relative Revenue Position of the Various Provinces, and Thus to Aid the Poorer Provinces.* The present (1962–67 period) formula is based upon the estimated yield of certain standard taxes in the various provinces.[7] The amounts given to each province per capita are designed to equal the difference between the per capita yield of the standard taxes in that province and the national average per capita yield. Thus, only those provinces whose tax capacity is less than the national average would receive grants. However, it is also provided that no province can receive less than the amount obtained under the 1957–62 formula, whereby the grants were designed to bring the per capita yield up to that in the two wealthiest provinces. In 1963, all provinces except Ontario and British Columbia receive equalization grants, totaling $162 million, the largest amounts, per capita, going to the poorer provinces.

3. *Stabilization Grants.* Grants are given to assure that the yield from the standard taxes of the equalization formula plus the equalization grants does not fall below 95 per cent of the unconditional grants of the two preceding years. In 1963, no stabilization grants were necessary. This rule is designed to protect provincial revenues in a period of depression.

4. *Special Grants to Newfoundland and to All the Atlantic Provinces in Recognition of Their Weaker Financial Position.* In 1963 the Newfoundland grant was $8 million, the Atlantic provinces grants $35 million.

This system, provided for a five-year period commencing in 1962, replaces the previous tax rental agreement system. During World War II the federal government, in order to obtain exclusive jurisdiction over income and estate taxes, offered payments to the provinces in exchange for their elimination of their own taxes in these fields. The wartime agreements were renewed, with some variation in structure, in 1947 and 1952, and with substantial differences, in 1957. Initially, the amounts paid the provinces were allocated on the basis of place of collection, but they were gradually altered in part into an equalization system designed to equalize the revenue position of the provinces. After the war period, Quebec did not participate in the agreements, and Ontario did so only to a limited extent. The system was effective in meeting the needs of the poorer provinces and lessening multiple taxation largely because of its flexibility and voluntary character, which allowed adjustment to changing conditions. However, the over-all effectiveness was lessened by the reluctance of Ontario and Quebec to participate fully. Furthermore, the long-standing

---

[7] Personal and corporate income taxes and successions duties, at specified percentages of the federal taxes, plus one half of the revenue from natural resources.

philosophy that the Dominion has an obligation to aid the provinces financially led to begging for funds on the part of the provinces and political maneuvering in the negotiation of new agreements. The provinces complained of loss of financial autonomy.

For these reasons, therefore, substantial changes were made in 1957, and in 1962 the government ended the tax rental agreements. It continued, however, the equalization grant program distinct from the tax agreements and provided for an abatement of federal personal and corporate income taxes up to specified amounts, as noted in Chapters 13 and 14. Also, the federal government continues to collect, free of charge, the income taxes of those provinces so desiring, provided that the bases of the taxes are identical to that of the federal tax. Quebec collects its own personal and corporate income taxes, and Ontario its own corporate tax; in all other instances, federal collection has been accepted. Thus the evils of multiple taxation are still largely avoided, but the provinces have greater autonomy. In the estate tax field a 50 per cent abatement (tax credit) is provided for provincial taxes, or if none is levied, half the federal estate tax revenue derived from the province is returned to the province.

On the whole, the trend of the last ten years has been away from the close fiscal integration of provincial-federal relations of the war years. The consequence has been an increased role of the provinces in the determination of tax policy, but a decline in the ability of the federal government to make tax adjustments for purposes of general fiscal policy. However, the wastes of duplicating tax administration are still largely avoided, and the equalization-stabilization grants serve to meet two of the major problems of intergovernmental fiscal relations.

The provinces also make some use of block grants to the municipalities, to provide them with additional revenue from sources other than the property tax, and equalize somewhat their revenue opportunities.

### The British Block Grant System

Great Britain has made some use of block grants for several decades. There are two major types. Rate deficiency grants provide annual payments by the national government to those municipalities with assessed value of property less than a certain amount per capita. Secondly, general grants are given to all local governments, with an allocation formula based on population, number of school children, and other factors. The amounts are not assigned for specific purposes, the use being discretionary on the part of the local councils; but in practice, most of the money is used for educational purposes.

## Australian Block Grants

Australia has for five decades provided unconditional grants to the three states with the weakest fiscal position—Tasmania, Western Australia, and South Australia. The amounts of the grants have been determined by the Commonwealth Grants Commission on the basis of study of the relative financial position of these three states compared to the others, without the use of a precise formula. The grant system has operated without the political maneuvering characteristic of the Canadian grant system, with acceptance of grants based on economic criteria without attempts to gain larger sums through political pressure.[8]

[8] See E. J. Hanson, *Australian Commonwealth Grants Commission* (Toronto: Canadian Tax Foundation, 1960).

## REFERENCES

### GENERAL

COMMISSION ON INTERGOVERNMENTAL RELATIONS. *Report to the President.* Washington, D.C.: U.S. Government Printing Office, 1955.
  The report of an extensive study of the problems of intergovernmental fiscal relations, by a commission appointed by the President.

BIRCH, A. H. *Federalism, Finance and Social Legislation.* Oxford: Oxford University Press, 1955.
  A review of intergovernmental fiscal developments in various countries, with emphasis on the field of social legislation.

COMMITTEE ON INTERGOVERNMENTAL FISCAL RELATIONS. *Federal, State and Local Government Fiscal Relations.* Washington, D.C.: U.S. Government Printing Office, 1943.
  The most complete study that has been made of the intergovernmental problems in the United States.

MAXWELL, J. A. *The Fiscal Aspects of Federalism in the United States.* Cambridge: Harvard University Press, 1946.
  A historical survey of the significance of the federal system for the development of the fiscal structures.

ADVISORY COMMISSION ON INTERGOVERNMENTAL RELATIONS. *Coordination of State and Federal Inheritance, Estate and Gift Taxes.* Washington, D.C.: U.S. Government Printing Office, 1961.
  An analysis of the intergovernmental relations in the death duty field.

————. *Measures of State and Local Fiscal Capacity and Tax Effort.* Washington, D.C.: U.S. Government Printing Office, 1962.

MAXWELL, J. W. *Tax Credits and Intergovernmental Fiscal Relations.* Washington, D.C.: Brookings Institution, 1962.
  Emphasis on the tax credit device, but with review of experience with other solutions to the problems.

NATIONAL BUREAU OF ECONOMIC RESEARCH. *Public Finances—Needs, Sources and Utilization*, pp. 79–274. Princeton: Princeton University Press, 1961.

HICKS, U. K., *et al. Federalism and Economic Growth*. London: George Allen and Unwin, 1961.
The question of the significance of federal government structures for economic development.

MAXWELL, J. A. *Federal Grants and the Business Cycle*. New York: National Bureau of Economic Research, 1952.

JOINT ECONOMIC COMMITTEE. *Federal Expenditure Policy for Economic Growth and Stability*, pp. 163–220. Washington, D.C.: U.S. Government Printing Office, 1957.
A series of papers on questions of intergovernmental fiscal problems.

CANADIAN EXPERIENCE

DEHEM, R., and WOLFE, J. N. "The Principles of Federal Finance and the Canadian Case," *Canadian Journal of Economics and Political Science*, Vol. XXI (February, 1955), pp. 64–72.

MOORE, A. M., and PERRY, J. H. *Financing Canadian Federation*. Toronto: Canadian Tax Foundation, 1953.
The most complete analysis of Canadian experience.

BURNS, R. M. "Recent Developments in Federal-Provincial Fiscal Arrangements in Canada," *National Tax Journal*, Vol. XV (September, 1962), pp. 225–38.
An excellent review of the developments in recent years.

CANADIAN TAX FOUNDATION. *Summary of Federal-Provincial Tax Arrangements*. Tax Memo. No. 31. Toronto, May, 1962.

SMILEY, D. V. *Conditional Grants and Canadian Federalism*. Toronto: Canadian Tax Foundation, 1963.

# Chapter 25

## THE OVER-ALL ECONOMIC EFFECTS OF THE EXPENDITURE AND TAX SYSTEMS

The preceding chapters have reviewed the nature and effects of the expenditure and tax systems individually. But a complete understanding of the significance of governmental financial activities for the functioning of the economy requires an analysis of the combined effects of expenditures and taxation. To this question the present chapter is devoted.

## THE EFFECTS OF TAXES

### The Purchasing Power Effects

The taxes themselves (ignoring, for the moment, the use of the revenues) constitute extractions out of the flow of purchasing power and thus reduce the amounts which are available for consumption or saving. Essentially, they divert a portion of the flow of the national income stream away from savings and private sector consumption. This distributional, or purchasing power, effect in itself reduces the total volume of private consumption expenditures and the amount of savings made, and alters the ratio between consumption and savings. It is likely that a substantial portion of the taxes is borne out of funds which would otherwise be saved, especially in the upper income levels, and, as a consequence, the percentage of disposable income consumed rises. Furthermore, the taxes almost inevitably reduce the total volume of investment, partly by lessening the funds available for this purpose and partly by reducing the level of consumption and thus the profitability of additional investment. Some forms of taxes directly reduce the return from investment.

The personal income tax extracts the purchasing power directly from individuals, either before it reaches their hands when withholding is used or shortly after they receive it. The corporation income tax absorbs the funds directly from the business enterprises. If the corporations reduce dividends, the final effect is much the same as that of a personal income tax. If the tax is paid out of funds that would otherwise have been added to surplus, there occurs a direct reduction in savings, and the volume of investment made by the firms may be reduced. If the tax is shifted in the form of higher prices, the effect is the same as that of a sales tax.

A sales or excise tax will tend to shift forward to the consumer and thus is extracted from the purchaser in the form of an addition to the price which he pays. In the terminology of a number of writers, a wedge —the tax—is driven between the price received by the seller and that paid by the buyer. If such a tax is not shifted, it reduces the incomes of the owners of the businesses (or, in the case of a corporation, the surplus, if dividends are not affected). If the tax causes factor prices to decline, the effect is much the same as that of an income tax.

A property tax is extracted in the same manner as a year-end income tax so far as homeowners are concerned, the primary difference being the base upon which liability is calculated. The portion on business property, including farm land, is in part extracted from the income of the owners, but primarily (except with land) from the consumers of the products and thus in the same fashion as a sales tax.

### The Announcement Effects

Not only does the collection of taxes have a direct purchasing power effect in reducing the amount of money available for consumption and saving, but the taxes also have *announcement* effects. The collection of the taxes, in various forms, may result in modification of behavior, by affecting the incentives for various actions, in addition to the necessary reduction in consumption or saving due to the purchasing power effect. These announcement effects have been discussed in the previous chapters and need only be summarized here. A personal income tax, for example, may alter the willingness of persons to work and thus may alter the labor supply, both in total and of particular types. It may lessen the willingness to undertake business development and expansion, and may particularly discourage risky ventures. A corporation income tax may likewise affect investment incentives, and it may alter the legal form of conduct of business, the type of financing, and the nature as well as the level of activities conducted. Excise taxes may alter relative consumption patterns, because some goods are made relatively more expensive compared to others. Excise or sales taxes applying to producers' goods will affect the choice of techniques of production. Property taxes may have much the same effect as excises, because one particular use of purchasing power, namely, for housing, is rendered relatively more costly than others, compared to the situation without the tax. The exact nature and degree of these announcement effects are very difficult to determine.

## THE EXPENDITURES

On the other side of the picture, expenditures of the governmental revenues restore to the income stream the amounts extracted by the taxes. A portion goes directly to individuals in the form of transfer payments, such as old-age pensions, without the acquisition of factor units by the government, and re-enters the income stream as it is spent by the recipients. Most of the revenue is used to acquire factor units and commodities necessary for the government to perform its services. The amounts paid for goods flow to business firms and, in turn, are paid out by these firms into the income stream in exchange for factor units. The amounts paid by the government to workers and other factor owners re-enter the income stream directly and immediately. In general, therefore, government expenditures tend to restore the flow of purchasing power (although not necessarily the actual spending) to the level which existed before the taxes were extracted, if the amounts of taxes and expenditures are equal. The situations in which there is a net surplus or deficit will be discussed in subsequent chapters.

Expenditures, as well as taxes, have announcement effects in addition to purchasing power effects, which may directly alter the supplies of various factors. Persons who receive transfer payments, such as relief or old-age pensions, may be less willing to work, and thus the labor supply will fall. On the other hand, some transfer grants, such as aid for dependent children, may allow persons to gain greater education and thus eventually increase the over-all quality of the labor supply. Conservation projects may make a greater supply of natural resources available. Expenditures on education temporarily lessen labor supply by holding children in school and permanently lessen the amount of unskilled labor available. But they lead eventually to an increase in the amount of skilled labor. The increased profits of businesses which result from the governmental expenditures not only provide greater funds for investment purposes but also increase the incentive for additional investment by business firms. Some governmental expenditures, such as those on highways or electric power facilities, may directly increase the profitability of some types of investment. Other services alter consumption incentives, since the relative desirability of various goods will be changed. Good highways increase the incentive to buy cars and lessen the desire to travel by rail. Good fire protection lessens the need to buy fire extinguishers.

## NET EFFECTS OF TAXES AND EXPENDITURES

With a balanced cash budget, the expenditures restore to the stream of purchasing power the exact amounts which the taxes take from it. Nevertheless, the expenditure-revenue program as a whole has very significant net effects upon the functioning of the economy. These effects will be grouped into three categories: distribution of purchasing power, allocation of resources, and the level of national income.

### Effects on the Distribution of Income

There are several ways in which the programs affect the distribution of purchasing power among various persons in the economy. In the first place, as a result of the extensive use of income taxes, wealthier persons are made to pay substantially more for the governmental services than are the lower income groups. If these services could be privately produced and sold at uniform prices and were acquired in the same manner as at present, the wealthy would pay considerably less and the poor more. More realistically, the lower income groups would not be able to acquire as many units, and their real incomes would be less. Or if the services were not produced at all and the resources were employed in producing other goods sold at uniform prices, the higher income groups would receive a much larger share of the national product. The net effect is that the poor receive considerably greater real income and the wealthy receive less than they would receive if the government did not carry on the activities. Education provides an excellent example of a governmental service which greatly increases the real income of the lower income groups, not only through the benefits of the education itself but through increased earning power as well. The benefits from the services, such as national defense, which accrue to society as a whole, cannot be allocated to individuals except on a purely arbitrary basis. But if they were not produced by governments and the resources were used to provide goods benefiting individuals directly, the real incomes of the wealthy would be greater, relative to those of the poor, than they now are, unless it is asssumed that these governmental services convey most of their benefits to the wealthy.

Secondly, certain governmental activities, such as old-age pensions and relief programs, directly increase the money incomes of the lower income groups. Since these payments are financed by taxes borne to a substantial extent by the higher income groups, the net result is a redistribution of purchasing power in favor of the lower income groups. Over the years, this type of government activity has increased substantially.

Thirdly, the conduct of production by the government may tend to level out factor incomes. The fact that the highest salaries in governmental organizations tend to be much less than salaries for comparable tasks in private enterprise and the fact that no earnings go to stockholders tend to lessen over-all differences in income when the government takes over an activity from private hands or increases the sphere of its sector. For example, if highways were provided by private toll road companies, salaries of top employees would, without question, exceed the salaries of the government officials supervising the highway system, and substantial profits might be paid to a few wealthy stockholders.

Several studies have been made in recent years of the effects of tax and expenditure systems upon the distribution of income. One of the most complete is that by John H. Adler, the over-all results of which are reproduced in Figure 32. The 45-degree line represents a perfectly equal

FIGURE 32

REDISTRIBUTION OF INCOME THROUGH THE FISCAL SYSTEM, 1946–47

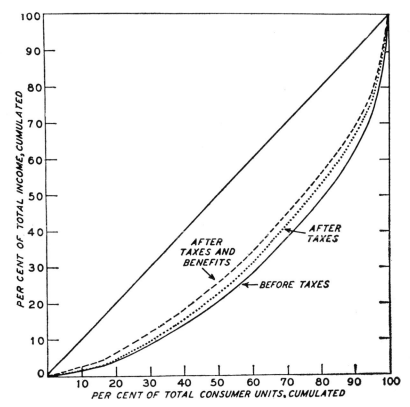

SOURCE: Kenyon E. Poole (ed.), *Fiscal Policies and the American Economy* (copyright, 1951, by Prentice-Hall, Inc., New York), from chap. viii, by John H. Adler, p. 399. Reproduced by permission of the publisher.

distribution; the degree of curvature of the line showing the actual pattern of distribution demonstrates the degree of inequality. The line which shows the distribution after taxes and benefits from governmental activities are taken into consideration is much closer to the 45-degree line than is the curve of distribution before these items are considered, and thus the extent of inequality is shown to be reduced by the present tax and expenditure system. The lowest income groups gain very substantially; the under-$1,000 income class experiences an estimated 73 per cent increase in real income as a result of the expenditure-tax program, whereas the over-$7,500 income class experiences a 22 per cent decline. In other words, for this group the money values of the benefits received are much less than the taxes paid. The higher income groups would experience a still greater decline. The income groups between $2,000 and $7,500 find their positions largely unchanged, since the gains from the governmental activities offset the burdens of the taxes.

A more recent and complete study of the distribution of tax burdens by income groups, without reference to benefits, has been made by R. A. Musgrave and his associates at the University of Michigan. The over-all results are indicated in Figure 33. The tax structure as a whole is shown to be progressive, but the distribution is almost proportional in the lower

FIGURE 33

DISTRIBUTION OF OVER-ALL TAX BURDEN BY INCOME CLASS,
ALL LEVELS OF GOVERNMENT, UNITED STATES, 1954

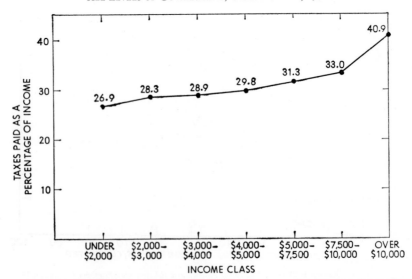

SOURCE: R. A. Musgrave, "The Incidence of the Tax Structure and Its Effects on Consumption," in Joint Committee on the Economic Report, *Federal Tax Policy for Economic Growth and Stability* (Washington, D.C.: U.S. Government Printing Office, 1955), p. 98.

income brackets. These groups are affected very little by the federal income tax but are subject to substantial payments of sales, excise, and property taxes, which are distributed in relatively regressive fashion. Were it possible to break down the $7,500-and-over class, a much higher degree of progression would be manifest in the upper range of the scale.[1]

A study was made by Irving J. Goffman of the distribution of Canadian taxation by income class for 1957.[2] The results are illustrated in Figure 34. The federal tax structure was found to be progressive throughout, the municipal structure somewhat regressive, and the provincial structure more or less proportional. The over-all result is a U-shaped curve.

A similar and very exhaustive study for Great Britain was made by A. M. Cartter.[3] He found that British taxes as a whole had a highly pro-

FIGURE 34

EFFECTIVE RATES OF CANADIAN TAXES BY INCOME CLASS BY
LEVEL OF GOVERNMENT, 1957

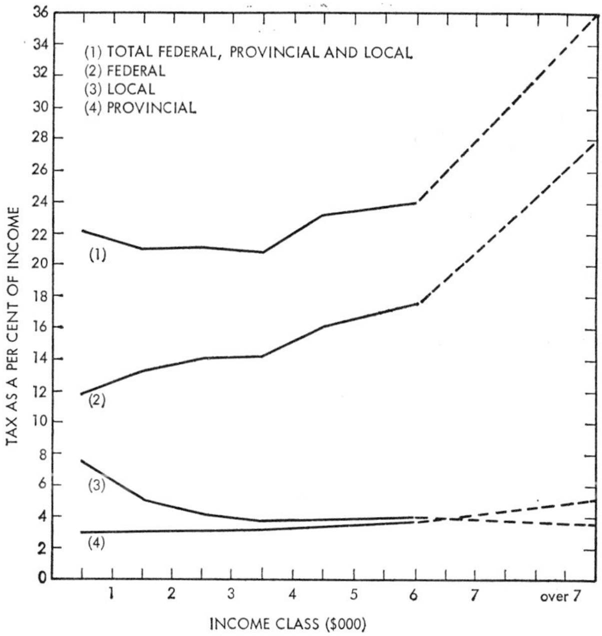

(1) TOTAL FEDERAL, PROVINCIAL AND LOCAL
(2) FEDERAL
(3) LOCAL
(4) PROVINCIAL

TAX AS A PER CENT OF INCOME

INCOME CLASS ($000)

[1] Two other studies which give somewhat different results are those by J. R. Beaton, "Family Tax Burden by Income Levels," *National Tax Journal*, Vol. XV (March, 1962), pp. 14–25; and G. A. Bishop, "The Tax Burden by Income Class," *National Tax Journal*, Vol. XIV (March, 1961), pp. 41–58.

[2] I. J. Goffman, *The Burden of Canadian Taxation* (Toronto: Canadian Tax Foundation, 1962).

[3] *The Redistribution of Income in Postwar Britain* (New Haven: Yale University Press, 1955).

gressive effect, constituting on the whole 24.5 per cent of the incomes of the lowest income groups and 106.6 per cent of the highest. On the other hand, the expenditure programs benefit the lower groups much more than those in the higher levels, relative to incomes. The extent of redistribution was found to be much greater than in the United States.

In these studies, arbitrary assumptions must be made about distribution of benefits, incidence of taxes, and income distribution, which lessen the significance of the results. Perhaps the greatest difficulties are encountered if an attempt is made to consider benefits as well. One problem is their valuation. As a practical matter, it is necessary to value on the basis of cost, yet it may be argued that the benefits may exceed the cost, in the sense that the community would be willing to pay a sum larger than this for the services. Secondly, and more seriously, since many governmental services benefit the community as a whole, any allocation of their benefits to individuals by income group is, of necessity, arbitrary. Even such activities as education, for example, are difficult to allocate. The actual procedure followed by Adler was to allocate benefits of the nondivisible services, such as national defense, on the basis of per capita income. The same procedure was followed with respect to highways, while a per capita basis was used for education.

Likewise, with regard to taxation, certain arbitrary assumptions are necessary. One problem is that of uncertainty about the incidence of various taxes. The most serious question concerns the corporate income tax. Musgrave, in his basic case included in the results noted above, assumed that one third of the tax is shifted to consumers and two thirds is borne by the shareholders. This assumption is, of course, highly arbitrary. Even the incidence of payroll, property, sales, and excise taxes is by no means entirely certain. Furthermore, once assumptions are made about incidence, there are also difficulties in determining the distribution of burden by income class. For example, if it is assumed that corporation income taxes are borne by the stockholders, the determination of burden of the tax by income group is hampered by the lack of adequate information about distribution of dividends by income group. If it is assumed that sales and excise taxes are shifted, there still remains the problem of ascertaining the typical expenditures on the taxed articles by income class. Accordingly, the results of the studies cannot be regarded as precise; but nevertheless, the general conclusions would appear to have some significance.

Apart from the general effects on distribution of real income by income class, the tax and expenditure structure unquestionably alters the relative real incomes of individuals in particular income groups. For example, if a person makes substantial use of liquor and tobacco, the greater burden to which he will be subject will alter his relative real income compared to a person who does not use these commodities. Persons who succeed in evading or avoiding income taxes gain in comparison to those who pay fully. To the extent that corporation income taxes are not shifted, the relative real income of corporation stockholders is reduced relative to other groups. These individual readjustments are of very substantial importance, but it is difficult to generalize about them.

### Effects on Resource Allocation

Secondly, the tax-expenditure structure has very significant effects on the allocation of resources or, in other words, on the product mix which comprises national product. These effects arise out of several features of the tax-expenditure system. Changes in resource allocation due to direct government intervention, such as the prohibition of the sale of marijuana, are not considered, because they are not results of the expenditure-tax program as such.

In the first place, the tax and expenditure programs, as noted, have some effect upon the relative supplies of various factors. Highly progressive income taxes may check the flow of persons into highly paid jobs and thus maintain a greater supply in the lower paid occupations. On the other hand, expenditures on educational services increase the supply of trained labor and reduce that of unskilled types. Conservation programs may reduce the current supply of natural resources but increase the amounts available over a long period. Taxes which penalize risky undertakings will lessen the number of persons willing to start businesses in these fields. These modifications in factor supplies will affect factor prices and thus the relative outputs of various commodities, since varying proportions of particular factors will be required for the production of different goods.

Secondly, the announcement effects of certain taxes result in a direct shifting of purchases and thus of output. The most obvious case is that of excises, which discourage the consumption of the taxed goods and increase the relative advantages of consuming other goods. Whether the output of the other goods will actually rise or fall depends, of course, upon relative demand elasticities and the use of the funds by the government.

Thirdly, the tax-expenditure system alters the savings-consumption ratio and thus the relative output of consumption goods and capital goods (assuming full employment). On the whole, the downward redistribution of income and the tendency of many persons to absorb taxes of all types out of funds which would otherwise be saved reduce the percentage of national income saved, although perhaps less than has usually been argued. Progressive personal income taxes, corporate income taxes, and estate taxes are particularly responsible for results of this type. The exact effect depends upon the particular types of taxes used, the marginal propensities to consume at various income levels, the reactions of the taxpayers to them, and the manner in which the recipients of the government expenditures employ the money.

Fourthly, the purchasing power effects of the taxes will alter consumer purchasing patterns, because income elasticities of various goods differ. Consumption of marginal commodities, those least preferred, will be most severely curtailed. The over-all redistribution of income will produce substantial shifts in purchase patterns; the purchase of yachts and fur coats and Cadillacs will be reduced, while the output of basic necessities is likely to be increased as a result of the transfer payments to the lower income groups. The net result is a shifting of output away from the goods purchased primarily by the wealthy to those purchased to a greater extent by the lower income groups.

Fifthly, the provision of the governmental services will reduce the output of goods which are substitutes for the governmental services and will increase the output of goods which are complementary to the services. The provision of better highways, for example, lessens the demand for and the output of railway service but increases the demand for gasoline. Some of the activities, such as education, modify persons' preferences for various goods.

Finally, and most important, the provision of the collective governmental services inevitably increases the total amount of such services utilized by society and lessens the total output of noncollective goods. Most governmental activities are undertaken because the services either would not be produced at all or would be produced in very inadequate quantities by private enterprise, and the undertaking of them by the government thus increases their relative use in the economy and decreases the relative output of other goods. This is particularly true of national defense, which would not be provided by private enterprise. As the government undertakes defense activities, the output of automobiles and houses and other privately produced goods is, of necessity, reduced below the levels which could otherwise be attained. So long as full employment is maintained, government activity is conducted at the expense of private production because fewer factor units are available for private sector production. Assumption by the government of activities such as electric power production, with governmental output of the service comparable to the output which would be produced by private firms, does not alter the composition of national product; but most activities of government in a market economy are not of this character. In general, our national product is made up to a much greater extent of national defense activities, education, highway construction, rivers and harbors improvements, and the like than it would be in the absence of the governmental activities and thus, of necessity, with full employment, to a smaller extent of new homes, refrigerators, and so forth.

## The Level of National Income

Finally, the tax-expenditure structure exercises some influence upon the level of national income, both in real and in monetary terms. The real level of national income depends in part upon the quantity and quality of resources and techniques available, and in part upon the extent to which available resources are fully employed. In turn, the level of employment, trends in the general price level, and thus the monetary figure of national income depend upon the relationship between aggregate spending and total output. This question will be discussed in detail in the next chapter, with only a brief summary at this point.

Governmental expenditures and taxes may influence the level of national income in two ways: (1) They may alter the supply of factors; and (2) by affecting the level of spending, they may alter the extent to which full employment is attained, as well as the general price level.

1. *Effects upon Factor Supply.* As indicated above, factor supplies may be altered by both the revenues and the expenditures; for example, educational activities, by increasing skill and training, may raise the output possible from a given quantity of factors. Taxes may alter the labor supply, either upward or downward, and they may affect the skill and efficiency of management. These changes affect the total output which is attained at a given level of employment. The educational, public health, resource conservation, reclamation, and highway programs, on the whole, make possible, over the years, a greater potential output (though perhaps reducing it in the short run by lessening factor supplies currently available). Progressive income taxes, if carried too far, may seriously restrict the output levels.

The effect of the tax-expenditure structure in altering the savings-consumption ratio likewise affects the potential output level. At full-employment levels the maximum possible output is reduced over the years by the lower ratio of output of capital goods to consumption goods during the current year. As indicated in earlier chapters, this effect does not necessarily interfere with the attainment of optimum economic welfare.

2. *Effects on the Level of Employment.* The possible effects upon the level of employment—the extent to which factors are fully utilized—

may be very significant. The effects of the taxes and expenditures upon the level of employment come about through their influence upon the total volume of spending in the economy, which is the direct determinant of national income and employment. An increase in total spending will bring about a rise in national income, primarily in real terms so long as resources are unemployed, and primarily in monetary terms once full employment is reached. A decline in aggregate spending will tend to lower the level of national income, partly in real and partly in monetary terms, except in an inflationary period, when it may merely reduce inflationary pressures.

Aggregate spending includes not only consumption and investment (including net foreign investment), but government spending on goods and services as well. An increase in government spending, not offset by an equivalent decline in private spending, will bring about an increase in total spending, while a decrease in government spending which is not offset will reduce total spending. In the former case, national income will rise; in the latter case, it will fall. Government spending, as such, is primarily expansionary, while tax collections are contractionary, since they reduce the amounts which persons have available for consumption and investment. But the expansionary effects of the spending and the contractionary effects of the taxes do not necessarily offset one another exactly. If taxes and expenditures are equal, the sum extracted from the income stream by the government is equal to the amount restored to it. But this does not necessarily insure that the total volume of spending will remain unchanged. Private spending will not necessarily be reduced by exactly the same amount by which government spending is increased, since the taxes may not reduce consumption and investment by the exact magnitude of the collections. The exact effects upon aggregate spending will depend upon the over-all effects upon the consumption-savings ratio and the net effects of the program upon investment, as explained in detail in the next chapter.

*a*) *Effects on the savings-consumption ratio.* Almost inevitably, the tax and expenditure program will alter the savings-consumption ratio by increasing the percentage of income spent on consumption, partly because of the generally downward redistribution of national income and partly because of the tendency of persons to absorb tax burdens out of savings residuals. Certainly, the collection of taxes from the wealthy and the payment of the money to old people with low incomes will raise the over-all propensity to consume. With other activities the effects are less marked, but the use of progressive taxes and the importance of the benefits of many governmental activities to the lower income groups suggest that the percentage of income saved will fall.

The exact effects, of course, depend on the types of taxes, the purposes for which the funds are spent, the manner in which the expenditures are distributed over various income groups, and the particular reactions of the taxpayers and the expenditure recipients. The greater the extent to which the taxes bear on the wealthy, the greater will be the reduction in saving. This is also true the greater the extent to which the taxes are borne out of undistributed corporate profits, which represent a portion of total savings. On the other hand, taxes which particularly burden the lower income groups will be borne largely, but by no means entirely, at the expense of consumption. Sales and excise taxes give some incentive to curtail spending, especially if the tax is regarded as temporary. This result, together with the relatively regressive distribution of burden of these taxes, will bring about a smaller curtailment in savings than that produced by the income taxes. The purposes for which the governmental expenditures are made also affect the results. The greater the extent to which the money is paid to persons in the lower income levels, the greater is the likelihood that the percentage of national income consumed will rise.

*b) Effects on the volume of investment.* The increase in the percentage of income consumed will exert an expansionary influence upon the economy, because the decline in private consumption spending due to the taxes will be less than the amount of the increase in government spending. However, the net effect of the governmental program upon aggregate spending depends also upon the changes in investment spending which occur. If this spending is reduced by an amount equal to the reduction in net savings, there will be no net change in aggregate spending, despite the higher percentage of national income consumed. If the decline in investment is less than the decline in savings, aggregate demand and national income will tend to rise. If the investment decline is greater, aggregate demand will fall.

The effects upon the volume of investment are complex. In part, investment is dependent upon the current volume of consumption purchases. Thus the rise in the percentage of income consumed will tend to maintain investment and further the expansionary tendencies. But on the other hand, the taxes take away funds from firms which are desirous of expanding and make the undertaking of the investment more difficult. Furthermore, progressive taxes may interfere with the incentives of businessmen to undertake investment and of individuals to supply equity capital to businesses. The expenditure of the tax revenues by the government tends, of course, to restore the investment funds to the businesses. But some net adverse effect on investment may remain, particularly if the taxes burden firms able to expand only with their own capital, and if business decisions are greatly affected by the taxes.

In other ways the tax and expenditure program may also affect investment. Certain types of governmental activities, such as highway construction, may increase the profitability of private investment. On the other hand, if the government receipts are spent for the establishment of commercial enterprises which compete with private businesses, the consequent contraction of the firms affected and the general fear of government competition created by the activities may result in significant declines in investment.

The exact effects upon private investment expenditures will depend on the types of taxes used, the purposes for which the money is spent, and the psychological reactions of persons to both the taxes and the expenditures. Highly progressive income taxes are particularly likely to affect investments; sales and excise taxes will have a minimum direct effect, though they will have greater indirect effects through their curtailment of consumption.

In summary, the over-all tax-expenditure structure, with a balanced budget, probably has net expansionary effects. The percentage of national income consumed is almost certainly increased. While the taxes reduce both the funds for investment and the incentives to invest, the increased consumption-plus-government-expenditures figure tends to increase investment. Unless the effects of the taxes upon investment are very drastic, it is unlikely that investment will fall sufficiently to offset the increase in the sum of governmental plus consumption spending; and thus, aggregate spending and national income will be higher—in dollar terms only if full employment would have been attained in the absence of the government activities; in real terms, if it would not have been.

3. *Direct Effects on Factor Costs.* In one other way the tax-expenditure program may affect the monetary level (and possibly indirectly the real level) of national income. Particularly with full employment, but possibly without, tax increases may produce increases in factor prices as the factor owners attempt to maintain their real incomes. Strong unions, for example, may succeed in maintaining real wages by pushing up money wages when taxes are increased. Sales taxes especially tend to increase wages, because of their direct effect upon the cost-of-living index. Personal income tax increases reduce take-home pay and may likewise produce demands for higher wages. General wage increases push up the

entire price level—monetary conditions permitting—and thus raise national income in monetary terms.

## THE CONCEPT OF LIMITS OF TAXATION

The effects noted in the preceding paragraph suggest that as governmental activities reach progressively higher levels, a situation may be encountered in which further increases in expenditures, even if accompanied by comparable or greater increases in taxes, will produce continuous inflation. This thesis was popularized by Colin Clark,[4] who has maintained that once expenditures and taxes reach a level which is equal to 25 per cent or more of national income, further increases are inevitably inflationary. Clark maintains that once taxes reach this level, an increasing number of persons in the economy will insist on further increases in factor prices as taxes are raised, incentives will be affected, production will suffer, and employers will be less resistant to wage increases. His conclusions are reached by some rather inconclusive statistical evidence in the post-World War I period and by economic analysis.

Actually, there is extremely little evidence to bear out the 25 per cent (or other percentage) rule. The statistical evidence is very meager. The actual effects are dependent upon the type of tax structure, the purpose of the government expenditures, the general reactions of the taxpayers to high tax rates, the relationship of marginal to average tax rates, the length of time the high rates have been in effect, the reaction of the people to the usefulness of the expenditures, and other factors.[5] In one country the breaking point may be reached at 10 per cent; in another, at 50 per cent.[6]

The general thesis of Clark and others has some merit, in pointing out that if taxes are pushed indefinitely higher, a point may be reached at which the inflationary influences will exceed the deflationary effects; once this point is reached, progressively greater difficulties will ensue for the government and the economy as a whole. But circumstances affect the location of this point to such a degree that no single figure can possibly be useful.

[4] See "Public Finance and the Value of Money," *Economic Journal*, Vol. LV (December, 1945), pp. 371–89; "The Danger Point in Taxes," *Harper's Magazine*, December, 1950, pp. 67–69.

[5] A good critique of the Clark point of view is to be found in the article by J. A. Pechman and T. Mayer, "Mr. Colin Clark on the Limits of Taxation," *Review of Economics and Statistics*, Vol. XXXIV (August, 1952), pp. 232–42.

[6] See the article by A. Morag, "The Limits of Taxation," *Public Finance*, Vol. XIV, No. 1 (1959), pp. 68–84.

## REFERENCES

JOINT COMMITTEE ON THE ECONOMIC REPORT. *Federal Tax Policy for Economic Growth and Stability.* Washington, D.C.: U.S. Government Printing Office, 1955.

JOINT ECONOMIC COMMITTEE. *Federal Expenditure Policy for Economic Growth and Stability.* Washington, D.C.: U.S. Government Printing Office, 1957.

EISNER, G. *Kaufkraftübertragungen durch öffentliche Financen.* Winterthur: P. G. Keller, 1956.
    A review of the studies of governmental redistribution of income in various countries.

TAX INSTITUTE. *Limits of Tax Capacity.* Princeton, 1953.
    A symposium.

# PART VIII

Government Borrowing and

Fiscal Policy

| Chapter | THE ECONOMICS OF |
| 26 | GOVERNMENT BORROWING |

Governments, like individuals and corporations, may at times obtain funds for current use by borrowing. This source of revenue is, of course, a provisional one, in the sense that its use gives rise to obligations which must be met from taxes or other current sources. The distinguishing characteristic of borrowing, in its usual form, is its voluntary nature, as contrasted to the compulsory features of taxation. The government offers its securities to the public in much the same manner as a corporation does, and persons are free to purchase them or not, as they wish. If they do so, they suffer no net diminution in their wealth, as occurs when they pay taxes; in exchange for their money they receive bonds or other securities which bear interest and which will ultimately be paid off. The government, in turn, receives money for use in meeting its obligations but incurs a liability for the payment of interest and the repayment of principal in the future.

## ECONOMIC EFFECTS OF BORROWING

The economic effects of a program of government expenditures financed by borrowing are somewhat different from the effects of a similar program financed by taxation. In the first place, under the assumption of full employment, borrowing will almost certainly result in a greater relative reduction in private investment and a lesser reduction in consumption, relative to the adjustments with tax financing. Taxes inevitably impinge in large measure on consumer spending; borrowing absorbs funds which primarily would be saved, and if the expenditure-borrowing program is not to result in inflation, the government borrowing must be offset by an equivalent decline in private investment (given the level of consumption), or inflation will occur. This result can be brought about by monetary policy if it does not occur automatically.

Secondly, borrowing, as such, will on the whole have less contractionary effect upon aggregate demand in the economy than taxes raising the same amount of money. Thus, typically, a program of expenditures financed by borrowing is likely to have a greater net expansionary effect on the economy than a program of the same magnitude financed by taxation. There are two specific reasons for the difference. In the first place, the voluntary character of borrowing increases the likelihood that it will absorb funds which would be saved in any event, rather than curtail consumption. In the second place, because the lending is voluntary and does not reduce the net wealth of the lender, the borrowing is much less likely to have adverse incentive effects such as those which taxation may produce. On the other hand, these consequences may be offset in particular instances if the borrowing and the growth of the debt create fears about the financial stability of the government and lessen private spending, especially for investment purposes.

### The Sources of Funds

The exact effects which the borrowing method of financing may have upon aggregate demand, and thus on the level of national income and employment, will depend in large measure upon the source of the borrowed funds. Major sources will be considered briefly.

1. *Borrowing from Individuals.* If an individual purchases government bonds, some readjustment in his consumption pattern or in the use of his accumulated savings must occur. In rare instances the person may curtail consumption in order to buy the bonds. But this action is unlikely, because of the voluntary character of the lending, except in war periods, when strong pressures may be exerted to induce persons to reduce spending and buy bonds. Otherwise, the purchase of bonds represents a diversion of current or previously accumulated savings into the government bonds from other uses.

There are several alternative uses of savings from which the funds may be diverted into government bonds. In the first place, the person might have used the funds for expansion of his own business had he not bought bonds. Secondly, the funds may be diverted from idle cash balances in which persons would have kept their wealth if the bonds had not been available. But the mere existence of the bonds will not lure funds from either business expansion use or idle balances unless the new bonds offer special advantages not available with existing issues or unless the sale of the bonds raises the market interest rate. Direct diversion from use for business expansion is particularly unlikely, as few persons will abandon profitable expansions merely because government bonds become available, unless they offer very significant advantages over present issues.

The third and most likely alternative is the diversion of the funds into government bonds from other securities, which would have been purchased or held if the government bonds had not been issued. As explained later in the section, this diversion will tend to depress security prices, raise the interest rate, and also make the sale of additional stock more costly to corporations. These effects, in turn, will tend to lessen business expansion, at least to a limited extent, and lure idle funds into the purchase of securities.

In summary, when government bonds are sold to individuals, there is likely to be very little direct effect in curtailing either consumption or business investment. The bonds will be absorbed in large measure out of funds that would have been used to buy other securities and perhaps in part from idle balances. The diversion from other securities and the fall in their prices may indirectly have some contractionary effect; this reaction will be considered after the review of the other sources of funds, since the effect is common to all of them.

2. *Borrowing from Financial Institutions Other than Commercial Banks.* In practice, a large portion of government bond issues is sold to various financial institutions, such as insurance companies, mutual savings banks, etc., as well as to commercial banks, discussed in the next section. When the nonbank financial institutions buy government bonds, in part they may simply reduce their cash balances. But in large measure, they are likely to buy the government bonds instead of other securities. This action, just like the reduced purchase of bonds by individuals, will tend to depress bond prices and raise the interest rate, as discussed in later sections. Finally, the increased holdings of bonds will lessen somewhat the funds available for direct loans to business firms, for purchase of new security issues, for loans for home construction or investment in housing projects, and the like. If the volume of such loans is reduced, there will be some net contractionary effect. But it is doubtful that this effect will be significant; the greater volume of government bonds available will not necessarily cause these institutions to allocate their funds between the low-return, low-risk government bonds and the higher return, higher risk loans for private use in a different manner. A significant effect is likely, as in the case of individuals, only if the government issues offer special advantages over present issues or if their sale raises the interest rate on low-risk investments.

3. *Borrowing from the Commercial Banks.* The commercial banking system, unlike other financial institutions, is capable of creating purchasing power. When the banking system has excess reserves, it can make additional loans up to an amount several times as great as the amount of

the excess reserves. The credit creation is made possible by the fact that amounts loaned by a bank are typically added to the borrowers' accounts and, in turn, paid to persons having accounts in other banks. So long as the sums are not actually drawn out as cash, they remain as reserves for the banks and thus serve as the basis for further expansion of loans.

Accordingly, if the commercial banking system has excess reserves, it can absorb an amount of government bonds considerably greater than the excess reserves without curtailing other loans. The purchasing power to buy the bonds is essentially created rather than being merely transferred. Thus, the program produces no contractionary effect at all. On the other hand, if the banks do not have excess reserves, they cannot buy government bonds without curtailing other loans, and the effect of the sale of bonds to them is much the same as that of the sale to other financial institutions.

4. *Sale of Bonds to the Central Banking System.* Finally, the government may sell bonds directly to the central banking system—the Federal Reserve banks in the United States and the Bank of Canada in Canada. This action creates purchasing power in the same manner as does the sale of bonds to the commercial banks. The amounts borrowed are credited to the accounts of the government with the Federal Reserve banks. When these accounts are drawn upon by the government and the amounts paid to other persons, the recipients will typically deposit the sums in their own banks and thus increase the total deposits of the commercial banks. Thus the purchasing power which the government spends is created, with no curtailment of funds available for other loans. Accordingly, there is no contractionary effect at all.

In addition, the borrowing actually increases the reserves of the member banks. When the checks drawn by the government on its newly created deposits are deposited by the recipients and cleared by the member banks, the amounts constitute additions to the member-bank reserves, since the checks are directly payable by the Federal Reserve banks. Accordingly, the lending powers of the member banks are increased. If the banks actually increase their loans, aggregate demand is increased, and the borrowing itself, quite apart from the expenditure of the funds by the government, is responsible for an expansionary effect on the economy.

### Security Price Changes, Consumption, and Investment[1]

Another element in the picture of effects is the significance of the decline in security prices for the propensity to consume. To the extent to

[1] See the article by E. R. Rolph, "The Incidence of Public Debt Operations," *National Tax Journal*, Vol. IX (December, 1956), pp. 339–53.

which security prices are affected by the increased demand for loanable funds, the current monetary value of security issues will fall; persons will consider themselves to be less wealthy, and thus to some extent may reduce consumption, particularly of durable goods. This effect is likely to be much greater than any direct influence of the borrowing in leading persons to reduce consumption in order to buy bonds, and is independent of the specific sources of the loans.

In similar fashion, to the extent that durable capital assets compete with securities for persons' liquid wealth, the higher interest rates may lessen the purchase (and thus construction) of such assets, with a consequent decline in investment. Thus, for example, the higher interest rates may reduce construction of new apartment buildings.

## The Net Effects of Borrowing upon Consumption and Investment Spending

It is now possible to summarize the over-all effect of government borrowing upon aggregate spending. Curtailment of consumption spending is likely to be slight, except in wartime borrowing programs in which substantial pressure is applied to individuals to reduce consumption and buy bonds. Otherwise, the effects upon consumption depend upon the effect of lower security prices in causing persons to consume less, and upon the special advantages (e.g., redemption rights) which the new securities might offer. Expenditures for new housing may be curtailed if financial institutions reduce lending for such purposes, but they are not likely to do so on any scale unless the interest rate on the bonds rises sharply.

There is a somewhat greater possibility of adverse effect upon investment. The sale of bonds to commercial banks having excess reserves and to the Federal Reserve System does not reduce the funds available for business expansion and therefore should not curtail investment at all (apart from general adverse psychological effects created by the borrowing, discussed below). In these cases the purchasing power is essentially created. On the other hand, the sale to commercial banks having no excess reserves and to nonbank commercial institutions lessens the amounts which these institutions have available for loans to business. The sale of bond to individuals reduces the funds which they have for expansion of their own businesses, for the lending of money for expansion, or for the purchase of stock in new enterprises. But so long as the interest rate is not affected and the new bond issues have no particular advantages over existing securities, the net effect in restricting private investment is likely to be slight.

However, the lessened demand for corporate securities (or in other words, the increased business-plus-governmental demand for loanable funds) will tend to lower security prices and thus drive up the interest rate and make the sale of additional common stock more costly to the existing owners. Both these effects may restrict private investment. However, if the central banking system is committed to a policy of preventing sharp increases in the interest rate, it will undertake open-market purchasing of bonds and thus prevent any rise by making the supply of money capital perfectly elastic. The effect in this case is the same as if the bonds had been sold to the central banking system initially, and the process is in a sense money creation, rather than true borrowing. Furthermore, even if the interest rate does rise, the deterring effect on investment may be slight; there is much evidence that the demand for money capital for investment purposes is affected very little by interest rate changes. The very large volume of investment undertaken with funds obtained from earnings is particularly insensitive to the interest rate.

On the whole, especially with present-day central banking policies, which prevent sharp increases in the interest rate, the government borrowing is not likely to have a very significant contractionary effect on total investment. The reduction in investment will be greater to the extent to which:

1. The increased demand for loanable funds increases the interest rate.

2. The volume of investment is sensitive to interest rate changes.

3. The new government bonds have special advantages (such as redeemability) over existing securities.

4. The commercial banks do not have excess reserves.

5. The bonds are sold to purchasers other than commercial and central banks.

6. Investors curtail loans for business expansion in order to buy government bonds.

There will be no contractionary effect at all if the bonds are sold to the central banking system, to the commercial banks if they have excess reserves, or to lenders who purchase them out of funds which would otherwise lie idle.

Apart from these possible direct effects upon investment, there is one indirect way in which borrowing may exert a direct contractionary effect on the economy. The growth of the debt may give rise to fear of increased taxes in the future or fear of some sort of national bankruptcy, which may reduce private investment and, in limited instances, consumption. The profitability of investments running over a period of years will appear to be less if it is felt that the borrowing will result in higher taxes or in collapse of the credit position of the government. The fact that the fears about the instability of the financial structure of the government may be completely unfounded does not prevent them from influencing the volume of investment.

### The Net Over-All Effect on National Income of an Expenditure Program Financed by Borrowing

Since, under usual circumstances, the borrowing of funds will have little contractionary effect upon the economy, the net effect of a program of government expenditures financed by borrowing is almost certain to be expansionary. The degree of expansionary effect, furthermore, will be greater than that arising from the financing of the same expenditures by taxation. Borrowing will have little effect upon consumption and typically no great effect on investment, while, in contrast, any program of taxation is certain to have substantial contractionary effect. The only instance in which the over-all effect is likely to be contractionary is that in which the borrowing creates great fear of the future financial stability of the government.

In conclusion, it should be noted that the expansionary effects of a borrowing-financed program are due basically to the expenditure of the funds rather than to the borrowing itself (except in part when the bonds are sold to the central banking system). The borrowing itself is likely to have a slight contractionary effect, not an expansionary one. The common statement that "borrowing is inflationary" is merely an abbreviated and somewhat misleading way of saying that a program of government expenditures financed by borrowing is likely to have a greater inflationary effect than a similar program financed by taxation.

### Effects upon Resource Allocation

The borrowing, in itself, has little effect upon resource allocation and thus the composition of national product; it does not have the numerous effects upon allocation which taxes produce. However, to the extent that borrowing curtails business investment, the relative output of capital goods, compared to total output, will be less. This is particularly true of borrowing during full-employment periods. Furthermore, the decline in investment is likely to be greater in some industries than in others, and thus the relative output of various types of capital goods and consumption goods will be altered. The allocation effects of the expenditures are not affected by the method of financing used.

## ECONOMIC EFFECTS OF THE DEBT

Distinct from the economic effects of the financing of an expenditure program by borrowing are the effects upon the economy which result from the existence of the debt, once it has been incurred. Analysis of these effects will be facilitated by a brief review of the nature of government debt. The securities represent claims of the bondholders against the government and thus against the taxpayers of the country. From the standpoint of the owners the bonds constitute personal wealth. But they do not comprise a portion of the real wealth of society, because their value as personal wealth is offset by the claims which they represent against the taxpayers. So long as the debt is held within the country, the real wealth of the country is neither increased nor decreased by the existence of the debt. Society is neither poorer nor richer as a result of the debt, although, as explained in later paragraphs, the existence of the debt may affect both production levels and income distribution. To the extent that the debt is held by persons in other countries, it constitutes a claim of foreigners against the people of the country. The payment of this claim and of interest on the obligations necessitates a larger excess of exports over imports than otherwise and thus lowers the real standard of living (assuming full employment).

If the amounts represented by an internally held debt had not been borrowed, but government expenditures of the same magnitude had been covered by taxation, the personal wealth in the form of the bonds would not exist; persons would have valueless tax receipts or canceled checks instead of bonds. On the other hand, the government, and thus the taxpayers, would have no obligations outstanding against them. If, however, in the years in which the debt had been incurred, government expenditures had been sufficiently low that they would have been covered by existing tax rates, individuals would have had more purchasing power available for other uses. To the extent to which business expansion would have been more rapid, the privately owned real wealth of the country would have been greater today than it is. But the difference cannot be charged to the borrowing method of financing, but to the different levels of government expenditures. It is, of course, possible that had the government expenditures been at a lower level, national income would have been lower because of unemployment, and the amounts would never have been received as income at all.

Nevertheless, while the existence of an internal debt does not mean that the real wealth of the country is less, the debt may have very significant effects upon various aspects of the economy.

## Effects upon Consumption

In the first place, persons consider themselves to have greater private wealth than they would if the debt had not been incurred. There are two exceptions. First, if the government debt results in a sufficiently lower level of all security prices to offset the value of the government bonds, that is, if the total value of all security holdings is no greater than it would be if the government debt were not incurred, private wealth is, of course, no greater than otherwise. Secondly, if all taxpayers discount their tax liabilities created by the debt back to the present, personal wealth will not appear to be greater. But these are unlikely circumstances. Typically, individuals who hold the bonds consider these to be portions of their personal wealth, which they would not have if the government expenditures had been financed entirely by taxation, but they are not likely to take into consideration the claims which the bonds represent against them as taxpayers. Accordingly, they are likely to desrie to spend somewhat higher percentages of their current incomes. This effect of the existence of the debt, therefore, is to increase the percentage of total income which is spent on consumption and thus to exert an expansionary influence on the economy. However, it also reduces the potential rate of capital formation, and thus the possible rate of economic growth.

## Effects upon Investment

The effects on investment are more complex. To the extent that business firms or persons wishing to start businesses have bonds, they are able to obtain additional funds for business expansion without difficulty. Furthermore, the existence of the debt makes the government reluctant to permit substantial increases in the interest rate; the rate may thus be held to lower levels than would otherwise prevail, with consequent encouragement to investment. On the other hand, if the existence of the debt generates fears about the future stability of the credit of the government, businesses may be somewhat more reluctant to undertake long-term investments.

## Liquidity

Not only does the existence of the debt increase personal wealth over what it would have been had the expenditures been financed by taxation, but it also provides persons with highly liquid assets, ones which can be converted into cash at any time with little danger of loss. Accordingly, individuals can increase their spending more quickly than they could if they had equivalent wealth in other forms. This was demonstrated in 1950, when fears of shortages of goods led to sharp increases in spending, financed in part by the redemption of savings bonds.

Furthermore, when the banks hold large amounts of government bonds, they can increase their reserves at any time by the sale of bonds. Accordingly, they can escape from the effects of restrictive credit control policies imposed by the central banking system, unless government bonds are allowed to drop well below par. But the existence of the debt, with its heavy interest burden, makes the government very reluctant to allow government bond prices to fall.

### The Interest Obligations

The existence of the debt gives rise to a continuing interest obligation. The gross annual payment is about $9 billion in the United States (1963), although the net cost is somewhat less, because the interest is subject to income tax. Unless the debt is to be allowed to increase indefinitely, taxes must be higher by the amount of the interest payments than they would otherwise be. The collection of the tax revenue and its use to pay interest are significant in several ways. The payment results in some redistribution of income, since the correlation between tax liability and bond ownership is not exact. A study by D. C. Miller indicated that in the United States the lowest income groups and the highest groups receive more in interest than they pay in taxes to cover the interest payments, while the middle income groups pay more than they receive.[2] The lack of adequate knowledge of tax incidence reduces the validity of the conclusions. Certainly, however, some redistribution occurs, although its exact character is unknown.

The higher taxes necessitated by the debt aggravate such adverse incentive effects as the taxes may have, and these are not offset by the interest payments. Whether the tax and interest payment program has a net contractionary or an expansionary effect upon the economy depends upon the relative propensities to consume of the taxpayers and the bondholders, and the effects of the taxes upon investment. Since a large portion of the bonds is held by persons in the higher income levels, the net effect is certainly less expansionary than most governmental tax and expenditure programs, and could easily be contractionary. On the whole, the interest burden on the internally held debt is likely to be disadvantageous from the standpoint of economic development.

2 *Taxes, the Public Debt, and Transfers of Income* (Urbana: University of Illinois Press, 1950).

## THE CASE FOR BORROWING

The question of the case for the use of borrowing must be divided into two segments, the first relating to the choice for the use of some method of financing other than taxation (or current charges), the second relating to the choice of borrowing in preference to the other nontax source, namely, the creation of money.

### Borrowing versus Taxation

There are three primary situations in which the use of taxation for the financing of governmental noncommercial activities may be regarded as objectionable.

1. *Periods of Unemployment.* The strongest case against the use of taxation is to be found in periods of depression. Basically, the primary reason for financing government activities by taxation is the need to reduce private spending in order to free resources for governmental use. Failure to do so results in an excess of aggregate spending over output and thus, in full-employment periods, in a tendency toward inflation. But in a period of depression, there is essentially no competition between the government and the private sector for resources and no need, from the standpoint of resource utilization, to check private use of resources by curtailing private spending. In such a period, therefore, to the extent that taxes are employed, private sector production is reduced still further, and unemployment is aggravated. Accordingly, there is strong justification for financing by means other than taxation. The problems of depression fiscal policy will be considered further in Chapter 30.

2. *War Periods.* Some use of nontax sources is almost essential during a major war. In a period of all-out war the total real burden is so great that collection of the funds via taxation could have disastrous effects upon production and thus interfere with the primary objective of winning the war. Likewise, complete use of taxation would place a crushing burden on persons whose incomes had not increased, since the taxes would cut drastically into their long-accustomed living levels and burden lightly those whose incomes had risen sharply but who were still accustomed to lower levels of living. These persons have substantial surpluses over current spending, which can be reached by borrowing much more effectively than by taxation. The primary goal, in an all-out war, is to confine civilian production to the minimum necessary for living standards sufficient to maintain physical health and civilian morale. But to force civilian spending down to this level by taxation would inevitably force some persons

below the level, since it is impossible to devise a tax structure which could accomplish the intended goal with respect to all persons. Thus the government is faced with the alternatives of a lower level of military activity and a balanced budget or a higher level and some nontax financing. In terms of accepted objectives the latter is the preferable alternative.

3. *Nonrecurrent Expenditures.* Smaller units of government are often subject to heavy, nonrecurrent expenditures for public improvements which will last over a period of years. The financing of the entire cost by taxation would result in extremely severe burdens in a short period and is considered inequitable between present and future taxpayers. The use of borrowing (in this case the only nontax source available) allows the spreading-out of the expenditures over a period of time and greater stability in tax rates. Furthermore, if taxation is used, the activities are not likely to be extended to the optimum, since persons will tend to discount heavily the benefits in future years, whereas the tax burden is direct and immediate. If a new high school building had to be financed entirely by current taxation in a small district, the voters might never approve it at all. On the other hand, if current routine expenditures are financed by borrowing, they are likely to be carried too far, in terms of optimum levels, since the benefits are immediate, but the costs, as the taxpayers see them, are pushed off to the future.

There is little justification, however, for borrowing for capital improvements merely because the particular projects will last over long periods, if roughly comparable amounts are to be spent each year. If a city is to pave thirty-five blocks of streets each year, nothing is gained (and total costs are increased) by borrowing; the mere fact that particular streets will last for long periods is not actually significant for the choice of methods of financing, except to the extent that the use of taxation may, at least during an initial period, hold the level of expenditures unreasonably low.

A closely related situation is that of borrowing for acquisition of capital equipment for government-operated commercial enterprises. If the cost of the equipment is to be paid for by the users of the services rather than by the taxpayers, it is essential that the funds be borrowed and ultimately paid off out of revenues.

## The Choice between Borrowing and the Creation of Money

If taxes are not to be employed, the government has two alternatives: borrowing or creation of money. The latter method has two advantages: It has no contractionary effects whatsoever (except possibly from psychological reactions to the use of this technique), and it does not give rise to interest charges or problems arising out of servicing and retirement of debt. Therefore, in periods of depression, in which nontax methods are used in order to lessen contractionary effects of the raising of funds, the case for creation of money is particularly strong. Borrowing is objectionable because it does exercise some contractionary effect, although this is weaker than the effects of taxation.

However, even in depressions, there are at least two objections to the policy. Particularly if the money is created simply by printing currency, serious loss of confidence in the government might result, since this policy has so long been associated with irresponsible finance and runaway inflation. The other is the great painlessness of the technique, which might make governments, once accustomed to it, reluctant to return to the use of painful taxes once full employment had been attained. There is, however, an intermediate technique, which has the form of borrowing, but actually involves money creation, that is, borrowing from the central banking system. This method has virtually all the advantages of paper money issue, since there is no contractionary effect, and the nominal interest payments may be recaptured for the government by absorbing the earnings of the central banking system. On the other hand, the psychological reactions are likely to be much less serious, particularly because most people do not understand the difference between this type of borrowing and other forms. However, the similarity to paper money issue is so close that governments have typically attempted to avoid the policy, at least in a direct fashion, although indirectly they have followed it by having the central banking system maintain interest rate levels by open-market buying concurrent with new government security issues.

In full-employment periods, money creation, whether by currency printing or central bank loan techniques, is objectionable for several reasons in addition to those applicable in depressions. In war periods, for example, the borrowing is a necessary evil, and the more contractionary it is, the weaker will be the inflationary pressures. Money creation will feed the inflationary fires, not only directly but by facilitating commercial bank credit expansion. In the financing of long-range improvements, the paper money technique is objectionable because it would make the projects appear too advantageous—virtually costless—and thus such activities would be extended too far. This portion of the governmental sector would grow too large relative to the sector financed by taxes, and to the private sector of the economy.

Thus, in full-employment periods, borrowing is always preferable to money creation; in depression periods, however, there is a stronger case for money creation, and the use of borrowing will necessitate a larger deficit to obtain a given degree of recovery. If society regarded money creation as acceptable and there were no danger of irresponsible use of it, the case for it would be strong. Under existing attitudes, its advantages are weakened by the possibility of general loss in confidence, and subsequent misuse of the policy. Because of psychological factors, the central-bank-borrowing form of money creation is preferable to the printing of additional paper money.

## THE OBJECTIONS TO BORROWING AS A SUBSTITUTE FOR TAXATION

The objections to the employment of borrowing as a substitute for taxation can be classed into two groups, those which are relevant to the financing by borrowing and those which are related to the debt itself. The former group applies even more strongly to financing by money creation than to borrowing, while the latter is significant only for borrowing.

### Inflationary Consequences

From the standpoint of the economy itself the basic objection to borrowing is the increased inflationary pressure which results from the choice of this method of financing in preference to taxation. In periods of full employment, when expenditures are financed by borrowing, the contractionary effects of the borrowing will almost certainly be weaker than the expansionary effects of the spending and also weaker than the contractionary effects of taxes. As indicated earlier in the chapter, to a large extent the bonds may be purchased out of savings without discouragement to private investment, especially in periods of optimism which characterize inflation. The result is an increase in total spending and thus a further increase in inflationary pressures.

However, the differences between borrowing and taxation can be exaggerated. To the extent that taxes are absorbed out of savings without effect on investment, no anti-inflationary pressure is created. As explained earlier in the chapter, borrowing may exert some contractionary effect, especially if it raises the general level of interest rates. While, on the whole, a borrowing-financed program can be expected to have a greater expansionary influence than one financed by taxation, the difference is one of degree rather than kind, the exact relative effects depending upon the sources of borrowed funds, on the one hand, and the types of taxes used, on the other.

This objection to borrowing is relevant only in periods of full employment. In depression conditions, no curtailment of private spending is necessary to free resources for governmental use, and there is no danger of inflation.

## Capital Formation

Under conditions of full employment the financing of government activities by borrowing will almost certainly mean a greater relative reduction in capital formation than would occur with tax financing, since the impact upon the private sector will be almost entirely on savings. Thus, central bank action to reduce investment will be required, or inflation will occur. As a consequence, the rate of potential economic growth will be reduced. If the government expenditures are undertaken for capital formation, there will be no net loss, but the over-all rate of growth will be below that possible with tax financing.

## Control of Expenditures

A third objection to borrowing is its relative painlessness; the fact that additional expenditures financed by borrowing do not give rise to immediate tax increases may result in governmental activities being carried beyond optimum levels. When taxation is employed, legislative bodies will take into consideration the adverse reactions of the community to the taxes as well as the favorable reactions to the benefits from the services. If borrowing is employed and little attention is paid to its possible future consequences, there is no offsetting factor to the gains from the additional services, and thus the activities may be extended unreasonably far. The classic example of this type of reaction is to be found in the behavior of the states and localities during the last century, when they could borrow freely. Very large sums of money were borrowed and used for purposes of very doubtful value to society. In some instances the debt burdens became so great that the governments were unable to meet them. There is no assurance that optimum levels of government expenditures will be attained with taxation, but there is greater danger that a suitable balancing of gains and costs will not be attained if borrowing is freely used as a source of revenue.

## The Objectionable Consequences of the Existence of the Debt

There are also serious consequences arising from the existence of the debt, as well as those which result currently from the financing of expenditures by borrowing. In the first place, the debt give rise to interest charges, which, as previously indicated, necessitate higher taxes, unless a continuous increase in the debt is to occur. The tax and interest payment program, on the whole, probably has a net detrimental effect on the economy.

Secondly, as noted, in periods of full employment the existence of the debt tends to aggravate inflationary tendencies. Because persons regard the bonds as personal wealth and ignore the claims on themselves as taxpayers arising out of the debt, they are likely to consume a greater percentage of their income than otherwise. The high liquidity of the bonds enables individuals to increase their spending and banks their lending very quickly and easily, as pointed out in an earlier section. The large debt makes the government reluctant to allow the use of anti-inflationary monetary policies; any increase in interest rates results in a greater interest burden for the government as existing securities mature and are refunded.

Thirdly, the debt may increase to limits beyond the ability of the government to meet the obligations and thus impair its credit standing and possibly endanger the entire financial structure of the country. With the federal government the dangers are less, because of the great taxing capacity and the ability of the government to borrow from the banks and the central banking system if it cannot obtain funds from other sources. But if the point is reached at which individuals become unwilling to buy government bonds, the bank borrowing will have particularly inflationary effects.

The problem is much more serious with the states and localities, which have limited taxing capacities, no power over the central banking system, and no powers to print money. During depression years especially, many local governments reach the point at which they cannot meet bond obligations out of tax sources which they are authorized to use or can effectively administer. During the thirties a number of jurisdictions were unable to meet their obligations, and default ensued; eventually, in the United States, bankruptcy laws were amended to provide for readjustment of debt in such circumstances.

These various limitations suggest that borrowing as a source of revenue should be confined to those cases in which strong specific justification exists. The most obvious case is that of a severe depression (assuming that a policy of money creation is not employed), when the gains in the form of assistance to recovery would appear to outweigh the disadvantages. In periods of full employment, there is strong justification for limiting borrowing to two situations: (1) periods of all-out war, in which maximum war potentials cannot be realized if all activities are financed by taxes, and (2) nonrecurrent expenditures of local units for capital improvements, which cannot be covered by taxation without excessive temporary tax rate increases.

## Does Borrowing Shift Burdens of Governmental Activities to Future Generations?

A long-debated question is whether the borrowing method of financing shifts burdens to future generations. The traditional popular argument is obvious: If taxes are used, persons pay for the activities now. If funds are borrowed, the present generation escapes, and the burden rests on persons in future generations paying interest and principal. Most economists have argued that this reasoning is fallacious, but a few have supported the popular traditional argument.[3]

Criticism of the traditional popular argument takes several lines. In the first place, it is argued that the real burden of governmental activities (except for incidental effects of tax collections, etc.) must be borne during the period in which the expenditures are made, since it is this period in which resources are diverted from private to public sector use. The real burden of a war consists of the use of materials, manpower, and the like to produce war material instead of civilian goods, and this is borne during the war in the form of reduced consumption and investment (and perhaps increased effort), regardless of the method of financing employed. The borrowing method affects the future generations in two ways only. To the extent to which it reduces the rate of capital formation, as noted earlier in the chapter, the stock of capital goods and the potential level of national income in future generations will be less. Secondly, the borrowing method creates some problems for the future generations in the form of adverse effects on the economy from the taxes necessary to pay interest and principal, inflationary or deflationary effects of the existence of the debt, etc. But there is no shifting of the basic burden to the future; while future generations inherit the obligation to pay interest and principal on the debt, they also inherit the bonds themselves. Thus, when interest and principal payments are made, there occurs only a transfer within the future generations, and no real burden. Except for the capital-formation and incidental effects of the taxes, there is no reduction in real income in the future generation.

In terms of usual concepts of "burden" of governmental activities, this argument is clearly valid. The attack upon it by Buchanan centers around the question of the meaning of the concept of "burden," which Buchanan interprets in terms of individual attitudes toward their economic well-being rather than in terms of changes in private sector outputs

---

[3] See the book by J. M. Buchanan, *Public Principles of Public Debt* (Homewood, Ill.: Richard D. Irwin, Inc., 1958), for a discussion of the question and a defense of the traditional popular point of view.

and real income. Buchanan argues that during the period in which the governmental activities and borrowing take place, no burden of any kind is created; individuals voluntarily exchange liquid funds for government bonds, instead of consuming or acquiring for investment purposes private sector output of equivalent value. No one feels himself to be any worse off. When the bonds are repaid in the future generation, funds are taken from the taxpayers to pay the bondholders; the former feel themselves to be worse off (as essentially they are, because they have less disposable income), while the bondholders do not feel themselves to be any better off, since they have merely exchanged bonds for cash.

This line of reasoning may be criticized for overemphasis on the individuals directly involved. At the time the governmental activities are undertaken, the persons who buy bonds are neither better nor worse off than they would have been had they put their liquid wealth in other investments. But some persons in the economy must experience less private sector real income, since, assuming full employment, the governmental activities reduce private sector output. At the time of bond repayment, some persons must experience an increase in real income to offset the loss experienced by the taxpayers, since total real income in society remains unchanged (apart from the generally recognized incidental effects of the taxes). No real loss occurs in this subsequent generation. In large measure, the persons benefiting are those whose security holdings are made more valuable because the sums obtained from debt retirement are used to buy other securities, thus driving their prices upward.[4]

### Debt Limitation Laws

The basic objections to government borrowing as a means of financing have been generally accepted for many years; thus, frequently the rights of governments to borrow have been restricted by constitutional provision. This is not true, however, of the federal government, which is

---

[4] A widely quoted article by W. G. Bowen, R. G. Davis, and D. H. Kopf, "The Public Debt," *American Economic Review*, Vol. L (September, 1960), pp. 701–5, seeks to prove that some shifting forward is possible. A. P. Lerner, in an article entitled "The Burden of the Debt," *Review of Economics and Statistics*, Vol. XLIII (May, 1961), pp. 139–41, shows how the Davis conclusions arise from a peculiar definition of generations. An extensive analysis of the question is to be found in the article by Franco Modigliani, "Long Run Implications of Alternative Fiscal Policies and the Burden of the National Debt," *Economic Journal*, Vol. LXXI (December, 1961), pp. 730–55. To Modigliani, burden may shift to future generations because government borrowing used in lieu of taxation reduces the current rate of capital formation to a greater extent than taxes, thus reducing the income from capital in future generations.

See also the article by C. S. Shoup, "Debt Financing and Future Generations," *Economic Journal*, Vol. LXXII (December, 1962), pp. 887–98.

specifically authorized by the Constitution to borrow money, and no significant limitations are attached. In recent decades, however, Congress has established a debt ceiling beyond which the administration cannot go, largely in the belief that this is an effective device for limiting governmental spending. In practice, Congress has been willing to raise the ceiling when urgent need for additional borrowing develops.[5] The January, 1963, limit figure is $308 billion.

During the last century, most of the states imposed rigid limitations on the borrowing powers of the state governments by means of constitutional provisions and, in addition, restricted local government borrowing powers.[6] In most states, borrowing by the state government is permissible only for specified purposes, and the issuance of bonds beyond a small figure requires endorsement by popular vote or constitutional amendment. Only five states have no restrictions. Local governments can usually borrow up to a sum equal to a specified percentage of total assessed valuation of property in the area. But even borrowing within this limit often requires a popular vote. The limits are absolute in some cases, but in others may be exceeded through popular vote, often more than a bare majority being required. In Canada, there are no restrictions on the borrowing powers of the provincial legislatures, but local governments are subject to restrictions comparable to those in the United States.

The state debt limits have not been highly effective. Various devices have been developed to escape them, primarily through the issue of revenue bonds of various types not subject to the restrictions.[7] They have, however, restricted the states from borrowing to meet depression deficits, and have led them to take action contrary to the goals of fiscal policy. The use of revenue bonds has significantly increased the total cost of borrowing; the interest rate has ranged from ½ per cent to ⅔ per cent higher than that on general obligation bonds in recent years.[8] Greater freedom for the legislatures to borrow would appear to be warranted. The local limits, on the other hand, have served a rather useful purpose in checking wanton local borrowing, although their inflexibility aggravates the depression problems of the local units. In recent years, local governments in some states, especially Pennsylvania, have commenced to avoid the debt limit laws by financing public improvements through revenue bonds issued by

---

[5] See the papers by H. L. Lutz and by W. W. Heller on federal debt limits in *Proceedings of the National Tax Association for 1958.*

[6] See B. U. Ratchford, "State and Local Debt Limitations," *Proceedings of the National Tax Association for 1958*, pp. 215–29.

[7] See A. J. Heins, *Constitutional Restrictions against State Debt* (Madison: University of Wisconsin Press, 1963).

[8] *Ibid.*, p. 84.

separate authorities, which are paid off out of tax revenues through contractual payments between the local unit and the authority. The most satisfactory solution for the local units is increased provision of temporary state and federal grants to them rather than relaxation of the debt limits. Some authorization to exceed the limits, however, may be justifiable, but complete elimination could easily result in excessive local borrowing. The popular vote requirement has considerable merit, although the greater willingness of the voters to approve bond issues in prosperity than in depression aggravates cylical changes in business activity.

## THE PRESENT DEBT

Figure 35 shows the total amount of federal, state, and local debt outstanding in the United States; by January, 1963, the figure of the federal debt had reached $306 billion. Figure 36 shows the relative importance of short-term and long-term federal debt, and Figure 37 indicates the holdings of federal securities by class of investor.

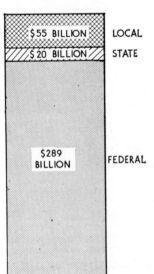

FIGURE 35

GOVERNMENT
DEBT BY LEVEL OF
GOVERNMENT,
JULY 1, 1961

$55 BILLION    LOCAL
$20 BILLION    STATE

$289
BILLION        FEDERAL

Most of the total governmental debt in the United States is federal debt, incurred almost solely for the financing of World Wars I and II, the high level of defense spending since 1945, and the depression of the thirties. Local debt is larger in total than state debt, mainly because the states conduct relatively few functions which have necessitated heavy borrowing. The great bulk of state and local debt is long-term in character; on the other hand, as of November, 1962, more than 40 per cent of federal debt consisted of obligations issued for periods of less than five years. The federal short-term obligations fall into three classes: Treasury bills, originally issued for periods of ninety days, but now up to one year; certificates of indebtedness, issued usually for periods of one year; and Treasury notes, with maturity from one to five years.

Approximately half of the state debt and 30 per cent of local debt consists of *revenue bonds*, which are not obligations of the taxpayers, but of the revenues from the activities which the bonds were issued to finance. These are

FIGURE 36

CHARACTER OF U.S. FEDERAL DEBT
OUTSTANDING, NOVEMBER 1, 1962

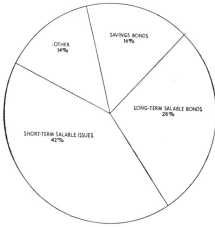

SOURCE: *Federal Reserve Bulletin.*

FIGURE 37

ESTIMATED OWNERSHIP OF U.S. FEDERAL
SECURITIES BY CLASS OF INVESTOR,
NOVEMBER 1, 1962

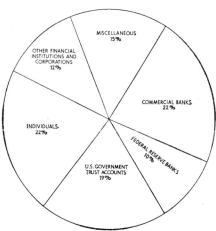

SOURCE: *Federal Reserve Bulletin.*

primarily toll roads at the state level and various public utilities at the municipal level. Some, however, are issued by special authorities to finance school buildings and other nonutility activities, the bonds being paid off by "rentals" paid by the local governmental units to the authorities. Revenue bonds are popular for two reasons: They are not subject to constitutional debt limitations, and they avoid placing any burden on the taxpayer. However, as noted, a substantially higher interest rate must be paid.[9]

As shown in Figure 37, only a small percentage of federal debt is held by individuals, about 22 per cent, of which about two thirds consists of savings bonds. Nearly 30 per cent of the debt is held by the government trust funds and the Federal Reserve banks, and thus is not in the hands of the public; in terms of the significance for the economy, it is the net debt outstanding, about $216 billion in November, 1962, which is of concern, rather than the gross amount.

The general significance of the debt depends also upon its relationship to the gross national product; this ratio has declined steadily over the last fifteen years despite the rise in the absolute amount of the debt. The ratio of the publicly held debt of GNP fell from 87 per cent of GNP at the end of 1947 to 44 per cent at the end of 1958 and 38 per cent at the end of 1962. Stated in reverse terms, so long as national debt increases each year less rapidly than GNP rises, its real significance in the economy falls.

## RETIREMENT OF DEBT

Retirement of debt, in the sense of a net reduction in the total amount outstanding, necessitates a surplus of taxes and other current revenues over governmental expenditures. Retirement may take the form of redemption of savings bonds, of payment of other issues as they mature, or of purchase of unmatured issues on the security markets.

### Economic Effects of Retirement

The economic effects of debt retirement are in many respects the opposite of those of borrowing. The making of the payments to the bond-holders may have some expansionary effect, because the assets of the holders are converted into more liquid form. But just as government borrowing probably has little direct contractionary effect on private spending, so the expansionary effect of the retirement is also probably rather limited.

When the retired bonds were held by individuals, the holders may in some cases spend a portion of the amounts received for consumption purposes. But this action is unlikely, since the receipts of money do not

[9] Note the article by E. Kurnow, "The Nonguaranteed Debt of State and Local Governments," *National Tax Journal*, Vol. XV (September, 1962), pp. 239–45.

in any sense constitute income but merely represent a change in form of wealth. If the persons had strongly desired to utilize this wealth for consumption purposes, they could have done so previously by redeeming or selling the bonds. Only the effect of the forces of inertia may result in the spending of the wealth at the time the bonds are retired. The holders may have had some interest in spending the amounts but did not bother to sell or redeem the bonds; once they are paid off in cash, they spend the money rather than reinvest it.

Of the amounts paid to individuals and financial institutions, a limited sum may be held in idle balances, but most of the money will be reinvested in other securities. As a consequence, some assistance will be offered directly to new investment by the availability of larger sums for the purchase of new securities or the making of direct loans to businesses. However, the money will primarily be used to buy existing securities; the increased demand will tend to raise security prices and lower the rate of interest, and thus encourage additional investment. If interest rates are already very low, there may be little change, a slight reduction in the interest rate resulting in a large attempted increase in the voluntary holdings of idle cash.

Retirement of bank-held debt is even less likely to have expansionary effects. If the banks had excess reserves before, the retirement of the bonds will merely reduce bank deposits and increase reserves. Some increase in bank loans may occur if reserves had been relatively low and the banks had been unable to make as many loans as they wished. Retirement of debt held by the Federal Reserve System has no expansionary effect of any kind and, as explained below, reduces member-bank reserves. Essentially, this action is equivalent to a reduction in the money supply.

On the other hand, the collection of the taxes necessary to provide the funds to retire the debt will inevitably have some contractionary effect on the economy, by curtailing consumption and investment. The exact effect, of course, will depend upon the types of taxes used. Those burdening the lower income groups will reduce consumption significantly; others will cut down the volume of investment to a greater extent. If the taxes are absorbed entirely out of idle funds, with no effect upon consumption or investment, there is no contractionary effect at all.

The combined effect of the collection of the taxes and the retirement of the debt is likely to be contractionary. The taxes almost inevitably produce some reduction in spending; on the other hand, the actual retirement of the debt, as indicated, is likely to have relatively little expansionary effect. The exact effect depends, of course, upon the type of tax used, the types of securities retired, and the reactions of their holders. The deflationary effect will be small if taxes are absorbed largely out of idle funds and if the revenue is used to retire debt owned by persons who spend a portion of the money when they receive it. On the other hand, the use of sales taxes to retire debt owned by persons who hold idle the amounts received will have substantial deflationary effect.

If the debt held by the commercial banks is retired and they do not increase private loans as a result of their improved reserve position, the purchasing power involved is essentially canceled. When the checks drawn by the taxpayers upon their accounts are cleared by the government and the amounts paid directly to the commercial banks, a net reduction in total deposits occurs. (The reader is reminded that bank deposits are the amounts the bank owes, not the amounts which it has.) However, if the banks do increase private loans, the old level of deposits will be restored.

The over-all effect of a program of collection of taxes and subsequent retirement of central-bank-held debt is a reduction not only in bank deposits but in bank reserves as well. When the checks in payment of taxes are cleared and the amounts are paid by the government to the Federal Reserve, the sums are subtracted from the deposits of the member banks with the Federal Reserve; these deposits constitute the legal reserves of the member banks. If the member banks do not have adequate excess reserves, they must curtail their loans. In this instance, not only the collection of the taxes as such but the use of the funds to retire the debt, as well, both have deflationary effects. If the banks have large excess reserves, no double effect is encountered.

### Debt Retirement Policies

The deflationary effects of the over-all program of retirement of debt and collection of the necessary taxes suggest that a national government cannot maintain a policy of systematic retirement of a certain amount of debt each year. When such a program has been attempted, the practical impossibilities of maintaining a budget surplus in depressions or wars and the realization of the adverse effects of debt retirement in a period of depression have prevented its continuation. On the other hand, retirement in periods of inflation not only eliminates a portion of the debt but also lessens inflationary pressures. It may be argued that a program of collecting a surplus without use of the funds to retire the debt would have an even greater anti-inflationary effect. But this policy would not eliminate the interest burden, and governments find it very difficult to retain surpluses; the political temptations which surpluses provide toward increased expenditures are tremendous.

A major question, however, over which there has been substantial debate is that of the importance of retiring the debt. Should the government make a strenuous effort to retire the debt as quickly as possible, so long as it can do so without causing or aggravating a depression, or should it regard the debt as relatively harmless, to be retired only when strong peacetime inflationary pressures make deflationary fiscal policy essential? The more conservative point of view stresses the desirability of retirement, while that represented, for example, in the writings of A. H. Hansen and A. P. Lerner, minimizes the undesirable effects of the debt and the need for retirement. This philosophy stresses the fact that the debt does not reduce the real wealth of the country and that interest payments are mere transfer payments from some persons to others within the country. Lerner, who sees no danger in continuous increases in the debt, suggests that interest should be met simply by additional borrowing, except in periods in which taxes are necessary for anti-inflationary purposes. Lerner and his disciples stress the fact that the basic economic function of taxation is to prevent inflation rather than to raise revenue to pay interest or for any other purpose. When taxes are not needed for this purpose, they should not be imposed, it is argued, the amounts necessary for payment of interest and other government obligations being raised by the printing of paper money or government borrowing.

The primary objection to the Lerner point of view is based upon the undesirable effects of the two alternatives available if the debt is allowed to continue. If interest is met by taxation, there may be adverse incentive effects and an increased tendency toward inflation. If the interest is financed by increased borrowing, the adverse psychological reactions may interfere with economic development. The generally inflationary effects of the existence of the debt make the control of inflation more difficult. If the debt is not reduced, it will almost certainly increase, even if the interest is covered by taxation, unless both depressions and wars can be avoided in the future. As indicated above, a breaking point of government credit might be reached. While bonds could always be sold to the banking system, severe inflation might occur if individuals became unwilling to buy them.

On the whole, there is substantial merit in a program of gradual retirement of the federal debt, so long as this can be done without precipitating or aggravating a depression. While the debt does not mean that the country is poorer than it would otherwise be, it does have a greater adverse than beneficial effect upon the economy.

The general attitude toward the national debt and the importance of its retirement has changed markedly in recent years. Prior to World War II, fear of the magnitude of the debt was very widespread, and was a factor checking recovery from the depression of the thirties. But since the war, despite the much larger debt, there is much less discussion of the need for retirement and much less fear of the debt. As a consequence, Congress has been unwilling to hold taxes high enough to insure surpluses. If this attitude persists, reduction of the debt will prove increasingly difficult, even in periods in which economic considerations justify budget surpluses. The Canadian postwar record of debt retirement has been much better.

### Retirement of State and Local Debt

State and local debt retirement has typically, at least in recent decades, been conducted on a systematic basis. When state and local bonds are issued, some system of retirement is usually required by law or constitutional provision. For many years the sinking fund method of retirement was most commonly employed but was not entirely satisfactory, largely because the funds set aside in the sinking fund to retire the debt were sometimes used for other purposes. Accordingly, there has been increased use of the serial issue method, under which the maturity dates are spread out over a period of years, a certain number of bonds coming due and being retired each year out of current revenues. Systematic retirement is almost essential for satisfactory local and, to some extent, state financial management; if strong pressures are not established to insure annual retirement, the governments will be inclined to neglect retirement entirely. It is neither possible nor desirable, however, for these governments to continue net reduction in debt during depression years; while the retirement programs are continued, they are often offset by new borrowing.

### Cancellation of Debt

The most extreme solution to the problem of government debt is deliberate default or cancellation. The federal government and the states, being sovereign so far as debt is concerned, can repudiate their debt if they wish, the bondholders having no redress. Four states have done so in the past, and some were temporarily unable to meet their obligations during the thirties.

This "easy" solution to the national debt, however, would be most inequitable between persons who had placed their wealth in government bonds and those who have other forms of investments. An unfortunate penalty would rest on those who had purchased savings bonds under government urging. Banks and other financial institutions hold so many government bonds that they would in large measure be destroyed by cancellation, unless they were permitted to reduce their own obligations to depositors, policyholders, etc. The general financial chaos which would result from these readjustments would have serious temporary effects upon the functioning of the economy. From a long-range point of view, future borrowing by the government would be rendered extremely difficult and would, almost of necessity, have to take the highly inflationary form of borrowing from the Federal Reserve. Cancellation of the debt cannot be regarded as a serious alternative to repayment or continuation. Repudiation of debts by national governments is almost unknown, except in the event of defeat in war or revolutionary overthrow of the government.

The legal position of local governments with respect to repudiation of debt is substantially different. Since they are municipal corporations rather than sovereign governments, they are not legally free to cancel their obligations. In the event of failure to pay, they may be sued, and appropriate orders may be issued by the courts compelling payment. The state laws provide the exact procedure in such cases. With respect to involuntary default, as noted above, a form of bankruptcy proceedings, with downward readjustment of debt payments, is provided for by federal law.

## DEBT POLICY

In this chapter the general questions relating to government borrowing have been considered without respect to specific borrowing and debt management policies which are desirable under different circumstances. These questions will be taken up in the two chapters on fiscal policy, of which borrowing and debt management policies are a significant part.

## APPENDIX—GOVERNMENT DEBT IN CANADA

Figure 38 shows the total amount of government debt outstanding in Canada. The federal debt, about $18 billion, is relatively smaller, compared to total national income, than the $302 billion debt in the United States. Provincial debt is much larger than local debt, in sharp contrast to the situation in the United States, and is a much larger fraction of the total than in the United States, largely because the provinces have undertaken far more public utility enterprises than the states. Figure 39 shows the relative holdings of the federal debt by type of investor. Most of the federal debt consists of bonds; short-term obligations are of much less importance than in the United States.

A substantial portion of provincial debt and a part of federal and local debt in Canada are designated as indirect debt, the bonds being direct

FIGURE 38

GOVERNMENT DEBT BY LEVEL OF
GOVERNMENT, CANADA, 1961

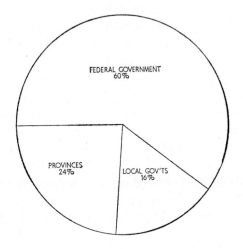

SOURCE: Bank of Canada, *Statistical Summary.*

FIGURE 39

OWNERSHIP OF FEDERAL DEBT, CANADA, 1961

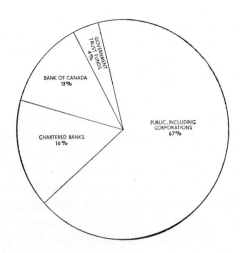

SOURCE: Bank of Canada, *Statistical Summary.*

obligations of various Crown (government-owned) corporations, primarily public utilities, which are guaranteed by the respective governmental units.

## REFERENCES

NOTE: Studies of debt management policies are listed at the end of Chapter 30.

ADAMS, H. C. *Public Debts.* New York: Appleton-Century, 1887.
The pioneer study of government borrowing in the United States.

BUCHANAN, J. M. *Public Principles of Public Debt.* Homewood, Ill.: Richard D. Irwin, Inc., 1958.
The most recent study of public debt, with emphasis on the thesis that borrowing does shift burdens to future generations.

COOKE, H. J. *The Role of Debt in the Economy.* Washington, D.C.: Public Affairs Press, 1961.

LERNER, A. P. "The Burden of the National Debt," in *Income, Employment, and Public Policy.* New York: W. W. Norton & Co., 1948.

MEADE, J. E. "Is the National Debt a Burden?" *Oxford Economic Papers,* Vol. X (July, 1958), pp. 163–83.

ROLPH, E. R. "The Incidence of Public Debt Operations," *National Tax Journal,* Vol. IX (December, 1956), pp. 339–53.

SIMONS, H. C. "On Debt Policy," *Journal of Political Economy,* Vol. LII (December, 1944), pp. 256–61.
A penetrating analysis of government debt.

———. *Economic Policy for a Free Society,* chaps. ix, x. Chicago: University of Chicago Press, 1948.
A further statement of the Simons position.

MUSGRAVE, R. A. *The Theory of Public Finance,* chap. xxiii. New York: McGraw-Hill Book Co., Inc., 1959.

Chapter

27

# INTRODUCTION TO
# FISCAL POLICY

Government expenditure and revenue programs inevitably have some influence upon the level of national income, in both real and monetary terms, as outlined in previous chapters. The expenditures themselves are almost certain to be expansionary, the exact extent depending upon the purposes for which the money is spent. The revenue collections tend to be contractionary, to a degree dependent upon the exact sources employed. On the whole, taxation is more contractionary than borrowing, and borrowing is more contractionary than the issuance of paper money. But there are wide ranges of effects within each of these categories; some types of taxation, for example, may be less deflationary than some forms of borrowing. The net effect of the combined revenue-expenditure program is likely to be expansionary, except in those cases in which the taxes have very severe effects upon incentives or borrowing gives rise to widespread fears about future financial stability.

## The Nature of Fiscal Policy

These effects have been recognized only in recent decades, and with this recognition has come the realization of the possibility of making deliberate adjustments in revenues and expenditures for the purpose of obtaining greater economic stability. To such adjustments the name *fiscal policy* is given. Prior to the decade of the thirties, government expenditures were regarded simply as the means of financing governmental activities, which in turn were evaluated strictly in terms of the direct benefits from the activities, without regard to any possible effects upon the level of national income. Taxes, on the other hand, were regarded solely as necessary means of financing the expenditures; while it was recognized that failure to use them might result in inflation, there was no recognition of the possibility of direct use of taxation as a means of fighting inflation. The rules about the need for annually balanced budgets were applied to governments in the same fashion as to individual households; thus, in a

508

period of depression, as government revenues fell, expenditures were reduced as well. When depressions or inflationary pressures developed, the only acceptable stabilization measure was monetary policy conducted through central bank operation.

During the depression years of the thirties, the theory of fiscal policy first developed, as an outgrowth of the long and severe depression and the failure of monetary policy to bring recovery. It was provided a strong analytical basis in Keynes's *General Theory of Employment, Interest and Money*, published in 1936. Governments began in an uncertain and halting fashion to attempt to use fiscal policy techniques, in the midst of bitter criticism by conservative adherents of the old balanced budget doctrines, who saw in fiscal policy a collapse in government credit and a permanent increase in the sphere of governmental activity. For a time, fiscal policy dealt only with unemployment problems, but with the coming of World War II, the other half of the analysis, that concerned with inflation control, was developed. Thus, by 1945, there was a substantial literature on the question, and widespread acceptance of certain basic tenets of fiscal policy, although there was great divergence of opinion on precise techniques and their effectiveness, and some die-hard resistance to the whole doctrine.

Basic to modern fiscal policy is the philosophy that the government cannot be subjected to the same rules as individuals, because of the effects which its action has upon society as a whole. Thus, for example, while individuals must reduce spending when their incomes fall, national governments not only do not have to do so, but should not do so, because such action will aggravate the general decline in economic activity. The secondary effects of government expenditures on national income levels are recognized, as well as the possibility of the use of tax measures as means of lessening inflationary pressures. The point is widely recognized that society can afford more, not fewer, governmental activities in depression than in prosperity, since in the former situation no diversion of resources from private production is necessary to permit increased governmental use of resources.

## ALTERNATIVE APPROACHES TO FISCAL POLICY

Despite the widespread acceptance of the general idea of fiscal policy, there are numerous divergent points of view, and substantial controversy, particularly over specific techniques and their effectiveness. These various points of view are grouped into three major classes, discussed in succeeding sections. To these may be added a fourth and purely negative approach, the traditional argument that fiscal policy should not be used at all, governments determining expenditure and tax policies in terms of the direct benefits and costs of the activities, and maintaining a balanced budget at all times. Essentially, the defenders of this point of view argue that fiscal policy is incapable of increasing economic stability. In depression, for example, basic readjustments in prices, wages, methods of production, and the like must occur before recovery will be self-sustaining. Governmental policies will interfere with these adjustments, and any revival artificially stimulated by government will quickly collapse. Governmental action will thus hinder, rather than aid, recovery. This attitude has become, to an increasing extent, a small minority point of view, in part because of the recognition that political considerations will not permit its acceptance by governments. When depressions develop, the pressures on governments to take action become so great that they cannot be resisted, and any government which attempts to do so will soon be turned out of office. But apart from the practical problem, the point of view that fiscal policy can be effective and should be attempted is much more widely accepted today.

### Functional Finance

The most extreme point of view on fiscal policy is that of the functional finance school of thought, which reached the height of its popularity in the late thirties and forties. A. P. Lerner is the best-known expositor. The functional finance approach argues that a prime factor in the determination of government expenditure levels should be the effect of the levels upon national income. Expenditures would be raised to bring full employment. The function of taxation is not to raise revenue for government but to check inflation; thus, only when inflation would otherwise develop should taxes be imposed. Borrowing likewise should be utilized only when it is desirable to make the private sector less liquid in the interests of restraining spending. When neither taxation nor borrowing are appropriate, government spending should be financed by money creation.

The chief criticisms of this extreme point of view center around the fear of adverse psychological reactions which would result from such policies, and the danger of extension of government spending to wasteful levels if no tie were maintained between expenditures and taxation. The doctrine is based upon an assumption that government policies can be determined by experts in a vacuum removed from political pressures and popular desires. This assumption is contrary to the basic approach to the determination of expenditure levels in democratic societies. Functional finance has a strong bias in the direction of expectation of continuing deflationary pressures, which may not be realized in practice.

### The Managed Budget Approach

The most widely accepted approach today may be called a managed budget policy; the traditional linkage between expenditures and taxes is maintained, but adjustments in both expenditures and taxes, and the relationship between them to attain greater economic stability, are considered to be desirable.

Various adherents to this general philosophy have taken divergent points of view about policies. One of the best-known points of view is that of Alvin Hansen, who did more than any other person to popularize the ideas of fiscal policy in the thirties. Hansen stressed increases in expenditures in depressions as the primary solution to unemployment. He did not regard the consequent deficits and government borrowing as objectionable, and argued that there was no more need to attempt to balance the budget over a period of years than in any one year. If periods of depression and inflation were of equal importance, this result might be obtained, but it is not at all essential, and Hansen expected depression periods to dominate, in light of his adherence to the secular stagnation point of view presented in Chapter 31.

A modification of this point of view gained particular strength in the Scandinavian countries, namely, that of planning for a balanced budget over a long-range period, but with deliberate incurring of deficits in depressions and surpluses in inflationary periods. The chief support for this variant of a managed budget policy was the argument that the failure to assure a long-range budget balance produces serious loss of confidence on the part of the business community in a depression, and thus interferes with the restoration of optimism necessary for recovery. The difficulty with the cycle balance approach is the danger that it may be unworkable if depressions greatly outweigh inflationary periods or vice versa.

The third version of the managed budget approach seeks to obtain economic stability without unbalancing the budget, by adjusting both expenditures and revenues in such a manner as to exert the desired expansionary or contractionary influence without incurring a deficit. Thus, in depression, expenditures would be increased, but taxes would be increased as well, with maximum use of taxes with the least deflationary influence. In periods of inflation, maximum use would be made of taxes giving rise to the strongest anti-inflationary influence. The primary advantage claimed for this approach is the avoidance of the growth of the debt, with consequent loss in confidence, and problems of interest and principal payments. But unfortunately, this policy would require a much larger over-all increase in government activities in depression, since the expansionary effect of the expenditure of a given sum financed by taxation is almost certain to be less than that of the same sum financed by borrowing. The greater increase in the scope of government activities might give rise to greater loss in business confidence than the growth in the debt.

### Automatic Stabilization—The Stabilizing Budget[1]

In the late forties, emphasis centered on a policy of primary reliance upon automatic stabilization, rather than deliberate discretionary changes in expenditures and revenues, as envisaged in the managed budget approach. The automatic stabilizers would provide what may be called "built-in flexibility," with automatic adjustments in expenditures and revenues taking place in such a manner as to bring about economic stability without deliberate governmental intervention. This approach is represented, for example, in the United States by the work of the Committee for Economic Development, a privately financed research organization established to analyze economic problems and policies.

Those who accept this point of view take cognizance of the effects which expenditure and revenue programs have upon national income and recognize that an annually balanced budget would aggravate economic instability and perhaps lead to increased waste in government spending. On the other hand, they fear the uncertainties which arise from deliberate managed budget policy and stress the forecasting difficulties, as well as the political obstacles, in the way of attainment of the goals of such a policy. Particular fear is expressed that the various programs undertaken in depressions will not be abandoned when full employment is reattained.

Under the automatic stabilization proposals, government expenditures would be determined on the basis of estimates of relative benefits and costs of various programs, and tax rates would be established at such a level as to provide a small surplus for debt retirement in periods of full employment. When business activity fell off, tax rates and expenditure programs, as such, would not be altered. But tax revenues, especially from the income tax, would fall sharply. Furthermore, the actual amounts of expenditures would rise, since under established relief, old-age pension, and farm-aid programs, increased payments would be made. More persons would be eligible to apply for relief, for example, and greater numbers of elderly persons would seek pensions, since their incomes would fall. As a consequence, a government deficit would develop, with a stimu-

[1] See the article by W. W. Heller, "CED's Stabilizing Budget Policy after Ten Years," *American Economic Review*, Vol. XLVII (September, 1957), pp. 634–51.

lating effect on business recovery. The deficit would be allowed to continue until it was eliminated automatically by return to full employment. In periods of inflation the sharp rise in income tax collections and declining need for relief and related payments would increase the budget surplus. The built-in flexibility features could be increased by a program of varying public construction expenditures on the basis of an index of business activity.

Automatic stabilizers, without question, have great value in lessening economic instability.[2] The great increase in the importance of such stabilizers in the governmental structure in the last two decades lessens the likelihood of extremely severe depressions in the future. Extension of these features may further lessen the need for uncertainty-creating direct measures. On the other hand, one major question may be raised about the feasibility of primary reliance on automatic stabilizers: Will they prove adequate to insure recovery from a severe depression and prevent price increases when inflationary pressures are strong? It is generally recognized that they could not be adequate in a war period. But it is extremely doubtful if they could offset strong deflationary pressures, since they come into operation only as a result of the decline in national income. This is not an argument against their usefulness and desirability but against complete reliance upon them.

## THE GOALS OF FISCAL POLICY

The appropriate goals of fiscal policy must, of course, be assumed; as with all goals, they cannot be ascertained by economic analysis, but reflect value judgments. The generally accepted goal of fiscal policy is that of attainment of greater economic stability, that is, the maintenance of a reasonably stable rate of economic growth without development of substantial unemployment, on the one hand, or of upward or downward movements in the general price level, on the other. In other words, real national product should continue to rise at a level permitted by changes in technology and factor supplies, and the general price level should remain reasonably stable. Such stability requires comparable rates of increase in aggregate demand and productive capacity. If aggregate demand outruns the rate of increase in output, inflation will result; if the former lags behind, unemployment will arise, and the actual rate of growth will not attain the possible maximum. Economic stability does not mean stability

---

[2] Their contribution in lessening the severity of the post-World War II recessions is demonstrated in the study by W. Lewis, *Federal Fiscal Policy in the Postwar Recessions* (Washington, D.C.: Brookings Institution, 1962).

in all sectors of the economy, since relative prices and outputs must be free to vary with changing technology, consumer preferences, and factor supplies, if optimum use of resources is to be realized.

### Full Employment

The avoidance of unemployment has typically been regarded as the primary goal. Failure to maintain full employment not only results in a less than optimum level of national income and rate of growth, but also gives rise to severe personal hardships for the persons affected. Elimination of unemployment allows the attainment of a higher level of economic welfare, since the gains to persons benefiting from the lessened unemployment are not offset by injury to others.

Some difficulties are encountered in the definition of the concept of full employment. Technically, the situation may be defined as one in which all factor units whose owners wish to have them employed at existing factor prices actually find employment, so that there is no involuntary idleness of resources, including manpower. Emphasis is usually placed upon labor, since unemployment of labor gives rise to the most serious social problems. It is sometimes argued that full employment should be defined as a situation in which demand for labor is constantly in excess of supply at prevailing prices, so that a person who loses one job can immediately find another and workers will have substantial choice of jobs. The first definition given, however, is the one most generally accepted.

Completely full employment, under either definition, is difficult to attain. At any particular time, there are of necessity some factor units which have lost employment and have not yet found new jobs, since the factor markets are not perfect. In practice, therefore, a situation of full employment may be regarded as one in which there are no significant numbers of factor units continuously unemployed for any period of time.

### Stability of the General Price Level

The second aspect of stability is the maintenance of a reasonably stable general price level. A sharp decline in the general price level makes difficult the maintenance of full employment, because of its adverse effect on expectations and its squeezing of profits. If the price decline commences and is expected to continue, individuals will delay buying durable goods, and business firms will postpone investment in anticipation of still lower prices. Because many costs do not vary with changes in the price level, business profits are squeezed, and expectations of businessmen are made still worse. A decline in real spending is almost inevitable.

Furthermore, a sharply declining price level produces a redistribution of real income which is considered contrary to generally accepted standards of equity. All persons who have obligations fixed in money terms find that their commitments have increased in real terms. Repayment of a debt by a farmer may take twice as many steers or bushels of wheat as the amount required at the time the money was borrowed. Creditors benefit, because the purchasing power of the dollars which they receive is greater.

On the other hand, sharp increases in the general price level also have adverse effects. While inflation aids in maintaining full employment and benefits some persons, it produces a capricious redistribution of real income, to the injury of many persons in the lower income groups, especially older persons living on fixed incomes. Labor strife is increased, and the persons taking actions which are detrimental to the best interests of society, such as hoarding of goods, are rewarded. Inflation lessens the efficiency of operation of the economy by encouraging hoarding, by both individuals and business firms, and interferes with the functioning of the accounting mechanism, especially with respect to check upon efficiency. Finally, inflation tends to become cumulative and, if long continued, may cause loss of confidence in the dollar. This, in turn, tends to speed up the velocity of circulation and could result in complete breakdown of the monetary and credit structure.

While the principle that the general price level should be reasonably stable is generally accepted, the determination of the exact trends which are most satisfactory from the standpoint of the welfare of society is difficult. It is sometimes argued that a slightly downward trend best serves the interests of the community as a whole, because the gains from increased productivity and lower cost would be shared among all persons in society instead of going chiefly to the workers in the industries affected. On the other hand, a downward trend would increase the difficulty of maintaining full employment because of its adverse effects upon investment and business optimism. Furthermore, such a trend appears to be impossible of attainment in the light of present-day union strength and policies.

A gradually increasing general price level has likewise been advocated, primarily because it would encourage investment and lessen labor strife, since annual money wage increases would be possible. However, this alternative would produce a gradual worsening of the economic position of the fixed income receivers. The case for this policy is increased if difficulty is encountered in maintaining full employment. The third alternative point of view, a compromise between the other two, regards a perfectly stable general price level as the optimum. The gains from greater productivity would go primarily to the workers in the industries, but the injury to the economic well-being of the fixed income groups would be avoided, as well as the dampening effect of declining prices.

Stability in the general price level does not mean stability of all individual prices. Constant changes in prices are essential if the price system is to perform its basic function of guiding the operation of the economy. Individual prices must be free to vary with changing demand and output conditions and changes in cost due to technological developments.

## The Possible Conflict of the Two Stability Requirements

Increased doubt has been raised in recent years about the compatibility of the two requirements of general price stability and full employment. The problem arises from the danger that a guarantee of full employment, if effective, would eliminate the major checks upon continued increases in the price level.

Even before full employment is reached, there may be some tendency toward price increases. Full employment of some resources will be reached before that of others, and thus individual prices will rise. Even if some labor is unemployed, firms will offer higher wages to induce workers to move. Labor unions may seek higher wages even when substantial unemployment still exists. As the economy moves closer to full employment, these forces become increasingly serious.

If a government is successful in completely preventing unemployment, both business and labor groups will realize that price- and wage-raising activities on their part run no risk of unemployment. Unions particularly are likely to attempt to force wages higher and higher; if the annual increases exceed the rise in productivity, the general price level will continuously rise. Apart from wage changes, general frictions in the economy will work in the same direction. Whenever demand shifts, for example, increases in the prices of the products for which demand has risen and of factors used in their production are not likely to be offset by declines in the prices of goods whose sales have declined. The net change is thus upward. Price level increases due to higher wages and other costs are very difficult to check by fiscal means, and any attempt to do so may precipitate a decline in production.

If dangers of price and employment declines are permanently eliminated, persons will have less incentive to save and to hold accumulated wealth in relatively liquid form. As a consequence, the percentage of income consumed and the volume of investment will tend to rise and increase inflationary pressures. It is impossible to assess the significance of this danger, particularly because inflationary pressures are constantly being offset by technological developments which lower costs. Some persons are sufficiently concerned about the danger to argue that the government should not seek to insure full employment but merely to hold unemployment to a reasonable minimum. Such a policy would avoid serious suffering but would exercise a restraining influence on labor union activity. Whether the dangers are sufficient to warrant this policy or not is doubtful; it may also be argued that a slight degree of inflation may be preferable to a small amount of unemployment. Meanwhile, however, there is no assurance that fiscal policy can actually succeed in preventing unemployment, let alone (in peacetime) cause inflation.

### The Goal of Economic Growth

In the last five years the stress in fiscal policy has shifted from primary concern with the prevention of unemployment and inflation to greater emphasis on economic growth. Thus the primary goal is now usually conceived to be the attainment of an optimum rate of economic growth, the avoidance of unemployment and inflation being considered as aspects of the broader goal. In mature economies, such as the United States, primary attention has been given to the relationship of the actual rate of growth to the potential rate permitted by the consumption-savings ratio, technological considerations, and other factors. In the less developed countries, stress has been placed on increases in the potential rate as well as the relationship of the actual and potential rates. This question will be considered at length in Chapter 31.

### Fiscal Policy and Resource Allocation

Emphasis upon these major goals of fiscal policy must not be allowed to overshadow a major long-run goal of government activity, that of assisting in the attainment of optimum allocation of resources. In the selection of fiscal programs, attention should not be given solely to their effects upon recovery but to the direct usefulness of the activities as well. Programs which yield no direct gain to society may be as successful in bringing about full employment as those which offer direct and immediate benefits, but the latter are obviously preferable. Thus the construction of completely worthless public works may stimulate recovery as successfully as the expenditure of the funds on projects which are useful to society, but there is obvious merit in selecting the latter. There is a tendency at times to concentrate attention solely on the recovery effects and to forget about other gains from the activities. However, if sufficient useful projects which do not compete with private enterprise cannot be found, the undertaking of useless ones is to be preferred to complete inactivity, if the program actually stimulates recovery.

Before attention is given to specific fiscal policies, it is desirable to consider briefly the relationship between fiscal policies and the major alternative governmental policies of attaining greater economic stability.

## THE ALTERNATIVES TO FISCAL POLICY

Governments have two primary alternatives to fiscal policy which they may use in attempting to increase economic stability. The first is monetary or credit policy; the second, which can be employed only as a weapon against inflation, consists of direct controls, such as the use of price ceilings, rationing, and allocation of materials. These various alternatives are not in conflict with one another but may all be employed as elements in a general program of economic stability. There are significant differences of opinion, however, about the relative effectiveness and desirability of the various programs.

### The Relation of Monetary and Fiscal Policy

The first technique which governments developed in an effort to lessen economic instability was monetary or credit control policy, which attempts to stabilize economic activity by lessening fluctuations in investment spending through control of the interest rate and the availability of bank credit. This control, in turn, is effected through central bank policy, which influences bank reserves and the total supply of money. In depression periods, open-market purchases of government bonds by the central banking system are undertaken in order to lower interest rates and increase bank reserves, thus facilitating expansion of credit and the money supply by the banks. Likewise, rediscount rates and bank reserve requirements are lowered to encourage bank lending. The increased availability of funds and the lower rate should increase business investment and thus stimulate recovery of economic activity. On the other hand, in inflationary periods, investment spending and thus inflationary pressures would be checked primarily by open-market selling of bonds, which would reduce bank reserves. In addition, rediscount rates and reserve requirements would be increased. All these policies tend to raise interest rates and check bank lending, thus restricting increases in the total money supply.

Four decades ago the belief that monetary policy alone could insure economic stability was widely accepted. But the experience of the thirties showed that lower interest rates and increased bank reserves have only limited influence in stimulating investment in periods in which most business firms are not willing to borrow for any purpose because profit prospects are so bad. Furthermore, it became evident that the interest rate could not be pushed below certain levels because additional amounts of money were merely held idle, once the return from lending fell very low. In other words, the demand for idle balances became almost perfectly elastic below a certain interest rate.

So far as inflation control is concerned, the most serious inflationary pressures of recent decades have been produced primarily by excessive governmental and consumer spending, relative to potential output at full employment. Investment spending was held rigidly in check during World War II by direct methods and, while not negligible in the postwar period, was a minor element in total spending. Under such circumstances, credit control policy is of limited value in checking inflation. When business prospects are good, very sharp increases in the rate may be necessary to check the total volume of investment, especially when most of the expansion is being undertaken without resort to borrowing. Under such circumstances, control of inflation by monetary policies is likely to be impossible without intolerably great increases in the interest rate.

This experience has made relatively clear the inadequacy of monetary policy in insuring economic stability and has led to increased attention to fiscal policy. But the limitations of monetary policy do not prevent it from being useful as an element in a general program of attaining economic stability. Monetary policy is much more flexible than fiscal policy, and is politically more acceptable, since it gives rise neither to government deficits in depressions nor to tax increases in periods of inflation. Mild recessions can probably be checked by interest rate reductions, and mild inflations by general tightening of credit. In major depressions the increased supply of money facilitates recovery once it starts, and in major inflations the tighter credit helps to reinforce fiscal policy. But in both depressions and inflationary periods of any severity, fiscal policy is a much more positive type of program.

### Direct Control Measures

In past wars, fiscal and monetary policies have proven incapable of completely checking inflationary pressures without objectionable effects upon production and insuperable political obstacles. The increases in government expenditures have been so great that tax and borrowing measures could not control inflation, particularly because of the concentration of inflationary pressures in certain segments of the economy. Accordingly, direct controls have been used as a supplement to fiscal and monetary measures. There is no counterpart of wartime direct controls in depression periods; while the government can forceably prevent increases in prices, it cannot compel increases in output by direct means.

Inflation period direct controls consist of the setting of price and wage ceilings, the allocation of materials among various lines of production, and the rationing of essential commodities which are particularly scarce relative to demand. These programs attempt to prevent inflation by direct interference with the operation of the price mechanism. Market forces are prevented from bringing about equilibrium of demand and output, the prices being held at artificially low levels and the available stocks of goods either being rationed or allowed to go to the first comers. If the program succeeds, persons are essentially compelled to save more than they wish to save, because they cannot purchase as many goods as they desire to buy, yet they cannot bid prices up.

Without question, direct controls can limit price increases, check speculative buying, and insure a more equitable distribution of particularly scarce goods. In a period of strong inflation caused by high defense spending, some essential articles may become so scarce that fiscal policy cannot possibly prevent drastic price increases, and direct controls may be the only alternative.

On the other hand, direct controls suffer from serious limitations, which suggest that their use be minimized and reserved for extreme emergency conditions. The fundamental objection is the interference by direct controls with the basic regulatory mechanism of the economy. When prices are held artificially low, demand exceeds the available supply, and rationing becomes necessary to prevent hoarding, waiting in line, and inequitable distribution of output. But rationing is hard to enforce and is often inequitable. If prices are controlled, they no longer guide production effectively. Price ceilings themselves are difficult to enforce, since both buyer and seller may find it advantageous to violate them. Black markets develop and channel supplies from legitimate outlets. Direct controls in large measure merely dam up purchasing power, and once they are eliminated, the accumulated demand drives prices up very rapidly. Political pressures often bring premature elimination of the controls.

The direct controls can be regarded only as emergency measures; even when they are used, the more effective the fiscal policy measures, the less will be the pressure on the controls, and the more effective they will be. Direct controls are not the painless methods they may appear to be at first glance.

## THE NATIONAL INCOME FRAMEWORK OF FISCAL POLICY

Modern fiscal policy is based upon the analysis of national income determination as it has developed over the last three decades. A brief summary of the analysis is necessary as a background for the discussion of fiscal policy.

The equilibrium level of national income is that at which total spending in the economy, namely, consumption, investment, and government spending, is equal to national income, as shown on Figure 40 by the intersection of the $C + I + G$ line with the 45-degree line. At any higher

FIGURE 40

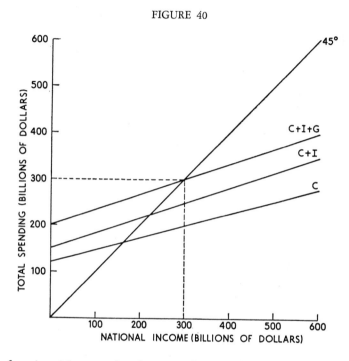

level of national income the $C + I + G$ line is below the 45-degree line, showing that total spending is less than national income; thus, some of the goods being produced cannot be sold, and hence production will be curtailed and national income will fall. If national income were temporarily less than the figure of $300 billion shown on Figure 40, $C + I + G$ would be above the 45-degree line, or, in other words, total spending would outrun the current rate of output. With less than full employment, national income would rise primarily in real terms; with full employment, in monetary terms. Thus, only if the current rate of spending—consumption, investment, government—is equal to the current rate of output can the rate of output and thus national income remain at current levels. At the equilibrium level, savings $(S)$ and investment $(I)$ will be equal. Since national income consists of $C + S + G$, and total spending of $C + I + G$, the totals can be equal only if $S$ equals $I$.

The equilibrium level may be at the figure of national income which will allow full employment, or it may be at a lower level. In the latter instance, there is a deflationary gap at full employment, in the sense that total spending at the full-employment level of national income is less than national income, and thus this level cannot be maintained. If, on Figure 40, the full-employment level were $400 billion, a deflationary gap would exist, and the equilibrium level would be lower than the full-employment level. If an inflationary gap exists, with total spending in excess of national income at full employment, the general price level will rise, and an equilibrium will be attained at a higher general price level.

Any increase in governmental spending not accompanied by an equivalent decline in private (consumption plus investment) spending will cause national income to rise, while any reduction not accompanied by an increase in private spending will cause a decline. Thus, to stimulate an increase in employment, the government can raise its expenditures or reduce taxes (which will increase consumption and investment); to check inflationary pressures, it can reduce its expenditures or raise taxes. This summary statement involves great oversimplification, of course, and more complete analysis will be provided in subsequent sections.

Not only will an increase in government expenditures with tax levels unchanged cause an increase in national income, but so will an increase in government expenditures accompanied by an equivalent increase in taxes, under usual circumstances, although the relative effect will be much less. The sum collected in taxes will be used to purchase goods and services in its entirety; thus, unless the marginal propensity to consume of taxpayers is 100 per cent, the government tax and expenditure program will cause a net increase in total spending in the economy (with the assumption that the propensity to consume of the recipients of the government expenditures is comparable to that of the taxpayers).

### The Multiplier

Under usual conditions, not only will an increase in government spending lead to an increase in national income, but the increase is likely to be several times the amount of the original expenditure. This is the familiar multiplier theorem, as applied to government expenditures. In its traditional form, the multiplier expresses the relationship between a given increase in investment and the subsequent increase in national income which results from it. For equilibrium to be re-established following an increase in investment, savings must rise by the amount of the increase in investment, since only when savings again equal investment can total spending again equal national income. But so long as the marginal propensity to save is less than one, national income must rise by a larger sum than the investment increase to bring forth the volume of savings necessary for equilibrium. The multiplier is, of course, the reciprocal of the marginal propensity to save. The multiplier concept can equally well be applied to an increase in government spending; if taxes remain unchanged, equilibrium can be restored only by an increase in national income substantially greater than the amount of the expenditure increase. If taxes are raised as well, the multiplier will apply only to the net increase in total spending arising from the combined tax and expenditure program.

The possible influence of the increase in government spending goes beyond the multiplier effect. The rise in national income will increase the profitability of investment, and once full utilization of existing equipment is reached, further rise in consumption will cause a sharp rise in investment, under the operation of the *acceleration* principle. The increase in investment generated by the consumption increase will, in turn, be subject to the multiplier effect, and the combined influence of the multiplier and the acceleration principle, reinforcing each other, may be sufficient to bring about full employment as a result of a relatively small continuing increase in investment or consumption.

While the multiplier analysis is useful in tracing the reactions to government spending increases, it is subject to several well-known limitations, which will merely be summarized here. As national income rises, the marginal propensity to save may rise, and thus reduce the size of the actual multiplier. The marginal propensity may differ widely among various groups in the economy, and it may be unstable, a feature which makes forecasting of the precise results of an increase in government spending impossible. Furthermore, the effects of the increased aggregate spending may be dissipated largely in price increases rather than raising output, particularly if full employment is approached.

The multiplier, of course, works both upward and downward. Once the increased government spending is cut off in the belief that recovery is under way, the process may operate in reverse, unless private spending picks up sufficiently to offset the decline in public spending. Or in a period of inflation, deliberate reductions in government spending or tax increases may hold down the price level for a time, but once they are eliminated in the belief that stability has been attained, inflationary pressures may break out again.


## THE INHERENT LIMITATIONS OF FISCAL POLICY

As suggested in the preceding sections, fiscal policy should be able to lessen economic instability through its influence upon total spending in the economy. But there are several major obstacles in the path of complete success of a fiscal stabilization policy.

### The Forecasting and Timing Problem

The most serious difficulty is that of accurately forecasting trends in economic activity and adjusting fiscal policies in terms of the trends. At any one time, with the present state of knowledge, it is impossible to make highly reliable forecasts about economic conditions a few months hence. As a consequence, it is impossible to time the fiscal policy for maximum effectiveness, especially in light of the time lag between the date of making a decision and that on which policy based upon it becomes effective. This is particularly true of public works projects, but to a lesser extent of other policies as well. There is always the danger of acting too soon in a recession and converting it into strong inflation, and of restraining mild inflation and bringing about a decline in activity.

There are also real differences of opinion about the correct timing. Many people argue that a small amount of fiscal stimulus applied early in a decline before optimism gives way to pessimism, or early in a period of inflation, will be far more effective than massive application at a later date. Others, particularly persons holding to the "readjustment" doctrine noted below, feel that a certain amount of "wringer application" is desirable before fiscal policy is applied, early use of the latter resulting in perpetuation of maladjustments requiring correction.

### Political Obstacles

Even if correct forecasting were possible, political considerations in a democracy are likely to prove major obstacles to the success of fiscal policy. In a depression, for example, the carry-over of the old ideas of balanced budgets constitutes an obstacle to quick action on the part of Congress, and the dislike of admitting that a depression is under way may make the administration reluctant to recommend strong and immediate action. Even partially effective fiscal policy may come about only after change of administration and balance of power in Congress.

In inflationary periods the obstacles are even more severe, because it is very difficult to convince legislative bodies of the need for government surpluses. Taxes are still traditionally regarded as means of paying for governmental activities, and the resistance is extremely strong against raising taxes for fiscal policy purposes. Even if Congress is sold on the policy, the general public may resist the increases, and bring about a change. The experience of the United States between 1947 and 1960 was very discouraging; Congress was simply unwilling to keep taxes high enough to restrict the inflationary influences. The Canadian policies were somewhat more satisfactory, partly because of the parliamentary form of government, but the government was bitterly attacked for its policies, which were a factor in the 1957 defeat of the Liberals.

There is always great danger that the political pressures of certain groups particularly injured by depression, inflation, or the normal process of dynamic growth may result in the introduction of policies, in the guise of fiscal policy measures, which may seriously retard adjustments necessary for continued growth. Thus, during the thirties, farmers were seriously affected by the depression, and succeeded in getting policies established which have perpetuated the *status quo* in agriculture and prevented the wholesale exodus of people from this field, which is imperative from the standpoint of long-term economic growth.

### Obstacles Arising Out of the Structure of the Economy

The difficulties are not solely ones of imperfect knowledge and political interference, but in part arise from features of the economy itself. In the first place, the national income analysis upon which fiscal policy is based is highly oversimplified, with no reference to relative changes in various sectors of th eeconomy. A decline may be concentrated in one sector of the economy, yet fiscal policy will spread its impact throughout the economy, perhaps providing little assistance to the sectors suffering the worst decline. Or price increases may be confined to certain industries, yet anti-inflationary fiscal policy, by reducing demand over a wide sector of the economy, may do little to check the price increases, and instead cause unemployment in many sectors. The old doctrine of readjustment, that is, the notion that the economy must be "squeezed through a wringer" by a depression, while not generally meaningful or valid, is of some significance in certain particular cases. In such instances, fiscal policy may prove to be only a temporary palliative, perhaps perpetuating the difficulty. Thus, if the decline in employment results from strong unions and monopolistic employers pushing prices up in one sector of the economy at a much faster rate than in other sectors, so that sales fall drastically in resistance to the higher prices, fiscal policy will do little or nothing to correct the situation (although, admittedly, the wringer process of depression may not, either).

The whole structure of fiscal policy is based upon the premise that changes in national income in dollar terms are caused by changes in aggregate spending, in conformity with usual national income analysis. But as considered at greater length in Chapter 29, a general price level increase may result from other forces—particularly the action of strong unions in pushing money wages up. Inevitably, fiscal policy will not work effectively in checking inflation from this source, as subsequently explained in detail. Similarly, tax increases themselves may generate cost increases and thus lose much of their anti-inflationary effectiveness. Fiscal policy assumes that factor prices are independent of tax collections, whereas, in fact, they may be greatly influenced by the latter.

Finally, the use of deliberate fiscal policy in itself introduces into the economy a new variable, that of uncertainty about the policies to be followed, which may be disturbing to the business world and to consumer behavior. This is most marked, for example, by the effects of anticipation of changes in excise tax rates, which alter the normal flow of purchases. But the whole range of fiscal actions generally adds to the uncertainty of business firms.

### The Mechanistic Nature of Fiscal Policy

Present-day fiscal policy calls for purely mechanistic adjustments based upon static equilibrium theory, designed to push up national income when it starts to fall, and to push down the price level when it starts to rise. What is required is a fiscal policy which will act directly and immediately to counteract developments in the economy which throw the actual rate of growth out of line with the potential rate at stable price levels.[3] In many respects the economy is inherently unstable; the task of attaining and then maintaining a stable and high rate of growth involves a very sensitive balance between aggregate demand and output capacity, coupled with flexibility to permit adjustments among sectors in the economy in response to changing conditions. But fiscal theory has not yet demonstrated how the governmental policies can be adjusted to attain these results—if, in fact, they are attainable. Modern built-in flexibility, particularly the progressive income tax with its fixed dollar exemptions, helps to dampen the swings. But these cannot reverse the undesired swings; they can merely dampen them. Deliberate fiscal policy today is a crude instrument, used often too late and too bluntly, which does nothing more than drive the economy by sheer force of dollar spending in one direction or another, rather than serving as a constantly operating mechanism to keep the actual growth rate from swinging away from the possible rate.

[3] One of the few attempts to analyze the problem of the relationship between fiscal policy and economic growth is to be found in an article by W. L. Smith, "Monetary-Fiscal Policy and Economic Growth," *Quarterly Journal of Economics*, Vol. LXXI (February, 1957), pp. 36–55.

The general question of fiscal policy in relation to economic growth will be considered in Chapter 31.

### State-Local Problems

In the United States and other countries, one of the major obstacles to effective fiscal policy is the perverse action of states and local governments, which carry on policies exactly opposite to that necessary for successful economic stabilization. In depressions, they cut expenditures, lay off workers, and raise taxes; while in inflationary periods, they increase their expenditures, borrow for building construction, etc. The only effective solution to this problem is increased financial co-ordination, with temporary federal grants in periods of depression.

In addition to these basic problems, there are certain other obstacles to the success of specific policies followed in depression or inflationary conditions, which will be noted in subsequent chapters.

These limitations do not warrant abandoning all fiscal policy, which, in fact, cannot be done, politically, until we have something better. Crude as modern fiscal policy is, it can serve as a major force in dampening down major swings, in conjunction with the automatic stabilizers. Every effort must be made not only to use it in the most satisfactory form, given the present state of knowledge, but also to educate people to its nature and purpose, in order to lessen the political obstacles in the way of most effective use.

## THE EMPLOYMENT ACT OF 1946

In 1946, Congress essentially committed itself to a policy of attempting to insure full employment, with the enactment of the Employment Act of that year. The key phrase stated, "it is the continuing policy and responsibility of the Federal government to use all practical means . . . to promote maximum employment, production and purchasing power." There was no specific mention of fiscal policy, but its use was obviously envisaged by the framers of the law. To facilitate the attainment of the goal, Congress established the Council of Economic Advisers to study current employment and production trends and make reports to the President, and the Joint Committee on the Economic Report (now the Joint Economic Committee) to appraise the reports of the council. This system has by no means worked to perfection, and for a time the activity of the council was seriously impeded by internal dissension and lack of influence. It was completely reorganized under the Eisenhower administration, and regained some prestige. But it has yet to play a dominant role in influencing fiscal policy.[4]

In Canada the government laid down a much more specific policy in 1945, in the statement, "The government will be prepared, in periods when unemployment threatens, to incur the deficits and increases in the national debt resulting from its employment and income policy, whether that policy in the circumstances is best applied through increased expenditures or reduced taxation" (*White Paper on Employment and Income,* 1945). There has been no establishment of any organization comparable to the Council of Economic Advisers in the United States.[5]

## REFERENCES

Extensive lists of references on various aspects of fiscal policy will be found in the next two chapters. A few basic reference are noted below.

KEYNES, J. M.  *The General Theory of Employment, Interest and Money.* New York: Harcourt, Brace & Co., 1936.

The theoretical framework of contemporary fiscal policy.

DILLARD, D.  *The Economics of John Maynard Keynes.* New York: Prentice-Hall, Inc., 1948.

A simplified restatement of Keynes.

HANSEN, B.  *The Economic Theory of Fiscal Policy.* London: George Allen and Unwin, 1958.

The most complete theoretical analysis of fiscal policy.

HOLMANS, A. E.  *United States Fiscal Policy 1945–1959.* Oxford: Oxford University Press, 1961.

POOLE, KENYON E. (ed.).  *Fiscal Policies and the American Economy.* New York: Prentice-Hall, Inc., 1951.

Chapter i presents a history of the theory and practice of fiscal policy.

"The Problem of Economic Stability," *American Economic Review,* Vol. XL (September, 1950), pp. 501–38.

A report on the problem of economic stability, prepared by a committee of the American Economic Association.

STRAYER, P. J.  *Fiscal Policy and Politics.* New York: Harper & Brothers, 1958.

Fiscal policy in light of political considerations.

[4] Note the papers of the symposium entitled "The Employment Act in the Economic Thinking of Our Times," *Proceedings of the American Economic Association for 1956,* pp. 96–144.

[5] For Canadian experience, see the paper by W. C. Clark, "Canada's Postwar Finance," *Proceedings of the American Economic Association for 1952,* pp. 1–18; and K. W. Taylor, "Fiscal Policy in Canada," *Proceedings of the National Tax Association for 1958,* pp 26–35.

SMITHIES, A., and BUTTERS, J. K. (eds.). *Readings in Fiscal Policy.* Homewood, Ill.: Richard D. Irwin, Inc., 1955.

A collection of major articles on fiscal policy, together with a very detailed bibliography.

JOINT ECONOMIC COMMITTEE. *Federal Expenditure Policy for Economic Growth and Stability,* Parts V, VI. Washington, D.C.: U.S. Government Printing Office, 1957.

A series of papers on fiscal policy and stability.

# Chapter 28

# FISCAL POLICY AND UNEMPLOYMENT

Unemployment, with its great individual hardships, is the worst evil which besets the modern economy, and thus prevention of it would constitute a major step in the direction of optimum economic welfare. Unemployment arises whenever gross national product drops below the level which allows persons to find employment for all factor units, and particularly their own labor, which they own and wish to have employed at current factor price levels. National product will fall below full-employment levels if total spending at such levels becomes inadequate to absorb the current rate of output. Such a decline may be caused by any of a number of developments, such as a slowing-down in the rate of increase of consumption in the economy, which causes investment to fall; by the completion of extensive investment programs by business firms; by an increase in the rate of interest; or by a general decline in business expectations about future profits. Once a decline commences, it tends to become cumulative, as the decline in national income reduces both investment and consumption, and the multiplier and acceleration principles accentuate the initial decline.

Recovery can come about only from an increase in total spending —consumption, investment, or governmental. This increase may occur automatically, for example, once inventories are seriously depleted and much equipment is worn out, so that investment commences to rise, or from a general increase in the propensity to consume. It may be stimulated by monetary policy, which lowers the interest rate. But this policy is now generally regarded as inadequate in periods of severe depression, and automatic recovery forces may come very slowly, once pessimism becomes widespread. Thus, governments inevitably turn to fiscal policy once a depression has continued for a time.

There are two general approaches to depression fiscal policy. The first attempts to increase private consumption and investment spending directly by lowering taxes and thus allowing more purchasing power to remain in the hands of the public. The second involves a direct increase in government spending itself.

## TAX REDUCTION AS A FISCAL MEASURE

A reduction in tax rates in a period of depression should stimulate spending by leaving more money in the hands of individuals and business firms for consumption and investment use, and by lessening the incentives given by the tax structure to reduce spending. The case for tax reduction is based primarily upon the consideration that when resources are not fully employed, taxes are not required to lessen private spending and thus free resources for government use, as they are in periods of full employment, since the resources which the government requires would otherwise be idle. Not only are the taxes not required to check private consumption, but their use will aggravate unemployment by reducing total expenditures. Accordingly, when a recession begins, immediate tax reduction may be of great assistance in checking the decline and stimulating recovery.

### Advantages of Tax Reduction

The tax reduction approach has several advantages over any program of increased government expenditures. In the first place, tax reductions do not increase the relative sphere of government activities in the economy, as do expenditure increases, and therefore should produce fewer adverse reactions and fears of government competition on the part of the business community. The problems and delays in finding suitable projects for government expenditures are avoided, as well as the "charity" aspects of direct relief programs. Expenditure of funds for administration of the program is not required. Tax reductions may be made effective quickly, if legislative bodies are willing to co-operate. The increased output of goods which results will consist directly and immediately of articles which individuals desire and are willing to buy, instead of government services and various public works projects, which may be of much less benefit.

### Limitations to the Effectiveness of Tax Reduction Programs

On the other hand, a tax reduction program is subject to several limitations, compared to a program of increased government expenditures. The gains—especially if income taxes are reduced—go to those still earning incomes rather than to the persons who not only greatly need the assistance but will spend most of any additional income received. Inevitably, a greater percentage of the sum of the reduced taxes will be saved than of an equivalent amount of additional expenditure; thus the dollar-for-dollar gain, from the standpoint of recovery, will be less with this method than with expenditure increases, unless the lower taxes greatly stimulate investment. The increased expenditures may not be distributed in such a manner as to provide assistance to industries or geographic areas which are particularly distressed.

In part as a result of the lesser effect on aggregate demand compared to that of increased government expenditures, tax reductions, even if carried to the extent of complete removal of all taxes, might be inadequate to bring recovery from a severe depression. In the situation in the 1930's, in which government expenditures and taxes were only a small fraction of national income, it is doubtful whether elimination of all federal taxes would have had any substantial effect. At the present time, however, total tax burdens are so great that reduction would be much more significant. If reduction or elimination of taxes proved inadequate, a system of negative taxes, whereby persons with incomes less than a certain figure would be entitled to receive payments from the government, could be introduced. This is essentially a form of expenditure increase and will be treated as such. Finally, a tax cut requires legislative action and thus admission by the administration that a recession is under way, whereas expenditure increases can be proposed on other grounds.

Apart from these relative weaknesses compared to expenditure increases, there are certain limitations common to both methods of stimulating recovery; in particular, the growth of the national debt may adversely affect business confidence, as discussed below. Likewise, just as expenditures may not be curtailed when recovery is attained, so the taxes may not be restored to higher levels. Acceptance of the principle that tax reductions facilitate recovery may also result in popular acceptance of the view that taxes are not needed at all, with consequent inflationary results, once full employment is attained. The politically popular aspects of fiscal policy—such as tax reduction—may be accepted by legislative bodies much more readily than the politically unpopular aspects.

### Forms of Reduction

If the principle of tax reduction is accepted as a depression fiscal measure, major questions must be resolved about the exact changes to be made. Consumption can most easily be stimulated by removing excises on goods of widespread use, since such taxes not only absorb purchasing power but discourage purchasing as well. Likewise, raising income tax exemptions or reducing lower income bracket rates should have a substantial effect on consumption purchases. On the other hand, if the primary effort is directed at investment, changes in higher bracket income and corporate tax rates may be more effective. Unfortunately, however, if investment prospects are bad, the volume of investment may be affected very little by the tax changes, and most of the additional savings will be held instead of being used for business expansion. Thus, no impetus will be given to recovery. Changes in corporate tax rates have a greater chance of success at the time a depression is starting and pessimism is not strong. Accelerated depreciation plans suffer the same limitations, although they are likely to be cheaper means (in terms of lost governmental revenue) of encouraging investment than a corporate income tax rate reduction. But in severe depressions, they are likely to do little good. On the whole, changes in excises and lower bracket income tax rates offer greater chances for aiding recovery, just as increases in these levies have the greatest anti-inflationary effect.

## INCENTIVE TAXATION

Numerous plans have been devised to provide deliberate incentive for persons to alter their behavior in such a way as to aid recovery. One of the most common has been the investment allowance or investment tax credit system, whereby business firms are permitted to deduct from income for tax purposes a portion of the cost of new capital equipment purchased during the period, without reduction in subsequent allowable depreciation charges. A modified form of this plan was introduced in the United States in 1962. Such a plan, by increasing both the funds available for expansion and the incentives to expand, should aid in raising the level of investment so long as business prospects are reasonably good. But in a severe depression, prospects are so bad that even 100 per cent tax credits would have little effect.

Another type of proposal provides a direct tax concession for firms increasing their rate of output over the previous period. This is suggested in the work of Knorr and Baumol,[1] and introduced in Canada in 1962, with profits gained from additional sales over the previous period subject to a 50 per cent tax rate reduction. Unfortunately, the plan is fraught with numerous administrative difficulties, and there is grave doubt that firms can profitably increase volume of sales in the face of inadequate demand merely because of a tax concession of this type.

More drastic proposals called for levying punitive taxes on firms unless they added certain numbers of employees. The problems created by this plan would be more serious than those of the previous one; the dis-

---

[1] See K. Knorr and W. J. Baumol, *What Price Economic Growth?* (Englewood Cliffs, N.J.: Prentice-Hall, Inc., 1961).

posal of the additional output would be the most troublesome. One version of this plan called for government purchase of the surplus, a policy fraught with obvious dangers, as has been demonstrated by experience with the farm programs. Under another form of incentive taxation a special tax would be levied on the portion of income saved (in contrast to the spendings tax, which would apply only to the portion spent). Administrative difficulties, especially the determination of the accuracy of reported figures of spending, would be comparable to those of the spendings tax.

Closely related were schemes for taxing idle money, in an effort to stimulate consumption or investment. The task of distinguishing between idle and active balances is a difficult one, and persons would tend to transfer their wealth from liquid form to bonds, a result which would accomplish little so far as recovery was concerned. There would also be a tendency to draw funds from bank deposits and keep them in idle cash, which would be difficult to trace. The holding-of-cash problem could not be solved without the use of a stamped money system, with the requirement that each piece of money would continue to be valid only if a stamp were attached to it each week or month. Thus, for example, the law might require that each $1 bill would be valid only if a one-cent stamp were affixed to it each Saturday.[2] These systems have often been advanced without careful analysis of all economic ramifications; the "musical chairs" aspects of the stamped money represent serious obstacles to its effective use. On the whole, while some of the less extreme proposals warrant further attention than they have been given, the use of more orthodox methods is less likely to produce uncertainty and loss of confidence, and may accomplish the same results with fewer adverse consequences.

## INCREASES IN GOVERNMENT EXPENDITURES

The type of depression fiscal policy which has received greatest attention in the past consists of various programs of increases in government expenditures designed to raise the level of aggregate spending in the economy. There are various purposes for which the expenditures might be made. At the one extreme, they can be given out as direct consumer grants, in themselves involving no purchasing of resources but providing funds to persons who in turn will spend them. Direct relief, supplements to unemployment compensation, and increased old-age pensions are examples. At the other extreme the expenditures may be made for extensive public

---

[2] Plans of this sort were first suggested by Silvio Gesell. They were embodied in the "Thirty Dollars Every Thursday" plan in California.

works, such as the power projects of the 1930's. In this case the government obtains labor and buys materials (typically at prevailing wage and price levels), and thus directly increases total spending. There are also intermediate programs, such as the WPA projects of the 1930's, in which persons are hired to work on minor projects not involving construction of extensive permanent improvements.

### Direct Relief and Other Cash Payments

Each type of policy has some advantages. The direct relief method can operate much more quickly and is more flexible than public works programs, which involve substantial delays in getting under way and cannot be stopped easily as full employment is reattained. Direct relief also avoids the serious tasks of finding suitable public works which will not compete with private enterprise, on the one hand, and yet be of some benefit to society, on the other. In addition, dollar for dollar, direct relief is probably more effective in stimulating recovery, since virtually the entire amount paid out will be spent on the output of the private sector of the economy. When money is spent on public works programs, a greater percentage is likely to be saved by the recipients, since the amounts will be paid out in larger sums to fewer people.

Relief, in its usual form, is often condemned because of its "charity" aspects. Continued dependence on relief is detrimental to the morale of the recipients, and results in loss of skills and possible loss of the desire to work. As a consequence, alternative proposals for direct payment of cash have been developed. In the 1957–58 recession, for example, serious consideration was given to a plan for providing supplements to unemployment compensation once the recipients had exhausted the benefits to which they were entitled. Because of the semi-insurance features of the unemployment compensation system, persons are entitled to draw benefits for only limited periods, and thus frequently lose their assistance at the time it becomes most needed. The provision of supplements from general revenues to extend the period would simplify administration, compared to the use of direct relief, and would lessen somewhat the charity aspects.

A much more far-reaching system would provide negative tax payments or cash subsidies; persons whose incomes fell below a certain figure would be entitled to draw "negative taxes" from the government, in an amount determined by number of dependents, actual income, etc. With such a system the charity aspects would largely be eliminated, but the incentive to attempt to find employment would be lessened, and strong safeguards would be required to prevent mass "chiseling." Any plan involving extensive outright cash payments for which nothing is rendered in exchange furthers the notion that the "government owes everyone a living" —a philosophy which could become very dangerous if widespread.

### Public Works

A system of public works avoids the charity and "something for nothing" aspects of all the cash payment systems, and serves to preserve the skills of the workers. An effective public works program not only may facilitate recovery but may yield some very useful projects to society at low real cost. If factors are unemployed, the use of them to construct major projects does not reduce the supply of factors available for private production, since their services would go to waste if the government did not use them. Accordingly, the projects cost society virtually nothing, except through some exhaustion of certain types of natural resources to provide the necessary materials, and can be justified even though the benefits would not be sufficiently great to warrant diversion of resources from private production in periods of full employment. In depression periods, not only are the marginal social costs of various projects reduced, because no curtailment of private production is required if they are undertaken, but the marginal social benefits are increased, because of the favorable effects of the programs upon the level of business activity.

Despite the advantages of public works, the delays in getting them under way make it almost impossible to depend entirely upon them. Governments are reluctant to undertake them early in a recession for fear that by the time they are started, the recession will be over, and they will generate new inflationary pressures. Once a depression becomes bad enough to make the need for them obvious, some other stopgap measures are required while they are becoming effective. Furthermore, public works cannot be distributed geographically in such a manner as to care for all unemployed. In addition, the task of finding suitable projects which do not compete with private enterprise is substantial. Finally, they are probably somewhat less effective, per dollar spent, in encouraging recovery than direct relief, since the money goes to a smaller number of persons, and more will be saved.

Since both direct relief and public works have certain advantages, a program combining both methods is likely to be more satisfactory than complete reliance upon either. There is some merit in making as extensive use of public works as possible, because of the direct benefits which the projects convey to society. On the other hand, some direct relief is almost essential, because of the delays in getting public works under way and the inability to adjust them on a geographical basis in terms of location of unemployment. Intermediate programs, such as those of the WPA, avoid the charity aspects of direct relief and have greater flexibility than public works, but yield fewer direct benefits.

Whether the additional expenditures are made for relief, public works, or minor projects, they provide more direct aid to the persons who are most severely affected by the depression than does a tax reduction program, and thus they constitute a necessary supplement to such a program. Nevertheless, the problems encountered in finding suitable projects and the "charity" aspects of direct relief suggest that as much use be made as possible of the tax reduction method as a means of stimulating recovery, up to the point at which further reductions have little effect in stimulating spending.

## THE LIMITATIONS OF DEPRESSION FISCAL POLICY

In terms of the theory of the multiplier and the acceleration principle, and in terms of ordinary common-sense observations about the effects of additional spending, the governmental fiscal policies outlined in the preceding paragraphs should provide a stimulus toward recovery and, in the case of public works, yield some useful direct by-products to society as well. There are, however, certain basic limitations to the effectiveness of the programs. Precise adjustment of the policies to attain the exact desired goals is difficult, and the programs adopted may have some adverse effects upon private spending, which partially offset the direct stimulus to recovery.

### Forecasting and Timing

The basic limitations which apply to all fiscal policy are, of course, relevant to depression periods. The difficulties of forecasting make it impossible to determine whether a decline in business activity is only a minor readjustment or the beginning of a major depression, and thus programs —particularly public works—may be undertaken too early or too late. Political considerations may seriously delay the establishment of programs, and then result in their being continued after the depression is over.

### Uncertainty

Closely related is the danger of the uncertainty created by the inability of businessmen to predict the policies of the government and the possible adverse effects of the programs themselves upon business confidence. During the depression of the 1930's the government fumbled around with various policies, trying first one and then another. Businessmen rapidly lost confidence and, since they did not know what to expect next, found it particularly difficult to estimate the desirability of programs of expansion. Some of the government activities involved or threatened competition between public projects and private enterprise, and thus checked private investment. Even if the competition is not actually significant, the fear of its spreading may produce adverse effects. Related also is the fact that the control of governments in depressions tends to shift to groups which are regarded as "leftist" by businessmen and which are likely to promote policies which do not create a political climate favorable to the business community. As a consequence, business expansion is discouraged. Finally, the usual methods of financing the fiscal policy, as discussed in the following section, are likely to lead to loss of confidence in the future.

If a deliberate fiscal policy can be planned and generally accepted in advance and carried through on the basis of the plans without constant changes, these dangers will be minimized. More planning should be possible in the future than was the case in the thirties, the first period in which the government sought to bring recovery from a major depression. Likewise, if the government can retain the confidence of the business community and avoid coupling fiscal policies with various other measures regarded as hostile to business, the program has a much greater chance of success. But the accomplishment of these results is not easy, in the light of general attitudes prevailing in a typical severe depression period.

### The Financing of the Program: The Growth of the Debt

A major obstacle to the success of depression fiscal policy centers around the problems of financing. Tax reduction, in the face of constant or rising expenditures, will inevitably create a deficit, and increased expenditures without higher taxes will, of course, have the same effect. In many respects the financing of government expenditures from borrowing in depressions is justifiable. As indicated above, the major economic function of taxes—to free resources from the private sector by curtailing spending—is not necessary when unemployment exists. Since curtailment of spending is not only unnecessary but will actually aggravate the problem of unemployment, a strong case exists for borrowing. During a period of decline, investment outlets are inadequate to absorb the entire volume of savings which persons desire to make. To the extent that this excess of planned savings is absorbed by the government by borrowing and used to cover government expenses, the decline can be checked and recovery started.

However, despite this basic justification for depression borrowing, it has certain repercussions which may serve to check the effectiveness of the recovery program. The greatest danger is purely psychological; if the growth of the debt lessens the confidence of the business community in the future stability of the government and the economy, private investment will be discouraged, even if there is little basis for the fear. In war periods, when confidence is good, little attention is paid to the growth of the debt. But in depressions, when pessimism is strong anyway, the reactions to the borrowing may be very serious. This consideration certainly played a major part in checking the effectiveness of recovery programs during the thirties.

Another possible limitation is the effect of borrowing upon interest rates; if these rise, some deterring effect would be placed upon private investment. This danger can be averted by proper monetary policy. Purchase of bonds by the central banking system, while in itself not a very effective way of stimulating recovery, can assure that interest rates will not be forced upward by the borrowing. Furthermore, if the government borrows from the commercial banks and these banks have large excess reserves, as is typical in depressions, no tightening of the money markets should result, even without central bank action.

As noted below, however, there are certain objections to borrowing from the banks. In addition to these limitations, the growth of the debt will lead to higher government interest burdens and make control of any consequent inflationary pressures more difficult. Finally, long-continued borrowing may result in general acceptance of the notion that a balanced budget is never necessary.

### The Financing of the Program: A Balanced Budget

Recognition of these limitations suggests consideration of the possibility of attempting to develop depression fiscal policy with a balanced budget.[3] Such a program involves equivalent increases in both government expenditures and taxation, and relies for its effectiveness upon the validity of the principle that a balanced budget exercises a net expansionary effect upon the economy. But as noted in Chapter 27, this policy would require a much greater increase in the sphere of governmental activities than a program involving borrowing, and thus the net adverse psychological effect on business confidence might be greater rather than less.

### The Financing of the Program: The Creation of Money

Since the primary goal of depression fiscal policy is that of increasing aggregate demand, it may be argued that the most logical method of financing is the one which has the least deflationary effect—namely, the

---

[3] The most complete discussion of such a program is to be found in the book by J. Hubbard, *Creation of Income by Taxation* (Cambridge: Harvard University Press, 1950).

creation of money. Such a policy would avoid the interest charges created by the debt and the general loss in confidence which may occur because of the growth of the debt.

If there was general acceptance of the money creation method of financing depression expenditures, this technique would have important advantages over both taxation and borrowing. But particularly the issuance of paper money for this purpose would give rise to fears about ultimate inflation and to general loss in confidence in the financial stability of the government, which could easily have more adverse effect upon business investment than the growth of the debt. There is, of course, the further danger that this method of raising money would prove to be so easy that governments would be unwilling to return to the more painful method of taxation once unemployment had been eliminated, and loss of restraint on government expenditures and inflation would result. But assuming financing responsibility on the part of the government, the real objection to the paper money method of financing in depressions is the purely psychological one of the upsetting effects upon general confidence in the government. The objection is also relevant, but less serious, to the technique of money creation by sale of bonds to the central banking system.

### Price Changes

A further obstacle to recovery by fiscal means is the tendency for prices to rise before full employment is attained. As signs of recovery appear, unions are likely to seek wage increases, or at least to recover previous reductions. Prices of farm products, determined in relatively competitive markets, almost certainly will rise, as well as prices of other goods whose output reaches capacity long before general full employment is attained.

These price increases are by no means wholly detrimental to recovery, since they are likely to assist in restoring a general feeling of confidence. Price rises typically benefit businesses as a whole, because of the tendency for costs to lag, and investment is stimulated. But nevertheless, in large measure the dissipation of the effects of increased aggregate demand in higher prices instead of greater output results in a smaller increase in real income and reduction in unemployment than would otherwise occur.

### Failure to Stimulate Self-Generating Recovery

One of the greatest hazards of depression fiscal policy is the danger that the economy will slip backward again once the stimulus of fiscal action is removed. As full employment is approached, it is obviously necessary to bring the depression fiscal policies to an end, or they may precipitate inflation. Thus, expenditures must be curtailed and taxes increased. If the recovery by this time has not become sufficiently self-generating, the withdrawal of the stimulus will cause a reverse action of the multiplier and the acceleration principle. In other words, spontaneous increases in private spending—particularly private investment—must be adequate to take up the slack created by the withdrawal of the government assistance. Whether this is likely to occur is difficult to state; the chief possibility for it rests upon the effects of the restored confidence upon the willingness of businesses to invest. If this is not adequate, the economy will slip back.

There is also the possibility that once high employment levels are reached, the total volume of saving will become so great that it will outrun investment opportunities, regardless of the degree of confidence. This possibility, based upon the so-called "stagnation" thesis, will be discussed below.

### The Problem of State and Local Finances in Depression

One of the major obstacles to successful fiscal policy, especially in a country with a federal governmental structure, is the fiscal "perversity" of states and local governments—the tendency of these units to follow financial policies which aggravate both depressions and inflations rather than help to control them.[4]

In periods of depression the states and localities tend to reduce their expenditures as their revenues fall, and thus aggravate the decline in total employment and output. For example, state and local expenditures for new construction fell from $2.5 billion in 1930 to $0.6 billion in 1935, a decline which largely offset the increases in federal expenditures on public works designed to facilitate recovery. One reason for this policy is the existence of limitations on state and local borrowing, imposed by the state constitutions or, in some localities, by state law. Moreover, local government credit is often not good in depressions, and additional bonds can be sold only at very high cost.

As tax revenues decline, the states and local governments have no alternative but to cut expenditures (or raise taxes). Actually, the economy can afford far more public improvements in depressions, when the social cost is low, than it can in prosperity, when resources are fully employed. Yet the financial circumstances of the states and localities are such that they are virtually compelled to follow exactly the opposite policies.

[4] The outstanding study of this problem is that of A. H. Hansen and H. S. Perloff, *State and Local Finance in the National Economy* (New York: W. W. Norton & Co., 1944).

During the thirties, many of the states were unable to balance their budgets despite attempts at economy, mainly because of increasing relief needs, and turned to new tax sources, particularly the sales tax. Increased taxation in depressions, especially the use of sales taxes, tends to aggravate the decline in total spending to much the same extent as does a reduction in government spending.

The solution to the problem of the perverse fiscal behavior of the states and local governments is difficult to find. These governments cannot be expected to undertake deliberate fiscal policy, because of their limited tax resources for meeting subsequent debt burdens and the leakage of benefits from such programs to outside areas. But it should be possible to develop methods of insuring that they can avoid action which will offset the effectiveness of the federal programs. Since these governments cannot meet the problems themselves, the only practical solution is a program of increased federal grants in depression periods, to meet current local and state government operating deficits, as well as to finance public works projects. Not only will this program allow the states and localities to continue their usual functions, but it will also facilitate better use of federal funds than would occur if the federal government devised ways of spending the money itself. Apart from routine operating expenses, the local governments have opportunities for many public works which are not within the sphere of activity of the federal government. Schools, hospitals, streets, sewerage systems, subways, and the like offer useful outlets for federal funds, and construction of them in depressions not only will aid in bringing recovery but will also avoid the need for undertaking them in inflationary periods.

### The Experience of the Thirties

The failure of the government to bring recovery during the decade of the thirties is often cited to demonstrate the ineffectiveness of fiscal policy. However, not until the mid-thirties, when the depression had become very severe and pessimism was strong, was any deliberate effort to use fiscal policy considered. A study by E. C. Brown[5] has shown that the combined effects of federal, state, and local government activities on aggregate demand (total spending) were substantially greater than in 1929 in only two years of the thirties (1931 and 1936), in which large pay-

---

[5] "Fiscal Policy in the Thirties: A Reappraisal," *American Economic Review*, Vol. XLVI (December, 1956), pp. 857–79. A. M. Sharp, in the article entitled "The Countercyclical Fiscal Role of State Governments during the Thirties," *National Tax Journal*, Vol. XI (June, 1958), pp. 138–45, indicates that the states themselves did not actually pursue a perverse policy. Primary difficulty apparently rests with the local governments.

ments were made under the veterans' adjusted compensation programs, which were not undertaken for fiscal policy purposes. The trend of the effects of government financial activities on aggregate demand was downward throughout the thirties. Thus, essentially, during most of the period, governments were aggravating the depression rather than aiding recovery, not because of fiscal policy, but because they were not actually using it at all. The federal government itself followed expenditure policies which increased aggregate demand, but these were largely offset by the increase in federal taxes in 1932, which virtually doubled the potential full-employment tax yield, and the net expansionary effect of the federal programs was more than offset by the action of the states and local governments in raising taxes.

### Other Recent Empirical Studies of Fiscal Policy

Several studies of the actual behavior of federal receipts and expenditures during business cycles have been made in recent years.

A long-range study by J. M. Firestone for the National Bureau of Economic Research for the period 1879–1958 showed the following major results:[6]

1. In the peacetime cycles other than those immediately after war periods, unbalanced budgets developed in depressions, and cash surpluses in periods of prosperity, despite the lack of any deliberate fiscal policy until the 1930's. The deficits and surpluses were due to changes in revenues rather than to countercyclical changes in expenditures.

2. The introduction of the income tax greatly increased the magnitude of the changes in budget surpluses and deficits from depression to prosperity and back to depression.

3. In the immediate postwar cycles, changes in government expenditures were primarily responsible for the deficit-surplus pattern.

A very detailed study of the fiscal policy in the post-World War II recessions by W. Lewis[7] concludes:

1. The built-in stabilizers made a significant contribution toward economic stability, producing deficits of substantial magnitude relative to the changes in gross national product. The timing has been good in terms of fiscal effects. The reversal of the stabilizers when recovery starts tends, of course, to impede recovery.

2. The direct stabilizers—the personal income tax, and unemploy-

---

[6] *Federal Receipts and Expenditures during Business Cycles* (Princeton: Princeton University Press for National Bureau of Economic Research, 1960).

[7] *Federal Fiscal Policy in the Postwar Recessions* (Washington, D.C.: Brookings Institution, 1962). See also the article by K. E. Poole, "The Role of Federal Fiscal Policy in the 1957–60 Business Cycle," *Journal of Finance*, Vol. XVI (March, 1962), pp. 17–37.

ment compensation and payroll taxes—made the greatest contribution. The corporate income tax accounted for a substantial change in the budget surplus position but had less effect on recovery.

3. Discretionary fiscal actions have been less helpful; there have been numerous constraints on the deliberate adjustments in revenues and expenditures for fiscal policy purposes. The major adjustments have been on the expenditure side, partly because these changes could be justified politically more easily on grounds other than those of counterrecession measures. Only in the 1948–49 recession did budget policy provide a significant positive contribution. The actions, where favorable, have been so delayed that they did not cushion the decline but did aid recovery. On the whole, they have been much less significant than the built-in stabilizers.

4. Expenditure changes were more attractive than tax cuts to the administrations because they did not require the government to admit that conditions were sufficiently serious to require corrective measures.

5. Major constraints on effective policy included campaign pledges which required contrary action, uncertainty about whether or not a recession was coming, fear of reducing business confidence by admitting that a recession was under way, concern over balanced budgets, trust fund financing, and others.

6. Definite improvements have occurred over the period in the acceptance of the need for fiscal policy to meet recessions.

## DEPRESSION FISCAL POLICY AND RESOURCE ALLOCATION

From the standpoint of the attainment of full employment, any net increase in aggregate spending is advantageous; it matters little whether the money is spent for milk for starving babies or for marijuana, for the construction of tuberculosis hospitals or for stone monuments to long-forgotten explorers. This principle, which has become rather generally recognized, may easily result in neglect of one almost universally assumed goal of government activity, namely, that of assisting in the attainment of optimum allocation of resources.

In the development of depression fiscal policies, it is important that the optimum resource use goal be kept in mind. In the selection of projects, priority should be given to those which offer the greatest chance of benefits to society. Unfortunately, a dilemma is often encountered because those projects which are most useful may be the ones most likely to compete with private enterprise. This is particularly true of housing developments, a type of improvement of great benefit to society, especially in the low-income areas of large cities. Unfortunately, government housing projects lessen private investment in the field. This dilemma is an inevitable product of the fact that the most useful goods—except those yielding their benefits to the community as a whole—are produced by private enterprise. If the government undertakes their production, it enters into competition with private businesses and interferes with business morale and private investment. Thus, in large measure the government must be confined to relatively (but not entirely) useless projects, once it exhausts the possibilities of additional activities in its usual fields of endeavor, and the unemployed must be put to work building monuments while persons urgently need new houses and automobiles. But unless some type of cooperative investment program can be devised between government and private business, the government must confine its activities to the less useful projects, or the whole recovery program may be undercut. But nevertheless, within the range open to government, every effort must be made to develop those projects which offer maximum gain to society.

## REFERENCES

From 1935 to 1950 a tremendous quantity of literature on depression fiscal policies was published. Only a few of the major references are listed below; those listed at the end of Chapter 27 are not repeated.

HANSEN, A. H. *Full Recovery or Stagnation?* New York: W. W. Norton & Co., 1938.
The development of the stagnation thesis.

———. *Fiscal Policy and Business Cycles.* New York: W. W. Norton & Co., 1941.
A strong defense of depression fiscal policy.

———. *Economic Policy and Full Employment.* New York: McGraw-Hill Book Co., Inc., 1947.

HAYES, H. G. *Spending, Savings, and Employment.* New York: Alfred A. Knopf, 1945.

LERNER, A. P. *Economics of Employment.* New York: McGraw-Hill Book Co., Inc., 1951.
Lerner, like Hansen, is a strong defender of depression fiscal policy.

VILLARD, H. H. *Deficit Spending and the National Income.* New York: Farrar & Rinehart, 1941.

*Policies to Combat Depressions.* Universities–National Bureau Committee for Economic Research Symposium. Princeton: Princeton University Press, 1956.
A series of papers on depression fiscal policy, with particular emphasis on specific techniques.

| Chapter | ANTI-INFLATIONARY |
|:---|:---|
| **29** | FISCAL POLICY |

 

Fiscal policy seeks not only to insure full employment, but also to maintain a relatively stable general price level. Anti-inflationary fiscal policy involves adjustments in government expenditures, taxation, and borrowing and debt management policies. The first two will be considered in this chapter, and the latter in Chapter 30. Borrowing and debt management policies involve a close interrelationship of governmental and central banking policy, and are sometimes classed as a third type of stabilization policy distinct from either fiscal or monetary policy.

## THE CAUSES OF INFLATION

A review of the forces responsible for inflationary pressures will facilitate an understanding of the operation of anti-inflationary fiscal policy. These forces may be grouped into two classes, namely, the demand-pull influences, which raise prices by increasing the demand for commodities and services, and the cost-push forces, which do so by increasing costs of production. While the two types of forces are interrelated and usually operate in conjunction with each other, they may occur separately.

### Demand-Pull Influences

The demand-pull influence is a manifestation of an excess of total spending (consumption, investment, and governmental) over the current rate of output at prevailing prices, in a situation in which full employment is attained. So long as factors are unemployed, an excess of aggregate spending over output will lead primarily to increases in output, without major changes in the general price level. But once full employment is approached, significant increases in output can no longer occur, and the pressure of the excessive demand is reflected almost entirely in price increases. The excess of aggregate spending over total output under such circumstances is known as the *inflationary gap*.

The development of an excess of spending over output may come about from an increase in any of the three elements which comprise total spending. Consumer expenditures may increase, as they did in the summer of 1950 and the early spring of 1951, when fear of a third world war was strong. Investment expenditures may increase sharply, as occurred on several occasions in the later decades of the last century and immediately after World War II. Finally, inflation may be due, as it often has been, to an increase in government spending without an equivalent decline in private spending. This is typical during a period of war or heavy defense spending. When government expenditures rise sharply, not only is the government competing for scarce goods and resources and thus bidding up their prices (unless there is an equivalent decline in private spending), but by pushing up factor prices and thus incomes, it increases private consumption at the same time that the output of consumption goods falls as resources are shifted to governmental production.

### Cost-Push Influences

The cost-push influences tend to raise prices by increasing costs of production. In part, these influences result from and reinforce the demand-pull influences; when aggregate demand is excessive, the prices of factors will be bid up, as well as the prices of the finished products. Factor price increases, of course, result in higher costs of production and thus lead to further price increases. In addition, full employment increases the bargaining power of labor unions and thus results in wage increases, which produce higher costs and lead to price increases. Even in a period in which there is no initial excess of aggregate demand, increased strength of union power may produce inflation by pushing up the general wage level. The higher wage incomes raise aggregate money demand and thus sustain (from the demand standpoint) the higher dollar volume of national income. Monetary adjustments to support the higher price level are of course necessary, as explained below.

Once inflationary pressures start, they tend to become cumulative. The wage-price spiral is the most familiar manifestation of the cumulative behavior. Higher prices lead to demands for higher wages, which in turn result in still greater price increases, and so on. Likewise, speculation in anticipation of further rises increases the tendency toward higher prices; cash holdings are reduced, and total spending is increased as persons buy up commodities in the belief that prices are going still higher.

### Braking Forces

As inflation continues, however, certain automatic braking forces come into operation. As prices rise, individuals and business firms commence to postpone purchases of durable goods in anticipation of lower prices in the future. The tendency of profits to rise faster than other incomes increases the share of national income going to the wealthy and cuts down the over-all propensity to consume. A rise in productivity increases output per factor unit employed. The built-in flexibility elements in the present tax structure tend to reduce private spending; the yield of a progressive income tax, with given dollar exemptions and brackets, increases at a more rapid rate than the price level rises.

A further braking force is an increase in interest rates caused by the inability of the money supply to carry on the larger dollar volume of transactions, unless central banking policy provides adequate adjustments in the money supply. Any increase in the general price level requires certain monetary adjustments. A higher general price level, with a given volume of output, requires either a greater supply of money (in the broad sense of the term, including commercial bank deposits) or a higher velocity of money. As prices rise, there is some automatic increase in velocity, as some idle balances will come into use. Increased business and governmental borrowing from the banks tends to raise the total volume of bank deposits. But if inflation continues, these automatic adjustments may prove inadequate, and the interest rate will rise sharply unless action is taken to prevent it from doing so. However, if the central banking authorities are committed to a policy of preventing significant increases in the interest rate, they will undertake open-market operations in order to increase bank deposits and bank reserves. The increased reserves enable the banks to make additional loans and thus to increase the money supply still further. Such a policy thus restricts the operation of the monetary braking force.

This discussion suggests that inflation could be prevented by aggressive central banking policy, which would take measures to insure that the interest rate did rise when inflation started, instead of adjusting the money supply upward so that the inflation can go on. But when inflationary pressures are strong and are due primarily to excessive consumer and governmental spending rather than to excessive investment, tremendous rate increases might be necessary to check the inflation. These increases would raise the burden of the government debt and interfere with investment in facilities needed for additional output of particularly scarce goods. In a mild inflation a policy of allowing some tightening of credit may help in reducing inflationary pressures. But this program cannot check a severe inflation without intolerable increases in the interest rate.

In the light of the possible inadequacy of the automatic braking forces and the limitations to the desirability of the use of severe credit restriction policies, fiscal policies have come to be recognized as the government's major weapon to check inflation (apart from direct controls, noted earlier).

## THE AIMS OF ANTI-INFLATIONARY FISCAL POLICY

If fiscal policy is to check inflation in a manner consistent with other accepted goals of governmental policy, the following immediate aims must be attained:

1. Curtailment of the volume of spending, in such a manner that costs of production are not increased.

2. Insurance of maximum incentives: for workers to work, for business firms to maintain optimum output, for transfer of resources toward most productive activities.

3. Distribution of the burden of the governmental activities in a fashion regarded as equitable.

4. Minimization of the problems created for the postinflation period.

In general, attainment of these goals requires (1) a maximum reduction in government expenditures consistent with the accomplishment of the desired governmental programs and (2) the use of revenue and debt programs most suited for the accomplishment of the aims. Expenditure adjustments will be considered first.

## FISCAL POLICY: EXPENDITURES

Since excessive aggregate spending is a primary cause of inflation, a reduction in government spending, which is one element in the total, will tend to lessen inflationary pressures. Unfortunately, however, the most serious inflation typically occurs in periods of high defense spending, in which large items of federal spending cannot be reduced if the goals considered to be of primary importance in such periods are to be attained.

### Curtailment of Activities

However, the presence of inflation makes particularly important a re-examination of expenditure programs, to eliminate waste in the conduct of the activities and to discontinue those programs which may be justifiable in periods of low employment but are not warranted in full employment. Subjective estimates of relative merits and benefits are always involved in such decisions, but a careful appraisal of the expenditures may call attention to ones which are marginal at best and submarginal in periods of inflation.

Secondly, inflationary pressures can be lessened if public construction of various types, such as the building of new post offices, can be postponed. Not only should federal projects be delayed, but those of the states and local units as well. Unfortunately, those governments are inclined to increase their public improvement expenditures in inflationary periods because their revenues are high and voters are willing to approve bond issues. Postponement becomes increasingly difficult if the inflationary pressures continue over a period of years.

### Subsidies

While increases in government expenditures in general tend to aggravate inflation, one type—namely, certain subsidies—may aid in checking inflationary pressures if they are used judiciously. In the first place, if certain basic commodities, such as steel, are in particularly short supply, subsidies to marginal producers which enable them to increase output may eliminate specific inflationary influences which have very widespread ramifications. If completely full employment is attained, total output cannot be increased, except to the extent that subsidies make possible the use of poor resources otherwise unprofitable to exploit. But the subsidies may lessen over-all inflationary pressures by increasing the output of particularly scarce strategic goods. The second type of subsidy consists of grants to producers of articles of necessary consumption to offset cost increases, so that these firms will not have to raise prices and thus increase the cost of living and set off general wage increases. Both types of subsidies were used in World War II.

It must be recognized that the subsidy payments in themselves are inflationary, since they result in increased purchasing power in the hands of the public. But if they bring about significant increases in output of very scarce goods, the increased supply will more than offset the greater demand. If the first type of subsidy noted above is to be successful, the payments must be made only for output which would not otherwise be forthcoming. Any form of blanket subsidy going to all firms in the industry is likely to do much more harm than good. Yet in practice, it is difficult to devise means of confining subsidies to cases in which they actually bring forth more output. Furthermore, any direct subsidy program is always an invitation to "chiseling."

From an inflation control standpoint the most effective type of subsidy is one applied to imports. Such a subsidy increases the domestic supply of the commodity without adding to domestic purchasing power. However, the gains may be partly lost through greater exports due to the increased ability of other countries to buy our products. Furthermore, the policy tends to "export" inflation to other countries and may lead to retaliation.

## FISCAL POLICIES: TAXATION

In the light of the obstacles to significant reductions in government expenditures, the most promising anti-inflationary fiscal measures are to be found on the revenue side of the picture. In turn, adjustments in taxation would appear to have the greatest chances of success, since taxes have a greater deflationary effect than other revenue sources. However, various taxes differ in their direct anti-inflationary effects and their influences upon incentives. Accordingly, the anti-inflationary effectiveness of the collection of a given amount of tax revenue will depend upon the types of taxes which comprise the tax structure. The major taxes will be reviewed from this standpoint.

### Increases in the Personal Income Tax

A tax on personal income reduces inflationary pressures by taking away from individuals purchasing power which might otherwise be spent. The chief merits of personal income tax increases include the ease of making such a change and the conformity of this method with accepted standards of equity. The same equity considerations apply to the use of income taxes as anti-inflationary measures as to their use as permanent elements in the tax structure. There are, however, certain objections on an equity basis. Persons able to evade or avoid income taxes escape appropriate burden. No burden is placed on persons contributing to inflation by spending large amounts from accumulated savings. On the other hand, persons with heavy fixed savings commitments, such as mortgage and life insurance premium payments, may be squeezed badly by the tax, despite the fact that these payments do not contribute to inflation. Nevertheless, on the whole, income tax increases conform with equity standards more satisfactorily than do most other measures.

From an administrative standpoint the income tax increases can be made quickly and easily, especially as a result of the use of the withholding system. No additional personnel are required for large returns than for small, although lowering of exemptions would increase the number of returns and produce some increase in costs.

From the standpoint of inflation control the income tax does absorb purchasing power that would in large measure be spent, and it does have a minimum effect on business costs, except to the extent that reductions in take-home pay lead unions to insist on wage increases. On the other hand, the tax gives no direct incentive to curtail spending and does not place a tax burden on persons who are able to evade the tax or who spend large amounts from accumulated wealth. But more seriously, the tax applies to all income rather than merely to that which is being used in a manner which increases inflationary pressures. Accordingly, the relative burden on persons saving large portions of their incomes is greater, compared to that on persons spending most of their income, than it would be with a tax which applied only to the portion of income spent. Thus a greater percentage of an income tax will be absorbed from savings than of a tax concentrated on the portion of income spent, and thus the anti-inflationary effect of the income tax will be less, per dollar of revenue, than that of a tax confined to spending. As one consequence, if given inflationary pressures are to be checked by the use of income tax increases, the tax rates must be higher than they would need to be with a tax having a greater effect in curtailing spending. Accordingly, the adverse effects on incentives to work and to produce will be somewhat greater.

The incentive effects of income taxation have been discussed in Chapter 12. Business optimism is so great, as a rule, in inflationary periods that the tax will not cause deliberate output curtailment. But there is somewhat greater danger of adverse effects on labor supply. The fact that incomes are rising during an inflationary period increases the likelihood that persons will cut down on overtime work and increase absenteeism when tax rates are pushed up; because the tax increase occurs when their incomes are rising, they are able to maintain existing levels of living despite the tax without the need for attempting to work additional hours. The net effects on total labor supply are difficult to determine. The higher tax rates will, however, definitely interfere with the flow of labor into other jobs.

Income tax increases will have a minimum effect on incentives and the greatest anti-inflationary effectiveness if they are concentrated on the lower income groups, through a reduction in exemptions and increases in the first bracket rates. This adjustment will not only lessen the danger of reduced labor supply but will lessen spending effectively, because these groups have little savings margin and must bear the tax largely through reduced consumption. However, this policy may be regarded as inequitable, since the poor are compelled to sacrifice items of consumption which are essential for a minimum living standard, while the wealthy are affected very little. This fundamental conflict between fiscal and equity considerations, which plagued the Roosevelt and Truman administrations, can be solved only by compromise.

In summary, income tax increases present the simplest and in many respects the most equitable means of checking inflationary pressures and are one of the first steps that can be taken when inflationary pressures develop. But the possibility of adverse incentive effects and the fact that considerable revenue is caught without anti-inflationary effects suggest that in event of severe inflation, other taxes must be considered.

### The Spendings Tax

The basic limitations to the use of income tax increases, namely, their application to income used for noninflationary purposes as well as that used for inflationary purposes, and their failure to provide any incentive to curtail spending, suggest the possible use of a spendings tax, which would apply at progressive rates to the portion of spending over and above an established minimum, with the exclusion of appropriate items such as medical expenses. As indicated in Chapter 15, the tax would be collected in conjunction with the income tax, the person being subject to spending tax on the excess of income received over the net increase in accumulated savings.

There are several primary merits, as contrasted to income tax increases. First, the amounts of income saved would not be included in the base, and thus the anti-inflationary effects of the collection of a given amount of revenue would be greater than if obtained from a tax based upon all income. It is true, of course, that even the spendings tax may be absorbed out of savings, even though it applies only to income spent. But the concentration of the burden upon persons spending most of their incomes would compel greater reduction in spending than would an income tax, which would impose greater relative burden on persons with large margins of saving. On the other hand, the spendings tax would lessen the tax pressure on persons with heavy fixed savings commitments.

Secondly, a penalty would be placed on spending, especially if the rate were highly progressive. Rates well over 100 per cent could be used; if, for example, a maximum rate of 200 per cent were set, the spending of $100 additional, once the top bracket was reached, would incur a $200 tax liability. Many persons would hesitate to undertake additional spending under such circumstances, and thus the percentage of income saved would tend to rise. It is impossible to establish this type of deterrent under an income tax. Likewise, the tax would place a penalty on spending from accumulated wealth, a result which the income tax cannot accomplish.

Minimum expenditures for family subsistence can be exempted much more easily than with a sales tax. On the basis of theoretical considerations alone, a spendings tax would be the most effective and equitable inflation control measure.

The limitations are largely administrative. As pointed out in Chapter 15, concealment of assets when the tax was introduced and eventual presentation of them as evidence of savings would be especially difficult to prevent. Adjustment of tax burden on the purchase of durable goods, such as houses, would be troublesome, as well as the attainment of equity between tenant and homeowner.

If it should prove possible to solve these difficulties, the tax should provide an extremely effective supplement to income tax increases and warrants serious consideration in the event of severe inflation in the future. In addition, a careful "selling job" is necessary to avoid the repetition of the rejection of the Treasury proposal after only a cursory examination by Congress in 1942.

### Commodity Taxes: General Considerations

In the light of the administrative difficulties of a spendings tax, the attempt has been made to accomplish in part the same results by levying taxes on the sale of commodities. Excise taxes have been extensively used and a general sales tax considered at various times. Taxes on the sale of commodities serve to check inflation in two ways: They provide a limited incentive to curtail consumption, because the taxes can be avoided by saving, and they take away purchasing power (to the extent that the taxed goods are bought) by driving a "wedge" between the price paid by the consumer and the price received (net of tax) by the vendor. The addition to the purchase price of the articles represented by the tax absorbs consumer purchasing power but does not become factor income directly, and thus has the effect of reducing total factor demand.

It is sometimes maintained that the argument that a tax can be deflationary by raising prices is contradictory. Actually, this is not the case. The usual inflationary price increase is self-generating; the higher money incomes due to the higher prices raise spending, increase prices still more, and so on. But the price increase due to the tax is not self-generating; it does not increase factor incomes over what they would otherwise have been but replaces nondeflationary borrowing, and thus retards the inflationary spiral. Just as the income tax reduces the purchasing power which a person has to buy goods from business firms, so a sales tax produces the same result by increasing the prices of goods purchased. As a consequence, a given total dollar expenditure will constitute a smaller payment to business firms (exclusive of the tax element which they pass on to the government) and will thus create a smaller factor demand.[1]

### Commodity Taxes: Excises

Excise and sales taxes affect inflationary pressure in somewhat different ways and thus must be considered separately. Hart and Brown have very conveniently divided excises into two groups, those which are primarily demand-shifting and those which are primarily demand-absorbing.[2]

1. *Demand-Shifting Excises.* Demand-shifting excises are designed to discourage persons from buying particularly scarce commodities. The tax is thus intended as a type of rationing device, to be employed in cases in which actual rationing is difficult. The policy will be effective, of course, only if the demand for the product is reasonably elastic. The excise tax on passenger transportation in the United States in World War II was largely designed for this purpose, along with other excises in both the United States and Canada. Denmark and other countries have made extensive use of excises for fiscal policy purposes.

A primary objection to the use of demand-shifting excises is the fact that they "ration" scarce goods to those persons with sufficient incomes that they are willing to buy them despite the tax. If the commodity is one of wide use and of considerable importance in the consumption patterns of lower income groups, this method of discouraging use is particularly inequitable. The excises are also somewhat clumsy devices for controlling the use of the articles. Since it is impossible to adjust them to accomplish the precise results, there is great likelihood that they will either do too much or not enough. An example of the former is the effect of the sharp increase in the Canadian excise tax on automobiles in 1950, which apparently cut purchases below the potential output and caused strenuous complaints on the part of the industry. Expectations of the levying of these excises will stimulate buying; expectations of repeal will reduce purchases

---

[1] Earl Rolph has argued that in an inflationary period a sales tax lessens inflationary pressures by preventing further increases in factor prices and thus by lessening money incomes in the same manner as an income tax. But this point of view inevitably produces the conclusion that any tax which checks inflation does so by lowering factor incomes, and ignores the very different incentive effects which arise with different types of taxes. The point of view that a sales tax checks inflation by raising prices is much more useful for analytical purposes (see E. R. Rolph, "A Proposed Revision of Excise Tax Theory," *Journal of Political Economy*, Vol. LX [April, 1952], pp. 222–39).

[2] A. G. Hart and E. C. Brown, *Financing Defense* (New York: Twentieth Century Fund, 1951), p. 48.

sharply.[3] One danger, which became manifest after World War II, is that demand-shifting excises levied during inflationary periods may be retained in periods in which they are no longer required. The tax on passenger transportation was not repealed until 1962 (air transport, 1963).

2. *Demand-Absorbing Excises.* Demand-absorbing excises, in contrast, are levied upon commodities of inelastic demand, with the primary purpose of absorbing purchasing power that would otherwise be used for inflationary spending. The basic dilemma encountered in the use of excises for this purpose arises from the fact that most commodities of inelastic demand are ones of widespread use, and thus the burden of a tax upon them will be distributed in the same regressive fashion as that of a sales tax. And unlike the sales tax, these excises are discriminatory among individuals according to their preferences for particular commodities. Likewise, regardless of the selection of commodities, some demand shifting is likely, with possible increases in demand for commodities in scarcer supply than those taxed.

On the whole, considerable doubt may be raised about the use of excises as devices of inflation control. The demand-absorbing variety, if used extensively, has much the same effect as a sales tax and is more discriminatory than the latter. The demand-shifting type is suitable only for commodities which have highly elastic demands, are not essential for customary living standards, are in very short supply, and are difficult to ration, if the latter policy be employed. In such a case the tax may be preferable to inequitable rationing or, if no rationing is employed, to sharp price increases which create large excess profits for the producers.

### Commodity Taxes: General Sales Taxes

A general sales tax is somewhat comparable in its anti-inflationary effects to those of a widespread system of demand-absorbing excises, taking purchasing power that would in large measure be spent for goods and services and thus further inflationary pressures.

1. *Merits.* The primary merits of sales taxes as anti-inflationary measures are comparable to those of spending taxes. The dangers of adverse incentive effects are less than those of income tax increases, in large measure because of the nonprogressive nature of the sales tax rate. If a

---

[3] In December of 1957 the development of widespread belief that the Canadian excise tax on automobiles was to be reduced brought car sales almost to a standstill.

A review of Canadian experience with excise taxes as an instrument of fiscal policy by Jared Sparks raises serious doubts about the desirability of such a policy, because of the great difficulties in ascertaining the rates which will accomplish the desired results, and the disturbing effects of anticipation of rate changes. See the article by J. Sparks, "Canadian Excise Taxes and Inflation Control," *Canadian Tax Journal,* Vol. VI (January-February, 1958), pp. 70–80.

ANTI-INFLATIONARY FISCAL POLICY · **557**

sales tax is compared with an income tax distributed in the same general fashion by income class, its relative advantage over the income tax is much less. However, there is still some net advantage, to the extent that persons wish additional income for savings purposes. These persons may be deterred from working by the income tax but will not be affected by the sales tax. But persons who wish additional income only for consumption purposes will be affected by the sales tax as well, because the buying power of a given amount of money income will be reduced by the tax.

The sales tax, like the spendings tax, does place a penalty on spending from accumulated wealth. It likewise gives some definite incentive to save more and spend less, especially if the tax is expected to be temporary. But the penalty on spending is much less than that provided by a highly progressive spendings tax. Some methods of making a sales tax progressive through a requirement that sales taxes be payable by the consumers only in tax stamps sold to them at rates progressive according to amounts spent during the year have been suggested but do not appear to be administratively feasible. Persons with high incomes and expenditures would have great incentive to buy stamps from persons with low income. The sales would be difficult to prevent, yet would sabotage the whole program. In addition, the stamps would be a source of great nuisance to consumers and vendors, and an elaborate system for control of amounts sold to persons would be required.

From an equity standpoint the sales tax has the merit of placing the tax burden on persons who escape income taxes and on those who spend from accumulated wealth. Furthermore, the sales tax places a relatively heavy burden on persons who spend large percentages of their incomes in order to maintain high levels of living in the face of shortages. This group can justifiably be penalized, since their action aggravates the inflation.

*2. Limitations to Sales Taxes as Anti-inflationary Measures.* On the other hand, a sales tax does not distinguish between high rates of spending necessary to maintain minimum living levels in the face of adverse circumstances and those which represent deliberate maintenance of levels higher than typical for the income group when many goods are scarce. The result is the placing of a penalty on those persons whose circumstances require them to spend high percentages of income, particularly persons with very low incomes, large families, persons living in high-cost areas, and the like.

The regressive distribution of burden can be mitigated, as discussed in Chapter 17, by exemption of food and other basic commodities or by some form of personal exemption. But tax administration is complicated by so doing, inflationary effectiveness is weakened, and new inequities are created. On the whole, sales taxes with these exemptions are better than ones without, but they are nevertheless by no means entirely equitable.

But the most serious limitation of the sales tax as an anti-inflationary measure is its tendency to produce wage increases and thus stimulate further inflation. The sales tax directly increases the cost of living and thus leads to demands for higher wages. When wage contracts contain escalator clauses, the sales tax will produce automatic increases by raising the index of living costs. Even without such clauses the higher cost of living increases the upward pressure on wages. Any attempt to exclude the sales tax element in prices from the index will encounter serious political obstacles. Even if exclusion were feasible, the pressures on wages would not be eliminated but merely lessened.

In addition, there are certain problems involved in the internal structure of a sales tax which limit its effectiveness as an anti-inflationary device. It is administratively impossible to establish a truly general sales tax applying to all consumption expenditures; those of necessity exempt, such as for housing, personal servants, etc., would serve as outlets for spending shifted from taxed categories, and inflationary pressures upon them would increase. The inability to exclude from a sales tax all items purchased by business firms, as discussed in Chapter 17, is a complicating factor. Taxation of these purchases would create inflation-aggravating pyramiding and would necessitate adjustments of price ceilings if these were in effect.

A final objection to the use of a federal sales tax as an anti-inflationary measure is the danger that a tax introduced in such a period will remain in use after inflationary pressures are over.

In summary, a sales tax is definitely inferior to a spendings tax as an anti-inflationary measure but is much easier to administer. The sales tax should have less adverse effects on work incentives than income tax increases and would prove somewhat more effective, per dollar of revenue, in controlling inflation than the income tax if wage increases can be prevented. But a sales tax without exemptions distributes the burden in a fashion discriminatory against persons finding it necessary to spend high percentages of their incomes, while any modifications designed to meet this problem complicate administration and create other inequities.

3. *Desirable Characteristics of an Anti-inflationary Sales Tax.* Should a sales tax be used as an anti-inflationary measure, certain specific characteristics are desirable if the objectives are to be attained. The use of the retail form of sales tax is almost essential if the tax is to be introduced for the first time or its rate increased in the inflation period, in order to avoid the problems of pyramiding that are particularly likely when de-

mand for commodities is strong. Only the retail form of tax can be applied directly to the final selling price and quoted separately to the buyer as a means of impressing the tax element upon the individual purchaser.

Secondly, exclusion, so far as feasible, of goods used in further production is desirable, to avoid not only the general disadvantages of taxing such items discussed in Chapter 17 but also cost increases.

Thirdly, the scope of the tax should be as broad as possible, consistent with the avoidance of excessive burden on persons compelled to spend large percentages of their incomes. Use of either a personal exemption or an exemption of food may be justified on this basis. Multiplication of exemptions lessens both the ease of administration and the effectiveness of the tax in controlling inflation.

### Corporation Income Tax Increases

Another alternative measure is that of increases in the corporate income tax. Such an increase is deflationary in two primary ways. First, to the extent that dividends are reduced, individual spending is lessened, at least to a limited degree. Secondly, the funds for business expansion are curtailed, with consequent checking of investment. This factor is not of importance in a major war, when investment is of necessity controlled by the government directly through allocations, but may be of some significance in a nonwar inflationary period.

Actually, however, the anti-inflationary effect is not likely to be great. Because of the concentration of stock ownership in the higher income levels, little check upon consumption can be expected per dollar of corporation tax revenue. The effects upon investment are diverse. The checking of investment, in itself, is deflationary, since investment is one element in aggregate spending. But to the extent that the investment would have allowed greater output of particularly scarce goods in a later period, the over-all effect might have been advantageous. On the other hand, increased investment in facilities which are already ample has no such redeeming effect. In 1950, for example, additional investment in steel mills would have produced ultimate anti-inflationary effects, while additional construction of service stations would have been entirely inflationary. But taxes cannot distinguish automatically between the two types of investments. Thus the checking of investment, to the extent to which it occurs, may easily have as much adverse as beneficial effect. Increases in the corporate tax, just like the excess profits tax noted below, also have the disadvantage of weakening incentives toward efficiency.

On the whole, corporation income tax increases are not particularly effective weapons in an inflation control program. In many cases, they must be introduced as elements in political compromises, designed to make the personal income tax increases more palatable to the workers; in wartime, they do serve to lessen the growth of the national debt and may weaken demands of unions for wage increases justified on the grounds of high profits.

### Changes in Depreciation Allowances

In addition to changes in the rate of the corporate tax, other adjustments in the tax may improve its anti-inflationary effectiveness. One is the alteration of the rate at which capital equipment may be depreciated for tax purposes. During World Wars I and II a system of accelerated depreciation, which allowed the writing-off of equipment in a shorter period than normal, was introduced in order to encourage corporations to undertake investment in war production facilities or in ones designed to aid the conduct of defense activities, which might be usable for only a short period of time.

In 1951, Canada commenced the use of the reverse policy of deferred depreciation as a means of checking investment which was regarded as particularly inflationary.[4] Under the rules established, firms were denied the right to depreciate new capital equipment during a four-year interval, unless specific approval of the Department of National Revenue was obtained, except in certain industries in which over-all expansion of output was desired. The provision was eliminated at the end of 1952 because of lessened inflationary pressures. Despite the short period of operation, there is evidence that the measure significantly reduced investment and thus contributed to the checking of inflation.[5] A deferred depreciation policy has the great advantage of selectivity, since it can be applied to investment which is regarded as unessential, but not to that necessary to increase output of basic scarce commodities. There are administrative problems in the operation of the selective mechanism, but these are not insurmountable.

### The Excess Profits Tax

An excess profits tax applies only to earnings of amounts in excess of those defined to be normal. Such a tax will have even less restrictive effect on consumption than the corporate tax, since it is less likely to affect dividend rates. Likewise, to the extent that it actually rests on truly "ex-

---

[4] See H. D. McGurran, "Deferred Depreciation," *National Tax Journal*, Vol. IV (December, 1951), pp. 299–304.

[5] See M. W. Sharp, "Deferred Depreciation," *Canadian Tax Journal*, Vol. I (May-June, 1953), pp. 277–83.

cess" profits, it will have less deterring effect on investment than will the corporate income tax, which affects earnings from all investments. To the extent that investment is checked, the same considerations are relevant as those applying to investment-checking influences of the corporate tax. On the other hand, the excess profits tax gives firms a definite incentive to increase expenditures on activities yielding a long-term return, such as good-will advertising, and lessens the incentives toward maintenance of maximum efficiency. As a consequence, inflationary pressures are increased.

The case for an excess profits tax during inflationary periods must rest primarily upon the equity case of recapture of profits, of particular importance in war, and upon the political necessities of obtaining acceptance by labor unions of higher personal income taxes and wage stabilization policies. As a direct anti-inflationary measure the tax is very weak.

## THE OVER-ALL TAX LEVEL

In the preceding pages the relative anti-inflationary effectiveness of various taxes has been discussed. But a distinct question is that of the desired over-all tax level, compared to the expenditures. In other words, to what extent is a balanced budget or a budget surplus required if inflationary pressures are to be eliminated? No precise answer to this question is possible, since the answer depends in part upon the types of taxes used and in part upon the exact nature and inflationary effects of the government expenditures. It also depends upon the magnitude of the expenditures relative to national income and upon the relationship between total spending (consumption and investment) in the private sector of the economy and the output of goods available for private sector purchases.

### Various Possible Situations

First, suppose that in the private sector of the economy, total spending (consumption plus investment) would exactly equal current output, in the absence of government activity or, in other words, that planned savings and planned investment in the private sector of the economy were exactly equal, with full employment. If government expenditures and revenues are equal, and if the expansionary effects of the expenditures are equal to the contractionary effects of the raising of the revenues, price and output stability will be maintained. But if the expansionary effects of the expenditures exceed the contractionary effects of the taxes, as is likely, inflation will develop despite the balanced budget, and a budget surplus will be required to maintain the existing price level. If private sector spending is tending to outrun output available for private sector use, as has occurred at times in the postwar period, a government surplus will be required to check inflation, even if the governmental financial activities with a balanced budget have no net expansionary effect.

On the other hand, if planned investment in the private sector is lagging behind the amounts which persons wish to save and thus total private spending is less than current output, inflation may be avoided even with a government budget deficit. In some of the postwar years in the United States, there was little inflation despite government deficits, a result which suggests that in the absence of the high level of government spending and the deficits, there might have been a tendency toward unemployment. The net expansionary effects of the governmental expenditure and revenue programs were merely offsetting deflationary influences in the private sector of the economy. However, as government expenditures reach progressively higher levels, there is increased danger that inflation will be stimulated even with a balanced budget, as the high level of expenditures will probably stimulate private production to a greater extent than the taxes check it. The higher the level of government expenditures, the greater is the likelihood that a budget surplus will be required to check inflation, unless governmental activities are of such character as to discourage private investment.

However, even if inflationary pressures are present in the private sector of the economy, it may be possible to check inflation without a budget surplus if the tax structure is made up of elements which have strong contractionary effects. Thus, extensive use of a high-rate spendings tax and deferred depreciation policies might so reduce private spending that price stability could be obtained despite a budget deficit.

Thus, in summary, the extent to which a balanced budget will hold inflation in check will depend upon:

1. The net inflationary pressures present in the private sector of the economy or, in other words, the relation between total private sector spending and total private sector output.

2. The contractionary effect of the tax system, which, in turn, is dependent upon the types of taxes used and the effects which these taxes have upon spending.

3. The expansionary effect of the government expenditure program, which, in turn, is largely dependent upon the purposes for which the expenditures are made.

In both the literature and the public discussion of inflation, altogether too much emphasis has been placed upon the balancing of the budget, as such, as both a necessary and a certain means of checking inflation. There is no particular magic about taxes, as compared to borrowing, that insures that the financing of all expenditures by them will check inflation. On the whole, of course, taxes are more deflationary than borrowing. But some types of taxes are little better than borrowing and in some instances may even be weaker. The point of budget balance has no particular significance from the standpoint of inflation control, although it does, of course, with respect to the growth of the debt.

## THE WEAKNESSES OF ANTI-INFLATIONARY FISCAL POLICY

A co-ordinated program of expenditure reduction and tax increases should exercise a restraining influence upon inflationary pressures. But there are serious obstacles in the way of complete control of inflation by this means, especially if inflationary pressures become strong.

### Tax-Generated Cost Increases

A major weakness is the danger that tax increases, at least beyond a certain point, will commence to generate cost increases, and thus lose their anti-inflationary effectiveness. The resistance of the taxed groups to a reduction in their disposable incomes may result in increases in factor prices, which will nullify the effects of the collection of the taxes in reducing total spending. This danger is greatest with the sales tax because of its direct impact upon the cost of living, but it may occur with the income tax as well. Reduction in take-home pay resulting from the tax may lead unions to demand and receive higher money wages, which in turn lead to price increases. The resistance of employers to money wage increases is often not strong in periods of prosperity. Of all possible levies, the spendings tax probably offers the least danger of generating factor price increases. Once inflation goes on for a time, each group seeks to protect itself from the effects of both inflation and tax increases designed to prevent it by means of escalator clauses in factor price contracts. The result is a reinforcement of inflationary pressures and a grave threat to price stability, one which fiscal policy is powerless to overcome.

### Cost-Push Inflation

Closely related is the inadequacy of fiscal policy as a means of combating inflation which is generated primarily by cost increases. Fiscal policy is based upon the assumption that inflation results basically from excessive spending, and seeks to control it by checking spending. But if the inflation is rooted primarily in continued wage increases brought about by union action and furthered by markup pricing practices of many business firms, fiscal policy is almost powerless. Drastic action might reduce total spending so sharply as to bring down the general price level, but not necessarily prices in those sectors in which the greatest increases had occurred, and only at the cost of a large volume of unemployment. Of the two evils, unemployment and inflation, most persons would presumably prefer the latter. In any event, drastic fiscal action of this type is not likely to be carried on.

### Political Limitations

One of the greatest obstacles to the successful use of anti-inflationary fiscal policy is that of obtaining appropriate action by legislative bodies. In periods of inflation the pressures to increase rather than reduce government expenditures are strong, and the opposition to tax increases may prevent action to insure the necessary budget balance or surplus. It is particularly difficult to sell the notion of the need for taxes in excess of expenditures in periods of inflation, as witnessed by American experience in the years after World War II. Just as in the thirties, fiscal policy failed to be effective not because of the manner in which it was used, but because it was not really used at all, at least to an adequate degree. Successful fiscal policy in the future will require an extensive process of education of both Congress and the public. The problem is somewhat less difficult but by no means absent in a country with a parliamentary form of government.

## CONCLUSION

In a relatively mild inflation generated by excessive spending relative to output at full employment, prompt fiscal measures should be successful in dampening the general price increases. A budget surplus will probably be necessary, the surplus being used to retire debt—preferably, from an inflation control standpoint, that held by the central banking system. In a period of very strong inflationary pressures generated by high defense spending, fiscal policy may serve as a useful restraining influence, but it is not likely to be capable of controlling inflation singlehanded. In an all-out defense effort, civilian goods output must be reduced to the minimum necessary to preserve the ability and willingness of the community to carry on production. But an attempt to reduce spending to this level by taxation would undoubtedly force many persons below it, particularly those lacking liquid assets to supplement disposable income, and those who would be forced far below accustomed living standards because their incomes had not risen. Borrowing must be relied upon to some extent, and direct controls used to supplement fiscal policy for particularly scarce goods, and to prevent general wage and price increases. Even if fiscal policy were economically capable of controlling the inflation, political interferences would probably prevent completely effective use of it.

The type of inflation least amenable to fiscal policy is the gradual, long-continuing variety experienced after World War II, in which the spiral of wage increases went on year after year. Even if fiscal policy were feasible politically, it could probably not stop the inflationary spiral without causing serious unemployment. Yet direct controls are not acceptable politically or economically, since continued use over a period of years would seriously interfere with the basic regulatory mechanism of the economy.

## REFERENCES

HART, A. G. *Defense without Inflation.* New York: Twentieth Century Fund, 1951.
> The best brief analysis of inflation–its causes, effects, and control.

HART, A. G., and BROWN, E. C. *Financing Defense.* New York: Twentieth Century Fund, 1951.
> The best available review of the relative anti-inflationary effects of various tax measures.

SHOUP, C.; FRIEDMAN, M.; and MACK, R. *Taxing to Prevent Inflation.* New York: Columbia University Press, 1943.
> An analysis of the anti-inflationary effects of various taxes, in the setting of World War II.

CHANDLER, L. V., and WALLACE, D. H. *Economic Mobilization and Stabilization.* New York: Henry Holt & Co., 1951.
> A series of papers on inflation control problems.

DIRECTOR, A. (ed.) *Defense, Controls, and Inflation.* Chicago: University of Chicago Press, 1952.
> A symposium volume on various approaches to inflation control.

GOODE, R. "Anti-inflationary Implications of Alternative Forms of Taxation," *Proceedings of the American Economic Association for 1951,* pp. 147–60.
> An analysis of the relative anti-inflationary effectiveness of various taxes.

MORAG, A. "Deflationary Effects of Outlay and Income Taxes," *Journal of Political Economy,* Vol. LXVII (June, 1959), pp. 266–74.
> A comparison of the anti-inflationary influence of the two types of taxes.

# Chapter 30 | DEBT MANAGEMENT

By the term *debt management* is meant the adjustment of the structure and composition of the national debt to attain desired objectives. This adjustment involves decisions by the government about the types of securities to issue in order to raise money by borrowing and to refund existing securities. Management involves such questions as the term for which the money is borrowed, the interest policy, salability of securities, redeemability, and other aspects.

Debt management rests primarily with the Treasury, subject, of course, to the rules imposed by legislation. Congress, however, is less inclined to specify detailed rules for debt management than it is to specify details of tax legislation. While debt management is regarded primarily as a Treasury function, the Federal Reserve System is inevitably involved to a substantial degree; the type of open-market operations which it conducts affects Treasury policy, and close co-ordination is usually attained. The question of policies designed to influence the over-all level of market interest rates are regarded as elements in monetary policy, rather than debt management.

## THE GENERAL APPROACH

Apart from cyclical aspects to be noted below, there are two major approaches to the general policy of debt management. The first may be called the "tailored to the market" doctrine. Debt management seeks to attain two primary goals: (1) to induce illiquidity, that is, to encourage the lenders to keep wealth in the government bonds rather than spend the sum and thus contribute to inflationary pressures, a goal of primary concern during periods of full employment, and (2) to minimize the interest cost. As noted in Chapter 26, the program of payment of interest from tax collections has adverse effects upon the economy; therefore, minimization of the interest burden is desirable. Thus, it is argued, the debt structure should be tailored to meet the desires of a wide variety of investors in order to tap all potential sources at lowest over-all interest cost, consistent with obtaining a desired degree of illiquidity.[1] There will be some optimum pattern which will allow the desired degree of illiquidity at lowest cost.

The critics of this point of view, who include such distinguished economists as Milton Friedman,[2] argue for a much simpler debt structure, with only two or three issues—savings bonds, one type of short-term issue, and one type of long-term issue, preferably in perpetuity. One reason for a simple structure is the difficulty of attaining the optimum pattern outlined in the "tailored" approach. Likewise, it is argued, the government should leave the task of adjusting its securities to market needs to private financial intermediaries which would buy the standard government issues and sell a variety of their own issues to the public. The task of debt management would be simplified, and co-ordination of the work of the Treasury and the Federal Reserve facilitated.

### Long- versus Short-Term Borrowing—The Major Issue

A basic issue in debt management is that of the relative desirability of long- and short- term borrowing, and of shifts from one to the other for fiscal policy purposes. Long-term debt offers several advantages. Constant refunding is avoided, with possible need for Federal Reserve support at a time when monetary policy dictates a reverse policy. The liquidity of long-term debt can be reduced by Federal Reserve action to bring down the prices of the bonds, and the prices can be increased in depression periods to increase liquidity. Short-term obligations are of necessity highly liquid, and extensive short-term holdings create a major threat of sharp increases in consumer spending and a strong argument (for interest cost reasons) against anti-inflationary monetary policy.

Short-term borrowing, on the other hand, is typically but not always cheaper; this is particularly true in depressions, when there tends to be a great surplus of money available on a short-term basis. The high degree of liquidity is also an advantage in depression periods, when increased spending is desirable.

Accordingly, it was widely argued that countercyclical fiscal policy

[1] This position is to be found in the writings, among others, of Earl Rolph; for example, "Principles of Debt Management," *American Economic Review*, Vol. XLVII (June, 1957), pp. 302–20.

[2] See *A Program for Monetary Stability* (New York: Fordham University Press, 1960), chap. iii.

requires a shift to short-term obligations in periods of depression in order to increase liquidity, and to long-term obligations in periods of inflation, in order to reduce liquidity and raise long-term interest rates. However, it has been stressed by Warren Smith and other students of the question[3] that the shift from short-term to long-term securities, or vice versa, in itself has relatively little effect. The benefits from long-term securities are not created by the shift to these securities but by the policy of having a large portion of the debt consist of them at the time inflationary pressures arise. Accordingly, the debt should be refunded into long-term securities at the time such borrowing is cheapest, namely, in the midst of depression. Short-term borrowing should be avoided in such periods despite the current low interest rates, because such borrowing is subject to interest rate increases as recovery proceeds, and because of the disadvantages of having the debt in such form in full-employment periods. The disadvantage of having the debt in relatively liquid form in depressions can be offset by Federal Reserve action which holds up the prices of government securities.

On the other hand, any attempt to shift the debt in periods of inflation to longer term securities will result in higher over-all interest burden and will accomplish little in terms of inflation control. Virtually no government will in practice push such a program very far, because of the higher interest costs resulting, as demonstrated by the behavior of the Eisenhower administration on this issue. Initial attempts to lengthen the time periods of the security holdings were soon abandoned because of higher interest costs. Any new borrowing necessary in inflationary periods should be made on a short-term basis, with refunding into long-term issues when interest rates decline.

## BORROWING POLICIES IN PERIODS OF INFLATION

Specific attention will now be given to the types of borrowing policies which will minimize inflationary pressures when resort to borrowing becomes necessary in full-employment periods. Such procedure is most likely to occur in a period of high defense spending, when for economic or political reasons it becomes impossible to finance entirely by taxation. The extent to which inflationary pressures will be minimized depends in large measure upon the sources of the funds, as well as the types of securities issued, the inducements given to buy and to hold securities, and the interest rate policies followed.

3 See W. L. Smith, *Debt Management in the United States*, Study Paper No. 19, Joint Economic Committee, Congress of the United States (Washington, D.C.: U.S. Government Printing Office, 1960).

## Voluntary Purchase of Bonds by Individuals

To the extent that bonds can be sold to individuals, inflationary pressures are likely to be less than if the bonds are sold to other buyers, particularly the commercial banks. In the first place, only if the sales are made to individuals is there any chance of significant reduction in consumption spending. Appropriate sales policies may induce some persons to reduce current consumption in order to buy bonds. Even if this result is not attained, the liquidity of the bond buyers is reduced. Wealth invested in bonds is less likely to be spent than wealth held in the form of cash or bank deposits, especially if the owners of the bonds are given some inducement to hold their securities. Finally, the sale of bonds to individuals avoids the creation of purchasing power and the complications for subsequent credit control which arise from sale to the commercial banks.

Maximum attainment of the advantages of sale of bonds to individuals requires the realization of three goals:

1. Sales of bonds to individuals must be as large as possible, with minimum sale to financial institutions.

2. Individuals must be given maximum incentive to curtail consumption and buy bonds.

3. Maximum inducement must be provided to hold the bonds which are purchased.

Unfortunately, the policies which will best attain each of these goals are somewhat conflicting. Policies which will allow maximum sales, for example, may interfere with the provision of maximum incentive to hold the bonds purchased. Some compromise among the various policies becomes necessary.

1. *Inducements to Buy Bonds and Forgo Consumption.* Several inducements can be given to encourage persons to forgo consumption and buy as many bonds as possible. In the first place, interest rates higher than prevailing levels may be offered. The higher rates will probably have little effect in leading persons to spend less and save more, but they will induce persons to forgo liquidity and place more of their wealth in bonds instead of in cash and bank deposits. The extent to which higher rates will produce this result depends upon the elasticity of demand for securities relative to interest rate changes or, in other words, the elasticity of individual liquidity preferences. If higher rates induce little shift from idle balances, the Treasury's interest burden will be increased without much net gain in the way of reduced liquidity.

The higher interest rates will also encourage persons to sell other securities in order to buy the new government securities, action which will depress security prices and check private investment to a limited extent. This effect is of little importance during a period in which investment is controlled by allocations of materials. The shifting-away from older government bond issues to the new higher rate issues has a somewhat undesirable effect on the government bond market and produces losses for holders of existing government securities.

Secondly, guarantee of bonds against decline in selling prices will increase their attractiveness. This result can be attained by making the bonds redeemable; with this provision, bond purchasers know that they can obtain money at any time from the redemption of the bonds without danger of loss, and thus will be more willing to forgo liquidity. Unfortunately, the granting of the privilege of redemption lessens the extent to which the bonds will be held.

Finally, direct pressures, through advertising, bond drives, payroll deduction plans, etc., can be used to induce persons to cut consumption and buy bonds. The success of these is difficult to predict; unfortunately, in many cases, if persons are "high-pressured" into buying bonds, they will sell other securities (or redeem bonds previously bought), without any change in consumption patterns or net loss of liquidity.

2. *Inducements to Hold.* If a borrowing program is to reduce individual liquidity, some inducement to hold the bonds is highly desirable. The most obvious method would be to make them both nonmarketable and nonredeemable, but such a procedure would interfere drastically with their sale and thus defeat the first aim of the borrowing program. A second and more feasible device is that of providing a scale of interest rates which adjusts the actual rate of interest received to the length of time the bonds are held, the maximum rate being obtained only if the bonds are held to maturity. Interest considerations cannot have a tremendous effect upon bond retention but may exercise some influence, especially if the penalties on early redemption are relatively severe. Investors could be given the choice of bonds with a heavy penalty for early redemption but with a high interest rate, or bonds with lesser penalty but lower maximum interest rate. To the extent that persons bought the former type, the over-all liquidity would be more effectively reduced, but the availability of the second type would facilitate sales to persons unwilling to sacrifice liquidity.

As an alternative, if bonds are made marketable and are allowed to drop below par, persons will be induced to hold them. If they sell, they will lose a portion of their capital, whereas if they hold the bonds until maturity, the full amount will be paid. But some question may be raised about the equity of this procedure, and if it is anticipated by the bond purchasers, they will be less willing to buy.

Finally, various pressures to hold, such as advertising, may be applied. These are of doubtful significance unless they are very drastic. Redemption could be made very unpleasant, through the use of complicated and inconvenient procedures or publication of the names of persons redeeming bonds under the heading of "unpatriotic citizens." But such devices would interfere with sales and would be unpopular politically.

3. *World War II Experience.* The experience of the United States during World War II is of interest as a basis for consideration of possible future policies. Canadian practice was very similar to that in the United States. In both countries, in an attempt to increase bond sales and reduce personal liquidity, an interest rate somewhat higher than prevailing levels was set on the savings bonds, which were designed for sale to individuals. But in order to prevent the use of the higher rate from depressing the prices of existing securities, the bonds were made nonsalable, and a maximum holding per individual was prescribed, while other lower rate bonds were available in unlimited amounts. Secondly, the savings bonds were made redeemable at will, and thus their attractiveness was increased, since not only were they highly liquid, but the redemption feature (with nonsalability) guaranteed against any decline in principal value. This policy was particularly designed to avoid the unhappy consequences after World War I, when Liberty bonds fell well under par.

Thirdly, the interest was payable only at redemption or maturity. By this means the cost to the Treasury of making payments was minimized, and immediate payment of interest into the income stream was avoided. Redemption values (and thus effective interest rates) were established in such a manner that the actual annual interest yield increased progressively the longer the bonds were held. In other words, if the holder redeemed the bonds after a couple of years, the rate which he received was much less than the full annual rate, which was obtainable only if the bonds were held to maturity.

Finally, substantial pressures were applied to persons to buy and hold bonds. Extensive advertising programs, bond drives, and quotas were used, with great reliance placed on the payroll deduction system. If a worker could be induced to authorize a bond deduction each month, the forces of inertia were placed on the side of continued bond purchases.

Without question, the program had some success. But it proved impossible to get more than roughly 25 per cent of the total debt into the hands of individuals. Furthermore, without doubt, most of these bonds were bought out of funds which would have been saved in any event. The purchase of bonds did reduce individual liquidity, however.

### Mandatory Lending

The limited success with the savings bonds suggests that some form of mandatory lending program might have been much more effective. In Canada a program of this type was attempted.

Before discussing the proposal further, it is necessary to distinguish clearly between compulsory saving, in the true sense, and compulsory lending, since the former phrase has often been used when the latter is meant.[4] Under the former a person would be required to save a certain percentage (probably progressive according to income, with a minimum exemption) of his income annually; this would be, of necessity, new savings, and no net liquidation of accumulated wealth would be permitted. In contrast, compulsory lending merely requires the payment of a sum to the government, in addition to regular taxes due, in exchange for a promise of repayment in the future. The taxpayer may be given nonsalable bonds as evidence of this promise or merely a receipt for payment. Compulsory lending may be called "refundable taxation," particularly if no issue of bonds as evidence of the promise of repayment is provided, but the taxpayer is merely given the promise that the supplement to the regular taxes will eventually be returned to him.

Of these two alternatives, compulsory saving would obviously be more effective in curtailing spending but would be tremendously difficult to administer, because of the problems involved in insuring that other assets were not liquidated. Compulsory lending would be less effective as an anti-inflationary device, since persons having previously accumulated liquid savings could spend these amounts if they wished to continue previous spending levels, and thus they would not actually be forced to increase their net savings. But on the other hand, the program would be relatively simple to administer, especially if operated as a supplement to the income tax, and would inevitably reduce total spending. Persons having no margin of accumulated saving would be forced to curtail spending, and others would hesitate to liquidate existing holdings. For many persons the net effect would be merely a transfer of wealth from liquid form to nonsalable bonds or refundable tax receipts, since they would have saved the amounts anyway; but their liquidity would be

---

4 Some authorities believe that a compulsory lending program was killed in the United States in the forties by applying the unpopular name "compulsory savings" to it. Had the program been called one of "refundable taxes," it would have been much more popular politically.

reduced, and they would be prevented from spending this wealth until the end of the inflationary period.

The program would have less direct anti-inflationary effect than an increase in income taxes bringing in the same amount of money, since many persons would consider the amounts as additions to their wealth and maintain spending at higher levels than they would if they received only valueless tax receipts. But nevertheless, the program has certain advantages over income tax increases from the standpoint of over-all fiscal policy. The fact that the payments would eventually be refundable should lessen the adverse incentive effects, to the extent that persons would seek additional income for purposes of saving and recognize the amounts taken from them under the program as constituting increments to their savings. Persons are more likely to do so if they are actually issued bonds than if they are merely given tax receipts and a promise of eventual repayment; Canadian experience with the latter technique in World War II was not reassuring.

A further advantage, compared to further income tax increases, is that of equity. The refunding feature would alleviate the heavy burden placed on the lower income groups and create a backlog of purchasing power for use in any subsequent depression. It likewise would help to meet the problem of taxpayers' fixed savings commitments under sharp income tax increases, since some of these commitments could be allowed as credits against compulsory lending liability. The program would provide a broader and more equitable distribution of bonds than that obtained with a voluntary system.[5]

---

[5] In the United States the suggestions for compulsory lending during World War I did not receive serious attention, in part because of inept handling by the Treasury Department. The so-called "Victory Tax" (a supplement to the income tax, without exemptions) did have a refundable element, as did the excess profits tax.

In Great Britain, compulsory lending, based upon the suggestions of J. M. Keynes, was introduced in 1941, as a supplement to the income tax. The benefits were confined largely to the lower income groups because of the setting of a maximum amount refundable to any taxpayer. Apparently, the workers differentiated very little between the ordinary taxes and the refundable portion, and thus little was gained from the program with respect to incentive effects.

Canada introduced its compulsory lending system in 1942. One half of income taxes paid were made refundable after the war, with a maximum refund of 8 per cent of the income for single persons, 10 per cent for married couples, or $800 and $1,000, respectively, whichever sum was less, with 1 per cent of income or $100 added to the maximum refund for each additional dependent. Because of these limits, only about 15 per cent of income taxes paid were actually refundable. Offsets for various other contractual savings commitments, such as insurance and payment of debt on residential property, were allowed, but not purchases of government bonds. Interest of 2 per cent was paid; a fixed schedule of repayments after the end of the war was specified. Just as in Great Britain, the average taxpayer apparently did not differentiate between the tax and the refundable portion, and thus the system did not avoid

Should compulsory lending be used, there are several major questions to be considered. One is that of the base; while actual experience is confined to an income basis, others, such as spending, could be employed. A second is the question of whether offsets of other amounts saved, as allowed in Canada, are desirable. These complicate administration considerably, but they do mitigate one of the worst inequities of high income taxes in inflationary periods—the "squeezing" of persons with heavy contractual savings obligations. A third question is that of whether interest should be paid. Regardless of the specific base employed, various questions arise about the exact determination of liability. The effectiveness of the system could be greatly increased if liquid wealth were taken into consideration as well, and thus some characteristics of compulsory saving (as distinguished from lending) introduced, but this is very difficult to do administratively.

### Fixed Purchasing Power Bonds

After World War II, in both Canada and the United States the persons who had bought savings bonds suffered heavily from declines in the value of the savings involved due to inflation, while persons who had invested in land, durable goods, or common stocks during the war came out much better financially. There is danger that in future inflationary periods the fear that the inflation control programs will not succeed, and thus that prices will continue to rise, may interfere seriously with the sale of bonds. Accordingly, Sumner Slichter and others have suggested a fixed purchasing power bond, one payable in dollars of given purchasing power (as determined by the appropriate price index) rather than in a constant number of dollars.[6] This plan would eliminate the danger of losses from inflation and thus make the bonds more attractive than the

---

the adverse incentive effects of higher nonrefundable income taxes. As a consequence of these incentive effects, in the form of absenteeism, unwillingness to work overtime, and "loafing on the job," the government abandoned the system in 1944, before the war ended. This experience suggests that in any future use of the system, sharp differentiation of taxes and compulsory loans is essential, even if substantial personnel are required to insure immediate issuance of bonds.

One example of nonwar use of compulsory lending is provided by Ghana, which instituted such a system in 1961 to increase funds available for economic development. The liability is related to income and the tax collected in conjunction with the income tax. Nonsalable bonds are issued.

For a survey of British and Canadian experiences, see W. W. Heller, "Compulsory Lending: The World War II Experience," *National Tax Journal*, Vol. IV (June, 1951), pp. 116–28.

[6] See R. Goode, "A Constant Purchasing Power Savings Bond," *National Tax Journal*, Vol. IV (December, 1951), pp. 332–40.

present bonds, if inflation were anticipated. It might prove feasible to restrict redemption (or at least attainment of full advantage of the constant purchasing power feature) until some time in the future. This provision would encourage persons to hold the bonds until maturity and thus lessen inflationary pressures.

The primary disadvantage of the plan centers around the relationship between present securities and the new; if there was strong fear of inflation, great shifting of investments would occur, with considerable disorganization of security markets. This tendency could be minimized by limiting individual purchases, in the same manner as the savings bond issues.

Another objection is the psychological one that issuance might serve as notice that further inflation was anticipated and lead to a sharp spurt in buying. In addition, the system might weaken the pressures on the government to take other measures to check inflation. If inflation did occur, the government payments would be sharply increased, a matter of considerable concern if inflationary pressures were continuing. It would likewise keep the bondholders from "feeling poorer" as the price level rose, a reaction which serves now to dampen their spending and the inflationary pressures. A fixed purchasing power bond system would add one more "escalator" feature to the economy and thus serve to aggravate inflation when the latter actually got under way.

### Sales of Bonds to Nonbank Financial Institutions

In a major war, it has proved impossible to sell all bonds to individuals; as a consequence, if necessary funds are to be obtained by means other than creating money, some sales must be made to financial institutions. A large market is normally available with nonbank financial institutions, such as insurance companies and mutual savings banks. Sales to these may lessen somewhat the willingness and ability of these institutions to make private loans. The chief advantage of sales to them is the avoidance of the creation of purchasing power, which occurs when the bonds are sold to commercial banks.

### Sales of Bonds to Commercial Banks

When sales to individuals and nonbank financial institutions are inadequate, sales to commercial banks become necessary, unless the government is willing to resort to direct loans from the central banking system. As explained in Chapter 26, the commercial banks are able to create the purchasing power, so long as they have excess reserves, and no deflationary effect at all is exerted by the loans which they make to the government. On the other hand, this type of borrowing has no less direct deflationary effect than the borrowing of idle funds from individuals or nonbank corporations. The latter type of borrowing, however, does lessen the liquidity of the lenders, whereas borrowing from the commercial banks has no such effect, if excess reserves are ample.

Perhaps the most unfortunate aspect of borrowing from the banks is the fact that the banks themselves are placed in the position of having a large supply of very liquid assets, which they can dispose of at any time. This situation interferes seriously with postwar credit control, because of the ability of the banks to replenish their reserves by the sale of the bonds.

In practice, it proved necessary to rely during World War II to a substantial extent on bank borrowing. In part, this policy was desirable in order to facilitate an increase in the money supply necessary for the larger volume of transactions. But in addition, other bond purchases were inadequate, and thus the banks were relied upon to absorb all amounts that could not be sold to nonbank sources, in order to avoid the adverse psychological effects which would arise out of failure to sell all bonds offered. To insure necessary bank participation, the banks were not required to hold reserves against government deposits, and the central banking systems took measures to insure that the banks always had adequate reserves as their nongovernmental deposits increased.

On the other hand, measures were taken to hold bank sales to the minimum. Many issues were restricted to nonbank holders, primarily to keep the banks from earning large amounts of interest on purchasing power which they created. Maximum quotas were set in some instances for bank purchases, and the savings bond issues were pushed as much as possible. During most of the war the government succeeded in avoiding excessive bank sales, but toward the end, such great quantities went into the hands of the banks that there was a tendency toward general declines in the interest rate.

### Sale to the Central Banking System

The final resort in borrowing is the sale of bonds directly to the central banking system—the Federal Reserve banks in the United States. Governments typically have attempted to avoid this type of borrowing for two reasons. In the first place, this procedure directly increases the reserves of the member banks. When the government borrows from the Federal Reserve and draws checks on the deposits created for it in the Federal Reserve, these checks are deposited in commercial banks and, when cleared, increase the reserves of the banks and the power of the member banks to make loans. Thus the borrowing is in itself directly inflationary, if the commercial banks actually make additional loans on the basis of their greater reserves. The second consideration is a purely psychological one; central bank borrowing so closely resembles the printing of paper money as a source of revenue that governments hesitate to use this method for fear of adverse public reactions.

Actually, in World War II the Federal Reserve and, in Canada, the Bank of Canada stood ready to buy government bonds on the open market at any time, in order to insure against a decline in price. As a matter of fact, the Federal Reserve was compelled to absorb a substantial quantity of bonds, in part to assure that the commercial banks had adequate reserves to absorb all issues not otherwise sold and in part to replace cash lost by the banks into circulation, due to a larger volume of transactions. There is actually very little difference in effect, except the psychological ones, between direct sale to the Federal Reserve and indirect sale via the commercial banks. But the direct method was not used.

A few authorities, particularly E. A. Goldenweiser, argued that the government should have sold directly to the Federal Reserve instead of to the commercial banks, with adjustment of reserve requirements in such a manner as to "freeze" the additional reserves gained by the member banks and thus prevent their use as a basis for credit expansion. By this method the bonds could have been kept out of the commercial banks, and thus the excessive liquidity and freedom from credit control avoided, as well as the demand to protect bond prices from falling in the postwar period. In addition, the government's interest charges could have been materially reduced. The success of this program would have depended primarily upon the success with which the additional reserves could have been frozen and the psychological reactions to this type of program

## OTHER ASPECTS OF BORROWING POLICY

Apart from the problems related to the sources of funds, there are two major questions which must be considered in determining exact borrowing policy. One is the question of the time periods for which securities are issued; the second is that of the interest rate.

### Short- versus Long-Term Borrowing

In strong inflationary periods in which the interest rate has been held down to preinflation levels, as in World War II, short-term borrowing is disadvantageous for several reasons. Short-term securities provide maximum liquidity and thus are least effective in freezing purchasing power. Secondly, the constant refunding is a source of considerable nuisance and expense. If the securities are not replaced by long-term securities prior to the time interest rates are permitted to rise, the over-all interest costs will rise. On the other hand, the short-term securities can tap some funds from individuals unobtainable on a long-term basis, and thus lessen the need for resort to sources which are more inflationary. In practice, in World War II the United States government relied heavily on short-term issues, which comprised 23 per cent of the debt at the end of the war.

On the other hand, as noted early in the chapter, in an inflationary period in which interest rates are permitted to rise in order to check inflation, short-term borrowing is advantageous, since it allows the government to meet its borrowing needs without making long-term commitments at high interest rates. The relatively liquid nature of the short-term securities is a disadvantage, but may well not be a significant one so far as actual effects upon spending are concerned.

### The Interest Rates

Unlike private borrowers, the government is not at the mercy of the current market rates, since, in conjunction with the central banking system, it has the power to adjust the market rate, within limits. But a basic dilemma is obviously encountered; lower interest rates reduce costs of borrowing but lessen the effectiveness of the inflation control program. Low rates are inevitably somewhat less successful than higher rates in drawing funds out of liquid holdings of individuals and businesses (and thus increase reliance on bank borrowing), and they also are less restrictive on business investment. In determining interest rate policy in inflationary periods, the government must obviously consider the effects of the program upon the economy, as well as upon its own borrowing costs.

During World War II the United States government essentially froze interest rates at levels prevailing at the beginning of the war, except for the somewhat higher rate paid on savings bonds, discussed in a previous section. So far as the long-term marketable issues were concerned, it was recognized that a higher rate would have relatively little effectiveness as an anti-inflationary measure in periods in which business investment was rigidly controlled. On the other hand, any increase would depress the selling prices of existing issues and increase the interest burden of the government. Thus the rate was set at 2.5 per cent; in order to avoid postponement of buying in anticipation of higher rates, the government announced that it would maintain this rate throughout the war, by appropriate Federal Reserve action if necessary. This policy was adhered to throughout. All things considered, it is likely that this program was the most satisfactory; it is doubtful whether higher interest rates during the war, within reasonable limits, would have had much anti-inflationary effect.[7]

The United States policy on short-term rates proved to be much less satisfactory than its long-term program. The short-term rates were also frozen at prewar levels, ⅜ per cent for ninety-day bills and ⅞ per cent for treasury certificates with from nine- to twelve-month maturity. The low rates were favored partly as a means of minimizing interest costs and partly in order to hold down bond yields. It was generally believed that low short-term rates help to maintain low long-term rates. Unfortunately, however, once the government pledged the maintenance of the 2.5 per cent rate on long-term bonds, the gains to investors from buying short-term securities largely disappeared. The normal relative advantages of the short-term investments, namely, their greater liquidity and minimum danger of capital loss, were lost once the long-term bonds gained the same features through essential guarantee of their prices. Thus the market for short-term securities largely vanished, and the Federal Reserve was forced to absorb large quantities of the amounts offered on the market. But the low-rate policy was continued throughout the war.

## DEBT MANAGEMENT IN MILD INFLATIONARY PERIODS

As explained above, in periods of heavy defense spending, government borrowing is essential if the primary objectives are to be attained. But in mild inflationary periods, such as in the years immediately following World War II, it should be possible to maintain surpluses and thus reduce the debt. The surpluses not only aid in restricting inflation but also eliminate from the economy the disturbing influences of the debt. In the period after World War II, however, substantial defense activities and strong political demands for tax reductions greatly restricted the hands of the governments in reducing debt.

Apart from debt retirement, other policies employed with respect to the debt may have substantial effects in the control of inflation. The most significant of these is the interest rate policy, a question widely debated in the United States after World War II. This is a question of monetary policy rather than debt management, but will be reviewed briefly.

[7] In Canada, interest rates were considerably higher at the beginning of the war than the rates in the United States. When the war started, the government deliberately lowered the rate in order to lessen the interest costs. In 1939 the average yield on government issues was 3.5 per cent, while in 1945 it was 2.6 per cent. The low rate was maintained by purchases of bonds by the Bank of Canada and the chartered banks when necessary.

### Interest Rate Policy

It may be argued that increases in the interest rate (and the accompanying decline in the prices of existing bond issues) constitute an effective anti-inflationary weapon in nonwar inflationary periods. This point of view was accepted by most economists[8] after World War II, as well as by the Federal Reserve System. A higher rate may be anti-inflationary in several ways. Most importantly, the decline in federal bond prices below par makes the holders—especially the commercial banks—reluctant to sell them prior to maturity. Thus the ability of the banks and other financial institutions to expand loans at will by disposing of government bonds is seriously checked, and the over-all credit control policy becomes more effective. Secondly, the higher market interest rate will discourage some private investment. Thirdly, individuals, as well as institutions, will be encouraged to hold the bonds instead of selling them to obtain funds for consumption or business expansion. Fourthly, the higher rate may induce some individuals to buy additional bonds and thus not only lessen their liquidity but get some of the bonds out of the hands of the banks.

### The Treasury–Federal Reserve Controversy

However, in the postwar period the Treasury strongly opposed any policy which would have raised government interest rates. The Treasury was interested, directly and immediately, in minimizing the government's interest burden. The basic economic argument for the Treasury's point of view was the claim that declines in bond prices and higher interest rates would have little real effectiveness in checking inflation. In the first place, the large volume of current investment financed by surplus funds which the corporations had on hand from profits would not be deterred by the interest policy. Secondly, it is even doubtful whether investment financed by borrowing is very sensitive to minor changes in the rate. If the bonds were allowed to drop below par, it is true that the banks would be less willing to sell them in order to increase loans. But the significance of this effect upon the volume of investment may not be great. In addition, it was argued that in the postwar inflation the principal inflationary pressures arose from consumer and government spending; accordingly, a very great reduction in investment would be required to curb the inflation. Such a reduction would have some undesirable effects, since increases in the output of particularly scarce goods would be checked. Tighter credit, like tax increases, does not differentiate between investment which is particu-

---

[8] See, for example, the article by L. V. Chandler, "Federal Reserve Policy and Federal Debt," *American Economic Review*. Vol. XXXIX (March. 1949), pp 405–29

larly inflationary and that which ultimately contributes toward the checking of inflation by bringing about increases in output of goods in short supply.

This argument is not easily resolved. It is certain that higher interest rates would have some deflationary effect. If the Federal Reserve System had not supported government bond prices, continued high levels of consumer and government spending could have caused sharp increases in interest rates and tightening of credit, because the money supply would have become increasingly inadequate. But whether the over-all anti-inflationary effects would have been sufficiently great to warrant the added interest cost is a matter of debate. The author is inclined to accept the Treasury point of view.

An alternative to higher interest rates which has been frequently proposed is a plan which would require the banks to keep a secondary reserve of government bonds in addition to their normal reserves. This policy would essentially freeze a substantial sum of bonds in the hands of the banks and have much the same effect as a further decline in bond prices. Such a plan has been favored by the Federal Reserve banks but has never been carried into effect, primarily because of the opposition of the commercial banks, which fear the effects of such a program on their earnings.

### Canadian Policy

In Canada the controversy never reached the sharpness that was encountered in the United States, although there were diverse points of view. Bond prices were held relatively constant until 1950, after which they were allowed to rise by open-market selling, the basic rate going from 2.75 per cent in June, 1950, to 3.5 per cent by June, 1952. The increase was thus considerably greater than that in the United States, in conformity with the Canadian government's policy of making thorough use of various inflation control devices. As in the United States, rates were driven up rather sharply in 1956 and early 1957, only to be relaxed as business activity commenced to decline. No open disagreement between the government and the Bank of Canada occurred in the postwar years, except for an exchange between the president of the bank and party leaders in the 1958 campaign over the bank policies in tightening credit in 1957.

In 1960 and 1961, however, a sharp difference of opinion developed between the Bank of Canada and the government; the bank, convinced that inflationary pressures were still strong, pursued a high-rate policy, whereas the government, more concerned about unemployment and increased output, sought a lower rate. When the bank refused to give way, the government took the unprecedented action of ousting the governor of the bank.

### Refunding Policies

Anti-inflationary debt management also requires effective refunding policies. Since the short-term obligations are much more liquid than the long-term, especially if the latter are allowed to fall below par, replacement of short-term by long-term securities facilitates inflation control, although at the expense of higher interest costs.

Likewise, refunding of bank-held debt by borrowing from other sources helps to check inflationary influences if the banks do not relend equivalent amounts. Even if they do, the fact that the bonds have passed out of their hands facilitates reinstatement of effective credit control over a period of time. The United States government had considerable success in this program after World War II; commercial bank holdings fell from $93 billion in 1946 to $57 billion in 1951. Not all of this change was a result of deliberate policy, as some represented disposal of the bonds by the banks in order to make other loans.

A special refunding problem arose with the savings bonds. When these were issued during World War II, it was widely believed that by the time they came due, the country might be in a depression and that their repayment, from funds obtained from other sources of borrowing, would facilitate recovery. In such periods, some of the bondholders would spend the amounts received, whereas most of the funds borrowed from other sources would otherwise have been idle. Actually, however, the bonds commenced to mature in a period in which inflationary pressures were continuing. Accordingly, the government provided for an automatic extension of time, the interest continuing to accrue.

## DEBT MANAGEMENT POLICIES IN DEPRESSIONS

The problems of borrowing policies and debt management are less serious in depressions than during periods of inflation. Depressions are characterized by large idle balances and excess bank reserves, because of the limited investment opportunities. If the government borrows these funds or new current savings which would not find outlet in investment (and thus would tend to depress the economy still further if the government did not spend equivalent amounts), the borrowing, in itself, will have no contractionary effect at all. If there is any tendency toward tightening of money markets, central bank open-market purchasing of bonds will restore an adequate supply of funds.

With regard to the exact source of funds, it is obviously not desirable to attempt to get individuals to sacrifice consumption in order to buy bonds, as it is during war periods. On the other hand, the borrowing of otherwise idle funds from individuals and financial institutions has no contractionary effect. The commercial banks can purchase almost unlimited amounts of government bonds, so long as their reserves are maintained at high levels by central bank action. But there is some merit in holding sales to these banks as low as possible; if the banks acquire large quantities of government bonds, their lending policies are difficult to control in any subsequent inflationary period, since they can obtain additional reserves at will by the sale of bonds.

Sale of bonds to the Federal Reserve would have the merits of minimizing the deflationary influence and increasing commercial bank reserves at the same time. The only limitation is the purely psychological one of interfering further with general business confidence. There is actually very little difference in effect between direct sale of the bonds to the Federal Reserve and sale to the public at the time the Federal Reserve is acquiring the same volume of bonds through open-market purchasing. The only difference is the purely psychological one; sale to the Federal Reserve too closely resembles the printing of paper money.

So far as existing debt is concerned, retirement is out of the question in depressions, because of its deflationary consequences. As bond issues mature or savings bonds are cashed in, they must be replaced by new loans. Few refunding difficulties are likely to be encountered, because of the ready availability of liquid capital and the resources of the central banking system. The existence of the savings bonds, which may be redeemed at will, is itself a factor in the economy which facilitates recovery.

## REFERENCES

MURPHY, H. C. *National Debt in War and Transition.* New York: McGraw-Hill Book Co., Inc., 1950.
    A complete survey of World War II debt policies in the United States, from the Treasury viewpoint.
ABBOTT, C. C. *The Federal Debt.* New York: Twentieth Century Fund, 1953.
    A detailed analysis of the significance of the national debt.
HART, A. G. *Defense and the Dollar.* New York: Twentieth Century Fund, 1953.
    Monetary and debt policies in inflationary periods.

ROLPH, E. R. "Principles of Debt Management," *American Economic Review*, Vol. XLVII (June, 1957), pp. 302–20.

An analysis of the determination of the optimum debt structure in terms of interest cost and desired deflationary effect.

SMITH, W. L. *Debt Management in the United States*. Study Paper No. 19, Joint Economic Committee, Congress of the United States. Washington, D.C.: U.S. Government Printing Office, 1960.

One of the best analyses of debt management.

MUSGRAVE, R. A. *The Theory of Public Finance*, chap. xxiv. New York: McGraw-Hill Book Co., Inc., 1959.

# Chapter 31

# GOVERNMENT FINANCE
# AND ECONOMIC GROWTH

One of the most significant trends in economics and politics in recent years has been the great emphasis placed on the question of economic growth, that is, the annual rate of increase in total output. In the United States the emphasis is in part a product of the cold war and the desire to maintain a rate of growth comparable to that of the Soviet Union. In less developed areas of the world, such as Africa, the numerous newly independent states are extremely anxious to raise their standards of living in a short period of time to the levels of the more mature economies. This increased attention to growth has shifted emphasis in public finance from more traditional questions and fiscal policy problems relating to unemployment and inflation to those of stimulation of growth.

### Potential versus Actual Growth Rates

A distinction must be made between the potential growth rate of a country and the actual rate. The potential rate is the maximum which can be attained, given the basic determinants:

1. The rate of technological development, which influences the output possible per unit of labor and other resources.

2. The trends in population: in number, age composition, education, experience, and the like.

3. The trends in the availability of natural resources: exhaustion of existing supplies, development of new ones, etc.

4. The rate of capital formation at full employment. Increased output is made possible primarily by accumulation of a greater stock of capital goods. In turn, the potential rate of capital formation is controlled by the percentage of national income saved at full-employment levels. Real investment is of necessity limited to the volume of savings at full employment if general price level stability is to be attained.

The actual growth rate, that is, the path followed by the economy, cannot, of course, exceed the potential rate. But it may lag behind. One possible cause is the failure to use available technological developments, organizational skills, and the like. But the more significant one is the failure to attain full employment, due, in turn, to inadequate aggregate demand in the economy, as outlined in the previous chapters.

### The Goals of Economic Growth

There are therefore two major questions relating to goals in this field. The first is the question of the optimum potential rate of growth. Of the various determinants of this rate, the most significant one over which governments can exercise influence is the rate of capital formation. The question of the optimum is therefore primarily the question of the desired allocation of output between present and future consumption. This decision, as on all questions relating to goals, must be based upon value judgments—the thinking of contemporary society on the question—and cannot be derived by scientific analysis. It would appear from everyday observations that there is prevailing sentiment in such countries as the United States and Canada for a somewhat higher rate of growth than has been occurring—perhaps one or two percentage points more. In the underdeveloped countries of the world, there is widespread desire for a much more rapid rate of growth than is being attained. The second goal, on which there is little disagreement, is that of insuring that the actual rate of growth coincides with the potential rate.

Attention will be given in the next section to growth in mature economies, and in the following one to the underdeveloped economies.

## THE MATURE ECONOMIES

The term *mature economy* is used in reference to such countries as the United States, Canada, and the countries of western Europe, in which more or less complete use is made of available technology, and the stocks of capital goods relative to national income and the per capita real incomes are relatively high compared to other areas.

### Increase in the Potential Growth Rate

Under the assumption that such societies wish a higher potential growth rate than that now attained, there are several types of tax and expenditure policies which may be employed to attain this goal:

1. Aid to research, to speed technological development. Such aid may take the form of special tax concessions, like the new Canadian rule which permits firms to deduct 150 per cent of the cost of certain research

expenditures. Or governments may undertake, directly or through grants, various types of basic research.

2. Further increases in the levels of education.

3. Most significantly, an increase in the potential rate of capital formation by increasing the percentage of national income saved at full-employment levels. There are several possible approaches, some of which have been discussed in earlier chapters:

*a*) Shift in tax burden from higher to lower income levels. Under the assumption that persons in the higher income groups save greater percentages of their incomes, such a shift will result in an over-all increase in the percentage of total income saved. Some reaction of this type is almost inevitable. But studies in recent years of marginal propensities to save suggest that the differences in these propensities between high and low income levels are less than has typically been believed, and thus the effects would be less than anticipated.[1] Some reduction in taxes at very high income levels, however, would perhaps have substantial effect. Reductions in the corporate income tax may have significant effect on corporate savings.

Unfortunately, such a shift may run counter to accepted standards of equity, particularly if the magnitude of the shift is substantial.

*b*) Shift from the income basis to the expenditure basis, through the greater use of commodity or expenditure taxes. Such a shift is likely to transfer burden to the lower income groups, and also provide some definite incentive to save more and spend less. The sales tax does the former; the expenditure tax, which can be made highly progressive, is of course more effective from an incentive standpoint. The net effect of such a shift depends upon a number of factors, but particularly upon the purposes for which money is saved, and expectations about future tax changes. If the savings are made now for expenditures to be undertaken in the immediate future when the tax is still in effect, the shift to an expenditure basis will have little effect. The shift will have greatest effect if the savings are made as a permanent reserve or if it is expected that the taxes will be temporary.[2]

---

[1] For a summary, see T. R. Beard, "Progressive Income Taxation, Income Redistribution, and the Consumption Function," *National Tax Journal*, Vol. XIII (June, 1960), pp. 168–77.

[2] For discussions of the question, see M. A. Willemsen, "The Effect upon the Rate of Private Savings of a Change from a Personal Income Tax to a Personal Expenditure Tax," *National Tax Journal*, Vol. XIV (March, 1961), pp. 98–103; A. R. Prest, "The Expenditure Tax and Savings," *Economic Journal*, Vol. LXI (September, 1959), pp. 483–89; and A. Morag, "Deflationary Effects of Outlay and Income Taxes," *Journal of Political Economy*, Vol. LXVII (June, 1959), pp. 266–74.

*c*) Increased budgetary surpluses. One simple method is to increase the tax level relative to government expenditures; the surplus acquired can be made available for private borrowing via government debt retirement. To the extent to which the funds would have been spent on consumption, there is a net increase in savings in the economy as a whole.

As will be pointed out later, these policies designed to increase savings may greatly aggravate the problem of attaining the potential rate of growth.

### The Actual Rate

Typically, the more pressing problem of the mature economy is to insure that the actual rate of economic growth coincides with the potential rate, concurrently with the maintenance of a reasonably stable general price level. First, this relationship will be attained only if there are no disincentives preventing effective utilization of the best available techniques and methods of organization, or the supplying of optimum labor-hours. Furthermore, it will be attained only if aggregate demand—total expenditure—in the economy grows at exactly the same pace as full-employment output. If expenditure fails to keep up with output, sales will lag below output, production will decline, and unemployment will prevent attainment of the potential growth rate. Or if total demand outruns output, inflation will occur. There are three major potential sources of a lag:

1. A tendency for investment to lag behind savings, because the increasing stock of capital goods reduces the marginal productivity of capital and the rate of profit. Since capital tends to rise faster than labor supply, profits will tend to fall, unless the rising quantity of capital equipment is offset by sufficiently rapid technological change, or by continually improving expectations about the future, the latter a remote possibility at best. This doctrine of declining profits, which has been stressed by various writers for centuries, is the basis, for example, of the analysis by Challis Hall, in the most complete study yet made of the relationship of fiscal policy and growth.[3] Inadequate investment also played a major role in the stagnation thesis popular in the 1930's, which attributed the lack of investment opportunities to a lag in technological change, an increase in capital-saving inventions, the decline of the frontier, and other factors.

2. A tendency for saving to rise more rapidly than national income as income continues to rise. This long-popular doctrine has been largely destroyed by empirical studies which show the absence of any such tendency. But it represents a possible cause in a society in which consumer wants become satiated at certain levels.

[3] *Fiscal Policy for Stable Growth* (New York: Holt-Rinehart, 1960).

3. Autonomous changes in total spending, caused, for example, by the ending of a period of high defense spending.

Regardless of the cause of a cyclical movement, it may be very difficult for the economy to level off at the full-employment rate of growth because of the acceleration principle; as the rate of expansion slows down as full employment is attained, a fall in investment is likely, with consequent decline in business activity.

Thus the primary general aim of tax and expenditure policy, so far as attainment of the potential growth rate is concerned, is to offset the operation of the forces within the economy which tend to restrict investment below the full-employment levels of savings, and to nullify the influence of extraneous influences which push the economy off the potential growth path. The latter goal requires the use of policies discussed in the fiscal policy chapters, adjusted in terms of the specific circumstances. The present discussion will center on the longer range issue of maintaining an adequate volume of investment. In the last five years, in both the United States and Canada, there would appear to be a definite investment lag.

### Structural Reforms to Increase Investment

Certain types of structural reforms in the federal tax and expenditure structure are suggested to aid in increasing the volume of investment and thus the likelihood of holding the actual growth rate to the potential rate.

The first is a shift in relative tax burden off the higher income groups, and off business income generally. Those in the higher income groups are the ones most likely to undertake business development and expansion; the lower the taxes on them, the greater the incentive to do so, and the greater the quantity of funds which they have available for the purpose. Reduction in the corporate income tax and still more lenient treatment of capital gains should also facilitate investment. A general tax differential in favor of property income would do so as well. These are, in general, the same policies which would increase the potential rate of saving.

However, these policies, other than perhaps a reduction in the very top-level income tax brackets, run so obviously contrary to usually accepted equity standards that their use on any scale is almost unconceivable. More lenient treatment of property income compared to labor income violates the basic equity rules relating to equal treatment of equals. Furthermore, as noted below, such a policy will aggravate the task of maintaining aggregate consumption demand needed to justify the high level of investment activity.

Another type of change in the tax structure consists of special tax concessions for new investment. Increased carry-over of losses is significant in reducing the risk element. Accelerated depreciation, with higher deductions in the first years, also lessens risk and increases the supply of working capital. Investment credits or tax credits for new investment provide a direct incentive to undertake investment. This is particularly true if the concessions are confined to net increases in the firm's investment (total investment less depreciation), although this type of credit gives no reduction for modernization. Unfortunately, except for the risk-reducing element, this type of change is not likely to provide continuing incentive for additional investment; it is a type of policy which is most effective when it is first introduced. Demand for the commodities produced with new capital is over a long period the prime determinant of the volume of investment. It would appear that only continued liberalization of the concession policies could provide a continuing stimulus of any magnitude.

### Over-all Budget Adjustments to Increase Spending

While structural changes primarily affecting investment may have some influence in holding investment to high levels and thus facilitating attainment of the optimum growth pattern, they may prove to be inadequate. The general alternative is one of policies designed to increase total demand—particularly consumption demand—by adjustments in the over-all levels of government expenditures and taxes. An increase in the government deficit will almost certainly increase aggregate demand, since the expenditure of the funds by the government will not be offset by an equivalent decline in private spending under usual circumstances. The effect will be maximized if the funds to cover the deficit are created by the central banking system. Or similar results can be obtained by maintaining the same level of government deficit but increasing both government spending and taxation; the taxes will typically reduce spending less than the amount collected because some will be absorbed from savings without an equivalent decline in investment. Each approach has certain merits; the deficit approach involves a smaller increase in the scope of the government sector but, on the other hand, involves a continuous increase in the government debt. Either taxes, which have repressive incentive effects, must be increased to cover the interest, or the debt must be allowed to grow still faster, with adverse psychological effects. Another alternative to increased consumption is a shift in tax burden from high-income groups to lower groups.[4]

[4] A partial or perhaps complete substitute for this approach is increased use of central bank open-market buying, which will continue to lower the interest rate and encourage investment. The problem, however, is that it is extremely difficult to drive the rate of interest below certain levels.

The basic difficulty with this general approach is that it runs directly contrary to the goal of increasing the potential rate of growth by increasing the portion of national income saved. Resort to a program of deficits, or to one which reduces the taxes on the lower income groups, will without question increase total demand in the economy, but at the expense of a higher potential rate of capital formation.

Thus the basic dilemma of government policy to maintain a high, stable rate of growth is apparent. Any increase in the percentage of national income saved and any general shift in tax burdens away from investment income will make more difficult the task of holding the actual rate of economic growth on the path of the potential growth, if there is any tendency toward inadequate total demand. Thus, compromise among the conflicting aims is necessary. Certain adjustments in tax policy, particularly reduction of very high marginal income tax rates which yield little money, and special concessions to business investment, may help significantly in holding up the volume of investment. But if these fail, some reduction in the potential rate of growth by acceptance of a lower ratio of savings to national income at full employment appears to be essential. Otherwise, the potential rate cannot be attained.

This discussion suggests the two schools of thought on reform of the federal tax structure. That represented, for example, in the writings of Dan Throop Smith[5] urges liberalization of taxation as affecting the higher income levels and business investment, and increased reliance on commodity taxation primarily affecting the lower income levels, on the basis that tax concessions to investment will aid growth, without being offset by the adverse effect on consumption caused by the relatively heavier burden on lower income groups. The other approach stresses the need for holding up the level of consumption and thus opposes any general shift in relative tax burdens to the lower income levels.

### More Extreme Proposals

One of the more extreme proposals is that of Knorr and Baumol,[6] which was introduced in Canada in revised form in 1962.[7] The corporation income tax would be replaced, under the proposal, by a value-added tax, under which special tax concessions would be provided for firms increasing output. Thus, transfer of resources to growing firms would be

[5] *Federal Tax Reform* (New York: McGraw-Hill Book Co., Inc., 1961). Smith is much less extreme than others who take the same general approach.

[6] See K. Knorr and W. J. Baumol, *What Price Economic Growth?* (Englewood Cliffs, N.J.: Prentice-Hall, Inc., 1961).

[7] See W. C. Shakespeare, "Canadian Income Tax Amendments in 1962," *Canadian Tax Journal*, Vol. XII (January–February, 1963), pp. 19–29.

facilitated, and firms would be given particular incentive to seek out new markets. The relative tax penalty on nongrowing firms would cause a shift of resources away from them. The program would be accompanied by fiscal measures designed to maintain adequate total demand; the authors argue, however, that maintaining demand alone is not adequate, and some pressure must be placed on firms to expand or shift resources into new and expanding fields. The Canadian version involves tax concessions under the income tax to firms which have increased sales over the previous year. Administrative problems relating to definition of increased output without question are serious; there is also some doubt about the effectiveness of this type of approach in increasing output. The basic issue is: Can output increases be brought about by any means other than growing demand for the firm's products?

### Continuing Inflationary Pressures

The discussion of the preceding paragraphs has been based on the assumption of continuing inadequacy of investment and thus of total demand. Another possible situation is one in which there is no deficiency in total demand, but instead continuing full employment and some inflationary pressures. Under these circumstances, the goal is primarily one of increasing savings at the expense of consumption. Tight general fiscal policy, with relatively high general tax levels affecting the typical family, will discourage consumption. At the same time, low-interest rate policy brought about by the central banking authorities will facilitate a high level of investment. While low interest rates probably have little effect in stimulating investment during severe depressions, they probably have substantial effect under full-employment conditions. If inflationary pressures are particularly strong, resort to an expenditure tax may be warranted to reduce consumption still more.

If, however, continuing inflation is a product of the pressure of labor unions on wages rather than excessive demand, it is very difficult to prevent it by fiscal or monetary policy without creating substantial unemployment, and perhaps not even then. Any reduction in aggregate demand will simply push the economy below full-employment levels. Musgrave argues that the only potential fiscal policy solution to this problem is one which will bring a higher rate of capital formation, to allow productivity to rise more rapidly and thus avoid the necessity for price increases in response to wage increases. This, however, may also be difficult to attain without the use of policies which will result in inadequate consumer demand. On the whole, the problem of labor-induced inflation probably cannot be controlled by fiscal measures.

## THE DEVELOPING ECONOMIES

The problems of the developing economies of the world are substantially different from those of the mature economies. These countries are characterized by low per capita incomes compared to the mature economies—as low as $100 per year, for example; heavy reliance on subsistence agriculture; primary reliance for exports on a few basic farm crops; very limited levels of education; a small stock of capital goods compared to the labor supply; and in many, a very slow rate of growth over the centuries. All have access to modern technology, but are able to make little use of it. There are, of course, major variations among the developing areas; the southeast Asian countries, for example, are greatly overpopulated compared to food supply, whereas tropical Africa is not. Parts of South America suffer from large, poorly utilized land holdings, while in many parts of Africa, there is not private ownership of farm land. Cultural traditions are major obstacles to development in some areas, but not in others. Democratic government does well in some countries and has failed miserably elsewhere. But the common characteristics are of sufficient importance that some generalizations about public finance in such economies are useful.

The primary economic goal of these countries is to raise very sharply the level of per capita real income to bring it in line with the levels in the mature economies. Such an increase requires two major developments. The first is rapid improvement in levels of education and technical and organizational skills. The second is a much higher rate of capital formation, which will increase the stock of capital goods and permit introduction of modern technology. Since these changes have obviously not occurred automatically, governments must play a major role in their accomplishment.

### Governmental Activities and Expenditures

It is not possible to analyze in detail the various government activity and expenditure programs designed to bring rapid economic growth, but some brief review is possible. One of the characteristics of the last decade has been the establishment of development plans which seek to establish a co-ordinated program of government activity for a period of several years. The more elaborate plans include not only the governmental activities themselves, but also data of projected growth in the private sectors of the economy as well, aided by various government programs. The major fields in which increased government activities are regarded as imperative are noted below.

1. *Education.* One of the most urgently needed programs in many of these countries is increased education. While many have made great strides in recent years—Ghana, for example has 90 per cent of the children of primary school age in school—they still have a long way to go. In Uganda, for example, in recent years there have been about six hundred high school graduates a year, with a population of 6.5 million. The shortage of teachers is, of course, a serious bottleneck in most of the countries. Increased educational levels must be accompanied by increased economic development generally, or persons completing higher levels of education may not be able to find employment requiring these levels, to the detriment of morale.

2. *Public Health.* A major obstacle to increased production in many countries is the prevalence of endemic diseases, which greatly reduce work capacity. Governmental health programs may pay extremely high dividends in the form of increased output.

3. *Transport.* Improved rail and highway facilities are imperative to facilitate economic development and integration of the regions of the developing economies. These activities must under the circumstances be in government hands.

4. *Improvements in Agriculture and Lessened Dependence on Subsistence Production.* Most agricultural production in these countries (except on plantations) is operated on a small-scale, primitive basis. Improvements can be brought about primarily only by governmental assistance, in the form of agricultural extension work, eradication of the sources of livestock disease, particularly the tsetse fly, research for improved crops suitable to the areas, improved land tenure systems, and in some instances establishment of farm co-operatives.

5. *Industrial Development.* The rule is now almost universally accepted that industrial development must be fostered in developing economies, even in those which have few comparative advantages for industry. An attempt to bring a sharp increase in living standards with primary dependence on agriculture alone is extremely difficult; under such conditions, most goods necessary for higher living standards must be imported, and the ability to import is severely restricted by inadequacies of world markets for the farm produce of these countries. Industrial development is likewise necessary to provide employment opportunities commensurate with growing educational levels.

There are two primary approaches to the question of the role of government in industrial development. The countries use a combination of the two, but with varying emphasis. The first is direct governmental undertaking of major industrial enterprises, particularly those which will convey important secondary benefits to the economy but are not directly profitable to private enterprise, particularly in light of the high-risk element in a newly developing and perhaps politically unstable economy. Many of the countries have established development corporations which directly or indirectly undertake industrial activity. The other alternative is for the government to concentrate on encouragement to private enterprise. There are various forms of such assistance, such as provision of a portion of the capital, granting of tax concessions, outright subsidies, and the like, as well as tariff protection, which is often of utmost importance. The traditional economic arguments against tariff protection require reconsideration when applied to a developing economy; the important secondary benefits of new industry, the need for lessened reliance on basic primary production, and the competition of established producers in other countries warrant the use of tariffs which would be objectionable in developed economies.

The decision on the relative role of governmental production and governmental encouragement to private enterprise cannot be made on any doctrinaire basis, but must be made in light of the relative advantages of the two approaches in each particular circumstance. It is important for governments to keep in mind, however, that if private investment is to be encouraged, all steps must be taken to provide safeguards for these investments. This task is sometimes difficult to do under the political conditions of a newly developing country.

### Financing of Economic Growth

As noted in the previous section, more rapid economic growth requires provision of higher levels of education and other basic governmental services, as well as a higher rate of capital formation in production facilities, whether in private or governmental hands. Except to the extent to which unutilized or underutilized resources can be employed, growth requires the transfer of resources from consumption (or use in aspects of capital formation not significant for economic growth) to government or to private capital formation. The only other possible alternative is foreign investment, which allows increased importation of capital goods, but this is usually limited in potential amount. While it is the transfer of resources which is significant for growth, this is facilitated by the transfer of funds from savers to government or private enterprise; this transfer avoids the necessity for credit creation to offset the sums being hoarded.

The primary instrument for the transfer of funds to the government for the financing of governmental services or development projects is, of course, taxation. Taxes not only can force a curtailment of consumption, but also may be used to discourage investments not regarded as significant for development, and to provide incentives to alter economic behavior in such a way as to aid growth, such as to save more, enter the market sector from subsistence agriculture, work longer periods, etc. However, the potential dangers from taxation, which are present in all countries, are particularly hazardous in the developing economies. In the first place, there is a relatively limited potential margin between actual incomes and subsistence incomes, and unless the taxes are framed carefully, there is the danger of driving people below subsistence. Secondly, there is particular danger of adverse effects on incentives to work, to save, and to develop businesses under the circumstances of such an economy, and any such adverse effects are particularly serious in their consequences. In other words, without careful framing of the tax structure, undesirable incentive effects will outweigh the favorable ones. As a matter of fact, the extent to which the tax structure can be framed in such a way as to obtain advantageous rather than undesirable effects will be a major factor in influencing the rate of economic development. One of the major problems is that the type of taxation which most satisfactorily recovers for the government a portion of the gains from the rising national income—the income tax—is the form most disadvantageous in terms of incentives. One final major consideration affecting the development of a tax structure in a developing economy is the unsuitability for a highly developed tax structure of what may be called the general tax environment. The low levels of literacy, inadequate record keeping, limited personnel with the training necessary for tax administration and audit, limited use of bank accounts, the importance of subsistence production, and, in some areas, low levels of integrity make operation of the tax systems more difficult.

Given the general background and the problems, brief review will be made of the potential use of the major forms of taxes under such circumstances:

1. *Income Taxation.* The income tax offers several advantages. It can tap more equitably the above-subsistence income and be made progressive relative to the size of the surplus. The yield will increase more rapidly than the growth of national income. The tax catches the unearned income produced by growth, such as speculative gains and increases in land values, more effectively than other methods. In countries in which a relatively small proportion of the population gains a high percentage of the total income, the tax can have important redistributive effects.

Unfortunately, effective administration of an income tax with a broad coverage is extremely difficult under the typical conditions of a developing economy. Accurate reporting of income for a large sector of the population is impossible to attain. Furthermore, the tax, especially with high marginal rates, is almost certain to have some effect in discouraging investment, and perhaps even work. Even if these effects are not significant, the tax certainly provides no incentive to save more and spend less, and is likely to be borne in considerable measure out of funds which would in any event be saved. All things considered, therefore, it is necessary to confine the income tax in its usual form to the middle and higher income levels, thus excluding the typical family from the tax, and to limit the degree of progression in the rate structure. Thus the yield potentials are limited. Except in special circumstances, in which there is a substantial middle and higher income group, it is difficult for a developing economy to obtain more than 20 per cent of its revenue from an income tax, and many such countries get much less than this.

2. *The Personal Tax.* In order to apply some form of direct taxation to all adults in an effort to lessen dependence on indirect taxation and increase tax consciousness, a number of developing economies have introduced levies known as personal taxes, either on a flat poll tax basis or with some degree of graduation up to the income level at which the income tax commences. A minimum payment is required of all persons except the destitute, freed by administrative action. No exact determination of income is made, but the taxpayers are placed in rate groups by local assessment committees. One goal of the taxes has been to force subsistence farmers to make some sales on the market or to obtain jobs in order to gain money income with which to pay the tax. The taxes are important as steppingstones to more widespread coverage of income taxation.

3. *Corporate Taxation.* In many developing countries the corporate tax offers greater revenue potential than the personal income tax, because of the importance of large and often foreign-owned companies. Taxation of corporate profits in part absorbs funds which would otherwise be used for expansion, and does little to reduce consumption; thus, restraint in their use is desirable. But to some extent the tax will prevent the earnings from escaping to overseas owners of the companies.

In order to reduce the impact of corporate taxes on private business investment, various concessions are frequently made by developing countries. These may take the form of very liberal "carry-forward of loss" provisions, and accelerated depreciation, as in the mature economies. Or they make take the form of "tax holiday" or "pioneer companies" legislation, as in Porto Rico, Nigeria, and elsewhere. Under this type of program, complete tax exemption is provided for new firms for the first ten years or so of their operation, provided their applications are approved by the appropriate government agency as essential for economic development. The greatest difficulties have been administrative: the delays in approving applications and the problems of establishing suitable criteria for action. The programs can, theoretically, be used to direct investment into those lines which offer greatest benefit for economic development, but in practice, it is difficult to ascertain such investment in any scientific way. There is always some doubt about the effectiveness of the policy in luring additional industry beyond that which would have come anyway. The most significant effects are perhaps the psychological ones, of indicating a favorable government attitude toward private enterprise. The success of Porto Rico in luring new industry by tax considerations is likely to be due much more to the freedom of Porto Rican firms from United States income tax, although they enjoy duty-free entry to the United States market, than it is to the Porto Rico concessions.

4. *The Expenditure Tax.* Since one of the prime goals of tax policy in a developing economy is the encouragement of saving, it may be argued that the expenditure tax is preferable to income taxation. Such a tax not only gives a definite incentive to save, but also has less adverse effect upon investment. The savings influence will, of course, be largely lost if the tax is expected to be permanent and the funds are saved to buy taxable goods in the future. The main obstacle is administrative; the tax is even more difficult to operate than the income tax, and thus its use must await the attainment of some minimum level of education and record keeping.

5. *Customs Duties.* Levies on imports offer several major advantages from a revenue standpoint. They are very easy to administer, apart from minor problems with smuggling. They are basically consumption levies, and thus do not directly reduce the earnings from work or business development. Since they raise the cost of consumption of luxury and semiluxury goods, they provide some incentive to increase saving; in fact, Ghana has used duties for this deliberate purpose. Since the duties do not apply, usually, to the basic necessities, the burden distribution accords reasonably well with accustomed standards of equity. Finally, they can be used to curb heavy importation of luxury goods which creates foreign exchange difficulties for developing economies; thus the foreign exchange is made available for capital goods imports which are significant for economic growth. On the whole, customs provide governments with substantial revenues not otherwise obtainable in a developing economy.

However, the merits can be overstated. So far as incentives are concerned, to the extent to which persons seek higher incomes for the purpose of acquiring luxury goods, as may be typical in an economy emerging from a backward state, a high tax on the commodities, which pushes them out of reach of many people, may have as adverse incentive effects as an income tax. Sharp increases in customs can produce riots and political in-stability, as in Ghana and British Guiana in 1961 and 1962. Some dis-crimination among the consumers of various types of goods is inevitable, since uniformity of burden on all luxury consumption is impossible. Pyra-miding of tax and application of tax to some producers' goods are hard to avoid.

Despite these limitations, customs are in fact the chief revenue source of virtually every developing economy, with a few exceptions such as Rhodesia. But as a country develops, inevitably the relative reliance on customs falls as income taxes grow and domestic production comes to constitute a higher percentage of total economic activity.

6. *Sales and Excise Taxes.* Use of general sales taxation is not likely to be satisfactory in the early stages of a developing economy. The nature of retailing in these areas, with relatively small shops and lack of records, is such that a retail sales tax, the most satisfactory form, is impossible of use. So long as a high percentage of nonsubsistence goods is imported, the customs duty approach is more satisfactory than wholesale or manufac-turers' sales taxes. Beyond a certain point, however, a wholesale or value-added tax extending through the wholesale level becomes preferable to customs duties to insure tax from domestically produced goods.

Excises become useful on such commodities as liquor and tobacco products as domestic production of them develops, as usually occurs at an early stage in economic growth. As long as luxury items which might be subject to excises are imported, duties are simpler to operate than excises. If, ultimately, a general sales tax is not established, there may be a case for some excise taxation of domestically produced luxuries.

Motor fuel taxation is appropriate at an early stage, to provide bene-fit-based support for highway development and facilitate allocation of resources between railways and highways.

7. *Export Duties.* A characteristic of the tax structures of many newly developing economies is the taxation of exports of a few basic agri-cultural or mining products. These are important revenue sources in a number of such countries. The products taxed are frequently exported by governmental or government-controlled marketing boards, so that admin-istration of the taxes is simple. Since the prices of these commodities are determined in world markets, the net effect of the taxes is to reduce the income of the producers. One major advantage of the taxes is that when world market prices of the products are high, the government is able to obtain large sums of revenue for development purposes which would otherwise largely be used for consumption, with inflationary influences on the domestic economy.

On the other hand, there are major objections. Since the tax is directly related to output, the net effect may be to cause the producers to reduce the output of these major export crops, and perhaps even return to subsistence farming. The taxes are discriminatory among the producers of export and nonexport crops. The revenues are likewise highly unstable, because of the instability of the world prices of the goods.

8. *Property Taxation.* Since economic rent of land is a true surplus, it may be argued that land taxation offers the least danger to incentives for economic development, per dollar of revenue, and even taxation of buildings is less detrimental than direct taxation of income from them. Land taxation may also be used to break up large estates where these are an obstacle to growth, or to force more intensive cultivation. These taxes also recover for the government a portion of the sharp increases in urban land values which accompany rapid growth. The lump sum nature of land taxation, once assessed, is in general an incentive to increased production and efficiency, rather than a deterrent.

Unfortunately, there are several major obstacles in the way of effective property taxation in many developing economies. In some areas, as in tropical Africa, there is little private ownership of land and a tradition against charging rents for the use of communally owned land. In other jurisdictions the obstacles are mainly political; the dominant group in the government is often representative of the landowner class. But on the whole, this approach to taxation offers important advantages to developing economies.

*Summary.* On the whole, a developing economy is likely to rely heavily on customs duties, which, if properly devised, can provide a relatively equitable distribution of tax burden and substantial curtailment of consumption, without unless pushed too far, detrimental effects upon production. But there is likewise merit in developing direct taxation, of necessity crude for the lower income levels, but in the more sophisticated income tax form at the higher levels. But incentive considerations dictate that the levels be lower than in mature economies. Deterrent effects of corporate taxation upon economic development can be minimized by liberal loss carry-over and accelerated depreciation provisions; special tax concessions can be used in theory not only to reduce adverse tax effects but also to guide investment into desired lines. In practice, however, in developing economies they are difficult to administer effectively.

The expenditure tax may have a role in some developing economies, especially if there is a small high-income class devoting its incomes to luxury consumption instead of economic development. Land taxation can yield substantial funds for development without adverse economic effects. The precise tax structure must, of course, be developed in terms of the exact circumstances of the particular economy.

### Government Borrowing

The government of a developing economy may resort to borrowing under several sets of circumstances. Money markets are often not well organized in such economies, and a substantial portion of savings may be hoarded. Government savings bond programs may tap these hoards, or money creation through central bank borrowing will create equivalent amounts of purchasing power. Compulsory borrowing systems, as used in Ghana in conjunction with the income tax, may encourage savings without the potential adverse effects on incentives of equivalent income tax increases, provided that the persons distinguish between the borrowing and taxation, which they may not do. Further domestic borrowing, particularly from the central bank, is likely to produce inflationary consequences. This, in turn, provides funds for development at the expense of fixed income receivers and consumption generally, and is sometimes regarded as preferable to a lesser rate of development. But inflation, if long continued, as in some South American countries, discourages savings and disorganizes the functioning of the economy, and is on the whole detrimental to economic growth.

Borrowing by the government from outside the country permits the importation of capital equipment necessary for economic development, without giving foreign investors control over domestic industry. But it inevitably gives rise to subsequent problems of interest and principal payments, and most governments of developing economies therefore prefer to use it with some discretion.

## APPENDIX—SOCIAL CREDIT

An even more extreme point of view on the question of inadequacy of purchasing power is represented by the social credit movement. For centuries the idea has persisted that income is inadequate to buy all goods produced; the writings of the pre-Marxian socialists particularly stressed this thesis. But the classical economists demonstrated rather conclusively that income and output are, of necessity, equal and thus that purchasing power cannot fall below the current rate of output. More recent work in national income analysis has provided more precise reasoning. But the contrary point of view has persisted and was given revived strength by the writings of Major C. H. Douglas, a retired British engineer. Douglas argued that purchasing power was inevitably inadequate to buy all goods produced, primarily because depreciation costs and payments for materials are elements in price but do not become incomes. Accordingly, he argued for "social credit," a program of regular governmental payments to all persons, designed to increase total spending to adequate levels, the funds to be obtained by the printing of paper money.

The Douglas movement gained no significant following in the United States,[8] but in Canada, it became a force of some moment. The center of the Canadian movement was Alberta, a province very severely affected by the depression. William Aberhart, a Calgary high school principal and director of the Prophetic Bible Institute, became a convert to the Douglas ideas, coupled them with a severe denunciation of the banks as the primary source of evil in society, and expounded them in his religious radio broadcasts. After failing to sell the existing government in Alberta on the ideas, he developed his own Social Credit Party, which swept into power in Alberta in 1935, on a platform of paying $25 a month to all adults.

The problem of how to make these payments, in the light of the bankrupt condition of the province and the lack of power of the provinces to issue money, was an immediate dilemma and produced a violent internal dispute in the Social Credit Party. Faltering steps were taken to carry out the promises, particularly by introducing measures designed to check the powers of the banks. But all the social credit legislation was held invalid by the courts or disallowed by the lieutenant governor, and no payments were actually made. The coming of the war and prosperity diverted attention from the "social dividends." The Social Credit Party remains in power in Alberta and has gained control of the government in British Columbia, but relatively little is said today about the social credit doctrines, except in occasional reference to the basic defects in the monetary system and the fact that the federal government has prevented the provinces from carrying out the proposals.[9]

The fallacy in the Douglas reasoning is so obvious that it hardly needs refutation; to the extent that amounts equal to depreciation charges are reinvested in new capital equipment, there is no shortage of purchasing power. Failure to reinvest such amounts, if not offset by equivalent new investment, will, of course, reduce aggregate demand and lead to a decline in output. But the difficulty is one not of a basic inadequacy of purchasing power but of insufficient profitability of investments. Payments for materials become incomes to the owners of the factor units used

---

[8] Other schemes substantially similar gained at least regional strength; the "Thirty Dollars Every Thursday" program in California was related.

[9] Upon the death of Major Douglas in 1952, Alberta's Premier Manning stated: "His analysis of the basic defects in our present monetary system proved correct." Unfortunately, few persons except social crediters would agree with this pronouncement. In 1957, Alberta commenced to pay an annual oil and gas royalty payment, amounting in that year to $20 per person and in 1958 to $17.50, as a "social dividend."

in producing them. Any program of continuous payments of substantial sums of printed money to individuals, except in a period of depression, would produce runaway inflation.

## REFERENCES

### GENERAL

HALL, CHALLIS. *Fiscal Policy for Stable Growth.* New York: Holt-Rinehart, 1961.
The most thorough study of fiscal policy as related to growth in a mature economy.

KNORR, K., and BAUMOL, W. J. *What Price Economic Growth?* Englewood Cliffs, N.J.: Prentice-Hall, Inc., 1961.
A plan of drastic tax reform for economic growth.

MUSGRAVE, R. A. *The Theory of Public Finance,* chap. xx. New York: McGraw-Hill Book Co., Inc., 1959.

PEACOCK, A. T. *Analytical Concepts of Fiscal Policy with Special Reference to Developed Economies.* Colectânea de Estudos, No. 15. Lisbon: Centro de Estudos de Estatística Económica, 1962.

SMITH, W. L. "Monetary-Fiscal Policy and Economic Growth," *Quarterly Journal of Economics,* Vol. LXXI (February, 1957), pp. 36–55.

### DEVELOPING ECONOMIES

CHELLIAH, R. J. *Fiscal Policy in Underdeveloped Countries.* London: George Allen and Unwin, 1960.
Primary reference to India.

INTERNATIONAL BANK FOR RECONSTRUCTION AND DEVELOPMENT. Series on *Economic Development* of various countries. Baltimore: Johns Hopkins University Press.
Recent volumes include Tanganyika (1959) and Uganda (1961).

PREST, A. R. *Public Finance in Underdeveloped Countries.* New York: Praeger, 1962.

PHILIPS, PAUL A. M. VAN. *Public Finance and Less Developed Economy.* The Hague: Nijhoff, 1957.
Primary reference to Latin America.

SLESINGER, R. E. *"Fiscal Policy Considerations for Underdeveloped Economies,"* *Kyklos,* Vol. 15, No. 3, 1962, pp. 624–34.

WALD, H. P. *Taxation of Agricultural Land in Underdeveloped Economies.* Cambridge: Harvard University Press, 1959.

# INDEX

# INDEX

*This book has been set in Intertype Garamond
12 and 10 point, leaded 1 point. Part and chapter numbers and titles are in Futura Medium.
The size of the type page is 27 by 46½ picas.*